EDGAR W. BUTLER
UNIVERSITY OF CALIFORNIA, RIVERSIDE

T5-BPZ-864

HARPER & ROW, PUBLISHERS
New York, Hagerstown, San Francisco, London

Sponsoring Editor: Dale Tharp
Project Editor: Ralph Cato
Designer: Michel Craig
Production Supervisor: Stefania J. Taflinska
Photo Researcher: Myra Schachne
Compositor: Ruttle, Shaw & Wetherill, Inc.
Printer: The Murray Printing Company
Binder: Halliday Lithograph Corporation
Art Studio: Harold Spitzer, architect
        J & R Technical Services, Inc.

301.36
B985u

Photography credits: 7 Stoy, DPI   10 Smallman, DPI   12 Krathwohl, Stock, Boston   18 John and Kathy Marchael   19 Shelton, Monkmeyer   21 Joel Gordon   30 New York Public Library Picture Collection   32 Menzel, Stock, Boston   33 Menzel, Stock, Boston   36 New York Public Library Picture Collection   41 New York Public Library Picture Collection   42 New York Public Library Picture Collection   54 Reeberg, DPI   60 New York Public Library Picutre Collection   61 Monkmeyer   64 Flying Camera, DPI   66 Monkmeyer   72 French Embassy Press & Information   74 Herwig, Stock, Boston   77 Conklin, Monkmeyer   80 George Gardner   83 Merrim, Monkmeyer   84 Gross, Stock, Boston   106 Brody, Stock, Boston   107 Fujihira, Monkmeyer   109 Joel Gordon   111 Zimbel, Monkmeyer   112 Greenberg, DPI   127 Forsyth, Monkmeyer   129 Steffee, DPI   138 John and Kathy Marchael   144 Silberstein, Monkmeyer   150 New York Public Library Picture Collection   151 New York Public Library Picture Collection   153 New York Public Library Picture Collection   160 Zimbel, Monkmeyer   162 Michel Cosson   165 Strickler, Monkmeyer   167 Lau, Photo Trends   169 Mark Chester   178 Dietz, Stock, Boston   183 George Gardner   190 Wide World   192 Joel Gordon   205 New York Public Library Picture Collection   215 Joel Gordon   217 Almasy, WHO   218 Beckwith Studios   220 Wide World   222 Charles Gatewood   232 Wide World   235 Wide World   260 Joel Gordon   264 George Gardner   270 George Gardner   278 George Gardner   281 Forsyth, Monkmeyer   285 Bonnie Freer   286 Wide World   291 George Gardner   302 Joel Gordon   304 Patterson, Stock, Boston   307 Wide World   311 New York Public Library Picture Collection   316 Wide World   319 George Gardner   331 Wide World   332 Wide World   336 Joel Gordon   344 Mannheim, DPI   347 Sapieha, Stock, Boston   352 Joel Gordon   366 Wide World   368 Charles Gatewood   371 Charles Gatewood   383 Beckwith Studios   386 George Gardner   391 Culver   397 Joel Gordon   413 Brody, Stock, Boston   419 Forsyth, Monkmeyer   423 Wide World   434 Charles Gatewood   441 Wide World   446 Saidel, Stock, Boston   450 Wide World   461 Falk, Monkmeyer   462 Charles Gatewood   463 BART   465 Wolinsky, Stock, Boston   466 Charles Gatewood   468 Wilks, Stock, Boston   474 Granger Collection   475 Caraballo, Monkmeyer   477 Beckwith Studios   485 Mark Chester   486 Public Archives of Canada   490 George Gardner   493 Jensen, Monkmeyer   496 Virginia Hamilton   503 General Motors

URBAN SOCIOLOGY: A Systematic Approach

Copyright © 1976 by Edgar W. Butler
All rights reserved. Printed in the United States of America. No part of this book may be used or reproduced in any manner whatsoever without written permission except in the case of brief quotations embodied in critical articles and reviews. For information address Harper & Row, Publishers, Inc., 10 East 53rd Street, New York, N.Y. 10022.

Library of Congress Cataloging in Publication Data

Butler, Edgar W
  Urban sociology.

  Bibliography: p.
  Includes indexes.
  1. Sociology, Urban.   I. Title.
HT151.B85   301.36   76-22518
ISBN 0-06-041106-6

81-710

URBAN SOCIOLOGY

URBAN
SOCIOLOGY
A SYSTEMATIC APPROACH

This book is dedicated to
Pattie, Brian, and Tracey Butler

BASIC ORGANIZATION OF THE TEXT

CONTENTS

Urban Sociology *is designed to provide a systematic approach to the study of urban society, especially in the United States. It was written primarily as a textbook for undergraduate urban sociology courses. However, the author trusts that students of various fields—such as urban studies, urban planning, urban political phenomena and government, geography, and social activism—will find the book equally useful inasmuch as it shows how a variety of seemingly diverse phenomena are interrelated within the urban complex. Similarly, it demonstrates that not all urban regions are alike, that there is a variety of areas within the city, and that there are causes and consequences of differences among cities and intracity areas, all of which affect the organization of the urban region and the population that lives there.*

This volume systematically pulls together a range of new ideas and information as well as some relevant research that has been largely ignored in the past. It utilizes and describes various frames of reference, orientations, and theories involving urban phenomena and evaluates this framework in light of available research. Thus theories are not presented in a vacuum. Nevertheless, due consideration is given the fact that, while nonresearchers rigidly adhere to many of these frames of reference, systematic researchers find some of them to be inadequate.

The approach of Urban Sociology *is eclectic in nature. Although heavy emphasis is placed upon the work of sociologists, other appropriate research* has been utilized to broaden the perspective. Whenever the evidence appears to warrant it, a tentative statement is made about the relative merits of one orientation over another. Some of the material is standard fare; yet most of what is presented is new—the method of presentation has brought together a great diversity of theories and the research necessary to evaluate those theories systematically.

Although the pace of changes in the urban environment is rapid, much of the work accomplished by earlier urbanists is still applicable. On the other hand, the author fully appreciates that in this text, like any other on the subject, a few sections will be out of date by the time of its publication. Because the basic plan of Urban Sociology does not rely upon specific time-bound information, appropriate portions of the text may be emended by classroom discussion as scientific knowledge increases, without necessarily throwing other aspects of the presentation off balance. This is as it should be.

In brief, this volume fits a vast array of studies into a systematic framework that primarily, but not exclusively, emphasizes urbanization and its impact, variation among urban complexes and cities, and variation within urban places and cities. It brings into consideration other factors such as population composition, social organization, environment, technology, cultural values, behavior, and attitudes—especially their spatial element. Similarly, there is an emphasis on the temporal aspects of urban life as they are affected by and affect these other factors. The material in this volume has been successfully used in urban ecology, urban sociology, and urban problems courses at the University of North Carolina, Chapel Hill, and the University of California, Riverside.

My appreciation is especially given to students who have, in the past, posed the penetrating questions that forced me to reexamine my statements and to clarify my thoughts. Also, two former graduate students, Gerard J. Hunt and John H. Freeman, have been supportive, and I appreciate the contributions they have made to my intellectual growth. Maurice D. Van Arsdol, Jr., Georges Sabagh, F. Stuart Chapin, Jr., J. Richard Udry, and Amos H. Hawley—all have left their imprint on me through what I consider extremely fortunate and satisfying academic and personal relationships. Although each of them may not necessarily agree with particular aspects of what I have included in this volume or my interpretation of materials, I am sure they will recognize, in various sections of the book, their impact upon my thoughts about urban phenomena. I want to thank S. John Dackawich and Wilfred G. Marston, who read an earlier draft and made valuable suggestions—some of which I was able to incorporate into the final version. I owe my very special thanks to Alma Heyse, who has gone through the manuscript many, many times. Also, my thanks to Dale Tharp, Ralph Cato, and Michel Craig at Harper & Row, as well as to Claire Komnick for her expert copyediting of the manuscript. Finally, I would like to express my profound debt to the many researchers and authors who granted permission to quote from their works and to many others whose work was drawn upon in all sections of this book. They are the foundation that made this book possible.

Edgar W. Butler

URBAN
SOCIOLOGY

INTRODUCTION

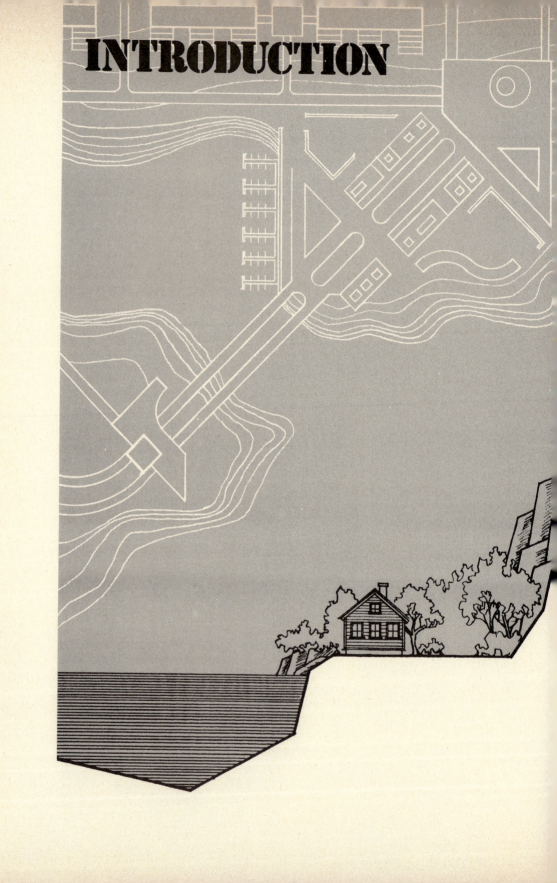

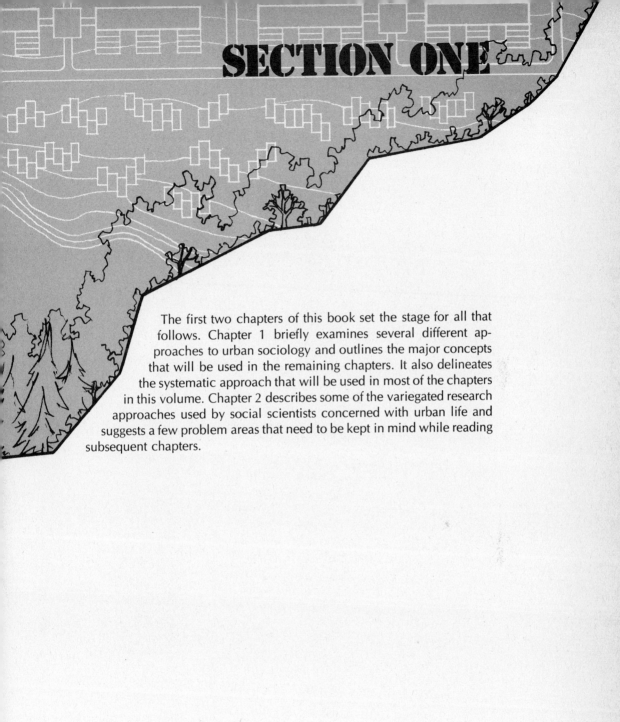

SECTION ONE

The first two chapters of this book set the stage for all that follows. Chapter 1 briefly examines several different approaches to urban sociology and outlines the major concepts that will be used in the remaining chapters. It also delineates the systematic approach that will be used in most of the chapters in this volume. Chapter 2 describes some of the variegated research approaches used by social scientists concerned with urban life and suggests a few problem areas that need to be kept in mind while reading subsequent chapters.

CHAPTER 1
APPROACHES TO URBAN SOCIOLOGY

INTRODUCTION

Urban sociology is one of the broadest and most eclectic of all sociological fields. It tends to overlap geography with its emphasis on spatial distributions; political science with its emphasis on political behavior, power, and decision making; economics with its perspective on public policy, taxation, and public expenditures; and anthropology with respect to the culture of groups. Many interests of the urban sociologist and ecologist also overlap those of city planners, social workers, and various specialists in education, race relations, housing, and urban rehabilitation (Gist, 1957). Perhaps as a result of its eclectic nature, there is a need to clarify and refine many of the basic concepts in the field: community, the city, urban, urbanism, urban society, urbanization, industrialization, modernization, and so on. Currently, a major problem is that these concepts are loosely defined and used indiscriminantly by students of urban phenomena (Sjoberg, 1959).

Another major problem facing those who study communities and urban places is how to make general statements that are widely applicable despite the many gradations in size and other characteristics that differentiate one urban community and place from another. One possible approach is to construct "ideal types" and make broad statements about each. Another possibility is to determine some of the important empirical dimensions that are so general that they apply to all communities regardless of differences existing among them. Both of these approaches have their adherents. Stein (1960) followed the first approach when he used the three analytical concepts of *urbanization, industrialization,* and *bureaucratization.* Schnore (1958), on the other hand, concentrated on population size and density, since these kinds of data presumably are available for all communities and subdivisions within them. Dewey (1960) brought both of these approaches together in an attempt to bridge the gap and showed that the cosmopolitan nature of a place is not necessarily related to size or density.

From a local community approach, Warren (1963) has suggested four dimensions that could be used as a frame of reference: (1) *local autonomy*—dependence and independence upon other units or communities; (2) *coincidence of service areas*—the extent to which the service areas of local units (stores, churches, schools, etc.) coincide or fail to coincide; (3) *symbolic identification with a common locality*—a sense of local identification. (Is the local area an important focal point for the individuals living in it or is there a lack of attachment or of belonging?); and (4) *social system dimension*—the structural relationship of the various local units (both individuals and subsocial systems) to each other. In some communities the sentiments, behavior patterns, and social system connections are highly interrelated; in others they may be very weak.

From another broad perspective Sjoberg (1959) suggested four primary theoretical orientations in urban sociology, which differ according to the variable that is given primacy—*the city, cultural values, technology,* or *power.* These concepts are discussed in some detail because they are used throughout the book.

THE CITY

Geographers have considered the location and settlement of cities as a *dependent* variable—that is, something to be explained. On the other hand, the city as a key *independent* variable in *explaining* some types of ecological patterns and behavior has been stressed by sociologists and ecologists of the so-called Chicago School, as represented by Park, Redfield, and Wirth. In this view certain spatial and temporal patterns are functionally necessary to the continued existence of an urban community.

From this perspective the spatial structure of the urban complex, such as the clustering of people and institutions, is examined. People are seen as being differentially distributed or segregated in space, and, generally, the larger the population concentration, the more numerous and variegated are the social institutions in a particular city or urban area. A focus on the spatial aspects of the city may stress almost any demographic characteristics of the population or any other statistically ascertainable factor: people on welfare rolls, percentage of married females working, crime rates, income inequality, or what kinds of cities and subdivisions of cities have had more successful community chest or United Fund campaigns. It should be noted that rural communities as well as urban communities may be studied in their spatial and structural aspects.

In this view there is also a focus on the social organization of the city and the social psychology of its inhabitants (Reiss, 1956: 108). Typical research has centered questions such as the following: (1) What makes cities grow? (2) Is the city reproducing itself? (3) Do cities follow a regular pattern of growth? (4) Is the slum a disorganized area? (5) What is the pattern of race relations in cities? (6) What happens to local institutions and populations when cities grow?

A variety of ecological patterns has accompanied the rise of cities.

The heterogeneity of land use, transportation, and people is shown in this photograph of busy Tremont Street and Park Street Church opposite the Commons in Boston.

Wirth's position (1938) was that the impact of the urban community was reflected by size, density, and heterogeneity and that these factors were considered key determinants of social organization, attitudes, and behavior. Redfield (1941) assumed that heterogeneity and lack of privacy were primary characteristics of the city. In addition, Wirth typified urban life by secularization, secondary-group associations, increased segmentation of social roles, and poorly defined norms that lead to alienation. Wirth and his followers considered these as "effects" of urban development, which were to be kept distinct from the consequences of cultural values or industrialization, which were assumed to be a constant. According to this perspective, then, all cities, both past and present, should display these characteristics.

The primary limitation of this approach is that it exaggerates, even for the United States, the degree of secularization and disorganization that supposedly typifies urban communities. Axelrod (1956) and Whyte (1956), among other critics, claim that cities are highly organized and that many informal networks of social relationships were overlooked by earlier writers. Lewis (1959), for example, notes that in Mexico City urbanization was not accompanied by destruction of the social and moral order. More recently, Suttles (1968) has demonstrated that the slums of Chicago are highly organized.

An additional criticism of Wirth and his followers is that they neglected to consider the city as being influenced by the total sociocultural system—that is, the city as a *dependent* variable. Cities may be created purposively or otherwise, and their ecological distributions and social norms may be determined by institutional spheres external to any particular city. Social power as a variable becomes relevant here. Also many early writers considered folk or primitive societies to be closed independent systems, whereas urban communities were assumed to be dependent upon their hinterlands for survival. Sjoberg (1959) suggests that, logically, comparisons should be made between folk and urban *societies* or between rural and urban *communities*.

Other criticisms of the Wirth approach suggest that the city may be a positive force in social change, but the precise role needs further specification and greater attention must be given to the influence of social organization. Further comparative studies of cities in a variety of societies are needed. One of the most urgent requirements in urban sociology is a reformulation of the theoretical approach that regards the city as an independent variable.

In viewing the city as an independent variable, we can discern three primary subclassifications of writing and research: (1) communities as wholes, (2) as types, and (3) the social processes and dimensions that are specific to the community and that distinguish it as a sociological category from other kinds of social structure (Simpson, 1965).[1]

Communities as Wholes

Research on communities as wholes has been primarily an anthropological endeavor; the Middletown (Lynd and Lynd, 1929, 1937) studies are excellent examples. Most research in this area consists of case studies of a single community or urban complex, and very often there is little awareness of the need to contrast obtained results with those from other communities. The work done so far tends to be noncumulative, although occasionally an investigator will use case study material to illustrate certain points. For example, Stein

---

[1] It should be noted here that Simpson was concerned specifically with community research. We have extrapolated his classifications to include that of urban complexes. It is rather difficult to separate conceptually in many instances the distinction between community and urban, which again points up the need for clearer theoretical and conceptual specification.

(1960) in his study of urbanization, industrialization, and bureaucratization, used case studies to illustrate his theory, and Walton (1966) used a host of case studies to compare the results of reputational and decision-making methodological approaches to urban power structures.

Recently there has been some emphasis on studying urban complexes as a social system. Focus in this approach is on delineated subsystems within the city or urban place, on determining how these subsystems are interrelated to larger systems, and on indicating how some parts of the local system are part of the larger system called nation.

Communities as Types

Efforts have been made to explain a wide range of behavior on the basis of a typological classification scheme of communities. In contrast to research on communities as wholes, the study of communities as types is by its very nature *comparative*. The analytical focus has been on heuristic-invented types (Weber, 1958; Wirth, 1938) or on empirical types such as those derived from an analysis of the economic and/or occupational structure (Duncan et al., 1960; Nelson, 1955, 1957) or the population and housing structure (Price, 1942; Hadden, 1965). Some work has also been directed at describing types of areas within metropolitan regions (Shevky and Bell, 1955; Van Arsdol, Camilleri, and Schmid, 1961). Simpson (1965) essentially has suggested bringing together the heuristic-invented and empirical approaches by splitting up global notions of invented typologies into separate variables. He would then examine how these notions are related in the real world, and would finally put them back together into theoretically meaningful typologies. His suggestion probably is a reaction against the evident lack of feedback between theory and research to date.

Community-Specific Processes

What makes up the realm of community processes is essentially a definitional and conceptual problem. Warren (1963) has pointed out five major functions of community that fit under this rubric: (1) production-distribution-consumption, (2) socialization, (3) social control, (4) social participation, and (5) mutual support.

1. *Production-Distribution-Consumption.* All institutions in the urban complex, whether industrial, business, professional, religious, educational, governmental, or whatever, provide goods and services. When and to whom goods and services are distributed and consumed in the production-distribution-consumption of goods and services are important considerations. Similarly, changes in conditions that bring about alterations or changes from one institution to another are important processes.

2. *Socialization.* Socialization is the process of transmitting prevailing knowledge, social values, and behavior patterns to its individual members. At early ages the nuclear family and, increasingly as one grows older, peer groups

Las Vegas is representative of a recreational type city with a specialization in gambling and entertainment.

and the school system become important transmitters and socializing agents.

　　3. *Social Control.* Social control is the process by which a group influences the behavior of its members toward conformity. Informal social control agencies are the family, kin, peer groups. Formal social agencies, such as the school, church, and government, are becoming increasingly important. Government is especially pertinent here, since it has the ultimate coercive power — incarceration or loss of life. Informal groups, of course, continue to control membership through formal sanctions up to and including exclusion.

　　4. *Social Participation.* The interaction of people — their association

with one another and their behavior in regard to each other—is an important sphere of community processes. Generally, social participation is divided into institutionally related behavior along informal lines such as family, kin, and neighbors and formal associations such as religion, voluntary organizations, and participation in the economic structure (Hunt and Butler, 1972). Another slightly different focus is on interactional networks and processes such as conflict, competition, cooperation, and so on. A third point of view stresses "activity patterns" of individuals (Chapin et al.)

Kaufman (1959) has listed the following as primary areas of investigation in social interaction: (1) the degree of comprehensiveness of interests pursued and needs met, (2) the degree to which action is identified with locality, (3) the relative number and significance of local associations, (4) relative number, status, and degree of involvement of residents in association with others, (5) the degree to which action maintains or changes the local society, and (6) the extent of organization for action in various kinds of behavioral activities.

Social participation, of course, is closely associated with socialization and social control mechanisms. Early in most people's lives the group having the widest participation is the family, followed, for many, by the church and church-related organizations. It does appear that participation in informal and formal voluntary organizations, with kin, co-workers, neighbors, and friends, varies by age and social class and other factors. Research focusing on social isolation in urban areas and the relationship between the individual and mass society has been relatively neglected to date.

5. *Mutual Support.* This consists in giving help in time of need. Traditionally, family, kin, and neighbors have been the major sources of mutual support. Some of these functions appear to be in the process of being transferred to public agencies (Litwak and Szelenyi, 1969).

CULTURAL VALUES
The cultural value orientation has clashed with the one outlined previously. This frame of reference explains social behavior and ecological organization in terms of *cultural values*. Firey's work, *Land Use in Central Boston* (1947), and the Middletown studies are examples of this orientation. Du Wors (1952) studied several different New England communities located near each other and described the value system of one community as being "sporty," or at best having a constellation of dominant values including a high respect for the fine arts and learning and, at worst, an irresponsible emphasis on hedonism; nearby was a community that he identified as "thrifty," which at best was characterized by a high sense of responsibility for community and financial stability and, at worst, by a narrowness identified with strict puritanism. Similarly, Vogt and O'Dea (1953) examined two southwestern communities. They characterized one as a community of "cooperation" and the other as a community of "individual independence." This study showed how marked differences in the effectiveness of community organizations and behavior and atti-

This view of Boston at night shows the impact of cultural values upon transportation, buildings, and the organization of the city.

tudes of individuals was related to their acceptance of definitions of life situations based upon certain value premises.

The use of comparative data suggests that values not only have relevance for land use but also affect, in part, whether urban centers will arise at all and to what extent they will grow. Values can influence a city's size, the heterogeneity of its areas, and its population density—all key variables in the Wirth approach. Also, the values of influential people such as bankers, politicians, planners, and others are important in determining how an urban complex grows and develops.

There can be little quarrel that values are a critical independent variable in accounting for differences among and within urban places. However, it is necessary to point out that the precise relationships between values and the ecological structure of urban centers and the behavior of individuals are difficult to determine. What is needed are more empirical comparative studies of a variety of urban places and areas within them.

TECHNOLOGY

An emphasis on technology assumes that it is an important factor in determining the location of places and the ecological and social organization within them. Furthermore, technology is viewed as having an impact upon behavior through the varying kinds of influence industrialization exerts on the traditional value system (Blumer, 1964). Industrialization, an advanced form of technology, takes place primarily within an urban setting.

Most efforts focusing upon technology as a key concept have dealt with establishing the requirements of industrial cities and the kinds of behavior associated with a large-scale, rational economic organization, a fluid class system in which achievement rather than ascription of such characteristics as race, sex, age, and so forth, is emphasized, a loosely organized conjugal family system, mass education that stresses science and technology, and extensive mass communication.

All of these facets appear to be interrelated, but the present state of knowledge is such that one cannot be confident of generalizations that indicate how they are related. This partly is a result of extrapolating too freely from the experience of the United States. The American system emphasizes certain traits, and these may not be invariant. Also, other factors have not been studied thoroughly, such as religion, power, and environment. An additional difficulty is that it has never been clearly specified whether or not mature industrial-urban systems and those in the process of industrialization and/or urbanization are different. These aspects of industrialization and urban development need to be studied because it appears that an authoritarian state is more likely to flourish in a society that is seeking to industrialize and urbanize than one that has already reached this goal. Historically, it appears that once a high degree of industrialization-urbanization is reached, it is doubtful that a small elite can maintain a monopoly of power in that society.

POWER

Social power, or the ability of certain organizations, groups, or individuals to manipulate other organizations, groups, and individuals, results in differential organizational and distribution patterns that are substantially related to ecological patterns, economic competition, social stratification, and, at the individual level, the extent of life opportunities. Thus power is of special interest—especially who has power, who uses it, and for what purposes.

The impact of external power sources on urban places is a neglected area, and we cannot assume that cities, organizations, or individuals function in isolation. Power, then, can be considered as an important factor in understanding the social life of communities and urban centers. For example, both local and extralocal power decisions have an impact upon a city's ecology and social structure. In turn, a city's ecology and social structure influence interaction patterns, communication, and other individual social behavior within that urban center.

FRAME OF REFERENCE

Most of the orientations and concepts discussed so far will be utilized throughout the remainder of this book to aid us in understanding urban phenomena in the United States.[2] Each of the individual frames of reference, orientations, or theories sensitizes us to observe certain phenomena that are related to or exist in urban society. However, none of them fits or helps describe urban areas in their entirety. The systematic approach used in this book allows the utilization of these approaches and orientations at various times when they are appropriate to the subject matter under discussion.

The systematic framework used in this book may at first glance appear deceptively simple. It is possible in any given theory — or research effort oriented toward a specific aspect of urban phenomena — to utilize more specifically generated propositions (although even in these more limited approaches this is not often accomplished) and hypotheses and to adopt a specific research method. However, in a textbook of this nature, a broader framework is necessary so that a variety of orientations and research methods can be drawn upon. Accordingly, this volume attempts to fit in an orderly manner as much as possible of the following into each topical area under discussion: (1) urbanization and its (possible) impact; (2) variation *among* urban complexes and cities; (3) variation *within* urban places and cities; and (4) other factors such as population characteristics, social organization, environment, technology, value, behavior, and attitudinal factors that appear to be relevant to a specific analysis.

The *spatial distribution* of these four generalized areas of systematic analysis is especially emphasized. This focus is not necessarily one that requires "geographical determinism" or attributing "cause" to such distributions. However, there are two factors related to spatial distributions. First, virtually all phenomena associated with urbanization, urbanism, and urban places are differentially distributed in space. Thus space becomes one organizing element along which phenomena can be viewed. Second, any explanation of human behavior in urban environments must account for the differential spatial distribution of phenomena, such as racial populations, or, in my opinion, it cannot be considered an adequate theoretical explanation.[3]

[2] This book substantially ignores other societies — a deliberate omission. Since there is so much material available on urban areas in the United States, it is premature, in my opinion, to carry out a cross-cultural work. However, this book has laid the groundwork for cross-cultural urban studies, and I urge students to examine the research done in this area.

[3] For an extended discussion of the role and significance of spatial distributions in urban areas see Timms (1971).

Many will also detect in this volume an emphasis on the *temporal* facets of urban society. But temporal aspects receive less emphasis and are less discernible at points only because substantial up-to-date theoretical and research efforts by social scientists are still needed; thus there is not enough material to draw upon. Future work in the temporal aspects of urban life will, of course, add substantially to the knowledge base utilized in this book and allow expanded discussion and analysis.

In summary, this volume fits a vast array of studies into a systematic framework that primarily, but not exclusively, emphasizes urbanization and its impact, variation among urban complexes and cities, variation within urban places and cities, and brings into consideration other factors such as population composition, social organization, environment, technology, cultural values, behavior, attitudes, and so on, especially their spatial elements. Similarly, there is an emphasis on the temporal aspects of urban life as it affects and is affected by these other factors.

BIBLIOGRAPHY: Articles

Axelrod, Morris, "Urban Structure and Social Participation," *American Sociological Review,* 21 (February 1956): 13–18.

Blumer, Herbert, "Industrialization and the Traditional Order," *Sociology and Social Research,* 48 (January 1964): 129–138.

Dewey, Richard, "The Rural-Urban Continuum: Real but Relatively Unimportant," *American Journal of Sociology,* 66 (July 1960): 60–66.

Du Wors, Richard E., "Persistence and Change in Local Values of Two New England Communities," *Rural Sociology,* 17 (September 1952): 207–217.

Hunt, Gerard J., and Edgar W. Butler, "Migration, Participation and Alienation," *Sociology and Social Research,* 56 (July 1972): 440–452.

Kaufman, Harold F., "Toward an Interactional Conception of Community," *Social Forces,* 38 (October 1959): 8–17.

Litwak, Eugene, and Ivan Szelenyi, "Primary Group Structures and Their Functions: Kin, Neighbors, and Friends," *American Sociological Review,* 34 (August 1969): 465–481.

Nelson, Howard J., "A Service Classification of American Cities," *Economic Geography,* 31 (July 1955): 189–205.

Nelson, Howard J., "Some Characteristics of the Population of Cities in Similar Service Classifications," *Economic Geography,* 33 (April 1957): 95–108.

Price, Daniel O., "Factor Analysis in the Study of Metropolitan Centers," *Social Forces,* 20 (May 1942): 449–455.

Schnore, Leo F., "Social Morphology and Human Ecology," *American Journal of Sociology,* 63 (May, 1958): 620–634.

Simpson, Richard L., "Sociology of the Community: Current Status and Prospects," *Rural Sociology,* 30 (June 1965): 127–149.

Sjoberg, Gideon, "Urban Community Theory and Research: A Partial Evaluation," *American Journal of Economics and Sociology,* 14 (January 1955): 199–206.

"Special Issue: Urban Studies," *American Behavioral Scientist,* 6 (February 1963): 3-54.

Van Arsdol, Maurice D., Jr., Santo Camilleri, and Calvin Schmid, "An Investigation of the Utility of Urban Typology," *Pacific Sociological Review,* 4 (Spring 1961): 26–32.

Vogt, Evon Z., and Thomas F. O'Dea, "A Comparative Study of the Role of Values in Social Action in Two Southwestern Communities," *American Sociological Review* 18 (December 1953): 645–654.

Walton, John, "Research Note: Substance and Artifact: The Current Status of Research on Community Power Structure," *American Journal of Sociology,* 71 (January 1966): 430–438.

Wirth, Louis, "Urbanism as a Way of Life," *American Journal of Sociology,* 44 (July 1938): 1–24.

BIBLIOGRAPHY: Books

Chapin, F. Stuart, Jr., Edgar W. Butler, and Frederick C. Patten, *Blackways in the Inner City,* Urbana: University of Illinois Press, forthcoming.

Duncan, Otis Dudley, W. Richard Scott, Stanley Lieberson, Beverly Duncan, and Hal H. Winsborough, *Metropolis and Region,* Baltimore, Md.: The Johns Hopkins Press, 1960.

Firey, Walter, *Land Use in Central Boston,* Cambridge: Harvard University Press, 1947.

Gist, Noel P., "The Urban Community," in Joseph B. Gittler (ed.), *Review of Sociology,* New York: John Wiley & Sons, 1957, pp. 159–185.

Hadden, Jeffrey K., *American Cities: Their Social Characteristics,* Chicago: Rand McNally & Co., 1965.

Hannerz, Ulf, *Soulside: Inquiries into Ghetto Culture and Community,* New York: Columbia University Press, 1969.

Lewis, Oscar, *Five Families,* New York: Basic Books, Inc., 1959.

Lynd, Robert S., and Helen M. Lynd, *Middletown,* New York: Harcourt, Brace and Company, 1929.

Lynd, Robert S., and Helen M. Lynd, *Middletown in Transition,* New York: Harcourt, Brace, 1937.

Redfield, R., *The Folk Culture of Yucatan,* Chicago: University of Chicago Press, 1941.

Reiss, Albert J., Jr., "Urban Sociology," in Hans L. Zetterbert (ed.), *Sociology in the United States of America,* Paris: UNESCO, 1956, pp. 107–113.

Shevky, Eshref, and Wendell Bell, *Social Area Analysis,* Berkeley and Los Angeles: University of California Press, 1955.

Sjoberg, Gideon, "Comparative Urban Sociology," in Robert K. Merton, Leonard Broom, and Leonard S. Cottrell, Jr. (eds.), *Sociology Today,* New York: Basic Books, 1959, pp. 334–359.

Stein, Maurice R., *The Eclipse of Community,* Princeton: Princeton University Press, 1960.

Suttles, Gerald D., *The Social Order of the Slum,* Chicago: University of Chicago Press, 1968.

Timms, Duncan, *The Urban Mosaic: Toward a Theory of Residential Differentiation,* Cambridge, England: Cambridge University Press, 1971.

Warren, Roland L., *The Community in America,* Chicago: Rand McNally & Company, 1963.

Weber, Max, *The City,* translated and edited by Don Martindale and Gertrude Neuwirth, New York: The Free Press, 1959 (Paperback).

Whyte, William H., Jr., *The Organization Man,* Garden City, N.Y.: Doubleday and Company, Inc. 1956.

CHAPTER 2
RESEARCH APPROACHES OF URBAN SOCIOLOGY

INTRODUCTION

In carrying out community and urban studies, researchers have used a variety of methods and techniques. Research methods range from participant observation, such as the Liebow (1967) and Hannerz (1969) studies of black life in Washington, D.C.; surveys of various populations such as the Middletown Study of Mental Health in the Metropolis (Srole et al., 1962); and the use of secondary sources of data such as the U.S. Census of Population and Housing (Duncan and Reiss, 1956). These research endeavors range from descriptions of social life in one area within an urban complex to very sophisticated statistical analyses of all places in the United States. In other words, the use of methods and techniques is highly variable, and the urban specialist must at least be aware of a large number of research methods and techniques.

Research methods and techniques tend to be different and vary substantially according to the threefold division of interest pointed out earlier, that is, focus upon places as a dependent variable, an independent variable, or as a setting for research. It should be noted that in some instances the methods and techniques overlap. Further, some investigators do not make explicit from what perspective they are approaching their studies, nor do they make explicit their research methodology.

RESEARCH APPROACHES

The variety of community research approaches was reviewed several years ago by Arensberg (1954). He pointed out that one major focus of research has been on the spatial-temporal descriptions of communities. This perspective generally examines geographic distributions of diverse factors such as land use patterns, the place of work as a nucleus, the journey to work, questions of who goes where and when, analyses of central business districts, segregation (most typically of blacks, but this concept applies to all social categories, i.e., the

This grain elevator in Atalissa, Iowa, is an important item in the functional analysis of Atalissa. It shows the interrelationships of transportation, the hinterland, and the community to the environment.

aged, income levels, social classes) and population change. Most emphasis has been on the *spatial* aspects to the neglect of the *temporal*. Temporal analysis involves changes over time. Community and urban sociologists, as well as most other behavioral scientists, generally have neglected the study of change, and there are relatively few techniques to examine change effectively.

When the approach to community and urban centers focuses on the study of the location of places and urban complexes, and the reasons for these locations, statistical analyses utilizing census data and other information collected by governmental and private agencies are utilized. This particular interest has led to a functional analysis of communities. Loesch, Christaller, and others (see Chapter 4) were early identified with this interest. They examined the location of communities with respect to each other, the relationship of communities to the environment, the relation of the hinterland of an area to the central place, and the influence of transportation upon place location.

Eldridge (1956) has noted that one of the most basic problems in urban research is the definition and delineation of adequate and meaningful geographic units of analysis. Research has been varied, with research in the United States centering on states, counties, standard metropolitan statistical areas, central cities, census tracts,[1] enumeration districts in 1960, or block groups in

---

[1] *Census tracts* are small areas into which large cities and metropolitan areas have been divided for statistical purposes. Tract boundaries were established cooperatively by local committees and the Bureau of the Census and were generally designed to achieve some uniformity of population characteristics, economic status, and living conditions. Initially, an average tract had about 4000 residents. Tract boundaries were established with the intention of being maintained over a long time so that comparisons could be made from census to census.

Information about cities, neighborhoods, and the people in them may be obtained by face-to-face interviews on the street, as shown here, or at places of residence.

1970, which are smaller subdivisions of census tracts, and other kinds of units such as blocks. Some authors have argued that all of these are artificial units and the unit of analysis should be "natural areas" (Hatt, 1946). *Natural areas* are those delineated by certain specified characteristics, such as demographic character, value/belief systems, behavior, and so on; typically, they have no relationship to formal or legally defined boundaries such as the central city or census tract boundaries.

DATA SOURCES

The major source of statistical data up to the present has been censuses. The U.S. government conducts a housing and population census every 10 years and reports data on a number of different-sized units. In addition, other kinds of data are gathered by various federal agencies, as well as various other kinds of data.[2] There are many administrative statistics available for some jurisdictions; these include political administrative units, educational districts, vital statistical areas, and so forth. Survey data are available for certain samples

[2] Census data for all of these units for every standard metropolitan statistical area, central city, and so on, are generally available in the documents section of most college libraries.

of the population through private and governmental facilities. Another major source of data is locally conducted surveys by agencies.

Theories and conceptual perspectives currently are attuned to static notions when they should be concerned with dynamic process. Current needs in research are to develop adequate taxonomies of cities, urban places[3] and of areas within cities and urban complexes. Urban specialists must be more acutely aware of the time dimension; that is, they should carry out longitudinal as opposed to cross-sectional studies. While current statistical techniques appear to be highly sophisticated, they are hardly developed in the areas of measuring change or time-related statistics (Duncan et al., 1961). The time dimension is important also in longitudinal studies because they involve the conflict between studying natural areas versus comparable areas over time as defined by the census or by other political bodies. Natural-area boundaries presumably shift with the concept or variable under consideration, and they change as the population shifts or moves about differently over time. Using comparable areas as the unit of analysis on the other hand means maintaining boundary integrity, but units within the boundaries may change at differential rates.

There is a need to go beyond case studies and focus on comparative studies. For example, rather than having a case study of a power structure of one urban place, it would be useful to know how power structures of various kinds of urban complexes differ (if indeed they do) according to some structural base such as the division of labor. Related to all of the comments made so far, there is a parochial focus on the United States, with a neglect of cross-cultural studies.[4] How useful for analyzing other societies is a conceptual apparatus based upon the experience of the United States? In most cities in the United States, for instance, the poor tend to live in transitional zones near the Central Business District (CBD), whereas in some American cities such as Raleigh, North Carolina, and Riverside, California, they live to some degree in the outer city or on the periphery. How do we account for these empirical differences? Our concern here, then is a theoretical and methodological one: Can one legitimately generalize from localized, that is, U.S.-based, case studies to other nations? In other words, is there any *external validity* in generalizations based upon this country's experience? Here we face head on the problem of proper units of analysis, the time dimension, and the generality of findings.

As noted in Chapter 1, communities, urban complexes, and areas within urban places and cities have been considered as independent variables.

---

[3] *Place* refers to a concentration of population, regardless of the existence of legally prescribed limits, powers, or functions. Most places are incorporated as cities, towns, villages, or boroughs. In addition, larger unincorporated places outside urbanized areas have been delineated, and those having populations of 1,000 or more are treated in the same manner as incorporated places of equal size. Also, unincorporated places in urbanized areas that have 10,000 inhabitants or more and an expression of local interest in their recognition are treated as incorporated places.

[4] As we noted in Chapter 1, this book also is parochial in the sense that it focuses on the United States. However, the systematic framework can be applied to other societies.

In contrast to censuses and surveys, some researchers observe and record city life from a more personal vantage point, such as this photographer recording a day in the life of an alcoholic.

They are thought of as determinants of attitudes and behavior. This leads to comparisons between rural and urban people and/or comparisons of differences within metropolitan complexes, that is, differences between the behavior of central-city residents and suburban residents, or differences in various areas within the urban complex classified along some specified dimension such as the extent of familism or social rank (Shevky and Bell, 1955). Censuses are most often utilized in these studies, although survey data are used as well as an occasional combination of other research techniques.

Other theoretical and methodological problems are involved in determining how to separate and define the notions of homogeneity-heterogeneity and changes in them. An area may be homogeneous according to one dimension, for example, a population dimension — sex. However, change may be occurring in other population characteristics, for example, age.

The third major orientation of those interested in communities and urban areas uses them only as a locale for the study of various kinds of value systems, attitudes, or behaviors — research *within* an urban setting. The focus is not on why places are located where they are or how different kinds of places may influence attitudes and behavior — these are regarded as givens — but on various kinds of behavior and phenomena within urban places, such as mental illness, crime, poverty, voting, and fertility. Research techniques range from participant observation, surveys, and statistical data to use of official records.

Little work has been accomplished so far dealing with the ecological

context or situations of persons holding different attitudes or having varying behavior patterns. A few social mobility and organizational studies, approach this
kind of analysis, however, and a major study by the Swedish sociologist Harald
Swedner (1960) is most relevant for our purposes. All of these studies have
been concerned with a central bone of contention in the social sciences,
namely, the separation of *individual* and *structural* or *contextual* effects upon
attitudes and behavior. This is a level-of-analysis problem which argues that
the individual but not ecological areas or aggregated information is the proper
focus of scientific inquiry. In this book we utilize studies of individuals, census
tracts, through larger units such as cities and larger urban complexes. Robinson
(1950; but also see a rebuttal, Menzel, 1950) has argued that the social sciences can advance only on the basis of concepts and empirical observations
based on descriptive properties of *individuals,* such as height, income, color, or
race (Van Blaaderen, n.d.), or, if you will, trees in the forest. However, in this
book we are concerned with the trees (individuals), as well as their context —
the forest (cities, urban complexes, census tracts).

   Some social scientists, then, use units of analysis other than the individual. This may seem to be a minor problem, but it actually gets at the very
basis of many of the differences that currently divide social scientists. Are
organizations, cities, census tracts, groups, and so on, useful units of analysis in
the social and behavioral sciences, or can we deal only with individuals? In this
book we assume that all of these aspects of social life are viable units and we
use all of them. However, we will make explicit what our units are as we shift
our focus on societies to cities, to areas within cities, and to individuals.

   Several other methodological problems of importance should be noted
though we will not deal with them specifically. There is the problem of how
one can interrelate various data sets, for example, how data obtained in a survey compare with U.S. census data or with other kinds of information (for a
good example see Van Arsdol et al., 1964). Also, perspectives concerned with
urban places as a dependent variable, an independent variable, or only as a
setting for research are highly varied, result in different research methods and
techniques, and utilize different theoretical and conceptual approaches to phenomena. This problem is, of course, one faced by all the sciences: What in the
world is it that we are studying, and what approach shall we take? Are we going
to study the community, urban or urbanism, or industrialization and/or modernization, characteristics of individuals, or attitudes and perceptions?

SUMMARY

   In our presentation so far in Chapters 1 and 2 we have very briefly discussed several perspectives on community and urban phenomena. A more
elaborate discussion of the city, cultural values, technology, and power as key
variables was undertaken in Chapter 1. While we recognize the need to incorporate into urban sociology more cross-cultural studies, we will focus on the
urban society and research concerned with the United States, although not

exclusively. Historically, sociologists as well as other social scientists, have tended to study segments of urban social and ecological phenomena rather than the totality. Similarly, much of the literature only uses the community or urban complex as a laboratory for testing theories or hypotheses not specifically related to these units (Sjoberg, 1959). In future discussions we will keep in mind whether we are considering communities and urban places as *dependent* or *independent* variables or as a *setting* for certain kinds of research endeavors studying human behavior.

In subsequent chapters we expand many of the notions discussed so far in relation to urban location, growth, and types and the differentiation among and within rural, suburban, and urban areas. Additional chapters focus on community, social stratification, political behavior, the sacred (religion), and alienation. In considering social problems in the urban complex, we will try to determine whether problems are universal to all communities, cities, urban areas, and societies or whether they are peculiar to certain types of communities, cities, and/or societies. The section on urban problems includes a chapter on environmental hazards such as air and water pollution, and other chapters examine physical and mental illness, slums and poverty, urban renewal and rehabilitation, crime, riots and violence, and government in relation to services. The implications of taking the city, values, technology, or power as key variables in *explaining* these social problems of the urban complex are pointed out.

Finally, the last two chapters are devoted to urban planning and the urban future. The planning chapter examines the basic processes of urban planning especially as it involves active citizen participation in the process of making policy decisions. The last chapter of the book examines some possible futures of the urban environment, with special attention being paid to viable alternatives.

BIBLIOGRAPHY: Articles

Arensberg, Conrad M., "The Community Study Method," *American Journal of Sociology*, 60 (September 1954): 109–124.

Bogue, Donald J., "Economic Areas as a Tool for Research," *American Sociological Review*, 15 (June 1950): 411–416.

Bopegamage, A., "A Methodological Problem in Indian Urban Sociological Research," *Sociology and Social Research*, 50: 2 (January 1966): 235–240.

Eldridge, Hope Tisdale, "The Process of Urbanization," in J. J. Spangler and Otis Dudley Duncan (eds.), *Demographic Analysis*, Glencoe, Ill.: The Free Press, 1956, pp. 338–343.

Foley, Donald L., "Census Tracts and Urban Research" *Journal of the American Statistical Association*, 48 (December 1953): 733–742.

Hatt, Paul, "The Concept of Natural Area," *American Sociological Review*, 11 (August 1946): 423–427.

Hollingshead, August, "Community Research: Development and Present Condition," *American Sociological Review*, 13 (February 1948): 136–146.

Menzel, Herbert, "Comments on Robinson's Ecological Correlations and the Behavior of Individuals," *American Sociological Review,* 15 (October 1950): 674.

Robinson, William S., "Ecological Correlations and the Behavior of Individuals," *American Sociological Review,* 15 (June 1950): 351–357.

Van Arsdol, Maurice D., Jr., Georges Sabagh, and Francesca Alexander, "Reality and the Perceptions of Environmental Hazards," *Journal of Health and Human Behavior,* 4 (Winter 1964): 144–153.

Van Blaaderen, Maris Andreas N., "Human Ecology and Robinson Ecological Correlations," unpublished paper, Department of Sociology, Washington State University, n.d.

BIBLIOGRAPHY: Books

Butler, Edgar W., *Urban Society: A Cross-Cultural Perspective,* forthcoming.

Dogan, Mattel, and Stein Rokkan (eds.), *Quantitative Ecological Analysis in the Social Sciences,* Cambridge: M.I.T. Press, 1969.

Duncan, Otis Dudley, and Albert J. Reiss, Jr., *Social Characteristics of Urban and Rural Communities, 1950,* New York: John Wiley & Sons, Inc., 1956.

Duncan, Otis Dudley, Ray P. Cuzzort, and Beverly Duncan, *Statistical Geography: Problems in Analyzing Areal Data,* Glencoe, Ill.: The Free Press, 1961.

Gibbs, Jack P. (ed.), *Urban Research Methods,* New York: D. Van Nostrand, 1961.

Hannerz, Ulf, Soulside: *Inquiries into Ghetto Culture and Community,* New York: Columbia University Press, 1969.

Hauser, Philip M. (ed.), *Handbook for Social Research in Urban Areas,* Ghent, Belgium: UNESCO, 1965.

International Urban Research, *The World's Metropolitan Areas,* Berkeley and Los Angeles: University of California Press, 1959.

Lenski, Gerhard, *The Religious Factor,* Garden City, N.Y.: Doubleday and Company, Inc., Anchor Books, 1961.

Liebow, Elliot, *Tally's Corner,* Boston: Little, Brown and Company, 1967.

Shevky, Eshref, and Wendell Bell, *Social Area Analysis,* Berkeley and Los Angeles: University of California Press, 1955.

Sjoberg, Gideon, "Comparative Urban Sociology," in Robert K. Merton, Leonard Broom, and Leonard S. Contrell, Jr. (eds.), *Sociology Today,* New York: Basic Books, 1959, pp. 334–359.

Srole, Leo, Thomas S. Langner, Stanley T. Michale, Marvin K. Opler, and Thomas A. C. Rennie, *Mental Health in the Metropolis: The Midtown Manhattan Study,* New York: McGraw-Hill, 1962.

Swedner, Harald, *Ecological Differentiation of Habits and Attitudes,* Lund, Sweden: CWK Gleerup, 1960.

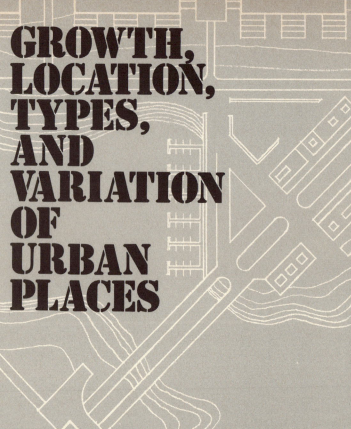

GROWTH, LOCATION, TYPES, AND VARIATION OF URBAN PLACES

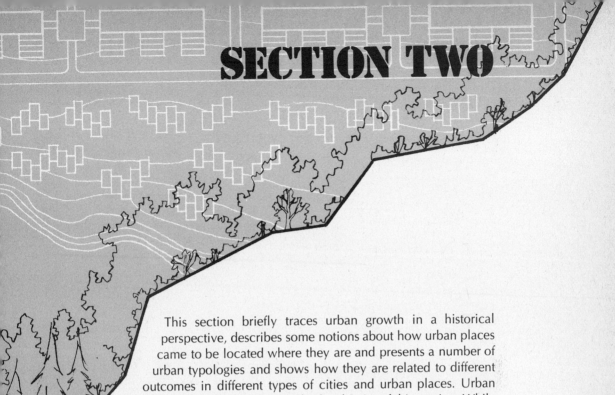

SECTION TWO

This section briefly traces urban growth in a historical perspective, describes some notions about how urban places came to be located where they are and presents a number of urban typologies and shows how they are related to different outcomes in different types of cities and urban places. Urban places as the unit of analysis is the focal point of this section. While Chapter 3 traces urban growth and city development from the Greek and Roman empires to contemporary America, the major emphasis is on urban growth and development as it has occurred in the United States. Chapter 4 describes several different perspectives or theories of urban and place location and views urban places primarily as a dependent variable. It also presents information that demonstrates how applicable these perspectives are to city and place location in the United States. And like Chapter 3, Chapter 4 primarily focusses on cities and urban places as the unit of analysis and for the most part ignores differentiation within them, which will be covered in Section III. Chapter 5 explores a number of typologies that consider cities and urban places as entities, and it demonstrates, in addition, how these typologies and differing characteristics of cities and urban places have consequences for the city and its residents. This chapter primarily views urban places as having characteristics that affect the residents, for example, an independent variable.

Section II, then, sets the stage for the examination in later sections of differentiation *within* cities and urban places. Whenever possible, discussions in subsequent chapters will describe cities and urban places in terms of the characteristics and typologies examined in this section.

CHAPTER 3
URBAN GROWTH IN HISTORICAL PERSPECTIVE

INTRODUCTION

The first population concentrations appear to have come into existence under favorable environmental conditions that allowed a diverse agricultural economy. As surpluses grew, trade among settlements became institutionalized and defense of the settlement became a necessity. Apparently, the first non-agricultural occupations were defense and administrative special-ties. Other gradually occurring changes related to population concen-tration were the creation of taxation and capital accumulation, construction of public buildings, the establishment of a hereditary ruling class, writing, artistic expression, the development of arithmetic, geometry, and astronomy, and the emergence of the practice whereby the requirement of resi-dence, as opposed to kinship, was used as the basis for membership in the community (Childe, 1950–1951).

While there is some controversy over when major places first ap-peared, there is general agreement that the earliest urban places were located in Mesopotamia. Some of these urban places had as many as 24,000 inhabi-tants (Childe, 1946). These cities were surrounded by walls, and the center typically contained a palace, a temple, other religious buildings, and storage facilities for agricultural products. The main marketplace was located outside of the walls.

Generally, these urban places maintained power and kept the local hinterland secure from outsiders. The only way in which places could exist was for surrounding agricultural districts to produce more than they consumed so that urban people would be able to use the surplus for food and trade. In addi-tion, spoils from war and plundering added to the wealth of the city. Overall, there was little heterogeneity in people or in occupations in these early cities. Government and religion were closely intertwined, and a leader in one was a leader in the other. Since this was before the development of wheeled vehicles, transportation was by man himself or beasts of burden.

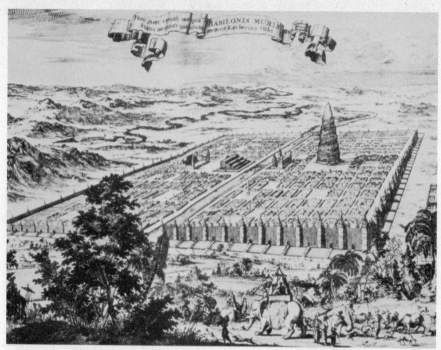

Athanasius Kircher's seventeenth century reconstruction of Babylon in ancient Mesopotamia shows the walls, the legendary Tower of Babel, the ziggurat, or sacred building, and the hanging gardens. Babylon formed a square about 5 miles on each side. Note the elephants and camel in the foreground as beasts of burden. Such modes of transportation coupled with agricultural surpluses in the surrounding countryside enabled cities like Babylon to prosper.

Many of these places were located at strategic locations such as on trade routes, where trade routes crossed, or at important water locations. Where transportation routes intersected and different forms of transportation were used to transport goods, for instance, from water to land, and/or where goods changed owners, urban places grew quite rapidly in size. As a result of invasions, environmental changes in rivers and harbors, and foreign domination, many cities grew, lost population, grew again, and some eventually disappeared altogether.

GREEK CITIES AND THE ROMAN EMPIRE

As late as the sixth century B.C., Greek cities were agriculturally oriented and primarily fortresses where the population could protect itself from recurring invasions. Gradually, the Greeks turned to trade and piracy, and Athens became the political and trading center of the developing Greek city-states. The city became more heterogeneous in occupational composition with an increasing division of labor. Artisans, merchants, mariners, and traders from other lands became commonplace. Athens has been estimated to have covered slightly over 600 acres, less than 1 square mile, and to have had a population of 124,000, although others have reported that it had a larger population (Jones, 1966: 142–145).

Accompanying the development of trade were the diminution of bartering and the increasing usage of coins and credit. Social class differences became more pronounced than previously as wealth was drawn to Athens. Citizenship was on a hereditary basis, and citizens had many more rights than noncitizens. Even this early in history the excess rural population migrated to the cities, creating urban population problems. Subsequent colonization of other lands, such as Southeast Asia and Egypt, was one mechanism used to reduce the overpopulated Greek cities.

Compared with Greece, the city was of primordial importance in the Roman Empire. Rome itself contained a highly dense and more heterogeneous population than previous cities. Social forces pushed dwellings together and multistoried apartments were built. Rome in the first century A.D. was composed largely of 6- to 10-story *insulae*, the prototype of the modern tenement building (Passonneau, 1963: 13). Merchants became more specialized in the goods that they sold, and areas within the city became devoted to specialized functions. Social organization became more refined, lower-level manufacturing began, and guilds were organized by artisans and merchants. Rome, the largest of the early cities, covered 5 square miles. Its population size has been debated, with estimates ranging from 1.2 million or 240,000 per square mile (Gibbon, 1932, Vol. II: 346) to 350,000, or 65,000 per square mile, a rather dense population by current standards (Russell, 1960). Hawley (1971: 33–35) suggested that these estimates err on the liberal side, since land productivity and irrigation limitations meant that only in exceptional circumstances could a place grow beyond 33,000 in population during this era.

Goods, tax monies, and agricultural products flowed into Rome from the far-flung empire. There were slaves, as well as laboring classes, and the poor in the city. Roads were primarily for use by the military and were a means of controlling the hinterlands. As Rome expanded its empire, hundreds of towns were established. Many of these towns were primarily military at first but grew into more permanent and heterogeneous settlements. Many towns grew into cities, becoming somewhat autonomous communities governing themselves as well as the surrounding territory. "Geographically, the empire was a mosaic of city territories" (Jones, 1966: 237). City size varied principally according to the extent of administrative responsibility and the size and population of the territory governed.

By the fifth century A.D. the decline of the empire was apparent. Population in city territories decreased because of famines, war, and rampant disease. The empire was no longer able to protect itself or its citizens from repeated invasions of "barbarian hordes" and the Vandals from Africa. Towns

The Alcazar in Segovia, Spain, and these ramparts in Avila are representative of the walled and fortified cities of medieval times.

reverted to agricultural enterprises, and population density decreased to pre-Roman Empire levels (Gibbon, 1932).

Population movement within and among Greek and Roman cities was more or less restricted to military and religious purposes although trade flourished. Religious and social participation was for the most part divided along social class boundaries, and social stratification was clearly defined. Little social mobility occurred in these early city-states, and power rested with religious and military elites. Environmental hazards were substantial, and epidemics produced large-scale illness and mortality. Little information is available about the poorer classes or about crime, suicides, violence, and so on, in these early city-states.

FEUDAL AND MEDIEVAL CITIES

The Roman Empire disintegrated by the fifth century A.D. Until 300 or 400 years later, life was centered on subsistence agriculture and land was divided into feudal domains. Lords controlled the land, which was allocated to warriors who subdivided their allotments into sections for persons of lesser status. At the bottom of the social stratification network were serfs. Warriors, craftsmen, agriculturists, laborers, and serfs — all were under the bondage of the lords (Pirenne, 1937: 40–41). Each stratum paid its dues to the next higher stratum. "Every man had an assigned place and tradition was the arbiter of disputes" (Hawley, 1971: 40). In Europe the permanent settlements that continued to exist were remnants of the Roman Empire. They were dependent upon agriculture and were fortified to protect the lords or ecclesiastics who resided there. Transportation networks deteriorated following the collapse of the empire. In addition, transportation for very long distances was extremely

difficult because of the need for armed guards as well as the necessity to cross multiple feudal jurisdictions that exacted tolls for safe passage.

From the fifth through the fifteenth century changes gradually took place. Trading never completely vanished, and it continued to experience slow growth until the Crusades, which exposed Europeans to the Moslem world. Showing the way, the Crusaders brought back Eastern goods and ''a host of contrasting ideas about standards of consumption, the uses of money, techniques of doing things, and the propriety of alternative ways of life'' (Hawley, 1971: 46). When the innumerable obstacles to trade were gradually overcome, trade once again began to flourish.

The population declined after the fading away of the Roman Empire, but then began a slow but steady growth. Towns became the focus of trade through fairs, and merchants began settling outside of the walls—the first suburbs! As illustrated in Figure 3-1, many of these suburbs in turn built walls, so that some towns had successive fortifications. The importance of trade began to be recognized by the lords, and the ruling classes began protecting merchants residing outside the walls as well as on roads and waterways. Many established towns increased in size, and new urban places came into being. After a period, towns were judged on the basis of their commercial activities.

Then, as now, environmental factors were important determinants of town location, growth, and the extent of commercial activity. Towns were located where trade routes crossed, especially land-and-water crossroads, and many towns along trade routes flourished. An accessible harbor or navigable river helped even though substantial tolls were exacted. Many towns that survived the decline of the Roman Empire did not survive the trade revival and increased societal population growth because they were not on the trade routes

Figure 3-1. The Growth of St. Gallen in the Middle Ages. This city in northeastern Switzerland developed around a Benedictine abbey founded in the early seventh century. Its increased political and economic importance in the Middle Ages followed four centuries of renown as an educational center north of the Alps. The tenth-century city walls and gateways are clearly shown in the old print above. The photograph below depicts the medieval city core that is still standing within the modern city of today. *Print from H. Boesch et al.,* Villes Suisses à Vol d'Oiseau, *Bern: Kümmerly & Frey, 1963. Photo Courtesy of Swiss National Tourist Office.*

and they faded from view or became relatively unimportant.

Technological changes made possible some of the town growth. The moldboard plow began to be used extensively around the ninth century, making possible the tilling of formerly undeveloped land and an increase in the availability of surplus agricultural products. Similarly, agricultural productivity was increased by adapting different crop rotation plans, which, in effect, doubled agricultural production. Each of these developments required social cooperation among a number of individuals, and this change in social organization may have been more significant than the technological innovations. The moldboard plow, for example, required a certain number of oxen to draw it; thus several persons had to form a cooperative to ensure sufficient oxen power. Further, land had to be redistributed so that newer forms of crop rotation would be put into practice. in addition, land transportation costs were reduced substantially by introduction of the horse collar, tandem harness, and horseshoes (White, 1940: 141–146), which permitted an increased use of horses in pack-trains during both dry and wet weather conditions.

As municipal autonomy was won through the efforts of merchants, power passed from landed feudal lords to the merchants. Civil law evolved, uniform penal codes were written, many tolls and fees formerly extracted from merchants were abolished, and jurisdictions were consolidated (Pirenne, 1939: 170). Merchants broke the hold of the landed aristocracy, and the local municipalities they helped form became the cornerstone of many of the major changes in people's independence in future years. Cities began to exert direct power over rural territories and smaller places. The economy became town oriented. Cities in some instances grew to over 20,000 inhabitants and were spread throughout Europe (Russell, 1960: 57).

Within the walls of feudal cities the primary focus was on religious life, and religious and political buildings dominated. Walls within many feudal cities ensured the segregation of ethnic groups and others considered as undesirables. The elite isolated itself from the nonelite in the center part of the city, where the greatest protection was available. In contrast, the poor and the "undesirables" lived on the periphery along with many of the merchant class. While cities tended to have either an open square, or plaza, or a broad straight thoroughfare that served as a focus of city life, most streets and passageways were narrow, just barely wide enough to allow animals and people to circulate within the city (Sjoberg, 1955: 183; 1960: 96). A substantial part of the work that took place in the city occurred in the place of residence; therefore, work and residence were not separated. "The feudal city's land use configuration was in many ways the reverse of that in the highly industrialized communities" (Sjoberg, 1960: 103).

The problems of waste disposal and of furnishing an adequate water supply were difficult to surmount. In view of these kinds of conditions it is no surprise that, periodically, large-scale illness, plague, and death occurred in these cities. Beginning in the 1340s, the Black Death was carried into Europe by Italian traders (East, 1966: 317), and on and off for the next several hundred

Plague decimated the populations of cities and wiped out entire families. Fearing for the lives of their children, some parents of plague-ridden households evacuated their children to the country to save them from the ravages of urban epidemics.

years epidemics decimated entire populations of cities. After the Black Death era the population expanded from about 100 million in 1650 to 187 million in 1800 (East, 1966: 392).

Feudal and medieval cities, like their modern counterparts, required an agricultural hinterland producing a surplus, a transportation network to facilitate the movement of goods, and an increasing division of labor to manufacture goods for trading. Changes in agricultural production and transportation modes occurred slowly, but as technology became more sophisticated, the division of labor became intensified. In England during the eighteenth and nineteenth centuries these changes all came together to produce the first Industrial Revolution.

During the Middle Ages period of city building and rebuilding, the requirements of defense and communications limited the area of cities. As in Rome, high, closely packed tenements were the standard dwellings for most of the population of medieval Paris, the cities of Renaissance Italy, and most of the other cities in Europe. The working-class quarters of the newly developing industrial cities of Edinburgh and Birmingham, England, may have consisted of the "most depressing and unsanitary environments man have ever invented" (Passonneau, 1963: 13).

THE INDUSTRIAL REVOLUTION
AND THE GROWTH OF URBAN PLACES

Many of the major forms in urban places can be traced to the impact that changing technology made possible through more efficient transportation modes and industrialization. This point of view has led some to categorize cities as "preindustrial" or "industrial" (Sjoberg, 1955). Comparatively few cities in the United States had their beginnings before the nineteenth century and could be considered as industrial in nature. At the beginning of the nineteenth century only 4 percent of the population lived in cities of 8000 or more population. Part of the reason that cities did not grow as rapidly before the nineteenth century as they did thereafter was because of the excessively high death rates then prevalent in cities. Migration from the countryside "did little more than fill the vacant places caused by death" (Weber, 1899: 233). The ability of the countryside to replace the city population appeared to be true no matter what percentage of the urban population died as a result of epidemics and plagues.

A reduction in the death rate was necessary for the growth of cities in the United States. It resulted in higher rates of natural increase (more births than deaths = population increase). In addition, a large influx of migrants from the countryside to the cities and immigrants from other lands populated both city and rural areas. Death rates in early large cities of the United States were substantially higher than in smaller cities, and all sizes of cities had higher death rates than rural areas (for data on New England in 1892 see Weber, 1899: 344–346). Moreover, these death rate differentials appeared to hold for all ages, with increasing death rates correlating with increasing city size. However, Weber, (1899: 348) concluded that "excessive urban mortality is due to lack of pure air, water and sunlight, together with uncleanly habits of life induced thereby. Part cause, part effect, poverty often accompanies uncleanliness: poverty, overcrowding, high rate of mortality, are usually found together in city tenements." Nevertheless, he also concludes that there is "no inherent eternal reason why men should die faster in large communities than in small hamlets, provided they are not too ignorant, too stupid, or too selfishly individualistic to cooperate in the security of common benefits." "The real checks upon the growth of population in previous centuries were war, famine, pestilence, and unsanitary cities involving particularly high infantile mortality" (Weber, 1899: 155). Thus medical and sanitary progress reduced several of these checks: Pestilence and unsanitary conditions resulting in lower (infant) mortality and the Malthusian limitations on population growth were no longer applicable to the United States. Thus, in any evaluation of urban growth it is necessary to consider the general increase of population, since urban areas could be growing at the same or different pace than the population as a whole (Weber, 1899: 155).

At the beginning of the United States when settlement was taking place, usually the first objective upon reaching the Atlantic shore was to found a community that would serve as a means of mutual protection and as a base from which the surrounding countryside could be colonized (Schlesinger, 1940). Almost all early colonial towns were planned, with a town square, wide streets, and shade trees. Most early colonial cities—Boston, New York, Norfolk, Savannah, Philadelphia, Baltimore, and Charleston—were seaports. While social stratification in early colonial towns approached a caste structure, by the mid-1700s class boundaries were not clear, although certainly they still existed, and a great deal of social mobility was taking place. As colonial places became larger, social organization became increasingly complex, and the beginnings of what were to become severe urban problems a century later had already appeared. In addition, public schools became mandatory in some colonies, and voluntary organizations proliferated.

At the beginning of the nineteenth century, larger American cities were tied to the dominant water transportation mode of the times and were located, for the most part, along sea coasts; their economies were still primarily extractive. Piers in these cities were the focus of commercial activity, and main streets terminated at the piers. Also, many places grew at the *fall lines* of rivers, where water power was available for utilizing "the industrial secrets which sharp-witted Americans had recently filched from Britain" (Schlesinger, 1940).

At least up until the early 1800s, American cities were characterized by a relative lack of congested areas, dark alleys, slums, and, for the most part, crime. Before long, however, the existence of slums was being reported, and New York City and Boston had areas inhabited only by the poor. As cities grew larger, so did their problems. Few streets were paved, and mud was a prominent feature during wet weather. A number of personal journals by writers visiting and living in cities of the mid-1800s report that animals roamed the city streets freely, and at least one writer observed that without these animals, which served as garbage disposals, the streets would have been choked with filth. Similarly, cities of this era were virtually without sewage facilities. (New York created its department of sewers in 1849, one of the first cities in the country to do so.) It is not too surprising then that epidemics occurred frequently in early cities. Diseases that could be carried by the water system or by ditches and streets polluted by garbage were especially evident. Among the diseases that reached epidemic proportions were dysentery, typhoid, and typhus. Large-scale epidemics of cholera, which is spread primarily through water contamination, occurred in 1832, 1849, and 1866. Yellow fever, transmitted by mosquitoes that propagate in fetid pools of water, claimed many lives at the turn of the century and lasted in northern cities until around 1825. Yellow fever epidemics decimated thousands (4000 in Philadelphia in 1793), and in 1847 in New Orleans it claimed over 2000 lives and over 8000 during the summer of 1852. The large-scale epidemics and the resulting high mortality rates led many people of this era to suspect that increasing congestion and density of the population were responsible; others had different opinions: "In the early years of the century poverty like disease was ordinarily considered the result of an individual's moral failure" (Glaab and Brown, 1967: 90–91).

Early cities were characterized by inadequate traffic and transportation facilities. As cities grew and became more dense and crowded, a more complicated and sophisticated administrative system was needed to handle the complex problems that change was creating in the institutions of society. City government in the early United States was alternatively viewed as being very good and then, conversely, virtually beyond redemption. The large increase in the urban population, of course, created tremendous problems and, as we noted earlier, made it mandatory that new forms of social organization be created to solve the problems generated by larger-sized cities. Similarly, changing technology intensified urban problems and created new forms of social organization. Governmental costs increased faster than the population because the demand for municipal services in the cities made capital investment a necessity. Many functions not performed previously or performed formerly by private organizations fell to the city government and required expanding facilities.

As poverty and slums grew in the cities, there was a corresponding increase in crime rates. The rising crime rate forced a change in the social organization of cities. In the past, cities had used a combination of day policemen and part-time hired "night watchmen," both of who had little train-

Davidson College Library

ing and typically did not wear uniforms; but in 1844 they followed the lead of New York City in abolishing this informal system and using a single body of policemen. This change in social organization was further modified when boards of police commissioners were established and for the first time, over bitter opposition, policemen were required to wear uniforms. While crime increased in cities, violence on a large scale also occurred in a number of different places. Many of these violent episodes were between workers and their organizers, and employers. Other public services, such as fire protection, water, and sewage, gradually came under the jurisdiction of municipal governments. In addition, bridges, streets, streetlights, sewage facilities, educational facilities, and so on, all required large capital outlays that had to be paid by the residents of cities. The demands for these new and expanded services and a lack of institutionalized means in dealing with them led to large-scale graft, and only gradually did reform governments come into being that attempted to deal with these problems.

Up until 1830, urbanization barely kept pace with the diffusion of hundreds of thousands of settlers into the unsettled (by whites) back country, and, at most, 10 percent of the population lived in what could be considered towns, and fewer people than that lived in urban places. There was extremely rapid growth of cities four decades prior to the Civil War. Statistics showed at least fivefold increases in city growth while rural areas doubled their population. By 1860 over 20 percent of the population was living in urban places (2500 people or more). Towns and cities of this era were still "walking towns" —with few exceptions it was still possible to cross the city on foot in one day (Wade, 1963: 67–68).

By the time of the Civil War, maritime trade was still important; however, new cities had been developed and older cities began vying for interior trade. Manufacturing was beginning to be important, and in some of the larger cities as many as one in four workers was engaged in a manufacturing occupation, while in some smaller places virtually all of the labor force was so engaged. Urban growth continued after the Civil War, and mass transit made its appearance in the form of horse-drawn cars and buses and, finally, in commuter train service. These modern forms of transportation opened for residential development the areas surrounding cities, and larger suburbs came into being. In addition, development of the steamboat helped western commerce, and many new places came into being while others already in existence grew substantially. However, some places that had previously been important were not located so as to take advantage of the new transportation modes, and they decreased in size.

After the nineteenth century the excess of births over deaths and extensive immigration, along with other factors noted previously, resulted in large-scale urban population increases in the United States that were much higher than rural population increases. From around the mid-1800s through the first decade of the twentieth century, the United States became highly urbanized.

This street scene from Valparaiso, Chile, is representative of the horse-drawn buses used in U.S. cities after the Civil War.

Major contributing factors were economic forces that were made significant by the Industrial Revolution, major technological innovations, especially in manufacturing and transportation, and newly emerging economic networks among cities, the solution of some transportation problems, and the increased productivity of agricultural enterprises (Weber, 1899). Also, it should not be forgotten that the population increased threefold from around 31 million in 1860 to almost 92 million by 1910; the urban population (living in places of 2500 or more) increased from 6 million in 1860 to almost 45 million in 1910, or from 19.8 to 45.7 percent, respectively. New York City's population in 1790, when the first U.S. census was taken, was 33,000. By 1869 its population had grown to almost a million persons. Philadelphia grew from 33,000 in 1790 to slightly over one-half million in 1860. The increasing size of such places as Baltimore and Boston and the greater number of urban places were accompanied by the emergence of a national system of cities and increasing specialization in function. Virtually every city that subsequently has become a major place in the United States was established before or during this period.

The importance of transportation in the location of cities was further reinforced during this historical period. While earlier cities had been limited by the location of adequate harbors or navigable rivers and lakes, the emergence of railroad technology permitted the building of places (indeed required new places for refueling and water supplies) that had previously been outside the major transportation networks. The rise of Kansas City, Missouri, as a western railroad center and regional metropolis supplies one of the best examples of the

These emigrants departing for the United States from Naples, Italy, around 1876 are embarking upon typical ships of the era. Such vessels were crowded with people, and the density of passengers aboard ship was often equal to that shown on this dock.

influence of available real estate, local promotional efforts, and railroad location to the growth of individual cities in this era of booming regional development (Glaab and Brown, 1967: 114–115). The construction of a railroad bridge across the Missouri River at Kansas City assured its growth. Coincidentally, it should be noted that Leavenworth, Kansas, was vying for the same transportation network and influence as Kansas City. Subsequently, Leavenworth's growth has been small compared to that of Kansas City, now one of the major cities in the United States. Most cities of the Far West were founded as commercial centers, and railroad and real-estate developers were prominent in establishing their locations. Thus during this era when the urban network was substantially completed, it was influenced by the then prevailing technology and dominant transportation modality—the railroads.

While rapid urbanization of the United States was occurring, the pattern of life in these communities became altered. Cities not only absorbed large population increases, but technological changes accompanying this demographic phenomenon required changes in the human institutions of the family, religion, education, government and in how people viewed their world. Demographic changes were a result of two migrations—migration into cities from the rural areas of the United States and immigration from abroad, primarily Europe (Davis, 1966). The U.S. census reported that between 1900 and 1910 there were almost 12 million new city residents. Of these, 41 percent were immigrants from other nations; about 30 percent were migrants from rural areas in the United States; and slightly less than 22 percent were the result of natural increase—excess of births over deaths in cities. The remainder of the increase (7.6 percent) was a result of incorporating previously fringe areas into the city proper. Nevertheless, it should be noted that in spite of these substantial increases in the urban population, the rural population in the United States increased in *absolute* numbers even though the percentage decrease in rural population was substantial.

The impact of the immigration to the United States is shown by the following:

> In 1890, New York (including the still legally separate municipality of Brooklyn) contained more foreign born residents than any city in the world. The city had half as many Italians as Naples, as many Germans as Hamburg, twice as many Irish as Dublin, and two and a half times the number of Jews in Warsaw. In 1893, Chicago contained the third largest Bohemian community in the world; by the time of the First World War, Chicago ranked only behind Warsaw and Lodz as a city of Poles. Notable also was the fact that four out of five people living in greater New York in 1890 had either been born abroad or were of foreign parentage [Glaab and Brown, 1967: 139; used by permission].

These immigrant populations did not live all over the city but formed immigrant neighborhoods and ethnic ghettos. The impact of immigration was greater on eastern seaboard cities than on western and southern cities.

Around 1850 several technological innovations occurred that made it possible for cities to grow upward by constructing taller buildings as much as horse-drawn buses, and later railroads, had made it possible to expand horizontally into vacant land surrounding the city. Horizontal expansion was greatly aided by the electrification of the railways. Cast-iron columns made it possible to build higher buildings, the first skyscrapers; the invention of an efficient elevator helped move people up and down faster in these higher buildings. So while earlier cities were rather compact and expanded populations lived near their sites of work, with the advent of the electric railway around the turn of the century the more modern city began its outward expansion in earnest, and accompanying it, of course, were the first large-scale suburban developments. Early suburbanites, like those today, were primarily from the middle and upper strata of society. It should be noted here that as cities grew and expanded upward and outward, areas of formerly high population concentrations lost population; this is probably because the central part of the city was taken over by commercial and office buildings rather than because of any particular dissatisfaction with city life by the inhabitants. In other words, this loss of population in formerly densely populated areas was a consequence of intensified land use and central district land becoming too valuable for residential use.

In summary, during the nineteenth century several different trends were apparent. First, there was an increase in the number of large urban places as well as in the total population living in urban areas. Second, growth within larger urban places was greater than growth elsewhere—that is, larger metropolitan areas were growing at a faster rate than smaller urban places and rural areas. Third, substantial population growth began to occur outside of the city limits proper, and the suburbanization of the United States began. Another great leap in suburban population took place in the 1920s when the automobile became a major mode of transportation. Thereafter, the population became increasingly decentralized; and as the metropolis expanded outward, clearly defined suburbs came into being. It should be noted that most of these new suburbs also were located adjacent to earlier forms of transportation, such as electrified railway lines. Later suburbanization, of course, followed these earlier suburban developments, and again technology made possible grade separations, synchronized stoplights, and freeways and thruways for use by larger suburban populations.

Weber (1899: 158–160) noted two different processes taking place in the urban environment: (1) *differentiation,* or an increase in heterogeneity out of originally homogeneous conditions; (2) *integration,* or a growing interrelation and interdependence of parts. Thus increasing differentiation in the urban millieu, for example, territorial specialization, implies changes in territorial units but also means that these changing territorial units must be linked together—integrated—and this is accomplished through transportation systems, communications networks, and the various social systems and institutions comprising the complex social organization of the metropolis.

TWENTIETH-CENTURY
URBAN AND METROPOLITAN GROWTH

In the United States in 1800 only about 6 percent of the population lived in urban places, and on the eve of the Civil War in the 1860s only one city contained more than a million residents—New York; Philadelphia had one-half million, and Baltimore 250,000. By 1920 over one-half of the people in the United States were living in urban places. A sharp rise in birth rates and declining death rates gave an added push to the suburbanization process in the 1920s. In the 1920s and 1930s suburban development, virtually without interruption, dominated the economic, social, and political life of the United States (Wade, 1963: 75). The automobile was important in this suburban expansion. Previously, as we have already noted, the shape of urban growth was more or less determined by the capacity of public conveniences to transport the populace. Thus early suburban expansion occurred along railroad lines that radiated out from the commercial core. The automobile made possible a different kind of expansion not bounded by railroad lines; the old confinements broke, and

TABLE 3-1
U.S. Population Growth: 1790–1970

YEAR	TOTAL POPULATION	URBAN TERRITORY^a	IMMIGRANTS
1790	3,929,000	24	
1800	5,297,000	33	
1820	9,618,000	61	8,385
1840	17,120,000	131	84,066
1860	31,513,000	392	153,640
1880	50,262,000	949	457,257
1900	76,094,000	1,737	448,572
1920	106,466,000	2,722	430,001
1940	131,954,000	3,464	70,756
1950	151,326,000	4,741	326,867
1960	179,323,000	6,041	265,000
1970	203,212,000	7,062	373,000

Sources: Historical Statistics of the United States: Colonial Times to 1957, U.S. Department of Commerce, Bureau of the Census, Washington, D.C., 1960; and U.S. Bureau of the Census, *Statistical Abstract of the United States: 1973* (94th ed.), Washington, D.C., 1973.
^{a} 2,500 or more.

"urban sprawl" began in earnest. Along with urban sprawl the appearance of a shrinking revenue base for the cities came into focus for the first, but not last, time.

As westward expansion took place, there was a continued increase in the proportion of the population classified as urban except for the decade between 1930 and 1940, during which the urban percentage remained virtually the same. However, the increasing urbanization of the population began anew during the 1940s, probably a result of World War II, and by 1970 well over 70 percent of the American population lived in urban areas.

Larger cities, and the areas around them, continued to grow, and by 1970 there were over 25 urban complexes containing more than a million inhabitants; there were over 50 places with more than one-half million population, and several hundred urban areas with a population of 100,000 or more. This means, then, that there are actually many more cities 100,000 or more in size because many cities of this size are virtually lost as suburbs surrounding larger central cities such as New York, Chicago, and Los Angeles. As the population in the United States increased, a larger and larger proportion of the total population lived in urban areas. Table 3-1 illustrates the expanding total population of the United States and the increase in the number of urban territorial units, based on places with 2500 or more inhabitants. Regionally, the northeastern part of the country was the first to urbanize, and it has maintained its urbanization lead over the rest of the country. During the 1950–1960 decade, however, 5 million urban residents were added to the Californian population, and this population growth continued between 1960 and 1970. Similarly, urban areas in the South, especially Florida, and the West grew rapidly.

The increasing urbanization of the population and the coalescence of some population concentrations into contiguous urban areas has led to the notions of conurbation and metropolitanism. The term "conurbation" has been used to describe areas that previously had been distinct political and geographic units but whose population grew and joined together to form dense population masses on a scale far greater than any past cities or urban places. While typically political jurisdictions remained the same, geographic separation no longer existed (Mumford, 1955: 391).[1] The metropolitan concept includes a large central city and a much larger surrounding geographic area with a population whose social and economic activities form a more or less integrated system revolving around the central city. The more densely inhabited areas in the metropolitan complex, including the central city or cities, and the surrounding closely settled territory, make up what the U.S. Bureau of the Census calls "urbanized areas."

The metropolitan notion was made an official part of the U.S. census, and in 1950 the designation Standard Metropolitan Area (SMA) was used to denote such areas. In 1960 it was changed slightly to Standard Metropolitan Statistical Area (SMSA). By 1970 over two-thirds of the population lived in SMSAs, as delineated by the census. So we now must not only consider the urbanization of the population but its metropolitization as well. Metropolitan areas have grown faster than the rest of the United States. Thus migrant streams to cities, along with natural increases, have resulted in larger and larger proportions of the population living in metropolitan areas, especially those along the sea coasts—the East, the Gulf, and the West—and the Great Lakes.

Metropolitan areas outside of the central city have grown at a much faster pace than the central city, and in some instances the central city has actually lost population. In other cities certain areas within the central city have lost population while the central city as a whole has actually gained population. Some have suggested that the central city is in a state of decline. More appropriately, upon examining land use changes taking place in the city and the total metropolitan complex, it becomes apparent that the central city is not declining but that its function and form are changing. Even in those central cities not losing population there are some areas losing residential population; but rather than the land remaining vacant, its function is changing to more intense use and form for purposes such as offices, shopping centers, convention centers, and so on.

In more recent decades, metropolitan areas have experienced the greatest population gains, but while central cities of some smaller SMSAs grew, either minor increases or actual declines occurred in central cities of medium and larger SMSAs. Some central cities claimed growth, but upon closer inspec-

---

[1] One gets the distinct impression from Mumford's comments that the formation of conurbations was a calamity for the human race.

tion many times this was shown to be a result of the annexation of formerly unincorporated territory. Areas outside the central city have had substantial absolute and percentage increases, especially in larger metropolitan areas. Growth patterns have been greatest in the Old South, the Southwest, and on the West Coast, with substantial portions of their increases coming from net migration (more in- than outmigrants). One very obvious pattern that has been established over the past three or four decades is the increasing proportion of blacks in the population living in central cities, and of chicanos especially in the West and the Southwest (see Grebler et al., 1970: 115).

The twentieth-century metropolitan area is the product of extensive application of science to industry, the diffusion of electric power, and the advent of the automobile. Compared with earlier forms, it is the product of the accelerating technological revolution that permeates virtually all phases of life. The combination of electric power, the automobile, and modern communications technology set in motion centrifugal forces that simultaneously diffused population and industry widely over the landscape and permitted larger agglomerations of both (Hauser, 1965: 4).

Besides the notion of cities, suburbs, and fringe areas joining to form metropolitan areas, now metropolitan areas of the United States are coming together and forming the megalopolis. The *megalopolis* is made up of a number of metropolitan areas. One example of a megalopolis is the northeastern seaboard, which covers all or most of the states of Massachusetts, Rhode Island, New Jersey, and Maryland and the District of Columbia and substantial sections of New York, Pennsylvania, and Delaware and some parts of New Hampshire and Virginia. The total area is well over 50,000 square miles and contains about one out of every five persons who live in the United States. Add to this megalopolis the one developing along the Los Angeles-Orange-Riverside-San Bernardino-San Diego counties of California, and the Chicago complex, and one out of every three persons in the United States lives in a major megalopolis.

This brief survey of the origin and development of cities is based in part on legend, myth, speculation, and archeology and in part on the known origins of cities that have emerged during the period of recorded history. Four factors dominate the discussion of urban growth: (1) the size of the total population; (2) the control of natural environment, (3) technological development, and (4) developments in social organization (Hauser, 1965; Duncan, 1959). We now turn to the social organization of the population.

URBAN GROWTH AND SOCIAL ORGANIZATION

As the population became increasingly urbanized, specialization in social organization became more and more prominent. While originally the family had met virtually all of its own needs, including producing most of its own food, in some early cities increasing specialization accompanying urbanization resulted in the breaking down of such familial functions. Changing technology made it difficult for household enterprises to compete with larger-scale manufacturers. The loss of the productive function of the family was accompanied by radical changes in the family. Most family members were no longer part of the labor force, and "children were converted from a valuable resource to a charge against a wage or salary income" (Hawley, 1970: 121). No longer did the family unit process most of the food and make clothing; no longer was it the focus of recreational activities.

As the family lost functions and became more specialized, other institutions of society also became more specialized. Practically all families and their members had to develop an increasingly wider social space. Population movement and circulation were required more and more if the family was to survive. Thus family members were exposed to a wider world beyond the immediate family and neighborhood. A great deal of movement took place within cities from one area to another. Spatial movement, both migration to the city and movement within the city, resulted in a breakdown in many instances of kinship networks, mutual aid by neighbors, and primary group social controls on behavior.

The emergence of mass urban society, of increasing specialization and differentiation, ultimately resulted in a variety of homogeneous areas within the metropolitan complex with differing degrees of people interacting with each other—or "neighboring"—and a whole variety of life styles unlike those known previously. Social participation patterns changed markedly, and voluntary organizations became for many the centers of social interaction, with a decline in extended family and friend participation. Participation in and adherence to the traditional religious order declined and for many became nonexistent. For others religious participation became devoid of religious content and was used as another kind of voluntary organization.

Severe social stratification existed in early cities; as cities and urban areas in the United States grew, old social class distinctions became blurred. Nevertheless, it was clear then, as it is today, that all cities in the United States have areas that most residents can point out as being lower, middle, or upper class. The extent of social mobility increased as urbanization and industrialization in the United States occurred on a large scale and new sources of social power came into being. The greater social mobility that took place cannot be minimized just as it must be emphasized that rural migrants took over lower-level positions in the city and helped the city dweller to move up the social class ladder.

As urbanization of the United States occurred, government and its services became more specialized and increasingly took more of the earned dollar. Governmental complexity, overlap, and inefficiency became a way of life. Environmental hazards, slums, poverty, deteriorated housing and neighborhoods, and crime and violence—all became significant problems in the United States during the nineteenth and twentieth centuries. Planning became a byword, and in spite of the planning that did take place in many metropolitan areas, urban problems continued to proliferate.

WORLD POPULATION GROWTH

Elsewhere, outside of the United States, the population of the world also continued to grow and now approximates in excess of 3 billion persons. Population growth has been especially rapid during the twentieth century, and if the current rate of growth continues, the worldwide population will double in approximately 35 years. Obviously, rate of population growth is not the same in all parts of the world. In general, industrialized countries, such as the United States, have lower growth rates than less industrialized areas of the world. Currently, rates of population growth at the societal level, with very few exceptions, are simply the difference between birth and death dates and do not reflect international migration. Formerly, of course, the populations of some nations, among them the United States, grew quite rapidly because of migrants from other countries.

When we compare the growth rates of urban areas in various countries, the particular definition that each country uses becomes important. The most common definition of urban is based on population size, with the 100,000-population mark coming closest to the notion of *metropolitan* areas. Metropolitan development has been concentrated in the most industrialized nations, although some nonindustrialized nations also have large proportions of their populations living in metropolitan regions. In many countries it is interesting to note the extent to which the population is concentrated in the largest city—sometimes called the primate city. For example, in Uruguay almost one out of every three persons lives in the major, largest city, Montevideo.

Where do all of these urbanites come from? Davis (1966) suggests a threefold answer: (1) Formerly classified rural areas grow enough in population to be reclassified as urban places. (2) An excess of births over deaths results in population growth. (3) People moving from rural areas to the city increase the urban population. All of these reasons relate to either *natural growth,* an excess of births over deaths, or *migration.* Davis relies mainly on migration of people from rural areas to urban areas to explain growth.

Originally, the explanation offered for rural to urban migration was increased opportunities present in the city as a result of advancing technology, that is, industrialization. Urbanization has been occurring in almost all countries of the world, however, many of which have a low level of industrial development. In some newly developing countries the rural population is growing at a faster rate than the fast-growing urban population. In those countries the primary explanation is natural increase. On the other hand, in some countries the rural population increase is substantially lower than the increase in urban areas. The general explanation for this phenomenon is that, in contrast to earlier points in time, birth rates are fairly comparable between urban and rural people but the death rate is lower in cities because of the more extensive utilization of medical facilities and public health measures, which in turn produce a reduced mortality rate. Reduced mortality results in an excess of births over deaths and ensures an ever-expanding urban population unless birth rates are reduced or deaths increased.

BIBLIOGRAPHY: Articles

Childe, V. Gordon, "The Urban Revolution," *Town Planning Review*, 21 (1950–1951): 3–17.
Russell, Josiah C., "The Metropolitan City Region of the Middle Ages," *Journal of Regional Science*, 2 (No. 2, 1960): 55–70.
Schlesinger, Arthur M., "The City in American History," *Mississippi Valley Historical Review*, 27 (June 1940): 43–66.
Sjoberg, Gideon, "The Preindustrial City," *American Journal of Sociology*, 60 (March 1955): 438–446.
Wade, Richard C., "The City in History—Some American Perspectives," in Werner Z. Hirsch (ed.), *Urban Life and Form*, New York: Holt, Rinehart and Winston, 1963, pp. 59–79.
White, Lynn, "Technology and Invention in the Middle Ages," *Speculum*, 15 (1940): 141–156.

BIBLIOGRAPHY: Books

Childe, V. Gordon, *What Happened in History*, New York: Penguin Books, 1946.
Davis, Kingsley, "The Urbanization of the Human Population,' in *Cities, A Scientific American Book*, New York: Alfred A. Knopf, 1966, pp. 3–24.
Duncan, Otis Dudley, "Human Ecology and Population Studies," in Philip M. Hauser and Otis Dudley Duncan (eds.), *The Study of Population: An Inventory and Appraisal*, Chicago: University of Chicago Press, 1959.
East, Gordon, *An Historical Geography of Europe*, London: Methuen & Company, 1966 (fifth ed.).
Gibbon, Edward, *Decline and Fall of the Roman Empire*, Vol. II, New York: Modern Library, 1932.
Glabb, Charles N., and A. Theodore Brown, *A History of Urban America*, New York: Macmillan Company, 1967.
Grebler, Leo, Joan W. Moore, and Ralph C. Guzman, *The Mexican-American People*, New York: The Free Press, 1970.
Hauser, Philip M., "Urbanization: An Overview," in Philip M. Hauser and Leo F. Schnore (eds.), *The Study of Urbanization*, New York: John Wiley & Sons, 1965, pp. 1–47.
Hawley, Amos H., *Urban Society: An Ecological Approach*, New York: Ronald Press, 1971.
Historical Statistics of the United States: Colonial Time to 1957, Washington, D.C.: Bureau of Census, 1960.
Jones, A. H. M., *The Decline of the Ancient World*, New York: Holt, Rinehart, and Winston, 1966.
Mumford, Lewis, "The Natural History of Urbanization," in W. O. Thomas, Jr. (ed.), *Man's Role in Changing the Face of the Earth*, Chicago: University of Chicago Press, 1955, pp. 382–398.

Passonneau, Joseph R., "Emergence of City Form," in Werner Z. Irsch (ed.), *Urban Life and Form*, New York: Holt, Rinehart and Winston, 1963, pp. 9–27.

Pirenne, Henri, *Economic and Social History of Medieval Europe*, New York: Harcourt Brace Jovanovich, 1937.

Pirenne, Henri, *Medieval Cities*, Princeton, N.J. Princeton University Press, 1939.

Russell, Josiah C., *Late Ancient and Medieval Population*, Philadelphia: American Philosophical Society, 1958.

Sjoberg, Gideon, *The Preindustrial City*, New York: The Free Press, 1960.

Weber, Adna F., *The Growth of Cities in the Nineteenth Century*, Ithaca, N.Y.: Cornell University Press, 1963 (original publication date was 1899).

Weber, Max, *The City* (trans. and ed. by Don Martindale and Gertrude Neuwirth), New York: The Free Press, 1958.

CHAPTER 4
LOCATION OF URBAN PLACES

INTRODUCTION

The location and the distribution of cities and urban settlements have been studied since the beginning of the nineteenth century. These studies typically view city location as a *dependent variable*. That is, why are cities and urban settlements located where they are? The study of urban places is important because location is related to the *type* of urban place (as explored in the next chapter), and it helps explain the variation among urban places and within them as well. For example, a city such as Birmingham, Alabama, is located near natural resources necessary for steel manufacturing; thus we have a manufacturing city. On the other hand, Des Moines, Iowa, is more of a central place or market city primarily servicing a local hinterland. A service city implies a substantially different function *and* internal differentiation of social classes, and so on, than a manufacturing city.

Four somewhat overlapping frames of reference have dominated the study of the location of urban places. First was the emphasis placed explicitly or implicitly on the central place notion, which suggests that places perform services for surrounding areas—their hinterlands or influence areas. Second, focus has been placed on the importance of transportation places, that is, places that perform break-of-bulk and allied services along transport routes supported by areas that may be at remote distances but are closely connected because of the strategic location of the city on transport channels prevailing at any given moment. Third, specialized function places perform one service, such as mining, or several services, such as a military garrison or a recreation city, for large numbers of the population. Fourth is the urban hierarchy notion, which in many respects is closely allied to the central place orientation.

CENTRAL PLACE THEORY

The work of von Thünen, first published in 1826, postulated that under ideal conditions of an entirely uniform land surface a city would develop in the

The kinds of work available in a city depend to a considerable extent on city type. Thus steelworkers are found only in such cities as Birmingham, Pittsburgh, and Fontana, California.

center of the land area and concentric rings of land use around the city. Subsequently, Christaller argued that a certain amount of productive land is necessary to support an urban place. In general, this idea assumes that the larger the city the larger its supporting land, or hinterland. This relationship is reciprocal, since

> there should be cities of varying size ranging from a small hamlet performing a few simple functions, such as providing a limited shopping and market center for a small contiguous area, up to a large city with a large tributary area composed of the service areas of many smaller towns and providing more complex services, such as wholesaling, large-scale banking, specialized retailing, and the like [Ullman, 1941].

Services oriented toward the surrounding hinterland are termed "central functions" and places performing them are central places. According to von Thünen's orientation, each of these hinterlands would be circular in nature with the city at the center. Lösch (1938), however, suggested that the best shape to fill all of the geometric space is hexagonal. Other features of central place theory as modified by Christaller are as follows:

1. The basic function of a city is to be a central place providing goods and services for a surrounding tributary area. The term "central place" is used

because to perform such a function efficiently a city locates at the center of minimum travel of its influence area.

2. The centrality of a city is an indication of the degree to which it is such a service center; the greater the centrality of a place, the higher its "order," that is, the greater its influence upon surrounding areas.

3. Higher-order places offer more goods, have more establishments and kinds of businesses, larger populations, tributary areas, and tributary populations, do greater volumes of business, and are more widely spaced than lower-order places.

4. Low-order places provide only low-order goods, such as foodstuffs, to low-order influence areas; these low-order goods are generally necessities requiring frequent purchasing with little consumer travel. Moreover, low-order goods are provided by establishments with relatively low conditions of entry. Conversely, high-order places provide not only low-order goods but also high-order goods sold by high-order establishments with greater conditions of entry. These high-order goods are generally "shopping goods," such as television sets and appliances, for which the consumer is willing to travel longer distances, although less frequently. The higher the order of goods provided, the fewer the establishments providing them, the greater the conditions of entry and trade areas of the establishments, and the fewer and more widely spaced the towns in which the establishments are located. The number of businesses increases as their order diminishes. Since higher-order places offer more shopping opportunities, their trade areas for low-order goods are likely to be larger than those of low-order places, since consumers have the opportunity to combine purposes on a single trip, and this acts like a price reduction.

5. Central places can be arranged in a hierarchy comprising discreet groups of centers. Centers of each higher-order group perform all the functions of lower-order centers plus some central functions that differentiate them from and set them above the lower order. A consequence is the "nesting" pattern shown in Figure 4-1 of lower-order trade areas within the trade area of higher-order centers, plus a hierarchy of routes joining the centers.

Figure 4-1 illustrates Christaller's hexagonal network of urban places and also shows how smaller and larger places are "nested" to give differing but overlapping influence or hinterland areas. Table 4-1 gives the ideal distance apart whereby places would be given a uniform flat land surface, the population of each kind of place would have, the size of its tributary area, and the population of the tributary area according to central place theory. Thus the size, spacing, and functions of places all are interrelated.

An evaluation of the central place theory must focus on two different aspects. First, at least in the idealized model, there is the explicit notion of a system of places distributed in a rather specific geometric form (see Figure 4-1). Second, there is also the explicit notion of tributary, hinterland, or influence areas that are characteristic of each place. Conceivably, central place theory could be an accurate description of one aspect but not the other.

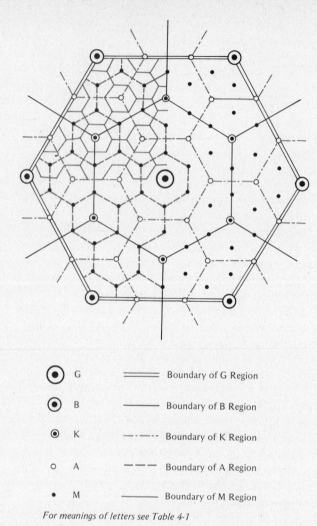

◉	G	═══════ Boundary of G Region
◉	B	──────── Boundary of B Region
⊙	K	─·──·──· Boundary of K Region
○	A	─ ─ ─ ─ Boundary of A Region
•	M	──────── Boundary of M Region

For meanings of letters see Table 4-1

Figure 4-1. Christaller's Hexagonal Network of Urban Places.

Christaller and Lösch, both German, were aware of the empirical distributions of places and population in Germany at the time of their writing; thus it is not too surprising that much of what they describe roughly fits the distribution of places for at least a part of Germany during the beginning of the twentieth century. However, whether the central place frame of reference fits other societies and other times is a crucial question. Ullman (1941) notes that "Many nonindustrial regions of relatively uniform land surface have cities distributed so evenly over the land that some sort of central-place theory appears to be the prime explanation."

TABLE 4-1
Towns and Hinterland in Germany: Distance, Size, and Population[a]

CENTRAL PLACE	TOWNS		HINTERLAND	
	DISTANCE APART (KM.)	POPULATION	SIZE (SQ. KM.)	POPULATION
Market Center (M)	7	800	45	2,700
Township Center (A)	12	1,500	135	8,100
County Seat (K)	21	3,500	400	24,000
District City (B)	36	9,000	1,200	75,000
Small State Capital (G)	62	27,000	3,600	225,000
Provincial Head City	108	90,000	10,800	675,000
Regional Capital City	186	300,000	32,400	2,025,000

[a] Used by permission and adapted from Edward Ullman, "A Theory of Location for Cities," *American Journal of Sociology*, 46 (May 1941): 853–864.

According to Thomlinson, "research indicates that the scheme is not too different from existing urban networks in many of the Midwest and Great Plains states in the United States. On the other hand, it is not well suited to coastal areas with river-mouth sites or to mountainous sections (where there are relatively few cities anyway)" (1969: 129). In spite of the still current discussions of central place theory (including this one), very little research has actually been accomplished testing the hexagonal network hypothesis. The most that can be said at this point is that there is a possibility that central place networks may grossly fit the hexagonal distribution in certain parts of the world, including parts of the United States. It should be noted that where the distribution apparently does approximate that suggested by the theory, one of the given conditions of a relatively uniform land surface is met, and, typically, these very same regions are predominantly agricultural in nature, with the central places being primarily service centers.

A number of studies have been accomplished that have investigated hinterlands, tributary or influence areas of places. Virtually all of these studies show that the hinterlands of a place can be measured along a variety of dimensions. As an example, an elaborate study of the "ecological differentiation of habits and attitudes" conducted in Sweden by Swedner (1960) shows that places are differently related to the surrounding area, that hinterland or influence areas vary by place, and that services within any given place have varying tributary areas depending upon the service provided. For some services the hinterland is relatively large, for instance, the newspaper from the larger place in the region studied, whereas the cinema's, the pharmacy's, and the hairdresser's hinterlands were smaller though still larger than those of churches, sports grounds, and grocery stores. Not one of these service hinterlands has a hexagonal or concentric shape; on the contrary, their shapes are variegated and

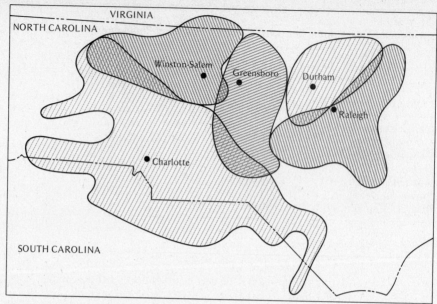

Figure 4-2. Out-of-Town Accounts for Selected Department Stores in Raleigh, Durham, Greensboro, Winston-Salem, and Charlotte. Each shaded area represents the generalized shape of the charge-account area of the indicated city based on the locations of towns of 500 or more population with at least 20 charge accounts per 1000 inhabitants. *Used by permission, Chapin, 1965.*

directional in the sense that the hinterland of most of the services extends geographically much farther in some directions than others, thus resulting in elongated shapes.

Patterns of service utilization also have been studied for the North Carolina Piedmont region by Pfouts (1962). His analysis suggests that each of the major cities in the industrialized Piedmont region has a rather clearly defined hinterland area, although it varies somewhat by the service measured. Also, his analysis shows quite clearly that there is an overlapping of hinterlands and that in no case could they be described as circular or hexagonal. As Figures 4-2 and 4-3 indicate, there is a variety of shapes that varies by place, service, and how that service is differentially measured.

From a central place theoretical perspective, population size alone is not a true measure of the importance of a place. It is the central place aspects that make the city important. How large a hinterland does the place serve? From this orientation one might predict that certain places would decrease or, at the minimum, not grow if technology changed or if the demand for certain kinds of services changed. The dieselization of the railroad had such an effect on some places (Cottrell, 1951); similarly, we might expect that with better roads and automobiles many small towns that formerly served as local service

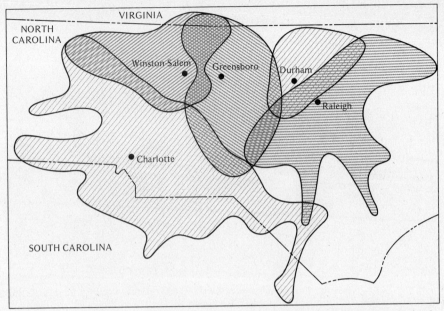

Figure 4-3. Out-of-Town Charge Accounts for Selected Department Stores in Raleigh, Durham, Greensboro, Winston-Salem, and Charlotte. Each shaded area represents the generalized shape of the charge-account area of the indicated city based on the locations of towns of 100 or more population with at least 15 charge accounts per 1000 inhabitants. *Used by permission, Chapin, 1965.*

centers would decline in importance. It is thus assumed that the centralization of activities and population in larger centers, tied to technological changes taking place, especially in transportation, might result in a decline of smaller places (Fuguitt and Thomas, n.d.).

Since Christaller's contribution the theory has evolved in several different ways. Lösch showed how a complete economic landscape can be created, based upon a general concept of hierarchies. He suggested an economic landscape characterized by densely developed and sparsely developed sectors radiating from the metropolis. While a hierarchy of transport routes exists in this landscape, places performing the same number of functions do not necessarily provide the same types of functions. More recently, Berry and Garrison (1958) have shown how the theory may also apply to the arrangement of business centers within cities.

Criticisms of the theory have revolved around the arguments that (1) central place theory is not a general theory of location for all cities (i.e., it only applies to trade centers); (2) it must be supplemented by theories applying, for example, to industrial cities; (3) the patterns of hexagonal trade areas in the ideal model illustrating the principle of marketing are not found in reality; and (4) it assumes a flat geographic surface without any major topographic breaks.

The importance of water transportation resulted in canals being built for the transportation of agricultural products and goods between the east and the west. In this 1874 etching, a side-wheel steamship on the Hudson River acts as tow for a group of grain barges en route from the New York State Canal to New York City.

Rather than being a general theory of cities, central place theory is a theory of location of tertiary activities or services. It is more limited than Christaller originally thought because other principles are needed, yet more general because it also applies *within* cities. Indeed, no one really expects to find an ideal case anywhere in the real world.

A further criticism is that there is no steplike hierarchy, but rather a continuum. Placing these criticisms in context, they accept the general features of Christaller's statement but reject the specific ideas of groups, steps, and regularly ordered nesting. Whether or not such a criticism is valid can only be answered by carrying out more extensive empirical work.

TRANSPORTATION AND URBAN LOCATION

The brief historical development of urban places and locations presented in Chapter 3 illustrated the importance that waterways and other transportation modes played in early urban settlement patterns. Virtually all of the first great urban concentrations were located on navigable rivers or at locations suitable for seaports, and this has also been true of the United States. Later, when technology made possible the building of larger and larger vessels, which could not navigate the same waters as earlier sailing vessels had, many of these seaports declined in importance. Some places that were located at the fall lines of rivers were able to maintain some importance because of their power-producing capabilities.

A break-in-transportation is illustrated by this facility located in Portland, Oregon, which is used to transfer products and goods between ships and railroad or truck carriers.

One of the first theories of place location emphasizing transportation was advanced by Cooley (1894). He stated that "population and wealth tend to collect wherever there is a break in transportation." Duncan and others (1960: 25) note that the break-in-transportation and central place notions are not necessarily completely separate ideas. Cooley observed that breaks in transportation may occur at a center where commodities are brought together for larger-scale movements. Given a uniform land surface and uniform transportation modes, it could be expected that central place and transport places would coincide; however, since these conditions seldom, if ever, prevail, the feature of transport places probably is a specific site factor. Especially in earlier times but even today a water site that can handle cargo-carrying vessels is a prime location for urban growth.

Transport routes alone do not produce a city, but, as Cooley noted, where break of bulk occurs—such as transferring goods from larger ships to smaller vessels or from one mode of transportation to another, say, from ship to rail—an urban center is likely to develop. Ullman (1941) gives an example of the simple break-of-bulk and storage ports of Port Arthur-Fort William at the head of Lake Superior. They are surrounded by unproductive land, yet "they have risen at the break-of-bulk points on the cheapest route from the wheat-producing Prairie Provinces to the markets of the East."

Cooley also pointed out the special importance of waterways to early settlement patterns. Duncan and others (1960) followed up Cooley's notions and reported the breakdown (presented in Table 4-2) of the distribution of central cities of 100,000 or more by the census year in which they first attained that

TABLE 4-2
Distribution of Standard Metropolitan Areas with Central Cities of 100,000 or More by Census Year in Which That Size Was First Reported, by Type of Location, United States: 1950[a]

| | | TYPE OF LOCATION | | |
YEAR	ALL SMSAS WITH CENTRAL CITIES OF 100,000 OR MORE	SEA OR LAKE COAST	NAVIGABLE RIVER	ALL OTHER LOCATIONS
1820–1840	3	3	0	0
1850–1880	14	9	5	0
1890–1920	42	10	14	18
1930–1950	35	10	8	17
Total	94	32	27	35

Source: Used by permission. Otis Dudley Duncan et al., *Metropolis and Region* (1960: 24).

size. Table 4-2 illustrates the importance, even the recent importance, of waterways in the growth and location of the larger cities in the United States. While the influence of waterways appears to be diminishing, over one-half of the cities that reached the 100,000 size between 1930 and 1950 still were located on waterways. Cooley, of course, was aware of other forms of transportation and their relationship to locations of settlements.

After the development of railroad technology, for instance, both in the United States and elsewhere, some strategic locations were along railroad lines. The railroad brought with it a migrant population and fixed intervals at which fuel and water stops had to be made. These in turn brought into being many places; and where repair shops and exchange points — break of bulk — were necessary, larger urban settlements came into being. Cottrell (1951) later illustrated the influence that the technological change from steam to diesel locomotives had upon the elimination of some of these places. Railroad centers no longer needed to be so close together for fueling and watering purposes, and after the advent of the diesel locomotive many settlements either vanished or in some instances were able to survive by changing their functions; that is, they continued to exist but, typically, as *smaller* places.

Location along streetcar and electric railway lines also was an important influence in settlement patterns *within* metropolitan areas. For example, in the Los Angeles region (including Orange, Riverside, and San Bernardino counties), the big Red Cars (Crump, 1962) of the Pacific Electric Railway laid down the basic grid for that region. Figure 4-4 is a map of the rail lines of the

Figure 4-4. Lines of the Pacific Electric Railway in Southern California. *From Crump, 1970, by permission of the author.*

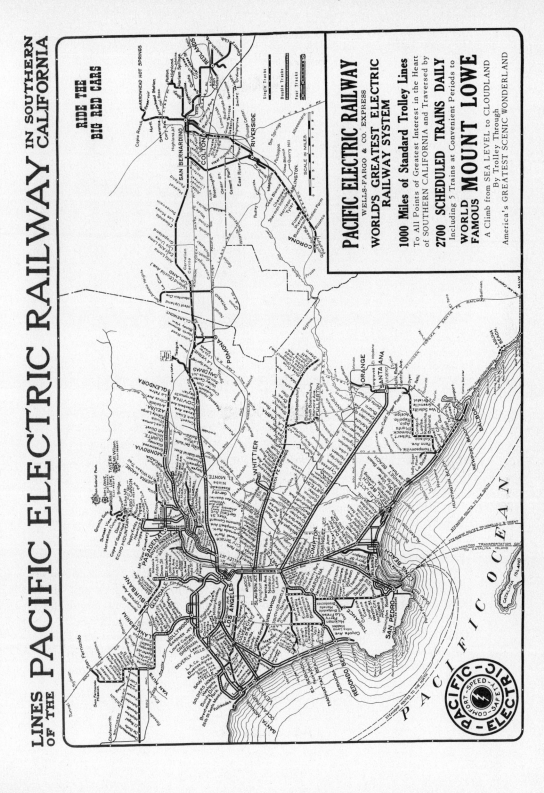

Locations near the interchanges and access ramps of interstate highways, thruways, and freeways are key locations desired for both commercial enterprises and residential locations. Such locations will undoubtedly be the focal points of future growth. Note the once-rural farm in lower left that has been swallowed up by suburban housing developments.

1920s and 1930s; this is essentially a map of the current major freeways in that region.

Highways too have become important in place location. The rapid growth of the interstate highway system might be expected to have an extensive influence upon the future settlement of new places and the growth of some small places (Cook, 1968).

In summary, it is quite apparent that changes in transportation technology influence the pattern of urban settlements. The development of metal hulls and engine-powered ships changed the importance of many early cities in the United States; later, the growth of railroads brought into being many places, some by necessity for water and refueling and others by speculation of railroad and real-estate people. Subsequently, changing technology made possible the development of the diesel engine. Trains could make longer trips without water and refueling, thus leading to the decline of many former railroad towns. The automobile and widespread development of highways resulted in a shift away from railroads and a filling in of interstitial sites between railroad lines. Finally, the growth of the interstate highway system and the increasing importance of air travel probably will help shape urban settlement patterns of the future.

SPECIALIZED FUNCTIONS AND URBAN LOCATION

Aside from central place locations and the stress upon transportation, there are places that are unusual in the influence that highly localized resources or environmental conditions have in the establishment of their location. These *specialized function places* may be recreational centers, political capitals, garrison cities, or places that have certain natural phenomena such as mineral ores nearby. For example, cities such as Scranton and Wilkes-Barre and other closelying towns are specialized coal-mining centers developed near anthracite coal deposits. "Pittsburgh and its suburbs and satellites form a nationally significant iron-and-steel manufacturing cluster favored by good location for the assembly of coal and iron ore and for the sale of steel to industries on the coal fields" (Ullman, 1941). Resort cities such as Miami, which developed as a result of a favorable climate and beach, also fall into the specialized function category. These cities will be further described under specialized function places in various typologies that we will discuss in the next chapter on city and urban typologies.

Ullman notes that, once begun, a specialized function place acts as a nucleus for similar and related activities. Once the city develops along certain specialized lines, it may require satellite services and industries. Plants may be required for making specialized parts. Thus, New York City has a large-scale clothing manufacturing industry, Grand Rapids is known for its furniture, and one usually thinks of automobiles when Detroit is mentioned. In the case of a resort community, ancillary services come into being to meet the needs of the large visiting population.

Specialization in function requires a varying division of labor and may result in a completely different social climate in cities with different specialized functions. In the next chapter on city and urban typologies we describe some places with specialized functions in more detail. Virtually every typology that is discussed has a congeries category of specialized cities indicating that these types have to be considered in any theory of urban and place location.

THE URBAN HIERARCHY

The hypothesis that cities fall into some kind of hierarchical arrangement "implies that a collection of cities, if properly delimited, may be regarded as a *system*" (Duncan et al., 1960: 6, italics in original). The hierarchy notion elaborates upon the concept of central place discussed earlier in this chapter. Central place theory assumes places of varying sizes performing a variety of services and serving different hinterlands. Intensive study of cities leads us to the conclusion that there is an urban hierarchy in the United States closely related to size of place.

Explicit recognition of the notion of a "system of cities" has come about only within the past two or three decades. This recognition represents the convergence of a number of different approaches to cities but always includes

Political capitals tend to be specialized function places surrounding a capitol like this one in Des Moines, Iowa.

some reference to the hierarchical aspect of the system (Duncan et al., 1960: 47). Obviously, the central place theory is relevant here, since it has an explicitly elaborated hierarchical scheme of places such as market hamlet, township center, county seat, district city, small state capital, provincial head city, and regional capital city. Thus population size, the spacing of centers, and a hinterland are specified for each level of the hierarchy.

In addition, there are at least three other kinds of approaches that have been prominent: (1) classification of centers according to levels in the hierarchy, (2) the "rank-size" rule, and (3) the correlates of city size.[1] Those who have empirically examined centers according to size category determine the kinds of services and goods that are available by different sizes of places. Thus a place of a given size category is expected to have specified levels of employment in banking, insurance, wholesale trade, daily newspapers, a university or college, and a certain size hospital. Smaller places in the hierarchy are expected to have less employment or none in these areas of endeavor and smaller facilities or none at all and perhaps a specified number of facilities such as banks, shopping facilities, theaters, and so on. (See Swedner, 1960, for an elaborate empirical illustration of the distribution of goods and services by size of place.)

Rank-size adherents note that beginning with the largest city the

[1] This section borrows heavily from Duncan et al., (1960), Chap. 3: "The Urban Hierarchy." Also see Hauser (1963: 5).

TABLE 4-3
The Actual Number of Urbanized Areas of 100,000 or More in the United States as of 1950 and the Calculated Number Using the Pareto Curve Formula

SIZE	CALCULATED	ACTUAL
1,000,000+	12.5	12
500,000−	12.1	13
300,000−	15.3	17
200,000−	20.8	18
150,000−	19.8	22
125,000−	15.9	16
100,000−	23.6	21

Sources: Used by permission. See footnote 2 for the Pareto curve formula; data are from Duncan et al., 1960: 53.

frequency of cities increases as size decreases. This relationship is mathematically constant. The earliest work on rank-size was accomplished by the application of Vilfredo Pareto's inverse exponential law of income distribution to the distribution of cities by size. Subsequently the Pareto notion was slightly altered for all nations except those with a primate city, to suggest that a second-ranked city should be one-half as large as the biggest city, the third-ranked city one-third as large, and so on.

Duncan and others (1960: 53–54) present an example of an approach patterned after Pareto to discern an urban hierarchy. Using 1950 U.S. census data for the 119 urbanized areas of 100,000 or more inhabitants, they used the formula for the Pareto curve[2] to determine whether they fit empirically. Table 4-3 illustrates the number of urbanized areas in specified size intervals deduced from an application of the formula as compared with the actual number; the data suggest that they found a rather high correlation.

For these data as well as other analyses based upon the formulas of Pareto or Zipf, the rank-size rule does reasonably well in giving a good fit to the empirical distribution of cities in different countries and at varying times. As cities grow, it might be assumed that the rank-size rule would be violated; however, it appears that once the distribution of cities is operative, "individual cities grow larger as the system enlarges, but the over-all shape of the urban distribution remains approximately the same" (Thomlinson, 1969: 140).

The final approach that Duncan and his colleagues suggested is the examination of the correlates of community size. This work, as they noted, has not relied upon any particular scheme of a hierarchy but simply uses size as a basis for classification. According to them, "if social and economic characteristics of cities can be shown to vary with community size in a systematic fash-

[2] The Pareto formula is as follows: $y = Ax^{-a}$, where x is the number of inhabitants of a community (size), y is the number of cities of size x or larger, and A and a are empirical parameters estimated from the size distribution; in the example presented in Table 4–3 (from Duncan et al., 1960: 53), the formula is $y = 10^6 \times 9.8528\ x^{-.98356}$.

ion, any viable theory of urban hierarchy must be able to account for such relationships or at least show that they are not incompatible with assumptions of the theory" (Duncan et al., 1960: 55). As a result of analyses using 1950 industry composition data, they concluded that there is an urban hierarchy in the United States insofar as manufacturing is concerned, while there is a regional (northeastern, north-central, southern, and western) hierarchy in services. Thus in their view there is a hierarchical system of cities in the United States that "is more or less adequately indicated by city size."

In an elaborate analysis of 1950 U.S. census data, Duncan and Reiss (1956) showed that there are many systematic differences in age and sex characteristics, race and nativity, marital status and family characteristics, mobility, education, labor force and occupational characteristics and income by size of place. As an example, median cash income is directly related to size of place, and they note that this relationship holds for subcategories by sex, age, race, and region of the United States (p. 37). Further, there is some evidence to suggest that the degree of income inequality is inversely related to size of place; this is only one example of the many differences they reported.

CONCLUSIONS

Given the evidence presented in this chapter, it seems reasonable to agree with Duncan et al., who stated: "It appears to be a workable hypothesis that nearly every city has a more or less standard repertoire of functions performed for its own inhabitants and for its immediate continuous 'hinterland' — comprising the area which it serves and upon which it depends most closely, in conformity with the central-place scheme" (1960: 5). Nevertheless, in evaluating their analyses of different approaches to the urban hierarchy, they concluded that "the differentiation and specialization of service trades with increasing city size can be explained to only a small degree by principles stemming from the central-place scheme" (Duncan et al., 1960: 80, italics in original). They further note that at least three other principles must be added:

1. "Conditions of life in large cities generate certain 'needs' or 'tastes' not typical of small cities."
2. "As city size increases, certain services performed by households or business units for themselves are demanded in sufficient quantity to support specialized units supplying them."
3. "With increasing city size, services performed by generalized units are taken over in part by units specialized in a restricted line of services."

A limitation of the central place system is "the failure of actual conditions to conform with the assumption of the system"; also, "the number and boundaries of categories in the system are necessarily arbitrary to greater or lesser degree" (Duncan et al., 1960: 49). Duncan and his colleagues (1960: 27) further suggested that the extraordinarily large variety of geographic settings and locations of cities may lead one to "despair of success in accounting for locational-functional patterns except in terms of specific historical analysis of individual places." Another major complication is that over time different factors may describe why any one place is where it is located, why it has grown, and why other locales do not have a place, or may have declined. Further, a prerequisite for attaining large size may be diversification of activities accompanied by several locational advantages. In addition, Duncan and others (1960: 29–30) described "the complex and contingent" character of events leading to a founding of a city, its subsequent growth and the "structural elaboration" that occurs over time, and how "the evaluation of the city's locational advantages must be periodically revised as essentially new locational influences come into play."

Thus we must conclude that although there are several theories of urban and place location, the most they do in their current state is to sensitize us to some factors of the subject. They leave us with some currently unexplained statistical uniformity that apparently underlies the distribution of urban places.

BIBLIOGRAPHY: Articles

Berry, Brian J. L., and W. L. Garrison, "Recent Developments in Central Place Theory," *Papers and Proceedings of the Regional Science Association,* 4 (1958): 107–120.

Cook, Daniel W., "Cosmopolis: A New Cities Proposal," *New Mexico Quarterly,* 38 (Summer 1968): 83–89.

Cooley, Charles H., "The Theory of Transportation," *Publications of the American Economic Association,* 9 (May 1894): 179–208.

Cottrell, W. Fred, "Death by Dieselization: A Case Study in the Reaction to Technological Change," *American Sociological Review,* 16 (June 1951), 358–365.

Fuguitt, Glen V., and Donald W. Thomas, "Small Town Growth in the United States: An Analysis by Size, Class and by Place," unpublished paper, n.d.

Hauser, Philip M., "Urbanization: An Overview," in Philip M. Hauser and Leo F. Schnore (eds.), *The Study of Urbanization,* New York: John Wiley & Sons, 1965, pp. 1–47.

Lösch, August, "The Nature of Economic Regions," *Southern Economic Journal,* 5 (1938): 71–78.

Pfouts, Ralph W., "Patterns of Economic Interaction in the Crescent," in F. Stuart Chapin, Jr. and Shirley F. Weiss, (eds.), *Urban Growth Dynamics,* New York: John Wiley & Sons, Inc. 1962, pp. 31–58.

Ullman, Edward, "A Theory of Location for Cities," *American Journal of Sociology,* 46 (May 1941): 853–864.

BIBLIOGRAPHY: Books

Chapin, F. Stuart, Jr., *Urban Land Use Planning,* Urbana, Ill.: University of Illinois Press, 1965.

Crump, Spencer, *Ride the Big Red Cars,* rev. ed., Corona del Mar, Calif.: Trans-Anglo
      Books, 1970.
Duncan, Otis Dudley, and Albert J. Reiss, Jr., *Social Characteristics of Urban and
      Rural Communities,* 1950, New York: John Wiley & Sons, Inc., 1956.
Duncan, Otis Dudley, W. Richard Scott, Stanley Lieberson, Beverly Duncan, and Hal
      H. Winsborough, *Metropolis and Region,* Baltimore, Md.: The Johns
      Hopkins Press, 1960.
Swedner, Harald, *Ecological Differentiation of Habits and Attitudes,* Lund, Sweden:
      CWK Gleerup, 1960.
Thomlinson, Ralph, *Urban Structure: The Social and Spatial Character of Cities,* New
      York: Random House, 1969.

CHAPTER 5
CITY AND URBAN TYPOLOGIES—
AND THEIR CONSEQUENCES

INTRODUCTION

Historically, it appears that cities and urban centers have had different functions, and as these functions changed, there have been rises and losses of population. Almost all cities have had administrative agencies through which nonagricultural needs were met. Prehistoric towns probably came into being to serve as places of protection during times of attack and crisis. Somewhat later, it appears that population concentrations were located primarily along waterways and caravan routes where trade was prevalent. Specialization subsequently began with a few towns becoming regional administrative centers. Locations where land and water trade routes intersected became strategic points, and life was highly organized in these centers.

By the time the Greek Empire had emerged, cities began to expand their trade and administrative functions and city-states were becoming more complex. City size continued to increase, and Rome, evidently the largest city at that time, had an extraordinary administrative organizational structure so that it could control its far-flung empire. The Roman Empire primarily consisted of city territories whose size and importance depended mainly on the extent of its administrative responsibility. After the decline of the Roman Empire there was an era during which towns and cities reverted back to earlier forms; however, beginning with the revival of trade several centuries later, places once again began to grow and became more complex and differentiated from each other. Eventually, of course, the New World was "discovered" and immigration took place to the Western hemisphere.

The colonization of the United States resulted in the building of many new places, and as the frontier expanded, other places came into being; many of them began to grow large and perform different functions. As urbanization and industrialization took place in this country, places became more specialized and differentiated from each other. Finally, social scientists began to realize that in urbanized societies, such as the United States, places serve different

Le Mont Saint-Michel in France had an ideal location for protection against attack during the twelfth through sixteenth centuries, when the great church was constructed. It could be supplied by land at low tide and by sea at high tide.

functions and can be classified in many different ways.

> What a city does depends so closely on where it is that function and location seem like the two sides of a coin. Deep-water ports are busy with commerce and trade. An urban concentration of chemical industries arises in a valley endowed by nature with bituminous coal deposits, pools of petroleum, pockets of natural gas, sources of brines and an abundance of water. "Gateway" cities collect the produce of agricultural belts and distribute it over wide regions [Duncan et al., 1960: 23].

Other types of places depend upon different kinds of environmental characteristics that lead to increasing specialization.

In addition, technology has an impact on location as it does on function. Perhaps even more fundamentally, although at times it may be forgotten or ignored, a society must have values that make cities and/or population concentrations useful to it before cities can come into being (Bendix, 1959). Further, it should be noted that not all good locations are being utilized for cities. Also, what is now considered a poor location may in the future be considered a good one, depending upon changing technology and social values. The complex relations among location, environment, technology, and values suggest that the opportunity for different *types of cities* certainly exists.

Typologies of cities generally assume that *latent* dimensions underly the characteristics of cities. They have as their goal the reduction of *within-category differences,* that is, producing types of cities that are as much alike as possible along the dimensions considered important; thus the differences that exist are *among* types of cities. Classification of cities and metropolitan areas can be accomplished in many different ways: by using many different criteria, one or a variety of dimensions, and different methodological techniques. However, city typologies are useful only if we learn more about cities in the process.

Typologies and classification systems help us to learn more about cities: (1) They summarize and compress a great deal of available information into a systematic framework so that order is possible; (2) They assist in identifying phenomena of strictly local and of more general distribution; (3) They are an indispensable step toward a realistic assessment of a better community; (4) They help locate the key dimensions that describe the city; (5) They provide the basis for a data framework that can examine changes in the city over time; (6) Used judicially, they can be an important element in policy and decision making; (7) They facilitate hypothesis testing; and (8) They may provide guidelines for the selection of specific types of places for sampling frameworks (Arnold, 1972: 370–372; Berry, 1972a: 1–2).

In addition to all of the facets pointed out previously, perhaps the most important potential use of the variety of city and metropolitan classifications and typologies available is in explaining other differences in cities — that is, to utilize city type as an *independent* variable. Thus, there is a wide variation in how much cities spend on health, education, and so on. Further, there may be systematic difference in how cities are spatially arranged, for example, racial minorities and lower social classes by type of place. However, Schnore and Winsborough suggest that ''these classificatory schemes have been sadly underemployed in urban research. The determinants, concomitants, and consequences of city functions have *not* been carefully explored by scholars in the field of urban studies'' (1972: 125).

Urban places may be classified according to age, size, shape, demographic composition, street pattern, density, land use, dependence, function, and by an array of other factors, such as power structure, government type, and so on. Thus, diverse frameworks have been used as a starting point for attempts at putting together meaningful classifications of places and cities. One approach has been to classify cities by functional type based primarily upon the dominant economic activity taking place there. Harris (1943) followed this approach when he grouped each city on the basis of economic activities as measured by occupational statistics. Others (Price, 1942) have used a variety of indicators to approach the problem of describing cities. We shall discuss these orientations shortly and give some early and more recent examples of the *functional typology* and the *multivariate typology* approaches to city classification.

More than educational services are provided in a university city. These students at Xavier must also have shelter, must purchase food and clothing, and require the availability of recreational services.

FUNCTIONAL TYPOLOGIES[1]

Harris (1943) argued that it had been long recognized that cities differed in their functions, but, generally, the criteria for such classifications were sadly lacking: A variety of writers had loosely identified cities as industrial, commercial, mining, university, and resort towns (Gist and Fava, 1964: 80) while others referred to them as manufacturing or production centers, centers

[1] Each author's own terminology is used in describing the specific studies reviewed in this chapter. This is made necessary by the fact that some of the studies examined used central cities as the unit of analysis while others use urbanized areas, SMSAs, and counties. In summary discussions, I shall use the term "city typologies" although the reference may be to a variety of studies using these slightly different units of analysis.

of trade and commerce, political and administrative centers, cultural or educational centers, health or recreation centers, and military cities. Harris set out to quantify city types by classifying them on the basis of the economic activity that was of the greatest importance in each one. He recognized that "all large cities are more or less multifunctional, and the classification of a city as industrial does not imply the absence of trade." But general types are distinct. Harris classified cities of 10,000 or more inhabitants in 1930 by using census information regarding employment of persons in the labor force. The criteria he specified and the types he reported are shown in Table 5-1.

Manufacturing cities were the most numerous, comprising some 44 percent of the metropolitan districts and 43 percent of smaller centers. Harris specified two subcategories of manufacturing centers; first, cities with a predominant manufacturing base and, second, cities with important manufacturing activity that is definitely secondary to other functions. The largest American city primarily devoted to manfacturing in 1930 was Detroit; examples of smaller, predominantly manufacturing cities were Reading, Flint, and Winston-Salem. Cities with extensive manufacturing, but of secondary importance, were Philadelphia and Buffalo. In 1930, most of the manufacturing cities were located within a "manufacturing belt" east of the Mississippi River and north of the Ohio, with narrow extensions stretching through the southeastern United States along the Piedmont and the Great Valley. Only 19 of the 258 manufacturing cities were outside of the manufacturing belt, and these outside cities were those that primarily dealt with treating products whose bulk or perishability is reduced by manufacture (lumber, fruit, vegetable and fish canneries, iron, copper, and oil).

Just over 100 cities in 1930 were classified as *retail centers*. These were generally smaller cities outside the manufacturing belt, and over one-half of them were near the eastern margin of the Great Plains, the agricultural center of the United States. A few centers were located in the South and the West. *Diversified centers* function as both trade and manufacturing centers; they tend to be the largest metropolitan centers. *Wholesale cities* are of two distinct types: those that are engaged in assembly and those that are engaged in distribution. Smaller cities, such as Riverside and Redlands, California, fall into the assembly category—agricultural products. Distributing wholesale centers are usually the largest cities serving a wide region; the principal cities of this type are New York, Chicago, and San Francisco. Thirty-two cities were classified as *transportation centers*. Eighteen of these were railroad centers, and 14 were ports. *Mining* predominated in 14 places, and 17 places were classified as *university towns*. *Resort and retirement* towns were located primarily in warm southern climates.

Harris neglected other types of places, although he did recognize their existence. He specifically pointed out regional centers that served a wide tributary area (serving as a central place?), political capitals, garrison cities, professional centers, and specialized places such as fishing, lumbering, and farming centers. He concluded by pointing out that different functional types of cities

TABLE 5-1
Criteria Used by Harris in Classifying Cities

MANUFACTURING CITIES M' SUBTYPE.
Principal criterion: Employment in manufacturing equals at least 74 percent of total employment in manufacturing, retailing, and wholesaling (employment figures).
Secondary criterion: Manufacturing and mechanical industries contain at least 45 percent of gainful workers (occupation figures). Note: A few cities with industries in suburbs for which no figures were available were placed in this class if the percentage in the secondary criterion reached 50. (N = 118)

MANUFACTURING CITIES M SUBTYPE
Principal criterion: Employment in manufacturing equals at least 60 percent of total employment in manufacturing, retailing, and wholesaling.
Secondary criterion: Manufacturing and mechanical industries usually contain between 30 percent and 45 percent of gainful workers. (N = 140)

RETAIL CENTERS (R)
Employment in retailing is at least 50 percent of the total employment in manufacturing, wholesaling, and retailing and at least 2.2 times that in wholesaling alone. (N = 104)

DIVERSIFIED CITIES (D)
Employment in manufacturing, wholesaling, and retailing is less than 60 percent, 20 percent, and 50 percent respectively of the total employment in these activities, and no other special criteria apply. Manufacturing and mechanical industries with few exceptions contain between 25 percent and 35 percent of the gainful workers. (N = ?)

WHOLESALE CENTERS (W)
Employment in wholesaling is at least 20 percent of the total employment in manufacturing wholesaling and retailing and at least 45 percent as much as in retailing alone. (N = ?)

TRANSPORTATION CENTERS (T)
Transportation and communication contain at least 11 percent of the gainful workers, and workers in transportation and communication equal at least one-third the number in manufacturing and mechanical industries and at least two-thirds the number in trade (occupation figures). (Applies only to cities of more than 25,000 population for which such figures are available.) (N = 32)

MINING TOWNS (S)
Extraction of minerals accounts for more than 15 percent of the gainful workers. (Applies only to cities of more than 25,000 for which such figures are available.) For cities between 10,000 and 25,000 a comparison was made of mining employment available by counties only with employment in cities within such mining counties. Published sources were consulted to differentiate actual mining towns from commercial and industrial centers in mining areas. (N = 14)

UNIVERSITY TOWNS (E)
Enrollment in schools of collegiate rank (universities, technical schools, liberal-arts colleges, and teachers colleges) equaled at least 25 percent of the population of the city (1940). (N = 17)

RESORT AND RETIREMENT TOWNS (X)
No satisfactory statistical criterion was found. Cities with a low percentage of the population employed were checked in the literature for this function. (N = 22)

Source: Used by permission. Adapted from Harris (1943: 88); N's, where given, were added from the original text.

Fewer than 8 percent of American manufacturing cities lie outside of the manufacturing belt running east of the Mississippi and north of the Ohio. This view of Lehighton, Pennsylvania, is characteristic of the smaller type of city devoted predominantly to manufacturing.

exhibit differences in the factors affecting their location. The central-location theory, in which centrality within a productive hinterland is stressed, is illustrated best by the distribution of wholesaling centers, which are usually large cities centrally placed within a wide area, and of retail centers, centrally placed within a smaller area. By way of contrast, in the rise of mining and resort centers site factors either mineral resources or climate are of greater importance than central location. Industrial cities are intermediate in that both location factors of convenience to markets and raw materials and site factors of power and labor are important; they exhibit diffusion within a clearly defined manufacturing belt.

Following the lead of Harris, Nelson (1955) developed a more systematic classification system based upon standard statistical notions that specified when cities should be given a specified kind of label; he classified cities by calculating the standard deviation for each of nine activity groups in each city. He assumed that the proportion of labor force engaged in performing a service is the best means of measuring the distribution of that activity. It is one of the few measures that is easily comparable from activity to activity or from year to year (Nelson, 1955: 189).[2] He selected nine major categories to represent the

[2] Unfortunately, Nelson used a poor statistical measure. He should have used the *coefficient of variability*, given the unusual frequency distributions by activity.

services performed in a city: mining, manufacturing, transportation and communication, wholesale trade, retail trade, finance, insurance and real estate, personal service, professional service, and public administration.

In 1950 the performance of manufacturing services occupied the largest proportion of the labor force (27 percent) in the 897 U.S. cities of 10,000 or more, and 20 percent of the labor force was in retail trade. Thus these two activities accounted for almost one-half of the labor force. Professional services accounted for about 11 percent of the urban labor force in the same year.

Generally speaking, the percent of the labor force in retail trade, professional service, and mining varied inversely with city size; that is, the percentages decreased according to city size. Manufacturing showed greater variation than any other activity, ranging from 5 percent in one city to 65 percent in another. Retail trade also varied, with a range of 6 to over 36 percent. Other activities fall into what may be considered a third general type; most cities have a fairly low percentage in the activity; then, in each instance, there were a few other cities in which these services were performed by a high proportion of the labor force. As an example, professional service was performed by about 6 to 12 percent of the labor force in most cities, by 30 to 40 percent in a few cities, and by 60 percent in several other cities. A brief description of the service classification by Nelson is presented next. For a more complete description see his original article. The population characteristics of the following cities are summarized from a subsequent article by Nelson (1957).

Manufacturing cities accounted for more than one-fifth of all cities, in spite of the fact that in order to be classified as such, a city had to have over 43 percent of its labor force employed in manufacturing. Manufacturing cities were strongly localized in the area north of the Ohio River and east of the Mississippi River—in the manufacturing belt and along the flanks of the Appalachian Mountains, just as they were in 1930. In no other category are cities so highly localized. Very few *retail-center cities* are found in regions in which manufacturing cities were concentrated. The largest concentration of retail centers was in a broad belt between the Mississippi River and the Rocky Mountains. California and Florida also contained important concentrations.

Eighty-one cities in the United States were outstanding in the proportions of their labor forces involved in *professional services*. Over 60 of these were the sites of colleges or universities or had a college or university nearby. Other professional cities tended to be those where an unusually large proportion of people were involved in hospital work. Professional centers were widespread, with at least one in almost every state; with only one exception, they had under 100,000 population.

Transportation and communication cities were primarily railroad associated; usually they were small cities that were division and junction points along main railway lines. *Personal service* cities were located primarily in Florida, California, Arizona, and Nevada. Generally, for one reason or another, these cities attracted a large transient or at least a semitransient population.

Public administration centers were almost exclusively of two types: either political capitals or cities near large military installations—garrison cities.

Wholesale trade places were actually of two major categories: those that serviced areas of intensive agriculture producing crops that require picking, sorting, and packing. California, Texas, and Florida claimed most of these places. Whosesaling, in the traditional sense as distributing points for bulk goods, such as groceries, hardware, drugs, and so on, were usually larger cities. *No* cities in the manufacturing belt were classified as wholesaling places, which otherwise were widespread. *Finance, insurance,* and *real-estate* cities were widely scattered over the country. Most of these cities were insurance centers, with a few dominated by real estate and several by finance.

Mining occupied fewer people than any of the other types of activities mentioned previously. Obviously, most mining activity takes place primarily where mineral deposits are found.

Two hundred and forty-six cities that did not have a sufficiently high proportion of any single activity category to receive one of the other classifications were referred to as more or less "average" cities. Generally, these cities were located in the northeastern and southeastern parts of the country, except for Florida.

In a similar study Jones (1953) reported that in 1950 almost one-third of the 992 U.S. cities with over 10,000 population were manufacturing cities (50 percent or more employment in manufacturing or related activities and less than 30 percent in retail trade); one-fifth were industrial or diversified cities with manufacturing dominating but softened by extensive retail trade; another one-third were retail cities (employment in retail trade greater than that in any other activity). The remaining 13 percent of cities were predominantly special cases of mining, transportation, education, government, or resort cities. He also divided cities into employing, dormitory or balanced cities serving both as an employment center and as a dormitory. The distinction between employment and dormitory places becomes important in a later chapter in our discussion of suburbs and the journey-to-work.

A Typology of Metropolitan Regions and Functions

Duncan et al. (1960) studied metropolitan regions in the United States by focusing on two different approaches. First, they emphasized what they considered the two *major functions* of metropolitan centers: One was national credit that showed the flow of credit and loans through Federal Reserve Banks, plus other large lending institutions. They noted that the flow of money falls into a hierarchy, with a few very large metropolitan centers making up the major part of the national credit and loan market, while lower in the hierarchy other metropolitan places progressively make fewer nonlocal loans and their "credit hinterland" is progressively smaller (see Chapter 6 of Duncan et al., 1960, for flows of funds among cities). The other function related to the volume of *wholesaling* and *commercial* activity as measured by sales and receipts from

The major national metropolis in the United States is New York City. This aerial view of Manhattan (looking north) shows Wall Street, the center of the financial district. The two waterways—the East River to the right, the Hudson to the left—are historically related to the wholesaling and commercial activity of the city. Most merchant ships dock across the bay in Brooklyn, leaving Manhattan Island to expand continually as a financial center (note the vast land-fill project at the far left).

business services. These two distributions were found to be very similar and concentrated in the same metropolitan centers, thus resulting in a national credit and wholesaling and commercial hierarchy.

In addition, Duncan et al. examined the distribution of industrial activities, as measured by "value added by manufacture." Value added by manufacture is the market price of goods completed minus the cost of materials used in the manufacturing process. They concluded that manufacturing is not as important as credit and wholesaling and commercial activity in defining metropolitanism, and they further argued that the influence of this activity is much different and more important than that of manufacturing.

Their second approach consisted of constructing "industry profiles" for all SMSAs in the United States of 300,000 or more population in 1950. The industry profiles included all types of employment, not only manufacturing. Additional related information concerned the extent to which the local hinterland or other regions supplied raw materials and received finished goods and services. The industry profiles made use of the "index of dissimilarity," which also has been extensively used to measure racial segregation in cities. Table 5-2 presents the results of Duncan et al.'s analyses according to metropolitan functions and regional relationships.

National Metropolis (N)

The two major national metropolises are New York and Chicago. Only slightly less important are Los Angeles and Philadelphia, which have an addi-

TABLE 5-2
Classification of Standard Metropolitan Areas of 300,000 or More Inhabitants According to Metropolitan Functions and Regional Relationships

NATIONAL METROPOLIS (N)
New York
Chicago
Los Angeles (Nd)
Philadelphia (Nd)
Detroit (Nm)

DIVERSIFIED MANUFACTURING WITH
METROPOLITAN FUNCTIONS (D)
Boston (Dn)
Pittsburgh (Dn)
St. Louis
Cleveland
Buffalo
Cincinnati

DIVERSIFIED MANUFACTURING WITH
FEW METROPOLITAN FUNCTIONS (D—)
Baltimore
Milwaukee
Albany-Schenectady-Troy
Toledo
Hartford
Syracuse

SPECIALIZED MANUFACTURING (M)
Providence
Youngstown
Rochester
Dayton
Allentown-Bethlehem-Easton
Akron
Springfield-Holyoke
Wheeling-Steubenville
Charleston, W. Va.

REGIONAL METROPOLIS (R)
San Francisco (Rn)
Minneapolis-St. Paul
Kansas City
Seattle
Portland
Atlanta
Dallas
Denver

REGIONAL CAPITAL, SUBMETROPOLITAN
(C)
Houston
New Orleans
Louisville (Cd)
Birmingham (Cm)
Indianapolis (Cd)
Columbus
Memphis
Omaha
Fort Worth
Richmond (Cd)
Oklahoma City
Nashville
Jacksonville

SPECIAL CASES (S)
Washington
San Diego
San Antonio
Miami
Norfolk-Portsmouth
Wilkes-Barre-Hazleton
Tampa-St. Petersburg
Knoxville
Phoenix

Source: Used by permission; Duncan and others (1960).

tional emphasis on diversified manufacturing. Detroit is the fifth national metropolis, with an emphasis on specialized manufacturing.

Diversified Manufacturing
with Metropolitan Functions (D)

While these metropolitan centers are highly diverse, manufacturing dominates and various kinds of products are produced. There is generally a highly skilled labor force and ready access to needed raw materials. No one industry or function dominates the center—such as the automobile industry in Detroit, with at least one but usually more large-scale manufacturing types of enterprises being present, usually with several industries in each type. These metropolitan centers are readily identified as a financial center of some importance, and each may have a Federal Reserve Bank.

An example of this type of metropolitan center is Boston. In 1950 Boston consisted of the entire county of Suffolk and parts of four other counties. Its 1950 SMSA population was 2,369,986, and its central city population was 801,444. It is a seaport, the capital of Massachusetts, and has a Federal Reserve Bank. Boston produces products that require few raw materials but highly skilled labor and technical knowledge: printing, banking, electrical equipment, education, and hospitals (all of these occupy over 3 percent of Boston's labor force). Other cities in this category include Pittsburgh, St. Louis, Cleveland, Buffalo, and Cincinnati.

Regional Metropolis (R)

The most significant functions of a regional metropolis are related to its somewhat immediate hinterland, which determines what activities will be prominent. San Francisco-Oakland is an example of a regional metropolis; it consists of six entire counties—Alameda, Contra Costa, Marin, San Francisco, San Mateo, and Solano. It is a seaport and a Federal Reserve Bank city; its most significant activities are those tied to the commercial, financial, and administrative functions performed for its agricultural hinterland, the Pacific and Intramountain states. Primary activities include the canning of fruits, vegetables, and seafood. One-fifth of the labor force is employed in service industries for nonlocal activities—transportation. If Duncan et al. were to replicate their research using 1970 data, San Francisco would undoubtedly qualify as a national metropolis (N), since it is a strong financial and commercial center.

Another example of a regional metropolis is the Atlanta SMSA, which is made up of three counties—Cobb, DeKalb, and Fulton. Its 1950 population was 671,797, with 331,314 residing in the central city. Atlanta is the state capital and a Federal Reserve Bank city. Its most important functions are commerce, finance, transportation, wholesaling, and governmental administration. About one-fifth of the labor force is involved in nonlocal service industries, for example, transportation. Other cities in this category are Minneapolis-St. Paul, Kansas City, Seattle, Portland, Dallas, and Denver.

The major industry of many cities is closely tied to their hinterland. This stockyard, drawing cattle from nearby hinterland areas, is typical of those located in several mid-western regional capitals.

Diversified Manufacturing
with Few Metropolitan Functions (D—)

These cities are not highly developed in metropolitan functions, for instance, with regard to credit flow and wholesaling and commercial activity; they do have a high level of manufacturing although it is not necessarily specialized in any one industry or product. They have many local services to complement manufacturing. Few cities of this type base their activities on resources in their immediate hinterlands. Hartford, Connecticut (SMSA, 358,081; central city, 177,397) is an example. It is located on a navigable river and is the capital of Connecticut. Its labor force is predominantly in service industries: security and commodity brokers, insurance, state public administration, machinery, and hospitals. Other cities in this category are Baltimore, Milwaukee, Albany-Schenectady, Toledo, and Syracuse. It is interesting to note in relation to the transportation theory of the location of cities that all of the national metropolises, cities with diversified manufacturing with metropolitan functions, and cities with diversified manufacturing with few metropolitan functions are located on navigable waterways.

Regional Capital, Submetropolitan (C)

Submetropolitan regional capitals are metropolitan centers with a close relationship to the local hinterland. Each city also seems to have a dominant industry, for example, Houston, oil; Omaha, livestock; Richmond and Louisville, tobacco; Memphis, grain; New Orleans, sugar and seafood. They are centers oriented toward personal services and commercial activity for its

Some cities have one unusual and specific dominant activity. Miami Beach is such a place, specializing in recreation. This dominant activity influences its labor force composition, its land use, and the lifestyles of its inhabitants.

hinterland. Most are branch cities of the Federal Reserve System; one is a Federal Reserve Bank city. These cities specialize in one type of transportation, and specialization in almost all other phases of activity is less than for the other types of metropolitan centers discussed so far.

Birmingham, Alabama, is an example of a submetropolitan regional capital. Its SMSA population in 1950 was 558,928, and 326,037 persons resided in the central city. It is a Federal Reserve Bank branch city; the labor force is primarily in iron and steel industries, coal mining, and transportation. Birmingham is closely tied to its hinterland and uses raw materials located nearby: iron ore, coal, and flux for the iron and steel industries. In addition, it serves as a commercial and wholesale center.

Specialized Manufacturing (M)

In these centers there is an extreme concentration of manufacturing activity, with a low level of trade and service activity. The work force is primarily in one or two specialized activities. There is a lack of metropolitan functions, that is, of credit and wholesale and commercial activity. Generally, they do not rely upon nearby resources. Virtually all of the centers are located in the manufacturing belt region of the northeastern United States. An example is Rochester (SMSA, 487,632; central city, 332,488), consisting of one county located on Lake Ontario and New York's Barge Canal. The labor force is predominantly in photographic and professional equipment, surgical tools, and so on.

Special Cases (S)

These cities are varied and generally have one specific dominant activity. In the governmental sphere Washington, D.C., has 27 percent of its labor force in government and 4 percent in printing and publishing. San Diego, San

Antonio, and Norfolk-Portsmouth are examples of primarily garrison cities. San Diego has 8 percent of its labor force on the federal payroll and 7 percent in aircraft and parts. San Antonio has 11 percent on the federal payroll and 5 percent in wholesale trade, primarily meats. Norfolk-Portsmouth has 12 percent of its labor force involved in federal activities and 7 percent in ship repair and building.

Miami is a special case that is primarily devoted to entertainment and recreation, with 4 percent of its labor force devoted to air-transport services and 5 percent to hotels and lodging places. Wilkes-Barre has 23 percent of its labor force in coal-mining activities; Knoxville has 9 percent in apparel and accessories, and Phoenix has 9 percent involved in service industries.

Conclusions

It is worthwhile, of course, to consult Duncan et al. for a more detailed elaboration of each metropolitan center. In summary, they show quite clearly that a national metropolis (N), a regional metropolis (R), or a regional capital (C) includes almost all instances in which it seems meaningful to think of a continuous hinterland in its ordinary use as a tributary or influence area surrounding a central place. They note that while each of these types of metropolitan regions has a hinterland, the size varies from that of New York City, with its hinterland virtually being all of the United States and much of the rest of the world, to regional capitals with their more limited and localized influence areas. In addition, they note that hinterlands "are overlapping and interpenetrating rather than discrete and clearly demarcated" (p. 18).

Manufacturing centers — D, D—, and M — on the other hand, are clearly different from the N-R-C metropolitan centers because it is inappropriate to refer to a particular hinterland for them. Special cases (S) include most places having highly specialized and unusual industry profiles and, as we noted previously, resort communities, transportation centers, garrison cities, among others. Duncan et al. hypothesized that the extent of special cases would have been greater had they extended their inquiry to smaller SMSAs. This speculation should be kept in mind when we examine multivariable typologies in the next section.

MULTIDIMENSIONAL TYPOLOGIES

Eventually, social scientists began to realize that there was more to urban character than could be explained on the basis of simple economic or functional differences, and this in turn led to many dimensions and variables being added to the classification and typologies of cities (Berry, 1972*b*: 16). One of the first attempts to classify cities empirically and systematically in the United States through the use of multiple dimensions was made by Price (1942). He examined 93 cities with populations of 100,000 or more in 1930. Using factor analysis and some 15 social and economic variables, he identified 4 factors that appeared to describe these cities. The results of his analysis can be interpreted as follows:

Factor I: Maturity

This factor is highly correlated with those characteristics thought of as defining "typical" larger metropolitan centers, that is, population size, median rentals, age of city, and percentage of employed making income-tax returns. Larger cities, such as New York, Chicago, Washington, Boston, and San Francisco, rank high on this factor.

Factor II: Occupational Structure of Cities

Primary elements associated with this factor are the percentages of employed in service industry, of increase in population, of the population between the ages of 15 and 50, of the population 10 years and longer gainfully occupied, and of gainful workers; female and median-size family. This factor defines the extent to which a city is or is not a service center or, negatively defined, the dominance of industry. Cities that rank high on the index are New York, Washington, Atlanta, Memphis, Dallas, and Flint (service centers), while Gary and Youngstown rank low.

Factor III: General Level of Living

The sex ratio, median monthly rent, percent of population between 15 and 50, percentage of female workers, and wages per wage earner are variables that define a general-level-of-living factor. Industrial cities tend to rank high, with the exception of textile manufacturing towns in New England and the South; highest-ranking cities are Gary, San Francisco, New York, and Flint.[3]

Factor IV: Trade Volume

Only two characteristics, wholesale and retail sales per capita, define the trade volume factor. Highly ranked cities are Kansas City, Missouri, San Francisco, Boston, Paterson, and Dallas.

Price suggested that additional analyses by others would determine whether these factors are generally applicable to all cities.

Using 1960 U.S. census data, Perle (1964) followed up Price's analysis and reported substantially the same factors. She concluded that the same underlying dimensions characterized cities in the United States in 1930 and 1960, although the importance of the factors varied slightly. Standard-of-living and maturity and size factors were statistically similar, but the occupation structure factor was much more important in 1960 than in 1930. This last is the most important variable. Perle followed up her factor analysis with a discussion of the various types of cities as follows:

Group I: National Metropolises[4] are the older, larger industrial cities of New York, Chicago, Detroit, and Philadelphia that perform metropolitan functions. A few cities with less than 1 million are diversified manufacturing centers

---

[3] It would have been interesting if *percent in unions* had been added as a variable.

[4] Group titles were added by me and are based upon the discussion of Perle and her reference to Duncan et al.'s monograph on *Metropolis and Region* (1960).

with definite metropolitan functions. Of the 14 cities in this category, none is located in the South.

Group II: Regional Capitals are smaller, old industrial towns; most have a population of less than 500,000 and a less diversified economic base than Group I. Differences between national metropolises and regional capitals seem mainly to be a function of size and degree of industrial diversification. The 22 cities in this group are spread throughout the United States, but only 3 — New Orleans, Fort Worth, and Houston — are from the South.

Group III: Regional Cities with Specialized Industrial Bases are old cities that are larger than Group II cities but smaller than Group I's. Many are regional metropolises and serve as a focus for a larger area than that of Group II. Only 1 — Miami — out of a total of 21 cities is located in the South, with the remainder scattered over the United States.

Group IV: Specialized-Function cities tend to be smaller; some function as regional capitals, others as ports, and still others are supported by the military or the government. They are, in general, older capitals of the South and southern borderlands or in the older Northeast. Five out of seven are southern — Savannah, Columbus, Corpus Christi, El Paso, San Antonio.

Group V: Older Specialized-Function Places are similar to those of Group IV and are primarily southern cities — Memphis, Richmond, Chattanooga, Knoxville, Nashville, Birmingham, and Jacksonville.

Groups VI and VII: Newer Specialized-Function Places are newer, smaller regional capitals of the South and the West. They are diversified in occupational structure and have experienced rapid growth in post–World War II years. They reflect the shift of industry to the South and the West. They all have populations of less than 250,000. Some are dependent upon government expenditures for their rapid growth, and most of them are highly specialized. Fourteen out of 23 cities in Group VI are southern: Atlanta, Oklahoma City, Dallas, Shreveport, Little Rock, Charlotte, Winston-Salem, Mobile, Tulsa, Austin, Montgomery, Baton Rouge, Jackson, Tampa; in Group VII, however, only 3 cities — Lubbock, Amarillo, and Greensboro — out of 12 are southern.

Group VIII: Highly Specialized Places are usually the suburbs of larger industrial complexes, or satellite cities.

If we divide the eight groups into three major categories, we have the following:

1. The *industrial metropoli,* within which the main differences are those of size and manufacturing diversity.
2. The *older regional capitals* of the South and the Northeast.
3. The *newer regional capitals,* which are cities serving a highly specialized function and experiencing rapid post–World War II growth.

More recently, Berry (1972b) carried out a factor analysis to determine the "latent" or hidden factors that underlie cities in the United States. The first factor that he identified was the "functional size" or aggregate economic power of cities within the nation's urban hierarchy. A rather large number of individual variables comprise this factor: number of inhabitants, labor force composition measures, employment levels, area of the city, and date the city passed 100,000 population (age of city). Cities that rank highest for this factor are the larger cities (about 32 in all) in the United States, for instance, New York City, Chicago, Los Angeles, Cincinnati, Fort Worth, and Buffalo. One of the key dimensions correlated with this factor is the date when a city passed 100,000 population, indicating that the largest current cities are those places that were fortunate enough to achieve earliest eminence.

A second factor was labeled "socioeconomic status of community residents," with a variety of income measures, housing values, housing conditions, and employment levels and unemployment rates comprising this factor. Cities at the extremes of this factor with the lowest and highest socioeconomic status were smaller places. At the upper end of the factor, Scarsdale, New York (median income $22,177), Winnetka, Illinois (median income $20,166), and Glencoe, Illinois (median income $20,166), were ranked first, second, and third. At the lower end of the scale were Mercedes, Texas (median income $2,395), Eagle Pass, Texas (median income $2,435), and Weslaco, Texas (median income $2,604). Because of their size, major central cities all had average status scores and encompassed a variety of income levels that resulted in a median income.

A third factor reported by Berry is "stage in life cycle." This factor includes median age, percent of aged population (65 and over), fertility rate, household size measures, percent of homes built between 1950 and 1960, and rate of growth. The most "youthful child-rearing" places were Carpentersville, Illinois, Thornton, Colorado, and La Puente, California, while the most "elderly" communities were Miami Beach, Beverly Hills, and Lake Worth, Florida.

Two factors revolved around ethnic status, with one factor consisting of nonwhite dimensions plus two crowding variables (1.01 or more persons per room), and percent of married couples *without* their own households. A second ethnic dimension was concerned with the foreign-born population but also included the percent of elementary schoolchildren in private schools, single-family housing units (SFHU), and the percentage using public transport. Some of the cities high on the factor were high on several other factors already mentioned: Miami Beach (elderly), Eagle Pass, Texas (low income), Weslaco, Texas (low income). Obviously, *different* foreign-born populations make up the Texas communities and Miami Beach's. With only 2 exceptions, all 16 communities ranked highest on the "Native American" end of this factor were located in Texas or Ohio.

Recent population growth — as measured by population stability, mobility and migration variables, and the vacancy rate of rental units — indicates that Scottsdale, Arizona, and many cities in California and Florida were the fastest-growing places, whereas most of the "stable" cities are located in the northeastern section of the United States, for example, New Hanover Township, New Jersey, Lansdowne, Pennsylvania, and New Hyde Park, New York. Interestingly, another factor reported by Berry was "recent growth in employment." This factor had virtually no overlap with rapid-growing communities, with only 1 California city appearing among the list of the top 16 growing places and the remainder being primarily a mid-western phenomenon.

Two factors revolved around labor force participation: One was primarily concerned with female participation in the labor force and included the cumulative fertility ratio and the nonworker/worker ratio. Of the 20 cities ranked highest in female participation in the labor force, 15 are located in the South; places with the least female participation in the labor force are scattered around the country. The second factor involving the labor force centered on a negative relationship between elderly working males and commuting to work outside the county of residence. Most of the places ranked high on this factor were metropolitan suburbs housing high proportions of independent businessmen; a few were isolated towns in peripheral regions from which many individuals in the active younger age groups had emigrated.

In addition to the preceding, Berry concludes that cities in the United States are differentiated according to their economic bases, but in "every case the towns displaying high degrees of functional specialization tended to be quite small . . ." (p. 33). He reported five different types of specialized economic places: manufacturing towns, mining towns, college towns, military installations, and service centers. Manufacturing towns primarily are located in the northeastern manufacturing belt, although a few cities in the South and the West were so classified. Mining towns are spread out more but cluster in the Southwest and Minnesota. College towns, on the other hand, are quite widespread throughout the United States. About one-third of the military installations are in California and the remainder are rather widespread. "Finally, relatively uniformly distributed throughout the West and South are towns functioning primarily as local service centers. Conversely, the midwestern and northeastern sections of the country, along with Piedmont area, are characterized by towns of specialized function" (p. 44).

Berry (1972b: 46–47) argues that in a nation that is "fully metropolitanized" the important elements of economic differentiation are applicable at the metropolitan level but not at the city-wide level. Thus he hypothesizes that a classification of cities on economic dimensions currently will separate only relatively small communities from each other. "It follows that the traditional economic approach to city classification is of minimal and declining relevance" (p. 47).

A Typology of Nonwhite Populations in SMSAs

In examining types of metropolitan areas by their nonwhite populations, Meyer (1972) notes that the distribution of nonwhites among cities is quite complex. As a result of his analysis, he used seven dimensions to describe variation among nonwhites, primarily blacks, and showed "the importance of caution in generalizing about Black Americans from studies of single cities," since there is a great variation from one metropolitan area to another. He allocated SMSAs to broader types based upon factor scores, and he reported six key types of SMSAs: northeastern, Texan, Deep South, North Carolina-Florida, declining industrial (small northern industrial), and young-family industrial (small northern industrial).

Those SMSAs classified as Deep South are primarily located in Arkansas, Louisiana, Alabama, Georgia, South Carolina, and Tennessee, although one Texas SMSA (Beaumont-Port Arthur) and one North Carolina city (Raleigh) are included in this category. This type "is merely support for the accepted view that Black Americans who live in the South participate in a similar set of social and economic institutions, whose most distinguishing characteristic is low socioeconomic status" (p. 88). In the North Carolina-Florida type are the textile and furniture industries of the Piedmont in North Carolina and the important tourist industry cities in Florida. Richmond, Virginia, was also included in this type. Texas, according to Meyer, is a special case for two reasons: (1) Its growth occurred after the Civil War, and (2) blacks in Texas compete with chicanos (Mexican-Americans) for low-status occupations. It should be noted that there may be more to this category than Meyer attributes, since both Knoxville and Nashville, Tennessee, which do not have large chicano populations, are included in this type. He gives some indication that the age structure may be of importance in defining this type, since all of these cities have relatively older black populations: ". . . young families are unlikely to move to, or remain in Texan SMSA's."

The northeastern SMSAs have a high rate of multifamily-dwelling living and female employment at the operative level. On the other hand, the small northern industrial SMSAs have young families, with males likely to be employed as craftsmen and operatives, although living in older housing and having a high probability of unemployment. "The curious occurrence of high unemployment with high employment in manufacturing exists in cities with stable or declining manufacturing establishments and expanding Black populations. Since they face job discrimination and are usually low in seniority, Black males have high rates of unemployment." The young-family industrial SMSAs show that blacks are highly differentiated even among small industrial northern SMSAs.

Missing from the Meyer typology are the Pacific Coast and larger SMSAs. He argues that since these SMSAs did not closely resemble each other on the dimensions he used in his study, this, in effect, means that any assumption that all large black ghettos are similar is highly inaccurate.

A Typology of Suburbs

Following procedures established by factor analysts, Walter and Wirt (1972) examined suburbs to determine whether there are systematic differences or types. According to them, four essential components describe suburbs in the United States. The first factor, *affluence,* includes the traditional measures of *social class*—years of schooling, income, and labor force composition. The second factor is related to *recent growth;* variables describing this factor include fertility, young age, and so on, perhaps representing stages in the life cycle as well as rapid growth. The third factor is primarily and almost exclusively described by the percent of foreign-born persons and employment in manufacturing or, in other words, "ethnically homogeneous suburban enclaves with a labor force employed in heavy industry." The fourth factor appears to be described by a population that is housed in rental apartment buildings. These "suburbs" of course are only listed as suburbs because they are located outside the central city; if one used definitions of suburbs other than the political boundary of the central city, these suburbs probably would be classified as "cities."

Conclusions

All of the typologies described above assume that there are underlying dimensions that characterize different kinds and types of cities and metropolitan areas. The frame of reference and the methodology used in research delineating these types generally have as their primary purpose differentiating cities that are alike or unalike on one or more dimensions. A number of early and contemporary examples of approaches to city typologies were given in some detail in order to illustrate the various methodologies and their results. In some respects this chapter is only a necessary preliminary discussion for the next section, in which city typologies are related to *outcome* dimensions. There typological results are treated as independent variables "causing" different outcomes such as in spatial distributions of social classes, ethnic minorities, the quality of life, expenditures for health, education and welfare.

It should be noted that the methodologies used in the classification of cities have changed significantly over time, and typologies are now viewed as serving a variety of purposes. Further, the evolving process of building city typologies is a continual search for better descriptions of the underlying dimensions of cities (Arnold, 1972: 375). The next major advance in this area probably will be in examining changes in types of cities across time and the effect, if any, that these changes have upon the "outputs" examined in the next section.

CONSEQUENCES OF CITY AND URBAN VARIATION

In the previous section it was demonstrated that there are systematic differences among cities and metropolitan areas in the United States. What is the significance of this? One of the major concentrations of current urban theory and research is attempting to show that systematic differences among cities and metropolitan areas have major consequences for people living in various types of places. The assumption tested in these studies is that various types of cities and metropolitan areas are systematically related to differences

---

FIGURE 5-1
A Model of the Consequences of Metropolitan and City Variation

---

EXTERNAL CONDITIONS ———→	CITY AND METROPOLITAN ————→ CHARACTERISTICS	POLITICAL SYSTEMS ————→

A. Physical environ-
ment
	A. Types
	  1. Functional
	  2. Multidimensional
		A. Forms of government

B. National and state
economics
	B. Individual character-
	istics
	  1. Size
	  2. Age of city
	  3. Demographic
	    composition
	  4. Economic base
		B. Social Stratification

C. State and federal political policies and structures		C. Legal boundaries of jurisdiction and representation

---

Source: This "model" was suggested by Dawson and Robinson (1963: 266); Dye (1966) and Paulson et al. (1969).

---

in spatial distributions of social classes, ethnic minorities, and public policy outcomes such as the quality of life, expenditures for health, education, and welfare, fire and police protection, and so on. It would be fortunate indeed if we could interrelate city typologies with such differences. However, extremely few of these kinds of analyses have been carried out to date. As a substitute, we will review some literature that has investigated outputs and relate them to specific variables, such as city size, density, age structure, income levels, education, and so on, that characterize cities, and have been used as key dimensions in typological studies.

Concern with public policy outcomes leads us directly to ideologies related to who has social power, who should control the economy, how much economic concentration there should be, to what extent there should be a freely competitive market, and, most relevant for our discussion, how responsive the social environment should be to the "needs of the people" (Fowler, 1958). We will devote most of our discussion in this section to city characteristics other than power. In a later chapter, however, we will return to several of the studies used here and relate *urban power structures* to many of the very same outputs.

Generalized models have been proposed by several political scientists who rely primarily upon the political character of the city (Dawson and Robinson, 1963; Dye, 1966) to explain social policy outcomes. Sociologists and others have viewed the process from a wider frame of reference than the politi-

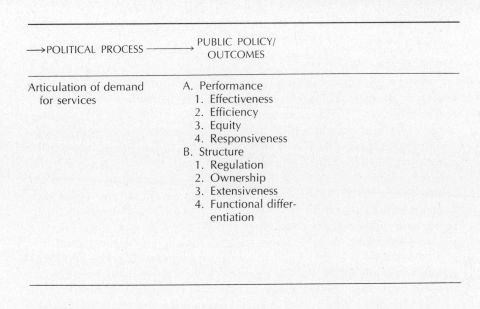

Articulation of demand
for services

A. Performance
1. Effectiveness
2. Efficiency
3. Equity
4. Responsiveness
B. Structure
1. Regulation
2. Ownership
3. Extensiveness
4. Functional differ-
entiation

cal scientists and generally have included a greater range of dimensions. However, virtually none of these approaches uses functional or multidimensional typologies as key independent variables, but they depend more upon individual characteristics of cities—such as size, when a city reached a certain size, demographic composition, or some aspect of the political system—to explain the differences in public policy outcomes.

Figure 5-1 provides a framework for understanding these approaches and the research that has been carried out to date and reported in this section. It assumes that there are conditions external to the city and metropolitan area that influence outcomes or social policy. These conditions may be whether or not there is money available for antipoverty programs, urban renewal, or redevelopment; they may also depend, for example, on whether the United States is at war or peace or in a period of economic prosperity or depression. Thus recognizing the possible importance of external conditions forces us to realize, if nothing more, that these factors may be important at the local level. If they are uniformly applicable, however, no variation at the local city level may be attributed to these external conditions.

Our major concern in this section is, to determine the extent to which there is variation or differences in public policy and outcomes by city, urban, and metropolitan characteristics; and, of course, which external conditions may be differently important to cities and must be considered for some outputs. Political systems and political processes may be considered as intervening factors or as outcomes of city characteristics—that is, dependent variables. Out of deference to political scientists these aspects are shown in Figure 5-1 as intervening variables.

City and Urban Variation and the Location of Social Classes

One possible consequence of city and metropolitan variation is a difference in how social classes are ecologically distributed in the city. Schnore and Winsborough (1972), using the *Municipal Year Book* typology, tested two hypotheses. First, manufacturing cities exhibit a greater degree of concentration of low-status people than do diversified cities or retail-trade centers. The authors also hypothesized a gradient, with manufacturing cities showing the greatest concentration and with declining concentrations through diversified centers to retail-trade centers. Unfortunately, they did not include special category places in their analysis. Second, "the greater the importance of manufacturing in a city's economy—as measured by the manufacturing ratio—the greater the preponderance of low-status people within its political limits."

As a result of their analysis of urbanized areas, Schnore and Winsborough concluded that manufacturing cities tend to be chiefly inhabited by persons with lower-level educations. Diversified cities show a mixed pattern, and retail-trade centers tend to have a concentration of persons with higher-level educational attainment. In addition, in comparing central cities with the rest of the urbanized area—that is, suburbs—they found that manufacturing centers clearly have higher suburban status but this suburban superiority progressively declines from one type to the next until, in the case of retail-trade centers, the central cities themselves have a higher socioeconomic status than their suburbs. Analyses using the manufacturing ratio instead of the functional typology produced similar results but not as clean-cut as those obtained with the latter; even so, the authors conclude that the manufacturing ratio may be more useful in statistical analyses.

These varying patterns of suburban and central-city socioeconomic status by functional type of urbanized place mean that the overall statistical relationship between economic status and suburban location should be low. In additional statistical analyses, Schnore and Winsborough noted that as boundaries of central cities vary to include more of the urbanized area's population, the percentage of the city's population that is higher in status rises more rapidly than does that of the suburbs (p. 141). They argue that the main factors in suburban growth are the extent of manufacturing (as measured by the manufacturing ratio) and of deteriorating and dilapidated housing in the central city, both of which make it unattractive to higher-status persons (p. 142). In addition, the possibility of a location outside the central city, for example, space and housing availability, obviously is important. Further, Schnore and Winsborough cogently argue that suburbanization and nonwhite residential segregation are two rather separate processes because with their statistical analyses they can "explain" suburbanization on the basis of using "data for the total population" without resorting to nonwhite data (pp. 142–143).

In summary, they concluded, as their original hypotheses stated, that the type of city makes a substantial difference in the residential distribution of social classes, at least insofar as comparison between the central city and the rest of the urbanized population is concerned. For further study they argued that the manufacturing ratio is a more useful predictor than the functional typology they used. Finally, they noted that they were dealing with an *intrinsically longitudinal* problem—the spatial sifting and sorting of social classes over time—with purely *cross-sectional data*. We also might add that they were viewing social class distributions in urbanized areas very broadly—central cities versus the rest of the urbanized areas, whereas data are available that allow more detailed analyses (e.g., census tracts) within both the central city and the suburbs as well as comparisons between them.

Urban Variation and
Community Welfare and City

Investigations interrelating the characteristics of cities and community welfare have all reported systematic variation; however, they diverge in emphasis and in the variables that are believed to account for these differences. Fowler (1958) noted that many of these studies are influenced by the investigator's ideology. Three hypotheses tend to dominate: (1) Small-business industrial structures will provide higher levels of welfare than big-business structures, other relevant factors remaining relatively constant; (2) local pluralistic power structures will produce higher levels of welfare than local monolithic power structures; and (3) "type of industry" has an equal, if not greater, effect on welfare than do other industrial structure variables, other relevant factors remaining constant (this is paraphrased from Fowler, 1958: 42).

Fowler tested these hypotheses on 30 small New York State cities ranging in size from 10,000 to 80,000 population, matched according to size and manufacturing ratio. Local welfare was measured by an index called the *General Social Welfare* (GSW) score made up of 48 rankings combined into the following 11 major welfare subcomposites: (1) income, (2) income security, (3) consumer purchasing power, (4) home ownership, (5) housing adequacy, (6) health needs, (7) health facilities, (8) literacy, (9) adequacy of educational provision, (10) political expression, and (11) municipal wealth and service. He did not include some of the more traditional welfare measures such as expenditures for public welfare assistance, and so on.

In contrast to the hypotheses tested, Fowler (1958, 1964) reports that higher levels of community welfare are associated with concentration of employment in large-scale industry, heavier durable-goods industry, absentee ownership, and some industrial diversification. Concentrated power structures (see Chapter 11 for further discussion of power structures) are associated with high welfare levels. Sample cities with big-business structures tend to have higher welfare levels because of their relationship to "the technically advanced nature of modern industry." Some of the reasons he posited are as follows: (1) Big-business cities have a more advanced technical mode of production that demands large numbers of highly skilled and thus higher-paid personnel; (2) since these local establishments are part of a large national organization, the particular locations selected by them were the result of careful site selection and long-term capital investment, thus making more tax revenue available for public services; and (3) the big-business plant draws ancillary industries with similar highly skilled and highly paid personnel. In addition, higher welfare levels are associated with the following gross socioeconomic and demographic variables: occupational distributions, large net population increase, a low degree of industrial unionism, and higher proportions of white, native-born, Protestants.

Fowler noted that even the largest industrial structures have extralocal pressures on them to make expenditures for community welfare. While he tended to discount local influence, his work supports the notion that city characteristics are systematically related to variations and differences in community welfare outputs. Fowler's work contrasts with that of Mills and Ulmer (1946) and others in the direction of findings but not in the fact that there is variation in community welfare outcomes by city characteristics. The main deficiency of Fowler's work is that he used only smaller cities in New York State for his research. Given the time and resources, a replication of his study on a wider basis might require some qualifications in regard to the impact that big-business industrial structures have upon local community welfare. Nevertheless, it is highly unlikely that the hypotheses of Mills and Ulmer will be supported.

In a study more specifically related to public welfare, Turk (1970) reported that for the 130 incorporated cities in the United States that had a population of more than 100,000 inhabitants in 1960, those with a previous history of outside funding established antipoverty organizations more often than cities that did not have a previous history of outside funding. Once established, however, there was little variation in extent of funding. He noted that, in general, the greater the capacity for local organization in a city, the greater its capability for manpower organization. While he did not stress characteristics of cities in regard to antipoverty expenditures, his data show that density, democratic vote, welfare expenditures, and educational expenditures are positively associated with per capita antipoverty expenditures, and age of city, migration, and educational level are negatively associated with poverty fund expenditures.

Perhaps the most interesting feature of Turk's analysis is that the extent of need (in his terms, demand), or poverty level, in the city is *unrelated to poverty fund expenditures*. This result is virtually identical to that reported by Paulson et al. (1969), who analyzed antipoverty fund expenditures at a completely different level—the 100 counties of North Carolina, only 6 of which have cities large enough to be considered as an SMSA (central city of 50,000 or more). Both of these studies suggest that while some cities and counties that had antipoverty programs may have needed them, the cities and counties that needed them the most were the least likely to have them! In North Carolina counties the major factor associated with antipoverty expenditures, as well as local and state welfare expenditures, was the *percent of white unemployed* (Paulson et al., 1969: 26).

Urban Variation and Urban Renewal

Hawley (1963) in studying urban renewal hypothesized that cities would be in different stages of urban renewal — such as the planning, execution, and completion stages — depending upon the characteristics of the cities. His argument was that the greater the concentration of decision making, the more likely the city would have reached the execution stage in urban renewal; cities with other than a concentrated decision-making structure would have a lack of attempted renewal; and dropout cities would be intermediate in concentration of decision making. Thus as concentration of decision-making structure varies, so does the likelihood of urban renewal success. Concentration was greatest in old cities, mayor-council cities, manufacturing centers, large-plant cities, and cities located in the Northeast. In contrast to Hawley's study, Clark (1968) studied urban renewal in 51 cities in the United States and reported that urban renewal expenditures are positively associated with a decentralized decision-making structure. Similar findings were reported by him for general budget expenditures. Both of Clark's results disagree with Hawley's research of urban renewal and with virtually all other studies analyzing outputs.

The conflict between Clark's and other studies may concern how centralized decision making was measured. For example, Hawley used the MPO ratio — managers, proprietors, and officials to the rest of the labor force — whereas Clark used the extent of *reported* participation and overlap of participation on specific issues by

> eleven strategically placed informants in each community: the mayor, the chairmen of the Democratic and Republican parties, the president of the largest bank, the editor of the newspaper with the largest circulation, the president of the chamber of commerce, the president of the bar association, the head of the largest labor union, the health commissioner, the urban renewal director, and the director of the last major hospital fund drive [p. 579].

Centralized decision making was determined by extent of *participation:* The larger the number participating, the greater the decentralization and the *overlap* of persons who participated in decisions concerned with various issues. The less the overlap, the more decentralized was considered the decision-making structure.

In an extension (1972) of his earlier analysis Clark utilized the same individual characteristics of cities, carried out a factor analysis, and interrelated these characteristics and factors to urban renewal expenditures. As a result of the factor analysis, he reported that the two factors characterizing "rapid population growth" and "early stages in the life cycle" (new suburbs with young people) are negatively associated with urban renewal. He also added the individual city characteristic of "age of community" to his analysis; age of city displaced poverty and population size as important dimensions in predicting urban renewal expenditures. Still unexplained, however, is why the percentage of Catholics remains the most important single characteristic related to urban renewal expenditures. Both the percent Catholic and age of community characteristics may be surrogates for some as yet undetermined underlying dimensions of cities.[5]

City and Urban Variation and Water Fluoridation

Pinard (1963) hypothesized that cities with certain kinds of characteristics are more likely than others to have apathetic and/or opposition forces to the leadership of the city. The degrees and patterns of support, apathy, or opposition are largely influenced by characteristics such as the size of the city, its rate of growth, its racial and ethnic composition, its occupational and power structure, and the condition of its labor market, for instance, unemployment. He reported that wherever there is a separation of the leadership and the lower segments of the system, there is probably a body of unattached citizens that oscillates between apathy or systematic opposition to the leadership. Indicators of this are the extent of unemployment and the rapidity of growth, and these characteristics are linked negatively to fluoridation. Thus Pinard suggested that cities that have a larger middle class are more likely to oppose fluoridation of the water supply than are lower-class communities, and retail cities are more likely to oppose fluoridation than industrial cities. Similarly, the larger the proportion of native white, for example, the more homogeneous the city, the more likely fluoridation referendums are to be approved by the voters.

Conclusions

The study of the consequences of city characteristics and types upon the ecology and the social life of the people living in them is in its infancy. As we have shown in this section, few studies have systematically interrelated city characteristics and typologies to outputs in these varying kinds of cities. Most of the studies carried out to date have utilized individual dimensions of cities rather than broader-based typologies. All of the studies reported in this chapter strongly indicate that future research using city and/or metropolitan typologies will prove extremely fruitful.

[5] A somewhat similar unexplained important phenomenon in some studies not referred to in this chapter is the importance the *percent of foreign-born* has in some statistical analyses concerned with policy outputs.

BIBLIOGRAPHY: Articles

Bendix, Reinhard, "Industrialization, Ideologies, and Social Structure," *American Sociological Review,* 24 (October 1959): 613–623.

Clark, Terry N., "Community Structure, Decision-Making, Budget Expenditures, and Urban Renewal in 51 American Communities," *American Sociological Review,* 33 (August 1968): 576–593.

Dawson, Richard E., and James A. Robinson, "Inter-party Competition, Economic Variables and Welfare Policies in the American States," *Journal of Politics,* 25 (May 1963): 265–289.

Fowler, Irving A., "Local Industrial Structures, Economic Power, and Community Welfare," *Social Problems,* 6 (Summer 1958): 41–51.

Harris, Chauncy D., "A Functional Classification of Cities in the United States," *Geographical Review,* 33 (January 1943): 86–99.

Hawley, Amos H., "Community Power and Urban Renewal Success," *American Journal of Sociology* 68 (January 1963): 422–431.

Nelson, Howard J., "A Service Classification of American Cities," *Economic Geography,* 31 (July 1955): 189–210.

Nelson, Howard J., "Some Characteristics of the Population of Cities in Similar Service Classifications," *Economic Geography,* 33 (April 1957): 95–108.

Paulson, Wayne, Edgar W. Butler, and Hallowell Pope, "Community Power and Public Welfare," *American Journal of Economics and Sociology,* 28 (January 1969): 17–27.

Perle, Sylvia, "Factor Analysis of American Cities: A Comparative Study," unpublished master's thesis, University of Chicago, Department of Geography, 1964.

Pinard, Maurice, "Structural Attachments and Political Support in Urban Politics: The Case of Fluoridation Referendums," *American Journal of Sociology,* 68 (March 1963): 513–526.

Price, Daniel O., "Factor Analysis in the Study of Metropolitan Centers," *Social Forces,* 20 (May 1942): 449–455.

Turk, Herman, "Interorganizational Networks in Urban Society: Initial Perspectives and Comparative Research," *American Sociological Review,* 35 (February 1970): 1–19.

BIBLIOGRAPHY: Books

Arnold, David S., "Classification as Part of Urban Management," in Brian J. L. Berry (ed.), *City Classification Handbook: Methods and Applications,* New York: Wiley-Interscience, 1972, pp. 361–377.

Berry, Brian J. L., "The Goals of City Classification," in Brian J. L. Berry (ed.), *City Classification Handbook: Methods and Applications,* New York: Wiley-Interscience, 1972a, pp. 1–8.

Berry, Brian J. L., "Latent Structure of the American Urban System, with International Comparisons," in Brian J. L. Berry (ed.), *City Classification Handbook: Methods and Applications,* New York: Wiley-Interscience, 1972b, pp. 11–60.

Clark, Terry N., "Urban Typologies and Political Outputs," in Brian J. L. Berry (ed.), *City Classification Handbook: Methods and Applications,* New York: Wiley-Interscience, 1972, pp. 152–178.

Duncan, Otis Dudley, W. Richard Scott, Stanley Lieberson, Beverly Duncan, and Hal

H. Winsborough, *Metropolis and Region,* Baltimore, Md.: The Johns Hopkins Press, 1960.

Dye, Thomas R., *Politics, Economics and the Public: Policy Outcomes in the American States,* Chicago: Rand McNally and Co., 1966.

Fowler, Irving A., *Local Industrial Structures, Economic Power and Community Welfare,* Totowa, N.J.: The Bedminster Press, 1964.

Gist, Noel P., and Sylvia F. Fava, *Urban Society,* 5th ed., New York: Thomas Y. Crowell, 1964.

Jones, Victor, "Economic Classification of Cities and Metropolitan Areas," *The Municipal Year Book: 1953,* Chicago: International City Manager's Association, 1953, pp. 49–47.

Meyer, David R., "Classification of U.S. Metropolitan Areas by Characteristics of Their Nonwhite Populations," in Brian J. L. Berry (ed.), *City Classification Handbook: Methods and Application,* New York: Wiley-Interscience, 1972, pp. 61–93.

Mills, C. Wright and Melville J. Ulmer, *Small Business and Civic Welfare,* Report of the Special Committee to Study Problems of American Small Business, U.S. Senate, 79th Congress, 2nd Session, No. 135, Washington, D.C.: U.S. Government Printing Office, 1946.

Schnore, Leo F., and Hal H. Winsborough, "Functional Classification and the Residential Location of Social Classes," in Brian J. L. Berry (ed.), *City Classification Handbook: Methods and Applications,* New York: Wiley-Interscience, 1972, pp. 124–151.

Walter, Benjamin, and Frederick M. Wirt, "Social and Political Dimensions of American Suburbs," in Brian J. L. Berry (ed.), *City Classification Handbook: Methods and Applications,* New York: Wiley-Interscience, 1972, pp. 97–123.

DIFFERENTIATION

SECTION THREE

Section Three presents some contrasts among rural, suburban, and urban areas. It describes several different approaches to differentiation *within* cities and urban areas, examines population redistribution or residential movement within cities and urban complexes, and relates these population movements to within-urban differentiation. This section also describes daily and/or intermittent circulation within cities and urban complexes in the journey-to-work and for other activities. Furthermore, the social stratification system of urban society in the United States and social mobility experiences are explored, as well as urban power structures and their consequences. The material presented in this section primarily is concerned with differentiation *within* cities and urban complexes. Thus it should be clearly noted that the unit of analysis has shifted from that presented in Section Two, which focused upon cities and urban places as the unit of analysis. Section Three is based on the traditional ecological position that social differentiation inevitably emerges as cities and urban areas increase in size. Thus the competition for desirable spatial locations results in an increasingly spatial differentiation. That is, individual areas within the urban complex are becoming increasingly homogeneous while the urban area, as an entity, is becoming more heterogeneous.

Chapter 6 shows that there are population, behavior, and attitudinal differences among people who live in different kinds of locations. Even though these differences may be diminishing, as some argue, others still obviously remain. While Chapter 6 focuses on rural, suburban, and urban contrasts, Chapter 7 more systematically evaluates several different frames of reference that have been utilized to delineate various areas within urban complexes. Some examination of the utility of each of these approaches is also included in Chapter 7. Chapter 8 examines why people move, where they move, and shows how residential mobility influences within-urban-area differentiation — that is, how areas within the city or urban complex become different from each other. Chapter 9 has as its purpose the demonstration of the impact that the general circulation of the population has upon the changing daily character and differentiation of various areas within the urban complex.

Chapter 10 explores some of the assumptions of stratification systems and how urbanization and other conditions such as the spatial distribution of social classes in urban complexes are associated with stratification in the United States. In addition, some of the consequences of stratification systems are examined. Chapter 11 extends the notion of social stratification systems in urban society to urban power structures. This chapter describes different kinds of power structures that have been reported to exist in cities and urban complexes in the United States, who belongs to them, and some of their consequences.

CHAPTER 6
RURAL, SUBURBAN, AND URBAN CONTRASTS

INTRODUCTION

A great deal of speculative and research literature has contrasted rural and urban people. The basic assumption is that rural and urban differences in the physical environment, community size, and, proportedly, social environment are expected to lead to different values, norms, behavior, and attitudes. Most of this comparative literature generally ignores variation within rural areas and cities. In the 1920s, research contrasting suburbanites and urbanites began to emerge. In this chapter we will present some rural-urban contrasts and suburban-city comparisons. In the following chapter we will explore differentiation within *suburban* and *city* areas and describe the variety of areas *within* the metropolitan complex.

RURAL-URBAN CONTRASTS[1]

The distinction between urban and rural places is generally based upon size of place measured in terms of resident population. On the other hand, it has been argued that the difference one should be concerned with is not the size of population but "individual outlook" (Stewart, 1958). As a consequence of these different perspectives, in this section we shall first examine demographic differences between urban and rural places based upon several definitions that primarily rely upon population size. Second, we shall determine whether there are systematic differences in attitudes, behavior, and value systems by population size. If an individual's outlook is influenced by the size of his place of residence, urban or rural, then in fact, urban and rural people in general continue to have different individual outlooks.

Population Characteristics

In contemporary newly developing nations, fertility in both urban and rural communities is generally high, with indications that there is no uniformity

[1] For a discussion of different types of rural communities see Edwards (1959).

While some observers argue that rural-urban differences are diminishing, it is still quite clear that demographic and density factors continue to maintain rural images, as in this dairy region of Wisconsin.

in those fertility rates that are consistently measured. In most non-Western countries urban fertility rates are below rural ones in about half the cases; in the remaining countries there is no apparent difference, or urban fertility appears to be higher than rural fertility. Further, whatever differences do exist in these countries with respect to population growth are mainly the results of *infant mortality* rather than fertility.

In Asia and the Far East, evidence shows that death rates of the population in general, and particularly of infants, are higher in cities than in rural areas, but the evidence is neither clear nor consistent. In Latin America, in fact, mortality is lower in urban than in rural areas. There is some difficulty in drawing a firm conclusion about urban-rural differences in general mortality, especially in developing regions.

In the experience of the West great declines in fertility were first evident in urban areas. With the emergence of urbanism as a way of life, rational decision making was extended to size of family, and fertility was deliberately controlled by some population segments in the urban region. Within urban areas, family planning originated among the elite, the better educated, and higher-income groups, and then diffused downward to other population segments. Obviously, however, not all of the poor and uneducated in urban areas are controlling their fertility.

In the United States differences in urban and rural fertility have been evident throughout the history of the nation. Fertility generally has been lower in urban than rural areas. Hauser (1965: 32 ff.) has reasoned that this is a result

As a result of immigration and high fertility among the native population, these multi-storied government resettlement buildings in Hong Kong are jammed with people.

of early selective migration to urban areas that brought a disproportionately large number of men into cities, thereby contributing to low, urban fertility. It should be noted, of course, that this is not true of many contemporary cities in the United States, since they have more females than males. It is true that birth rates have at times gone up in urban even more than rural areas during historical fluctuations in fertility. However, the general pattern of lower urban fertility seems to persist in the United States. Fertility variation by urban, rural nonfarm, and rural farm populations is shown in Table 6-1; this table illustrates fertility in the United States by race and rural-urban residence from 1970 U.S. census data. The rural farm fertility ratio was lower than the urban ratio, whereas, the rural nonfarm fertility ratio was higher. However, if the fertility ratio is divided into anglo, black, and chicano populations, it becomes apparent that a substantial part of this differential is the contribution made by chicano women. For the anglo and black populations, the rural farm fertility ratio is actually lower than the urban one. In contrast, the rural nonfarm fertility ratio for all populations is much higher than that for the urban or rural farm populations, although the largest differences are noted for minorities.

The emergence of the city, in some measure, was a function of rapid

TABLE 6-1
Fertility in the United States by Race and Rural-Urban Residence, 1970

	FERTILITY RATIO[a]							
	TOTAL		WHITE		BLACK		SPANISH HERITAGE	
	1000 WOMEN	1000 WOMEN EVER MAR-RIED	1000 WOMEN	1000 WOMEN EVER MAR-RIED	1000 WOMEN	1000 WOMEN EVER MAR-RIED	1000 WOMEN	1000 WOMEN EVER MAR-RIED
Total	326	453	325	446	330	502	456	633
Urban	315	444	—	—	322	482	451	624
Rural Non-farm	372	490	—	—	378	620	503	716
Rural Farm	287	410	—	—	314	585	438	659

[a] Children ever born to women aged 35–44.

Source: U.S. Bureau of the Census, *United States Summary*, 1970.

population growth. In the West the city has become the point of origin and diffusion of fertility control measures such as birth control pills. Urbanism in technologically advanced areas increasingly holds forth the prospect of deliberate control of population growth. It appears, however, that the city in newly developing countries has given little evidence of playing a similar role. Nevertheless, if the concerted efforts currently under way are to achieve fertility control, it may be anticipated that major successes in developing areas will first occur in urban rather than rural areas. If past experience is an indicator of what will happen in developing areas, the upper socioeconomic levels/upper social classes will be those who will first control their fertility and then the techniques will be diffused to the lower socioeconomic and lower-class population segments.

Apparently, very little residential movement takes place among rural areas. In the United States over the past century, and especially the past four or five decades, a mass exodus from rural to urban areas has taken place. A generation ago, many people in urban places had grown up on farms; however, this is less often true now. A much larger proportion of urbanites today have never had the experience of living on a farm or in a rural area.

Attitudes and Behavior

Aside from demographic data, Glenn and Alston (1967) used information gathered from a variety of national surveys reporting rural-urban differences in values, attitudes, and behavior. They provided empirical evidence

Graffiti and court athletics are two of the major forms of recreation participated in by urban children and adolescents.

that farmers and their families are relatively more prejudiced, ethnocentric, isolationist, intolerant of deviance, opposed to civil liberties, distrustful of people, traditionally religious, ascetic, work oriented, puritanical, uninformed, favor early marriage and high fertility and are less happy than urban people.

Swedner's (1960) review of a large number of studies that reported rural and urban differences can be summarized as follows: City children, in contrast to rural children, have better personal adjustment, are more rational, have better ability to make ethical adjustments, are more resourceful in group situations, have more freedom in adolescence, and, it appears, are less neurotic, less introverted, more dominant, more confident, and more sociable than rural children. In addition, the general level of family life is reportedly better in urban than rural areas. On the other hand, it appears that more urban girls drink and smoke, consider their homes unhappy (which is in contrast to the Glenn and Alston reported surveys) and were less likely to receive firm, strict discipline in their homes. There was also less consistency in child rearing.

Swedner also reported a number of studies that contrasted rural and urban differences in mental illness. It should be noted, however, that most figures on mental illness vary by definition, since diagnostic categories are not reliable, nor are data gathered uniformly. Most of the studies are biased toward the lower social class because they use public agency records. Most studies, even with these limitations, indicate no actual increase in the rate of mental illness over time, whether rural or urban or for younger age groups. Some recent national metropolitan data gathered in 1966 and 1969, however, using the same population and the same measure of mental well-being, suggests that, in fact, there was an increase in mental illness between 1966 and 1969 (Kaiser et al., forthcoming).

Insofar as other social deviations are concerned, *reported* crimes are higher in cities than in rural areas. Murder rates are higher in rural areas, while most other kinds of crime occur less frequently. Urban crime is likely to affect property; suicide seems to be somewhat inversely related to murder, which means suicide rates are higher in urban than rural areas. Reported sex deviation is higher for men in cities than in rural areas, whereas no differences are reported between women in urban and rural areas. The argument generally presented is that social ostracism is more frequent and more severe for women than for men who deviate sexually. Changing sexual patterns are developing in the United States, however, for both men and women. Deviation is more likely to be visible in rural areas, where there is more personal social control and less formal control; this also may be changing because of the spatial mobility of the population and changing values in regard to sexual behavior.

SUBURBAN-CITY CONTRASTS

Douglass (1925) suggested that suburban growth is associated with the growth of urban civilization. That is, as population increases, suburban growth requires either vertical building, an increase in surface population density, or spreading out onto previously unsettled land. Thus suburban growth can be thought of as a centrifugal spin-off from the city occupying former rural areas. The literature on suburban growth continually focuses on and reinforces the notion that selective population segments live in suburbs and that suburban movement is based upon peculiar social psychological and motivational stances that stress family privacy and independence. In the United States the first spurt of suburban growth appears to have been around 1910 and was associated with the advent of electric railways and streetcars. Later suburban growth owes much to the development of the automobile and street construction.

Definitions of Suburbs

The concept of suburbs remains largely ambiguous and undefined. Douglass (1925) defined the suburbs as ''that belt of population which lives under distinctly roomier conditions than is the average lot of city people, but under distinctively more crowded conditions than those of the adjoining open country, is suburban, whether lying within or outside the city.'' This criterion emphasizes *density of population*. More often used in current discussions and descriptions of suburbs is the operational definition of whether a population resides within the political boundary of the central city or outside of its boundaries but yet nearby in the metropolitan and/or urbanized area. In the United States ''nearby'' is generally defined as being within the SMSA but outside the central city. This definition also includes those residential areas that are located outside the city but are tied to it.

"Open space for children," "light and air," and "privacy" are the major reasons given by people who move to such urban developments as are found here in Westchester, New York. Note the tendency to block out one's backyard neighbors with dense trees and hedges.

Generally, the currently accepted notion points to the intermediate population density of suburbs between rural areas and the central city and being outside the limits of the city; suburbs also are dependent upon the city as a source of necessary goods and services and as a place of employment. According to this definition, there are "suburbs" like Hamtramck and Highland Park, which are completely enclosed by Detroit, or the city of San Fernando,

One of the features of living in a "dormitory" suburb is commuting to the city. These Connecticut commuters from New Canaan and Stamford are waiting — somewhat impatiently — for the New York and New Haven Railroad to take them into New York City.

which is likewise surrounded by Los Angeles. By political boundary definitions, well over 100 cities larger than 50,000 population fall into this classification. This is a very real definitional problem, since the very same city, apart from a much larger central city, would itself be a central city, have its own suburbs, and be classified as a SMSA. Another problem inherent in the political definition of suburbs is that cities are not uniform in the size of area and proportion of population living in the central city. El Paso, Texas, in 1970 had a population of 322,000 but only 37,000 suburban residents; similarly, the Utica-Rome SMSA had 139,000 people living in the central cities, with over 200,000 suburban residents by political definition.

Generally, however, the larger the size of the metropolitan area, the smaller the proportion of land and population that is in the central city. While using political boundaries to delineate suburbs has its problems, it may be very meaningful to study governmental organization and interrelationships, political processes, and so on, by the use of political boundaries.

Shryock (1964) has suggested an alternative definition of suburbs that includes the relative *proportion of multiple-family housing units* (MFHU) and *distance to civic center* (or Central Business District — CBD) as primary indicators. A location close to the civic center and with a high proportion of MFHUs would be considered as urban, and its opposite as suburban. How close lying a location with a low proportion of MFHUs would be classified or, how far away a location with a high proportion of MFHUs would be classified has not been specified. Hoover and Vernon (1959) have pointed out that population density, physical area characteristics, land use, and age of housing might be used in delineating city and suburban areas (also see B. Duncan et al., 1962).

As an alternative way of delineating suburbs, Martin (1956) has characterized the *definitive* characteristics of suburbs as being an ecological position outside of the central city, a high rate of commuting to the central city, smaller size, and a lower density of population. *Derivative* characteristics—that is, factors that may characterize suburbs but are not essential to suburban status—are a low proportion of unrelated individuals, a high proportion of young married adults, many young children, middle class, middle income, and homogeneity in values and attitudes.

The assumed homogeneity in values and attitudes has led some writers to elaborate upon suburbia as a new way of life. Focus on suburbia as a style of life stresses the near-identical ranch houses, neat lawns and streets, two-car garages, and large numbers of children. Each family reportedly resides only temporarily in the suburb because heads are promoted and thus as families become upwardly mobile, they move to more prestigious suburban addresses. Activities include extensive neighboring, organizational participation, and children-oriented activities. Commuting to the city by the head of household is common and the mother is primarily responsible for child rearing. The importance of religion is stressed as is a change in political affiliation from Democrat to Republican. Available evidence suggests that this description, or what has been called the "myth of suburbia" (Berger, 1960), is not universally true of all suburbs.

Unfortunately, various definitions must be used throughout any discussion of contemporary American suburbs. We will point out which definition we are using at any particular time. (For an extended summary and bibliography of the literature, see Pryor, 1968.)

Growth of Suburbs

Suburban settlements are not new, for the very earliest cities, as we have seen, had suburban inhabitants or persons who lived outside of the walls. The Mesopotamian city of Ur is estimated to have had a population of 34,000 inhabitants, with at least as many more living in its suburbs (Sirjamaki, 1964: 35). The residents of these suburbs contrasted with the city dwellers; the latter were the royalty, military, priests, government workers, and, later, merchants. As trade developed during the eleventh century, cities began to expand, and merchants and others who depended upon large-scale trade settled outside of the walled cities in suburbs, which several hundred years later were also enclosed by walls.

In the United States this trend was apparent from the very beginning of early settlements, and it intensified during the construction of the first railroads during the 1840s, which allowed people to live farther away from their workplaces. At the beginning of the twentieth century, larger U.S. cities had large-sized suburban settlements. Early suburban residents were typically the more wealthy who were looking for space, fresh air, and privacy and who established permanent homes along railroad lines then radiating out from the cities. The development of streetcar and subway lines made it possible for the middle classes to follow suit (Chinitz, 1964: 27). As the automobile became more prominent, interstitial areas became inhabited and earlier suburban areas either became part of the city or at least looked like it. From 1900 to 1920 central cities in U.S. metropolitan areas grew more rapidly than suburbs (though this may have been because of the extensive annexation of adjacent suburbs taking place then). Since 1920, annexation has declined, and suburban areas have grown more rapidly than central cities in U.S. metropolitan areas (Sirjamaki, 1964: 116–128).

Suburbs have become especially prominent in the United States since the end of World War II as accretion at the city's periphery became the dominant mode of metropolitan growth. This growth has been cited as one of the major social changes of the twentieth century — the emergence of large-scale, mass-produced suburbs. It has affected both countryside and city: the countryside by land use changes from agrarian to housing and services; the city in that it has been deserted by some inhabitants in their "flight to the suburbs" (Brunner and Hallenbeck, 1955).

An argument has developed over the suburbs' reason for being. According to the *motivational* argument, suburbs exist because they combine the advantages of both country and city. Emphasis is placed upon escape from the city with a dislike of its lack of privacy and space, because it does not have a place for a garden or for children to play; emphasis also is placed upon the romantic ideal of "country living," in the suburbs (Whetten, 1951: 322–325). The desire to own a home, coupled with the belief that doing so is cheaper than renting, also has played some part in the motivational explanation (Martin, 1956). On the other hand, in periods of rapid population growth the bulk of housing construction takes place where level and relatively unencumbered land suitable for the mass production of homes is available, that is, the countryside adjacent to or near cities. This explanation of the growth of suburbs is in keeping with the economic opportunity theory that associates movement to the cities with job availability in cities. These approaches do not necessarily conflict and may only be two different ways of viewing a phenomenon that undeniably does exist.

Closely related to the growth of suburbs, from either perspective, is the growth and availability of transportation. As we have noted previously, the first large suburbs in the United States were associated with the growth of the railroads in the 1840s. The suburban dweller of that era had to live close to the railroad or stage line. Later, of course, the automobile helped to fill in the interstitial areas between trolley lines. As automobiles increased in number, the use of freeways and parkways not only supplemented rail transport but, in some instances, replaced it entirely. Undoubtedly, as population continues to grow in the future, so will suburban expansion.

TABLE 6-2
Urban and Rural Residence, 1950, 1960, and 1970: The United States

		PERCENT		
		1950	1960	1970
	Total	100.0	100.0	100.0
Urban		64.0	69.9	73.5
Urbanized areas		45.8	53.5	58.3
Central cities		32.0	32.3	31.5
Urban fringe		13.8	21.1	26.8
Other urban		18.2	16.4	15.2
Rural		36.0	30.1	26.5
Metropolitan Residence				68.6
Nonmetropolitan Residence				31.4

Sources: U.S. Bureau of the Census, various published reports, 1950, 1960, and 1970.

Suburban-Urban Differences

A number of generalizations concerning differences between city and suburban areas and between city residents and suburbanites have appeared in the literature. Most of them have limited empirical substantiation and have been described in terms of a number of varied general concepts.

Since 1950, the U.S. census has used the term "urban fringe" for all territory within urbanized areas but outside the central city.[2] In standard census usage, these areas are considered suburbs. In 1950, as shown in Table 6-2, 64 percent of the population was urban, and by 1960 this percent increased to 69.9, and by 1970, to 73.5 percent. The major growth occurred in areas considered as an urban fringe or a suburb. Between 1950 and 1960 population in central cities increased in absolute numbers, although proportionately they had less population in 1960 than they did in 1950 even though they had a greater absolute population. Central cities continued to experience losses between 1960 and 1970. The proportional growth in urban population took place within the urban fringe, which increased from 13.8 percent of the population in 1950 to 21.1 percent in 1960, or an increase in absolute numbers from about 21 million to almost 38 million; the urban fringe population grew to over 54 million by 1970.

Results of the 1950, 1960, and 1970 censuses show that both the central city and the suburbs have an excess of females, with the excess being slightly larger in central cities in 1950 and increasingly larger in 1960 and 1970. In 1950, 1960, and 1970 the central-city population tended, on the average, to be older than the suburban population, and as with female-male

[2] See U.S. Census of Population: 1960. *Type of Place. Final Report* PC(3)-1E. Washington, D.C.: GPO, 1964, p. xi, for 1960 data; for 1950 data see Duncan and Reiss (1956); for 1970 data see any summary or state report.

ratio the descrepancy between central city and suburb increased with the former's median age remaining about the same but with the latter's median age decreasing.

Contrary to popular belief, the fertility ratio (ratio of the population under 5 to 1000 women aged 15–44) of the suburbs is typically higher than that of the central city. In the city it was 452 in 1950 and 513 in 1960; in the suburbs it was 534 and 571, respectively. Similarly, the dependency ratio (ratio of the population under 20 and 65 and over to the population aged 20–64) was smaller for the city than the suburbs. This difference was not great, and dependency ratios tend to be made up primarily of different population components in the central city and the suburb. Cities have an excess of persons 65 and over, and suburbs have an excess of younger persons, and the dependency ratios of both cities and suburbs seem to be increasing.

Between 1950 and 1970 the proportion of black population in the suburbs remained almost the same but increased substantially in the cities. Discrepancies in black-white distribution are more marked for smaller urbanized areas, and central cities had lower levels of educational attainment and lower incomes than suburbs. Concomitantly, the city has an overabundance of service and clerical workers, while the suburbs have an excess of professionals and managers. Residential mobility was nearly equal for both central city and suburb although there were slight differences regarding points of origin.

As Duncan and Reiss for 1950 noted (1956), there are some differences in these relationships when size of place and regions are examined separately. Nevertheless, the overall conclusion is that differences reported between central cities and suburbs are part of a general pattern. It further appears that this pattern continues to exist and is growing stronger as time passes, which leads inevitably to the conclusion that the central city increasingly is becoming polarized from its suburbs.

According to Berger's "myth of suburbia" (1960), then, suburbanites tend to reside temporarily in a neighborhood because they are upwardly mobile and are awaiting promotions and job transfers. There is a suggestion of a never-ending cycle of residential moves, moves that are generally made from a poor residential area to a higher-status neighborhood. Furthermore, there is an assertion that suburbanites are more highly educated and have higher-prestige occupations than their urban counterparts. Other features of the myth involve appreciation of home and neighborhood and the familism of the suburbanite.

Factors Influencing Suburban Growth

The earlier stages of the decentralization of cities in the United States represented families moving to the suburbs from the city. Similarly, the post–World War II era found mass-produced suburbs being populated by many married couples who were having children in substantial numbers. At this stage births helped account for a greater than ever proportion of the increasing suburban population. It was noted earlier that the suburban population, demographically at least, contrasts somewhat with the city population. Even though suburban movement includes people with a wide range of social and economic characteristics, there does appear to be a concentration of persons in certain categories, and more and more of the suburban population have had previous suburban living experience. Thus while there are differences in suburbs, there apparently is a selectivity of population taking place as the urban complex expands. Currently, families moving to the suburbs are likely to be composed of anglo adults who are in the early stages of the life-and-family cycle, who either bring large numbers of children with them or give birth to them once they have arrived in the suburbs.

Reasons given for moving to the suburbs invariably include primary reference to them as more desirable places than the cities for raising children and as being less congested places for youngsters to play in. Occasionally, a statement is made that few desirable houses and/or neighborhoods are available in the city. Others report that it is cheaper to live in the suburbs because land costs less and taxes are lower, although this may be a misperception inasmuch as it may actually cost more to live in suburbia than in the city.

These all are social psychological reasons advanced by respondents for their moving. Another reason given for the growth of suburbs and fringe areas is that this is where contractors have built new houses. After available space in the city is used up, expansion tends to be at the periphery. Another alternative is to increase density in the city by increasing crowding of the existing housing supply through building vertically. Vertical expansion, of course, is limited by the technology available at a particular time — and most people want more space, not less.

Specialization in Suburbs
Types of Suburbs
Suburbs in the United States have been classified as *residential* or dormitory, *industrial,* and *mixed* (Cole, 1958: 169). Schnore (1956) evolved a tenfold classification system, although he eventually simplifies his scheme into *industrial* and *residential* suburbs (also see Schnore and Winsborough, 1972: 134–136). He characterized industrial suburbs as employing centers that attract workers from other parts of the metropolitan area (also see Douglass, 1925). They are primarily located in the heavily industrialized areas of the northeastern and north-central sections of the United States. Residential suburbs, which are found in metropolitan areas of all regions of the country, serve as dormitories, and local retail trade is the dominant activity. The larger the central city, the greater the frequency of residential suburbs. They tend to be smaller than industrial suburbs.

There are some communities adjacent to the central city that are classified as suburbs under some conditions but not others. For example, Martin (1956: 448) states that "communities located adjacent to larger urban centers

but providing jobs for their own residents as well as others are classified as satellite cities rather than suburbs." Satellite cities appear more frequently in metropolitan areas with smaller central cities and tend to be older and larger than
residential suburbs. Typically, they have lower rents than residential suburbs
and probably are lower in the social class hierarchy (Schnore, 1957: 123).

Literature on suburbs in the 1950s focused mainly upon organization-
man residential-type suburbs (Whyte, 1956). Only recently have others pointed
out that "working class," lower-middle-class residential suburbs exist (Berger,
1960; Gans, 1967). Earlier we showed that there are differences between residents of the central city and suburb. Here we are concerned with *variation
within suburbs*. A particular suburb may be internally homogeneous but very
different from other suburbs. That is, residents of any given suburb probably are
pretty much alike in regard to family type, age composition, social class, and so
on, but in another suburb the residents also may be homogeneous, but the two
suburbs may have substantial differences between them.

Levittown—located near Mitchell Air Force Base and the commercial
air operations of Kennedy and La Guardia airports in the New York metropolitan area, as well as near several aircraft-producing firms—was one of the first
large-scale suburban developments to be systematically studied (Gans, 1967).
At the time of the study, only three black families and several oriental families
lived there. The implication is that ethnically, occupationally, and according to
social class, Levittown was homogeneous.

Public Services: Expansion and Problems

As suburban communities expand, conflict may be engendered between newcomers and longer-term residents. Besides bringing themselves,
newcomers usually introduce new ideas about schools, water systems, playgrounds, and other public services—all of which have the effect of increasing
the local tax load. The social cleavage may become so deep that reorganization of the local government may be required.

The concentration of families with children in the suburbs has increased the demand for more school facilities and teachers. Municipal services
have either had to be greatly expanded or, in some instances, built in their entirety. Expansion of public water and sewage systems to replace private facilities and enlarged police and fire protection services have been necessitated. All
of these services are expensive; and residential suburbs without an industrial
base must place heavy taxes on housing and land to provide them. Thus a basic
problem appears to have engendered conflict between central city and suburban residents: the raising and spending of resources.

The first attempt to help a city overcome its financial plight was to
annex the surrounding territory. Until the 1920s, annexation at least doubled
the 10 largest cities in size. Political opposition to this practice developed, and
since then annexation has proceeded at a much slower pace. More recently,
stress has been placed on the abolition of political boundaries and the need for

consolidation, merger, and county-metropolitan government. Some public corporations including central cities, residential and industrial suburbs, and unincorporated places have been formed to build bridges, tunnels, and airports; transit authorities have consolidated some metropolitan transportation networks.

Class and Social Mobility

Most suburbs have a middle- and upper-middle-class population. Nevertheless, there are aristocratic suburbs inhabited by wealthy families, quaint and picturesque country villages, mass-produced suburbs, more expansive rural areas of part-time farmers and nonfarm dwellings; and there are even a few black suburban ghettos (Whetten, 1951: 325–326).

The social class factor combined with the life cycle accounts for much of the variation between city and suburb. The extensive social participation in the suburbs is associated with the family stage of the life cycle, and with the norms of child rearing and parental role found in the upper working class, the lower middle class, and locally oriented portions of the upper middle and upper classes. According to Gans (1968: 74–75), this *is* the suburban way of life, and it is based primarily on class and age rather than ecological position in the metropolitan complex.

Stress has been placed upon the transient nature of suburbs and its relationship to upward social mobility (Whyte, 1956). The United States in general has had an increase in higher-status positions, which reportedly are associated with the shifting about of the population. Many suburbs are not only middle class, but they also are places where transiency and upward mobility have been institutionalized. Despite this prevailing view, many residents of suburbs have been reported as not being socially mobile, nor are they expected to be in the future (Berger, 1960: 18).

Suburbanism as a Way of Life

We have already noted the demographic selectivity of suburbs. Others have pointed out further that contemporary suburbs in the United States tend to be middle and upper middle class and, for the most part, white. Some writers have been led to emphasize the familistic nature of suburban living. Most suburbanites are nuclear-family members (father, mother, and at least one child). Indeed, the reasons most often given for making a suburban move relate to children and familistic values (Bell, 1958). There is, then, a focus in daytime activities upon the nurturance of children. Organizational affiliations and activities of the mother appear to be child oriented. Upper-middle-class mothers chauffeur their children around in order to expose them to the proper experiential and educational opportunities (Gans, 1968: 72).

It has been hypothesized that a suburbanite can be differentiated from others, since his or her personality is characterized by configurations more typical of urban social systems than rural. Similarly, Fava (1956) argues that, in addition to demographic factors in suburban living, there are social psychological aspects that serve to indicate the existence of a "suburban way of life"; and Jaco and Belknap (1953) have hypothesized that a new "fringe family" form has emerged in areas adjacent to but outside of cities. In addition, Martin (1956) suggests that living in the suburbs appears to have an important influence on patterns of social relationships and participation.

On the other hand, at least for some, movement to suburbia by working-class persons has not resulted in profound changes in basic behavior.

> They were still overwhelmingly Democrats—they attended church as infrequently as they ever did; like most working class people, their informal contacts were limited largely to kin; they neither gave nor went to parties; on the whole they had no great hopes of getting ahead in their jobs; and instead of a transient psychology, most of them harbored a view of their new suburban homes as paradise permanently gained [Berger, 1968: 435].

Since the advent of the mass-produced suburbs primarily began after World War II, children may be the only "true" products of modern suburbs, since they were the first residents who lived there during their formative stages.

Suburban-City Socioeconomic Contrasts
Socioeconomic status differentials between central cities and suburbs vary somewhat systematically with the size of urbanized area. The larger the urbanized area, the more likely suburbs are to be higher in socioeconomic status than the central city. An opposite result obtains for smaller urbanized areas, with the central city having a higher socioeconomic status than suburbs (Schnore, 1963: 78; 1962; Smith, 1970). Some cities, such as New York, Chicago, and Philadelphia, show a pattern of higher-status suburbs, while Los Angeles is different from these three cities in that *persons at the top and at the bottom* of the educational ladder are overrepresented in the central city (Schnore, 1964: 167). However, these four large cities only represent two of six different relations between urban and suburban populations. Tucson (along with 13 other cities) represents an almost complete "reversal" of that of New York, Chicago, and Philadelphia, with lower-status residents (as measured by educational attainment) living outside of the central city or, as Schnore (1964) points out, "*the exact reversal of the common image of suburbia.*" Ten other cities, for example, Albuquerque, have similar central city-suburban relationships, but the difference is not as quite as marked as for those cities typified by Tucson.

Los Angeles "*is actually the modal type,*" since 70 out of 200 urbanized areas in the United States have an overrepresentation at the upper and lower end of the social class scale. Three other types are relatively similar in that they fit the notion that suburbs are of higher socioeconomic status than the central city. Finally, there are four cities—Memphis is one—that do not fit any of the foregoing categories.

These patterns vary from one census division to another, with cities in New England, the Middle Atlantic area, and the East North Central region most closely demonstrating the hypothesis that central cities are of lower social status than their suburbs. The modal type with a concentration of upper- *and* lower-status residents in the central city is concentrated in the South Atlantic region and especially in the West South Central and Mountain regions. In a somewhat similar analysis of SMSAs having populations of 300,000 or more in 1960, but using occupational rather than educational differentials, metropolitan areas that have central cities in which white-collar occupations are over-represented tend to be smaller, newer, southern retail-trade centers with a lower population density, and less likely to be on a principal waterway than are other areas. An opposite type has an underrepresentation of higher occupational levels in the central city; these cities tend to be older, larger, with greater population density and to be "water-based, break-in-transportation centers" (Goldsmith and Stockwell, 1969: 393–394).

Furthermore, in more sophisticated statistical analyses it appears that date of settlement (or age of city) is better than size or any other tested variable in predicting central city-suburban differentials in socioeconomic status—with "older" cities more likely to have lower socioeconomic status than their suburbs, while "younger" cities are more likely to have higher status than their suburbs. Thus it is incorrect to characterize all suburbs as being higher in status than the central city.

Farley (1964: 39) argues that most studies only demonstrate that cities and their suburbs differ in composition at one point in time, and this "cross-sectional approach does not reveal how these differences developed nor does it indicate whether cities and suburbs are becoming more alike or dissimilar in composition." To support his criticism of these other studies he examined changes in suburbs over time. As a result of his *change analysis,* he argued that cities and suburbs are becoming more dissimilar in composition over time (p. 39). "Generally, the suburban areas have shown not only more rapid growth in total numbers but *proportionately greater increases in population of higher socioeconomic status"* (italics added). In addition, he proposed that existing lower-status suburbs and those currently growing are essentially industrial suburbs, with the lower-status population being attached to the large-scale decentralization (suburbanization) of manufacturing that is taking place. Notwithstanding this decentralization, he noted that particular suburbs retain their individual socioeconomic levels for long periods of time. Even in those instances when rapid population growth takes place, the socioeconomic characteristics of the suburb does not change substantially. Schnore and Pinkerton (1966) agreed that residential redistribution according to socioeconomic differences are occurring but note that there are substantial regional differences and that age of the city and population size are important factors in the extent to which socioeconomic differences between central city and surburb occur.

Conclusions

There is a growing concensus that suburban development is a continuation of past urban growth patterns. That is, suburban growth is associated with the expanding metropolitan population and is related to the need for additional vertical or horizontal expansion of the city. Adhering to this perspective does not require that we negate the view that there are demographic differentials between the central city and the suburb nor that there may be different ways or styles of life in each. There continues to be some question over whether these different styles of life are a consequence of the move from central city to suburb or whether they are a continuation of the style of life either lived in the city or desired by its residents. The suburban way of life is attractive to large segments of the population, and "suburban orientation" is strongest for those persons who previously have lived in the suburbs (Zelan, 1968: 408).

Various studies suggest that on the average the socioeconomic levels of suburban areas are higher than those of central city populations; yet most of the same research indicates that there is a large socioeconomic diversity of suburbs. Similarly, there is ample evidence that socioeconomic differentiation between central cities and suburbs is closely associated with the total urbanized area according to population size and when the city was first settled. Virtually ignored, however, in almost all of these studies is the role played by the *annexation* of former suburban areas by the central city in producing current differences between central city and suburbs (for an exception see Smith, 1970).

Several decades ago, Whetten (1951) identified a number of problems for research in suburbanization. Some progress has been made on "further identification and classification of suburban populations into meaningful groupings or community types," "the extent and selectivity of the migration," and social status and the suburban movement. But relatively little information is as yet available concerning the "impact of suburban living on personality" and the extent to which suburbanites realize their aspirations by moving to the suburbs. Similarly, more research concerning the relations of outlying areas to the central city is needed with some focus on social conflict in suburban areas as well as among various peripheral areas and the central city. Finally, future research should be concerned with longitudinal studies, since they allow a process orientation and the evaluation of trends.

BIBLIOGRAPHY: Articles

Duncan, Beverly, Georges Sabagh, and Maurice D. Van Arsdol, Jr., "Patterns of City Growth," *American Journal of Sociology,* 67 (January 1962): 418–429.
Edwards, Allen D., "Types of Rural Communities," in Marvin B. Sussman (ed.),

Community Structure and Analysis, New York: Thomas Y. Crowell Company, 1959.

Farley, Reynolds, "Suburban Persistence," *American Sociological Review,* 29 (February 1964): 38–47.

Fava, Sylvia F., "Suburbanism as a Way of Life," *American Sociological Review,* 21 (February 1956): 34–37.

Glenn, Norval D., and Jon P. Alston, "Rural-Urban Differences in Reported Attitudes and Behavior," *Southwestern Social Science Quarterly,* 47 (March 1967): 381–400.

Goldsmith, Harold F., and Edward G. Stockwell, "Occupational Selectivity and Metropolitan Structure," *Rural Sociology,* 34 (September 1969): 387–395.

Jaco, E. Gartley, and Ivan Belknap, "Is a New Family Form Emerging in the Urban Fringe?" *American Sociological Review,* 18 (October 1953): 551–557.

Martin, Walter T., "The Structuring of Social Relationships Engendered by Suburban Residence," *American Sociological Review,* 21 (August 1956): 446–453.

Pryor, Robin J., "Defining the Rural-Urban Fringe," *Social Forces,* 47 (December 1968): 202–215.

Schnore, Leo F., "The Functions of Metropolitan Suburbs," *American Journal of Sociology,* 61 (March 1956): 453–458.

Schnore, Leo F., "Satellites and Suburbs," *Social Forces,* 36 (December 1957): 121–127.

Schnore, Leo F., "City-Suburban Income Differentials in Metropoligan Areas," *American Sociological Review,* 27 (April 1962): 252–255.

Schnore, Leo F., "The Socio-Economic Status of Cities and Suburbs," *American Sociological Review,* 28 (February 1963): 76–85.

Schnore, Leo F., "Urban Structure and Suburban Selectivity," *Demography,* 1 (1964): 164–176.

Schnore, Leo F., and James R. Pinkerton, "Residential Redistribution of Socioeconomic Strata in Metropolitan Areas," *Demography,* 3 (No. 2, 1966): 491–499.

Smith, Joel, "Another Look at Socioeconomic Status Distributions in Urbanized Areas," *Urban Affairs Quarterly,* 5 (June 1970): 422–453.

Stewart, Charles T., Jr., "The Urban-Rural Dichotomy: Concepts and Uses," *American Journal of Sociology,* 64 (September 1958): 152–158.

Whetten, Nathan L., "Suburbanization as a Field for Sociological Research," *Rural Sociology,* 16 (December 1951): 319–329.

BIBLIOGRAPHY: Books

Bell, Wendell, "Social Choice, Life Styles, and Suburban Residence," in William M. Dobriner (ed.), *The Suburban Community,* New York: G. P. Putnam's Sons, 1958, pp. 225–247.

Berger, Bennett M., *Working-Class Suburb,* Berkely and Los Angeles: University of California Press, 1960.

Berger, Bennett M., "Suburbia and the American Dream," in Sylvia F. Fava (ed.), *Urbanism in World Perspective: A Reader,* New York: Thomas Y. Crowell Company, 1968, pp. 434–444.

Brunner, Edmund de S., and Wilber C. Hallenbeck, *American Society: Urban and Rural Patterns,* New York: Harper & Bros., 1955.

Chinitz, Benjamin, "City/and Suburb," in Benjamin Chinitz (ed.), *City and Suburb: The Economics of Metropolitan Growth,* Englewood Cliffs, N.J.: Prentice-Hall, 1964, pp. 3–50.

Cole, William E., *Urban Society,* Cambridge, Mass.: Riverside Press, 1958.

Douglass, Paul H., *The Suburban Trend,* New York: The Century Company, 1925.

Duncan, Otis Dudley, and Albert J. Reiss, Jr., *Social Characteristics of Rural and Urban Communities, 1950,* New York: John Wiley & Sons, 1956.

Gans, Herbert J., *The Levittowners: Ways of Life and Politics in a New Suburban Community,* New York: Pantheon Books, 1967.

Gans, Herbert J., "Urbanism and Suburbanism as Ways of Life: A Re-evaluation of Definitions," in Sylvia F. Fava (ed.), *Urbanism in World Perspective: A Reader,* New York: Thomas Y. Crowell Company, 1968, pp. 63–81.

Hauser, Philip M., "Urbanization: An Overview," in Philip M. Hauser and Leo F. Schnore (eds.), *The Study of Urbanization,* New York: John Wiley & Sons, 1965, pp. 1–47.

Hoover, Edgar M., and Raymond Vernon, *Anatomy of a Metropolis,* Cambridge, Mass.: Harvard University Press, 1959.

Kaiser, Edward J., Edgar W. Butler, and Ronald J. McAllister, *The Urban Nomads,* forthcoming.

Schnore, Leo F., and Hal H. Winsborough, "Functional Classification and the Residential Location of Social Classes," in Brian J. L. Berry (ed.), *City Classification Handbook: Methods and Applications,* New York: Wiley-Interscience, 1972, pp. 124–151.

Shryock, Henry, Jr., *Population Mobility Within the United States,* Chicago: Community and Family Study Center, 1964.

Sirjamaki, John, *The Sociology of Cities,* New York: Random House, 1964.

Swedner, Harald, *Ecological Differentiation of Habits and Attitudes,* Lund, Sweden: GWK Gleerup, 1960.

Whyte, William H., Jr., *The Organization Man,* New York: Simon & Schuster, 1956.

Zelan, Joseph, "Does Suburbia Make a Difference: An Exercise in Secondary Analysis," in Sylvia F. Fava (ed.), *Urbanism in World Perspective: A Reader,* New York: Thomas Y. Crowell Company, 1968, pp. 401–408.

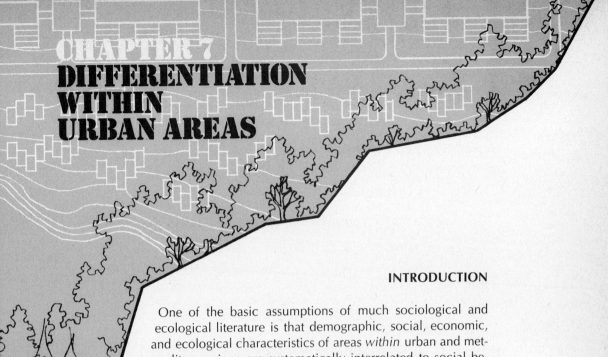

CHAPTER 7
DIFFERENTIATION WITHIN URBAN AREAS

INTRODUCTION

One of the basic assumptions of much sociological and ecological literature is that demographic, social, economic, and ecological characteristics of areas *within* urban and metropolitan regions are systematically interrelated to social behavior, demographic factors such as fertility, infant mortality, ethnic residential segregation, and to informal and formal social participation, aspirations, and so on. These characteristics have in turn been found to be associated with different measures of mental health, alcoholism, suicide, personal disorganization, family disruption, delinquency, and retardation (Goldsmith and Unger, 1970: 1–2). In this chapter we shall examine some frames of reference that have been developed to account for the variety and types of areas found within the metropolitan complex, as well as pertinent research endeavors for each perspective. First, the "traditional" theories—Burgess' concentric zone theory, Hoyt's sector theory, and the multiple nuclei theory—are described. Then several more recently developed frames of reference are explored in some detail. Density and ethnic, racial, and age segregation in the United States are also explored.

CONCENTRIC ZONE, SECTOR, AND MULTIPLE NUCLEI THEORIES
Concentric Zone Theory

Growth and differentiation in metropolitan areas in the United States has been described by Burgess (1924) as occurring in gradually extended concentric zones. This spatial patterning represents a more explicit and simplified statement of the ideas of Hurd. Drawing primarily from his study of Chicago, Burgess advanced the notion that, in the absence of counteracting factors, the modern city in the United States takes the form of five primary concentric zones.

Zone 1: The Central Business District (CBD).

Zone 2: The zone in transition. An area surrounding the CBD that includes areas of residential deterioration caused by encroaching business and industry from Zone 1.

Zone 3: The zone of independent workingmen's homes. An area largely constituted of neighborhoods of second-generation immigrant settlement in northern cities.

Zone 4: The zone of better residences. Residential areas of middle-class native-born Americans, small businessmen, and so forth.

Zone 5: The commuter's zone (30–60 miles from the CBD in large cities).

These zones were assumed to be a product of radial expansion taking place from the CBD of the central city. Burgess also identified two additional zones: Zone 6, which is made up of agricultural districts within commuting distance of the CBD, and Zone 7, which includes the hinterland of the city. As a result of growth and expansion, the city necessarily must be reorganized spatially, and each inner zone extends its spatial area by invading the next outer zone. It is quite clear, then, that Burgess conceived his theory as a dynamic one that describes the process of city growth and differentiation over time. He considered radial expansion to be the primary factor, but not the only one, that determines city structure. He noted that topographic features, such as rivers and hills, and transportation arteries introduce distortions into the zonal pattern, so that no city perfectly exemplifies concentric zones. However, Burgess assumes these concentric patterns to be dominant and explicitly discernible, with only minor variations, in all cities in the United States.

The concentric zone theory assumes a growing city. Quinn (1950: 116–137) identified additional implicit assumptions of the theory. He observed that *heterogeneity* of zones requires the presence of widely varying population categories such as the foreign-born, different races, a division of labor reflected in different occupations, and social classes. Quinn also identified the assumption of a particular kind of economic base—that is, a mixed commercial-industrial city, because the zonal descriptions explicitly include areas of commerce and industry.

Further, Burgess assumed an efficient transportation system that was equally utilitarian for all parts of the city. Recently, Schnore (1965: 354) pointed out that the zonal theory also explicitly describes a *geometry of space*. It assumes a primary CBD and that the supply of space increases away from the center where space is at a premium; a corollary of limited core space is that it is more valuable than space elsewhere in the city. The competition for this rare space is generally won by those having economic power. Similarly, occupancy patterns vary according to economic power: The wealthy voluntarily choose where they want to live, and leftover housing is available to the working and lower classes and to ethnic and aged populations.

Probably the most valuable space in Atlanta, Georgia, is this area stretching south from Peachtree Center in the heart of the city.

The concentric zone theory has been widely accepted by social scientists without enough critical examination. On the other hand, critics of the theory argue that zones do not always exhibit similar spatial distributions and in many instances there are no semblances of zones at all in some cities. In addition, critics have suggested that a distinction should be made between zones and gradients, or even concentric zones. It is possible for distinct zones to exist in a city but not to form gradients (Quinn, 1950: 116–137). Another critical point is that of internal *zonal homogeneity* as opposed to *zonal heterogeneity*. Quite explicitly, the Burgess theory describes homogeneous zones; however, Davie (1937) and Hoyt (1939) reported considerably zonal heterogeneity in the cities they studied (for information on industrial location see Reeder, 1953). Further, Firey (1947) has shown that survivals of earlier land use occur because of symbolic attachments and these survivals distort the gradient. Each of these criticisms suggests that the zonal theory may be applicable for some cities but definitely not for others.

Using 1940 census data, Blumenfeld (1949) tested the concentric zone theory for the city of Philadelphia and reported that despite the fact that the city "is divided by the fall line into two radically different topographic zones, the coastal plain and the piedmont," it shows a rather consistent concentric pattern. Nevertheless, he described three rather than five or seven zones. He delineated a small central core in the city center, a main urban area extending beyond the inner core to a distance of about eight miles, and not yet fully urbanized fringe areas beyond the eight-mile zone. Using a variety of indicators, he reported "an extraordinary consistency within the main urban area confirming strongly the dominance of the concentric pattern" (p. 212). The line dividing the main urban area from the fringe areas in particular clearly shows, over several decades, the expansion of the urban area. However, he argued that to understand the concentric zone theory fully, comparative *longitudinal* data for entire metropolitan regions would have to be examined.

The Sector Theory

A variation of the Burgess concentric zone theme describes a slow outward movement from the core of the city along transportation lines that results in *sectors*—a star-shaped city. The sector theory (also sometimes known as the "axial" theory) was an outgrowth of a study conducted by Hoyt (1939) for the Federal Housing Administration. He found that most residential areas within urban areas in the United States tended to be distributed in a definite manner with respect to *commercial* and *industrial* districts of the city. As a result, Hoyt argued that the general spatial pattern of cities in the United States can best be characterized as sectors rather than concentric zones. These sectors are like wedges radiating out from the CBD along *transport routes*. Residential areas grow outward along rather distinct radii, and growth on the arc of a given sector tends to take on the character of the initial growth in that sector.

Hoyt hypothesized that the location and the movement of high-rent residential areas are the most important organizing factor in urban growth and that the movement of these areas tends to pull the growth of the city in the same direction. High-rent areas usually move forward from the center of the city along a specified avenue or radial line that predicts future high-quality residen-

This view shows the importance of the Kaw (foreground) and Missouri (left) Rivers and the highway system that both links and separates Kansas City, Missouri (in the distance) and Kansas City, Kansas (foreground). Note the growth along transportation arteries away from the central city.

tial growth along the same radial. New construction of upper-class residential areas would be located on the outward edges of the old high-rent area; as high-quality areas move outward along a sector, lower rental groups would move in and occupy the housing that was formerly occupied by higher-income classes. Thus while the Burgess concentric circle theory suggested that high-rent residential areas encircle the outer rim of the city, the sector theory hypothesizes that they move out in several sectors from the center to the periphery.

Hoyt summarized his studies by the following:

1. Industrial areas do not develop around the CBD but along railroads, waterfronts, near outskirts of the city. They have stringlike expansion; that is, they follow transportation lines.
2. High-class areas are not located in the last concentric zone but only in one or more sectors.
3. High-grade residential areas originate near retail and office centers but tend to follow established lines of travel toward

another already established nucleus—preferably on high ground free from the danger of floods, or along bays, lakes, rivers, and so on.

4. Higher-priced residential neighborhoods tend to grow toward the homes of community leaders. They also tend to grow toward the section of the city that has free open country beyond the edges and away from "dead-end" sections that are limited by natural or artificial barriers to expansion.

The major criticism of the sector theory has been that it overemphasizes the importance of high-rent residential areas and underestimates the importance of zoning in shaping the urban area.

The Multiple Nuclei Theory

According to other theorists, as an urban area grows, it is differentiated into *multiple nuclei,* which are specialized but do not necessarily form concentric zones and which are not necessarily interconnected to form sectors. Harris and Ullman (1945) contended that in many cities land use patterns do not focus solely on a single center such as the CBD but on multiple centers that are quite discernible. These multiple nuclei reflect a combination of at least the following four factors:

1. Certain activities require specialized facilities.
2. Certain like activities come together because they all profit from concentration.
3. Certain unlike activities are detrimental to each other.
4. Some activities are unable to afford the high rents of more desirable sites in the city.

Conclusion

Of these three theories the concentric zone frame of reference has the most adherents despite ardent criticism. Critics of both the sector and the multiple nuclei theories, however, have been less severe than those of the concentric zone theory. There are ample indications though that city growth and differentiation are more complex than any of these theories postulates. We shall return to the concentric zone, sector, and multiple nuclei theories after we have discussed some more recent developments that attempt to explain urban growth and differentiation.

SOCIAL AREA ANALYSIS

The Burgess concentric zone model and the sector and multiple nuclei theories view the city in isolation from the rest of society. So far these theories have not been found adequate for general descriptive and predictive usage. In the late 1940s Shevky and Williams (1949) made explicit the need to examine urban growth and differentiation as a product of trends in the organization of society. Subsequently, Shevky and Bell (1955) suggested that as a society industrializes, there are changes in the "rate and intensity of social relations," "differentiation of function," and "complexity of organization." These notions were derived from Clark's (1940) hypothesis that as industrial development takes place, an increasing percentage of the population becomes employed in manufacturing and construction and thereby in trade, transportation, communication, and other services. In addition, changes in the scope of social interaction and dependency are viewed as aspects of society increasing in scale. Thus the city is not viewed as molding modern society, but rather as being molded by the economic and social changes taking place in society.

Although no one has seriously questioned the assumption that changes take place in the organization of a society as it industrializes, support for the Shevky-Bell model has been something less than enthusiastic (Hawley and Duncan, 1957). However, none of the studies undertaken to date has tested many of the major elements of the model primarily because time studies are necessary to determine its validity and applicability (Butler and Barclay, 1967). Specifically, no one has tested the notion that as a society increases in scale, its component areas—and presumably this means areas *within* the metropolitan complex as elsewhere—become more specialized and differentiated and individual areas become more homogeneous while the metropolis as a whole becomes more heterogeneous.

Udry (1964) notes that as society increases in scale, three interrelated processes supposedly occur:

1. Occupational structure shifts from a large proportion manual to clerical, supervisory, and managerial, resulting in general improvement in economic status and social rank. An index combining indicators of occupational status, educational level, and rent is suggested as an appropriate measure of this process.

2. Industry will shift from primary (extractive and agricultural) to secondary (manufacturing) to tertiary (service) production, which is accompanied by urbanization, that is, people concentrating in cities. A consequence is change in family life, as measured by fertility rates, the percent of females in the labor force, and the percent of single-family housing units.

3. Social organization becomes more complex, and this will be reflected in more complex and differentiated spatial organization. Increased segregation of functionally differentiated units will occur. Social and ethnic units especially will become more segregated.

The city from this perspective, then, is seen as a product of the complex whole of society. Society is viewed in a temporal framework in which dominant trends are changes related to the movement from a rural to an urban and industrial form. These changes are described as being part of the *increasing scale* of society. Increasing scale is characterized by three trends: (1) changes in the distribution of skills, (2) changes in the organization of productive activity, and (3) changes in the composition of the population. Social differentiation becomes more marked over time, that is, with increasing scale. Each trend contributes to the process of social differentiation.

The changing distribution of skills leads to a more definitive ordering of groups in society according to the socioeconomic status of each occupation; changes in the organization of productive activities are associated with changes in styles of living in which increasing scale is characterized by a decline in family life; changes in population lead to residential concentrations of similar — usually ethnic — types.

Impressive to date is the fact that most cross-sectional empirical examinations have shown the typology to be useful and meaningful, despite its critics, in describing the mosaic of areas that make up a metropolitan complex. Various "cluster analyses" of cities have consistently produced results that closely approximate those postulated by the social area analysts — both in the United States and elsewhere.[1] On the other hand, virtually none of the studies conducted so far has tested the theory by utilizing trends over time. In other words, how do areas within the metropolis change over time? They are *supposed* to become, according to this theory, more differentiated. As the city itself becomes more heterogeneous, *subdivisions within it should become more homogeneous.*

Social area adherents postulate three dimensions of differentiation that are required to explain variation in areas of cities in the United States: (1) social rank, (2) urbanization/familism, and (3) ethnicity-segregation.

Social Rank

Every social area analysis study has isolated a socioeconomic factor that most often accounts for the largest proportion of variation. That is, it explains more of the differences that occur among areas than any other dimension or factor.

Familism/Urbanization

Another factor relates to family size and age composition. It may be interpreted as describing "residential environments for different kinds of families at different stages of their life cycles" (Abu-Lughod, 1969: 202). In a few cities this factor appears to be mixed with social rank.

Segregation

The ethnicity factor is the least independent of the three dimensions and has been reported very rarely outside the United States. This may be because of the cities selected for study both in and outside the country; it may be related to the selection of variables; or, obviously, it may be representative of the *real* world in the United States and elsewhere.

---

[1] For example, see the studies of McElrath (1962) for Rome, except for segregation; Herbert (1967) for Newcastle, except for segregation; and Abu-Lughod (1969) for Cairo.

Classification Process

1. Each area within a given city (census tract, etc.) is allocated a *score* on each of the three constructs designed to measure degrees of social differentiation among area populations.

2. Adjacent or contiguous areas with similar scores are grouped together into "social areas" that present a mosaic of distinctive districts in the metropolitan complex; for example, areas A_1, A_{11}, and A_{36} in the following table are "high" on urbanization and "low" in social rank, while areas A_2 and A_{17} are the opposite. Other areas in any given city would be classified in these and the other categories.

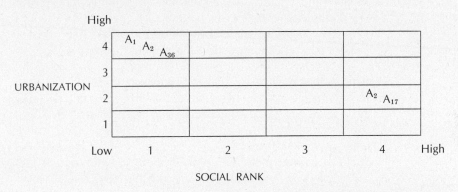

Social area adherents claim that the theory is simple in statement; serves as an organizing principle; it is theory linked and permits the derivation of testable propositions; it is precise in its specifications and permits observed agreement; and it represents a continuity with similar formulations that it aims to replace.

Uses of social areas analysis, according to Bell (1959), are as follows:

1. *The Delineation of Areas.* By applying these methods to the available data on American cities, it is possible to delineate systematically urban neighborhoods and communities having different social characteristics. Such a delineation has descriptive value to the social scientist and city planner alike.

2. *Comparative Studies at One Point in Time.* Comparative studies of the social areas of different cities at one point in time can be made. The social area distributions of neighborhoods in different cities can be compared to determine patterns differentiated by the regions in which the cities are located, the sizes of the cities, their chief economic functions, their relative ages, topographies, ethnic compositions, transportation bases, and segregation patterns.

3. *Comparative Studies at Two (or More) Points in Time.* Within a given urban area the extent of change over time can be determined. New neighborhoods appear, they grow and develop, they become old, and at times they change completely.

4. *A Framework for the Execution of Other Types of Research.* The framework can be used to study diverse factors such as neighborhood differences and individual attitudes and behavior ranging from suicide, voting, religious preferences, and mental disorder to personal morale, and so on.

5. As a tool for urban field studies, the typology serves a number of functions:
   a. It can be used as an aid in selecting neighborhoods and urban subcommunities for intensive study on the basis of informed judgments concerning the social position of a given area in the larger urban metropolitan complex.
   b. It provides an integrative frame for urban subcommunity field studies by codifying and ordering a large mass of data.
   c. It permits the investigation of the combined or independent effect of personal and unit characteristics of a neighborhood.

Criticisms of the Social Area Analysis Approach

A criticism of social area analysis is that it is presented as a dynamic system while the indexes describe a static pattern of differentiation (Van Arsdol et al., 1961: 26). Social area analysis indexes appear to offer no empirical or logical advantages over the more often used individual census measures although individual census tract measures give considerably better results (Van Arsdol et al., 1961: 30).

While Van Arsdol and others (1962) report that their analyses of 10 cities (with 2 exceptions) follow the Shevky model, *"The results of our factor analyses do not confirm Shevky's theory for the reason that the indexes and their composition are not deducible from the theory"* (p. 11). They do agree that the analyses offer "a certain pragmatic support" (p. 11). Thus the major criticism voiced by Van Arsdol and his associates is that the theory does not specify how one gets from it to actual data analyses, although they are willing to subscribe to the notion that the theory has some pragmatic utility (also see Hawley and Duncan, 1957).

Research Results

In a study comparing Los Angeles and San Francisco, results substantiate, to some degree, the claims of social area adherents that the typology is a useful technique for making intercity comparisons. The structures of similar-type social areas in the two cities were very much alike in 1940 (Bell, 1953), since by comparing the "sex ratio of every social area made up of Los Angeles census tracts with the sex ratios of the social areas made up of Bay Region tracts, it may be observed . . . that the characteristic sex ratios of the social areas in the two regions were similar" (p. 45). Thus we have the conclusion that *similar social areas, whether in Los Angeles or San Francisco, have similar sex ratios*. In addition, the age structure of similarly classified areas in the two cities were substantially the same.

Others have shown that residential mobility/stability helps account for variation in areas within urban complexes. Similarly, homogeneity has been found to be "highest for the group which constituted a small minority (10 percent or less) of the population in a census tract, whether the group was white or nonwhite" (Klee et al., 1967).

Sophisticated statistical factor analytic studies based on social area analysis variables have also been carried out. Such analyses of 1940 census tract data for Los Angeles and the San Francisco Bay Region were consistent with the social area description of the three key indexes (Bell, 1955). Similarly, statistical analysis for a set of 10 cities—Akron, Atlanta, Birmingham, Kansas City, Louisville, Minneapolis, Portland, Providence, Rochester, and Seattle—showed that when data for the 10 cities were combined, they conformed to the social area analysis description of differentiation in cities. When individual cities were analyzed, two of them did not follow the social area analysis pattern (Van Arsdol et al., 1958).

Abu-Lughod (1969) reviewed many social area analysis studies and concluded that, with only several exceptions, a *social rank* factor is always isolated and that it accounts for most of the variation in the structure of cities. She also notes a uniformity in previous studies of linkages among variables that could be considered as measuring the familism/urbanization factor, for example, family size and age composition. She noted that the single-family housing unit (SFHU) variable is culturally bound, since it was not useful in her study of Cairo. She suggests that the best measures of the familism factor are the fertility ratio, the dependency ratio, and the proportion of one- and two-person families.

Longitudinal Examinations
of the Shevky-Bell Model

Most of the major elements in the Shevky-Bell model concern trends and changes in society and how they are reflected in the components of the society. Most tests of the model have been cross-sectional, however, and thus have not examined its key aspects. Udry's longitudinal study (1964) of the nine census regions of the United States, 89 SMSAs, and Ohio's 88 counties resulted in his asserting that the social rank dimension emerges quite clearly in all units of analysis but that the urbanization/familism dimension is barely discernible and the segregation axis does not exist at these levels.

Conclusions

Although the theoretical relevance of social area analysis has been questioned, it does appear appropriate, at the minimum, to accept the constructs of social rank, urbanization/familism, and segregation as useful dimensions for describing the census tract structure of most American cities (Goldsmith and Unger, 1970: 5). In addition, Anderson and Egeland (1961) studied four cities that in 1950 were about the same size and had roughly circular shapes: (Akron, Dayton, Indianapolis, and Syracuse) to eliminate the possibility of major geographic disturbances. They concluded that familism/urbanization within each of these cities was clearly a concentric phenomenon with those areas (census tracts) located nearest the city center being the most urbanized. Social rank (they call it *prestige value*), however, was found in sectors, although in each of the cities they were not oriented toward the same direction from the city center. Cities, they concluded, may be combined to study urbanization, but they must remain separate for the purpose of studying social rank even though in each city social rank was clearly a *sector* phenomenon. They concluded then that "the principal findings of this study are that urbanization (at the tract level) varies primarily concentrically or by distance from the center of the city, while prestige value (or social rank) varies primarily sectorially, with very little distance variation" (Anderson and Egeland, 1961: 398). McElrath's (1962) study of Rome, Italy, tends to support this concentric and sector notion, although Cedar Rapids has been described as having sectors and multiple nuclei (Hartshorn, 1971).

HOOVER-VERNON
The Model

Another model of urban area differentiation has been advanced by Hoover and Vernon (1962). As a result of observations over 35 years and covering 22 counties that constitute the New York metropolitan region, they hypothesized that most variation among both individual households and urban areas can be accounted for by job type, income, and age structure of households. These three characteristics also are influential in the development of homogeneous neighborhoods.

Hoover and Vernon pointed out that there is not just one high-density commercial center, but many, of different orders of magnitude. They postulated an undulating theory of urban differentiation that takes into consideration a full range of variables such as age of population and housing and land use characteristics. The key variable appears to be *age of settlement,* which depends upon unspecified conditions. Once settlement occurs, it becomes the independent variable that is postulated as setting in motion an evolutionary process including most, *but not all,* areas within the metropolis.

Given the location of a particular job or class of jobs, Hoover and Vernon noted two conflicting trends that influence individuals in their choices of residence. On one hand, there is the desire for easy access to jobs and other urban amenities. On the other hand, this advantage is counteracted by an increase in population density, which is usually disliked by individuals. Thus there is a push away from the central city and a pull to "spacious" living in the suburbs. From the determinants of residential choice, Hoover and Vernon postulated a five-stage theory of areal differentiation. They are described as follows and are illustrated in Figure 7-1.

FIGURE 7-1
Hoover-Vernon Housing Cycle Imputed Housing Characteristics

STAGE	DATE OF SETTLE-MENT	AGE OF HOUSING	PERCENT			
			MULTIPLE-FAMILY HU's	RENTER-OCCUPIED HU's	CON-VERTED HU's	HOUSE-HOLD SIZE
1 — Building Up	10	new	very low	very low	none	very large
2 — Transition	10–19	young	low	low	none	large
3 — Downgrading	20–29	middle aged	medium	medium	medium	medium
4 — Thinning Out	30–39	old	high	high	high	small
5 — Renewal	40–49	new	very high	very high	none	?

Stage 1: Residential development of single-family housing units.

Stage 2: A transition stage in which there is substantial new construction and population growth but in which a high and an increasing proportion of new housing is in apartments, with an increase in average density.

Stage 3: A downgrading stage in which old housing, both single and multifamily, is being adapted to greater density use than it was originally designed for. In this stage there is usually little actual new construction, but there is some population and housing growth through conversion and crowding of structures.

Stage 4: Thinning-out stage, or the stage in which density and dwelling occupancy are gradually reduced. Most of the shrinkage comes through a decline in household size in these neighborhoods, but the shrinkage may also reflect the merging of dwelling units, vacancy, abandonment, and demolition. This stage is characterized by little or no residential construction and by a decline in population.

Stage 5: Renewal

As shown in Figure 7-1, the first stage is one of residential development of single-family housing units on land devoid of dwellings. Density of population during this *building-up* stage increases rather rapidly. During the second or *transition* stage, substantial new construction and population growth occur, but an increasing proportion of the new housing is in the form of apartments, with a resulting further increase in *population density*.

During the *downgrading* stage — the third stage — little new construction occurs. However, existing single- and multiple-family dwellings are converted to accommodate more inhabitants than they were originally constructed

Abandonment and demolition prior to urban renewal is one stage of the Hoover-Vernon approach to growth and decline in urban neighborhoods. It appears that this burnt-out building on the Lower East Side of New York City is in "stage 4" — awaiting demolition.

for, and consequently population and density continue to increase. At this time, minority groups may replace former residents. In the *thinning-out* stage, Stage 4, a decrease in population size and density occurs both because of a decline in household size and also through merger, abandonment, and demolition of housing units. At the end of the cycle is the *renewal* stage, or Stage 5. Obsolete housing is replaced by new housing, which then enters the cycle anew, or the land is withdrawn into other uses. If housing is constructed, overall population density may not be affected much although population composition will change. Renewal may be piecemeal, or it may be general as a result of public intervention.

An examination of the Shevky-Bell and the Hoover-Vernon models leads to the conclusion that the latter implicitly assumes many aspects of the former. For example, both models assume the concept of homogeneous areas differentiated from other areas. The Hoover-Vernon model though is in some ways the more flexible of the two in that changes in the composition of neighborhoods are expected, whereas this possibility is not explicitly discussed by the Shevky group. The implication of the model is that housing and population change together, although the housing cycle seems to be the primary criterion of the different stages that Hoover and Vernon identify in neighborhood evolution.

Upon closer examination it appears that at times the housing and population cycles may be independent of each other. For example, as Firey (1947) has shown in his study of Boston and as Hoover and Vernon have noted, neighborhoods may remain in the same stage of development almost indefinitely. During several decades of housing stability, obviously either the demographic characteristics of the inhabitants or the actual inhabitants would change. Theoretically, the reverse process also could occur. A major difficulty with the Hoover-Vernon approach is the lack of delineation of the time span of the individual stages in the model.

Research Results

In order to test the Hoover-Vernon model it is necessary to use some index of *date of settlement*. Beverly Duncan et al. (1962) used an index of two dwelling units per acre to designate a built-up tract. But because tracts are drawn to equalize population rather than area, it is possible that large tracts designated as not built-up may contain built-up areas equal to or larger than smaller tracts that are so classified. Furthermore, much intensive urban land use may not be residential. Tracts that contain heavy concentrations of manufacturing, transportation, office facilities, and so on, may be classified as not built up. Beverly Duncan et al. however, reported only three tracts in Los Angeles that were classified as built up but that had not satisfied their criterion by 1950. On the other hand, the two dwelling units per acre, they argued, permit most hilly and mountainous areas to achieve this density criterion for a built-up area.

Another prerequisite for testing the Hoover-Vernon model (also, it should be noted, the social area model) is that boundaries of areas within the metropolitan complex being studied have remained *comparable* over time. That is, the outer perimeters of the areas must not have changed, or otherwise the changes that have occurred may be changes in several different areas rather than in a specifically bounded one. Beverly Duncan et al. (1962) thus constructed a "comparability grid" that used consistent boundaries over time for Los Angeles between 1940, 1950, and 1960 to examine the Hoover-Vernon model.

As a result of their study, it appears that densities in Los Angeles areas settled prior to 1920 increased for 25 years after the date of settlement and then declined thereafter. Areas built up in the 1920s increased in population density for about 15 years, decreased after World War II, but then increased once again. In addition to these findings, B. Duncan et al. (1962: 422) noted that their data point up the "pitfalls" of generalizations obtained from cross-sectional data analyses; thus their longitudinal study is in their opinion much more valid than a cross-sectional one. They insisted that the expansion of the city can be only fully accounted for only if indicators of the historical growth context and already existing spatial configuration of built-up areas are included in the study.

Finally, they concluded that Los Angeles, in general, accords with Hoover and Vernon's formulation. Obviously, rapid growth was evident during the building-up phase. Then, over time, population increases in building-up areas, and eventually population declines as thinning out takes place.

A more recent study based upon the entire Los Angeles County metropolitan area (including the city of Los Angeles, as in the B. Duncan et al. study) has also suggested that the Hoover-Vernon model has substantial applicability to the whole region. Butler and Barclay (1967), following the lead of Hoover and Vernon and B. Duncan and others, used data for Los Angeles County (including that city) and examined the notion that certain population and housing characteristics would be found differentially distributed in the metropolitan area by date-of-settlement patterns. They hypothesized that the earliest settled areas would contain the highest proportion of older population and females in the labor force, a lower proportion of owner-occupied single-family housing units, and low fertility rates. Furthermore, they believed that the earliest settled areas would be characterized by lower social levels as measured by occupational and educational status and by housing value and median rent paid for housing, as well as by higher spatial mobility rates and proportion of minorities such as blacks and chicanos.

As a result of their analysis, they concluded that change did occur rather systematically in Los Angeles (the county and the city) and that these changes varied according to date of settlement. Broad support was given to the Hoover-Vernon model, while more limited support was given to the Shevky-Bell model.

Although these and virtually all other frames of reference emphasize the homogeneity of urban areas, this emphasis may be misplaced, since these longitudinal data show that the discussion should revolve around the *relative* degree of homogeneity in urban areas, which changes over time. For example, most first-settled areas—and, therefore, the oldest areas of the city *and* the county—characteristically have fewer young children, more older people and blacks, fewer single-family housing units, more persons in lower-level occupations, lower housing values as reflected in price and rents, and a lower percentage of owner-occupied housing units. Yet these same areas have reached their current state by going through transitional stages without ever being completely homogeneous. At the initial stages the black and the aged populations decrease, and then, as time goes on, a steady increase occurs as housing becomes older and begins to deteriorate. Similarly, at the initial building-up stage, the proportion of white-collar workers typically increases but gradually decreases thereafter. In addition, housing characteristics and tenure change over time. In early stages the proportion of owners increases and then decreases as areas go through various transitional stages. It always appears that populations and housing are only in a state of relative homogeneity and most areas are in a rather constant state of flux.

ATHEORETICAL TYPOLOGIES OF AREAS WITHIN URBAN REGIONS

In addition to the more theoretically based descriptions of the internal structure of urban regions in the United States, a number of investigators have used individual variables similar to those already described to derive empirical types of urban areas by utilizing scaling techniques (Green, 1956) or sophisticated statistical methods such as factor analysis. These statistical approaches can be considered as attempts to find the underlying uniformities or regularities of areas within urban complexes. A few of these statistical works have generated ex post facto theories, and in some other instances they appear to confirm aspects of earlier discussed theories.

Research Results

Carey (1966) examined Manhattan, New York, using 33 population and housing dimensions derived from the 1960 U.S. census. As a result of a factor analysis, he reports six different types of areas:

1. *A general Manhattan population-residence* factor is heavily influenced by population-size variables. Housing units are described as sound, though aging; the population is large and employed in retailing and services more than in the professions; female rather than male unemployment contributes more heavily to the description; racial variables, along with variables related to income and rent, contribute relatively little to this factor. Areas high on this factor are primarily located on the west side of Central Park, with smaller areas in central Harlem, and in lower Manhattan.

2. *The barrio or Spanish Harlem* (Puerto Rican core region) factor has a population with large numbers of elementary-school-age children and many high-school children. There also is a small black component. Workers are employed in the garment trades and to a smaller extent in eating and drinking places. Rents and family incomes are low. Housing is crowded, but there is a rather low density per acre; much of the housing is unsound. Few of the people in this area are employed in private households, as servants. Compared to an earlier study — as of 1950 — the area is relatively stable insofar as the core of the Puerto Rican population is concerned. The general location is northeastern Central Park. There are several unusual areas suggesting that in-depth studies are necessary to describe these areas fully. One tract has a cohesive colony of

longstanding Italians that forms an ethnic enclave that was still visible in 1966.

3. *The middle-income black* factor is one of the two types of areas clearly described by the *black population* variable. The population is employed in educational services or in private households (probably females). Density of population is low. Families have low median family income and low gross rent. Unemployment is not a problem, and there is a large school-age population. Its primary location is central and eastern Harlem. A careful comparison with housing maps of New York City shows that this region coincides to a remarkable degree with tracts where public housing developments have been placed.

4. *A black live-in servant* factor describes areas where many blacks are employed in private households and in other personal services. This may be a misnomer, for the area should really be divided into two parts: (1) blacks who live in with the wealthy, and (2) extremely poor blacks living in places with no or shared bathrooms, and so on. The poorest areas of Manhattan are included in this factor.

5. *Low-density transient residence* factor is used to refer to areas where population and housing-unit density are low. Median rent and family incomes are low; there are many individuals, that is, single persons. Much of the area is in other than residential use. The population tends to be nonblack and non-Puerto Rican. It is a transient white population.

6. *Rooming-house* areas are different from type 5 in that there is some employment in private households. The people pay relatively high rents yet occupy crowded quarters and share bathrooms. The location is west of Central Park.

A factor analytic study of Newark, New Jersey, using 48 variables—including most of those utilized in the Manhattan study—appeared to stress somewhat different dimensions than those in Manhattan (Janson, 1968). In addition, workplace location, land use, and assessed land value dimensions were included. Thus the studies, unfortunately, are not directly comparable. One type of area in Newark appears to correspond with Manhattan's barrio type and is labeled *Racial Slums* (or Social Rank-Race). High values on this factor indicate, among other things, many large families, many children, low income, few going to work by car, high unemployment, few old people, and a high proportion of unsound housing.

Another factor type was clearly defined as *Social Rank;* high-rent and home value, greater educational attainment, and a peripheral location characterized high scores on this dimension. Two other factors were reported by the author to be closely allied (although it might be instructive for the student to examine the original tables very closely) and stressed middle-age populations; one of these factors suggested areas containing Puerto Ricans and having commercial land use, with relatively high assessments. The other *middle-age* factor characterized areas as being non-Puerto Rican, having older housing and a higher percentage of women in the labor force. Another dimension included high proportions of adult males and a newly arrived young population; these areas were labeled as *mobile* areas. Finally, a *density and land utilization* factor is described as consisting primarily of public and semi-public land use, central location and large residential structures.

ETHNIC/RACIAL
AND AGE SEGREGATION[2]

Closely allied with the growth and internal differentiation of cities and urban complexes is age and ethnic/racial segregation. Currently, it appears that most cities and urban regions in the United States are becoming increasingly segregated along these dimensions. One of the earliest longitudinal studies of residential segregation conducted in Chicago showed that as the black population increased in numbers, it expanded into former all-anglo neighborhoods (Duncan and Duncan, 1957). At the same time, blacks tended to "pile up" in areas and neighborhoods already heavily populated by blacks, thus substantially increasing the density of already overpopulated areas. In Chicago, the black population generally moved radially outward from areas already heavily populated by blacks. The black movement into areas did not alter their socioeconomic character. Similarly, the outmovement of anglos and the in-movement of blacks did not alter social problems in the areas or increase them — these problems remained relatively constant regardless of population composition.

Blacks who first entered former anglo areas tended to be natives of the city and generally better off economically than those who remained behind in the predominantly black residential areas. Thus it appears that migrants from the South and rural areas moved into already well-established black neighborhoods. The differential distribution of natives and migrants in the black neighborhoods of Chicago suggests that there are substantial differences in black residential patterns. A study of Milwaukee (Edwards, 1970) confirmed this and showed that the residential segregation of black families in that city varied by income (also see Marston, 1969) and by stage of the family cycle. Black residential patterns resembled those of anglo populations. The greatest variation was found with families having higher incomes and couples with children who were living in areas contiguous to the black core. These areas may be serving as suburbs for wealthier black families with children.

In a more recent study Van Arsdol and Schuerman (1971) reported that in Los Angeles County the segregation of the Mexican-born and of nonwhites other than blacks decreased slightly over the past decades. As anglos moved to newly developed areas and neighborhoods in the urban complex, however, blacks tended to move into vacated areas, becoming more concentrated and segregated; these areas developed ghetto characteristics. As a result of their study, Van Arsdol and Schuerman concluded "that increased de facto segrega-

[2] Social class segregation is a topic of a subsequent chapter.

This view of a market street in Hong Kong shows high density of persons and housing units. The street probably supports a high density of persons per apartment—as well as per room—above the commercial stores.

tion can be expected in neighborhoods where there is a conversion, down grading, or a thinning out of housing units" (1971: 477). In newer developed areas, segregation is greater for blacks than for the Mexican-born or for nonwhites other than blacks. Blacks showed the greatest proportional increase in neighborhoods where they were already highly concentrated, a pattern not applicable to other minority populations.

Obviously, increasing segregation of blacks has a negative aspect insofar as assimilation of them into the population is concerned. The 1970 U.S. census showed that blacks were becoming increasingly suburbanized. But this is misleading because blacks who are suburbanizing are moving into older suburban areas with declining neighborhoods and deteriorating housing much like that available to them in central cities. In other words, some blacks are merely trading these kinds of conditions in the central city for a similar kind of environment in the outer city or the suburbs (also see Farley, 1970). Van Arsdol and Schuerman argued that their Los Angeles County data "support our contention that ethnic residential segregation is not confined to the central city but pervades the entire metropolis" (1971: 478).

While there is no question that blacks are becoming more segregated from other populations in most urban complexes (Kantrowitz, 1969), it is less certain that other ethnic minorities also are becoming more segregated. On the other hand, it should not go unnoted that in many cities the aged may be more segregated than blacks.

DENSITY

One condition, but not a necessary one, associated with urban growth and differentiation, is density. Density of population has been reported to be related to a variety of social and urban problems (Hawley, 1972: 525). Not often discussed, however, are the potential positive benefits of density (Hawley, 1972: 526). The effects, if any, of density so far have been primarily extrapolated from *rat* studies. More elaborate density measures should include at least the following: (1) persons per dwelling unit, (2) persons per room, (3) persons per acre, and (4) dwelling units per acre, and so on (Galle et al., 1972). A fruitful area of future research and theory will be in unraveling the effects density has upon stress, mental health, morbidity, mortality, and so forth, when factors such as poverty and underprivileged status have been controlled (Hawley, 1972: 525).

CONCLUSIONS

Future work that is concerned with the city needs to emphasize more systematically the dynamic aspects of growth and differentiation, since it is painfully obvious that cities may in fact increase in population and areas within them become more variegated and assume different characteristics. On the other hand, some cities in the United States have already experienced population declines over the past decade. In the future similar losses of population may be experienced in some metropolitan complexes as a whole. All of the theories described in this chapter neglect these possibilities.

BIBLIOGRAPHY: Articles

Abu-Lughod, Janet L., "Testing the Theory of Social Area Analysis: The Ecology of Cairo, Egypt," *American Sociological Review,* 34 (April 1969: 198–212.

Anderson, Theodore R., and Janice A. Egeland, "Spatial Aspects of Social Area Analysis," *American Sociological Review,* 26 (June 1961): 392–398.

Bell, Wendell, "Economic, Family and Ethnic Status: An Empirical Test," *American Sociological Review,* 20 (February 1955): 45–52.

Bell, Wendell, "A Probability Model for the Measurement of Ecological Segregation," *Social Forces,* 32 (May 1954): 357–364.

Bell, Wendell, "The Social Areas of the San Francisco Bay Region," *American Sociological Review,* 19 (February 1953): 39–47.

Bell, Wendell, and Charles C. Moskos, Jr., "A Comment on Udry's Increasing Scale and Spatial Differentiation," *Social Forces,* 42 (May 1964): 414–417.

Bell, Wendell, and Scott Greer, "Social Area Analysis and Its Critics," *Pacific Sociological Review,* 5 (Spring 1962): 3–9.

Bell, Wendell, and Ernest M. Willis, "The Segregation of Negroes in American Cities, A Comparative Analysis," *Social and Economic Studies,* 6 (March 1957): 59–75.

Blumenfeld, Hans, "On the Concentric-Circle Theory of Urban Growth," *Land Economics,* 25 (May 1949): 209–212.

Butler, Edgar W., and William J. Barclay, "A Longitudinal Examination of Two

Models of Urban Spatial Differentiation: A Case-Study of Los Angeles,'' *Research Previews,* 14 (March 1967): 2–25.

Carey, George W., ''The Regional Interpretation of Manhattan Population and Housing Patterns Through Factor Analysis,'' *Geographical Review,* 56 (October 1966): 551–569.

Cowgill, Donald O., ''Trends in Residential Segregation of Non-Whites in American Cities, 1940–1950,'' *American Sociological Review,* 21 (February 1956): 43–47.

Cowgill, Donald, and Mary S. Cowgill, ''An Index of Segregation Based on Block Statistics,'' *American Sociological Review,* 16 (December 1951): 825–831.

Duncan, Beverly, ''Devolution of an Empirical Generalization,'' *American Sociological Review,* 29 (December 1964): 855–862.

Duncan, Beverly, Georges Sabagh, and Maurice D. Van Arsdol, Jr., ''Patterns of City Growth,'' *American Journal of Sociology,* 67 (January 1962): 418–429.

Duncan, Otis Dudley, and Beverly Duncan, ''A Methodological Analysis of Segregation Indexes,'' *American Sociological Review,* 20 (April 1955): 210–217.

Edwards, Ozzie L., ''Patterns of Residential Segregation Within a Metropolitan Ghetto,'' *Demography,* 7 (May 1970): 185–193.

Farley, Reynolds, ''The Changing Distribution of Negroes Within Metropolitan Areas: The Emergence of Black Suburbs,'' *American Journal of Sociology,* 75 (January 1970): 512–529.

Galle, Omer R., Walter R. Gove, and J. Miller McPherson, ''Population Density and Pathology: What Are the Relations for Man?,'' *Science,* 176 (April 7, 1972): 23–30.

Goldsmith, Harold F., and Elizabeth L. Unger, ''Differentiation of Urban Subareas: A Re-Examination of Social Area Dimensions,'' Mental Health Study Center, National Institute of Mental Health, November 1970.

Goldstein, Sidney, and Kurt Mayer, ''Comment,'' *American Sociological Review,* 29 (December 1964): 863–865.

Green, Norman E., ''Scale Analysis of Urban Structures: A Study of Birmingham, Alabama,'' *American Sociological Review,* 21 (February 1956): 8–13.

Harris, Chauncy D., and Edward L. Ullman, ''The Nature of Cities,'' *The Annals,* 242 (November 1945): 7–17.

Hartshorn, Truman A., ''Inner City Residential Structure and Decline,'' *Annals of the Association of American Geographers,* 61 (March 1971): 72–96.

Hawley, Amos H., ''Population Density and the City,'' *Demography,* 9 (November 1972): 521–529.

Hawley, Amos, and Otis Dudley Duncan, ''Social Analysis: A Critical Appraisal,'' *Land Economics,* 33 (November 1957): 337–344.

Herbert, D. T., ''Social Area Analysis: A British Study,'' *Urban Studies,* 4 (February 1967): 41–60.

Hoyt, Homer, ''The Structure of American Cities in the Post-War Era,'' *American Journal of Sociology,* 48 (January 1943): 475–481.

Jahn, J., Calvin F. Schmid, and C. Schrag, ''The Measurement of Ecological Segregation,'' *American Sociological Review,* 12 (June 1947): 293–303.

Jahn, Julius A., ''The Measurement of Ecological Segregation,'' *American Sociological Review,* 15 (February 1950): 100–104.

Janson, Carl-Gunnar, ''The Spatial Structure of Newark, New Jersey, Part I, The Central City,'' *Acta Sociologica,* 11 (1968): 144–169.

Kantrowitz, Nathan, ''Ethnic and Racial Segregation in the New York Metropolis, 1960,'' *American Journal of Sociology,* 74 (May 1969): 685–695.

McElrath, Dennis, "The Social Areas of Rome," *American Sociological Review*, 27 (June 1962): 376–390.

Marston, Wilfred G., "Socio-Economic Differentials Within Negro Areas of American Cities," *Social Forces*, 48 (December 1969): 665–676.

Reeder, Leo G., "A Note on the Burgess-Davie, Firey Differences Regarding Industrial Location," *American Sociological Review*, 18 (April 1953): 163–169.

Schmid, Calvin F., and Kiyoshi Tagashira, "Ecological and Demographic Indices: A Methodological Analysis," *Demography*, 1 (No. 1, 1964): 194–211.

Schmid, Calvin F., Maurice Van Arsdol, and Earle MacCannell, "Comment," *American Sociological Review*, 29 (December 1964): 866–867.

Schmid, Calvin F., Earle H. MacCannell, and Maurice D. Van Arsdol, Jr., "The Ecology of the American City: Further Comparison and Validation of Generalizations," *American Sociological Review*, 23 (August 1958): 392–401.

Schnore, Leo F., "Another Comment on Social Area Analysis," *Pacific Sociological Review*, 5 (Spring 1962): 13–16.

Schnore, Leo F., and Philip C. Evenson, "Segregation in Southern Cities," *American Journal of Sociology*, 72 (July 1966): 58–67.

Sjoberg, Gideon, "The Preindustrial City," *American Journal of Sociology*, 60 (March 1955): 438–445.

Sweetser, Frank L., "Factorial Ecology: Zonal Differentiation in Metropolitan Boston, 1960." Paper presented at Population Association of America, April 1965, Chicago.

Udry, J. Richard, "Increasing Scale and Spatial Differentiation: New Tests of Two Theories from Shevky and Bell," *Social Forces*, 42 (May 1964): 403–417.

Van Arsdol, Maurice D., Jr., "An Application of the Shevky Social Area Indexes to a Model of Urban Society," *Social Forces*, 37 (October 1958): 26–32.

Van Arsdol, Maurice D., Jr., and Leo A. Schuerman, "Redistribution and Assimilation of Ethnic Populations: The Los Angeles Case," *Demography*, 8 (November 1971): 459–480.

Van Arsdol, Maurice D., Jr., Santo F. Camilleri, and Calvin Schmid, "Further Comments on the Utility of Urban Typology," *Pacific Sociological Review*, 5 (Spring 1962): 9–13.

Van Arsdol, Maurice D., Jr., Santo F. Camilleri, and Calvin F. Schmid, "An Investigation of the Utility of Urban Typology," *Pacific Sociological Review*, 4 (Spring 1961): 26–32.

Young, Ruth C., and Olaf F. Larson, "A New Approach to Community Structure," *American Sociological Review*, 30 (December 1965): 926–933.

BIBLIOGRAPHY: Books

Bell, Wendell, "Social Areas: Typology of Urban Neighborhoods," in Marvin Sussman (ed.), *Community Structure and Analysis*, New York: Thomas Y. Crowell Co., 1959, pp. 61–92.

Burgess, Ernest W., "The Growth of the City: An Introduction to a Research Project," in Robert E. Park, Ernest W. Burgess, and Roderick D. McKenzie, *The City*, Chicago: University of Chicago Press, 1925, pp. 47–62.

Clark, Colin, *The Conditions of Economic Progress*, London: Macmillan Co., 1940.

Davie, Maurice R., "The Pattern of Urban Growth," in George P. Murdock (ed.),

Studies in the Science of Society, New Haven, Conn.: Yale University Press, 1937, pp. 133–161.

Duncan, Otis Dudley, and Beverly Duncan, *The Negro Population of Chicago, A Study of Residential Succession,* Chicago: University of Chicago Press, 1957.

Firey, Walter, *Land Use in Central Boston,* Cambridge: Harvard University Press, 1947.

Greer, Scott, and Ella Kube, "Urbanism and Social Structure: A Los Angeles Study," in Marvin B. Sussman (ed.), *Community Structure and Analysis,* New York: Thomas Y. Crowell Co., 1959, pp. 93–112.

Hoover, Edgar M., and Raymond Vernon, *Anatomy of a Metropolis,* New York: Anchor Books, 1962.

Hoyt, Homer, *The Structure and Growth of Residential Neighborhoods in American Cities,* Washington, D.C.: Federal Housing Administration, 1939.

Hoyt, Homer, *One Hundred Years of Land Values in Chicago,* University of Chicago, 1933.

Jonassen, Christen T., and Sherwood H. Peres, *Interrelationships of Dimensions of Community Systems,* Ohio State University Press, 1960.

Klee, Gerald D., Evelyn Spiro, Anita K. Bahn, and Kurt Gorwitz, "An Ecological Analysis of Diagnosed Mental Illness in Baltimore," in Russell R. Monroe, Gerald D. Klee, and Eugene B. Brody (eds.), *Psychiatric Epidemiology and Mental Health Planning,* American Psychiatric Association, Psychiatric Research Report No. 22, April 1967.

Quinn, James A., *Human Ecology,* Englewood Cliffs, N.J.: Prentice-Hall, 1950.

Schnore, Leo F., "On the Spatial Structure of Cities in the Two Americas," in Philip M. Hauser and Leo F. Schnore (eds.), *The Study of Urbanization,* New York: John Wiley & Sons, 1965, pp. 347–398.

Shevky, Eshref, and Wendell Bell, *Social Area Analysis,* Berkeley and Los Angeles: University of California Press, 1955.

Shevky, Eshref, and Marilyn Williams, *The Social Areas of Los Angeles,* Berkeley and Los Angeles: University of California Press, 1949.

Willhelm, Sidney M., *Urban Zoning and Land-Use Theory,* The Free Press of Glencoe, 1963.

CHAPTER 8
POPULATION REDISTRIBUTION AND URBAN DIFFERENTIATION

INTRODUCTION

In the process of urbanization, new places come into being and already existing places grow in population (Eldridge, 1956). Both of these aspects of urbanization require a redistribution of the population, that is, movement in space by individuals, families, and social groups. Also, the growth of suburbs, or any other area within the urban or metropolitan complex, requires a shifting about of the population; migrants from other urban and metropolitan complexes may move to a growing and expanding metropolitan area, or there may be a shifting about *within* the metropolitan complex. It is primarily through population redistribution, therefore, that places come into being, grow, expand, and become internally differentiated from each other along certain social and demographic factors, for example, race and age. It is *only* through geographic mobility or population redistribution that populations come to live in segregated neighborhoods; thus it is only by differential moving behavior that areas become homogeneously or heterogeneously distinguished from each other.

The United States, of course, is a product of immigration beginning with the first colonists and continuing through the great waves of immigration of the 1800s. After the immigrations ceased, substantial population redistribution in the United States continued, with extensive rural-to-urban migration taking place. Similarly, extensive population redistribution is a widely recognized phenomenon of post–World War II United States as mass-produced suburbs came into prominence. Currently, most of the population redistribution that occurs in this country is internal, that is, rural-to-urban migration, migration between urban and metropolitan complexes, and population redistribution within urban and metropolitan complexes expanding and reshaping them.

Decennial census data and other information published by the U.S. Census Bureau show that about 20 percent of the population in the United

The millions of immigrants to the United States during the nineteenth century were from many parts of Europe. Most of them settled in Eastern cities. Ten million such immigrants disembarked on customs piers between 1860 and 1890 (top). Optimism and anxiety were constant companions at the crowded receiving stations (below).

States annually change their places of residence. Currently, this means that at least 40 million persons are moving every year—changing one's residence is a way of life in contemporary America. In this chapter we will be concerned with *long-distance migration,* for example, the movement of individuals and families from rural areas to the city, and with moves from one urban complex to

Most immigrants found employment in the burgeoning heavy industry of the day. Here (top), slavic recruits for Pennsylvania coal mines await their train, and Russian Mennonite families (bottom) are quartered by their employer in a temporary barracks in central Kansas.

another urban area. In addition, residential movement within the metropolitan region — *intrametropolitan residential mobility* — will be examined because it is primarily through such population redistribution that metropolitan areas in the United States become more *or* less differentiated in their population characteristics, such as age, race, social class, income, and so on.

Most existing literature on spatial mobility is concerned with migration as a type of spatial movement. *Migration* is generally defined as a change of residence from one place to another while remaining within the same national boundaries; this type of residential movement is distinguished from local movement or intrametropolitan residential mobility within the same metropolitan area (Bogue, 1959). While approximately one out of every five American families changes its place of residence during any given year, long-distance migration accounts only for about 15–20 percent of these moves. In other words, 80–85 percent of annual shifts in residence are not migratory or long-distance in nature but occur within the same metropolitan region. Over one-half of these moves occur during the summer months.

IMMIGRATION AND URBAN GROWTH

Historically, the United States is primarily a nation populated by immigrants and their descendants—Puritans, Dutch colonists, prisoners, nee'r-do-wells, slaves from Africa, and so on. Beginning in the early 1800s, European immigrants began arriving in great numbers, this influx of people overshadowed any immigration that preceded it or has occurred since. While some early immigrants to the United States moved to rural areas, most of them moved directly to the larger eastern cities of the United States. They numbered well over 42 million people (through 1964), although some of them eventually returned to their countries of origin (Taeuber and Taeuber, 1958: 48–70).

The early nineteenth-century immigrants to the United States had a hard life. If they survived the diseases and sicknesses of the voyage across the ocean, they faced exploitation upon their arrival. A high proportion of the immigrants during this period entered the country through New York City, where many of them sought employment and remained. Overcrowding became prevalent, and "the density of the seven lower wards of Manhattan increased from 94.5 to 163.5 persons per acre in the period from 1820 to 1850" (Glaab and Brown, 1967: 93–95). Substantial numbers of people were living underground in cellars, and the emerging slums began to change the character of the city. Other immigrants, especially the Irish, fleeing from the potato famine of the 1840s, arrived in Boston where they faced similar dismal living and working conditions.

By 1890 New York contained more foreign-born residents than any other city in the world; it had as many Italians as Naples, as many Germans as Hamburg, twice as many Irish as Dublin, and two and one-half times as many Jews as Warsaw (Glaab and Brown, 1967: 139). The structure of many cities in the United States changed markedly as a result of the large influx of immigrants, and residential segregation of immigrants resulted in the formation of ethnic ghettos. In the new ethnic neighborhoods organizations of immigrants were formed, and former residents of many areas moved away under the onslaught of thousands and thousands of immigrants seeking housing.

The large-scale immigration to U.S. cities had a number of con-

These slaves from Africa arrived in Key West, Florida, in 1860 on the slave bark *Wildfire*. Note the limited quarters and the emaciated condition of the slaves.

sequences. In 1852 more than one-half of those requiring public assistance in eastern cities were Irish and German, and by 1860, 86 percent of "paupers" were of foreign birth (Glaab and Brown, 1967: 95). Closely associated with the growth of the immigrant population and slums in eastern cities was an increase in crime. In 1828, John Pintard, wrote to his daughter that "as long as we are overwhelmed with Irish emigrants, so long will the evil abound" (Glaab and Brown, 1967: 95). As we pointed out earlier, this is approximately when cities in the United States introduced formal police systems, partly in response to the increasing immigrant population and accompanying rise in crime.

A strong antiforeign movement existed in the United States during the depression years of 1837–1843, and the development of the Know-Nothing party in the 1850s was an indication of this attitude. Political and municipal change abounded during the period of the great immigration, and although it is difficult to establish a cause-and-effect relationship, many institutional changes in U.S. cities coincided with the large influx of immigrants. Increased public assistance, public and municipal services such as water, fire protection, and the maintenance of streets and roadways also became the standard rather than unusual features. Glaab and Brown (1967: 223) also implied that there was a close connection between bossism and immigration; the "bosses" served social welfare functions that were still primarily individual voluntary efforts and not yet formally institutionalized in the United States.

Another aspect of the great immigration was the increasing diversity found in American cities. With immigrants arriving from many different countries, speaking a variety of languages and practicing different social customs, the city became a virtual mosaic of all Europe (Ward, 1968). Most European immigrants were peasants and thus rural oriented. Nevertheless, one aspect of their homelands that they transplanted was reflected in native organizations, banks, and mutual-aid societies, which were organized according to ethnic and national backgrounds. These organizations served as part of "a complex institutional network providing means by which the immigrant could order his life in the American city" (Glaab and Brown, 1967: 142).

The early 1900s were the last years in which foreign migration contributed substantially to the growth of cities in the United States. Previously, over a million immigrants each year reached the shores of the country. This number dropped substantially during the next few years. Immigration began to rise again in 1920, but legislation in 1921 and 1924 set quotas and thereafter reduced annual immigration. Thus after this immigration era "cities grew largely through internal migration down to the 1940's when the birth rate of urban dwellers began to rise substantially" (Glaab and Brown, 1967: 286).

Many commentators of the era regretted foreign immigration to the cities; diaries and letters written then suggest that for many immigrants the city and its natives were cruel and bitter enemies. Of course, immigrants of this historical era settled primarily in larger eastern cities, so that interior, southern, and western cities were for the most part influenced later by this large European immigration. Thus, as Glaab and Brown point out, "the city where ethnic diversity flourished does not necessarily represent historical urban America" (1967: 141).

URBAN MIGRATION

There are primarily three migration streams to urban and metropolitan regions. One is unskilled, lower-socioeconomic-status individuals and families that migrate from a rural area to an urban complex. This migration ordinarily is made by persons who have a relative lack of knowledge about city life and the city's institutions. Some adjustment of rural-to-urban migration may be facilitated by "gate keepers" (Kurtz, 1966). The second migration stream consists of professionals and upwardly mobile corporate and governmental administrators of higher socioeconomic level who migrate from one urban region to another. A third and residual category holds persons with various population characteristics who move from one urban place to another reportedly for "better job opportunities," which may be real or imagined.

Rural-Urban Migration

Rural-urban migration was associated with the mechanization of agriculture, which substantially reduced the need for a farm labor force and, at the same time, expanded industrial, commercial, and service employment opportunities and made more jobs available in metropolitan areas. As we have already seen, the great population increases in American cities prior to the 1900s were substantially due to immigration, primarily from Europe. But at the same time there was a strong migration stream from the countryside to the city. Also, immigrants from foreign lands and rural-to-urban migrants appeared to have reproduced at a greater rate than the native urban population, thus helping further to populate the cities.

> Of 11,826,000 *new* city dwellers in 1910, some forty-one percent were immigrants from abroad, 29.8 percent were native rural-to-urban migrants, 21.6 percent represented natural increase, and the remaining 7.6 percent were the result of incorporation of new territories into existing cities. Vitually all demographic evidence indicates that the growth of cities in the period 1860 to 1910 was sustained by high birth rates on the farm, including the rural areas of Europe, and among people newly arrived in the city [Glaab and Brown, 1967: 135].

Several of the great rural-to-urban streams were made up of southern blacks, the first substantial one occurring in the late 1700s as slaves moved north to escape their southern masters. Then in the 1890s another spurt of black urban migration took place (Hamilton, 1964). In the early 1900s there was another mass black migration to major northern cities, especially New York, Philadelphia, Chicago, and Cleveland. In addition, the border cities of Baltimore and Washington, D.C., and midwestern cities such as St. Louis had a large influx of black population. To some degree, southern cities, especially Birmingham and Norfolk also had a substantial inmigration of rural blacks. This stream was brought about primarily by the cotton crop failure just prior to World War I and accompanied by an increased industrial labor demand in cities of the Northeast as a result of World War I (Groh, 1972: 50–51; Glaab and Brown, 1967: 286).

This northward urban migration by rural, southern blacks continued during the 1920s and 1930s and once again was intensified in the 1940s by the increased demand for industrial labor in northeastern and midwestern cities brought about by the advent of World War II. Like immigrants to the United States from foreign countries, black migrants from the South formed ethnic ghettos in receiving cities. From the very beginning these ghettos were more homogeneous and permanent than immigrant enclaves. Unlike European immigrant colonies, black ghettos did not break up over time but remained predominantly black in character and began to spread outward. Unlike foreign immigrants, blacks were unable to obtain adequate education and to become upwardly mobile in the class system. It is interesting to note that southern black migrants living in metropolitan areas outside of the South typically have higher incomes and less unemployment than blacks born in the North (Masters, 1972). This negative impact upon employment and income also was reported in a detailed study of Near Northeast, Washington, D.C. blacks (Chapin et al., forthcoming); apparently, then, some aspect of living several generations in northern cities leads to lower income for and employment of blacks. Masters (1972: 423) states that it is racial discrimination and that migrants are more willing than longer-term city residents to accept jobs that require longer working hours, strenuous physical labor, and/or require participation in lengthy training programs. Succeeding urban generations may not be willing to work as hard as migrants.

Intermetropolitan Migration

Intermetropolitan migration is the amount of population movement or redistribution between metropolitan and urban complexes. Intermetropolitan migration streams are selective in nature, since young adults just finishing school and those who are well educated and/or in professional occupations are more likely to migrate between metropolitan regions than the less well educated and those in middle- and lower-level occupations. One attempt to explain the migration streams relies upon economic pulls; that is, the metropolitan area attracting people is generally believed to offer greater socioeconomic opportunities. Thus people tend to move in the direction of the great centers of commerce and industry. Another approach was to examine migration differentials by family status, physical health, intelligence, and motivation. A third approach involves statements about the relationships between the volume of migration and *distance* between metropolitan areas. It argues that most people will move only a short distance and that the number of people migrating into an area is related to the number of people residing in other areas divided by the distance of these areas from the area of destination; or, alternatively, the number of migrants is proportionate to the product of their population divided by the shortest transportation distance. Stouffer (1940), on the other hand, suggested an "intervening opportunities theory," which states that the number of persons migrating a certain distance is directly proportional to the number of opportunities at that distance and inversely proportional to the number of intervening opportunities. Several systematic statistical tests of the intervening opportunities theory have led to conflicting results (see Galle and Taeuber, 1966; Karp and Kelly, 1971).

SPATIAL MOBILITY WITHIN
URBAN AND METROPOLITAN REGIONS
Residential Development Process

The spatial pattern of residential urban growth can be thought of as the result of a residential development process, which itself is a result of a complex of decisions and actions made by a multiplicity of individuals and groups (Butler and Kaiser, 1971). One manner in which the total process of urban development and residential mobility in the metropolitan region has been conceptualized is shown in Figure 8-1. This model suggests that there are a number of interlinked decisions and processes that must be considered in describing population redistribution *within* urban and metropolitan regions. First, there needs to be some consideration of the kinds of subdivisions and housing available for the potentially moving population. Second, a variety of households compromises the moving population, including newly formed households, immigrants to the metropolitan region, persons who want to upgrade their current housing, and those who are moving involuntarily because of conditions seemingly beyond their control. Third, for whatever reason a household may be moving, it still faces another decision — where to live after moving. A few families, of course, find a place where they want to live, and thus the moving decision has been made. The decisions made by predevelopment landowners to sell or not to sell their land and by residential developers to build housing units and where to locate subdivisions also are related to spatial mobility within metropolitan regions (Butler and Kaiser, 1971).

As shown in Figure 8-1, the supply of new single-family and subdivision housing units, for the most part, depends on the willingness of large landowners to sell their land and of developers to buy the land and put up new housing. In addition, other housing becomes available through isolated new construction and families moving — perhaps to new suburban subdivisions. Thus additional vacancies are created by the large-scale developments as many families abandon their former dwellings for the large-scale suburban tracts that have desirable housing and neighborhood attributes. The abandoned homes are then filtered down to the aged, the lower classes, and ethnic minorities. This may in turn change the neighborhood character with respect to ethnicity, age, and so on. Thus, residential movement has implications not only for individual households involved but also for the neighborhood and the differentiation of areas within the metropolitan complex.

This residential-choice model (for an extended discussion of other residential location models, see Butler et al., Appendix A, 1969) provides the basis for a linkage of the supply and demand of housing units. It provides the means

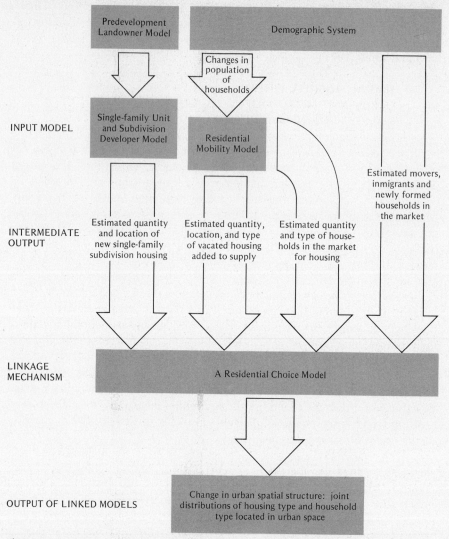

Figure 8-1.   A Linked Model for the Presidential Development Decision Process. *From Butler and Kaiser, 1971, by permission of Sage Publications, Inc.*

to allocate housing supply to the households or households to the supply of housing units.

For individuals and families the moving process has two stages that are influenced by household and property characteristics. Figure 8-2 illustrates some of the elements involved in the decision to move and in the selection of a new place to live. The first stage is the decision about the type of move—within the neighborhood, outside the neighborhood but within the metropolitan area,

FIGURE 8-2
Elements in the Consumer's Decision to Move and Selection of a New Household Location

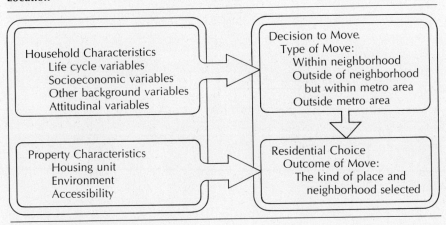

Source: Butler and Kaiser, 1971.

or migration out of the metropolitan complex. The second stage is the selection of a place to live within one of these contexts. Most of the time the household has some choice as to whether or not it is going to move and to which location. Obviously, some moves have elements of choice for only one stage, or, in a few instances, choice will be absent for both stages. In all except the latter case the two-stage choices involved can be thought of as separate but linked processes.

Decision to Move

Household and residential characteristics consistently shown to be related to the decision to move are the life cycle indicators of age of head, family type, household size, race, and past moving behavior (Rossi, 1955; Sabagh et al., 1969; Van Arsdol et al.,1968; Butler et al., 1964, 1969). Moving households tend to be larger, younger, full families with an eldest child under six (Long, 1972), or nonwhite. They also tend to have moved more recently than those not planning to relocate and to have migrated from out of state on the prior move or to have formed a new household. Socioeconomic status of occupation, location of the head's workplace, and expectations about staying on the present job are only slightly associated with residential moves. Households that are dissatisfied with their neighborhoods or housing units and those that have a higher social mobility (Leslie and Richardson, 1961) and social mobility commitment are more likely to have plans to move than their counterparts (Butler and Kaiser, 1971: 480–481). Some residential characteristics are related to moves. Families planning to move tend to be renters, those living in lower-quality housing and neighborhoods and in the central city.

A decision to move, if carried out, may require packing up and leaving kin, friends, and neighbors. When the world changes so abruptly, it's enough to dismay even a kitten . . . .

Movers also tend to live farther away from the head of household's workplace. This is the only type of accessibility related to prospective mobility. Accessibility to shopping, downtown, medical facilities, parks and playgrounds, school, and churches is not related to mobility. Most residential location models have some variant of accessibility of workplace as a key factor that is assumed to arrange the spatial distribution of households in a rational pattern. Accessibility to services and amenities also is included in some of these models as part of the trade-off between work accessibility and residential location. It should be noted too that in any particular metropolitan area any number of subareas of the metropolitan complex potentially have similar accessibility to workplace, services, and other amenities (see Butler et al., 1969). The problem remains of separating out the choice of a residential location over others with similar accessibility (Stegman, 1969: 28). Overall, accessibility plays a minor role in the decision to move (Thibeault et al., 1972; Kaiser et al., 1972).

In summary, it appears that: (1) There is a strong relationship between mobility and life cycle, such that younger families tend to be more residentially mobile (Rossi, 1955; Foote et al., 1960) and more migratory (Ladinsky, 1967; Beshers and Nishura, 1961). (2) Previous research indicates that individuals with higher educational attainment tend to be more residentially mobile (Leslie and Richardson, 1961) and more migratory (Schmid and Griswold, 1952) than individuals with lower educational attainment. (3) Rossi (1955) reported that larger families are more mobile than smaller ones. Ross (1962) confirmed this observation and further stated that many local movers report changes in family status as a principal reason for residence changes. Denton (1960), however, found no significant relationship between family size and distance moved. (4) The literature on socioeconomic status (or social class) and moving behavior is neither clear nor consistent. Rose (1958) suggested that persons of higher status will be more migratory than those of lower status and will move a greater distance for better job opportunities; the work of Goldstein (1954) and others seems to confirm this. A recent study, however, shows no significant relationship between spatial mobility and SES (Butler et al., 1969). (5) The role of duration-of-residence in moving behavior has only recently come to be recognized as an important factor (Taeuber, 1961). Persons who have been in their places of residence for a longer time are less likely to move than those who have a shorter duration-of-residence (McGinnis et al., 1963; Myers et al., 1967; Morrison, 1967, 1969).

The Search Process

The decision to move has no actual effect upon metropolitan differentiation. Rather, it is the actual search *and* relocation that result in varying residential and segregation patterns in cities. Once a family has reached the moving threshold, it becomes potentially mobile and may begin looking for another place to live. Ordinarily, the search process takes into consideration constraints — such as the amount of money available to the household, the available housing market, and household preferences in regard to geographical location such as the central city or suburb, the kind of neighborhood desired, and housing-unit preferences (Kaiser et al., forthcoming).

Where the household looks for a new place is in most instances directly related to the channels of information that are known to the family. Rossi (1955) reported that almost one-half of his Philadelphia sample households found their living places through personal contacts. Interestingly, he notes that

Of the several methods used to locate a different place to live, one is riding around in the car "looking," and another is engaging a real estate agent. Wedgwood House covered both contingencies. The probabilities are, however, that many of these apartments were let to seekers who heard about them by "word-of-mouth."

one-fourth of the families found housing through an accident or a "windfall," and about one-fifth found it by "riding around in the car." Similar results were found for a more recent national sample of persons who moved between 1966 and 1969 (Kaiser et al., forthcoming). Channels of information used by blacks and other minorities is much more severely limited and may result in their remaining in the ghetto when it is not a necessity (McAllister et al., 1972). Also, it should be explicitly recognized that not all neighborhoods and housing units within a household's awareness will be considered as viable opportunities. Some neighborhoods that do not have desirable characteristics will be eliminated from consideration prior to the search process. Of the suitable and desirable neighborhoods within the household's awareness, the family ordinarily must make a number of trade-offs among their choices and preferences, since no one single neighborhood may meet all of them.

One of the trade-offs least often made for most people is the cost of the unit, since cost constraints must be considered first in the search process by most families. Within a certain price range, the family may begin its search, considering its preferences and choices. However, Brown and Moore (1970) pointed out that after a certain number of units have been examined without satisfaction, the family may decide to remain where it is. On the other hand, upon finding one or more desirable locations, the family may decide to move. Another strategy, of course, is not to search extensively for housing and thus be less selective. In the national sample referred to earlier, fully one-third of the movers looked at only *one* place—the one they moved into. On the average, however, 10 housing units were viewed before the family decided upon the one they wanted. Some "recreational movers" looked at more than 50 housing units before moving.

Almost 70 percent of moving families in the national survey reported: "I made the decision to move and then started looking for another place to live." This response is considered as measuring a *push* out of the previous places of residence. About 17 percent reported a *pull* to their current places of residence: "I hadn't thought about moving, but I found this place and then made the decision to move." Nearly one-third of those families that only considered one place moved within their previous neighborhoods of residence. *Involuntary* movers ferret out more neighborhoods and houses than *voluntary* movers. Involuntary movers are pushed into the housing market, many of them without any particular reason for wanting to leave their previous places of residence.

In summary, the search for new housing and neighborhood often results in a residential move, and it is these moves that effect the structure and segregation patterns of urban regions. Generally, the searching process begins after the decision to move has been made; but there are some instances when a family, accidentally or otherwise, finds an alternative housing unit prior to deciding to move. For most the search for housing results from *pushes* (pressures to leave the present unit), balanced by constraints—such as costs, accessibilities, and so on—and *pulls* to different neighborhoods and housing units.

Residential Choice

One of the major dimensions of any residential move is the type of move in terms of distance. In a recent national study (Butler et al., 1969), 28 percent of last moves were within the same neighborhood; approximately 57 percent were outside the neighborhood but within the same metropolitan area; and only about 15 percent crossed a metropolitan boundary, a type that is ordinarily considered in migration studies (Butler et al., 1969: 9). Higher-income households, white households, households that previously owned their own homes, households having a low familism attitude or a low evaluation of the importance of one's neighborhood in getting ahead, and those moving because of a job change are most likely to move across metropolitan boundaries. Nonwhite, low-income, and rental households are more likely to move within the same neighborhood (McAllister et al., 1972). While general neighborhood dissatisfaction is associated with plans to move and sometimes with actual residential moves, specific complaints about crime and violence (Droettboom et al., 1971) and air pollution (Butler et al., forthcoming) are not related to subsequent moves out of a neighborhood.

The most consistent household characteristics related to selection of a new place are race and income. Lower-income households and blacks tend, more than others, to move shorter distances, locate in the central city, rent apartments, have fewer rooms, pay lower rent, or own cheaper housing. The weakest household characteristics for predicting the outcome of the move are age of household head, the attitudinal indexes of familism-consumerism, urban-versus-suburban orientation, social mobility commitment, and even a household's attitude about the importance of one's neighborhood for social mobility. It should be noted here that while the age of household head may be the single most important variable in predicting a move, it becomes relatively unimportant in predicting locational outcomes.

Previous residential experience, especially tenure—whether one owns or rents—provides a consistently strong relationship to residential choice. Renters are much more likely than owners to move, but they are also more likely to move shorter distances to locations in the central city, pay lower rents, and buy lower-value homes. Larger-size households and families that previously lived in larger units are more likely to move to larger units. Those who paid higher rent previously or owned more expensive residences are more likely than their opposites to do so again. As expected, renters are subsequently more likely to rent than are past owners.

Accessibility plays a relatively weak role in both residential mobility and choice (Thibeault et al., 1973). Although distance to work is a factor in some moves, no differences are generally found between movers and stayers with regard to accessibility to services and amenities such as grocery stores, shopping centers, downtown, doctors' offices, hospitals or clinics, parks, playgrounds, and elementary schools. With respect to accessibility after the move, whites typically obtain residences more accessible to services and employment than blacks, but there appears to be very little difference in accessibility to work, services, and amenities between central city residents and suburbanites, rich and poor, or renters and owners. There is little evidence that households improve their accessibility as a result of a residential move (Butler et al., 1969).

Residential Mobility Experiences

So far we have noted that extensive population redistribution within urban and metropolitan regions is a phenomenon that has been recognized since the end of World War II. Most research on this subject has focused upon explaining a household's entry into the geographic mobility process; other questions, such as what location a family will choose, have been somewhat neglected. Besides the whole range of decisions that affects population redistribution, there are *consequences* of residential moves both for the individual and his family as well as for the spatial configuration that makes up the metropolis.

Movement within local metropolitan regions accounts for at least four out of every five moves that are made. They are generally voluntary and are related to demographic and life cycle changes—especially the age of eldest child in the family. Some moves—ordinarily called forced, "situational," or in-

Many people who move want to own their own single-family home — like this one in Manchester, New Hampshire.

voluntary moves — result from dwelling-unit destruction, eviction, land taken by condemnation for urban renewal, and so on. They usually result from conditions that the household cannot control; in this category are included traditional forced moves but also moves associated with getting out of a place shared by others, with job change, new household formations, and retirements. Voluntary moves too may be related to constraints and pressures exerted on the household, but they are considered as an open choice made by the mover. It appears that approximately 60 percent of all moves are of the voluntary type (Abu-Lughod and Foley, 1960; McAllister et al., 1972).

According to a great deal of literature, most moves are from the central city to the suburbs — "the flight to the suburbs." However, in examining moves made by a national urban sample over a six-year period between 1960 and 1966, Butler et al. (1969) found that over one-half of the moves reported had the central city as their destinations. In fact, the two major destination areas were the *same* neighborhood in the central city and a different neighborhood in the same central city. Also, there was a small suburban-to-central-city stream (1.8 percent). Migrants to the central city from other metropolitan areas, towns, and rural areas accounted for almost 6 percent of moves, and 3 percent were newly formed households leaving the family of procreation or former single apartments. Only slightly less than 10 percent of moves could be considered as flight to the suburbs from the central city. Before the move to the 1966 place of residence, over 70 percent of the sampled households were renters; in their 1966 places of residence, however, only 40 percent were renters. Few owner households reverted to renter status, while over one-half of those who previously rented bought a home, with almost 80 percent of previous central city renters who moved to the suburbs buying homes. This suggests that at least part of the flight to the suburbs may be related to tenure status; if ownership opportunities existed in the central city, perhaps there would be less movement toward suburbs.

Households represented in the preceding study were followed up in 1969 to determine whether they had moved or stayed in their 1966 places of residence (Kaiser et al., forthcoming). Even though over one-third of the households moved during this period,[1] only 15 percent actually moved out of the metropolitan area, for example, were migrants; one-fourth of the moves were within the *same* neighborhood; about 40 percent moved to other neighborhoods in the same city (whether the central city or a suburban city); and about 20 percent moved to different places but within the metropolitan area. The suburban and ownership trends previously noted continued. There were fewer mobile households in suburban areas than in either the core of the city or the outer edges of the city. Most moves within the metropolitan complex took place within the same context; that is, central city residents tended to move within the central city and suburban residents moved to other suburbs. Migrants from a central city typically moved to another central city. Migrants from suburbs typically moved to a suburban location in the new metropolitan area of residence.

Race and Residential Mobility

Tilly (1962: 125) has pointed out that "America's racial minorities have generally done less long-distance migrating than have whites." A broader generalization was made by Lansing and Mueller (1968: 263), who stated that at the "present time geographical mobility is considerably lower among Negro than among white families in the United States" (also see Morrison, 1969: 18). In direct contrast Straits (1968; also see U.S. Bureau of the Census, 1969: 1) reported the following:

> In comparison with the white respondents, the Negroes had higher
> average rates of mobility: slightly over one half of the whites moved
> on the average less frequently than once every five years (that is,
> an annual rate of less than .20) while nearly three-fifths of the
> Negroes moved at least every five years.

Tilly focused on long-distance migration and, therefore, specifically related his

---

[1] If 20 percent of the households in the United States move each year, one might expect this figure to be greater than 35 percent recorded. Part of the difference is reflected in the number of families who make repeated or multiple moves (Goldstein, 1964). In this particular sample, 30 percent of the movers made more than one move between the interview in 1966 and the one in 1969; some (3 percent) made as many as five moves during this time period.

Many moves made by upper-middle and upper-class families to outlying suburban areas are to homes like this one, located in Rancho La Costa, near San Diego, California.

investigation to one type of spatial mobility. However, before a sweeping generalization like Lansing and Mueller's can be made, it is necessary to have information on all geographic moves, not only long-distance migration.

The apparent conflict between these statements is simply a matter of defining terms—in this case, geographic mobility. Actually, two different hypotheses have been examined. The first is that *blacks are less migratory* (in the classical sense of the concept) *than whites*, and the second is that *blacks are more residentially mobile within the metropolitan region than whites*. That is, although, in the United States blacks move more often than whites, the moves they make are most likely to be close to their previous places of residence or at least within the same metropolitan area (McAllister et al., 1972). Understanding the roles played by neighborhood and housing dissatisfaction, job changes, involuntary moves, and so on, sheds some light on which families move and why. But it does not explain *patterns* that emerge for different races: Why do blacks move locally more often than do whites? One recent explanation is that the social space of blacks is much smaller than that of whites and that blacks operate in an artificially constrained and much smaller environmental milieu than the typical white. Each person, it is suggested, can comfortably change residence only within the confines of his or her perceived social space. One cannot go outside of it without first becoming aware of the possibility to do so, and then only at the risk of personal strain or discomforting anxiety.

Black Americans—particularly those living in urban ghettos—have little or no opportunity to own their own property. Opportunities for them are circumscribed by the social situations in which blacks must live, and their options are restricted in such a way as to prevent them from being easily located and from living in neighborhoods and housing within their social space. Black families appear to be making repeated involuntary and voluntary moves in a nearly futile search for suitable housing and neighborhoods. That is, since their opportunity to buy is limited, so are their chances of moving into genuinely satisfactory neighborhoods and housing milieus in which they might be able to break the cycle of dissatisfaction (McAllister et al., 1972). Thus, in conclusion, the black family in urban America does not, and perhaps cannot, make a more extended search for available housing units. Such a search is not only limited by socioeconomic constraints, but it may also be a direct function of the perceptually limited life space the black man or woman has in this country. A black individual's opportunities to move outside the city into a suburban area are partially restricted by his or her own limited perceptions as well as by actual economic constraints and racial discrimination.

Recent census and survey data suggest, however, that a few blacks are moving to suburban locations, and especially to the periphery or outer edges of the city (Rosenthal, 1970; Farley, 1970). Nevertheless, the greatest amount of black replacement population (inmovers to vacated housing units) is still in the inner city. "Thus, there is certainly no *reversal* of the pattern of increasing concentration of Blacks in inner city areas" (Kaiser et al., forthcoming). Further, it is highly probable that blacks who are moving to the periphery of the city and the suburbs are moving into older, more deteriorated outer-city and suburban areas. Thus housing construction in the suburbs only has indirect influence upon blacks and other minorities by making new dwellings available for whites who abandon their older housing, which may in turn be filtered down to blacks, the aged, and other disadvantaged populations (Lansing et al., 1969; Butler et al., 1968).

A Note on Public Policy and Housing[2]

The influence local government has on a household's housing decision is weak and indirect. Many of the forces for change are beyond the control of local government, especially those socioeconomic forces affecting population trends, economic vitality, technology, and federal policies regarding the financing of new and used housing. Local governments, however, can directly interfere with the market through mechanisms such as open-housing laws and discouraging discriminatory private market practices, by public housing programs, and financial aids to consumers in the form of rent subsidies or mortgage insurance. To a lesser degree, local public policy can affect the course of change in built-up neighborhoods through zoning changes, the levels of services, and housing codes. By providing services, especially education, by protecting an area from incongruous uses, and by discouraging neglect of physical improvements, local government can encourage a higher environmental quality and thereby remove some of the cause for dissatisfaction and residential mobility. Further, much of the potential for maintenance levels is incorporated

---

[2] This section is taken from Butler and Kaiser (1971).

A prototype of the "defensive city" might be these protected condominium apartments located in Miami Beach, Florida.

into the quality of original planning and construction, which can be influenced at the local level.

Local government may have an indirect impact on residential movement and spatial allocation by influencing other agents in the residential development process — predevelopment property owners, developers, and financers. Zoning, the availability of urban services, and financing are important factors in development decisions. Especially important are site planning and the kinds of dwelling units, because the household's moving decision and residential choice are based in great part on the dwelling unit and the neighborhood rather than on accessibility and the larger environment.

Urban Problems and Population Redistribution

"Increasing rates of inner-city crime have prompted some pessimistic speculation about the potential effects of urban violence on the spatial structure of the American metropolis" (Droettboom et al., 1971: 319). Gold (1970) has suggested a model of the defensive city in which the central city would be sealed at night for protection and suburban neighborhoods would become safe areas protected from crime-prone populations by geographic distance and racial and economic homogeneity. However, in testing the notion that crime and violence lead to greater residential mobility, data from the national survey mentioned earlier (Butler et al., 1969; Kaiser et al., forthcoming), Droettboom and others (1971) reported that the individual's perception of violence in the neighborhood of residence has relatively little influence upon changes in residential location. The concern with crime and violence in the local neighborhood has not led to an exodus from those neighborhoods to the suburbs. Rather, the poor and blacks are more affected by local neighborhood crime and violence than middle- and high-income whites. It is also the former populations that are least able to escape the problem through residential relocation. Thus there may be a vast reservoir of potential movers in the local neighborhood areas most affected by crime and violence, but until economic and other constraints are removed, they will not be able to move to escape this crime and violence.

A similar analysis, using the same national sample of metropolitan households, examined the effect that the perception of air pollution as a serious problem in the local neighborhood has upon residential moves. As with the problems of crime and violence, awareness of air pollution has relatively little influence upon residential moves. The effect that does exist is stronger for whites than blacks, even though blacks are more likely than whites to live in areas of the metropolis most affected by heavy air pollution. Thus there is little evidence to suggest that crime and violence or air pollution are crucial factors in the decision of whether to move or in selection of alternative places of residence (Butler et al., forthcoming).

Analysis of other environmental hazards and their influence upon residential mobility probably would produce similar results (see Chapter 19 for more detail). That is, individuals may differentially perceive conditions as being a serious problem in their neighborhoods, yet they seem, incongruously, to be willing to tolerate these unsatisfactory conditions. "This may be because those most affected are the poor, the minorities, and the aged, and they are population segments least able to actualize desires and plans to move" (Butler et al., forthcoming).

Consequences of Residential Moves

Angell (1951, 1974) hypothesized that moving has negative effects upon social integration, since it ruptures the conditions that tie society together. This argument applies to areas (neighborhoods) as well as to individuals. This effect upon individual social integration also may occur for nonmovers in highly mobile areas where they must adjust to ever-shifting neighbors.

As noted earlier, it is through original settlement patterns and subsequent residential mobility that areas within urban regions become differentiated from each other. For many metropolitan areas this means an initial settlement of foreign and/or rural migrants near the CBD and subsequent movement outward as new populations of migrants enter these central slum areas (Freedman, 1948: 304). Part of the migrant zone serves as a receiving area for foreign and rural migrants; in addition, there are other areas within the city that are characterized by a great deal of residential mobility, even though there may not be much variation in the actual population composition of the area. In Chicago of several decades ago areas characterized by rural and urban migrants were concentrated contiguously and as a result made up a specific geographic area. The migrant zone in Chicago followed the principal transit lines and was marked by a higher than average proportion of apartments, rental furnished units, and a relatively high vacancy rate. Younger families are more likely to move out of the migrant zone than are older persons, and this leads in turn to a segregation of older persons in the migrant zone and also to zones of greater age homogeneity as population redistribution takes place. Similarly, differential migration and residential mobility patterns have led to socioeconomic differences between cities and their suburbs. Within some cities chronic decline of areas has led to the abandonment of whole neighborhoods or to the development of ghettos of disadvantaged persons (Morrison, 1972: 14–15).

For individuals the general assumption is that migration from the country to the city is difficult because of the accompanying changes and disruptions in the social order (Park, 1928). It also suggested that any move requires making new friends and adjusting to a new environment and this disrupts informal and formal social participation (Hunt and Butler, 1972). Movers, it is assumed, are more alienated, unhappy, and more likely to have poor physical and mental health than are nonmovers (Butler et al., 1973).

In testing some of these notions, in the Los Angeles SMSA it was found —when socioeconomic status and age were controlled—that migrants were less likely than natives to interact frequently with relatives, friends, and neighbors. On the other hand, this particular study did not find migrants any more unhappy or alienated than nonmigrants.

In a national study examining informal neighborhood visiting of women, McAllister and colleagues (1973) reported that women who move undergo a period of heightened social interaction in their new places of residence that eventually declines to a lower frequency but greater intensity. From the same study, it was noted, however, that formal organizational participation decreased for movers, while it remained relatively stable for stayers (Butler et al., 1973). This study also showed that the relative effect of moving upon the social participation of males and females was substantially the same. In contrast, there was a much greater apparent negative effect of moving upon the mental well-being of women. Evidently, the continued level of social interaction by residentially mobile females does not overcome all of the disruptive aspects of moving (Butler et al., 1973). This may partially be a result of the fact that the male typically enters quickly into a work role, and he is the one who establishes relationships with organizations and participates socially with co-workers. If upward social mobility is involved, the wife may also be required to learn new and different roles, many of which may be quite unfamiliar to her. "The resulting stress may be quite unapparent to her husband whose new work situation and continued formal associations may seem like natural progressions from his previous situations" (Hunt and Butler, 1972: 448).

Insofar as suburban moves are concerned, generally the move to the suburb results in relatively few, if any, changes in the way of life of a family (Gans, 1963). On the other hand, long-distance migration has been suggested as having a different effect upon families depending substantially on social class level. For example, middle- and upper-class families that move long distances typically do so under the auspices of the husband's work. In many instances, moving expenses are paid by the company employing him, and often a pay raise and/or promotion is involved in the move. Normally, the wife and children accompany the husband at the time of the move, and the change of location may seem more like an adventure than a disruptive personal or social experience. While the job may be new for the husband, the position probably involves meeting old acquaintances and joining or transferring memberships in similar-type social organizations.

Migration of lower-class families, however, typically involves substantially different circumstances. In most cases, the man migrates *for* work rather than *with* it. He probably, then, does not have a job when the family begins to move but must find one upon arrival at a new destination. The husband may have to leave his wife and children behind until he finds a job and saves up enough to send for them. There are few clubs and organizations that he can turn to for moral or social support, and thus the moving experience is one of stress (Hunt and Butler, 1972).

For some individuals — particularly for blacks and for migrants from rural to urban areas — a number of positive effects of migration have been noted (Morrison, 1972). These benefits are gains in income, occupational status, reduction in poverty, and a greater liklihood of gainful employment. Whether these effects are particularly related to the migration experience itself or a result of the favorable characteristics of the migrants themselves is a question that has not been clearly answered. In general, however, it appears that migrants are a somewhat select population: When compared to nonmigrants, they typically have greater aspirations, are better educated, and are more adaptable.

Some families move much more frequently than the general population, and such people may be better able to adjust to moves than people who do not move as often. These people also may serve as "integrators" for other people moving into the neighborhood (Toffler, 1970). Not all people in migrant or residential mobility zones in the metropolis move about — many are residentially stable, but they must adjust to the constant in- and outmovement of families and persons in the area. They also are affected by the population redistribution processes that take place in the metropolitan complex.

Finally, it is incorrect to characterize families in the United States as being "rootless." The nomad of the future may merely be households that are moving within circumscribed areas within the metropolis rather than willy-nilly throughout the country (Toffler, 1970).

BIBLIOGRAPHY: Articles

Albig, William, "Recording Urban Residential Mobility," *Sociology and Social Research,* 21 (January–February, 1937): 226–233.

Angell, Robert C., "The Moral Integration of American Cities, II," *American Journal of Sociology,* 80 (November 1974): 607–629.

Angell, Robert C., "The Moral Integration of American Cities," (Part 2) *American Journal of Sociology,* 57 (July 1951): 1–40.

Beshers, James M., and Eleanor N. Nishura, "A Theory of Internal Migration Differentials," *Social Forces,* 39 (March 1961): 214–218.

Brown, Lawrence A. and Eric G. Moore, "The Intra-urban Migration Process: A Perspective," *Geografiska Annaler,* Series B, 52B (No. 1), 1970.

Butler, Edgar W., and Edward J. Kaiser, "Prediction of Residential Movement and Spatial Allocation," *Urban Affairs Quarterly,* 6 (June 1971): 477–494.

Butler, Edgar W., Ronald J. McAllister, and Edward J. Kaiser, "Air Pollution and Metropolitan Population Redistribution," forthcoming.

Butler, Edgar W., Ronald J. McAllister, and Edward J. Kaiser, "The Effects of Voluntary and Involuntary Residential Mobility on Females and Males," *Journal of Marriage and the Family,* 35 (May 1973): 219–227.

Butler, Edgar W., Georges Sabagh, and Maurice D. Van Arsdol, Jr., "The Abandoned Environment: Residential Mobility and Alternative Housing and Neighborhood Character." Paper presented at the Pacific Sociological Association, San Francisco, April 1968.

Butler, Edgar W., Georges Sabagh, and Maurice D. Van Arsdol, Jr., "Demographic and Social Psychological Factors in Residential Mobility," *Sociology and Social Research,* 48 (January 1964): 139–154.

Caplow, Theodore, "Home Ownership and Location Preference in a Minneapolis Sample," *American Sociological Review,* 13 (1948): 725–730.

Droettboom, Theodore, Ronald J. McAllister, Edward J. Kaiser, and Edgar W. Butler, "Urban Violence and Residential Mobility," *Journal of the American Institute of Planners,* 37 (September 1971): 319–325.

Farley, Reynolds, "The Changing Distribution of Negroes Within Metropolitan Areas: The Emergence of Black Suburbs," *American Journal of Sociology,* 75 (January 1970): 512–529.

"Flight to the Suburbs," *Time,* March 22, 1954, p. 120.

Freedman, Ronald, "Distribution of Migrant Population in Chicago," *American Sociological Review,* 13 (February 1948): 304–309.

Galle, Omer R., and Karl E. Taeuber, "Metropolitan Migration and Intervening Opportunities," *American Sociological Review,* 31 (February 1966): 5–13.

Gold, Robert, "Urban Violence and Contemporary Defensive Cities," *Journal of the American Institute of Planners,* 36 (May 1970): 146–159.

Goldstein, Sidney, "The Extent of Repeated Migration: An Analysis Based on the Danish Population Registrar," *Journal of the American Statistical Association,* 59 (December 1964): 1121–1132.

Hamilton, C. Horace, "The Negro Leaves the South," *Demography,* 1 (1964): 273–295.

Henry, Andrew F., "Residential Turnover and Family Composition of Home Owners in Four Subdivisions in Nantick, Massachusetts," *Social Forces,* 31 (May 1953): 355–360.

Hunt, Gerard J., and Edgar W. Butler, "Migration, Participation and Alienation," *Sociology and Social Research,* 56 (July 1972): 440–452.

Jonassen, Christen T., "Relationship of Attitudes and Behavior in Ecological Mobility," *Social Forces,* 34 (October 1955): 64–67.

Kaiser, Edward J., Edgar W. Butler, Ronald J. McAllister, and Russell W. Thibeault, "Some Problems with Accessibility Standards: A Comparison of Household Preferences to Standards for Work, Shopping, and School Trips," *The Review of Regional Studies,* 3 (Winter 1972–1973): 111–123.

Kalback, Warren E., and George C. Myers, and John R. Walker, "Metropolitan Area Mobility: A Comparative Analysis of Family Spatial Mobility in a Central City and Selected Suburbs," *Social Forces,* 42 (March 1964): 310–314.

Ladinsky, Jack, "Occupational Determinants of Geographic Mobility Among Professional Workers," *American Sociological Review,* 32 (April 1967): 253–264.

Leslie, Gerald R., and Arthur H. Richardson, "Life-Cycle, Career Pattern, and Decision to Move," *American Sociological Review,* 26 (December 1961): 894–902.

Long, Larry H., "The Influence of Number and Ages of Children on Residential Mobility," *Demography,* 9 (August 1972): 371–382.

McAllister, Ronald J., Edgar W. Butler, and Edward J. Kaiser, "The Adaptation of Women to Residential Mobility," *Journal of Marriage and the Family,* 35 (May 1973): 197–204.

McAllister, Ronald J., Edward J. Kaiser, and Edgar W. Butler, "Residential Mobility of Blacks and Whites: A National Longitudinal Survey," *American Journal of Sociology,* 77 (November 1972): 445–456.

McGinnis, Robert, George C. Myers, and John Pilger, "Internal Migration as a Stochastic Process," 34th Session, International Statistical Institute, Ottawa, Canada, August 26, 1963.

Masters, Stanley H., "Are Black Migrants from the South to the Northern Cities Worse Off than Blacks Already There?" *Journal of Human Resources,* 7 (Fall 1972): 411–423.

Morrison, Peter A., "Duration of Residence and Prospective Migration: The Evaluation of a Stochastic Model," *Demography,* 4 (1967): 553–561.

Morrison, Peter A., "Theoretical Issues in the Design of Population Mobility Models," paper presented at the American Sociological Association, San Francisco, September 1969.

Myers, George C., Robert C. McGinnis, and George Masnick, "The Duration of Residence Approach to a Dynamic Stochastic Model of Internal Migration: A Test of the Axiom of Cumulative Inertia," *Eugenics Quarterly,* 14 (June 1967): 121–126.

Park, Robert E., "Human Migration and the Marginal Man," *American Journal of Sociology,* 33 (May 1928): 881–893.

Rose, Arnold M., "Distance of Migration and Socio-Economic Status of Migrants," *American Sociological Review,* 23 (June 1958): 420–423.

Rosenthal, Jack, "Black Exodus to Suburbs Found Increasing Sharply," *The New York Times,* July 12, 1970, pp. 1, 22.

Ross, H. Laurence, "The Local Community: A Survey Approach," *American Sociological Review,* 27 (February 1962): 75–84.

Sabagh, Georges, Maurice D. Van Arsdol, Jr., and Edgar W. Butler, "Some Determinants of Intrametropolitan Residential Mobility: Conceptual Considerations," *Social Forces,* 48 (September 1969): 88–98.

Schmid, Calvin F., and Manzer J. Griswold, "Migration Within the State of Washington, 1935–40," *American Sociological Review,* 17 (June 1952): 312–326.

Stegman, Michael A., "Accessibility Models and Residential Location," *Journal of the American Institute of Planners,* 35 (January 1969): 22–29.

Stouffer, Samuel A., "Intervening Opportunities: A Theory Relating Mobility and Distance," *American Sociological Review,* 5 (December 1940): 845–867.

Straits, Bruce C., "Residential Movement Among Negroes and Whites in Chicago," *Social Science Quarterly,* 49 (December 1968): 573–592.

Taeuber, Karl E., "Duration-of-Residence Analysis of Internal Migration in the United States," *Milbank Memorial Fund Quarterly,* 39 (January 1961): 116–134.

Thibeault, Russell W., Edward J. Kaiser, Edgar W. Butler, and Ronald J. McAllister, "Accessibility Satisfaction, Income, and Residential Mobility," *Traffic Quarterly,* 27 (April 1973): 289–305.

Van Arsdol, Maurice D., Jr., Georges Sabagh, and Edgar W. Butler, "Retrospective and Subsequent Metropolitan Residential Mobility," *Demography,* 5 (No. 1, 1968): 249–266.

Ward, David, "The Emergence of Central Immigrant Ghettoes in American Cities: 1840–1920," *Annals,* 58 (June 1968): 343–359.

BIBLIOGRAPHY: Books

Abu-Lughod, Janet, and M. M. Foley, "Consumer Differences," in Nelson Foote et al., *Housing Choices and Housing Constraints,* New York: McGraw-Hill Book Company, 1960, pp. 95–133.

Bogue, Donald J., "Internal Migration," in P. M. Hauser and O. D. Duncan (eds.), *The Study of Population: An Inventory and Appraisal,* Chicago: University of Chicago Press, 1959, pp. 468–509.

Butler, Edgar W., F. Stuart Chapin, Jr., George C. Hemmens, Edward J. Kaiser, Michael A. Stegman, and Shirley F. Weiss, *Moving Behavior and Residential Choice: A National Survey,* Washington, D.C.: National Academy of Sciences, 1969.

Chapin, F. Stuart, Jr., Edgar W. Butler, and Frederick A. Patten, *Blackways in an Inner City,* Urbana, Ill.: University of Illinois Press, forthcoming.

Denton, Alfred M., *Some Factors in the Migration of Construction Workers,* unpublished doctoral dissertation, Chapel Hill, N.C.: University of North Carolina, 1960.

Eldridge, Hope Tisdale, "The Process of Urbanization," in J. J. Spengler and Otis Dudley Duncan (eds.), *Demographic Analysis,* Glencoe, Ill.: The Free Press, 1956, pp. 338–343.

Foote, Nelson N., et al., *Housing Choices and Housing Constraints,* New York: McGraw-Hill, 1960.

Gans, Herbert, "Effects of the Move from City to Suburb," in Leonard J. Duhl (ed.), *The Urban Condition,* New York: Basic Books, 1963.

Glaab, Charles N., and A. Theodore Brown, *A History of Urban America,* New York: Macmillan Company, 1967.

Groh, George W., *The Black Migration: The Journey to Urban America,* New York: Weybright and Talley, 1972.

Kaiser, Edward J., Edgar W. Butler, and Ronald J. McAllister, *The Urban Nomads,* forthcoming.

Karp, Herbert H., and K. Dennis Kelly, *Toward an Ecological Analysis of Intermetropolitan Migration,* Chicago: Markham Publishing Company, 1971.

Kurtz, Norman R., *Gate Keepers in the Process of Acculturation,* unpublished doctoral dissertation, Department of Sociology, University of Colorado, 1966 (mimeo).

Lansing, John B., and Eva Mueller, *The Geographic Mobility of Labor,* Ann Arbor, Mich.: Institute for Social Research, 1968.

Lansing, John B., C. W. Clifton, and J. N. Morgan, *New Homes and Poor People,* Ann Arbor, Mich.: Institute for Social Research, University of Michigan, 1969.

Morrison, Peter A., *Population Movements: Where the Public Interest and Private Interest Conflict,* Santa Monica, Calif.: Rand Corp., August 1972 (R-987-CPG).

Palmer, Gladys, with Carol P. Brainerd, *Labor Mobility in Six Cities, 1940–1950,* New York: Committee on Labor Market Research, Social Science Research Council, 1954.

Rossi, Peter H., *Why Families Move,* Glencoe, Ill.: The Free Press, 1955.

Taeuber, Conrad, and Irene B. Taeuber, *The Changing Population of the United States,* New York: John Wiley, 1958.

Tilly, Charles, "Race and Migration to the American City," in James Q. Wilson (ed.), *The Metropolitan Enigma,* Cambridge, Mass.: Harvard University Press, 1968.

Toffler, Alvin, *Future Shock,* New York: Random House, 1970.

U.S. Bureau of the Census, *Current Population Reports,* Series P-20, No. 193. "Mobility of the Population of the United States: March 1968 to March 1969," Washington, D.C.: U.S. Government Printing Office, 1969.

CHAPTER 9
JOURNEYS AND CIRCULATION WITHIN URBAN AREAS

INTRODUCTION

In most cities in the United States the Central Business District has continued as daytime destination of commuters, shoppers, and so on, while residential areas have been undergoing considerable dispersal — the decentralization and suburbanization process. Not too long ago, U.S. factories were generally multistoried buildings surrounded by densely packed residences of workers. A lack of adequate transportation facilities discouraged dispersion. Today, however, workers are typically highly dispersed rather than being located near work; this necessitates a journey-to-work (Liepmann, 1944). Recently, industrial plants and facilities have been undergoing dispersal, a trend that may in the future once again drastically alter the spatial form of American cities.

A journey from one area to another involves movement from one differentiated and specialized area, for example, the place of residence, to another differentiated segregated, specialized area, the workplace. The movement back and forth between these distinct areas integrates or links the metropolitan complex into one great interrelated whole (Foley, 1954). About 1 out of every 5 metropolitan residents makes at least one trip to the CBD during each weekday, and about 1 in 10 is found in the CBD in the early afternoon hours when the peak accumulation occurs. This description best fits metropolitan areas with about 1 million population; for larger cities the ratios tend to drop; that is, a lower proportion of the total population makes trips to the CBD, while in smaller cities the ratios tend to be much larger, with a greater proportion of the population visiting the CBD. The ratios would be even higher if "only active adults were included in the population base figure" (Foley, 1952: 542–543).

In larger cities there is a marked difference between the spatial distribution of resident and daytime populations — they have been divorced (Foley, 1954). There is daily movement from places of residence to various other locations and then the return. Obviously, the most typical form of move-

The large number of commuters in this Boston subway station are waiting to go in either direction; later in the day, most of them will once again fill the station to go in the reverse direction. As Lewis Carroll's Cheshire cat wryly commented, to go "somewhere," all one has to do is pick a direction.

ment is the journey-to-work, which most often requires the use of some form of transportation because the workplace is not within walking distance. Journeys (trips) have been classified according to purpose — for instance, besides work, shopping, obtaining medical care, and so on — and according to origin and destination — residential, industrial, business, recreational, and so on. Roughly two out of every five trips from home have as their purpose reaching the workplace.

In the remainder of this chapter we shall be concerned with population journeys and circulation within urban regions. First, we shall focus on trips, especially the journey-to-work; second, we shall describe accessibilities to necessities and amenities; and, finally, we shall explore some more generalized notions of the activities of people in urban places.

JOURNEY-TO-WORK

"Traveling to work is a regular feature of a modern, urbanized, industrialized society and workers are accustomed to spending a considerable part of their time traveling to and from work" (Reeder, 1956: 56). Commuting to work has existed, no doubt, as long as population concentrations have, but the development of railroads first made it practical for a substantial proportion of the working population to live some miles from their workplaces. The automobile made possible further population deconcentration, and commuting to work now is an important characteristic of the daily life of millions of residents in metropolitan areas of the United States. The sum total of metropolitan workers who go to and from work each day is the major factor contributing to transportation bottlenecks that occur twice daily in most American metropolitan areas. Data on commuting and journeys are available from U.S. Bureau of Census publications, "origin-and-destination" traffic studies, management records (Schnore, 1960) and from household surveys conducted over the past several years (Butler et al., 1969).

Until recently the general assumption has been that there are forces that tend to minimize distance between home and workplace. By living close to work, so the argument goes, we can keep the physical effort, costs, time, and inconvenience of the journey-to-work at a minimum (Carroll, 1952). Recently, Catanese (1970) tested this hypothesis in Philadelphia and Milwaukee and showed in general that in 1960 fewer people were living closer to their jobs and more were living farther away from them than in 1946. He noted that suburban expansion resulted in more commuting and in more people living farther away from their workplaces.

Morgan (1967: 360) reported that "the amount of time people spend going to work and back is highest for those who live in central cities of the twelve largest metropolitan areas and least for those who live in outlying or rural areas." Generally, the larger the city, the longer the journey-to-work takes. In cities under 100,000 population most trips take no more than one-half hour. In New York City, on the other hand, two out of three workers spend at least 40 minutes going each way. People who live far from the urban center usually fall into two categories: (1) those with short commuting time, presumably working in the ring where they live, and (2) those with long commuting time, who presumably go into the central city to work. It should be noted that not all commuting is to the center of the city, and that one can travel farther with less time involvement in the suburbs. The speed of travel is slower the closer one gets to a congested center. Although mode of transportation may not be important in the length of trip, it becomes extremely important when one is concerned with *time*, because public transportation averages about one-half the speed of door-to-door automobile commuting (Morgan, 1967: 362).

The residential distribution of persons employed in central districts tends to approximate that of the entire metropolitan population (Carroll, 1952). That is, the population and residences of central-district workers are arranged about the core area in a constantly declining density. Persons employed in off-centered (not located in the central district) workplaces are concentrated most heavily in immediate or adjacent areas to them; the residential pattern resembles nucleated subclusters within the metropolitan complex. The first condition approximates the Burgess zonal hypothesis, while the second illustrates Hoyt's sector theory and/or Harris and Ullman's multiple nuclei notion.

In one of the very few statements in this regard, Carroll (1952) noted that if the foregoing distributions are accurate descriptions of metropolitan populations and their residences and workplaces, there may be systematic variation, by city type, of homes to workplaces, because heavily industrialized cities have much more large-scale employment in noncentral locations, which suggests much less population concentration and a more dispersed city than one that has as its primary purpose servicing a hinterland. The service-type city should have its population diffused in zones, whereas industrialized cities should be sectored or have multiple nuclei. Carroll offered the examples of Flint and Detroit as metropolitan centers in which off-center workplaces have a decentralizing effect.

The important variables of the length of time required to get to work are size of city and distance lived from the center. Education, race, region, home ownership, age, sex, and work hours are not related (Morgan, 1967). In Detroit, however, workers employed in higher-income occupations working in inner areas of the central city made longer journeys to work than others who resided outside of the inner city. Lower-income workers made shorter journeys-to-work and resided within or adjacent to areas to work regardless of the workplace location (Kain, 1962). Also, day-shift workers live closer to their workplaces than do those employed on other shifts (Schnore, 1960: 12). This suggests the hypothesis that cities in which there are places of employment with shifts around the clock—heavy manufacturing cities—will have a different distribution of workers and travel patterns than ones in which work is done primarily during daytime working hours, as, for instance, service centers.

Factory workers live close to work, whereas the pattern of residences of workers in the CBD tends to approximate that of the total city population (Carroll, 1949: 414). Obviously people who walk to work live close to their work. Public transportation users usually live two to six miles from work; but beyond that distance the time cost of travel by public transportation becomes prohibitive for factory workers. The willingness to move increases with distance from the factory, and older factories have a closer distribution of workers than new factories (Carroll, 1949: 417–418). Thus low-wage workers have economic constraints—that is, they must live close to their places of employment.

In general, the work force that is employed in the central city tends to live there; and the work force that is employed in the suburbs usually lives there. Nevertheless, there is considerable movement between the central city and the suburbs for the purpose of the journey-to-work (U.S. Bureau of the Census, 1963). About one out of four metropolitan workers crossed city boundaries in one direction or another for the journey-to-work in 1960 (Yu, 1972: 85). On the average, the central city gained one additional worker from outside it for every three workers who resided in it. The commutation rate to the central city, as reported by the census, is primarily a function of the city's historically determined boundary lines.

A high income presumably allows a family to live where it wishes, since economic constraints on place of residence are removed. As a result, some have hypothesized that families with higher incomes should be found near the central city where most jobs are located. An alternative hypothesis, however, is that families with higher incomes can live farther away from the central city because distance to work is not a constraint on their home location decision. As a result of analyses of commuting patterns in Philadelphia and Milwaukee, Catanese (1970: 455) concluded that the amount of intersuburban commuting by middle- and high-income families was much greater than previously believed and noted in the literature. These findings show that low-income families literally appear to be trapped in central areas and must usually commute away from them to workplaces. Workplaces appear to be following middle- and high-income families to suburban areas, but the amount of inter-suburban commuting indicates that work- and home places are not necessarily in the same suburbs. Thus his analyses show that both homes and jobs are decentralizing but not to the same areas.

The location of the workplace—that is, the attempt to minimize the journey-to-work—may have an important bearing upon a family's decision to move. However, in Milwaukee and Philadelphia only 6 percent of the families that moved gave this reason for doing so (Catanese, 1970: 447). Over a year's period of time, a few families did move closer to their work. However, most families in Philadelphia and Milwaukee moved farther away from their jobs in order to obtain better housing and neighborhoods. Further, Goldstein and Mayer (1964a) noted that the possibility of commuting extends the area in which job opportunities can be found without residential mobility. They argue, in fact, that when short-distance moves occur, they are independent of jobs and job changes, whereas a long-distance move almost necessarily involves a job change. But even after a long-distance move, it is not clearly established how close the family should live to the job.

Similarly, Hawley (1950: 337) has suggested that the daily journey-to-work might reduce moving within the local community. Reeder (1956: 62) implicitly agreed with this position and pointed out that the use of the automobile in the journey-to-work permits greater flexibility in the family's choice of a place of residence; thus a family may remain in one place of residence in spite of a job change. Aside from extremely wide threshold limits, work location appears to have little impact upon the specific neighborhood of residence of many families in metropolitan regions. While there are some notable concentrations of workers around employment centers, there is also extensive scattering of workers and their residences. Thus the notion that a family will always minimize distance and/or time in the journey-to-work appears to be inconsistent with the facts; the location of work has less influence now than formerly upon residential placement (Schnore, 1954: 337).

For a particular factory Schnore (1960: 14) reported data illustrating that distance commuted by employees may become longer over time and that as plant expansion takes place, workers come from longer distances; that is, an expanding labor market is created. However, Duncan (1956) reported that for the entire Chicago metropolitan area comparative data for 1916 and 1950 show a persistence of similar work-residence separation differences over time.

Mode of Transportation to Work

Seventy-three percent of Spokane, Washington, residents use an automobile to travel to work (Reeder, 1956: 59). Sixty-one percent of employed persons in New York City, however, travel to work by mass transit (Schnore, 1962: 491). Clearly, there are substantial differences by cities in the mode of transportation used to get to work. Schnore (1962) hypothesized three characteristics of cities that influence the travel mode used by their residents in getting to work: (1) *Size of the city* is important because "it determines the limits of the *market* for public transportation." (2) *Population density* helps in establishing an economy of operation and reducing per capita costs. (3) *Age of the city* — that is, when it first reached a large size (50,000 population) — is related to transportation mode especially if the city reached larger size prior to the widespread use and ownership of automobiles in the 1920s. "It might be expected that such cities would be better equipped with public transportation facilities, having been obliged to install and maintain mass transit systems before the turn of the century."

Schnore's analysis shows that all three of these characteristics are important factors, with the very largest cities (1 million or more inhabitants) having a greater proportion of their populations using public transportation, and cities with higher population densities having a greater use of public transportation than smaller ones and those with lower densities. But he ascribed the most importance to the age-of-the-city factor, which, when controlled, explains more of the differences among cities than the factors of city size and density. The three dimensions taken together statistically help explain about two-thirds of the variation in commuting modes. Other characteristics that probably are important in travel modes to work, both at the city level and in specific areas within the city, are the percent of minorities, employed females, and lower socioeconomic status (Schnore, 1962: 491).

Work Trips and the Black Ghetto

Findings of the major metropolitan transportation surveys in the United States quite consistently reveal that blacks have lower work-trip mobility than whites. Work-trip mobility among whites increases with rises in occupational status, but for blacks there is no consistent regularity between status and distance traveled to work (Wheeler, 1968: 108). Segregated housing obviously may affect the distribution of black employment and limit job opportunities away from the ghetto.

Meyer, Kain, and Wohl reported that, in both Chicago and Detroit, on the average blacks travel a shorter distance and incur less expense than do whites (1965: 146). Similarly, a Pittsburgh study of socioeconomic and racial variation in relation to spatial patterns of home and work showed that the

Some of these people in Gary, Indiana, are waiting for the bus while others are walking to their destinations. These two modes—walking and mass transit—are the dominant ones for most blacks living in cities.

length of the average work trip for whites was 3.45 miles and for blacks 3.05 miles (Wheeler, 1968: 107). Whites traveled farther than blacks in every occupational class except for service workers and laborers, in which blacks traveled farther. Black professionals and laborers must travel the longest distances to work.

The effect of residential segregation in restricting black employment in areas distant from the ghetto is clearly demonstrated in Pittsburgh, confirming Kain's findings for Detroit and Chicago. The reliance of blacks on mass transit magnifies the employment problem and also limits the jobs to which they have accessibility. Practically the only black population that escapes this limitation is black professionals, who are more dispersed than blacks in other occupational categories.

Some lower-status blacks have broken out of the "employment ghetto" (Wheeler, 1968: 112). But most people who work outside of the ghetto are probably involved in servant occupations. Since employment opportunities do not coincide with areas of the ghetto, some relatively long work trips involving *reverse* commuting are necessary, that is, from the inner city to the suburbs. Work-trip behavior of blacks is a response to racial discrimination rather than to residential location preferences as in the case with white workers.

From his study of residents of public housing in Chicago, Whiting (1952: 289) further reported that among blacks the need for good housing is so great that workers will travel long distances to work and change neighborhoods completely to obtain adequate residences and satisfactory neighborhoods.

After moving to public housing projects, black workers changed jobs in all directions but primarily to areas where public transportation was available. He also reported that many persons moving into public housing moved from substandard housing to low-rent housing even though they had to travel farther to work.

Most studies of black commuting primarily have been based upon larger cities and typically report average shorter-distance work trips for blacks than for whites. But in smaller cities blacks travel farther than whites because more of them are employed in the suburbs. In testing this hypothesis, using origin-destination data for Tulsa, Oklahoma, Wheeler (1969) found that virtually all blacks in Tulsa lived in a ghetto area adjacent to the CBD. They have longer work trips—on the average of approximately one-half mile longer—than do whites. Non-CBD trips make up this difference, since work trips of whites that terminate in the CBD are longer than those for blacks that terminate there. Thus the main component of longer work trips by blacks are trips made by females to non-CBD destinations. When time to work, instead of distance, is used as a measure, similar findings hold, although black females have greater variability in the time it takes to get to work than black males or whites. Black males take the longest time to get to work primarily because of the proportion who walk. Blacks who do not work in the CBD find themselves moving counter to major commuter streams. This, coupled with the low proportion of automobile ownership, means that blacks must either walk or use public transportation. The typical public transportation system is structured to get workers and shoppers to the CBD, and thus the routes and times are not convenient for non-CBD black workers. In order for blacks to come to terms with the urban environment, they must be able to increase their alternatives with respect to both residential and employment location (Wheeler, 1969: 177).

While a few blacks are moving out of the urban complex entirely, when they live in a smaller community, they tend to travel farther to work than whites. In semirural Michigan, blacks drive an average of 20 miles, 28 minutes, whereas whites drive an average of 6 miles, 13 minutes. Similarly, blacks travel farther than whites in the same community for gasoline, groceries, and clothing (Wheeler and Brunn, 1968: 228–229).

Meyer, Kain, and Wohl (1965: 155) concluded that it is reasonably clear that whites and blacks having similar workplace locations make a variety of residential choices and undertake different types of commuting trips to work. These residential and commuting patterns may well be a matter of choice by blacks and whites, as some have suggested, or it may be a result of differential opportunities for housing, with blacks being forced to live in the central city because of racial, occupational, and educational discrimination.

Interurban Variation in Commuting Patterns

According to Poston's (1972) analysis of 1960 U.S. census data for the country's 53 largest SMSAs, higher-socioeconomic workers tend to have more

TABLE 9-1
Commuting in Chicago, 1960

	NUMBER	PERCENT OF INVOLVED
Total Resident Workers	1,470,210	
Place of Work Not Reported	119,948	
Resident Workers (Reported)	1,350,262	79.3
Outcommuters	−100,049	−5.9
Noncommuters	1,250,213	73.4
Incommuters	353,123	+20.7
Total Workers (Reported)	1,603,336	94.1
Total Workers Involved	1,703,385	100.0
Net Commuting	+253,074	+14.8

Source: Forstall (1965: 101).

separation between their homes and workplaces than lower-socioeconomic workers. In all but a few of these largest SMSAs the higher the socioeconomic level of the city worker, the greater the degree of residential location in suburbs rather than the city. To measure variation in commuting to work in different cities, Forstall (1965) used the Employment/Residence Ratio (E/R) as a crude measure comparing the number of persons employed in a city, irrespective of residence, with the number of persons who live there. He further noted that there are *outcommuters* as well as *incommuters* and *noncommuters*. Table 9-1 presents 1960 data on commuting for Chicago.

As we made explicit earlier, Forstall pointed out that these data depend partially on the geographical (political) boundary that separates city from non-city (also see Sheldon and Hoermann, 1964). The importance of recognizing geographical boundaries is this: "A resident of east Minneapolis whose workplace is across the street in St. Paul is a commuter, while a resident of the outer reaches of the San Fernando Valley who works in downtown Los Angeles, more than 20 miles away, is not, because both his home and his workplace are within the same city." Keeping this caveat in mind, he presented data that indicate that, insofar as commuting is concerned, each large city appears to have a combination of distinct areas or neighborhoods possessing sharply contrasting commuting patterns.

Forstall also presented a "commuting classification of cities," which has two components: (1) the degree of *commuting self-sufficiency,* that is, the extent of noncommuting, and (2) the *balance between in- and outcommuting.* His classifications for self-sufficiency are as follows:

H = high percentage of noncommuters (85 percent or more).
M = medium percentage of noncommuters (60 to 85 percent).
L = low percentage of noncommuters (30 to 60 percent).
X = extremely low percentage of noncommuters (below 30 percent).

Only one city qualifies for the H Classification—El Paso, Texas. We used El Paso earlier (Chapter 6) as an example of a city that by virtue of its expansive city-limit boundaries and census definitions has virtually no suburbs and thus few suburban residents. This, of course, results in few commuters and its high classification under Forstall's system.

Under the M classification he subdivides cities into those having an incommuting rate substantially larger than that of outcommuting—ME; over one-half of the very largest cities are in this category, as well as Indianapolis, San Francisco, and Rome, New York. MB cities have a relative balance between in- and outcommuting; Phoenix, Albuquerque, Davenport, Erie, Beaumont, Portsmouth, Spokane, and Superior, Wisconsin, make up the total composition of this category. MF cities have significant fringe employment resulting in a large outcommuting component; three cities are so classified: San Antonio, Wichita, and Tucson.

Cities with a low percentage of noncommuters are subdivided into LE employing cities, LB balanced cities, and LD dormitory cities. The major extremes in the LE category are New York's borough of Manhattan, which has 17 times as many incommuters as outcommuters, Rochester, having 13 times as many incommuters as outcommuters, and East Chicago, Indiana, having 8 times as many incommuters as outcommuters. Examples of LB cities are Berkeley, California, and Elizabeth, New Jersey. LD dormitory cities include all four noncentral boroughs of New York City—Brooklyn, Queens, the Bronx, and Richmond.

Finally, the cities with the lowest percentage of noncommuters, or, alternatively, the *highest percentage of commuters,* are classified as follows: XE = employing cities that have major out- and incommuting components, with incommuting being most important—examples are Cambridge and Waltham, Massachusetts, Dearborn, Michigan, and Palo Alto, California. XB cities have a large commuting turnover but in- and outcommuting is roughly equal—examples are Anaheim and Compton, California, Cicero, Illinois, Passaic, New Jersey, Euclid, Ohio, and Falls Church, Virginia. Virtually all of these cities are relatively small, and none of them is the principal central city of an SMSA. XD, or dormitory cities, are places such as Warwick, Rhode Island, Garden Grove and West Covina, California, and Lakewood and Cleveland Heights, Ohio. These are the most extreme instances of outcommuting for all cities of over 50,000 population, but Forstall (1965: 107) believes that more extreme cities would appear if data were available for cities with fewer people.

Unfortunately, Forstall did not relate variation in commuting to city types; however, he did suggest that there is a tendency for southern and western cities and larger cities to have higher noncommuter components. While he did not indicate any reason for this, the explanation for western cities probably is that their city-limit boundaries include substantial land areas that would be categorized as suburbs in other parts of the country.

Consequences of the Journey-to-Work

Several negative consequences have been reported to be associated with a longer journey-to-work. For example, there are cities whose tax bases have been severely curtailed as a result of suburban expansion, and the problems of financing city services can probably be expected to multiply with the trend toward decentralization of the population and industry (Schnore, 1954: 336). In addition, the impact upon the psychological well-being of commuters and the social organization of suburbs has been stressed.

One consequence of the suburbanite's daily work trip is less cultural and voluntary organization participation in the community of residence. Scaff (1952) in his study of the effect of commuting upon residents of Claremont, California (a part of the Los Angeles metropolitan region), noted that in Claremont "a significant proportion of the young adult male population commutes to outside jobs." He reported that the flow of commuting was not toward the central city of Los Angeles but in all directions. One major effect of commuting to work was to have some males who participated in organizations in Claremont while most belonged to organizations near the place of work. Scaff noted that this has serious consequences for the local community, since local organizations are largely left in the hands of elderly retired people or women (p. 219). In addition, he reported that organizations are, without conscious effort, selective of educated and professional persons to the exclusion of the poor and minorities. He also showed a substantial relationship between longer-distance commuting to work and lowered participation in local organizations.

In summary, these studies suggest the hypothesis that working outside the place of residence reduces the extent of participation in local organizations. Further, as distance of commuting increases, social participation in local organizations decreases.

Intraurban Variation in Commuting Patterns

Using the social area analysis approach to the classification of intraurban areas, Goldstein and Mayer (1964b) studied commuting patterns of a number of different areas within the Providence and Pawtucket, Rhode Island, metropolitan region. They examined both socioeconomic-status differences and migration differences and their effects upon commuting to work. Generally comparison of journey-to-work patterns of central city residents by migration status shows minimal differences between nonmovers and those who had moved within the limits of the central cities (p. 281). They further concluded that some of these persons, despite moving to the central cities, continued to commute to their previous places of work. Movers into both central cities and suburbs travel greater distances to work than nonmovers and retain occupational ties with the areas of origin (p. 283).

Insofar as socioeconomic differentials are concerned, there is very little variation in commuting patterns by residents of central cities — except for the very lowest socioeconomic classification. Of all central city residents the lowest socioeconomic workers are more likely than others to hold jobs in the suburbs or in nearby satellite industrial cities of Woonsocket and Central Falls. Commuting patterns of suburban residents are more varied. About one-half of the highest-status suburban residents commute to the central city, whereas only 15 percent of the lowest-status workers do so. On the other hand, about one out of three highest-status suburban residents works in the suburbs, while almost one-half of the lowest-status suburban residents work there. Again, for the lowest-status suburban residents satellite industrial cities provide most noncentral city jobs. Goldstein and Mayer (1964b: 284) concluded that "traditional commuters from the suburbs to the cities consist largely of higher status workers who can afford both the cost of commuting to jobs in the city as well as the greater cost of living in high status suburbs." But more and more lower-status workers who are living in the suburbs also may work there or in nearby satellite industrial cities.

Schnore (1954) used a different perspective in studying commuter patterns in Flint, Michigan, when he examined where workers in the six largest principal industrial plants lived. Using distance zones (by miles), he found that the distribution of workers around the plants assumes a gradient pattern. Further, he showed that each plant drew workers from the distance zones in accordance with the number of employees in the plant, with larger plants having a greater local drawing power per 1000 local population. He noted that one of the smaller plants exerted a wider drawing power of employees than the others, which he attributed to its newness as one of the major industrial sites in the Flint area. Thus, as we have noted previously, the length of time a major plant has been located in the same place has some effect upon the residential distribution of its employees. The longer a plant has been located in one place, the closer more workers live to it.

Also, day workers in plants having different shifts approach the gradient system quite closely, with most workers living close to the plant. Those working on the remaining shifts, however, have an opposite distribution, and the number of residents increases as distance increases. This has led Schnore to suggest that those not working on the day-shift are "marginal workers" to the plant *and* to the industrial organization.

There is virtually no literature comparing the location of economic activities within urban areas and their relationship or influence upon the location of a residence. Perhaps the most sophisticated pertinent study done to date is the one carried out by Lowenstein (1965). He evaluated the journey-to-work by various industrial categories in a number of cities typed according to the Nelson typology described in Chapter 5.

Examining work trips by industrial categories, Lowenstein found that finance, insurance, and real-estate activities either were located in the core or were placed ribbonlike along major thoroughfares in residential areas. Thus work trips by employees involves trips to the CBD or to the same district in which the worker lives. Educational and medical facilities are located outside of the CBD, and the workers in many of these industries live downtown and have a downtown orientation; therefore, there is some commuting from the central part of the city to adjacent areas. The retail industry has a distribution similar to finance, insurance, and real estate, but the residential distribution of workers approximates that of the entire urban area.

Employees of personal business services are located downtown or near residential areas, although private household workers who are included in this category are distributed more into lower-class and minority areas. Transportation land use is distributed linearly in the metropolitan area, but workers live throughout the urban region, with many employees making long commuting trips to work from the region's outer reaches. In contrast, public administration activities are located in the core, though employees tend to live on the periphery; but yet they typically live within the city, since some cities require them to do so.

Manufacturing employees live in a variety of areas in the urban region, with residential patterns depending upon the size of the plant, the product produced, and linkages with supplies and customers. Few of these plants are centrally located, and the trips by employees are highly variable.

Lowenstein (1965: 263–264) noted that his study dealt with industry of employment as a key variable in determining residences and workplaces. He hypothesized, however, that size of a particular city, its age, and its economic base may have some bearing on the spatial distribution of residences and work places.

In view of the preceding discussion, Flint is almost an exclusively off-center industrial-type city and Providence and Pawtucket can also be considered as primarily industrial cities. Other types of cities, such as service centers, recreational areas, and so on, may have widely varying commuting patterns. Unfortunately, no detailed information is available. Nevertheless, it does appear that if decentralization of work opportunities, industrial or otherwise, continues in the future, more low-status people probably will be living in the suburbs. If these studies are generally applicable, lower-status workers who reside in the suburbs probably will work there also, while suburban higher-socioeconomic-status workers will continue to commute to the central city.

ACCESSIBILITY

Almost all current urban development models (see Butler et al., 1969, for a survey of these models) are based on a simple notion that new residential growth areas will be located as closely as possible to employment centers in order to minimize transportation costs. A great deal of empirical data and research indicate, however, that accessibility and accessibility satisfaction actually have little influence in residential relocations (see Chapter 8). In addition, national metropolitan sample data suggest that a large majority of families that have made a recent move to the suburbs are more concerned with *neigh-*

In addition to those who work at home or journey to work within an urban region, others constantly fly from one metropolitan area to another, keeping travel agencies, taxis, and airlines busy. The modern conception of "flying" is perhaps not what it once was, judging by the traffic backup of aircraft awaiting takeoff clearance at this airport.

borhood quality than with accessibility to other parts of the urban complex (Butler et al., 1969). Further, given the current configuration of land use in large urban areas, services and activities are more accessible to suburban residents than to city residents. Large numbers of suburban families do not have to tradeoff accessibility for savings in location rent—they can have both. Stegman (1969: 22), in fact, argued that the most rational choice of residential location is the suburb because of this increased accessibility.

In addition, an increasing minority of households are not tied to a specific work location. There are people who work at home—for example, housewives, writers, artists, photographers, telephone solicitors—and a larger number of workers who are not tied to a particular place of work. Included in this latter category are salesmen, handymen, girl fridays, truck drivers, and so on. Further, there are those who are peripherally involved in the labor force, such as welfare recipients and the unemployed, and those not in the labor force, such as "loafers" and the retired. These various categories of workers and nonworkers may account for as much as one-third of the adult population who do not actively participate in the journey-to-work as described in the previous section. Nevertheless, they do make many other trips such as for shopping, visiting health facilities, attending school and church, meeting friends, and so on.

While the time, distance, and costs of these other trips may not approximate those for making the journey-to-work, these other trips may have much more importance for many families. For example, a family may trade off traveling a longer distance to work by the head of the family for good accessibility to schools and/or a desirable neighborhood. Time distances to most services and activities (other than work) tend to group at the 5- to 10-minute distance. For example, almost two-thirds of the urban people interviewed in a recent national study lived 5 minutes or less from a grocery store; 87 percent of the families lived within 10 minutes of an elementary school, and over one-half of the population was less than 10 minutes from all services with the exception of hospitals—43 percent, downtown—32 percent, and work—29 percent. Of interest also is that virtually one-half of the population would like to be the same distance they are now from various services and work if they were to move; about 40 percent were indifferent. Thus very few people if they were to move want to move closer to various services—on the average, less than 10 percent (Butler et al., 1969).

Trips cross-classified by area of origin and destination, as already suggested, are primarily a result of an exodus from residential areas into industrial and commercial areas. Actually, three out of every four residents remain in residential areas. During most of the regular working hours, about 13 percent of all residents are found in the city's industrial areas and about 16 percent in the early afternoon peak are in commercial areas. By moving outward in concentric zones from the CBD, a changing ratio of daytime to resident population has been noted (Foley, 1954: 327):

ZONE	RATIO OF DAYTIME TO RESIDENT POPULATION
1	23.84
2	7.41
3	2.33
4	1.53
5	1.15
6	0.93
7	0.95
8	0.94

Trips for "social-recreational" purposes account for about one-fourth of all journeys. During weekdays, this is typically an evening trip. "Shopping" and "business" journeys are next in importance and tend to be afternoon activities. The number of commercial and social contacts in the city increase at a closer distance to the family home and decrease as distance becomes greater. Riemer (1959: 441–442) reported that the mean distance in Lakewood, California, for commercial contacts was 1.95, while it was 4.58 for social contacts, or over double the distance for commercial activities.

Low-income families are more likely than high-income families to prefer a favorably located residence over a superior neighborhood. Similarly, families without an automobile, those located in central cities, and older per-

The concentration of people in the CBD each workday requires an exodus from out-lying areas and results in traffic snarls, overcrowded sidewalks, and short tempers within the CBD.

sons give more significance to a location having good accessibility than to a quality neighborhood (Thibeault et al., 1973). According to a national urban sample, families who moved between 1966 and 1969 indicated four major destination points that they wished to live near: elementary schools (34.6 percent), head's workplace (19.7 percent), a shopping center (12.0 percent), and public transportation (8.4 percent). No other destination was reported as being most important by as much as 5 percent of the population. As shown in Table 9-2, upper-income families are more likely to view elementary schools and head's work as the most important destinations, while lower-income families are more likely to view access to public transportation and grocery stores, church, home of a relative, and a hospital or clinic as the most important desti-nations (Thibeault et al., 1973).

Most studies have reported that lower-income families reside closer to work than upper-income families. But in the national sample referred to previously, when the *time* it takes to get to work was examined, it was found that on the average it takes *longer* for lower-income people to get to work than upper-income people. Similarly, on the average, it takes longer for lower-income people to reach elementary schools, shopping centers, grocery stores, churches, hospitals-clinics, doctors' offices, downtown areas, and parks or playgrounds. Only with respect to the time it takes to reach a best friend's house is time *equal* for both upper- and lower-income persons (Thibeault et al., 1973). These differences are, in part, attributed to variation in mode of trans-

TABLE 9-2
Single Most Important Destination^a to Be Close to

| DESTINATION | PERCENT OF RESPONDENTS INDICATING DESTINATION AS MOST IMPORTANT | | |
| | UNCONTROLLED | CONTROLLED FOR INCOME | |
		LESS THAN $5250	$5250 OR MORE
Elementary Schools	34.6	30.1	36.5
Head's Work	19.7	15.0	21.7
Shopping Center	12.0	12.1	12.0
Public Transportation	8.4	10.7	7.5
Grocery Store	4.3	8.7	2.4
Church	3.7	6.3	2.6
Home of Relative	2.7	4.4	2.0
Highway	2.0	0.5	2.6
Hospital or Clinic	1.7	3.9	0.8
Doctor's Office	0.7	1.0	0.6
Home of Best Friend	0.6	0.0	0.8
Downtown	0.6	1.0	0.4
Fire or Police Department	0.3	0.0	0.4
Park or Playground	0.3	0.5	0.2
Not Available, Don't Know	7.9	5.3	8.9
N =	(699)	(206)	(493)

Source: Thibeault et al. (1973).

^{a} Question asked of 1966–1969 inmovers and outmovers only: "In selecting a place to live, what is the most important thing for your home to be close to?"

portation used, since lower-income families more often use public transportation and/or walk than do upper-income families. It is no surprise, then, that the same national study reported that higher-income families tend to be satisfied with their accessibility, whereas lower-income families tend to be dissatisfied with theirs. Similarly, it appears that longer trips are made by central city residents than by suburban residents (Stegman (1969). A substantial part of these income and central city/suburban differences is related to available and utilized transportation modes.

All of the studies surveyed suggest that destinations such as work and downtown are not as important in deciding where a family will live as literature has suggested. Thus accessibility to various amenities is not the primary reason for making a move or locating in a particular place of residence, though it is of some importance within a threshold.[1] Its importance is greater for lower-socioeconomic families than for upper-socioeconomic families. Finally, the ex-

[1] There may be a threshold of accessibility related to many services and amenities, but this threshold appears to be most important for accessibility to an elementary school (Butler and Kaiser, 1971).

isting spatial structure of metropolitan areas in the United States, combined with inadequate public and private transportation modes, along with income constraints, has precluded the attainment of accessibility desires by lower-income families (Thibeault et al., 1973) and the minorities.

Suburbanite's Use of the Central City

In a study of the high-status Philadelphia suburb of Radnor, slightly more than one-half of the residents could be called regular or frequent users (go into the city at least once a month) of the cultural and shopping facilities of the center city (Zikmund, 1971). However, almost one-fifth virtually never go downtown. Families with no children, of higher educational and occupational level, except for professionals, make more trips to and use the central city more than others. Also, people who live in suburban Radnor but work in the central city tend to use it for social and recreational purposes as well. Consistent with this, a high percentage of those who live and work locally in Radnor virtually never go into the central city (Zikmund, 1971: 193). The presence or absence of children influences the use of the central city by suburbanites. Further, professionals, middle-income, and middle-age populations use the city less than expected. These populations consist of families that have a stable home and community life and are more heavily involved in local activities. Newcomers to Radnor (less than two years of residence) use the central city more than longer term residents who have no use for the central city.

ACTIVITY SYSTEMS

"In its broadest sense, a study of urban activity systems is concerned with the patterned ways in which households and such institutions as firms, voluntary organizations and governments pursue their everyday affairs" (Chapin, 1974; Chapin et al., forthcoming). At the household level various activities that take place in day-to-day living form patterns describing activities common to whole aggregations of people. Two major focuses have been stressed in previous research. First, human activities are viewed as an economic phenomenon, and activity is assumed to be the result of utility-maximizing behavior in the allocation of time—a resource that needs to be kept in equilibrium (Becker, 1965). Another approach conceives human activities as outcomes of processes by which life-sustaining needs, such as sleep, food intake, and work, are met and in which culturally defined needs, such as social interaction, group participation, and recreation, are satisfied—all of which also helps to maintain the existing equilibrium (Hawley, 1950).

From both perspectives, activities are assumed to be distributed differentially throughout the metropolitan complex in patterned configurations, which are of special importance in the study of urban spatial structure. Chapin and Logan (1969) categorized systems of activities that revolve around the following: (1) income, (2) family, (3) recreation and relaxation, (4) religious and organizational participation, (5) socializing, and (6) subsistence (activities other than income-related ones). These systems of activities can be further broken down into a larger number of subsystems or different systems (for examples see Chapin and Logan, 1969, or Chapin and Hightower, 1965). Chapin and Hightower presented evidence, derived from a pilot study conducted in Durham, North Carolina, that socializing activities involve a spatially diffused and vastly different spatial pattern than that of recreation-relaxation activities, which are primarily passive and centered in the home. However, there are also spatial centers outside of the home and neighborhood where activities consistently take place. These spatial configurations are illustrated in Figure 9-1.

Using activity data from the national study to which we have previously referred (Butler et al., 1969), Chapin and Logan (1969) examined activities of household members according to: (1) the location of the activity, whether in or out of the home, (2) the degree of choice in selecting the activity, (3) the extent to which an activity was sociable, and (4) the extent to which it was active or passive. They reported that the daily activities of people are very similar, with little difference being found among races.

> *The daily activities of the various groups in the population as they are customarily divided are very much the same. A quick review of the frequencies shows that the most popular discretionary activities were television viewing and radio listening.* Over two-thirds of the sample engaged in one or both of these activities. Runners-up are activities—or the lack of them—characterized as resting, napping or taking it easy. About half of the respondents reported these. A little under a third did some sort of reading. Roughly 10 percent of the respondents had engaged in family activities, family visiting, and visiting in and out of the neighborhood. A little over 5 percent engaged in individual creative pursuits, casual diversions, church services, other church-related and organizational participation, various social activities not classified as "visiting," and in telephoning and correspondence. Education and sporting activities claimed the attention of about 2 and 3 percent, respectively [Chapin and Logan, 1969: 316].

The most noticeable differences reported are between heads of households and their spouses. As shown in Table 9-3, there are some outstanding differences concerning standard sex roles currently expected in traditional families. That is, spouses are much more likely than heads to devote time to child care, to child-centered activities, and to housework and shopping. Heads are more likely than spouses to have engaged in casual diversions—reading a newspaper, a magazine, or a book—or to have worked in the yard, on the home, and/or on automobile maintenance.

Because of the small differences in other comparisons, it appears that to explain differences in activity systems of households adequately we must include more than social and psychological variables. Chapin and Logan argued that the physical environment, including the facilities it offers and the

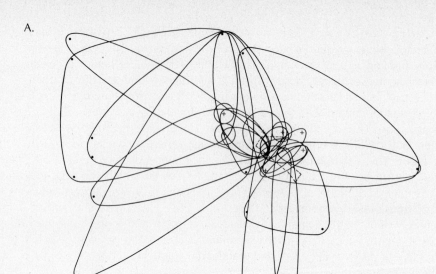

A.

B.

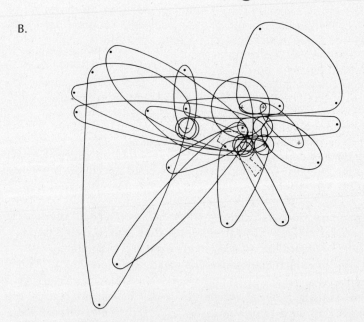

Figure 9-1. A. The Spatial Patterns of Recreation-Relaxation Activities.
B. Socializing Activities in CBD Census Tract 8, Durham, North Carolina. The tick
marks represent respondent homes and the dots, the locations of activities. *From the
revised edition of F. Stuart Chapin, Jr., Urban Land Use Planning.*

TABLE 9-3
Percentages of Heads of Households and Spouses Engaging in Activities[a]

ACTIVITY	PERCENTAGE ENGAGING IN ACTIVITIES	
	HEADS	SPOUSES
Child Care and Child-Centered Activities	8.5%	47.1%
Resting, Napping, and General Relaxation	55.0	42.6
Casual Diversions	6.8	6.2
Reading the Paper, a Magazine, or a Book	32.1	27.4
Watching Television or Listening to Radio	68.0	67.3
Socializing		
Visiting in Neighborhood	4.6	7.6
Visiting Outside the Neighborhood	7.0	8.8
Telephoning, Writing Letters	1.2	7.4
Shopping		
Convenience Goods	17.9	29.4
All Other Shopping	13.1	17.3
Health-Related Activities		
Sick at Home	2.6	1.4
Seeing, or Accompanying Others to, Doctor	4.7	8.3
Housework	18.8	91.0
Home, Yard, and Car Maintenance	22.2	9.2

Source: Used by permission of F. Stuart Chapin, Jr., and Thomas H. Logan and Resources for the Future, Inc.

[a] Survey instructions called for interviews with heads of households and spouses of heads on an alternating basis. If spouses were not present, the heads were designed to be respondents. The two classes of respondents split into 54 percent heads and 46 percent spouses.

costs it places on various activities, is instrumental in developing different activity patterns. The extent of time spent outside of the home was found to be related to the time spent on "gainful employment," the family, and its relationship to the life cycle, income, and social status. Interestingly, those working outside of the home spent more time in the home than those who did not work outside of the home in their "choice" discretionary activities. The elderly spend less time outside of the home than younger persons, and children appear to pull other household members outside of the home to their activity centers (also see Riemer, 1959). There are income differences as well, with those in the middle-income category ($5250 to $8750) and middle-status households spending more time outside of the home than other income or status categories.

The analysis presented by Chapin and Logan indicates that only about 7 or 8 percent of time spent on discretionary activities is in active pursuits (p. 324). The study also showed that the longer one spends at work, the smaller the proportion of the day devoted to choice activities; the authors also showed that those working longer hours are less likely to carry on out-of-home activities and socializing than are those working shorter hours or not working at all. Nonworking suburban housewives are the "leisure class," since they have a much greater time devoted to discretionary activities. On the other hand, women who are working outside of the home "carry a much greater share of household and family-related tasks than do the men" in these very same households.

Chapin and Logan further noted that the spatial aspect of activities, which could not specifically be analyzed in the national study, cannot be ignored. They concluded that outside work activity dominates the spatial routine when there are members in the household who are gainfully employed. Other activities, they suggested, fall into two different categories: (1) activities that clearly defined destination areas of concentration, including employment concentrations, retail centers, and commonly used community facilities such as schools, theaters, libraries, and so on, and (2) activities that are diffused in their spatial patterns. Spatially diffused activities include visiting and other forms of socializing and various kinds of unorganized recreational and leisure activities.

Activity Systems of Black Adults

In a study of the Near Northeast area of Washington, D.C., it appears that adults with higher incomes "are up and about for significantly longer hours of a day, spending significantly more of these waking hours on obligatory activities, and out of home than those from low-income households" (Chapin et al., forthcoming). In addition, black adults with higher incomes devote more of their time to obligatory activities than adults from low-income households, and higher-income adults spend more time in organizational participation than low-income adults. This activity emphasis reverses on weekends—primarily because of the more extensive church participation by low-income persons. Also, in discretionary activities low-income adults spend more time on social interaction and passive activities on weekends, but the reverse occurs during the week.

Working status has some influence upon how discretionary time is spent, with full-time workers spending less time on passive diversions and rest and relaxation than those not working full time. Similar to the earlier cited national sample study of activity systems, Near Northeast black women who are working experience the least amount of discretionary or choice activities. This appears to be true whether or not the working woman has children. Evidently, the male does not absorb many of the household duties such as housework and child care—at least not enough to equalize the use of discretionary time.

Chapin and others also examined the hypothesis that persons from households that make frequent moves show different patterns in their allocation of discretionary time than persons in households that do not move frequently. In testing this idea they found adults in the former group spent less time in social interaction and organizational participation and somewhat more time in passive kinds of pursuits than those in more settled households. Major sex role differences were noted, however, with females in mover households being more likely to engage in discretionary activity than males.

In general, differences in economic circumstances have relatively little impact upon the activity systems of the black residents of the Near Northeast in Washington, D.C. This tends to suggest that "living patterns in low-income society are void of social stratification of the kind found along economic lines in the larger society." Thus whatever differentiation in activity systems does exist in this black community would have to be examined along divisions other than income or social status. Chapin and his colleagues suggested that the separation is primarily between those who still believe that they will be able "to make it" in income and occupational status and those who no longer believe it.

Activity Systems of Children and Teenagers
Children living in a small town in the Midwest were found to cover a substantial portion of the town in carrying out their activities, and the territory that the children utilized gradually expanded as the child grew older. On a typical day each child made use of about 8 percent of the town's environment in the most prominent activities of socializing, playing, eating, working, and learning. Activities related to physical health, personal appearance, and so on, were minor. Activities varied from the "less reality-bound" in the younger ages to the "more reality-bound" activity patterns in older ages. Active coping with the world was dominant over passive viewing and feeling. The days of the children were "both extensively and intensively social," with about 80 percent of activities involving responses by others to the children. These social activities most often involved the mother and other adults rather than children.

An approximate spatial utilization of various settings in activity systems in this midwestern town is illustrated in Figure 9-2. The circles indicate various kinds of facilities in which activities take place, and the relative size of the circles approximates a rough activity utilization index. As an example, the number "6" in Figure 9-2 shows a major indoor entertainment center—the Midwest Theater. The circles attached by the same shading are indicators of other, but less important, indoor entertainment centers. The relative size of the circles, then, shows that the Midwest Theater is by far the main activity center for indoor entertainment in this midwestern town. Similarly, "5" indicates a main configuration of the activity of children in this town—with drug, variety and department stores all of about equally providing activity centers for the children. Unfortunately, it is impossible to present the entire catalog of activity centers for the town. It should be noted, however, that some 107 separate kinds of activity settings are shown in the figure, with the authors of this work listing some 585 subsettings within these larger activity forms.[2]

Black teenagers living in families with higher-level incomes in the

[2] For further exploration in the activity systems of midwestern children and the methodology of these kinds of studies, see Barker and Wright (1955) and Wright (1967).

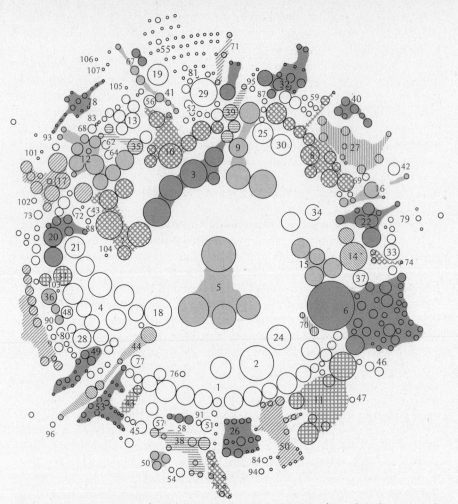

Figure 9-2. Base Map: Behavior-Setting Varieties. *From Wright and Barker, 1955, by permission of the authors.*

Near Northeast area of Washington, D.C., are similar to their parents in that they spend more of the total hours of the day up and about and on obligatory activities and time out of the home than teenagers living in families with lower-level incomes. Higher-level income teenagers spend a greater time being awake and in obligatory activities. The amount of time spent by both high- and low-income teenagers in discretionary activities is about the same; in addition, the kinds of discretionary activities are about the same regardless of income level. Teenagers whose families are moving frequently spend more time in social interchange than do settled families (Chapin et al., forthcoming).

BIBLIOGRAPHY: Articles

Becker, Gary S., "A Theory of the Allocation of Time," *The Economic Journal,* 75 (September 1965): 493–517.

Carroll, J. Douglas, Jr., "The Relation of Homes to Work Places and the Spatial Pattern of Cities," *Social Forces,* 30 (March 1952): 271–282.

Carroll, J. Douglas, Jr., "Some Aspects of the Home/Work Relationships of Industrial Workers," *Land Economics,* 25 (November 1949): 414–422.

Catanese, Anthony J., "Commuting Behavior Patterns of Families," *Traffic Quarterly,* 24 (July 1970): 439–457.

Chapin, F. Stuart, Jr., and Henry C. Hightower, "Household Activity Patterns and Land Use," *Journal of the American Institute of Planners,* 31 (August 1965): 222–231.

Duncan, Beverly, "Factors in Work-Residence Separation: Wage and Salary Workers, Chicago, 1951," *American Sociological Review,* 21 (February 1956): 48–56.

Foley, Donald, "Urban Daytime Population: A Field for Demographic-Ecological Analysis," *Social Forces,* 32 (May 1954): 323–330.

Foley, Donald L., "The Daily Movement of Population into Central Business Districts, *American Sociological Review,* 17 (October 1952): 538–543.

Forstall, Richard L., "Commuting Characteristics of Large American Cities," *Municipal Year Book,* 32 (1965): 98–111.

Goldstein, Sidney, and Kurt Mayer, "Migration and the Journey to Work," *Social Forces,* 42 (May 1964a): 472–481.

Goldstein, Sidney, and Kurt Mayer, "Migration and Social Status Differentials in the Journey to Work," *Rural Sociology,* 29 (September 1964b): 278–287.

Kain, John F., "The Journey-to-Work as a Determinant of Residential Location," *Regional Science Association Papers,* 9 (1962): 137–160.

Kaiser, Edward J., Edgar W. Butler, Ronald J. McAllister, and Russell W. Thibeault, "Some Problems with Accessibility Standards: A Comparison of Household Preferences to Standards for Work, Shopping, and School Trips," *Review of Regional Studies,* 3 (Winter 1972–1973): 111–123.

Morgan, James N., "A Note on the Time Spent on the Journey to Work," *Demography,* 4 (No. 1, 1967): 360–362.

Poston, Dudley L., Jr., "Socioeconomic Status and Work-Residence Separation in Metropolitan America," *Pacific Sociological Review,* 15 (July 1972): 367–380.

Reeder, Leo G., "Social Differentials in Mode of Travel, Time and Cost in the Journey to Work," *American Sociological Review,* 21 (February 1956): 56–63.

Scaff, Alvin H., "The Effect of Commuting on Participation in Community Organizations," *American Sociological Review,* 17 (April 1952): 215–220.

Schnore, Leo F., "The Use of Public Transportation in Urban Areas," *Traffic Quarterly,* 16 (1962): 488–498.

Schnore, Leo F., "The Three Sources of Data on Commuting: Problems and Possibilities," *Journal of the American Statistical Association,* 55 (March 1960): 8–22.

Schnore, Leo F., "The Separation of Home and Work: A Problem for Human Ecology," *Social Forces,* 32 (May 1954): 336–343.

Sheldon, Henry D., and Siegfried A. Hoermann, "Metropolitan Structure and Commutation," *Demography,* 1 (1964): 186–193.

Stegman, Michael A., "Accessibility Models and Residential Location," *Journal of the American Institute of Planners,* 35 (January 1969): 22–29.

Thibeault, Russell W., Edward J. Kaiser, Edgar W. Butler, and Ronald J. McAllister, "Accessibility Satisfaction, Income, and Residential Mobility," *Traffic Quarterly*, 37 (April 1973): 289–305.

U.S. Bureau of the Census, 1963, "Subject Reports: Journey to Work, Final Report," U.S. Census of Population: 1960. Series PC-2-6B, Washington, D.C.: Government Printing Office.

Wheeler, James O., "Transportation Problems in Negro Ghettos," *Sociology and Social Research*, 53 (January 1969): 171–179.

Wheeler, James O., "Work-Trip Length and the Ghetto," *Land Economics*, 44 (February 1968): 107–112.

Wheeler, James O., and Stanley D. Brunn, "Negro Migration into Rural Southwestern Michigan," *Geographic Review*, 58 (April 1968): 214–230.

Whiting, Robert F., "Home-to-Work Relationships of Workers Living in Public Housing Projects in Chicago," *Land Economics*, 28 (August 1952): 283–290.

Yu, Eui-Young, "Correlates of Commutation Between Central Cities and Rings of SMSA's," *Social Forces*, 51 (September 1972): 74–86.

Zikmund, Joseph, II, "Do Suburbanites Use the Central City?" *Journal of the American Institute of Planners*, 37 (May 1971): 192–195.

BIBLIOGRAPHY: Books

Barker, Roger G., and Herbert F. Wright, *Midwest and Its Children*, Evanston, Ill.: Row, Peterson and Company, 1955.

Butler, Edgar W., F. Stuart Chapin, Jr., George C. Hemmens, Edward J. Kaiser, Michael A. Stegman, and Shirley F. Weiss, *Moving Behavior and Residential Choice: A National Survey*, Washington, D.C.: National Academy of Sciences, 1969.

Chapin, F. Stuart, Jr., *Human Activity Patterns in the City: Things People Do in Time and in Space*, New York: John Wiley & Sons, 1974.

Chapin, F. Stuart, Jr., *Urban Land Use Planning*, Urbana, Illinois: University of Chicago Press, 1965.

Chapin, F. Stuart, Jr., Edgar W. Butler, and Frederick C. Patten, *Blackways in the Inner City*, Urbana, Ill.: University of Illinois Press, forthcoming.

Chapin, F. Stuart, Jr., and Thomas H. Logan, "Patterns of Time and Space Use," in Harvey S. Perloff (ed.), *The Quality of the Urban Environment*, Washington, D.C.: Resources for the Future, pp. 305–332.

Hawley, Amos, *Human Ecology: A Theory of Community Structure*, New York: Ronald Press, 1950.

Liepmann, Kate K., *The Journey to Work: Its Significance for Industrial and Community Life*, New York: Oxford University Press, 1944.

Lowenstein, Louis K., *The Location of Residences and Work Places in Urban Areas*, New York: The Scarecrow Press, Inc., 1965.

Meyer, John Robert, J. F. Kain, and M. Wohl, *The Urban Transportation Problem*, Cambridge, Mass.: Harvard University Press, 1965.

Riemer, Svend, "Urban Personality—Reconsidered," in Marvin B. Sussman (ed.), *Community Structure and Analysis*, New York: Thomas Y. Crowell Co., 1959, pp. 433–444.

Wright, Herbert F., *Recording and Analyzing Child Behavior*, New York: Harper & Row, Publishers, 1967.

CHAPTER 10
SOCIAL STRATIFICATION AND SOCIAL MOBILITY

INTRODUCTION

Evidently, in all societies there is social differentiation — that is, there are categories of persons that differ from each other in meaningful social ways. In urban areas of the United States differentiation involves the placement of individuals and families in social classes. *Social classes* are the strata of society in which its members are placed so as to produce a social hierarchy. In general, the social class, or social stratification, system recognizes some of the basic values of the society. Attached to each position and social class are prestige and esteem for its incumbents (Davis and Moore, 1945; Davis, 1942). The different positions and the unequal rewards attached to them may result in invidious comparisons. Stratification systems generally assume the following:

1. Differential positions occur in a variety of social structures, for example, in the religious, governmental, and economic spheres.
2. The rewards of these positions are of various types, for instance, financial gain, advantageous working conditions, and honorific value or "psychic income."
3. Some combination of all the rewards attached to any position constitutes the invidious value of that position and hence its prestige.
4. Total societal position is a summation of prestige, modified by the esteem bestowed by others as a reward for the manner in which the expectations associated with any given status are fulfilled.[1]

At different times and in different places, a large number of character-

---

[1] These are modifications (Reiss, 1961: 240) of more extensive statements made by Davis and Moore (1945) and Davis (1942). See Tumin (1953) for a critical analysis of these points. For an extensive review of social class from another perspective see Lasswell (1965).

istics have been used as the basis for class systems. These include: (1) authority; (2) power (political, economic, military); (3) ownership of property, relation to the means of production, control over land (as in the feudal estate); (4) income — amount, type, and sources; (5) consumption patterns and style of life; (6) occupation or skill, and achievement in it; (7) education, learning, wisdom; (8) divinity, relationship to the supernatural; (9) altruism, public service, morality; (10) place in "high society," kinship connections, ancestry (i.e., inherited position); (11) associational ties and connections; (12) ethnic status, religion, race. Which of these characteristics become the basis for stratification in a particular society (or rather, which combination of them, since the judgment typically gives differing weights to several of them) depends on what is considered particularly important to the society doing the stratifying (Berelson and Steiner, 1967: 72).

Positional rewards at the disposal of a society are listed by Davis and Moore (1945) as:

1. The things that contribute to existence and comfort
2. The things that contribute to humor and diversion
3. The things that contribute to self-respect and ego expansion

Weber (Gerth and Mills, 1958) identified three major aspects of social class or social stratification: (1) an economic or wealth factor, (2) a differential distribution of social honor or status — prestige, and (3) political power. Generally, the three go together; that is, the economic, or wealth, factor is associated with prestige and power. Measures of these dimensions of social class are usually consistent, and thus status crystallization or consistency occurs among these aspects of social class (Adams, 1953; Lenski, 1954).

The concept of social class suggests that individuals in one class are more alike than persons in other social classes; that is, there are relatively common traditions, values, habits, ideas, beliefs, and behavior patterns within a given social class that stand in contrast to those in other social classes. As an example, social classes have varying traditions, values, and behavior patterns regarding childrearing.

Unfortunately, the conceptualization of social class has been rather imprecise. Most social scientists in the United States follow Marx, to some degree or another, in almost invariably conceiving it as primarily consisting of people with different levels of wealth. On the other hand, the Marxian prerequisite of persons being "conscious" or aware of their common positions in society does not generally accord with current usage. Nowadays, whenever one refers to "the better people," "the rich," "the poor," "the better parts of town," and so forth, there is implicit recognition of different social levels or classes within society.

From the discussion so far, it should be apparent that social classes involve the ranking of individuals on a scale of superiority-inferiority according

This woodcut from an old medieval manuscript shows the most obvious form of social stratification. A noble is paying "homage," or swearing allegiance, to his king. Most modern stratification is more subtle.

to some commonly accepted basis of valuation in the society. In urban United States ranking ordinarily is based upon wealth. Generally, it has durability; that is, both the ranking and the criteria it is based upon are similar in nature over a long period of time. Some of the key status determinants in urban American society, besides wealth, are family lineage and race. These are *ascribed* characteristics; in other words, a person is born with them and it is relatively difficult, if not impossible, to change them. On the other hand, *achieved* characteristics such as educational attainment, occupation, and income (although it can be argued that there may be a great deal of heritability here also) are used as primary indicators of social class placement in this country. Thus wealth, extent of power, intellectual status, education, and other factors help determine one's social class. Complete reliance upon ascribed characteristics for social class placement generally results in a *caste* society. An opposite extreme of reliance upon achievement, of course, could result in a completely *open* society.

A dominant value expressed by many Americans is equality of opportunity. The door of opportunity is open to anyone, and hard work, intelligence, and talent, will be amply rewarded. Thus many people in the United States believe that one person's chances of succeeding are as good as another person's. That is, social class will be determined by achieved characteristics. However, Tumin (1953) regarded social inheritance (family lineage) and the "demand and supply" of positions in society as accounting more realistically for social stratification than other theories. That is, individuals with particular ascribed characteristics have advantages over persons with different ones, for example, with respect to race, sex, color, and so on.[2]

Measurement of social classes generally involves evaluating the *reputations* specific individuals or positions in society have that are commonly held by other members of that society. In the United States urban occupations are for the most part more highly evaluated than rural occupations. Another measure is *subjective identification,* or the manner in which a person compares positions, including his own, with other positions in the society. Also, social class placement has been measured by *objective* indicators such as income, years of educational attainment, occupational ranking, or some combination of these factors. How many social strata there are, how assignment of individuals to social classes is carried out, and how wide the strata are—these too must be taken into account.

All of these considerations are also important in determining movement among social classes, or *social mobility*. Social mobility may be measured from an intergenerational perspective, that is, sons (or, much less often, daughters) compared with their parents, most often the father; and from the point of view of a career (intragenerational) or of the changes in social class occurring during a person's lifetime.

Social class and social mobility are important because of the generally assumed differences that exist among social classes in behavior patterns and because some of these differences have consequences for the structure of cities, urban regions, and metropolitan areas. Social classes are differentially distributed throughout the metropolitan region, a fact related to many other social phenomena. It may help to explain the variety of differences—as in death rates, mental illness, crime, and personality—that currently exists in most urban and metropolitan regions in the United States.

SOCIAL STRATIFICATION
Urbanization and Other
Conditions Associated with Stratification

In broad historical terms Berelson and Steiner (1967: 76–77) summed up the growth and character of systems of stratification by looking at some of the more important determining conditions: (1) urbanization, (2) social change, (3) industrialization, (4) ethnic heterogeneity and migration, (5) ideology, (6) popular education, and (7) fertility rates.

---

[2] For an extended discussion of an approach distinguishing *social differentiation* from *social stratification* see Buckley (1958).

Urbanization

The more urbanized the society, the more complex and open the system. The city is more class-graded than the country, more differentiated in the types of social positions to be filled, more impersonal (so that family connections count for less), and so on.

Social Change

The more rapid the social change (usually induced by technological developments), the more open the system of stratification. In stable periods rankings based on different criteria are more likely to be equivalent, but rapid social change does "shake up" the class system. This is one of the reasons for the relative openness of the class system in the United States.

Industrialization

The more industrialized the society, the more complex and open the system of stratification. When more wealth is created, there are more types of positions to be held and hence more opportunities—more room at the top. At least in Western countries, including the United States, industrialization has shifted the basis of stratification from inherited wealth (ascription) to earned income (achievement) by downgrading lineage and nobility and upgrading individual producers.

Ethnic Heterogeneity and Migration

The more new populations become available for stratification, usually at the bottom, the more open the system. In this country, for example, almost every generation has had the benefit of rising atop new populations entering the system at the bottom—European immigrants in several waves, blacks migrating to urban centers, and migrant farmers. As such populations, usually ethnic in character, themselves become assimilated, they too begin moving up the class ladder.

Ideology

The more equalitarian the social philosophy of a society, the more open the stratification system. In turn, an equalitarian ideology is associated with the absence of a hereditary aristocracy; the lack of a feudal past, the presence of a frontier, the presence of deprived groups that are still considered active members of the society, the development of literacy, the growth of political participation, and the general improvement of the standard of living across classes.

Popular Education

The more widespread the system of education, the more open the system of stratification. The more a society emphasizes education, without at the same time permitting the right to an education to become the prerogative of special population categories, then the more likely it is that the interchange of ranks can continue; society becomes open. In such a society education could not be inherited. Most people in the United States now appreciate how important education is for increasing one's chances in life for success.

Fertility Rates

The greater the differential in fertility rates among classes, the more open the system. When the birth rate in the upper classes is less than adequate for their replacement, and the upper classes are not replenished from among their own ranks, then there is room for others to advance, Historically, upper classes have had lower fertility rates. But this difference is now becoming less apparent as the lower classes are becoming better informed about modern methods of birth control.

Intermetropolitan Variation in Social Stratification

Ordinarily, one does not think of cities, urban areas, or metropolitan regions as having a social class or being part of a social stratification network. In our earlier discussion (see Chapter 5) of different types of urban and metropolitan regions, however, we explored the notion of metropolitan dominance. Similarly, Vance and Sutker's (1954) work on the metropolitanization of the South shows four levels of metropolitan dominance: (1) dominant regional capitals, which are second-order metropolises nationwide—Atlanta and Dallas; (2) third-order metropolises—Houston, New Orleans, Memphis, Louisville, and Birmingham; (3) fourth-order metropolises—El Paso, Nashville, Charlotte, Jacksonville; and (4) subdominant places—San Antonio, Savannah, and Miami. There is a systematic relationship among these cities and metropolitan areas that places them in this rank order.

Vance and Sutker inferred rankings from the flow of goods, products, and economic resources, although differences in income, educational attainment, and occupation can also be examined. For example, Uyeki (1964: 73), using the social area analytic frame of reference (see Chapter 7), showed that between 1940 and 1960 the 22 cities that made up the Cleveland SMSA remained virtually the same insofar as social rank was concerned. That is, the social rank of the cities in 1940 was quite an accurate predictor of the relative rank in 1960. This was not quite as true for segregation and urbanization which had changed quite substantially.

Other studies have shown that the average level of attainment is positively related to city size. In addition, the community of residence apparently influences the income level of its residents. One explanation for differences in income levels among cities is that there are differing levels of occupational opportunities. This variation exists even when only very large cities are examined. Interestingly, it has been found that different population compositions match respective city occupational opportunity structures (Mueller, 1974: 665). Nevertheless, some argue that varying occupational structures do not differentially advantage or disadvantage their residents with regard to career opportunities and achievements (Mueller, 1974: 665). Migration is assumed to be a major factor in this match between resident composition and occupational structure and to make the occupational opportunity structure available for residents of disadvantaged cities, albeit evidently those residents with certain kinds of characteristics—at a minimum, with the willingness to migrate. There is some dispute, however, over the strength of the relationship between city size and income: Some describe it as very strong, while others believe that individual factors are more important and that the effect of city size is rather small when these are taken into account (Mueller, 1974).

Social Class in Urban and Metropolitan Regions

In preindustrial cities, as noted in Chapter 3, upper classes lived near the centers, whereas lower classes lived on the outskirts and, many times, outside the walls. In early towns and cities of the United States a similar relationship held, with an inverse relationship between social class and proximity to the center. Thus the concentration of slums and lower classes in the centers or cores of cities is more or less confined to the twentieth century (Thomlinson, 1969: 163). As the nation became more urbanized and as industrialism took place, a large working class came into being. As we saw earlier (Chapter 9), many of these workers lived near factories; however, as cities grew in size and modern transportation modes came into being, the working class became more decentralized, though it still lived in relatively homogeneous areas within the city or urban region.

Within the past few decades an increase in white-collar jobs and the professions has led to an expanding middle class, primarily living in suburbs. In the future, growing tertiary occupations (services, etc.) will probably alter social class distributions in cities and metropolitan regions in the United States. Common to all social class and social stratification networks in urban America is ethnicity or racial populations; black and chicano minorities especially are disproportionately distributed in lower social classes and live in highly segregated spatial areas within cities and metropolitan regions. Ethnic and racial differences, along with social class distinctions, are the most important elements making up the spatial separation of different areas within cities and metropolitan regions. Thus contemporary urban and metropolitan regions in the United States are a mosaic of social class areas and neighborhoods.

The Number and Size of Social Classes in Urban and Metropolitan Regions

How many classes are there in an urban and an industrialized society like the United States? There is no simple answer to this question. Some social scientists refer to six classes, others to three, and yet others argue that there is a continuum of social classes. Despite the inability of social scientists and the general population to agree precisely on the number of social classes, the existence of social classes in the United States is very real. Whether measured by indicators of income, education, occupation, or residential location, a number of value, attitudinal, and behavioral patterns have been exhibited by people in different social classes. Because of the blurring of social class lines, relationships between social class and other phenomena are probably attenuated.

One classic example of social classes in a city is the study of "Middletown" (Muncie, Indiana). Six classes, based primarily on occupation, were delineated there: (1) a very small "old" middle class, (2) a somewhat larger but still relatively small professional and small business class, (3) a larger middle class, (4) an aristocracy of the local labor force, (5) "the numerically overwhelmingly dominant group of the working class," and (6) the bottom marginal class (Lynd and Lynd, 1937: 458–460). An early study of "Yankee City" (Newburyport, Massachusetts) also reported six social classes, based upon prestige ratings by residents of the town. Yankee City (Warner and Lunt, 1941: 88) and a "Georgia Town" (Hill and McCall, 1950) had the following social class distribution:

	YANKEE CITY (PERCENT)	GEORGIA TOWN (PERCENT)
Upper Upper	2	}3
Lower Upper	2	
Upper Middle	10	15
Lower Middle	28	28
Upper Lower	33	28
Lower Lower	25	26

Virtually every study since Middletown and Yankee City has shown a strong relationship between prestige rating and occupational level; for example, over 80 percent of upper-uppers were professionals and proprietors, while almost 90 percent of lower-lowers were semiskilled and unskilled laborers in Middletown.

Different research techniques used in determining a person's subjective identification of the social class to which he or she belongs have resulted in somewhat different findings. Centers (1949) has shown that in two different national samples about 40 percent of the population says that they are in the middle class and slightly over 50 percent report being in the working class. However, these responses were based upon structured questions; that is, respondents were asked whether they belonged to the upper, middle, working, or lower classes. Gross (1953) has argued that this procedure is suspect, since respondents *must* identify with a class. He used two modifications in a study of Minneapolis residents and noted that when he asked a somewhat similar question leaving out the possibility of identification with the working class, that almost 80 percent of the population then identified themselves as middle class, 10 percent as lower class, and 5 percent as upper class. When an open-ended question was used that offered no categories to the respondent to consider, another distribution of social classes emerged. Thirty-one percent claimed to be middle class; 11 percent said they were of the working class; 20 percent did not know; and one person out of every seven said that social classes did not exist in Minneapolis. A few others claimed some kind of miscellaneous class membership such as the common, employer, or poor classes. On the other hand, the limited number of people claiming upper-class or lower-class status was consistent among all three ways of determining respondent self-classification; the *relative* high frequency of persons claiming middle-class status was consistent, and there were systematic differences in social class identification by residential area (Gross, 1953: 403).

Recent stratification studies tend to report fewer social classes than earlier studies. Quite often there is reference to (1) the upper class — the professionals, managers, officials, proprietors, and social leaders of the community; (2) the middle class — primarily white-collar workers; (3) the working class — craftsmen, skilled and semiskilled workers in the community; and (4) the lower class — manual and uneducated laborers, the unemployed, and those not in the labor force. Generally homemakers are attributed to the same social class as their husbands. In addition, of course, in many cities the elites (the "upper-uppers") and ethnic and racial populations have a separate status hierarchy within a distinct hierarchy of social classes.

Spatial Distributions of Social Classes Within Metropolitan Regions

The population in contemporary cities and in urban areas of the United States is spatially segregated along a number of dimensions, not the least of which is social class. Differences in metropolitan regions along class lines have been noted from gross comparisons between central cities and their suburbs and in more detailed analyses using smaller units (typically census tracts) within the metropolitan region. Of the large number of studies of the spatial patterning of the social classes of the urban population, most show quite conclusively that American cities have a regular pattern of the spatial distribution of social classes that persists substantially over time. As Barber (1957: 144) has suggested: "The type of dwelling place and its location within the local community are likely to be symbols of social class position in all societies." This is true because the local neighborhood is the scene of many important activities and intimate social interactions. Location of residence, of course, is both a determinant and a consequence of social class. One study, using residential location as an indicator of social class, listed seven categories ranging from the residential area of "highest repute" to slum areas and neighborhoods in "bad repute" (Warner, 1960).

In Chicago it appears that categories at the polar ends of the occupational scale are the most highly residentially segregated from others. Professionals and officials, managers and proprietors and laborers are more segregated than sales workers, clerical workers, craftsmen, operatives, and service workers (Duncan and Duncan, 1955). But there is a blurring of residential areas by occupation at middle-class levels. A segregation of social classes (as measured by occupation) similar to that of Chicago is implied by a study of Wilmington, Delaware (Tilly, 1961). In Wilmington, however, education was a more discriminating influence on residential segregation than was occupation.

Uyeki (1964) reported that Chicago and Cleveland have many striking similarities and as such they should show similar residential and social class patterns. Using 1950 and 1960 census data and a variety of indexes and statistical techniques, he concluded that, in fact, there is a remarkable consistency in residential patterns for the two cities, with similar industry distribution and socioeconomic characteristics, but differing in size. He also reported substantial stability of residential patterns of the major occupational categories in Cleveland from 1950 to 1960. Laborers have become more differentiated or segregated from other occupational classifications partly because of their relative lack of increase in income. His general contention is that "changes in residential pattern tend to occur for groups whose relative socioeconomic status is changing."

In Pittsburgh another study of residential location by occupational status also revealed that the two highest-level occupations (professionals and managers) and the two lowest-status occupations (service workers and laborers) are the most residentially segregated. Occupations in intermediate or middle-status levels are commonly found in all other residential areas, although there is some residential division by white-collar status. Thus these results are rather consistent with those presented for Chicago, Wilmington, and Cleveland. In addition, a study of Providence, a city declining in population, shows quite clearly that despite losses in population and residential shifts within the city that most areas substantially retained the same social class level in 1960 that they had in 1950. This appears to hold even though there was suburban growth that was quite heterogeneous in nature as working-class families of Providence participated in this suburban migration. The suburban migration by working-class families "slowed down the homogenization process inside the city" (Goldstein and Mayer, 1964: 53–54).

Vicksburg, a smaller southern city along the Mississippi and Yazoo rivers, has an arrangement of four social class residential areas that substantially follows the concentric zone notion of Burgess described in Chapter 7 (James, 1931). This concentric zone is modified by adjustment to ridges and valleys that intersect in the city; where these ridges and valleys exist, better classes of residence take the ridge tops, and poorer classes, the valley bottoms (also see Green, 1956).

A factor analytic study of three different-sized Indiana cities—Indianapolis, Columbus, and Linton — and three different-sized Arizona cities — Phoenix, Yuma, and Safford — shows that there is a general one-dimensional factor that describes stratification in these cities at a given time. This social class stratification is roughly equivalent in different-sized cities and towns in the United States (Artz et al., 1971). Further, there appears to be equilibrium among the various dimensions used to measure social rank or class. In other words, position in the economic hierarchy pretty much matches that in the political and prestige hierarchies. Whatever disequilibria do exist is associated with varying community size and conditions. Within these cities, residence by social class was a common characteristic of these cities and towns in the 1960s. The constant feature of rank stratification during this period was represented best by residence or neighborhood characteristics. Thus the neighborhood sets the "ecological conditions for social interaction, which select families by taste and affluence, and which serve to organize population conceptions of rank" (Artz et al., 1971). Apparently, though, neighborhoods and housing represent not the amount of resources available in every instance but how resources are spent. Similarly, some city-size variation exists: In smaller places, in addition to the neighborhood, subjective and reputational bases are important; in larger places occupation, education, and income are meaningful and utilized in placing others into a social hierarchy. Similarly, there is suggestion that when a city serves as a central place, e.g., both Phoenix and Indianapolis, as opposed to a manufacturing place, it produces different kinds of local as opposed to regional stratification systems.

Overall, these studies lead to the conclusion that one of the most constant features of rank stratification in cities and urban regions is the residence dimension. Michelson (1970: 114) goes so far as to suggest that the quality of housing is directly proportional to the social class of the family, as viewed in terms of occupational prestige. He notes that this is true for most white-collar and blue-collar workers whose incomes may be relatively similar; yet white-collar workers spend more of their income on housing, since housing is a symbol of "respectability." There also is some suggestion that residential pattern preferences are formed by childhood and adolescent experiences in which the father's occupation is an important factor. These childhood and adolescent experiences help account for some of the disparity that exists in residential neighborhoods and the occupations these children choose as adults. If when they were younger, for instance, they had lived in a lower-middle-class area and were upwardly mobile, they may still prefer living in a lower-middle-class area.

Social Elites
Elites have been reported to exist in many cities, but they are ordinarily outside of social class studies because of their inaccessibility to social scientists. However, a study of "Philadelphia Gentlemen" (Baltzell, 1958) suggests that they have the status of a quasi-caste. Family lineage, inherited wealth, and certain occupations appear to be necessary prerequisites to be considered as

part of this elite. It consists, then, of "old families," which are extended kinship systems that have a strong identification with each other and clan solidarity. Intermarriage among members of elite families is a regular occurrence and indeed is aided by the limited social contacts of elites with nonelites in the city. During most of the year, the elites live in a rather circumscribed geographical location known as the Main Line, consisting of several suburbs and sections within the city itself. During the summer vacation period, they tend to move to several specific resorts where they interact socially with each other and the elites from other metropolitan areas. Not only are they residentially segregated, but they are also restrictive in ethnic composition, virtually all of them being of Anglo-Saxon heritage. From the earliest ages they are exposed to the same private schools, belong to the same organizations and churches, and have circumscribed social circles (for a similar study of Bostonians see Amory, 1957).

Barber (1957) reported that in the marriage announcements of *The New York Times* the location of the family residence is always mentioned in the opening paragraph, and in many announcements several residences are indicated—a New York City address (or an upper-class suburb) and another seashore or country town address. Most metropolitan regions have areas that are considered as the "best places" to live and are readily identified in newspapers and by realtors. Obviously, at the other end of the scale, areas within the metropolitan region, especially in the inner city, are identified as slums and ghettos (see Firey, 1947, for a discussion of residential location as a symbol of social class).

Minority Social Stratification

Black social class has been examined by Drake and Cayton (1945) in Chicago.[3] They divided blacks into the upper class, of about 5 percent of the population, the middle class, which contained 30 percent of the population, and the lower class, which contained almost two-thirds of the blacks living in Chicago at that time. Upper-class blacks were in the professions such as medicine, law, social work and teaching, and in business. In addition, "shadies" who ran the rackets, prostitution, and so on, were included in this category. The middle class consisted of white-collar workers, postal clerks, porters, skilled craftsmen, some small businessmen, and others who consistently held respectable jobs. Lower-class blacks were primarily of recent southern origin and did the heavy labor of the city; and, of course, many others had no visible means of support. Thorpe (1972) argued that new social stratification studies need to be undertaken in the black community, since all of the earlier and current studies use white indexes of measurement, which are inappropriate.

A study of Los Angeles County in 1960 showed that the relationship between income and property value was quite high (r = 0.78) among whites

---

[3] For a discussion of black stratification during slavery see Moore and Williams (1942).

Wealth is a prerequisite for some items of consumption in our society; among them are a Rolls Royce, a seashore or resort residence, and access to the "best places."

(excluding chicanos) and low (r = 0.19) among nonwhites—80 percent black and 20 percent oriental (Thomlinson, 1969: 14). Thus higher incomes for blacks and orientals do not have the same effect upon social class distribution that they have for anglos.

Duncan and Duncan (1968) examined data from a national survey (N = 22,000) in regard to the impact minority status (other than black) has on occupational level and reported that for the most part discrimination in education and occupations does not exist. Where occupational differentiation does exist—for third-generation southerners and German Americans, it is because of educational underachievement. More severely limited were Latin Americans, who were handicapped in their competition for jobs by educational underachievement as well as discriminatory practices. Irish and Polish Americans had a somewhat preferential level of jobs compared with their level of education. Similarly, Russians and Czechoslovakians were above average in schooling and occupational level. Italian Americans enjoyed a better-than-average schooling but a lower-than-average occupational level. Thus overall only one instance of distinctly preferential position occurs with respect to competition for jobs. The advantaged population roughly approximates the Anglo-Saxon Protestants, which according to stereotype enjoy a favored position in American society (Duncan and Duncan, 1968: 363). Certainly there is no evidence that these individuals are overachievers in the school system even though their occupational success is greater than that of others with different social origins but with similar educational qualifications.

Consequences of Social Stratification

Ecological or spatial consequences, as we have already noted, produce distinctive social class characteristics in areas within metropolitan and urban complexes. Each area has been shown to be associated with some important demographic factors. First, differences in *life chances* have been systematically noted: The higher the social class, the less physical and mental illness (including suicide) and the longer the life expectancy. As Berelson and Steiner (1967: 83) pointed out, this is probably due to the nutritive, hygienic, and medical advantages that money and position can purchase. A host of studies (see Chapter 17 for more detail) leads to the general conclusion that socioeconomic differentials are crucial to the relationship between social class and mortality and illness. Antonovsky (1967) suggested that in the future, lower classes may be in an even more disadvantageous position, since medical care, especially preventive medicine, is increasingly becoming more expensive.

Infant mortality rates consistently varied by social class in early cities. Lower-class infants were more likely to die than middle- or upper-class infants. On the basis of his study of Syracuse, however, Willie (1959) argued that this social class differential has disappeared. Nevertheless, upon inspection of his data it appears that there remains a statistical association between infant mortality and some social class dimensions of areas. Thus he reported correlations of −0.19 through −0.36, which he interpreted as indicating "little association" between infant mortality rates and the socioeconomic-status level of ecological areas in Syracuse. He presented spatial distributions of infant mortality, which show that a patterning effect exists, but he discounted social class effects. Interestingly, his analysis disclosed some upper-level areas with high infant mortality rates and some lower-class areas with low infant mortality rates. Since these are ecological data, the unit of analysis is *area;* it would have been useful to his study if *individual* data had been available to determine the specific social class of infant mortality. In any case, Willie's research work is instructive, since it demonstrates that some variation exists in data interpretation by different social scientists.

In contrast to the Syracuse study, in New York City during the three years 1945–1947 infant mortality increased as the proportion of blacks in the neighborhood increased. Various socioeconomic factors appeared to influence infant mortality rates (Yankauer, 1950). A follow-up study, using data for 1953–1955, showed substantially the same results as the earlier studies, with racial differences in infant mortality continuing to exist and, by implication, social

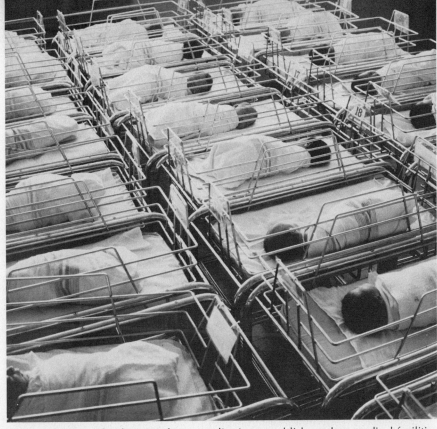

One mechanism of reducing infant mortality is to establish modern medical facilities which include maternity wards like this one. Of course, a carryover of reduced infant mortality is an expanded population.

class differences, with blacks, other minorities, and lower classes having higher rates than their counterparts (Yankauer and Allaway, 1958).

With regard to fertility, the upper and middle classes are less *fertile* than the lower classes. This is not to say that upper- and middle-class persons have less ability to have children (that is, are less *fecund*) but that because of the greater utilization of contraceptives and modern birth control techniques, they are less likely to have children than lower-class families. Also, there are child-rearing differences among the social classes. For example, middle- and upper-class children are more likely than lower-class children to be exposed to the latest "expert" fad or fashion in child-rearing practices, whatever it may be. Similarly, compared with the middle classes, there is less close supervision of children in the lower classes and more sex stereotyping.

Other research shows that, in general, higher-class persons are some-what taller, heavier, and of better health — both physically and mentally — when compared with those of lower social classes. Similarly, most studies of intelligence show that children in the former class score better than those in the latter — a result perhaps of systematic class biases inherent in tests.

The probability of going to college is linked to social class—and so is the specific college one attends. Few lower or lower-middle class students ever enter this gate to Yale University.

One of the main consequences of homogeneous social class neighborhoods is ensuring that children marry within the same social class as their families (Beshers, 1962; Hollingshead, 1950). Thus the class of person one dates and befriends, as well as the kind of churches, voluntary organizations, and so on, that he or she typically belongs to, is predetermined to a substantial degree. In addition, social class position is related to aspirations (Hyman, 1953), expectations, the probability of a person going to college, and what kind of occupational knowledge and opportunities one will be exposed to.

Some research has shown that there are social class differences in personality. Thus lower-class persons are reported to be more limited, restricted, and authoritarian than those of the middle and upper class. Similarly, social class has been reported to be linked with ability in self-direction and conformity to external authority (Kohn and Schooler, 1969). Finally, some research has suggested that rather large differences in life styles exist by social classes. Perhaps this is to be expected since the lower classes are bordering on or are below a marginal subsistence level, worrying about food and shelter while the affluent are flying around the world and many middle class individuals are concerned about their vacation cottages, boats, trailers, or campers and about where to go the next weekend.

In a study examining the relationships between prestige levels in the social stratification hierarchy and leisure-time behavior, results consistently show that leisure activities vary with social status and that the conception of people as being primarily spectators needs to be revised. Persons in the upper prestige levels tend to be quite active, attending theatrical plays, concerts, and lectures, doing community work, and entertaining at home. Middle-level persons tend to do more out-of-town visiting overnight, going to football games, playing golf, and working on an automobile, while lower-prestige level individuals may spend time in a tavern, visiting the zoo, going to a baseball game, playing poker, or driving around in the car for pleasure. At each prestige level, however, people devote most of their leisure time to nonspectator activities (Clarke, 1956: 305). The largest proportion of persons who spend their time in spectator leisure-time activities is at the middle level. Few people actually utilize commercial types of recreation; of those who do, the proportion is highest at the lowest prestige level and declines up the scale. More people spend time in craft activities (model building, sculpturing, painting, woodwork, etc.) than in commercial forms of leisure. Again, interest tends to vary with social prestige level, with lower-level individuals participating more in craft activities than upper-level ones. In examining a hypothetical instance of several more hours a day to participate in leisure-time activities, Clarke (1956) found that upper-level persons would use the extra time to work at their jobs while lower-level persons would use this additional time to rest and relax.

In view of foregoing discussion, then, being in the lower social classes means residing in less desirable areas of the urban complex. Thus lower classes, minorities, and, in many cities, the aged live in the worst areas of the city and are more exposed to the hazards of urban living, which include crime and violence, smog, heavy traffic, and so on. It is not too surprising, therefore, that there are consistently reported differences among social classes in mortality rates, physical illness, and other factors.

Further, there is little likelihood of social classes systematically mixing in neighborhoods in the future. Studies show that when extensive and large-range intermingling of social classes is attempted in a local neighborhood, it invariably fails. No matter how you as an individual may feel about it, evidently there is a rather restricted range in which local residents tolerate social class variation. Those with more money view the least valuable home in the neighborhood as setting the public image of the area, whereas residents in the lower social classes have considerable trouble adjusting socially to people of higher social classes (Gutman, 1963; Michelson, 1970: 194). Of course, these findings contrast with the egalitarian ethos that argues for heterogeneous neighborhoods; evidently, the major problem with heterogeneous neighborhoods in contemporary United States is that few people want to live in them despite their reported egalitarian "valves."

If social scientists are correct, most of these people in New York City's Shea Stadium are from the lower and lower-middle classes.

SOCIAL MOBILITY

Social mobility refers to the process by which individuals move from one social class position to another (Sorokin, 1927) or as the vertical movement of people between positions that are on different social class levels (Lipset and Bendix, 1963: 1–2). These social class positions, by general consent, have specific hierarchical values. Changes in social class (social mobility) have implications for differentiation within the metropolitan complex. Spatial mobility is usually assumed to be associated with social mobility.

Social mobility may be *upward, downward,* or *fluctuating*. Furthermore, a person may remain at a relatively *stationary* level. Two major facets of social mobility are *intragenerational* (career) and *intergenerational* mobility. *Intragenerational mobility* is defined as social class movement of the same person over time. Most typically observed in urban complexes are occupational changes, or the lack of them, over some specified time period used to measure the career social mobility of an individual. *Intergenerational mobility* is defined and measured as social class differences between father and offspring (typically a son, although the same logic applies to daughters) over time, with the father's longest-held occupation usually being used as the bench mark for measurement.

The *amount* and the *distance* of social mobility are sometimes distinguished (Schnore, 1961). *Amount* of social mobility is defined as the proportion of individuals who are upwardly or downwardly mobile or have a fluctuating pattern. The *distance* aspect consists of the number of steps upward or downward a given individual or group makes, which in turn depends a great deal upon social class conceptualization. For example, if a study utilizes manual/nonmanual categorization, the amount of social mobility will be the proportion of persons crossing that occupational boundary; however, the number of steps is limited to one. However, if three or more social classes are utilized (à la Warner, Drake, and Cayton, etc.), the amount also may vary, but the number of steps possible definitely increases, since there are four or five social class boundaries that may be crossed.

Stratification systems may be open or closed. In open systems people may move from one ranking to another; in closed systems they cannot or it is extremely difficult to do so. The ranks in the former are called classes; in the latter, castes. Both can exist at the same time within the same society. Classes may exist within a caste, as in the example of the Chicago black community. Caste membership is *hereditary* (ascribed), whereas class membership typically is subject to *achievements* by the individual. Caste distinctions are often enhanced by physically visible differences (e.g., skin color) and are often symbolized by caste marks or special dress (Berelson and Steiner, 1967).

It has often been stated that urbanized and industrialized societies such as the United States have more social mobility than agrarian or preindustrial societies. This is because industrializing and urbanizing societies are in the process of creating more opportunities. It has never been made clear, however, whether it is industrialization and urbanization occurring jointly that makes for increasing opportunities or whether industrialization is the primary dimension. A second factor associated with urbanization and industrialization is the breakdown of the traditional society and the former strict social class boundaries. Thus it is argued that industrialization and urbanization lead to an achievement-oriented society and create the motivation for upward mobility to fill expanding higher-level positions in society.

Social Class Placement and Social Mobility

Most studies of American social mobility stress its openness and upward mobility. Even in the United States, however, initial social class placement is primarily determined by parental social class, especially that of the father (for a contrasting view emphasizing the mother see Beshers, 1962). The individual inherits, by virtue of birth, social class placement from parents and all that this implies with respect to different kinds of socialization patterns that substantially determine the child's values, attitudes, and behavioral patterns. Similarly, expectations and aspirations are inculcated by parents. Thus the family is the training ground for later life, and the social class of the residential area in which the child grows up influences what social class one's friends, schoolmates, and peers will belong to, as well as what social mobility aspirations and expectations one will have.

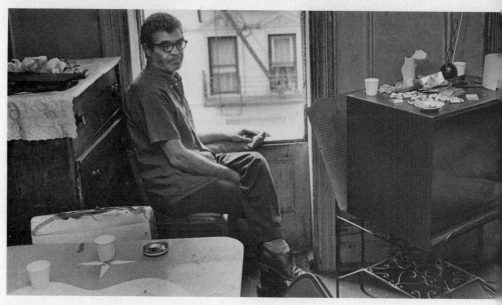

Without a substantial increase in income, it is doubtful if this man will be able to move into a better apartment or neighborhood—even if he wants to.

A great deal of stress in the sociological and general literature has been placed upon upward social mobility. Upward mobility is related to various social groupings and population categories that promote and inculcate in children learning, independence, and deferred gratification. Nevertheless, it should be noted that there is also substantial nonmobility, or stasis, and downward mobility in the United States, which must also be taken into consideration.

Intragenerational (Career) Mobility

Rogoff (1953) as well as others (Lipset and Bendix, 1963) have reported that there appears to be more upward than downward mobility in Western industrialized nations. Much of the upward mobility has been described as a result of *structural* needs. In a society undergoing substantial application of expanding technology, there is an increasing structural demand for people to be upwardly mobile, since the society itself has more upper-level positions opening up that it must fill. Structural mobility is contrasted with *individual* social mobility. When a society reaches a level in which it no longer has increasing numbers of higher-level positions being created but enters an era of structural equilibrium, the number of positions at each level remains substantially the same. At this time if a person is upwardly mobile, for example, it means that another person must be downwardly mobile. This is because the number of positions remains constant, upward and downward mobility are interrelated, and positions are not expanding, as would be the case, say, in a society with increasing upper-level positions being created by structural demand.

Actual studies of social mobility in urban areas in the United States show quite consistently that while social mobility does in fact occur, any given individual is most likely to remain in the same social class of birth or initial job entry — that is, to be *stationary*. Rogoff (1953: 21) in her pioneer study of Indianapolis reported that less than one-half of the persons moved out of the occupational class in which they had first held positions. What social class mobility does occur, then, is most likely to be of a one-step nature: that is, to occur between adjacent categories in the social class hierarchy.

The highest social class is the most stable. When social class is measured by occupational level, well over 90 percent of persons who first enter the professional and managerial level remain there throughout their careers, with few persons being downwardly mobile and an even fewer descending the scale from the highest to the lowest level. In the upper middle class it appears that around three-fourths of incumbents remain in that stratum, while about 10 percent are upwardly mobile and 15 percent are downwardly mobile. Similarly, stasis is reported for the lower middle class, with well over 60 percent remaining stationary and with somewhat more upward social mobility than downward social mobility. Because no downward mobility is possible in the lower social class, the only possibilities are to remain stationary, which over 60 percent do, and to be upwardly mobile, as are 35 to 40 percent of these people. Overall, leaving specific social class aside, the following 11-year social mobility experiences were reported for a population sample of households residing in the Los Angeles-Orange County SMSA as of June 1961: stationary (70.3 percent), upwardly mobile (19.0 percent), downwardly mobile (6.1 percent), and fluctuating pattern (4.6 percent) (Butler, 1966). Similarly, the Warner studies of Jonesville, Yankee City, and Old City show that the social class mobility was relatively slow and the range of movement was not very large.

DeJong et al. (1971) argued that there are no major differences in patterns of occupational mobility by sex. That is, those women who enter the labor force have about the same chances for occupational mobility that men have. Obviously, this conclusion is one that appears to conflict with some literature and the particular experiences of some females.

Intergenerational Occupational Mobility

The relationship between fathers' and sons' occupations defines intergenerational social mobility. Overall, in Los Angeles, two-thirds of sons were stationary — that is, they had the same occupational levels as their fathers; 22.2 percent were upwardly mobile, 7.1 percent downwardly mobile, and 4.2 percent had fluctuating patterns. Unlike career mobility in which the highest level has the least in- and outmobility, however, when comparing sons with fathers, the most difficult barrier to cross is that of the lowest occupational level, with almost two-thirds of sons having the same low status as did their fathers.

Sons with low- and high-middle-level fathers were most likely subsequently to remain in the same class and then to be in a lower occupational level, although some were also upwardly mobile. At least 40 percent of sons with low- and high-middle-level fathers subsequently were in lower levels than their fathers. Of course, this comparison contrasts some sons who are in the earlier stages of their occupational careers with their fathers, whose major occupational status has generally been achieved after a period of years in the labor force. Nevertheless, there is a strong suggestion that the extent of upward mobility may have been overplayed in our society. This is especially true, since there is a very high association between the occupational levels of sons during one period of time and their levels at a future date (Centers, 1948). Thus it is rather striking that only several reports cite the substantial amount of downward social mobility (Butler, 1966; Lipset and Bendix, 1963).

Insofar as intergenerational mobility of females is concerned, there appears to be relative stasis among middle-origin females. Thus, according to a recent analysis of four U.S. national surveys, the folklore and the impression one receives from the "scientific" literature that females marry up do not seem to be an accurate statement about this country. Females experience *less* favorable intergenerational mobility through marriage than do males through occupational attainment. The information from these surveys, in fact, shows considerable downward mobility on the part of females through marriage, and more females than males move downward across the nonmanual-manual line. This downward mobility of females has been suggested as working against the development of "working-class consciousness," since these downwardly mobile wives bring middle-class values to the marriage and in turn instill mobility aspirations in working-class sons and daughters through the socialization process (Glenn, Ross, and Tully, 1974).

Education and the Social Mobility Process

One of the major social institutions related to social mobility on an individual basis is education. The further people advance in the educational system, of course, the greater are their chances for higher-class positions. For lower- and lower-middle-class youth, education is virtually the only mechanism whereby one can advance in the social stratification hierarchy. The benefits of education go beyond those of the educational system itself, since it is biased: The higher one goes in the educational system, the more likely he or she will be exposed to students of the upper-middle and the upper-classes and thus become aware of social values, attitudes, and behavior patterns of the upper social stratum—all of which facilitates upward mobility once one leaves the educational system and enters the world of work. Thus there is more to becoming educated than attending an educational institution (Berelson and Steiner, 1967). In addition, Barber (1957: 398) has shown that not only does it make a difference that one has an education insofar as future and social class income are concerned, but it also matters which school is selected, for instance, an Ivy League school versus a midwestern college. Similarly, it should be noted that there are social class differences in the probability that a person will enter and finish college, which in turn affects the probability of social mobility by an individual (Sewell, 1966; Sewell and Armer, 1966; Wegner and Sewell, 1970).

Consequences of Social Mobility

Social mobility has been reported to have disruptive effects on primary interpersonal relationships that are dependent on face-to-face relations, to create stress and strain in the individual because of the need to adjust to new situations, new interpersonal relations, and new institutional structures (for an extended discussion see Blau, 1956). There is a frequent assertion that upward social mobility is associated with spatial mobility. When these occur together, it is argued, conditions for *anomie,* or alienation, are especially present. In one Detroit study it was found that upwardly mobile families were less likely to see friends, neighbors, and work associates than were the nonmobile in the same stratum. This difference disappeared after 40 years of age. Downward mobility produced no significant changes in interactional patterns. It should be noted specifically that this study did not evaluate the behavior of individuals prior to their upward or downward mobility and their behavior after such mobility, but rather compared the interaction of persons at one point in time who were mobile (Curtis, 1959).

Conclusions

In urban United States most studies of social mobility show that while upward mobility is not an unusual occurrence, most of it occurs between the lower and the middle classes; it takes several generations to go beyond this rather narrowly defined notion of upward social mobility. In addition, research shows that there is a great deal more downward social mobility than is generally acknowledged. The educational process does have profound influence upon social mobility potential, opportunity, and actual experiences. Finally, it is quite clear that social mobility experiences have social consequences for the individuals involved and for the social structure of cities and urban complexes.

BIBLIOGRAPHY: Articles

Adams, Stuart N., "Status Congruency as a Variable in Small Group Performance," *Social Forces*, 32 (October 1953): 16–22.

Antonovsky, Aaron, "Social Class, Life Expectancy and Overall Mortality," *Milbank Memorial Fund Quarterly*, 45 (April 1967): 31–73; also in E. Gartley Jaco (ed.), *Patients, Physicians and Illness,* 2nd ed., New York: The Free Press, 1972, pp. 5–30.

Artz, Reta D., Richard F. Curtis, Dianne T. Fairbank, and Elton F. Jackson, "Community Rank Stratification: A Factor Analysis," *American Sociological Review*, 36 (December 1971): 985–1002.

Blau, Peter M., "Social Mobility and Interpersonal Relations," *American Sociological Review*, 21 (June 1956): 290–295.

Buckley, Walter, "Social Stratification and the Functional Theory of Social Differentiation," *American Sociological Review*, 23 (August 1958): 369–375.

Butler, Edgar W., "An Empirical Examination of the Relationship of Vertical Occupational Mobility and Horizontal Geographic Mobility," unpublished doctoral dissertation, Los Angeles: University of Southern California, 1966.

Centers, Richard, "Occupational Mobility of Urban Occupational Strata," *American Sociological Review*, 13 (April 1948): 197–203.

Clarke, Alfred C., "The Use of Leisure and Its Relation to Levels of Occupational Prestige," *American Sociological Review*, 21 (June 1956): 301–307.

Curtis, Richard F., "Occupational Mobility and Urban Social Life," *American Journal of Sociology*, 65 (November 1959): 296–298.

Davis, Kingsley, "Conceptual Analysis of Stratification," *American Sociological Review*, 7 (June 1942): 309–321.

Davis, Kingsley, and Wilbert E. Moore, "Some Principles of Stratification," *American Sociological Review*, 10 (April 1945): 242–249.

DeJong, Peter Y., Milton J. Brawer, and Stanley S. Robin, "Patterns of Female Intergenerational Occupational Mobility: A Comparison with Male Patterns of Intergenerational Occupational Mobility," *American Sociological Review*, 36 (December 1971): 1033–1042.

Duncan, Beverly, and Otis Dudley Duncan, "Minorities and the Process of Stratification," *American Sociological Review*, 33 (June 1968): 356–364.

Duncan, Otis Dudley, and Beverly Duncan, "Residential Distribution and Occupational Stratification," *American Journal of Sociology*, 60 (January 1955): 493–503.

Glenn, Norval D., Adreain, A. Ross, and Judy C. Tully, "Patterns of Intergenerational Mobility of Females Through Marriage, *American Sociological Review*, 39 (October 1974): 683–699.

Goldstein, Sidney, and Kurt Mayer, "Population Decline and Social and Demographic Structure of an American City," *American Sociological Review*, 29 (February 1964): 48–54.

Green, Norman E., "Scale Analysis of Urban Structures: A Study of Birmingham, Alabama," *American Sociological Review*, 21 (February 1956): 8–13.

Gross, Neal, "Social Class Identification in the Urban Community," *American Sociological Review*, 18 (August 1953): 398–404.

Gutman, Robert, "Population Mobility in the American Middle Class," in Leonard Duhl (ed.), *The Urban Condition*, New York: Basic Books, 1969, pp. 172–184.

Hill, Mozell C., and Bevode C. McCall, "Social Stratification in Georgia Town," *American Sociological Review*, 15 (December 1950): 721–729.

Hollingshead, August B., "Cultural Factors in the Selection of Marriage Rates," *American Sociological Review*, 15 (February 1950): 619–627.

James, Preston E., "Vicksburg: A Study in Urban Geography," *Geographical Review*, 21 (April 1931): 234–243.

Lenski, Gerhard E., "Status Crystallization: A Non-Vertical Dimension of Social Status," *American Sociological Review*, 19 (August 1954): 405–413.

Michelson, William, "Potential Candidates for the Designer's Paradise," *Social Forces*, 46 (1967): 190–196.

Michelson, William, "An Empirical Assessment of Environmental Preferences," *Journal of the American Institute of Planners*, 32 (November 1966): 355–360.

Mills, C. Wright, "Middle Classes in Middle-Sized Cities," *American Sociological Review*, 11 (October 1946): 520–529.

Moore, Wilbert E., and Robin M. Williams, "Stratification in the Ante-Bellum South," *American Sociological Review*, 7 (February 1942): 343–351.

Mueller, Charles W., "City Effects on Socioeconomic Achievements: The Case of Large Cities," *American Sociological Review*, 39 (October 1974): 652–667.

Schnore, Leo F., "Social Mobility in Demographic Perspective," *American Sociological Review*, 26 (June 1961): 407–423.

Sewell, William H., "Community of Residence and College Plans," *American Sociological Review*, 29 (February 1964): 24–38.

Sewell, William H., and J. M. Armer, "Neighborhood Context and College Plans," *American Sociological Review*, 21 (April 1966): 159–168.

Thorpe, Claiburne B., "Black Social Structure and White Indices of Measurement," *Pacific Sociological Review*, 15 (January 1972): 495–506.

Tilly, Charles, "Occupational Rank and Grade of Residence in a Metropolis," *American Journal of Sociology*, 67 (November 1961): 323–330.

Tumin, Melvin, "Some Principles of Stratification: A Critical Analysis," *American Sociological Review*, 18 (August 1953): 387–394.

Uyeki, Eugene S., "Residential Distribution and Stratification, 1950–1960," *American Journal of Sociology*, 69 (March 1964): 491–498.

Wegner, Eldon L., and W. H. Sewell, "Selection and Context as Factors Affecting the Probability of Graduation from College," *American Journal of Sociology*, 75 (January 1970): 665–679.

Wheeler, James O., "Residential Location by Occupational Status," *Urban Studies*, 5 (February 1968): 24–32.

Willie, Charles V., "A Research Note on the Changing Association Between Infant Mortality and Socio-Economic Status," *Social Forces*, 37 (March 1959): 221–227.

Yankauer, Alfred, Jr., "The Relationship of Fetal and Infant Mortality to Residential Segregation," *American Sociological Review*, 15 (February 1950): 644–648.

Yankauer, Alfred, and Norman C. Allaway, "The Relation of Indices of Fetal and Infant Loss to Residential Segregation: A Follow-up Report," *American Sociological Review*, 23 (February 1958): 573–578.

BIBLIOGRAPHY: Books

Amory, Cleveland, *The Proper Bostonians*, New York: E. P. Dutton & Company, 1957.

Baltzell, E. Digby, *Philadelphia Gentlemen*, Glencoe, Ill.: The Free Press, 1958.

Barber, Bernard, *Social Stratification*, New York: Harcourt, Brace and Company, 1957.

Berelson, Bernard, and Gary A. Steiner, *Human Behavior*, shorter version, New York: Harcourt, Brace & World, 1967.

Beshers, James, *Urban Social Structure*, New York: The Free Press, 1962.

Centers, Richard, *The Psychology of Social Classes*, New York: Russell and Russell, 1961.

Drake, St. Clair, and Horace R. Cayton, *Black Metropolis*, New York: Harcourt, Brace, 1945.

Firey, Walter, *Land Use in Central Boston*, Cambridge, Mass.: Harvard University Press, 1947.

Gans, Herbert, *The Urban Villagers*, New York: The Free Press, 1962.

Gerth, H. H., and C. Wright Mills (trans.), *From Max Weber: Essays in Sociology,* New York: Oxford University Press, 1958.

Hyman, Herbert H., "The Value System of Different Classes: A Social Psychological Contribution to the Analysis of Stratification," in Reinhard Bendix and Seymour M. Lipset (eds.), *Class, Status, and Power,* Glencoe, Ill.: The Free Press, 1953.

Kahl, Joseph A., *The American Class Structure,* New York: Holt, Rinehart, and Winston, 1957.

Lasswell, Thomas E., *Class and Stratum,* Boston: Houghton Mifflin Company, 1965.

Lipset, Seymour M., and Reinhard Bendix, *Social Mobility in Industrial Society,* Berkeley and Los Angeles: University of California Press, 1963.

Lynd, Robert S., and Helen M. Lynd, *Middletown in Transition,* New York: Harcourt, Brace, 1937.

Michelson, William, *Man and His Urban Environment,* Reading, Mass: Addison-Wesley Publishing Co., 1970.

Reiss, Albert J., Jr., with collaborators, *Occupations and Social Status,* New York: The Free Press of Glencoe, 1961.

Rogoff, Natalie, *Recent Trends in Occupational Mobility,* Glencoe, Ill.: The Free Press, 1953.

Sorokin, Pitirim A., *Social Mobility,* New York: Harper & Brothers, 1927.

Thomlinson, Ralph, *Urban Structure: The Social and Spatial Character of Cities,* New York: Random House, 1969.

Vance, Rupert B., and Sara Smith Sutker, "Metropolitan Dominance and Integration," in Rupert B. Vance and Nicholus J. Demerath (eds.), *The Urban South,* Chapel Hill, N.C.: University of North Carolina Press, 1954.

Warner, W. Lloyd, *Social Class in America,* New York: Harpers, 1960.

Warner, W. Lloyd, and Paul S. Lunt, *The Social Life of a Modern Community,* Yankee City Series, Vol. 1, New Haven, Conn.: Yale University Press, 1941.

CHAPTER 11
URBAN POWER STRUCTURES

INTRODUCTION[1]

One of the most important influences upon contemporary cities and urban complexes is the national and local power structures. Power, as it is related to decision making in cities and elsewhere, is important in determining much of what is and is not accomplished in contemporary urban United States. *Power* ordinarily is defined as the capacity to command a particular behavior or performance. This capacity may belong to an individual—for example, one person may be able to command performance or behavior by another individual.[2] This social psychological view of power assumes that an individual's personal attributes permit him or her to control the behavior of others, especially in important decision-making processes in the community.

Power from a social system point of view entails the belief that every unit of human organization—family, voluntary organizations, and the urban complex—has inherent in it a system of power organized to facilitate the performance of a given activity or activities (Hawley, 1971: 210). *Power structure* (Walton, 1967) thereby is also defined as the characteristic pattern whereby resources are mobilized and sanctions employed in ways that affect an organization or a city as a whole. The urban complex from this view is then considered an organization of units that revolves around the notion of power. At the city or urban complex level an organization or "power group" may be able to command performance or behavior by other individuals or organizations. The individual level of command may perhaps be viewed more easily than when

[1] I wish to acknowledge the contributions that Professor Bert N. Adams, University of Wisconsin, and Professor Hallowell Pope, University of Iowa, made to several unpublished papers that form the basis of several parts of this chapter. They should not be held accountable, of course, for my interpretation of our joint efforts carried out several years ago.

[2] For a critique of this "simplistic" notion of power, see Bierstedt (1950) and Bachrach and Baratz (1963), who elaborate on the concepts of power, dominance authority, influence, manipulation, and force.

one organization is controlling another or when a monolithic power structure in a city is controlling it in regard to the kinds of social services, programs, or transportation networks that exist. In both instances, nevertheless, power and a power structure may be said to exist.

Sources of power (Lasswell and Kaplan, 1950) are found in the control of that which is valued by people in a society. Thus power tends to reside with individuals and groups controlling whatever the members of the society value. In our society, of course, this means that whoever controls the economic institutions holds power, influences decisions, and is able to implement them (Goldberg and Linstromberg, 1966).

The character of power in society undoubtedly has changed as urbanization has taken place. As society has become urbanized and industrialized, channels of communication have changed, and conflict between elitist adherents and democratic idealists has become an important issue in the United States. This conflict over decision making has generated a substantial body of literature and research, primarily in political science and sociology. As it turns out, this two-pronged research literature begins with different assumptions about decision making in contemporary America, and contrasting conclusions somewhat attenuate the confidence of what we report in this chapter.

Power structure studies have gone through several different stages: (1) the power-elitist stage; (2) the stage of pluralist counterstudies; and (3) a comparative community study stage (Clark, 1968). This latter stage has been concerned with city characteristics and outcomes as influenced by power structure type. Questions that have been asked and investigated by social scientists interested in power structures generally revolve around the following: (1) Is there a single, monolithic, hierarchically structured power system in communities in the United States, or are there different power structures, the number and nature depending on the characteristics of the local city's or metropolitan region's institutional system? (2) Who are the power elite (where they exist), and how do they exercise power in terms of decision making and control of institutional functions? (3) To what extent are there interlocking power positions that include power derived from economic, political, and social institutions? (4) In what way is a local city's power structure interlaced with regional and/or national power systems? (5) What methods or approaches are most effective in the study of urban power structures and with what results? In this chapter we shall examine some of the pertinent literature on these questions.

URBANIZATION AND POWER STRUCTURES

Virtually no studies exist of the impact of urbanization upon power structures.[3] However, early reports on developing cities suggest quite clearly that they contained elites, with a vast majority of the population not having any

---

[3] See Lenski (1966) for a historical and comparative treatment of "power and privilege."

FIGURE 11-1
Leadership System Types

I. Monolithic

M_1 Concentrated individually–Concentrated organization-ally
M_2 Diffused organizationally–Concentrated individually
M_3 Concentrated organizationally–Diffused individually

II. Countervailing Elites

Countervailing concentrations of previous monolithic sub-categories.

III. Pluralistic

Decision making, taking place within specific organizations by duly designated individuals who have the legitimate authority to make decisions in the specific areas under consideration

IV. Amorphous

Diffused individually and organizationally, with no discernible pattern

voice in the decisions affecting them. Subsequently, it appears that there has been increased participation in decision making by a larger population segment. Some argue that the two major transfers of economic power since the feudal period were brought about by changing technology, which disrupted the feudal order and transferred power to the corporate structure; the second change now in process is that of transferring power from the corporate structure to the government, especially the federal government (Goldberg and Linstromberg, 1966: 8).

TYPES OF POWER STRUCTURES

Most investigators tend to classify power structures into *monolithic* and *pluralistic* polar categories. Some research has suggested, though, that this dichotomy may be too simple and that clusters of "other" types might be found. The conflicting notions appear to center on the four possible types of leadership systems shown in Figure 11-1: (1) monolithic, (2) pluralistic, (3) countervailing elites, and (4) amorphous (for another approach see Agger et al., 1964).

The earliest sociological studies described a *monolithic* structure (sometimes called a pyramidal structure). In the monolithic model there are established repetitive and predictable patterns of decisions made by an elite group, generally regarded as the controllers of the economic sphere of the city. In other words, a single, solidary group controls decisions that are of city-wide scope; that is, we have an authoritarian model. Within the monolithic type three subtypes can be identified that involve the two major aspects of power as set forth by Weber (1947): (1) *personal attribute factors* and (2) power as part of *established authority*. These subtypes of monolithic structure are the concentrated individually and concentrated organizationally type (M_1), which implies

Chicago's mayor Richard Daley (left), shown here with Mayor Joseph Alioto of San Francisco, is purported by many to rule Chicago in a monolithic manner. Daley's government might be described as "M_1."

an extreme centralization of power; the diffused organizationally but concentrated individually type (M_2); and the concentrated organizationally and diffused individually type (M_3).

A *pluralistic* model (sometimes called a coalitional model) was proposed by Dahl (1961) and other political scientists. Their notion also includes an established, repetitive, and predictable pattern of decision making, but decisions are made by "legitimate" authorities, with the leadership varying according to the issues and being made up of fluid and interested persons and groups (Walton, 1967). That is, by leaders voted into office by the electorate or at least responsible to them, in other words, the democratic model. In this model, groups involved in making decisions are assumed to represent "the people" and are responsible to them, and although they may compete, they generally have an assigned and accepted area of decision making.

The third and fourth models, the *countervailing elite* and *amorphous* types, have been relatively neglected both by theorists (however, see Galbraith,

1952) and researchers. The countervailing elite or factional model consists of at least two, durable competing elites that are attempting to control city-wide decisions. It may include an economic elite on one side and local political officeholders and their technical staffs on the other side. The major difference between this model and the pluralistic one is the durability of factions; the degree of conflict is much greater and presumably involves different *value systems* and the resulting implications for decision making and issue outcomes. An amorphous power structure is one that has not solidified; it has a large number of competing interest groups and power centers but lacks a persistent pattern of leadership.

Crosscutting all of the foregoing are types of leaders. There are *concealed* and *visible* leaders. Visible leaders have been more closely associated with the pluralistic model, whereas concealed leaders have more often been associated with monolithic systems. Additionally, *symbolic leaders* are persons who, according to other leaders, do not have much power but are perceived by others (nonleaders) as being powerful persons in the community (Bonjean, 1963). Apparently, symbolic leaders are not limited to one of the types of leadership systems outlined previously (Miller and Dirksen, 1963), although they are most likely to be in a monolithic system. There is some evidence that the visibility of the leadership is a variable related to community characteristics (Bonjean and Carter, 1965; Preston, 1969: 46).

DELINEATION OF POWER STRUCTURES

Early sociological studies of community power structures dealt with individual personalities within one local community. This approach, or the so-called *reputational* approach, emphasizes perceptions of various "knowledgeables." These knowledgeables make a list of prominent leaders, who are then interviewed. Interviewed leaders in turn list other leaders, which creates a snowballing effect as more leaders are named. Focus in this type of study also is on the extent of interaction and a "voting" system for determining the most influential leaders. The person nominated most often by other named leaders is presumed to have more influence than those who receive fewer votes (Hunter, 1953).

Political scientists and others have criticized the reputational approach because of its emphasis on the perception of individuals rather than upon behavior in community political systems (Dahl, 1961; Wolfinger, 1960; Polsby, 1962; Sayre and Polsby, 1965: 127–134). These critics have asked the following questions: (1) Are reputations for power an adequate index of the distribution of power? (2) Even if the respondent's perceptions of power relations are accurate, is it useful to describe (political) systems by presenting rankings of leader participants according to their power? Perhaps the most potentially damaging criticism is that reputationalists "expect" a tight-knit, monolithic structure to emerge because of the influence their *ideology* has upon their research methodology. Thus, according to the critics, reputationalists are look-

ing for a monolithic structure and assume a static distribution of power and ignore goals, strategies, power bases, decisional outcomes, recruitment patterns,
and other similar types of questions (for reasoned critiques see Anton, 1963;
Danzger, 1964).

Political scientists and others, on the other hand, have more often studied issues and decisions. This approach focuses upon the political system of the
community and is dynamic in the sense that the decision-making process is
studied. Attention is paid primarily to political processes and persons who were
elected or appointed to their positions. The major criticism of this approach is
that it is primarily concerned with elective positions and decisions made by
persons in the government. There has not been an attempt to go behind the
scenes to determine whether there are other persons or groups holding power
over political officeholders.

Common to both perspectives is the consistency or pattern of *positions*
that community leaders hold. These positions *almost invariably* include company presidents, managers of absentee-owned corporations, bank presidents,
head cashiers of banks, a mayor or a city manager, a city attorney, a medical
association chairman, a bar association chairman, and a judge. *Typically*
included are people who hold the positions of school superintendent, school
board chairman, president of an influential union, newspaper editor, television
station manager, pastor of a prestigious church, police chief, united fund executive director, and so on.

Several investigators have used this information to advantage in their
studies of community power structures. That is, they assumed that persons in
certain positions are, by virtue of their positions, leaders in the community. The
reputational study of Booth and Adrian (1962) is especially notable here. These
investigators utilized knowledge of the close association between community
leadership and organizational positions to elicit other leadership information as
well as perceptions of community issues and decision making. This perspective, however, is based on the assumption that those holding positions of authority actually make key decisions, while those who do not occupy such positions do not make key decisions (Bonjean and Olson, 1964).

In an unpublished study, K. Miller mailed a questionnaire to a select
number of individuals representing organizational spheres in a large number of
cities in the United States. He developed a power typology and related it to
community characteristics. He did not, however interrelate these factors with
community decision making. Booth and Adrian replicated a much larger case
study of Lansing, Michigan, by utilizing only 14 interviews selected on an insti-
tutional- and organizational-position basis. They found an almost identical
number of leaders and structures as was found in a much larger and more time-
consuming study. Again, however, these investigators did not relate the leadership system to community decisions. Wilson, in a recent and as yet unpublished study of a number of cities throughout the U.S., utilized a mail ballot
technique to determine the leadership structure and the leaders' perception of

This meeting over transportation problems brought together many national leaders, all of whom were from one of the three institutional areas delineated by Mills and subsequent researchers.

issues, coalitions, decision making, and so on. His study, a valuable one, interrelated community characteristics, leadership systems, and decision making.

Researchers utilizing the reputational approach tend to find more centralized decision-making structures than researchers using other methods (Walton, 1966). This has been interpreted as method influencing research results and, of course, the resultant description of the city or community under investigation. Another plausible alternative is that perhaps researchers with different methodological bents select communities for study that match their predispositions, for example, a monolithic or a pluralistic power structure (Clark et al., 1968). If this is so, then a city's structural characteristics should explain more variation in power structure type than discipline of the researcher (Blankenship, 1964).

NATIONAL POWER STRUCTURES
Both C. Wright Mills and Floyd Hunter postulated the existence of a national power elite in the United States that influences policy both at the national and local levels. Mills (1959) said that this national power elite rules the country and makes important decisions on any given issue that is salient to itself. According to him the power elite consists of top people in the institutional hierarchies of the economy, the political order, and the military establishment. There is a "circulation of the elite" and thus a great deal of interchangeability among top leadership positions in these three spheres in the United States. A high-ranking military officer, therefore, might "retire" and become a high-level corporate officer, or, alternatively, a high-ranking banker may become an ambassador in the government's service. These people, as a rule, are wealthy, but Mills (p. 9) believes that their wealth is a result of their power rather than a cause of it. Further, he sees them as forming a "self-conscious" social class,

since they view themselves as being different from other people, and their behavior toward each other is distinctly different than that shown toward members of other classes (p. 11). Finally, Mills says:

> What I am asserting is that in this particular epoch a conjunction of historical circumstances has led to the rise of an elite of power; that the men of the circles composing this elite, severally and collectively, now make such key decisions as are made; and that, given the enlargement and the centralization of the means of power now available, the decisions that they make and fail to make carry more consequences for more people than has ever been the case in the world history of mankind.

Like Mills, Hunter (1959) argued that there is a top power elite in the United States that controls the decisions that affect the nation and local cities and urban regions. He used a variety of research techniques including most of the features of the snowballing reputational techniques, polls of national leaders, and extensive personal interviews. Hunter's view of the power structure in America is that the membership lists of the National Industrial Conference, the Committee for Economic Development, and the Business Advisory Council provide good starting points for anyone interested in a quick and partial rundown of national leadership (p. 33). Thus Hunter's conclusion parallels that of Mills when he says that there exists in the United States a single, monolithic, hierarchically structured power system and that this elite power group makes most of the decisions that greatly affect the country. Their decisions do not only concern local and national issues but international ones as well. Further, Hunter demonstrated that the national leadership is systematically interrelated with local power structures; that is, a network exists.

Because Hunter did not follow the general practice of using pseudonyms for leaders, his work can be utilized for various other analyses including the examination of personal characteristics of top leaders in the power elite (also see Lundberg, 1968). From his point of view government is only an instrument for the execution of policy, not its formation. Most top leaders, according to Hunter, are not political representatives but are those who raise political money and confer with others to find suitable candidates for public office. While political representatives listen to "the public," their focus is on industrial policy makers and their desires (p. 209). Rose (1967: 13) has criticized the eclectic methodology of Hunter by characterizing it as a series of "hit-and-miss sequences of techniques almost all of which have a built-in bias toward the industrial and commercial elite."

In a more recent assessment Domhoff (1967) asked the question: "Is the American upper class a governing class?" His analysis of the American upper social class led him to conclude that by all generally acceptable definitions of social class a national superclass exists in the United States. His analysis shows that this superclass owns a disproportionate amount of the wealth of the nation, receives a disproportionate amount of the country's yearly income, and controls the major banks and corporations that in turn control the economy. In addition, he argues that this upper class controls foundations, elite universities, the largest of the mass media, and important "opinion-molding associations" such as the Council on Foreign Relations, the Foreign Policy Association, the Business Advisory Council, the National Advertising Council, and so on. Similarly, he presented evidence that illustrates how the power elite, or members of the super-upper class, controls the executive branch of the federal government and, through it, regulatory agencies, the federal judiciary, the military, the CIA, and the FBI. According to Domhoff, the power elite does not control but merely influences the legislative branch of the federal government, as well as most state and city governments. Nevertheless, through its control of "corporations, foundations, elite universities, the Presidency, the federal judiciary, the military, and the CIA," it qualifies as a "governing class" (p. 11).

On the other hand, at least several social scientists believe that while there may have been at one time a single hierarchical ruling class, it has been replaced by "veto groups" and the dispersal of power (Riesman et al., 1956). Others believe that the power structure of the United States has been misinterpreted by those who say it is monolithic. Instead, the power structure of the United States should be viewed as

> highly complex and diversified (rather than unitary and monolithic), that the political system is more or less democratic (with the glaring exception of the Negro's position until the 1960's), that in political processes the political elite is ascendant over and not subordinate to the economic elite, and that the political elite influences or controls the economic elite as least as much as the economic controls the political elite [Rose, 1967: 492].

The overall conclusion by Rose is that the American power structure is extremely complex, with multiple influences coming into play in any decision (p. 493).

While the controversy continues over what kind of national power structure exists in the United States, it may be useful to examine material not directly collected to examine that issue. The *Report of the Federal Trade Commission on Interlocking Directorates* (1951) and Lundberg's *The Rich and the Super-Rich* (1968) are especially useful, since they use actual names for corporations and executives (as did Hunter). It remains, of course, for each individual to examine these data to determine whether they correspond to the point of view of a monolithic structure or a highly complex power structure (also see Allen, 1974).

TYPE OF CITY AND POWER STRUCTURES

Clark (1967: 291) has pointed out that one of the common assumptions of social scientists studying local community power studies is that all places are alike—"rural villages, commuter suburbs, central cities, vacation hamlets, and entire metropolitan regions all tend to be carelessly thrown together under the general rubric of 'community.'" Yet Wirth and other early sociologists pointed out that variation among cities occurs in industrial make-up, location in metropolitan region, age, national region of population, growth characteristics, size, density, and type (see Chapter 5). Characteristics of cities that might be related to the type of power structure are the degree of industrialization, population size, heterogeneity of population along ethnic, religious, and occupational axes, the scope of local government, the political party system, and the unionization of blue-collar workers, and the political and economic organization of the working class (Rogers, 1962). Similarly, political scientists and others have stressed that there are differences in cities according to the type of government, whether there are partisan or nonpartisan elections, the presence or absence of a city manager, and the age of the city.

Since elites may not yet be consciously organized in newly developing cities, public officials may be expected to dominate decision making. In larger and earlier developed cities a great variety of issues and group interests serves to limit the power of any one such group or issues-oriented organization. Thus, with their respective countervailing strengths, these groups tend to cancel each other out. Boskoff (1970: 234) proposed that as a result of such cancellation, power is accrued to public officials who act as power brokers among groups. He noted that public officials may be especially effective in such situations, since they have the "power of the purse." However, the larger, more developed, and more complex the urban area, the more likely decisions will be a result of "a series of exercises in collective interference or mutual checks on effective power" (Boskoff, 1970: 235). One perspective argues that these checks and balances lead to a pluralistic power structure. On the other hand, it may be that effective decisions are not being made because no individual or group is willing to risk a confrontation and lose the battle—that is, we have an amorphous structure. In the case of elected officials, losing a battle also may entail the loss of position. Thus the end result is inaction and indecision.

Absentee-owned corporations in some cities influence decisions that are made locally through the role executives from these corporations play in civic affairs. Generally, executives seek to protect the corporation's interests, and they tend to hold conservative and business-oriented values that cause them to influence policies in these directions. One such study of absenteed-owned corporations and their executives in Bigtown (Baton Rouge, Louisiana) suggests that while executives generally are attempting to further their corporate careers by participating in local decisions, at least some of them participate more extensively than necessary because they seem to be quite concerned with the "sorry state" of community services in Bigtown and wish to contribute improvement (Pellegrin and Coates, 1956). Nevertheless, since the executive depends upon his superiors for his career advancement rather than upon local individuals or institutions, his primary loyalty lies outside of the local community. If a conflict between the local community and corporation exists, the executive invariably tends to side with the latter.

From another perspective Duncan and Schnore (1959) hypothesized that cities of different size and functional type comprise significantly different areas for the struggle among contending power groups. Further, they believe that there are industrial-occupational differentials in concentrations of power that correspond to community size and place. "Dominance" within a community, according to Hawley (1950), ordinarily is associated with those functional units that control the flow of sustenance into it, power being defined as the "capacity to produce results." He argued that government in the United States plays a relatively passive role in the flow of sustenance to the local community; business and industry are the mediators of the community's external relations and derive power from this source, as well as from controlling local economic resources. Wealth is related to influence that can be turned into control over other resources, that is, personnel, or institutions, that can be utilized in decision making (also see Michel, 1964). Also, the local resources are often necessary for implementing decisions or for obtaining funds to qualify for some federal programs.

Local urban power structure studies should not only consider population growth and socioeconomic factors but also internal social diversity. Previous work in typologies, whether using metropolitan centers, counties, cities, or census tracts within SMSAs, invariably describes social diversity as a major factor. Basically, a plausible hypothesis is that the more heterogeneous the city, the more likely there is to be a pluralistic or amorphous power structure. Such systems are expected in heterogeneous communities and especially where there is a great deal of economic diversity. An amorphous system is expected to be heterogeneous in the previous sense and to be found in a city, possibly of large size, undergoing extremely rapid growth and other types of change. Nevertheless, some research points out that a rapidly growing urban area has a monolithic structure, while, according to most opinions, the structural differentiation that accompanies industrialization contributes to a pluralistic leadership system. Obviously, more research is needed to test these ideas.

Few have been particularly concerned with the interrelationship of leadership systems and policy or program outcomes. However, K. Miller's unpublished study interrelated structural indicators with a power structure dimension. His analysis was based on a general frame of reference that restricted the number of variables, each of which was hypothesized as being related to different types of power structures. Miller did not look for underlying dimensions as did previous investigators but interrelated individual variables with his power dimension.

Individual social structure indicators that have been suggested as being systematically associated with different types of power structures are as follows: (1) the MPO (managers, proprietors, and officials) ratio, (2) occupational distribution, (3) population growth, (4) urban population, (5) population size,

(6) extent and rate of industrialization, (7) economic complexity—the number of banks and the number and size of primary industrial units, (8) governmental type, (9) population diversity and stability, (10) population mobility, (11) poverty indexes, (12) dependent population—the unemployed, the young, and the aged, and so on, (13) ethnic diversity—both racial and of national origin, (14) density of population, (15) educational indexes, (16) age of place, (17) political conservatism, and (18) electorate involvement.

Characteristics reported to be associated with concealed power elites are cities with a large influx of population, greater poverty, and complexity. Walton (1967), summarizing a number of case studies, reported that region, population size, industrialization, economic diversity, and the type of local government were not found to be related to type of power structure. On the other hand, he showed that local ownership, lack of adequate economic resources, being an independent city (not a satellite), and the lack of party competition all suggest that a city has a pyramidal or monolithic power structure. Recently, Gilbert (1967) and Clark (1967) generated a number of propositions that suggest demographic, economic, legal, and political structure, social integration, and cultural and educational factors that vary by place and thus influence who governs, where, and when—for example, the urban power structure. Gilbert (1967) argued that self-contained places are becoming rarer, and as a result most local power structures are becoming less concentrated, that is, more pluralistic. However, her description of findings suggests that many cities have become amorphous in structure, diffuse, and fragmented: The only way to accomplish anything in them is for a strong leader to rise who is capable of pulling together disparate interest groups. In her study of power structures over time she made the following conclusions: Cities are increasingly becoming good government cities (reformed government) and more pluralistic in nature; they are continuing to have the same kinds of conflicts; the power of officials is decreasing, with an increasingly large proportion of cities having economic dominants at the upper levels of power; and there is no apparent trend in increased utilization of "experts" in the shaping of policy. Apparently it is extremely difficult for experts in government or the generally established pressure or interest groups to introduce innovation. However, there is some trend for ad hoc groups to develop innovative programs. Overall, Gilbert remarked, then, that "the evidence supports the notion that increasing scale of society is reflected in the political structure of local communities." Decision making is "less and less in the hands of a privileged few and is increasingly dependent upon the broker, be he elected official or not, who can bring together (to the extent he can bring together) various elements in the *community*."

Finally, Walton (1967) noted that when community consensus is limited, leadership tends to be more competitive. He further suggested that the more extralocal (what he calls the vertical axis) influence exists in a given city, the more competitive the power structure. Thus "to the extent that the local community becomes increasingly interdependent with respect to extra-community institutions (or develops along its vertical axis) the structure of local leadership becomes more competitive." Development along extralocal lines involves interdependence and the introduction of new interests and new insitutional relationships and thus injects competitiveness into the power structure.

Invariably, researchers suggest that more general knowledge about the characteristics of cities and urban areas needs to be obtained before we shall be able to understand how social structure affects leadership systems. This point of view tends to be supported by a study in which it was found that there was virtually no relationship between whether the discipline of the researcher was sociology or political science and the power structure type for 166 cities that had been the sites of previous power structure studies (Clark et al., 1968). On the other hand, this study showed that city characteristics such as type of place, partisan or nonpartisan elections, median age of population, and so on, were related to power structure type, although not at a level high enough for very accurate predictive purposes. The important finding, however, is that discipline and method of researcher were not important in predicting the power structure, whereas city characteristics had some significance (also see Gilbert, 1968: 226–227).

LOCAL POWER STRUCTURES

By far, most studies of power structures in the United States have focused on a single local community power structure. For example, these studies range from Atlanta, Georgia, at several different time periods to Burlington and Durham, North Carolina, Syracuse, New York, and Oakland, California. One of the very first studies of community power structures was carried out by the Lynds in the Middletown studies (1929 and 1937). In Muncie, Indiana, at the time of the first study, the Lynds reported that the power structure essentially consisted of one family, and from the 1920s through the 1930s this community power structure was continued by family sons. This particular family dominated the city in regard to its manufacturing, banking, hospitals, department stores, milk depots, political parties, churches, the newspaper; and it controlled the local airport. The concentration of power in one family does not exist to this degree in most other cities, but power concentrations are systematically reported by researchers.

Atlanta, Georgia

The study that set off a whole spate of power structure studies was carried out by Hunter (1953) for Atlanta, Georgia (called Regional City in his book), just after the end of World War II. This particular study showed that there were two power structures in Atlanta at the time: One consisted entirely of whites, and another power structure was identified in the black community, but it was beholden to the white power structure (also see Thompson, 1963, and Burgess, 1962). Hunter found that about 40 persons made up the power structure of Atlanta. They were primarily presidents of companies, chairmen of boards of corporations and/or institutions, and professionals, primarily lawyers. In addition, five of the persons were socially prominent and of inherited wealth. Most leaders knew other leaders, and many held interlocking director-ates in businesses and corporations; there were also many overlapping club memberships. Hunter reported links to national leaders as well, which later led him to carry out his previously mentioned national study of top U.S. leaders.

Top leaders of Atlanta did not hold offices in charitable, civic, or social organizations, but Hunter believes that they exercised power over those who did hold these offices, thereby keeping these organizations under their social power. Further, they exerted influence through organizations such as boards of corporations and by being presidents of banks, and so on. Hunter concluded that Atlanta was governed by a concealed economic elite. Most leaders in the power structure of Atlanta lived in one particular section of the city, that is, in the most desirable section, and the professionals in Atlanta lived in this area or other almost as desirable areas. Only one person considered as a leader or a high-level professional actually lived in what was classified as an undesirable residential area.

A decade or so after Hunter studied Atlanta another study of decision making in that city was published. It was not specifically a replication of the earlier study but was influenced by it (Jennings, 1964, see especially Chapter 8). In Atlanta at this later date it appeared that top-level influentials were highly politicized and involved in a moderate range of issues; however, there were issues in which top-level leaders were not involved. In addition, persons other than those considered as top leaders were involved in decision making over some issues. Thus, viewed in the text of a wide range of issues, it *appears* that Atlanta also had a general elite at the time of this study. But, this was not the case according to the author, since the city was actually dominated by "a num-ber of slightly to moderately competitive coalitions, *not dominated by eco-nomic notables,* exercising determinative influence in their own policy areas" (p. 161).

In this study, then, economic notables were important in the decision-making process, but they were not as important in the earlier study reported by Hunter. Nevertheless, in this later study economic dominants played signifi-cant roles in decision making in Atlanta, but there is a rejection of the idea that they prevailed over others in the city. However, Jennings notes that "we cannot deny the importance some of them have for decision-making in Atlanta" (p. 166).

Apparently, there is some overlapping membership among coalitions, which are linked together when some individuals participate in several dif-ferent decisions. One problem with this study is that no distinction is made concerning the *salience* of issues to influentials. Thus leaders may not actively participate in some decisions that are relatively unimportant to them. But if the issue, for example, taxes, was salient to the leadership, would the leaders then systematically influence the decision?

There are three possible explanations for the contrasting findings of the two Atlanta studies: (1) Changes in the structure could have occurred over time. (2) The authors had different orientations to the decision-making process. (3) The validity of the research techniques utilized in the studies can be questioned. There is some support for the argument for a change in power structure, since federal programs may have increased the impact local governmental officials had in obtaining such programs. Similarly, race relations have changed dramatically in Atlanta the past few years. Since these studies, a black mayor has been elected in Atlanta. However, these arguments were rejected by Jennings. Instead, he believed that Hunter emphasized decisions in regard to *fixing priorities,* thereby overlooking other phases such as initiation, planning, long-range conditioning of attitudes, persuasion, bargaining, promotion, and implementation (p. 163). Yet fixing priorities is perhaps the most important area of concern, and at least some of the other stages are not as important and are dependent upon previously fixed priorities.

Syracuse, New York

One study in this city showed that industrialists of locally owned firms made up the top of the power structure (Hodges, 1958), with government officials and politicians being subordinate. Several other studies reported, though, that a host of people, from a variety of institutions, has and wields power in Syracuse (Martin, Munger et al., 1961; Freeman et al., 1960). In fact, the monolithic power structure that "many knowledgeables in local affairs" believe to exist is a myth (Martin et al., 1961: 306). Even though one person, Mr. Syracuse, is quite consistently mentioned as exercising the key power and without whose "consent, tacit or explicit, nothing of importance can be done," "analyses of actual decisions taken with respect to public problems in the Syracuse metropolitan area do not support an interpretation based on the concept of monolithic power" (p. 306).

The use of several different procedures to determine top leaders in Syracuse resulted in the conclusion that top leaders do not converge on a single set of individuals. Reputation and position seem to go hand in hand, however; in addition, officers in organizations are substantially the same persons who have reputations as leaders (Freeman et al., 1963: 797).

Based on the relationship among reputation, position, and participation, leaders in Syracuse were classified as either (1) *institutional leaders,* (2) *effectors,* or (3) *activists.* Institutional leaders are "the heads of the largest and most actively participating business, industrial, governmental, political, professional, educational, labor and religious organizations in Syracuse" (Freeman et al., 1963: 797). These leaders were discovered by reputational, positional, or organizational participation. Institutional leaders are not active participants in community activities. Many effectors are employed by the institutional leaders, and "it seems likely that their activities are frequently guided by what they view as company policy" (p. 798). Finally, activists are people who lack an institutional power base but are active in voluntary organizations, clubs, and so on; through the commitment of time and effort they help to shape the future of the community. At one time, perhaps 30 years earlier, conditions were such that institutional leaders and effectors were the same people; but over recent decades there has been a broadening circle of participants in decision making.

Interestingly, data presented on participation in decisions by "won" and "lost" categories suggest that the dominant "winning" factions in Syracuse are the Republican party, the manufacturers association, real-estate interests, town government officials, and, to a lesser degree, the village weekly newspapers. The Democratic party, the CIO, and the League of Women Voters seldom, if ever, "won" a decision (1961: p. 309). Nevertheless, three conclusions are cited in this study: (1) A monolithic power structure does not exist in Syracuse. (2) There tends to be as many decision centers as there are decision areas, and decisions are fragmented among persons, agencies, and institutions. (3) There are many different kinds of community power.

Battle Creek, Michigan

Several studies of Battle Creek, Michigan (Community A), have been carried out. The first such study delineated a power structure much like the one that Hunter found for Atlanta (Belknap and Smuckler, 1956). Battle Creek was described as having a fairly concentrated manufacturing base, with a small proportion of minorities, as using a nonpartisan ballot, and as being conservative, and much like other Michigan cities in the same size category (about 50,000 population). Several different research techniques showed that approximately 15 individuals made up the power structure. One person in particular stood out — a lawyer, a former three-term mayor from a well-known family. In this city it appears that positions held in the city, for example, in industry, business, city government, organizations, and so on, were closely linked to how the public viewed leaders. The major exception to this was position in organized labor. Leaders were instrumental in most city activities, and their backing and approval were sought. Further, approximately 60 other persons were designated as second-echelon leaders. Overall, then, this study suggests a pyramidal model of a small core of leaders, a somewhat larger pool of secondary leaders, and a mass of nonparticipants or nonactives.

Several years later, in 1961, a replication of the power structure in Battle Creek was accomplished (Booth and Adrian, 1962). During these interim years, the economic environment in Battle Creek had deteriorated. The downtown was being vacated by businesses for more favorable locations even though parking was more than adequate. The city had a 10-percent decline in population, although the black proportion of population had doubled and the proportion of population that was working class decreased. Thus some of the important changes that had taken place during the seven years between the two studies regarded population and the environment (slum clearance, flood control, expressway development, and the "flight to the suburbs"). Also, more *city* leaders now lived outside the city limits. Twelve of the top 15 leaders belonged to the Mayfair Club.

Although the 1961 study did not use the same methodology as the earlier study, the results were substantially comparable. As in the earlier study, nearly all top 15 leaders held important organizational positions and still retained power (except for those who had died in the intervening years). Between 1956 and 1961, however, a split had apparently grown in the leadership of Battle Creek: The mayor, a labor union official, and one of the city councilmen were nonmembers of the Mayfair Club, and all three claimed to be members of the working class and representatives of its interests. "All three representatives of the labor point of view were avowed and outspoken opponents of the old city leadership . . ." (p. 288). Also apparent was the antagonism between these two factions. Was this city moving toward a countervailing elite model? Unfortunately, no additional follow-up studies of Battle Creek's power structure have been accomplished, so that the question remains unanswered.

Other Cities

Many case studies of other cities have been made. They suggest that there are variations in decision making, with some cities being described as monolithic and others as pluralistic. For example, a study of cities along the American-Mexican border showed that the reputational technique provided a good indication of perceived general influence apart from specific influence and that reputed leaders were deeply involved in general community decision making (D'Antonio and Erickson, 1962). While not every leader was involved in every decision, there was extensive overlap, and a small group made up largely of "Key Influentials" was involved in many major issues (p. 735). "Our findings suggest that a group of general community influentials did in fact exist in El Paso and that it's existence has had important consequences for the community during the 1950s." On the other hand, in a study of Lorain, Ohio, McKee (1958) suggested that there are multiple coalitions of individuals and groups that form in that city depending upon the issue at hand. Thus it appears that "the pyramidal model of the social order, with power and authority located at the apex, is inaccurate and misleading" (p. 369).

Another variation is reported in a study of an industrial suburb in which major plants had been absorbed by absentee-owned corporations. The managers of these plants did not meddle in local decisions, leaving them to be made by people other than the economic dominants (Schulze, 1958). This left an apparent power vacuum at the top leadership levels. The abdication of power by the corporations may have been a result of the feeling that the local community could have little effect on them. If the local community made a decision that adversely affected the corporations, they could probably use their *potential* power and threaten to leave the city (for a study of power in an unincorporated place see Gereffi, 1970).

Perceptions of Leaders

Self-conception and appraisal of leaders by others in the community were evaluated in Pacific Town, Washington (Abu-Laban, 1963). Evaluations of community leaders were made according to their: (1) influence, (2) ability to influence important changes (instrumentality), (3) belongingness in the leadership groups, and (4) community support. The results indicated that "leaders whose self-conception was one of high influence in the community were likely to have been highly appraised by the local residents" (p. 34). Similarly, the higher the appraisal of a leader by the community, the higher the evaluation he or she had of greater support from the community. In addition, highest-rated leaders were those who were perceived or identified as being influential in a number of issue-related areas: business and industry, education, religion, politics, municipal affairs, and personal matters. Thus there was no relationship between the *content* of issues and community evaluation. At least in this one city there appears to be a conjunction between community appraisal, leadership self-evaluation, and influence (for other approaches, see Ehrlich, 1967; Gamson, 1966; and Form and Sauer, 1960).

Social Control Techniques

Techniques used by power leaders are all well-known dimensions of social control. Cole (1958: 248) listed a number of these techniques and noted that negative controls such as intimidation are used only when there is no other convenient way of exerting social power (also see Schermerhorn, 1961: 36–39). Cole's list included the following:

1. The planning of strategy through association of power leaders with each other.
2. The deliberate selection of people by power structure leaders capable of "doing a job" or carrying out tasks.
3. The initiation of action by a small group of power leaders and the expansion of the circle of action to include the leaders of other groups.
4. The development and manipulation of a following as in politics and in the economic substructure supporting the power system.
5. The attempt to establish unanimity and value agreement through resolutions, propaganda, and appeals.
6. The witholding of response to an issue, organization, movement, and drive if it conflicts with the wishes and values of the power leaders or of the power structure.
7. The use of intermediaries, such as representatives from trade and professional organizations, who reflect and espouse the philosophy of the power leader or the power structure.
8. The manipulation of people through the use of compliments and flattery.
9. The use of incentives such as matched funds or "initial gifts."

10. The use of threats, pressure, and intimidation of dissenters, especially via the superiors of dissenters.

It has been argued that the actual application of sanctions is an admission of defeat by the so-called power wielder. Similarly, it is a defeat if the prior *threat* of sanctions fails to bring about desired behavior (Bachrach and Baratz, 1963: 635). In fact, applying sanctions may lend to a loss of power in that the coerced persons may recognize that they do not have to comply.

POWER STRUCTURES, COMMUNITY DECISIONS, AND ISSUE OUTCOMES

So far we have seen that in every community there are individuals who have considerable influence over community affairs, over *what* is considered as an issue and *how* issues are decided and decisions implemented. From an organizational point of view, occupational and other positions (e.g., lawyer and United Fund chairman, mayor and department storeowner) that people hold in the community are related to influence. Obviously, there is variation in the influence that each person exerts over others and over organizations. When considering community power, we should also examine the bases or *sources* of a person's influence, the number of persons who have influence, and, given the organizational aspect of power, the number of organizations involved in the utilization of power (Perruci and Pilisuk, 1970).

Communities confront numerous problems, some recognized by everyone, some by a few, and some generally unrecognized. In addition, there is variation in the extent to which community problems are considered as important issues: tax rates, fluoridation of water, crime and delinquency, industrial development, antipoverty programs, water, air, and soil pollution, and so on. A variety of outcomes can be specified for those problems that become issues: (1) discussion, no specifics, (2) actual proposals pending, (3) proposals rejected with opposition, (4) proposals dropped, (5) adopted, no opposition, and (6) adopted over opposition.

An important question is then: What issues are decided at what levels in the United States? "The initiation of issues and the decisions about them may occur at quite different levels in the power structure" (Schermerhorn, 1961: 100). In the initial stage there are three major areas of controversial issues. First, conflicts may arise over economic issues such as taxes and industrialization; second, disputes may arise over the form of government, representation in decision making, and so on; and third, conflict may arise over certain cultural beliefs and values, such as in educational philosophy and school desegregation (Coleman, 1957). An important question here is: ". . . what issues are not allowed in the area of public discussion and what problems are allowed to become part of the public realm?" "This problem is important because the selection of issues—at least public issues—precedes the making of decisions"

FIGURE 11-2
A Model of Decision Outcomes[a]

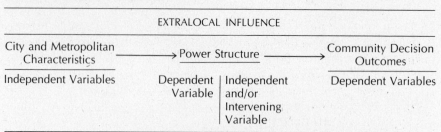

EXTRALOCAL INFLUENCE

City and Metropolitan Characteristics	→ Power Structure →	Community Decision Outcomes
Independent Variables	Dependent Variable | Independent and/or Intervening Variable	Dependent Variables

[a] See Figure 5-1 for a more elaborate model incorporating all of these as well as other factors. Also see Clark (1968: 18) for a model with more emphasis on political factors other than power.

(Schermerhorn, 1961: 101). Some grievances, conditions, and so on, in some places never become issues. This may be because individuals and/or groups effectively prevent them from doing so, which is, of course, another way of exercising power. While this may describe a *nondecision* or *nonevent,* in fact the process of nondecision making may be the same as decision making (Bachrach and Baratz, 1963). Thus many outcomes of urban power structures may not be observable, for example, the decision *not* to have an antipoverty or urban-renewal program.

A somewhat simplified model of the relationship of extralocal influence, community characteristics, and power structures to decision outcomes is shown in Figure 11-2. Many outcomes in any particular urban place are influenced in whole or in part by decisions made external to the local unit. That is, "policies and procedures of state or national organizations, by state and federal law, and by developments in the national economy" (Warren, 1956: 338) all influence community decision outcomes. Cities and other places in the United States "are simply points of geographical contact of criss-crossing networks of different organizations like the Presbyterian Church, the Grange, Rotary International, Standard Oil Company of New Jersey, Atlantic & Pacific, and so forth" (Warren, 1956: 388). Each of these private and governmental units influences decision outcomes at the local level. These extralocal influences limit local autonomy by regulations, charters, defining conditions of operations, and by administrative directives (Warren, 1963; see especially Chapter 8).

Issues vary in their relevancy for the leadership system, and in many instances they are perceived as being salient only if social change may become manifest because of a decision (Barth and Johnson, 1960). A model of the process including saliency and implications for structural change outcomes is shown in Figure 11-3. Since monolithic leadership structures control the number and shape of important decisions, a concentration of power results in sub-

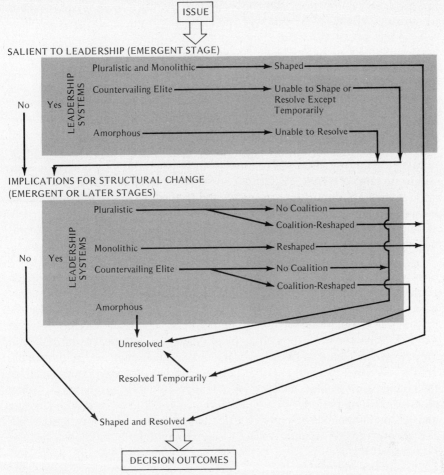

Figure 11-3.   Simplified Illustration of the Interrelationship of Leadership System Types, Program Saliency to Leadership, Implication for Social Change, and Issue Shaping and Resolution.

stantial activity or little activity as a result of leadership *consistently* influencing decision making on various types of issues in one direction. Therefore, two possibilities exist, depending upon the value system within the monolithic structure: The monolithic structure could effectively *block* most decisions, or, on the other hand, the power structure can actively seek and influence and direct programs in the community (Fowler, 1958). In both instances the element of control over community decisions is manifest. In monolithic communities if the issue is salient to the community leadership in the emergent stage, it is assumed that the program will be shaped and resolved in a fashion suitable to the leadership structure. At the emergent stage the community leadership structure probably will not become involved in the issue if there are no implications for structural change. On the other hand, if there are structural change implications in the proposed program either at the emergent or later stages, the issue becomes salient for the leadership and involvement results in a reshaping of the issue and/or proposed program.

Cities with a pluralistic power system probably offer the most opportunity for innovative problem solving. This is a result of their greater number of power centers, of the interlocking of these centers, and of a greater extent of interaction with each other. "For many issues this will mean the creation of an organization whose specific task is the implementation of the decision to innovate" (Aiken and Alford, 1970: 663) — housing authorities, welfare councils, and so on (also see Turk, 1970). Of course, the conditions that lead to the introduction of an innovation may not be the factors that are most conducive to high performance by organizations. Thus high performance may be more closely related to an additional factor of organizational autonomy — that is, having strong control over units concerned with the issue.

Both the countervailing elite and amorphous types are assumed to be *nearly incapable of reaching long-term decisions* or *sustaining decisions*. In the countervailing elite system this is a result of several centers of power alternately controlling community affairs. At times coalitions may be formed that will *temporarily* allow decisions to be implemented, but coalitions tend to be short term. Thus the countervailing elite model suggests a great deal of variability in the number and shape of decisions as the ebb and flow of power holding in the community fluctuates and as issues become more or less important to each of the countervailing elites. When there are approximately equal countervailing elites, alternating periods of dominance should result in programs undergoing changes in number, kinds, and shape. Extralocal community influences are expected to be greater upon this type of community than in the monolithic and pluralistic types.

In the amorphous type, inaction is a result of no decisions being made inasmuch as there are no major power centers but many *veto* groups. The large number of power centers have not coalesced into an effective decision-making or controlling system for community affairs, and/or there is a high level of citizen participation that generates conflict and ineffective decision making (Crain and Rosenthal, 1967). It is expected that such cities will stagnate; if there is activity, it is probably a result of the imposition by extracommunity forces.

While each of the foregoing indicated assumptions is testable and assumes *patterned* relationships between leadership structures and community decision making, and the consequent number and shape of community programs, little research has been carried out to verify such hypotheses. However, in Chapter 5, several different studies were examined that interrelated city and urban characteristics with a variety of outcomes. Therefore, in this section we shall review only several additional research efforts that illustrate how power structures have influenced outcomes.

Hawley (1963) has presented substantial evidence that the managerial component of the labor force (or the MPO ratio, which he uses as a measure of power) is associated with urban-renewal programs. Cities in the "execution" stage consistently had a higher degree of power than those in the "dropout" or "never in program" stage. The findings in an analysis examining public welfare and antipoverty expenditures, also using the MPO ratio as a measure of power, were just the opposite of Hawley's inasmuch as a high concentration of power was associated with such programs only *when* there was a high percent of white unemployed (Paulson et al., 1969). It should be noted that Hawley's sample consisted of larger cities, whereas the latter study used counties in a southern state as the unit of analysis (see Turk, however, 1970), and Williams (1973) has argued that the MPO ratio may not be a reliable and valid measure of power.

Other studies tend to show that general community characteristics account for variation in outcomes. For example, a comparative study of 51 cities in the United States showed the impact that the percent of Roman Catholics has on urban-renewal expenditures and on about two-thirds of all other budget items (Clark, 1968: 589).[4]

Finally, a more elaborate and complex formulation was advanced by D'Antonio and Erickson (1962: 375), who noted in their studies along the American-Mexican border that few cities had the monolithic power elite described by Hunter and others and that these cities also did not fit the pluralist model. A more apt description is that while there may not be a single power elite, there is a small group of persons whose influence is "general" and cuts across many issues, although at times these persons may be in contention with each other in regard to the outcomes of decisions. Again, whether this can be generalized or is a characteristic of border cities has not been determined; however, a study of 18 New England communities showed some very strong similarities (Gamson, 1966).

Long (1958) advanced a view contrary to all of these others: When cities and decision making are examined quite closely, there is *no* structured decision making. Long believes issues are resolved by the development of a system of unintended cooperation among interest groups and institutions. Unintentional coalitions deal with metropolitan problems from a limited perspective, that is, one confined to their particular interest or institutional

[4] This study is valuable insofar as it shows how comparative analysis is much more useful than case studies in studying power structure, community characteristics, and decision outcomes. Nevertheless, two major deficiencies probably influenced the results. First, the measure of power is such that all of the cities have monolithic structures, with only slightly varying degrees. Thus the discussion about centralized versus decentralized structures needs to be recouched in terms of degrees of centralized decision making. Second, some of the data are inconsistent — for example, budget expenditures are most highly correlated with the percent of population that is Roman Catholic; yet the author notes that there is a tendency for "a community to spend more than others nearby by taxing it's industries, is more a suburban than a general phenomenon" (p. 590). These two findings are incompatible, since most Catholics live in central cities and not in the suburbs. In any case, this study should be read but closely examined and carefully evaluated.

base. Thus he argued that the debate in the power structure literature is misplaced because it may have obscured the possibility that *no one is systematically making decisions*. From this point of view fragmentation and competitive patterns exist in community decision making.

Although this may appear to be the case, few studies have examined the full range of issues that come before a community and an individual decision maker. In addition, most of the issues and outcomes examined have been dramatic or controversial rather than of the everyday type that affect the local community. Similarly, few studies conducted so far have been comparative in nature; that is, they do not compare a large number of cities in regard to a variety of dramatic and nondramatic issues, decisions made in regard to them, and their subsequent outcomes (Rossi, 1957).

Notwithstanding the relative lack of knowledge, it is unfortunate that the flow of power structure studies, especially as they have been interrelated with outcomes, has slowed over the past few years. It still appears that a reliable and valid measure of power at the city and urban level needs to be developed.

BIBLIOGRAPHY: Articles

Abu-Laban, Baha, "Self-Conception and Appraisal by Others: A Study of Community Leaders," *Sociology and Social Research*, 48 (October 1963): 32–37.

Aiken, Michael, and Robert R. Alford, "Community Structure and Innovation: The Case of Urban Revewal," *American Sociological Review*, 35 (August 1970): 650–665.

Allen, Michael P., "The Structure of Interorganizational Elite Cooptation: Interlocking Corporate Directorates," *American Sociological Review*, 39 (June 1974): 393–406.

Anton, Thomas F., "Power, Pluralism, and Local Politics," *Administrative Science Quarterly*, 7 (March 1963): 425–457.

Bachrach, Peter, and Morton S. Baratz, "Decisions and Non-decisions: An Analytical Framework," *American Political Science Review*, 57 (September 1963): 632–642.

Barth, Ernest A. T., and Stuart D. Johnson, "Community Power and a Typology of Social Issues," *Social Forces*, 38 (May 1960): 29–32.

Belknap, George, and Ralph Smuckler, "Political Power Relations in a Mid-West City," *Public Opinion Quarterly*, 20 (Spring 1958): 73–81.

Bierstedt, Robert, "An Analysis of Social Power," *American Sociological Review*, 15 (December 1950): 730–738.

Blankenship, L. Vaughn, "Community Power and Decision-Making: A Comparative Evaluation of Measurement Techniques," *Social Forces*, 43 (December 1964): 207–216.

Bonjean, Charles M., "Community Leadership: A Case Study and Conceptual Refinement," *American Journal of Sociology*, 68 (May 1963): 672–681.

Bonjean, Charles M., and Lewis F. Carter, "Legitimacy and Visibility Leadership Structures Related to Four Community Systems," *Pacific Sociological Review*, 8 (Spring 1965): 16–20.

Bonjean, Charles M., and David M. Olson, "Community Leadership: Directions of Research," *Administrative Science Quarterly*, 9 (December 1964): 278–300.

Booth, David A., and Charles R. Adrian, "Power Structure and Community Change: A Replication Study of Community A," *Midwest Journal of Political Science*, 6 (August 1962): 277–296.

Clark, Terry N., "Community Structure, Decision-Making, Budget Expenditures, and Urban Renewal in 51 American Communities," *American Sociological Review*, 33, (August 1968): 576–593.

Clark, Terry N., "Power and Community Structure: Who Governs, Where and When," *Sociological Quarterly*, 8 (Summer 1967): 291–316.

Clark, Terry N., William Kornblum, Harold Bloom, and Susan Tobias, "Discipline, Method, Community Structure, and Decision-Making: The Role and Limitations of the Sociology of Knowledge," *The American Sociologist*, 3 (August 1968): 214–217.

Crain, Robert L., and Donald B. Rosenthal, "Community Status as a Dimension of Local Decision-Making," *American Sociological Review*, 32 (December 1967): 970–984.

D'Antonio, William V., and Eugene C., Erickson, "The Reputational Technique as a Measure of Community Power: An Evaluation Based on Comparative and Longitudinal Studies," *American Sociological Review*, 27 (June 1962): 362–376.

Danzger, M. Herbert, "Community Power Structure: Problems and Continuities," *American Sociological Review*, 29 (October 1964): 707–717.

Duncan, Otis Dudley, and Leo F. Schnore, "Cultural, Behavioral, and Ecological Perspectives in the Study of Social Organization," *American Journal of Sociology*, 65 (September 1959): 132–146.

Ehrlich, Howard J., "The Social Psychology of Reputations for Community Leadership," *Sociological Quarterly*, 8 (Autumn 1967): 514–530.

Form, William H., and Warren T. Sauer, "Organized Labor's Image of Community Power Structure," *Social Forces*, 38 (May 1960): 332–341.

Fowler, Irving A., "Local Industrial Structures, Economic Power, and Community Welfare," *Social Problems*, 6 (Summer 1958): 41–50.

Freeman, Linton N., Thomas J. Fararo, Warner Bloomberg, Jr., and Morris H. Sunshine, "Locating Leaders in Local Communities: A Comparison of Some Alternative Approaches," *American Sociological Review*, 28 (October 1963): 791–798.

Gamson, William A., "Reputation and Resources in Community Politics," *American Journal of Sociology*, 72 (September 1966): 121–131.

Gereffi, Gary A., "Dimensions of Community Power: A Study of an Unincorporated Town," *Sociological Focus*, 3 (Summer 1970): 43–64.

Gilbert, Claire W., "Some Trends in Community Politics: A Secondary Analysis of Power Structure Data from 166 Communities," *Social Science Quarterly*, 48 (December 1967): 373–381.

Goldberg, Kalman, and Robin Linstromberg, "A Revision of Some Theories of Economic Power," *Quarterly Review of Economics and Business*, 6 (Spring 1966): 7–17.

Hawley, Amos H., "Community Power and Urban Renewal Success," *American Journal of Sociology*, 68 (January 1963): 422–431.

Long, Norton E., "The Local Community as an Ecology of Games," *American Journal of Sociology*, 64 (November 1958): 251–261.

McKee, James B., "Status and Power in the Industrial Community: A Comment on Drucker's Thesis," *American Journal of Sociology*, 58 (January 1953): 364–370.

Michel, Jerry B., "Measurement of Social Power on the Community Level," *American Journal of Economics and Sociology*, 23 (April 1964): 189–196.

Miller, Delbert C., and James L. Dirksen, "The Identification of Visible Leaders in a Small Indiana City: A Replication of the Bonjean-Noland Study of Burlington, North Carolina," *Social Forces*, 43 (May 1965): 548–555.

Paulson, Wayne, Edgar W. Butler, and Hallowell Pope, "Community Power and Public Welfare," *American Journal of Economics and Sociology*, 28 (January 1969): 17–28.

Pelligrin, Roland J., and Charles H. Coates, "Absentee-Owned Corporations and Community Power Structure," *American Journal of Sociology*, 61 (March 1956): 413–419.

Perruci, Robert, and Marc Pilisuk, "Leaders and Ruling Elites: The Interorganizational Bases of Community Power," *American Sociological Review*, 35 (December 1970): 1040–1057.

Polsby, Nelson W., "Community Power: Some Reflections on the Recent Literature," *American Sociological Review*, 27 (December 1962): 838–847.

Preston, James D., "The Search for Community Leaders: A Re-examination of the Reputational Technique," *Sociological Inquiry*, 39 (Winter 1969): 39–47.

Rossi, Peter H., "Community Decision-Making," *Administrative Science Quarterly*, 1 (March 1957): 438–439.

Schulze, Robert O., "Economic Dominants in Community Power Structure," *American Sociological Review*, 23 (February 1958): 3–9.

Turk, Herman, "Interorganizational Networks in Urban Society: Initial Perspectives and Comparative Research," *American Sociological Review*, 35 (February 1970): 1–19.

Walton, John, "The Vertical Axis of Community Organization and the Structure of Power," *Social Science Quarterly*, 48 (December 1967): 353–368.

Walton, John, "Research Note: Substance and Artifact: The Current Status of Research on Community Power Structure," *American Journal of Sociology*, 71 (January 1966): 430–438.

Warren, Roland L., "Toward a Typology of Extra-Community Controls Limiting Local Community Autonomy," *Social Forces*, 34 (May 1956): 338–341.

Williams, James M., "The Ecological Approach in Measuring Community Power Concentration: An Analysis of Hawley's MPO Ratio," *American Sociological Review*, 38 (April 1973): 230–242.

Wolfinger, Raymond E., "Reputation and Reality in the Study of Community Power," *American Sociological Review*, 25 (October 1960): 636–644.

BIBLIOGRAPHY: Books

Agger, Robert E., Daniel Goldrich, and Bert E. Swanson, *The Rulers and the Ruled*, New York: John Wiley & Sons, Inc. 1964.

Boskoff, Alvin, *The Sociology of Urban Regions*, 2nd ed., New York: Appleton-Century-Crofts, 1970.

Burgess, M. Elaine, *Negro Leadership in a Southern City*, Chapel Hill, N.C.: University of North Carolina Press, 1962.

Clark, Terry N. (ed.), *Community Structure and Decision-Making: Comaparative Analyses*, San Francisco: Chandler Publishing Company, 1968.

Cole, William E., *Urban Society*, Boston: Houghton Mifflin Company, 1958.

Coleman, James S., *Community Conflict*, Glencoe, Ill.: The Free Press, 1957.

Dahl, Robert A., *Who Governs?* New Haven, Conn.: Yale University Press, 1961.

Domhoff, G. William, *Who Rules America?* Englewood Cliffs, N.J., 1967.

Freeman, Linton, et al., *Local Community Leadership,* Syracuse, N.Y.: University College of Syracuse University, 1960.

Galbraith, John, *American Capitalism: The Concept of Countervailing Power,* rev. ed., Boston: Houghton Mifflin, 1956.

Gilbert, Claire, "The Study of Community Power: A Summary and a Test," in Scott Greer, Dennis L. David, W. Minar, and Peter Orleans (eds.), *The New Urbanization,* New York: St. Martin's Press, 1968, pp. 222–245.

Hawley, Amos H., *Urban Society,* New York: Ronald Press, 1971.

Hawley, Amos H., *Human Ecology,* New York: Ronald Press, 1950.

Hodges, Wayne, *Company and Community,* New York: Harper & Row, Publishers, 1958.

Hunter, Floyd, *Top Leadership, U.S.A.,* Chapel Hill, N.C.: University of North Carolina Press, 1959.

Hunter, Floyd, *Community Power Structure: A Study of Decision Makers,* Chapel Hill, N.C.: University of North Carolina Press, 1953.

Jennings, M. Kent, *Community Influentials,* New York: The Free Press, 1964.

Lasswell, Harold D., and Abraham Kaplan, *Power and Society,* New Haven, Conn.: Yale University Press, 1950.

Lenski, Gerhard E., *Power and Privilege,* New York: McGraw-Hill Book Co., 1966.

Lundberg, Ferdinand, *The Rich and the Super-Rich,* New York: Lyle Stuart, Inc., 1968.

Lynd, Robert, and Helen Lynd, *Middletown in Transition,* New York: Harcourt, Brace, 1937.

Lynd, Robert, and Helen Lynd, *Middletown,* New York: Harcourt, Brace, 1929.

Martin, Roscoe C., Frank J. Munger, et al., *Decisions in Syracuse,* Bloomington, Ind.: Indiana University Press, 1961.

Mills, C. Wright, *The Power Elite,* New York: Oxford University Press, 1959.

Presthus, Robert, *Men at the Top,* New York: Oxford University Press, 1964.

Report of the Federal Trade Commission on Interlocking Directorates, Washington, D.C.: U.S. Printing Office, 1951.

Riesman, David, Nathan Glazer, and Reuel Denney, *The Lonely Crowd: A Study of the Changing American Character,* Garden City, N.Y.: Doubleday & Company, 1956.

Rogers, David, "Community Political Systems: A Framework and Hypothesis for Comparative Studies," in Bert E. Swanson (ed.), *Current Trends in Comparative Community Studies,* Kansas City, Mo.: Community Studies, Inc., 1962, pp. 31–48.

Rose, Arnold M., *The Power Structure: Political Process in American Society,* New York: Oxford University Press, 1967.

Sayre, Wallace S., and Nelson W. Polsby, "American Political Science and the Study of Urbanization," in Philip M. Hauser and Leo F. Schnore (eds.), *The Study of Urbanization,* New York: John Wiley & Sons, Inc., 1965, pp. 115–156.

Schermerhorn, Richard A., *Society and Power,* New York: Random House, 1961.

Smuckler, Ralph H., and George M. Belknap, *Leadership and Participation in Urban Political Affairs,* East Lansing: The Government Research Bureau, 1956.

Thompson, Daniel C., *The Negro Leadership Class,* Englewood Cliffs, N.J.: Prentice-Hall, 1963.

Warren, Roland L., *The Community in America,* Chicago: Rand McNally & Company, 1963.

Weber, Max, *The Theory of Social and Economic Organization,* trans. by A. M. Henderson and Talcott Parsons, Glencoe, Ill.: The Free Press, 1957.

ORGANIZATION OF URBAN LIFE

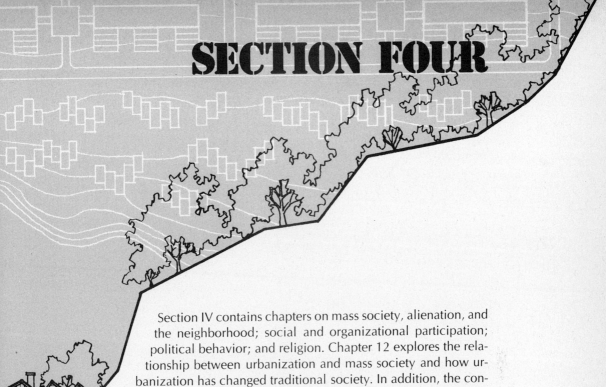

SECTION FOUR

Section IV contains chapters on mass society, alienation, and the neighborhood; social and organizational participation; political behavior; and religion. Chapter 12 explores the relationship between urbanization and mass society and how urbanization has changed traditional society. In addition, the concepts of community, neighborhood, and alienation are examined in relationship to urbanization. Chapter 13 examines social and organizational participation and shows how urbanization affects social participation; it also demonstrates the varieties of interaction with kin, neighbors, friends, and of expressive and instrumental voluntary organizations in urban regions. In addition, it shows how these variations in social participation patterns are linked to area of residence in the urban complex, social class, and ethnicity. The chapters on political and religious behavior explore in more detail the same kinds of spatial, social class, and ethnic factors upon such behavior in urban complexes. In addition, some of the common assumptions about political and religious behavior in contemporary urban areas of the United States are made explicit.

CHAPTER 12
MASS SOCIETY, ALIENATION, AND THE NEIGHBORHOOD

INTRODUCTION

The notion of the alienation[1] of man from society, especially in contemporary urbanized America, is a prevalent one today. The urban mode of life, it is believed, tends to create solitary souls, uproot the individual from his customs, confront him or her with a social void, and weaken traditional restraints on personal conduct. Personal existence and social solidarity in the urban society appear to hang together by a slender thread. There is the feeling that relations among people are based upon a pecuniary nexus and that the very existence of relations is capable of being disturbed by a multitude of forces over which the individual has little or no control. This has led to a sense of individual helplessness and a feeling of despair and estrangement from society (Josephson and Josephson, 1962).

Human beings are conceived as being unstable, inadequate, and insecure because they are cut off from the channels of social membership and clear beliefs. Further, rapid change and dislocation in society are followed by an increasing scale of personal disorganization. These dislocations and changes are considered as being in conflict with the desire for cultural participation, social belonging, and personal status. Clearly what exists here is a postulated conflict between what has been called "community"—that is, the family, the religious association, and the local neighborhood, and the intimate relationships generally reported as being found there—and the release of human beings from the boundaries of the community and the extensive "freedom" gained from this release. A concomitant of the release from community is the isolation of the individual from his or her cultural heritage, the isolation of individuals from their fellows, and the creation of sprawling, faceless masses—the mass society.

[1] A number of articles have dealt with the meaning of alienation: Nettler (1957), Seeman (1959), Dean (1961), Browning et al. (1961), McClosky and Schaar (1965), and Neal and Rettig (1967).

People may be literally surrounded by others yet feel profoundly isolated and alienated from society. This group of unemployment-insurance recipients surely have something in common, but they share no sense of "community."

As a result, Nisbet (1953) suggested that "increasingly individuals seek escape from the freedom of impersonality, secularism, and individualism." They look for community in marriage, in attachment rather than commitment to religion, in the psychiatrist's couch, in cults, and in pseudointimacies with others. A question of utmost importance, then, is: Where is man to find status and security? For some these are gained in the primary associations of family, neighborhood, and church; for others they are obtained in large-scale organizations. And some others who perhaps have economic security have few intimate, personal relationships—for them freedom from constraints has been obtained. In subsequent chapters we shall examine the extent of social and organizational participation, participation in neighborhood cliques, kinship patterns, and political and religious participation. In the remainder of this chapter the discussion will focus on the modern individual in mass society, the community, the neighborhood, and alienation.

MASS SOCIETY

Ordinarily, alienation is generally believed to have originated with the development of industrialization and the mass society. Mass society is characterized by the evaporation of moral bonds, the shriveling of kinship and traditional institutions and beliefs, and the isolation of the individual from his or her fellows; this characterization is supposed to typify modern Western society, including the United States (Shils, 1960). Thus the image of mass society is one of a territorially extensive society, having a large population, and being highly urbanized and industrialized. Power is concentrated, and often the masses are manipulated through the mass communication media. Civic spirit is poor; local loyalties are few; and basic social solidarity is nonexistent. There is no individuality, only egoism, and when isolation from mass society exists, it results in extremist responses (Gusfield, 1962). In this country mass society had its first great visibility between World War I and World War II, and without a doubt it is characteristic of the era since World War II.

Some of the characteristics of the mass society have led to a whole series of conditions that some people interpret as being responsible for the social problems that currently exist in the United States. Recently, Shils (1960) has pointed out another perspective on the mass society that has been relatively neglected. It is discussed at some length because it brings together the mass society and the neighborhood, or community (Wilensky, 1964). This contrary point of view, however, evaluates both the negative and positive aspects of mass society. In this view there is a nationwide market economy dominated by large nationwide corporations and by central governmental regulations or, in some other countries, by a socialistically planned economy. In either case the net results are the same. One positive result not ordinarily considered is the higher level of educational attainment, the higher degree of literacy, and the greater availability of cultural products such as newspapers, television, and records. Moreover, mass society has made the culture available to almost all of the population, whereas previously it had been available only to a small elite. One outgrowth of the mass society and the spread of its culture has been the idea of a common citizenship extending over a vast territory, for example, the United States. Thus the confines of kinship, caste, religious belief, and feudal boundaries have been broken down. The negative aspect of this breakdown has, some have argued, resulted in alienation of the population.

The mass society includes the entire population of the society in its central institutions. In contrast to traditional society, it requires a rather substantial consensus about the central social *institutions*. Hence, despite internal conflicts, within the mass society there is more sense of attachment to the society as a whole, more sense of affinity with one's fellows, more openness to understanding, and more common understanding among mankind than at any previous point in history. The mass society is not the most peaceful or orderly society that has ever existed, but it is the most consensual. Even today, of course, the elite and the masses do not have identical life styles, tastes, or outlooks, but the mass has more influence now than it did in earlier societies.

As a result of the growth of mass society, authority structures have changed markedly. Formerly, the authority hierarchy had direct control over the citizens, primarily exerted by tradition. Obviously, traditions continue to exert their influence, but they are less important now than formerly, more ambiguous, and more open to divergent interpretations. Those who have alternative life styles are both the product of the mass society and part of the problems that have arisen out of it. Earlier societies did not usually tolerate divergent life styles. The decline in traditional authority is shown by the less authoritative relationship of adults to children—a shift brought about by mass society and the cause of problems. Similarly, the increased freedom of the working classes, women, youth, and ethnic groups, as well as their emphasis on their rights, is both a product of the mass society and the cause of special and unique problems. The dispersion of the mass culture to a whole variety of ethnic groups and peoples was made possible by the greater stress on individual dignity and rights in mass society. Obviously, inequalities remain, partly as a carry-over of old traditions; but they are much less severe than in traditional society. Individuality, personal relationships, and love, while not original with mass society, have come to be regarded as part of the rights of everyone.

It has been argued that mass society has brought about a loss of individuality through the dull acceptance of what is readily available; and since what is readily available is so widespread, it produces mass mediocrity. Relatively speaking, however, mass society presents many more choices in more spheres of life than ever before—moreover, these choices are not made for the individual only by tradition, authority, and scarcity. Obviously, choices made may be unwise or ill considered, but they do exist; the individual in the mass society need not dumbly accept what has been handed down by tradition. Thus, it is argued, although a significant proportion of the population in every society has lived in a nearly vegetative routine, this proportion is much less in the mass society.

A two-handed aspect of mass society is that it is a welfare society. This means that the society pays more attention and concern to the well-being of its members. This, of course, is not necessarily related to the industrialization that has taken place nor necessarily to the poverty or other social conditions that exist and that many believe need to be solved. Rather, it is only in the mass society that problem conditions are considered as needing redress because concern for the well-being of its members exists.

Part of the alienation believed to exist in mass society is related to the nature of industrialized work. In earlier societies one did not have the time to be alienated, since survival depended upon how successfully work was done—for instance, hunting, farming, and so on. Without industrialization, mass society would not be possible, nor would the elaborate networks of communication and transportation. These networks permit heightened mutual awareness of the well-being and concerns of others in the mass society and have enlarged the internal population that dwells in the minds of people to include, for example, the national and international spheres. Byproducts of industrialization are the intellectual professions and the educational system. While deficiencies exist in the educational system, the mass society opened it up to virtually the entire population and exposed the human mind to the varieties of experience and to other people.

A paradox of the mass society made possible by its technology is the desire for achievement in occupational roles, which have at the same time become, for the most part, less important in the guidance of human behavior and status.

A contrasting view of the mass society characterizes it as alienated, without beliefs, atomized, amoral, conformist, rootlessly homogeneous, morally empty, faceless, egotistical, lacking in loyalty. Actually, of course, all of these facets do exist in mass society, but a great deal more also exists. It should be emphasized too that the mass society arose from a society that was inegalitarian, against a background of puritanical authority, local allegiances, traditional authority and social control structures, and an unbelievable poverty and drudgery of work.

Thus the world of modern urban man and woman in much of the literature is pictured as being separate and distinct from his and her counterparts in the past. Early sociologists pictured the megalopolis—the mass city—as being culturally heterogeneous, dominated by bureaucratic structures and mass media, and destroying the smaller units of society. More recently, however, the importance that organizations and social interaction (Nisbet, 1953) play in mediating the relationship of isolated individuals to the mass society has been stressed. Current literature emphasizes that the contemporary metropolis consists of different individual areas that are highly variable in the extent to which they have organizations and social interaction patterns that help mediate between the individual and the mass society. The mediating relationships are worked out in what are ordinarily thought of as informal social groups: sewing circles, peer groups, groups of neighbors, friends, relatives, and so on. Formal organizations include, among others, service organizations, child-oriented organizations, and the church.

URBANIZATION AND THE MASS SOCIETY

The trend toward a mass society began a number of years ago as changing technology made possible more efficient forms of transportation and, of course, the Industrial Revolution. The movement of vast numbers of people from the countrysides to the cities made it more difficult to form and maintain the highly integrated forms of social existence that are possible in isolated areas and small villages. Similarly, changes in traditional institutions, such as the family and church, reduced some of their impact and influence and increased that of the larger, impersonal community.

Improvements in transportation and the means of production resulted in a loss of basic economic security and security of owning a plot of land. Industrialization made labor appear to be merely another cog in the production wheel of goods and services, and workers felt a loss of individuality. The trend away from a folk society and toward a mass society had social aspects that have been noted throughout this book. Among them are the great migrations from the countrysides to the cities, the separation of workplace and residence,

Ordinarily, communities are considered to be small geographic places, like this New Hampshire village. Yet a community may consist of an ethnic area or a particularly close-knit neighborhood—such as one of long-time residents—within a large and multi-faceted city.

the increasingly large and complex settlements (e.g., the development of metropolitan complexes), the changing functions of the family—education, economic production, and so forth—and the changing roles of the church and other institutions of society (Rose, 1967: 181–212).

COMMUNITY

"Community" is a widely used term in the vocabulary of sociologists. Yet sociologists know only too well how ill defined and imprecise the concept of community really is. Hillery (1955) measured the depths of this confusion by examining a wide variety of definitions. Out of his work came the conclusion that the definitions of community are almost as varied as the number of sociologists who deal with the concept. Nevertheless, the extensive use of the term suggests that it attempts to define something that many people see as important. "Neighborhoods, suburban municipalities, and central cities, as well as the monastery and beehive, are spoken of as communities" (Bollens and Schmandt, 1965: 44).

Sociologically, communities may be described as having certain territorial limits and as being organized in some fashion to meet human needs. Other characteristics are face-to-face associations, a common way of life, common ends, means, and goals, social completeness and self-sufficiency, a collection of institutions, and an interdependent way of life. Other definitions assume a sense of identity, common values, terminology, and language, social control or power over members, and reasonably clear limits (social and/or geographical) of the community.

FIGURE 12-1
Selected Characteristics of Moral Communities and Mass Societies

MORAL COMMUNITIES (GEMEINSCHAFT)	MASS SOCIETIES (GESELLSCHAFT)
IDENTIFICATION	ALIENATION
Members of the moral community have a deep sense of belonging to significant, meaningful groups.	Members of mass society have a deep sense of being cut off from meaningful group associations.
MORAL UNITY	MORAL FRAGMENTATION
Members of the moral community have a sense of pursuing common goals and feel a oneness with other community members.	Members of mass society have a sense of pursuing divergent goals and feel no sense of oneness with other members of the mass society.
INVOLVEMENT	DISENGAGEMENT
Members of the moral community are submerged in various groups and have a compelling need to participate in these groups.	Members of mass society have no meaningful group memberships and feel no compulsion to participate in the collective activities of various groups.
WHOLENESS	SEGMENTATION
Members of the moral community regard each other as whole persons who are of intrinsic significance and worth.	Members of mass society regard each other as means to ends and assign no intrinsic worth or significance to the individual.

Source: Poplin (1972).

Some writers have discussed similar notions but used other terms: folk society (Redfield, 1930, 1947, 1955); moral communities versus mass societies; Gemeinschaft versus Gesellschaft; mechanical and organic solidarity (Durkheim, 1951). At their polar extremes these notions are illustrated in Figure 12-1).

As shown in Figure 12-2, this perspective also assumes that as size, density, and heterogeneity increase, the individual is seen as losing the capacity to integrate diverse elements of his or her existence into a recognizable, understandable, and manageable whole. As a result, much of the environment is depersonalized, and, it is believed, there has been a loss of control over it. According to this orientation, to regain control over the environment, and to have a feeling of belongingness, is to reduce its complexity, density, and size.

Finally, Hawley's (1950: 157–258) definition of community as "that area, the resident population of which is interrelated and integrated with reference to its daily requirements, whether contacts be direct or indirect," is closely allied to another concept extensively employed—neighborhood.

FIGURE 12-2
A Typology of Communical Units

	COMMUNAL UNIT		
	VILLAGE	CITY	METROPOLITAN AREA
DEMOGRAPHIC CHARACTERISTICS			
Size of Population	small (under 10,000?)	intermediate (10–50,000?)	large (over 50,000?)
Density of Population	low	intermediate	high
COMMUNITY-HINTERLAND RELATIONS			
Hinterland Population	small	variable	large
Community's Influence over Hinterland	limited	variable	extensive
Number of Community-Hinterland Ties	few	variable	many
SOCIO-CULTURAL CHARACTERISTICS			
Heterogeneity of Population	low	intermediate	high
Availability of Organizations and Services	limited	intermediate	extensive
Division of Labor	low	intermediate	high
Potential Anonymity of the Individual	low	variable	high
Predominant Character of Social Relations	primary	secondary	secondary
Predominant Type of Social Control	primary	secondary	secondary
Degree of Status Ranking on Basis of Overt Symbols	low	intermediate	high

Source: Poplin (1972: 29–59).

THE NEIGHBORHOOD

The community most frequently identified as a meaningful social unit in mass society is the neighborhood (Thomlinson, 1969: 181). Neighborhoods in mass society are important because they are (1) persistent forces affecting the personality and behavior of residents and (2) the character of a neighborhood is determined by its inhabitants.[2] According to the standard definition, not all areas within a metropolis or urban region qualify as a neighborhood. The meaning of neighborhood varies; however, descriptions of this concept usually involve at least three elements: (1) spatial proximity to some focus of attention; (2) physical or cultural differentiation from surrounding areas; and (3) intimacy

[2] For a general theoretical treatment of the concept of neighborhood see Keller (1968).

of association among inhabitants of an area.[3] For a neighborhood to exist in the metropolis requires that individuals be willing to limit leisure-time activities to those persons living within easy walking distance and willing to congregate within the residential neighborhood with like-minded and like-interested people. "Such conditions are the exception in the modern city" (Riemer, 1951: 43).

Is it possible for neighborhoods and neighboring to persist in the urban environment? Some believe that they cannot; but others who might agree that the traditional neighborhood is disappearing believe that they are merely developing into different forms. The city is a place where people reside in residential areas larger than neighborhoods rather than living in rural or village neighborhoods as in the past. As shown earlier (Chapter 9), urbanites may work, shop, and carry on recreational and religious activities away from their immediate neighborhoods. Personal friends may be scattered over a metropolitan region rather than in the neighborhood. Special-interest groups increasingly take up more time, energy, and money and leave less time for localized activities.

Where the elements of neighborhoods exist, they are strong forces affecting the personality and behavior of residents (Thomlinsòn, 1969: 181). Also, it has been noted that the reverse is true: "The character of a neighborhood is determined by its inhabitants." Nevertheless, not all areas within the metropolitan complex form neighborhoods under the common definitions of the term. At least one study suggested, however, that some areas within the metropolitan regions of Boston and Chicago (Ross, 1962) are viewed as neighborhoods by their residents. A commonly accepted name for the neighborhood existed and was recognized by the residents of the area as well as by many people residing elsewhere in the metropolis; generally, though, there was some discrepancy concerning the actual boundaries of the neighborhood, except when such boundaries were formed by barriers such as parks, rivers, and large streets. Names of areas were shown to have class and ethnic connotations, which were in agreement with census data. On the other hand, little use was made of local facilities except in common convenience items, and this localized use was common from area to area. Most sections of cities — and large portions of many cities — do not have neighborhoods in the standard sense (Thomlinson, 1969: 182). Rather, they are areas with an aggregation of individuals.

ALIENATION

A major element in the mass society perspective is alienation. The assumption that it is universal in our mass society has not been tested, and there is still a lack of consensus on a definition (Taviss, 1969). Particularly evident in

[3] This definition of neighborhood is similar to Hatt's (1946) conception of a *natural area,* which he defined as follows: "(1) A spatial unit limited by natural boundaries enclosing a homogenous population with a characteristic moral order and (2) a spatial unit inhabited by a population united on the basis of interrelatedness among its residents."

various definitions of alienation is the distinction between "alienation from self" and "alienation from society." In alienation from society the individual believes that the social system is oppressive or incompatible with his or her desires; self-alienation means that the individuals manipulate themselves in accordance with apparent social demands and feel incapable of controlling their own actions. "The socially alienated maintain distance from society, while the self-alienated engage in self-manipulatory behavior so as to eliminate this distance" (Taviss, 1969: 47).

From magazine stories at two different time periods (the 1900s and the 1950s), it appears the later period contained a higher proportion of stories with alienation themes. During this time span, however, social alienation themes decreased slightly; thus self-alienation showed a larger overall increase *and* a heightened intensity. "Contributing most heavily to this increase are the sense of lack of control over one's own behavior and the deliberate development of a particular style of response in order to influence or manipulate others" (Taviss, 1969: 51).

In a further refinement Faia (1967: 399) noted that alienation may be from society at large or from specific milieus within society, and the consequences of the two types of alienation may be quite different. Faia (1967: 390) has proposed the following two models:

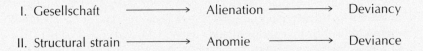

I. Gesellschaft   ⟶   Alienation ⟶ Deviancy

II. Structural strain ⟶ Anomie   ⟶ Deviance

The first model stresses the idea of anonymity, impersonality, social isolation, bureaucratization, and "urbanism as a way of life." The second model supersedes the first, according to Faia, because other theories that emphasize opportunity structures, differential association, and symbiotic relationships between deviant and normal social structures take into account self-alienation, social alienation, and alienation related to specific milieus with society.

Alienation has therefore come to mean many things. Among them is the feeling that people have when they cannot relate to the world around them. This may take the form of (1) estrangement from work, (2) feeling powerless in political affairs, (3) social isolation, and (4) cultural or value estrangement as a result of the breakdown of societal values (Seeman, 1971), and (5) generalized despair and distrust (anomia). One measure consistently used to measure *anomia*—alienation—is Srole's (1956) scale items,[4] which presumably measured the extent of *normlessness* of an individual, as originally conceived by Durkheim (1951).

---

[4] *Anomia* is normlessness at the individual level, whereas *anomie* is normlessness at the societal level. Not all authors make this distinction.

One strain of research (Model I) focuses on mass society with its emphasis on access to large-scale industrial bureaucratic structures; Model II focuses on class-oriented economic influences and opportunity structures. It has been noted, however, that there are managers in smaller enterprises and are owners in large-scale bureaucratic organizations (Nelson, 1968: 185). Thus a variety of possibilities exists, each suggesting somewhat different features in regard to alienation. The mass society approach assumes generalized alienation for workers, whereas a social class (economic) approach assumes that those who are *deprived* economically, whether they be workers *or* managers, are more likely to be alienated. For example, in a study of 28 Minnesota communities, it was generally found that owners were more likely to be anomic than managers — because of the latter's greater commitment to social and geographical mobility and higher economic status (Nelson, 1968: 191). But deprived owners tend to become antagonistic toward and reject the larger society, whereas anomia for managers is more related to their economic level. In general, this study showed that anomia was related more to economic deprivation (e.g., Model II) than access to bureaucratic structures.

While some argue that many workers in modern urban, industrialized societies are alienated from their jobs and employers, and that this is particularly evident for those workers whose jobs involve monotonous, unrewarding, and hard labor, Seeman (1971: 137) stresses that when propositions about alienation from work are tested, the supposed consequences generally do not materialize. Seeman (1971) found, in fact, that urbanites varied greatly in the degree of alienation and on four different types of alienation measures. As an example, those who exhibited work alienation did not necessarily also feel powerless. Thus he feels that the one-dimensional view of an alienated urbanite is incorrect and that of the various kinds of alienation, "powerlessness" has the most important consequences for individuals and society.

Urbanization and Alienation

Recently, it was reported that, on the basis of several different samples, community size and the powerlessness dimension of alienation are not associated. When a social isolation measure was used, a small correlation was found between community size and a sense of alienation. Attendance at meetings did not necessarily lessen the *feeling* of social isolation whereas having relatives living in the neighborhood did (Fischer, 1973). Thus overall this particular study *rejects* the idea that urbanism is associated very strongly with alienation. In another study of white Appalachians it was noted that under a variety of living conditions (urban and rural and migrant status) the level of anomia was relatively constant — between 32 and 35 percent. This same study, however, showed that rural southern migrants to Detroit had a lower percentage of anomics — 22 percent, while only 14 percent of native Detroiters were reported as such (Nelsen and Whitt, 1972: 382–383). These findings contrast directly, of course, with the hypothesis of increased alienation with urbanism.

There is less alienation in urban regions than in rural areas. One reason may be that for some rural people—like this West Virginia family—the hardships of day-to-day survival make problems like alienation too academic to think about.

An analysis of three upstate New York communities varying along urban-rural dimensions also casts doubt upon the assumption that anomia is more characteristic of urban than rural life (Mizruchi, 1969); it suggested that "differences between dwellers of large urban areas and those of less urbanized communities have often been exaggerated" (Mizruchi, 1960: 653).

Finally, a study of a city and a small county seat in a southeastern state found that the relationship between urbanism and anomia is a tenuous one. According to this study, the level of education accounts for apparent urban-rural differences in anomia among whites, while such differences do not exist at all for blacks (Killian and Grigg, 1962). More specifically, it was found that "Whites who place themselves in the upper or middle class are more likely to display high anomia if they live in the city rather than in the small town" (p. 664). On the other hand, black white-collar workers, if they live in rural areas, are more likely than other blacks to display anomia. Thus both position in the social structure and urban-rural residence may interact to influence anomia.

In summary, a simple proposition that mass society and/or urbanism is closely linked to alienation is not supported by current available research. There does appear to be some support for the idea that different socioeconomic circumstances and opportunity structures are linked to at least some types of alienation. Obviously, further theorizing and research are needed.

Variation in Alienation
Within Metropolitan Complexes

Given the extensive theoretical and speculative literature concerned with alienation, it is strange that so little information exists that examines alienation as it is spatially distributed in different areas throughout the metropolis. One study, using Srole's (1956) anomia scale, showed that such differences may systematically exist: Thirty-four percent of the residents, but only 15 percent of suburban residents of St. Louis were anomic (James, 1969: 194). The greater degree of anomia in the city was accounted for by those in the lower social classes. Also, gross differences between central city and suburb are somewhat misleading, since there is great differentiation among neighborhoods in both areas. On an individual level, persons with higher job levels, formal schooling, and household income were less likely to be anomic than their counterparts, leading to the conclusion that "disorganization" in the larger community and lower socioeconomic status on the individual level are associated with anomia (p. 195).

Somewhat similar results between the central city and the suburbs were reported for the Los Angeles SMSA, which showed that 45 percent of those residents were anomic, while in a suburb of the same SMSA the proportion of anomics was 36 percent (Miller and Butler, 1966: 404). Another study of four different areas of the Los Angeles metropolitan complex (Greer and Kube, 1959: 106–109), similar in socioeconomic status but varying along the social area dimension of urbanism (see Chapter 7), found that the more urbanized areas of Hollywood and Silver Lake had higher percentages of anomics (about 12 percent) than the more suburban areas of Eagle Rock and Temple City (about 9 percent). However, there was variation in the percentage of "semianomics" and "nonanomics," and thus there is some confusion as to whether or not urbanism within the metropolitan complex is closely linked with anomic status. The main determinant of anomia in this study appears to have been socioeconomic status and educational level, with those deprived of income and education being more likely than others to be anomic. Migrants to the Los Angeles metropolitan area generally were not any more likely than natives to be alienated; but lower-class migrants were more likely than natives to be alienated (Hunt and Butler, 1972).

In the Los Angeles metropolitan complex, when a sample of integrated middle-class blacks was compared with black ghetto residents, middle-class integrated blacks "had greater expectations for control of events that concerned them and less of a feeling of anomia." They also appeared to be oriented more toward the "mainstream" of society rather than toward segregated black institutions. "Alienation within the ghetto takes on a circular characteristic; not only is it a product of segregated living, it also acts to keep people locked in the traditional residential patterns" (Bullough, 1967: 477).

Finally, it appears that social class and education are closely linked to alienation. In a San Francisco study, for example, Bell (1957: 114) noted: "It seems clear from the results of this study that anomie is inversely related to economic status. This is true whether economic status is measured by individual or neighborhood variables." Similarly, anomia is related to social isolation. The relationship between neighborhood status and anomia indicates that the economic character of the neighborhood may play an important part in "sorting out persons having different degrees of anomie" (p. 115). Also, it appears that the neighborhood influence on anomia persists even when *individual* variables such as social participation, rural-urban background, age, and individual economic status are controlled.

Conclusion

Despite pleas for a decent burial (Lee, 1972), it is likely that alienation as a concept will continue to be used in sociological and urban literature. Meanwhile, it would be wise for those who read this literature to understand what the particular author may mean by the use of the term in the context of a particular study or essay. For example, "work alienation and powerlessness, two of the varieties of alienation most discussed in the contemporary literature, function independently (and generally in opposite ways): *high* work alienation and *low* powerlessness" tend to produce different kinds of behavior (Seeman, 1972: 15).

BIBLIOGRAPHY: Articles

Bell, Wendell, "Anomie, Social Isolation, and the Class Structure," *Sociometry*, 20 (June 1957): 105–116.

Browning, Charles J., Malcolm F. Farmer, H. David Kirk, and G. Duncan Mitchell, "On the Meaning of Alienation," *American Sociological Review*, 26 (October 1961): 780–781.

Bullough, Bonnie, "Alienation in the Ghetto," *American Journal of Sociology*, 72 (March 1967): 469–478.

Dean, Dwight G., "Alienation: Its Meaning and Measurement," *American Sociological Review*, 26 (October 1961): 753–758.

Faia, Michael A., "Alienation, Structural Strain, and Political Deviancy: A Test of Morton's Hypothesis," *Social Problems*, 14 (Spring 1967): 389–413.

Fischer, Claude S., "On Urban Alienations and Anomie: Powerlessness and Social Isolation," *American Sociological Review*, 38 (June 1973): 311–326.

Gusfield, Joseph R., "Mass Society and Extremist Politics," *American Sociological Review*, 27 (February 1962): 19–30.

Hatt, Paul, "The Concept of Natural Area," *American Sociological Review*, 11 (August 1946): 423–427.

Hillery, George A., Jr., "Villages, Cities, and Total Institutions," *American Sociological Review*, 28 (October 1963): 779–791.

Hillery, George A., "Definitions of Community: Areas of Agreement," *Rural Sociology*, 20 (June 1955): 111–123.

Hunt, Gerard, and Edgar W. Butler, "Migration, Participation and Alienation," *Sociology and Social Research*, 56 (July 1972): 440–452.

Killiam, Lewis H., and Charles H. Grigg, "Urbanism, Race and Anomia," *American Journal of Sociology*, 67 (May 1962): 661–665.

Lee, Alfred McClung, "An Obituary for 'Alienation,'" *Social Problems*, 20 (Summer 1972): 121–127.

McClosky, Herbert, and John H. Schaar, "Psychological Dimensions of Anomy," *American Sociological Review*, 30 (February 1965): 14–40.

McDill, Edward, and Jeanne Clare Ridley, "Status, Anomia, Political Alienation, and Political Participation," *American Journal of Sociology*, 68 (September 1962): 205–213.

Miller, Curtis R., and Edgar W. Butler, "Anomia and Eunomia: A Methodological Evaluation of Srole's Anomia Scale," *American Sociological Review*, 31 (June 1966): 400–406.

Mizruchi, Ephraim H., "Social Structure and Anomia in a Small City," *American Sociological Review*, 25 (October 1960): 645–654.

Neal, Arthur G., and Solomon Rettig, "On the Multidimensionality of Alienation," *American Sociological Review*, 32 (February 1967): 54–64.

Nelsen, Hart M., and Hugh P. Whitt, "Religion and the Migrant to the City: A Test of Holt's Cultural Shock Thesis," *Social Forces*, 50 (March 1972): 379–384.

Nelson, Joel I., "Anomie: Comparisons Between the Old and New Middle Class," *American Journal of Sociology*, 74 (September 1968): 184–192.

Nettler, Gwenn, "A Measure of Alienation," *American Sociological Review*, 22 (December 1957): 670–677.

Redfield, Robert, "The Folk Society," *American Journal of Sociology*, 41 (January 1957): 293–308.

Riemer, Svend, "Villagers in Metropolis," *British Journal of Sociology*, 11 (March 1951): 31–43.

Ross, H. Laurence, "The Local Community: A Survey Approach," *American Sociological Review*, 27 (February 1962): 75–84.

Seeman, Melvin, "Alienation and Knowledge-Seeking: A Note on Attitude and Action," *Social Problems*, 20 (Summer 1972): 3–17.

Seeman, Melvin, "The Urban Alienations: Some Dubious Theses from Marx to Marcuse," *Journal of Personality and Social Psychology*, 19 (August 1971): 135–143.

Seeman, Melvin, "On the Meaning of Alienation," *American Sociological Review*, 24 (December 1959): 783–791.

Shils, Edward A., "Mass Society and Its Culture," *Daedalus*, 89 (Spring 1960): 288–314.

Srole, Leo, "Social Integration and Certain Corollaries: An Exploratory Study," *American Sociological Review*, 21 (December 1956): 709–716.

Taviss, Irene, "Changes in the Form of Alienation: The 1900's Vs. the 1950's," *American Sociological Review*, 34 (February 1969): 46–57.

Wilensky, Harold L., "Mass Society and Mass Culture: Interdependence or Independence?" *American Sociological Review*, 29 (April 1964): 173–197.

BIBLIOGRAPHY: Books

Bollens, John C., and Henry J. Schmandt, *The Metropolis: Its People, Politics, and Economic Life*, New York: Harper & Row, 1965.

Durkheim, Emile, *Suicide*, trans. by John A. Spaulding and George Simpson, Glencoe, Ill.: The Free Press, 1951.

Greer, Scott, and Ella Kube, "Urbanism and Social Structure: A Los Angeles Study," in Marvin B. Sussman (ed.), *Community Structure and Analysis*, New York: Thomas Y. Crowell, Company, 1959, pp. 93–112.

Hawley, Amos H., *Human Ecology*, New York: Ronald Press, 1950.

James, Gilbert, "Community Structure and Anomia," in Scott Greer, Dennis McElrath, David W. Minar, and Peter Orleans (eds.), *The New Urbanization*, New York: St. Martin's Press, 1969, pp. 189–197.

Josephson, Eric, and Mary Josephson (eds.), *Man Alone: Alienation in Modern Society*, New York: Dell Publishing Company, 1962.

Keller, Suzanne, *The Urban Neighborhood*, New York: Random House, 1968.

Mizruchi, Ephraim H., "Romanticism, Urbanism, and Small Town in Mass Society: An Exploratory Analysis," in Paul Meadows and Ephraim H. Mizruchi (eds.), *Urbanism, Urbanization, and Change: Comparative Perspectives*, Reading, Mass.: Addison-Wesley Publishing Company, 1969, pp. 243–251.

Nisbet, Robert A., *The Quest for Community*, New York: Oxford University Press, 1953.

Poplin, Dennis E., *Communities: A Survey of Theories and Methods of Research*, New York: The Macmillan Company, 1972.

Redfield, Robert, *The Little Community*, Chicago: University of Chicago Press, 1955.

Redfield, Robert, *Tepoztlan: A Mexican Village*, Chicago: University of Chicago Press, 1930.

Rose, Arnold M., *The Power Structure*, New York: Oxford University Press, 1967.

Thomlinson, Ralph, *Urban Structure*, New York: Random House, 1969.

CHAPTER 13
SOCIAL AND ORGANIZATIONAL PARTICIPATION

INTRODUCTION

According to many early ecologists and sociologists, heterogeneity, specialization, anonymity, formality, and impermanence characterize urban life. The urban personality tends toward individualization, loss of tradition, artificiality, time consciousness, loneliness, and despair. More recently, it has been recognized that in fact there are many relatively stable, enduring, and highly structured relationships in all sections of the urban complex. Urban people have primary as well as impersonal and segmental social relations. Among primary relations, kin, neighbors and friends are the most prominent. There may be various reasons why kin, neighbors, or friends form the key primary relations of any given individual. Each of these also may form a mutual-aid network, although kin are the most likely to be systematically included in such a network. The social networks of urban dwellers, then, are highly complex and include relations both in and outside the neighborhood and community of residence.

In addition to kin, neighbors, and friends, voluntary-association participation is important to many individuals. Such participation may act effectively as a mediator between the individual and society; but there is general agreement that informal social participation with relatives, friends, neighbors, peer groups, and so on, is more important for most individuals. Many of these social relations are barely structured enough to make them identifiable; others are more structured but have no formalized rules, agreements, and designated purposes. Generally, social relations are undertaken for the emotional satisfaction afforded by intimate association with other individuals. It has been argued that if an individual participates in informal groups, it does not matter whether he or she does not belong to voluntary associations. A number of studies report, however, that many individuals extensively participate in informal groups *and* belong to organizations. In addition, many who do not belong to associations extensively participate in informal groups, most notably with kin. Informal social participation is reportedly influenced by ecological, demographic/structural, and social psychological factors.

In this chapter we shall examine social participation patterns of urbanites. The focus is on informal relations — kinship networks and neighboring and friendship patterns and voluntary-organization participation, excluding religious and political participation, which we shall examine later. In describing urban informal and voluntary participation, we shall systematically examine the following: (1) ecological differences — that is, differing interaction patterns by the types of urban places and areas within urban places such as the central city or the suburbs or by areal social rank; (2) demographic and structural differences — social class, race and ethnicity, family type, age, sex, and other such factors; (3) social psychological aspects of informal and voluntary-association participation that might help clarify ecological and demographic/structural differences in interaction patterns.

URBANIZATION AND SOCIAL AND ORGANIZATIONAL PARTICIPATION

During the nineteenth century, the family lost many of its functions which led to its undergoing radical changes, with increased social participation outside of the family. Status began to be derived more externally to the family rather than within it, and as the traditional extended family lost much of its reason for existence, the nuclear family became the mode. The female's functions became more diverse and isolated from the male's, and children were no longer members of a household labor force (Hawley, 1971: 120–122). As the United States became urbanized and industrialized, then, for most workers occupational pursuits were accomplished away from the home. Further, the family abdicated the responsibilities for education, religious instruction, making clothing, and baking, as well as for care of the elderly.

More recently, a variety of alternative family types has emerged in contemporary United States, and they appear to be gathering numerical strength. Nevertheless, the predominant family type continues to be the nuclear family — husband, wife, and their children, but other family types such as "street families" and single-person households are in the majority in some areas of the urban complex. Predominant family type varies by ecological position in the urban complex, by social class, and probably by other factors as well. As society became urbanized and industrialized, the roles that women played expanded beyond that of the traditional home labor force participant, and many rights and privileges formerly denied to women have become commonplace for them. Shifts in responsibilities have helped change many authoritarian families into more equalitarian ones, and, again, there has been increased social activity outside the home.

Finally, the emergence of "familism," especially in contemporary American suburbs, has been noted (Riesman, 1957). *Familism* is placing a high valuation on nuclear-family living, on the expenditure of time upon child-rearing activities (and on participation in child-oriented voluntary organizations) and on gardening. Familism has been hypothesized by Bell (1958) as being the main reason for most suburban moves.

TYPES OF URBAN PLACES AND
SOCIAL AND ORGANIZATIONAL PARTICIPATION

No study has had as its express purpose a comparative examination of variation in kinship interaction patterns in different kinds or types of urban places. Variation of kinship patterns by types of ecological areas *within* urban places is available; but this information is strictly limited, and data are more theoretical than definitive. Also, no studies have been conducted that evaluate the extent of differences or similarities of neighboring and friendship patterns in different types of metropolitan places, nor have many studies been conducted that systematically compare them according to size of place, region, and so forth. Conclusions we draw then, unfortunately, are based upon limited evidence. As such, then, these conclusions must be viewed as propositions for testing rather than systematically verified hypotheses.

A national study conducted in 1953 reported that 64 percent of respondents belonged to no voluntary association, excluding unions (Wright and Hyman, 1958). In another national study the proportion of adults belonging to at least one voluntary organization in larger urban places was 47 percent (over 250,000). The percentage belonging increased as the size of urban place decreased down to the category in which all communities were under 10,000 in which 68 percent belonged. However, village and farm residents were intermediate to residents of larger and smaller urban places in the proportion belonging to voluntary organizations (Hausknecht, 1962). Another national survey reported a different pattern. In general, small urban places had a higher proportion of families *without* voluntary-organization membership than families residing in urban places with a central city of 50,000 (SMSA) or more population. Further, residents of larger, not smaller, urban centers are more likely to have multiple memberships (two or more) (Wright and Hyman, 1958).

Another study reported results that also suggest that household heads are less likely to belong to voluntary organizations in large cities (Milwaukee and Buffalo) than in medium-sized (Dayton and Rochester) and small-sized (Saginaw, Michigan, and Rockford, Illinois) cities. Nevertheless, the proportion belonging to just one organization is similar for all city sizes, but the heads in medium- and smaller-sized metropolitan places are more likely to have multiple memberships (Hawley and Zimmer, 1970: 56).

VARIATION WITHIN URBAN PLACES AND
SOCIAL AND ORGANIZATIONAL PARTICIPATION

Within metropolitan places, neighborhoods differ in demographic composition, location within the metropolitan complex, and according to cultural and physical characteristics. Each of these factors may have some impact

The influence of parents and kin upon children continues to be extremely important in our society.

upon the social interaction that takes place both within and outside neighborhood. Fortunately, a number of studies have examined neighboring and friendship patterns by types of areas within metropolitan complexes; thus we are in a position to evaluate ecological differences in kinship interaction, neighboring, and friendship participation.

Kinship Networks[1]

Kinship networks are the web of relationships existing among familial statuses. Generally, they are characterized by long-term, relatively permanent ties and mutual aid; they play an important role in shaping the value systems and behavior patterns of the individual members. Over time, kinship networks ordinarily are bound by affectional ties, although certainly the influence of kin visiting habits established in early childhood years should not be entirely discounted.

The relationship between urbanization and family structure ordinarily assumes that the pressures of urban living discourage traditional extended-family systems and encourage the "modern" conjugal or nuclear family. The contemporary American family kinship system has been called by some the "modified extended family" because a number of nuclear families, even though not living with either the wife's or husband's kin, are able to maintain

[1] For extensive reviews and a bibliography related to kinship participation and associated factors, see Adams (1968 and 1970).

social ties, mutual aid, contact by telephone and letter, and visits by automobile and airplane, despite geographical separation. In addition, Litwak (1960) has hypothesized that the modified extended-family system helps achieve upward mobility for its members. In other words, geographical separation does not necessarily result in *social* separation from kin (Litwak and Szelenyi, 1969: 467–469), although attachments may grow weaker over time if families' members are spatially separated.

Neighborhoods
In 1950 Bell (1968) examined social participation in four different types of San Francisco neighborhoods. Using the social area frame of reference (see Chapter 7), he selected (1) Mission—a low-rent rooming-house neighborhood characterized by a relatively low socioeconomic status and relatively low score on the index of familism; (2) Outer Mission—a neighborhood of low-rent houses but high on the familism index; (3) Pacific Heights—with high-rent apartments and low familism; and (4) St. Francis Wood—with high-rent detached houses and high familism. Each of the areas was predominantly white, and only men were interviewed. A comparison of the neighborhoods along the familism dimension showed that social isolation from relatives varied inversely with familism. Even so, there were very few isolates in any of the areas, regardless of social rank or the extent of familism. As a result of these data, Bell concluded that relatives continue to be an important source of companionship and mutual support in urban places. Nevertheless, there was sufficient variation shown by neighborhood to conclude that participation with relatives varies by ecological character and neighborhood context within which the individual lives.

Demographic Factors
A number of demographic and structural factors have been reported to influence the extent of kinship networks in urban settings: social class, race and ethnicity, family type, age, sex, and so on. Each of these aspects will be explored in this section and their relative influence evaluated.

Social Class
Studies concerned with the prevalence of kinship patterns among urban families consistently report that visits with relatives substantially exceed those to friends or neighbors; further, this extensive visiting with relatives occurs at all social class levels (Axelrod, 1956). Because of less migration, working-class kin networks are generally less scattered geographically, and kin are more available, therefore, for frequent interaction (Young and Willmott, 1957). But there remains a controversy over which social class visits relatives most often. Dotson (1951) reported that New Haven, Connecticut, working-class nuclear families visit most members of their larger kinship groups— brothers, sisters, cousins, and in-laws, many of whom are not in the immediate

neighborhood but are in other areas of the metropolitan center. Further, he reported that the total participation patterns for almost one-third of his sample consist exclusively of kinship, and, in well over another half, kinship relationships represented the major feature of social life. Irelan (n.d.; 4) argued, though, that social isolation is a characteristic of low-income life styles.

Hannerz (1969: 34) demonstrated, however, that the social structure of the black ghetto is made up primarily of a multitude of connecting personal networks of kinsmen, peers, and neighbors. His view is amply supported by other ethnographies and autobiographies. According to him, these stable social relations tend to be differentiated by a number of roles, but primarily by age and sex. In addition, social networks fluctuate by life styles, which influence the *quantity* as well as *quality* of interaction.

Middle-class families in suburban Crestwood Heights (Toronto, Canada) are geographically separated from their extended kin and also are socially separated (Seeley et al., 1956). While this geographical distance frees families from responsibilities to relatives, it also deprives them of benefits that accrue to families living in close proximity. Another study suggested that among white Protestant middle-class families strong affectional and economic ties continue to exist between middle-aged parents and their children. Mutual-aid assistance such as gifts, loans, and baby-sitting, as well as nursing care during illnesses or childbirth, are exchanged by a vast majority of families; further, sons are given opportunities in the family business (Sussman, 1953; Litwak and Szelenyi, 1969). Middle-class parents have widespread involvement in activities—such as the PTAs, music lessons, the Boy Scouts, and so on—that they believe are related to the status and welfare of their children. Finally, Warner and Lunt (1941), in a study of Newburyport, Massachusetts, reported that upper-class families maintain close ties with their extended families.

Race and Ethnicity

Hannerz (1969) reports that social participation with relatives in the inner-city black ghetto (Winston Street, District of Columbia) is rather extensive. Similarly, well over one-half of the adults and teenagers in another black ghetto (Near Northeast, District of Columbia) have three or more households of relatives living in the district (Chapin et al., forthcoming). Feagin (1968) reported that 84 percent of Boston inner-city blacks had relatives in the metropolitan area; similar percentages of inner-city blacks having relatives nearby were reported for Philadelphia (Blumberg and Bell, 1959) and Highland Park, Michigan (Meadow, 1965). Further, teenagers are more likely to report having other relatives in the metropolitan area than are adults (Chapin et al., forthcoming). The greatest intensity of contact with relatives is with those living nearby, and there is a tendency for greater interaction with peer relatives than with older or younger ones (Feagin, 1970: 664). Teenagers report more social activities with relatives than do adults (Chapin et al., forthcoming).

Feagin (1968: 665) has proposed that there are more similarities than

Despite some popular beliefs and prejudices, the nuclear family is an important institution for most inner-city blacks.

differences in black and white patterns of kin contact. While Meadow (1965: 177) tends to agree, she suggested that neighborhood integration is greater for families with no relatives in the urban area (Detroit). In the early years of residence, however, those families with more kin contact, that is, with kin nearby, also do more neighborhood visiting, suggesting a hyperactive visiting pattern among some neighborhood residents. After several years of residence, however, this pattern is reversed, with more kin contact being associated with less neighborhood interaction (also see McAllister et al., 1973).

Scanzoni (1971: 135) noted that aid received by black relatives from kin is primarily financial (60 percent), and the remainder is advice and counsel. Feagin (1968: 663) reported that 24 percent of Boston blacks received aid such as financial assistance, business advice, and help during family illness; 22 percent reported giving such mutual aid. He further noted that 48 percent of families had received aid from their kinspeople in moving into their current places of residence. In addition, mutual aid by kin probably increases during an initial move into a new neighborhood of residence where relatives already reside. People tend to turn to relatives first for assistance and support during stress and rely upon the latter's established social patterns (Meadow, 1965: 178). Nevertheless, in spite of extended-family interaction and mutual aid, kin beyond the immediate nuclear family do not substantially influence related individuals in important decisions (Scanzoni, 1971: 135).

Generally, women's kinship ties exceed men's, and women report more interaction and feel closer to their kin than do men (Booth, 1972). Apparently, physical disability or health problems reduce kinship social participation by women, whereas this is not true for men. Also, a decline in kinship interaction for women is not accompanied by an increase in other types of social participation (Booth, 1972). Further, families with a behaviorally retarded member have reduced relative interaction (McAllister et al., 1973).

Insofar as social status is concerned, Roxbury-Boston higher-status respondents were somewhat more involved with their kin than lower-status respondents (Feagin, 1968: 663). In contrast, in the Near Northeast, Washington, D.C., adult and teenager participation with relatives did not vary by income level (Chapin et al., forthcoming).

Conclusions

Boskoff (1970: 162) has succinctly pointed out that the analysis of urban family forms and social relations are only at the threshold of sophistication. We must await the difficult task of disentangling the effects of ethnic background, length of urban experience, social status, stage in the family cycle, social competence of family members (McAllister et al., 1973) and so forth, on kinship social participation. Tentatively, it appears that kinship networks are of particular significance for working-class families, ethnic populations that continue to identify themselves as such, and upper-class families.

Neighboring and Friendship Patterns

Prevailing urban folklore is that little neighboring and informal visiting take place in metropolitan centers. But we shall see that actually a substantial amount takes place.

As we pointed out earlier, neighborhood and friend interaction are influenced by a variety of factors: ecological position and neighborhood character, demographic composition and structural characteristics of the people in the neighborhood, and social psychological factors. Further, as with kinship networks, friendships and cliques are not necessarily bound by the local neighborhood and may be based upon similarities in sex, age, social class, ethnic background, and religion. Church affiliation, particularly among blacks and middle-class whites is an important factor in generating close ties among some people. For some adults work or profession is important in forming friendship ties, and, of course, in many other instances, neighbors and friends are one and the same.

Ecological Context

One important influence upon social participation may be the ecological context within which the individual resides. This means that the neighborhood and its social composition may affect social participation independently of the effects of individual characteristics (Nohara, 1968). For example, suburban residents (Nassau County, New York) are less likely than residents of the central city (Manhattan and Queens) to join voluntary associations, and suburbanites tend to neighbor more than central city residents: "Neighboring gradually increases with distance from the city center" (Fava, 1958: 126). Nor do factors such as marital status alter this conclusion; that is, married persons living in the suburbs neighbor more than those living in the central city. In a somewhat similar study of residents of the Detroit metropolitan complex, participation with friends and neighbors increased with distance from the inner city and especially so when one crossed Detroit's city limits and examined participation in the suburbs. In addition, social participation was facilitated when relatively many persons with similar characteristics lived in the same neighborhood. While it appears that age, marital status, education, and migrant status also may influence social participation more than ecological zone of residence, it is important to note that "all exceptions to the tendency of increased suburban participation involve residents who do fit into the general pattern of the area" (Tomeh, 1964).

Using the social area frame of reference (see Chapter 7), Bell's study (1968: 140) of San Francisco revealed that men in neighborhoods of low familism were less likely to get together informally with neighbors than men of high familism, although an area with high familism *and* high social rank had the lowest neighboring of all. Friendship participation varied primarily by social rank, with the upper social ranks areas, despite different levels of familism, having the greatest frequency of visiting friends. Co-worker visiting varied only slightly by familism and social rank dimensions, with the area high on social rank and familism having the lowest level of participation with co-workers (also see Bell and Boat, 1957). Also, using the social area frame of reference, Nohara (1968: 186–197) concluded that various residential areas in a metropolitan complex represent different opportunities for social participation, while the social characteristics of individual residents represent their potential to avail themselves of these opportunities. Thus he noted that the primary influence upon the extent of neighboring in the St. Louis social areas he studied was the familism of the area, modified somewhat by economic and ethnic composition.

Social Class

In general, contacts with neighbors, friends, and co-workers tend to increase with higher social class. Dotson (1951) reported that most working-class families in New Haven rarely visit outside of their kinship networks, although a few have strong neighborhood ties. In Detroit only one-third of lower-class persons frequently visit with friends at least a few times a month, whereas three-fifths of upper-class people visit at least that often (Axelrod, 1956). In Lansing, Michigan, friends are about equally divided between neighbors and nonneighbors. Close neighborhood friendship patterns are more prevalent, however, in middle- and higher-class areas than in lower-class ones. The explanation for this phenomenon is that the greater average length of residence of higher-class families permits more intimate friendships to develop than is the case for the more residentially mobile lower-class families (Smith et al., 1954). Similarly, lower-class individuals in Evanston, Illinois, had fewer intimate friends and engaged in less visiting among friends than the middle and upper classes (Reissman, 1954). Further, lower-class persons in the same city tended to limit their social interaction more to immediate kin and the local neighborhood; and it appears that middle-class persons, on the whole, tended to dominate organizations, the intellectual life, and the voluntary-organization leadership of the community.

Race and Ethnicity

Black friendship patterns have been reported to vary by life style as well as by neighborhood (Hannerz, 1969). In the black Near Northeast neighborhood of the District of Columbia (Chapin et al., forthcoming) there are some persons who are virtually complete social isolates; others have friends only outside of the neighborhood, who, of course, act in competition with neighbors (Hannerz, 1969: 208). Feagin (1970: 307) has argued, though, that the friendship networks of blacks are encapsulated in the local neighborhood. In the Near Northeast this appears to be true for teenagers, about two-thirds of whose best friends live in the neighborhood. On the other hand, only about 30 percent of adults' best friends live in the neighborhood. Adults have a wider geographical range, which includes the entire Washington metropolitan area; but a teenager's best friend is most likely to reside in the immediate neighborhood or, in a few instances, elsewhere within the district. From this study it appears that adults have a greater choice of friends than teenagers because many of them have been freed from spatial limitations in their selection. There is some indication that more recent inmovers have a higher interaction rate with friends than persons who have lived in the neighborhood for a longer period of time (Feagin, 1970: 307); and in St. Louis it appears that black neighborhoods high in familism (see Chapter 7) also have greater neighborliness (Nohara, 1968).

Participation with friends is largely sex segregated and for most persons consists of routinized sociability with the same persons in the same location. Ihinger and Butler (1972) reported different kinds of interaction styles for teenage males and females. Primary activities that teenagers participate in with their best friends are going shopping, "hanging out," and doing homework together. Over one-half of the teenagers visit schoolmates as often as once a week. Male activities tend to be more diverse and less intimate and range from parties, traveling around by car or bus, meeting on the street corner, and talking on doorsteps and porches to meeting at "hangouts" (also see Hannerz, 1969, and Liebow, 1967). Females tend to spend more time together in or near the home with fewer participants and have more intimate, enduring relationships.

A substantial amount of socializing goes on at the door steps in black and chicano neighborhoods.

In the same study the primary activities of adults with friends were to go shopping or to church and to get together occasionally for meals.

No differences by income level were noted in this inner-city black ghetto for either adults or teenagers and the frequency of visiting best friend. But while there was no difference in area of residency of best friend by income level for adults, teenagers in the lower-income level, were more likely than those in the higher-income levels to have their best friends living in the immediate neighborhood than in the District of Columbia, the suburbs, or elsewhere. This contrasts somewhat with the work of Hannerz (1969: 209), who reported that most black teenage hangouts are outside of the immediate neighborhood.

Adults in the same Near Northeast area referred to earlier visited much less frequently with the neighbors than with relatives and friends, with only 27.6 percent visiting neighbors as often as once a week or more. Neighbors exchange few favors or give little advice on problems. As with best friends, however, teenagers' activities are much more localized, and they report a great deal more interaction with neighbors than adults: Two-thirds of the teenagers visited neighbor children at least as often as once a week. The more extensive

These young people live in South Bronx, New York, and are on their way to a street gang headquarters in the basement of a nearly empty building. This particular gang meeting attracted about 100 boys and girls on this afternoon. In neighborhoods dominated by street gangs, such meetings may be quasi-governmental, as well as social, in nature.

neighboring of teenagers compared with that of adults was also reported by Riemer (1959) for white children and their parents in the southern California suburb of Lakewood (Los Angeles SMSA). Teenagers there reported more exchanging of favors and giving of advice on problems than adults.

No differences by income status exist in interaction with neighbors for adults or teenagers in the Near Northeast. Also Greer and Kube (1959) reported that employed residents in four greatly different areas in the Los Angeles metropolitan area neighbor as much as those who stay home. Further, no differences according to income level or working status are apparent for teenagers visiting with schoolmates.

There are competitive factors for neighboring time such as working status, especially for females. The working female typically has less time available than nonworking females, and the time that she does have is more likely to be devoted to her family than in establishing friendships or visiting with neighbors (Meadow, 1965: 180; but also see Greer and Kube, 1959). Nevertheless, the major differences noted in black neighboring and friendship participation are generational, with teenagers being much more active with friends and neighbors than adults (for a similar statement see Hannerz, 1969: 34). Income status is not strongly associated with informal social participation patterns in the black community. However, the few differences that do exist suggest that a higher income facilitates a larger "social space" and contacts throughout a wide geographical area including the local neighborhood, the central city, and the entire metropolitan complex.

Another facet of black social participation in urban areas is social relations with whites. Blacks who have experienced extensive social relations with whites are those who are most likely to be seeking integrative housing and neighborhoods in the future; they are also those who are most likely to be able to make a satisfactory adjustment to an integrated living situation (Bullough, 1969).

In the Near Northeast study cited earlier, 37.3 percent of the adults had previously lived in an integrated neighborhood, while only 11.1 percent of teenagers had ever lived in a neighborhood with white residents. Adults have had more opportunity than teenagers to live in white neighborhoods. Nevertheless, we suspect that when these teenagers reach adulthood they will, as an aggregate, still have had less integrative living experience than that experienced so far by adults. The isolation of black teenagers from whites is further indicated by more adults than teenagers having white friends and visiting in a white person's home. *Almost one-half of the Near Northeast black teenagers had never been in a classroom with white teenagers!* Perhaps a manifestation of this lack of integrative experiences on the part of teenagers is reflected in the larger proportion of them (37.2 percent compared to 24.1 percent of the adults) who feel that they "cannot trust whites," and a greater proportion of teenagers than adults who feel that the District of Columbia police treat blacks worse than whites. No large differences in black and white relations exist by income or working status, although working and higher-income adults are more likely than nonworking and lower-income adults to report that blacks are treated worse than whites in the district.

There is a very real generation gap in the Near Northeast in the larger proportion of integrative experiences of black adults and, in contrast, a much greater distrust of whites by black teenagers. If one assumes that previous integrative experiences prepare one to live in integrated neighborhoods, adults in the Near Northeast are better prepared than teenagers, since they have had a larger number of integrative experiences, currently are more likely than teenagers to have white friends, and are more likely than teenagers to trust whites. The lack of integrative experiences of teenagers probably reflects the strict neighborhood and housing segregation in the District of Columbia and the metropolitan area. As the District becomes increasingly black, the expectations of any kind of integrative experiences will most likely decline unless conscious efforts are made to expand them. Ironically, McCord and others (1969: 142) pointed out that skid row is one part of the city where there is true companionship between black and white. Drunks eat, sleep, and drink together. Interestingly, there are no differences in integrative experiences, trust, or attitudes about police treatment, for either adults or teenagers, by working or income status.

Teenagers' fewer contacts with whites perhaps explains why more adults (25.7 percent) than teenagers (9.4 percent) report instances of discrimination directed personally against themselves. No differences in personal discrimination experiences were reported according to working status; yet both adults and teenagers at higher-income levels reported more personal discrimination than those at lower-income levels. This again may be related to the opportunity factor: A higher-income level permits a wider range of contacts in the metropolitan area, whereas lower incomes restrict outward movement from the immediate neighborhood. If one's life space is restricted to the Near Northeast neighborhood, he or she will not be subject to personal discrimination by whites — few whites live there and rarely do whites enter the neighborhood except for business purposes.

Ethnic populations other than blacks have been studied. For example, second-generation, lower-class Italian Americans living in an ethnic neighborhood of New York City have more friends, and more close friends, than first-generation persons. This is probably because the second generation has a wider range of social contacts with people at work and in other formal situations, increasing the chances of learning urban values and of having the opportunity to develop friendships. In addition, most second-generation Italian Americans have had a better command of the English language and an orientation toward activities outside of the family setting (Palisi, 1966). On the other hand, when the ethnic heritage of both intimate and nonintimate friends was examined by generation, friends of different generations did not vary by ethnicity, since virtually all of them were of Italian heritage. This is probably accounted for by the ethnic homogeneity of the neighborhood and the fact that residential proximity is related to the development of close and intimate friendship ties.

Peer Groups

Gans (1962) has shown how the social life of West End Boston Italians revolves around peer groups. These peer groups consist primarily of compatible kinspeople and friends of a similar age, social class, and specific interest. They meet in homes of participants, and most interaction consists of discussing celebrations, weddings, neighborhood activities, child-rearing practices, housekeeping, and gossip. These peer groups serve as an important integrating mechanism for the people in the community, and although they take away some of the privacy of the residents, individuals prefer them to "being alone."

Sex

In Bloomington, Indiana, Sweetser (1942) found that sex and age[2] are important, with individuals tending to be good friends only with members of the same sex, although acquaintances are not sex linked. One-fourth of both males and females never visit with neighbors; however, more females than males visit with neighbors on a daily basis (Berado. 1966: 301). Also, it ap-

---

[2] More pronounced than sex in intimate and aquaintance interaction is age. All ages tend preferentially to select their own age categories for both intimate and acquaintance interaction.

pears that white-collar husbands are more likely than their wives to initiate and maintain mutual friendships and to have more close friends (Booth, 1972). Children in Lakewood, a suburb of Los Angeles, neighbor more than their parents and men in this particular suburb tend to neighbor where their spouses had neighbored previously (Riemer, 1959: 440). Nevertheless, women — even when employed — see friends more often than do men. Also, women do more visiting outside of the neighborhood than do men (Butler et al., 1973: 222). In addition, in Lakewood female friendships are richer in spontaneity and confidences, and females do more things together on the spur of the moment. But men have more friends of the opposite sex than do women.

Voluntary-Organization Participation

Voluntary associations are highly specialized and explicitly organized groups composed of persons with a common interest that cannot be satisfied through individual behavior or by already existing forms of social interaction. They tend to function with a limited set of definitive objectives or interests, and they have a visible formal organization. In most instances, membership is voluntary, and entrance and withdrawal are dependent upon personal decisions of interest. Voluntary associations help mediate between the individual and the larger society. They have developed and attracted members for a variety of reasons. Some urbanites join them because of interests in literature, taxes, the poor, personal status and to enhance the opportunity for social mobility. Those who do not have enough personal contact elsewhere use voluntary associations as an occasion for interacting with others who share somewhat similar interests.

Most voluntary associations are semibureaucratic and have official positions, rules, records; and they may use parliamentary procedures at meetings. Even so, they are characterized by personal interaction among members. Meetings may occur quite frequently or only as often as once every six months. Nevertheless, there is a sense of continuity in an organization, and meetings serve to regularize the lives of its members.

Available literature indicates that a number of people belong to *many* organizations, while others do not belong to any. Further, only a few members of each organization attend every meeting and become intimately involved in the work of the association. This core of active participants tends to be made up of longer-term members. Many voluntary organizations in any urban complex are affiliated with counterparts in other urban areas, resulting in an interlocking of organizations on a regional, national, and international basis.

Formal organizations have several functions: (1) to confer social status upon individual members; (2) to give security and mutual support; and (3) to provide a link that connects the individual with the larger society, thus facilitating adjustment to the social milieu. Formal organizations represent a wide range of human activities, including professional, veterans, social, civic service, cultural, and, of course, religious and political activities. Every major study of formal organization participation in the United States reports that there are a large number of organizations available to the population; in fact, the extent and variety of these organizations have led to the characterization of this country as a nation of "joiners."

Integrative and Disintegrative Aspects of Voluntary Associations

The impact of formal organizations on the city or urban complex can be integrative or divisive despite what they may or may not accomplish for the individual. Organizations may promote cooperation in harmony, or they may promote competition and conflict. Many associations are differentiated upon the basis of race, ethnicity, prestige, or religion. Minnis (1959) reported that the most rigid distinction in New Haven was by race, with at least 90 percent of organizations being racially exclusive. In addition, some organizations restrict membership along several dimensions; a religious-ethnic organization, for instance, only admitted native-born Caucasian Protestants. Ordinarily, boundaries of formal organizations represent the deep social cleavages within the community. Litwak (1961) also has taken the point of view that extensive participation in voluntary associations is negatively related to neighborhood primary-group cohesion and thus may be dysfunctional from that point of view.

Types of Voluntary Organizations

Formal organizations have been classified into two major types, the expressive and the instrumental, according to their dominant objectives (Rose, 1953: 55–66). *Expressive* organizations provide opportunities for self-expression, creativity, and the exchange of ideas and are directed toward limited fields of interest. Examples are hobby clubs, literary societies, fraternal lodges, veterans organizations, and book clubs. Expressive organizations at times serve as a supplement to or as a substitute for primary-group relations. *Instrumental* organizations—such as political organizations, lobbying groups, taxpayers' associations, educational, professional, and medical organizations, and social action organizations—are more concerned with influencing other persons and organizations.

A somewhat similar typology has been suggested by Bell and Force (1956). They classified organizations into three broad types: (1) general interest —devoted to the broader public welfare rather than a specific segment of the community (Lions, Rotary, Kiwanis, etc.); (2) special-stratum interest—related to particularized statuses (veterans, unions, PTA, chamber of commerce, etc.); and (3) special individualized interests—involving a nonstatus interest (hobbies) or aiding others not represented by a particular stratum in society (charitable organizations for the retarded, crippled, etc.).

Using a somewhat more elaborate typology of voluntary organizations, Lieberson and Allen (1963) noted that there is a rough association be-

The members of this Omaha group are expressing themselves as well as having fun by participating in a local parade.

tween the size of a metropolitan complex and its rank as a center for headquarters of national voluntary associations. New York City has almost one-third of the national headquarters, followed by Washington, D.C., with 15 percent, and Chicago, with 11 percent. Thus nearly 60 percent of all headquarters of national organizations are located in three metropolitan areas. As these authors noted, this is not too much different from earlier studies reported for 1929 and during the 1950s. About one-half of welfare, public affairs, ethnic, and religious associations and national chambers of commerce have headquarters in New York City. Lieberson and Allen concluded that the headquarters of voluntary associations are differentially located in these three metropolitan regions because they are the focuses of the political, financial, industrial, communicative, and transportation systems of the United States. Similarly, organizations related to other activities are more spatially widespread depending upon their clientele and functions.

Voluntary-Organization
Participation Within Urban Places

Zimmer and Hawley (1959) found that residents of Flint, Michigan, have more voluntary-organization memberships than residents of its fringe area. Further, central city residents were more likely than fringe residents to belong to a union, to attend church, to be registered to vote, and actually to vote in elections. They noted that these differences remained when age, education, income, occupation, and how long the person has lived in the current place of residence were controlled.

In contrast, another study comparing two examples each of large, medium-, and small-sized metropolitan places showed that in the first two categories suburban residents were more likely than central city residents to belong to an organization and to have multiple organizational memberships. In the two smaller metropolitan places little difference existed between central city and suburban residents (Hawley and Zimmer, 1970: 56).

Using the Shevky and Bell social area typology to classify areas *within* metropolitan San Francisco, general-interest and special-stratum interest and special-individualized-interest associations (hobby groups and organizations for the underprivileged) were rarer in high- and low-ranking areas than in middle-ranking areas, although high-status males more often participate in general-interest associations, while low-status males more often belong to special-interest associations (unions, PTAs, etc.). Areas with high social rank tend to have a greater diversity of voluntary organizations than middle- and lower-ranking ones (Bell and Force, 1956).

Possible reasons for discrepancies in these studies are as follows: (1) Population size and economic structure of the area may have a varying influence reflected in different voluntary-organization patterns. A possible resolution of this problem, obviously, is to study voluntary-organization participation not only by population characteristics reported in this chapter but to extend these studies to include urban-area type based upon demographic, social structural, and economic variables as key factors. (2) Political boundaries influence what is called the central city and what is considered the suburbs or the fringe. In addition, different universes were studied; therefore, even if the sampling had been carried out properly, the results are from different populations. Unless the universes are similar, there will be different results. More consistent results probably would have been obtained if the urban areas had been systematically classified into one or more of the urban typologies discussed in Chapter 5.

Social Class
and Voluntary Associations

As we pointed out earlier, different categories of people differentially participate in voluntary associations in urban places. One of the major determining factors of such participation is status or social class. Middle and upper social classes have much greater involvement in associations than lower-class individuals, a difference that persists no matter what indicator is selected to measure it—salary (Freeman et al., 1957), income, education, occupation, subjective identification with a social class, and as we noted earlier, by social rank or status of neighborhood. Further, many studies report that people in middle and upper social classes are more likely than people in the lower classes to belong to multiple organizations. Moreover, there appears to be differences by social class in the types of associations one belongs (for example, see Boskoff 1970: 180–181, and Barber, 1957).

Race and Voluntary Associations

One reaches different conclusions on the prevalence of black and white memberships in voluntary associations depending upon the sources consulted. A number of years ago, Myrdal and others (1944) argued that blacks are "exaggerated" Americans in their relatively larger number of associations and their greater likelihood of belonging to associations. This associational pattern was considered by Myrdal and his associates to be "pathological," since black patterns of associational membership are a generation behind those of whites and because black associations attain little of what their members set out to achieve in them. Further, these associations (birthday clubs, Northside Squires, etc.) are primarily expressive and nonutilitarian in nature as opposed to more instrumental organizations such as the NAACP (Babchuk and Thompson, 1962: 653, and Dackawich, 1966: 74).

On the other hand, several national surveys indicate that a larger proportion of whites than blacks are members of voluntary associations (Hausknecht, 1962 and Wright and Hyman, 1958). Frazier (1957) found little participation in formal or civic clubs and organizations by blacks in urban areas but reported a substantial amount of voluntary activity and interest in informal, loosely organized social clubs. Drake and Cayton (1945) suggested, however, that while there is little voluntary-association participation other than churchgoing by lower-class blacks, the emerging middle-class black extensively participates in voluntary organizations. Olsen (1970) and Babchuk and Thompson (1962: 647–648) hypothesize that blacks are less likely than whites to participate in voluntary associations because more blacks than whites are lower class; but when class is controlled, the affiliation rates should be similar.

In fact, Orum (1966), using data from Detroit, Chicago, and a Washington, D.C., suburb, found that among blacks and whites at the lowest-class level, blacks are more likely to be affiliated with organizations than are whites. Evidence at the middle- and upper-class levels was less clear. Thus much of the difference observed between blacks and whites in voluntary organizational participation may be related to social class distinctions. Orum claimed that organizations mean much more to blacks who belong to them, since they offer a congenial environment for collective social activity. By contrast, whites view organizations as a mechanism for the enhancement of their prestige through belonging to the "right" kinds of organizations. Olsen further reported that when socioeconomic status is controlled, blacks are more likely to vote and are more active in voluntary associations than whites. His data also suggest, following Lane's (1959) hypothesis, that blacks who identify as members of the black minority tend to be more active than nonidentifiers.

Ethnographic studies have revealed little voluntary-association participation by blacks in urban areas. Hannerz (1969) describes four ideal-type life styles for adult ghetto residents and the different social interaction patterns for each. For the most part, "mainstreamers" (those who ascribe to and succeed in achieving dominant cultural goals, values, and goods) comprise the membership in the voluntary organizations that exist in the black inner city (PTA, church, community improvement projects, etc.). "Swingers" (young single or married adults) tend toward cosmopolitanism rather than localism, finding friends and acquaintances and participating in informal social events and parties throughout the city. "Streetcorner men" and "street families" center on informal interaction patterns in the local community and, with the exception of church, avoid formally organized activities. Hannerz' data corresponds closely with other social anthropological studies of ethnic ghetto life, such as those of Boston (Gans, 1962), Chicago (Suttles, 1968), and Washington, D.C. (Liebow, 1967).

In addition, Chapin et al. (forthcoming), using both survey and ethnographic research methodology, reported that black adults and teenagers of the inner city (Near Northeast Washington, D.C.) evidently are one of those population segments that does not participate very extensively in formal organizations. Other than participation in church-related activities, few adults or teenagers in the inner-city area they studied belonged to a voluntary association. Further, if the extent of participation in various organizations is used as an indicator of social cleavages within the community, few such cleavages are evident other than church versus nonchurch in the black inner city. Their point of view, however, was that voluntary organizations only very loosely reflect the basic social cleavages in the ghetto. They reported that very few adults belong to formal organizations and even fewer regularly attend meetings. Their results are in stark contrast to a Lincoln, Nebraska, sample of blacks of which 75 percent belonged to one or more voluntary associations, *plus* being affiliated with a church (Babchuk and Thompson, 1962: 650). The divergence between these two studies may be a result of different city size, black population size, and/or social class composition.

As Dackawich (1966: 77) has pointed out, participation by blacks in civil rights organizations is minimal, and there is even less participation in organizations that can be considered militant. Further, there is little participation in organizations that stress organized-protest strategies (Friedman, 1967). In the Near Northeast there is not much difference between adults and teenagers in the extent of belonging and attending meetings for civil rights or militant organizations. However, voluntary-organization participation by teen-agers is somewhat higher than for adults. Most studies agree with Hannerz (1969), who found that few residents of the black ghetto are members of volun-tary organizations.

In view of the low level of participation in formal organizations, excluding the church, the likelihood of participation in political organizations is very slight (see Dackawich, 1966: 74). Further, since few adults and teenagers belong to fraternal, civic, school, or civic rights groups or acknowl-edge membership in organizations that could be characterized as militant, probably no differences in such participation exists by working status or in-come level for such types of organizations. Few studies in this regard have made direct comparisons between blacks and whites, and it is difficult to ac-cept the hypothesis that when social class is controlled, black participation in voluntary organizations is much higher than that of whites (Dackawich, 1966: 74).

Multiple memberships are held by some adults and teenagers. Dacka-wich (1966: 77) hypothesized that the plurality of black memberships in volun-tary organizations would be in work-related special-interest organizations. In the Near Northeast this is not true. Further, Babchuk and Thompson's expec-tation (1962: 650) that there would be a slight relation between income and multiple membership was not upheld in that study.

In summary, there appears to be some question as to the importance of voluntary organizations for black inner-city residents. Opinions range from that of Myrdal, who called blacks "exaggerated" Americans because of their exten-sive organizational participation, to those who argue that ghetto residents are social isolates. Our conclusion is that few blacks belong to voluntary organiza-tions in the inner city. Even fewer residents belong to militant or civil rights organizations.

Sex and Voluntary Associations

The proportion of males that belong to voluntary associations varies over time and, evidently, according to metropolitan place as well as area within the metropolitan complex. Axelrod (1956) reported that 63 percent of males in Detroit belonged to voluntary associations compared with 77 percent in San Francisco (Bell and Force, 1956). On the other hand, Komarovksy's (1946) study conducted in New York City during the 1930s found that only somewhere around one-half of the males belonged to voluntary associations, other than the church. Generally, women are less likely to belong to organiza-tions than are men. Men belong to a greater variety of voluntary associations and are more likely to hold multiple memberships than are women, although men are less stable in their membership. Males typically belong to in-strumental-type organizations, whereas women are more likely to belong to expressive organizations, especially recreational and church-oriented groups. Women are less likely to belong to organizations while they have young children in the household, but when the youngest child enters school, they once again begin to join organizations (Booth, 1972).

Part of the variation in various studies may be attributed to the time in which the studies were carried out, part to sex differences, and part to the sample. Komarovsky's study, for example, was primarily carried out in the central city and during a depression.

Other Factors in Voluntary-Association Participation

Immigrants from other nations developed an elaborate network of ethnic-specific voluntary associations. In addition, rural-to-urban migrants have developed voluntary associations and used them to help throw off their old rural ways of life. Voluntary associations, then, may function as mediators between the old ways of doing things, whether in the old country or in rural areas; and they may help migrants adjust to the complexity and anonymity of urban life. But if these organizations are oriented toward maintaining the old ways of doing things, it is dubious whether they help migrants to adapt to urban life (Hunt and Butler, 1972: 449–450). This is especially so when ethnic voluntary-association participation is coupled only with intensive relative and ethnic friend interaction.

Migration and residential mobility, which are widespread in urban complexes, have been reported by some to influence voluntary-association participation, although others dispute this hypothesis. Wright and Hyman (1958) reported small differences between migrants and long-term residents in voluntary-association participation. On the other hand, a study of the Los Angeles suburb of Claremont, a college town, indicated that length of residence is related to associational membership (Scaff, 1952). Newcomers to Claremont participate less in various organizations than do old-timers. This study further showed that commuters, who also were more likely than old-timers to be new residents, participate less than noncommuters. The fact that Claremont is a college town may have influenced the results. Moreover, newer residents probably are those who live on the periphery of this suburb in newer housing tracts suggesting that the date of settlement of the neighborhood has an important influence upon the level of participation in voluntary associations.

Background characteristics of migrants—such as region of origin and rural-urban residence—also may influence the levels of voluntary-association participation. For example, Zimmer (1955) showed that membership in voluntary associations increases with length of residence and that younger migrants reach high levels of participation before older migrants do. In addition, migrants from rural areas have lower rates of participation than do those from urban and rural-nonfarm situations. His data further indicate that even after several decades of residence in the urban region rural migrants do not reach the level of participation of urban and rural-nonfarm migrants. Social class and educational differences are substantial among these migrants and also may have helped to account for differences in voluntary-association participation.

In addition, it is possible that other breaks or discontinuities in a person's life, for instance, severe economic deprivation, divorce, and so on, may lead to reduced social participation, although these factors have been left relatively unexplored to date (for an exception see Pope, 1964)

There is a relative lack of information on the social psychological factors involved in patterns of voluntary-association participation. Freeman and others (1957) suggested, on the basis of their Spokane study, that while social class differences are primary in patterns of voluntary-association participation, general satisfaction with the size and operation of the community, optimism about the community's future, and so on, are associated with multiple associational memberships. Another study (Dynes, 1957) conducted in Columbus, Ohio, disclosed that persons with sectarian religious beliefs belong to fewer non-church associations than those with a nonsectarian orientation to religion (that is, the separation of religion from other aspects of life).

CONCLUSIONS

It clearly appears that there is a vast array of different kinds of social and organizational participation in urban areas in the United States. Participation patterns vary according to areas within the urban complex as well as other factors such as social class, ethnicity, and sex.

BIBLIOGRAPHY: Articles

Adams, Bert N., "Isolation, Function and Beyond: American Kinship in the 1960's," *Journal of Marriage and the Family*, 32 (November 1970): 575–597.

Axelrod, Morris, "Urban Structure and Social Participation," *American Sociological Review*, 21 (February 1956): 13–18.

Babchuk, Nicholas, and Ralph V. Thompson, "The Voluntary Associations of Negroes," *American Sociological Review*, 27 (October 1962): 647–655.

Bell, Wendell, and Maryanne T. Force, "Urban Neighborhood Types and Participation in Formal Associations," *American Sociological Review*, 21 (February 1956): 25–34.

Bell, Wendell, and Marion D. Boat, "Urban Neighborhoods and Informal Relations," *American Journal of Sociology*, 62 (January 1957): 391–398.

Berado, Felix M., "Kinship Interaction and Migrant Adaptation in an Aerospace-Related Community," *Journal of Marriage and the Family*, 28 (1966): 296–304.

Blumberg, Leonard, and Robert R. Bell, "Urban Migration and Kinship Ties," *Social Problems*, 6 (Spring 1959): 328–333.

Booth, Alan, "Sex and Social Participation," *American Sociological Review*, 37 (April 1972): 183–192.

Butler, Edgar W., Ronald J. McAllister, and Edward J. Kaiser, "The Effects of Voluntary and Involuntary Residential Mobility on Females and Males," *Journal of Marriage and the Family*, (May 1973): 219–227.

Dackawich, S. John, "Voluntary Associations of Central Area Negroes," *Pacific Sociological Review*, 9 (1966): 74–78.

Dotson, Floyd, "Patterns of Voluntary Association Among Urban Working Class Families," *American Sociological Review*, 16 (October 1951): 687–693.

Dynes, Russell R., "The Consequences of Sectarianism for Social Participation," *Social Forces,* 35 (May 1957): 331–334.

Feagin, Joe R., "A Note on the Friendship Ties of Negro Urbanites," *Social Forces,* 49 (December 1970): 303–308.

Feagin, Joe R., "The Kinship Ties of Negro Urbanites," *Social Science Quarterly,* 49 (December 1968): 660–665.

Freeman, Howard E., Edwin Novak, and Leo G. Reeder, "Correlates of Membership in Voluntary Associations," *American Sociological Review,* 22 (October 1957): 528–533.

Friedman, Cyril R., "Attitude Toward Protest Strategy and Participation in Protest Groups Among Negro Americans," unpublished Ph.D. dissertation, University of Connecticut, 1967.

Hunt, Gerard J., and Edgar W. Butler, "Migration, Participation and Alienation," *Sociology and Social Research,* 56 (July 1972): 440–452.

Ihinger, Marilyn, and Edgar W. Butler, "Residential Mobility and Social Interaction Patterns of Black Urban Teenagers," paper presented at the Pacific Sociological Association, April 1972.

Komarovsky, Mirra, "The Voluntary Associations of Urban Dwellers," *American Sociological Review,* 11 (December 1946): 686–698.

Lieberson, Stanley, and Irving L. Allen, Jr., "Location of National Headquarters of Voluntary Associations," *Administrative Science Quarterly,* 8 (December 1963): 316–338.

Litwak, Eugene, "Voluntary Associations and Neighborhood Cohesion," *American Sociological Review,* 26 (April 1961): 258–271.

Litwak, Eugene, "Reference Group Theory, Bureaucratic Career, and Neighborhood Primary Group.Cohesion," *Sociometry,* 23 (March 1960): 72–84.

Litwak, Eugene, and I. Szelenyi, "Primary Group Structures and Their Functions: Kin, Neighbors, and Friends," *American Sociological Review,* 54 (August 1969): 465–481.

McAllister, Ronald J., Edgar W. Butler, and Tzuen-jen Lei, "Patterns of Social Interaction Among Families of Behaviorally Retarded Children," *Journal of Marriage and the Family,* 77 (February 1973): 93–100.

Meadow, Kathryn P., "Relationship of Neighborhood Friendship Formation to Other Types of Social Contact," *Journal of Intergroup Relations,* 4 (Summer 1965): 171–184.

Meadow, Kathryn P., "Negro-White Differences Among Newcomers to a Transitional Urban Area," *Journal of Intergroup Relations,* 3 (Autumn 1962): 320–330.

Olsen, Marion E., "Social and Political Participation of Blacks," *American Sociological Review,* 34 (August 1970): 682–697.

Orum, Anthony M., "A Reappraisal of the Social and Political Participation of Negroes," *American Journal of Sociology,* 72 (July 1966): 32–46.

Palisi, Bartolomeo J., "Ethnic Patterns of Friendship," *Phylon,* 27 (Fall 1966): 217–225.

Pope, Hallowell, "Economic Deprivation and Social Participation in a Group of 'Middle Class' Factory Workers," *Social Problems,* 11 (Winter 1964): 290–300.

Reissman, Leonard, "Class, Leisure, and Social Participation," *American Sociological Review,* 19 (February 1954): 76–84.

Riesman, David, "The Suburban Dislocation," *Annals of the American Academy of Political and Social Science,* 314 (November 1957): 123–146.

Scaff, Alvin H., "The Effect of Commuting on Participation in Community Organizations," *American Sociological Review,* 19 (April 1952): 218–219.

Smith, Joel, William H. Form, and Gregory P. Stone, "Local Intimacy in a Middle-

Sized City," *American Journal of Sociology,* 60 (November 1954): 279–289.

Sussman, Marvin B., "The Help Pattern in the Middle Class Family," *American Sociological Review,* 18 (February 1953): 22–28.

Sweetser, Frank L., Jr., "A New Emphasis for Neighborhood Research," *American Sociological Review,* 7 (August 1942): 525–533.

Tomeh, Aida K., "Informal Group Participation and Residential Patterns," *American Journal of Sociology,* 70 (July 1964): 28–35.

Wirth, Louis, "Urbanism as a Way of Life," *American Journal of Sociology,* 44 (July 1938): 1–24.

Wright, Charles R., and Herbert H. Hyman, "Voluntary Association Memberships of American Adults: Evidence from National Sample Surveys," *American Sociological Review,* 23 (June 1958): 284–294.

Zimmer, Basil G., "Participation of Migrants in Urban Structures," *American Sociological Review,* 20 (April 1955): 218–224.

Zimmer, Basil G., and Amos H. Hawley, "The Significance of Membership in Associations," *American Journal of Sociology,* 65 (September 1959): 196–201.

BIBLIOGRAPHY: Books

Adams, Bert N., *Kinship in an Urban Setting,* Chicago: Markham Publishing Company, 1968.

Barber, Bernard, *Social Stratification,* New York: Harcourt, Brace and Company, 1957.

Bell, Wendell, "The City, the Suburb, and a Theory of Social Choice," in Scott Greer, Dennis L. McElrath, David W. Minar and Peter Orleans (eds.), *The New Urbanization,* New York: St. Martin's Press, 1968, pp. 132–168.

Bell, Wendell, "Social Choice, Life Styles, and Suburban Residence," in William M. Dobriner (ed.), *The Suburban Community,* New York: G. P. Putnam's Sons, 1958, pp. 225–247.

Boskoff, Alvin, *The Sociology of Urban Regions,* New York: Appleton-Century-Crofts, 1970.

Bullough, Bonnie, *Social Psychological Barriers to Housing Desegregation,* Los Angeles: Center for Real Estate and Urban Economics, University of California, July 1969.

Chapin, F. Stuart, Jr., Edgar W. Butler, and Frederick C. Patten, *Blackways in the Inner City,* Urbana, Ill.: University of Illinois Press, forthcoming.

Drake, St. Clair, and Horace R. Cayton, *Black Metropolis,* New York: Harcourt, Brace, 1945.

Fava, Sylvia F., "Contrasts in Neighboring: New York City and a Suburban County," in William Dobriner (ed.), *The Suburban Community,* New York: G. P. Putnam's Sons, 1958.

Frazier, Franklin E., *The Negro in the United States,* rev. ed., New York: Macmillan, 1957.

Gans, Herbert J., *The Urban Villagers,* New York: The Free Press, 1962.

Greer, Scott, and Ella Kube, "Urbanism and Social Structure: A Los Angeles Study," in Marvin B. Sussman, (ed.), *Community Structure and Analysis,* New York: Thomas Y. Crowell Company, 1959.

Hannerz, Ulf, *Soulside: Inquiries into Ghetto Culture and Community,* New York: Columbia University Press, 1969.

Hausknecht, Murray, *The Joiners,* New York: Bedminster Press, 1962.

Hawley, Amos H., *Urban Society,* New York: Ronald Press, 1971.

Hawley, Amos H., and Basil Zimmer, *The Metropolitan Community: Its People and Government,* Beverly Hills, Calif.: Sage Publications, 1970.

Hollingshead, August B., *Elmtown's Youth,* New York: Wiley, 1949.

Irelan, Lola M. (ed.), *Low-Income Life Styles,* Washington, D.C.: U.S. Dept. of Health, Education, and Welfare.

Lane, Robert, *Political Life: Why People Get Involved in Politics,* Glencoe, Ill.: The Free Press, 1959.

Liebow, Elliot, *Tally's Corner,* Boston: Little, Brown and Company, 1967.

McCord, William, John Howard, Bernard Friedberg, and Edwin Harwood, *Life Styles in the Black Ghetto,* New York: Norton, 1969.

Minnis, Mhyra S., "The Patterns of Women's Organizations: Significance, Types, Social Prestige Rank, and Activities," in Marvin B. Sussman, (ed.) *Community Structure and Analysis,* New York: Thomas Y. Crowell Company, 1959.

Myrdal, Gunnar, *An American Dilemma: The Negro Problem and Modern Democracy,* New York: Harper & Row, 1944.

Nohara, Shigeo, "Social Context and Neighborliness: The Negro in St. Louis," in Scott Greer, Dennis L. McElrath, David W. Minar, and Peter Orleans (eds.), *The New Urbanization,* New York: St. Martin's Press, 1968, pp. 179–188.

Riemer, Svend, "Urban Personality—Reconsidered," in Marvin B. Sussman (ed.), *Community Structure and Analysis,* New York: Thomas Y. Crowell Company, 1959, pp. 433–444.

Rose, Arnold, *Theory and Method in the Social Sciences,* Minneapolis, Minn.: University of Minnesota Press, 1953.

Scanzoni, John N., *The Black Family in Modern Society,* Boston: Allyn and Bacon, Inc., 1971.

Seeley, John R., R. Alexander Sim, and E. W. Loosely, *Crestwood Heights,* New York: Basic Books, 1956.

Suttles, Gerald D., *The Social Order of the Slum,* Chicago: University of Chicago Press, 1968.

Warner, W. Lloyd, et al., *Democracy in Jonesville,* New York: Harper & Bros., 1949.

Warner, W. Lloyd, and Paul S. Lunt, *The Social Life of a Modern Community,* New Haven, Conn.: Yale University, 1941.

Young, Michael, and Peter Willmott, *Family and Kinship in London,* Baltimore: Penguin Books, 1957.

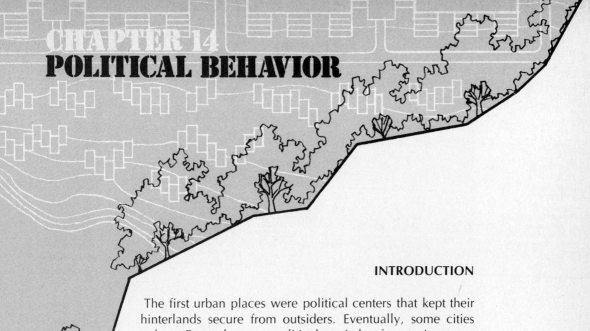

CHAPTER 14
POLITICAL BEHAVIOR

INTRODUCTION

The first urban places were political centers that kept their hinterlands secure from outsiders. Eventually, some cities such as Rome became political capitals of vast city-states. Quite clearly in those early city-states there were social divisions of elites who lived in one section of the city and of workers and slaves who lived elsewhere in the city or outside the protective walls. Some early political power struggles involved merchants against the landed aristocracy. After the merchants won, they assumed much of the power formerly held by the landed gentry. Gradually, more and more political rights were granted to larger population segments, and by the time of the colonization of the United States, voting and other political rights were being demanded by both those who owned property and those who didn't. As this country became settled, voting privileges were extended to virtually all white males. Presumably, after the Civil War these same rights were extended to black males.

Urbanization of the country continued as millions of immigrants began arriving from the Old World. During this time, the great "bosses" of the cities arose and, along with them, machine politics. It is not clear whether the massive urbanization or the flood of immigrants contributed most to the rise of bossism; indeed, it may have been a combination of both. During the 1920s, through the efforts of the League of Women Voters and other organizations and individuals, the right to vote was finally extended to women.

Also about this time a few scholarly studies of voting in the United States were undertaken. One of these early studies of political phenomena was Stuart A. Rice's book, *Quantitative Methods in Politics* (1928). This book, though written over 40 years ago, still is one of the most useful insofar as methodology and theoretical implications are concerned for the study of political behavior in metropolitan regions. Also, Heberle, in his book *Social Movements*

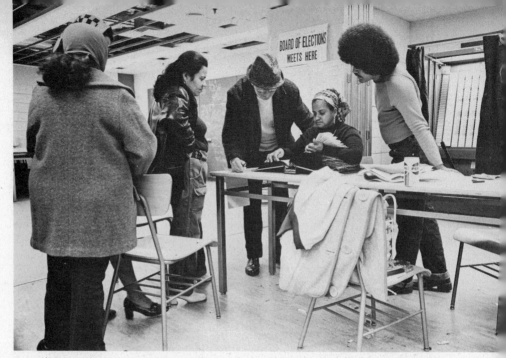

According to election researchers, the mute voting machine standing in this urban polling place can divulge much more than who is the winner and loser in a political contest. Voting behavior, Heberle argued, is the expression of an entire way of life.

(1951: 195–265), discussed political ecology at some length. He viewed political ecology as being

> election analysis with the purpose of investigation of multiple factors as the political phenomena requires more than the study of single factors. It is desirable to take into consideration the interrelation between various parties in each significant area and also to study complexes or constellations of factors in those areas.

He points out that the sociologist reverses the thinking of the politician—the political candidate knows approximately what social groups are his potential supporters. The sociologist, on the other hand, has election results by wards, precincts, and so on, compares election results with the composition of population segments within areas, and can *infer* which populations gave their support to a candidate or party. Political ecology, then, involves the study of complex political and social phenomena in their geographical distributions and interrelationships.

Heberle gives some general principles "about the ecology of social movements, and political parties" that can be used in the study of election returns: (1) The geographic characteristics of a region—topography, soil quality, resources, climate, physical accessibility, and nearness to markets by various routes—determine the development of the economy of that region—the kind and relative importance of agriculture, of manufacturing industries, commerce, transportation, and so forth; (2) the economy determines the economic class structure—the planters and sharecroppers, family farmers, renters, and hired help; factory owners and workers, and so on; (3) the economic class structure determines the nature of local, social, and political issues as well as reactions to national issues. In the city this general outline would be modified. There topography determines what locations may be considered most desirable for certain purposes—commercial, industrial, residential with subclassifications, and so forth.

Heberle also lists four tentative specific guidelines in the study of election returns: (1) The association between social classes, social movements, and political parties must lead to geographical differences in the relative strength of political parties and social movements if the class structure varies among areas; (2) constellations of political parties and social movements vary among areas, because social class structure varies and because parties and movements react to one another; (3) geographical variation in the strength of social and political movements and parties, especially among larger geographical regions, may be partly the result of differences in the political history of the regions; certain experiences in the past may affect the present attitudes, opinions, and preferences prevalent in a certain region; and (4) variation in ethnic composition of populations of various areas may result in differences in attitudes and opinions, intensity of participation in social movements, and in party strength.

Heberle (1952: 2) argued that voting behavior is an index of the level of social integration or disintegration of a society or subarea such as a city or urban region, and in many instances "political tendencies are an expression of the entire way of life of various groups of people." He noted, for example, that the main factor of political solidarity in the American South is the presence of rural blacks; in these areas a majority of votes are cast for candidates representing white supremacy. On the other hand, poorer hill areas, predominantly white in character, are areas where radical and reform movements grow and where demogogues arise and command votes.

Another illustration of voting as a reflection of an entire way of life is that most longitudinal studies of areas show that voting patterns are surprisingly consistent over time. Heberle's research conducted in Louisiana over a nine-decade period reported similar tendencies as in suburban Orange County, California, an area that grew from a relatively small population in 1950 to several million by 1970. Thus there is evidence to suggest that factional political attitudes and strength persist in the same ecological areas over long periods of time. Easton (1965) suggested that in the study of political behavior it must be recognized that physical boundaries are one important way of delineating political systems, although not necessarily the only way.

VOTING PATTERNS

While early research was ecological, most subsequent studies focused either upon individual decision making, the flow of information, and influence

The voter who chooses this candidate will probably do so, according to most studies, because his or her parents would have chosen similarly. Salisbury and Black would consider this tendency valid even as a voter relocates across the rural-urban line.

during campaigns or on attitudinal variables and the political content and implications of individual voting behavior (Sheingold, 1973). For example, *The People's Choice* (Lazarsfeld et al., 1944) is a survey study of Sandusky, Ohio, mainly concerned with decisions involved in making a choice of candidates and the effects of mass media upon that choice. The main hypothesis emerging from that study is that voters have a high degree of loyalty to a political party and hesitate to deviate from it. In addition, it was reported that (1) various personality characteristics seemingly had no significance as to what party a person belonged to; (2) personal influence was more important than the mass communication media on a person's voting behavior; and (3) the decision to vote for one party or another, or one candidate or another, was a group decision rather than a personal decision. The mass communication media, as already mentioned, seemingly had little effect as to what party or candidate a person voted for, possibly because only those who were already convinced of a particular party or candidate listened to the particular campaign. It also was found that "changers" had a low level of exposure to campaign propaganda and a low interest in the campaign and seemed apathetic. Factors most related to voting behavior in these studies were socioeconomic status, religion, and *rural-urban* residence (also see Berelson et al., 1954, and Campbell et al., 1954).

Interest in politics is related to the possession of political skills and a feeling of competence in politics, that is, a belief that one can actually affect the political process (Lipset, 1956: 46). When a person does vote, however, most studies show that at least three out of four persons vote for the same party that their parents did and that they seldom change from election to election. Party identification is important in predicting voting even when social class is held constant or controlled. In addition, it has been noted that participants in voluntary associations are more likely to be voters, to remain voters, and to become voters if they had previously been nonvoters than are nonparticipants (Maccoby, 1958: 532). Other factors such as rural-urban residence may not be as important as party identification in determining the vote (Salisbury and Black, 1963).

At the national level there has been a growth of two diametrically opposed voting trends: (1) Republican presidential candidates win the presidency, and (2) Democratic majorities carry both houses of Congress. They appear to be long-term trends, because this has been substantially the pattern since at least 1956 (Cox, 1960). These earlier results portended the current voter trend of crossing party lines at the state and local levels. Thus each election finds more and more crossing party lines in voting for various candidates and a larger and larger proportion of voters preferring to be labeled "independent" rather than Democratic or Republican.

Yet most studies indicate that the political affiliation of the populace is relatively stable and that many people vote for a party only because their parents, relatives, and so forth, voted for that party. Party loyalties are given a high priority and are relatively stable over a period of time. Nevertheless, there are departures from this point of view. Dissenters Bean (1940) and Ewing (1947), analyzed congressional elections from 1896 to 1944. Ewing showed very graphically that in 1928 the Republicans far outdistanced the Democrats, whereas in 1932 an almost complete reversal took place. Granted that a depression was an intervening variable in this case, how do we explain other fluctuations in voting results? For example, at the same time in 1928 when the Republican star was rising, the Democrats also were receiving an additional number of votes.

Fluctuations may be related to voter turnout. The South typically has a lower turnout than the rest of the United States, and this has been explained by mechanisms used to disfranchise blacks. Another factor related to lower voter turnout is social class: Cities having large lower-class populations report lower turnout rates than cities with smaller ones (Alford and Lee, 1968). Rate of population change also appears to be related to voter turnout, since as population growth increases, voter turnout tends to decrease. A monumental work by Key (1950) that traces the impact of different facets upon elections in the South pointed out that votes at the county level are not random events but are rather systematically distributed and show consistent *shifts* over time. In addition, his work demonstrated the systematic impact that a "home" candidate has on voting in his or her local county as well as in contiguous counties, where a candidate may be considered as a "friend and neighbor" regardless of political persuasion, slant on issues, and so forth.

Another possible explanation for the voting fluctuations that occur is that while the voter may be given a clear-cut alternative on a question and a clear-cut choice of candidates, the choices may not present the particular alternatives, nor the exponents of certain issues, that the voter would prefer (Rice, 1924: 21). Those on the opposite sides of a political issue "are only relatively likeminded—[they] may in fact possess many utterly dissimilar motives for their behavior." Thus attitudes held lightly may be easily changed. While economic interests are important, traditional and habitual attitudes in voting are even more significant (Rice, 1924: 32), but even these may be transcended during times of severe crisis or economic disaster or by other issues.

Similarly, Gosnell and Pearson (1939) were especially concerned with methodological problems as well as specific area voting patterns. They showed that most voters did not change their party affiliation. Those who did, however, had some individual and environmental factors in common. For example, in Iowa at that time switchers were predominantly dry (e.g., for prohibition), native white, and farmers who had suffered considerable losses in corn production.

The most frequently studied elections in this country are those that involve the general election of the President and, to some extent, mayors of larger cities. However, it should be noted that primary elections are important in determining who will eventually be elected President; in many areas in the South even today, winning the Democratic primary election is tantamount to being elected (Cutright and Rossi, 1959). Similarly, there are many other offices, bond elections, referendums, and so on, that are important to voters but little studied. Besides voting there are, of course, other levels of political activity. Some people are quite active in taking public positions on local governmental issues, in trying to persuade others on a personal level, and in attending meetings about issues.

URBANIZATION AND POLITICAL BEHAVIOR

Rice published a study (1924) of labor and farmer voting throughout the United States. He found that "progressivism" and "insurgency" are phenomena associated with areas in which taxpayers' payments are utilized in largest ratio for state and local ends.

With the aid of occupational information based on the 1950 U.S. census and voting data, MacRae (1960) studied occupations and the congressional vote for the period of 1940–1950 and showed contrasts between sectional and class politics. There was less participation at the congressional level than at the presidential level insofar as the total number of votes was concerned. The congressional vote was closely allied with party identification, displayed a more stable pattern, and was heavily influenced by issues and personal views. The last finding does not seem to be supported adequately by MacRae's data and conflicts with much other voting behavior research. In recent years high occupational status indicates voting for Republican candidates, and low occupational status, for Democratic candidates—a finding that does not necessarily hold for rural areas, however. Rural voting seems more closely allied to the traditions of the community. In other words, in smaller rural communities votes tend to be directed by tradition and local leaders, but not in urban areas, where class or occupation level is more important.

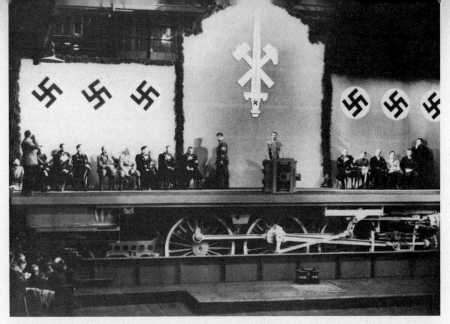

Adolph Hitler was one of the most influential political figures of the twentieth century. Like all successful demagogues, he knew how to appeal to the alienated and dissatisfied—and how to wield them into a powerful political movement.

MacRae's research has significance for further study: *the more homogeneous an area is in its traditions, values, and so on, the more likely it is to have a nonvariant voting record.*

Heberle (1951), in his studies of Louisiana voting, found that Huey and Earl Long's power was provided by poorer white farmers. Reports that city parishes and other factions that supposedly were Fascist in nature and supporters of the Longs did not bear out when the voting was analyzed ecologically. If a label were to be attached to the Longs, Heberle concluded, it would have to be almost the direct opposite, moderate Socialist. Heberle also mentioned a study concerning the southern part of the United States in which he tested the hypothesis that the southern Democratic party is held together solely by the black issue. In the main the hypothesis stood the test of his analysis.

TYPE OF URBAN PLACE
AND POLITICAL BEHAVIOR

Virtually no work has been done that compares the political behavior of people in different types of urban places. The little bit of information that does exist must be gleaned from research endeavors that only imply or allude to such differences. One such study of four Wisconsin cities—Green Bay, Kenosha, Racine, and Madison—showed that there is great variability among cities in party attachment. In addition, within each of the cities there are contrasts in voting patterns among the wards (Alford and Scoble, 1968 and 1969). The major structural factors related to local political involvement are social status (class), organizational activity, and homeownership. Not related were feelings of political efficacy, alienation, civic duty, goegraphical mobility, length of residence, and so on. Green Bay, a retail-trade center, had the largest proportion of Republicans; Racine and Kenosha, manufacturing cities, had the largest proportions of Democrats. Madison, which was considered a "professional" center because of the governmental and university facilities located there, had a mixed political base. Surprisingly, Alford and Scoble (1968 and 1969: 174) claimed that partisanship in these cities is associated with historical and political factors quite unrelated to their social composition despite the fact that the cities are of different types. The "immediate" sociopolitical milieu (to use their words) has little influence upon political involvement. Again, this is surprising because homeownership, for example, clusters in certain neighborhoods of the cities and certainly did influence local political involvement according to their analysis. Homeownership may be a good indicator of those persons who have specific interests at stake in the neighborhood and city and thus are more likely to be involved in the political process than are renters. These differences in political party affiliation, therefore, are exactly as one would predict given no other knowledge of the cities or of areas with them.

A large study of a sample of U.S. cities reported the mean percentage of persons of voting age registered to vote was 73.3 percent and the mean percentage registered to vote who voted was 81.6 percent (Kelly et al., 1967: 362). In general, the average rate of registration was highest in midwestern and western cities (82.5 and 80.7 percent respectively), intermediate in Northeast (76.1 percent) and Border cities (70.7 percent, and lowest in the South (55.9 percent). The range of registration rates is 90 percent plus in cities such as Berkeley, Detroit, South Bend, Seattle, Scranton, Lansing, Des Moines, Minneapolis, and St. Paul to less than 40 percent in Birmingham, Columbus (Georgia), Atlanta, Portsmouth (Virginia), Newport News, and Las Vegas, Nevada.

The main factors associated with voter registration are education and race. Typically, the larger the proportion of persons in the age category of 20–34 relative to other persons of voting age, the lower the proportion of registered voters in the city. Cities with a high population over 25 years of age and exceeding the educational level of the general sample also had higher registration rates. Cities with a high proportion of nonwhites (or blacks) had lower registration rates than those with lower proportions (Kelley et al., 1967: 364). However, differences in mean income levels appeared to have little effect upon registration results. These findings, coupled with those from other studies, suggest that education is much more important than income in determining registration percentages (also see Alford and Lee, 1968). However, variation in mean educational attainment explained much less variation in cities that had a permanent registration system, and it appears to a substantial degree that the regional differences noted earlier probably are a result of age, education, and race differences.

Some cities did not fit the general pattern of "expected" registration levels. This was partially accounted for by a large percentage of Catholics, which leads to an underprediction of registration, and in a few cities a substantial number of resident aliens resulted in an overprediction of registration. In addition, restrictive rules and procedures for registration certainly have an effect upon it as does limited competition among parties. Finally, it should be noted that all of the previously discussed factors demonstrate that variables other than socioeconomic ones operate at the city-wide level in the registration of voters (Kelley et al., 1967: 374), a conclusion somewhat in contrast to studies that have focused on the individual voter as the unit of analysis.

Other studies have shown that the "larger the population or voting population of political units, the smaller the vote cast relative to the population or voting population." In addition, rapidly growing cities or urban areas cast smaller relative votes than do cities whose population is either fairly stationary or changing slowly. Generally, a larger vote is cast for executive than for legislative or judicial offices, and in the political units there occurs sufficient parallelism, iteration, and time recurrence of action to indicate that their voting behavior is not chaotic (Titus, 1935: 19).

VARIATION WITHIN METROPOLITAN
COMPLEXES AND POLITICAL BEHAVIOR

As we have consistently noted, the metropolitan complex is made up of a mosaic of social worlds; it should be added that it also is made up of a mosaic of political units—counties, the central city, suburbs, unincorporated areas, and voting precincts. These political units have meaning to the residents in the metropolis because it is through them that they may indicate their preferences for candidates, bonds, referendums, reforms, and so on. Obviously, in a political sense the central city is a much different political arena from smaller suburbs or other political units. The city tends to generate a broad-gauged, impersonalized, larger-scale area of political action, whereas smaller suburbs and enclaves typically have more personalized political activities. This section reviews some of the literature dealing with election variability within metropolitan complexes and some of the related factors. Again, it should be noted that, unfortunately, most of the studies are cross-sectional rather than longitudinal (Boskoff, 1970: 265).

While some rule out the importance of ecological influences like region of birth and place of residence upon party preference and voting (Knoke, 1972), within most cities in the United States there are certain areas in which political support and opposition are concentrated. The way in which this support and opposition operate and whether they operate consistently or idiosyncratically are important to the city and its residents, because decisions on issues are affected. It is not necessary for these voting zones to be interpreted, as some analysts interpret them, as *determinants* of voting behavior. It is enough to recognize that they exist and contribute to the explanation of varying appeals with which politicians court the public for votes; and they provide a setting against which other aspects of the urban environment become more meaningful (Kasperson, 1971: 406).

Chicago

One longitudinal study of urban voting was undertaken by Kasperson (1971) for the city of Chicago during the mayoralty elections of 1951, 1955, and 1959. Chicago at that time was divided into some 50 wards, and aldermen were elected from these wards. Based upon an analysis of the spatial distribution of elections during these three mayoralty elections, four political regions were delineated: (1) the *core area,* which included wards in which the Democratic party obtained over 80 percent of the votes; (2) the *inner zone,* in which the Democratic party received over 60 percent of the votes; (3) the *outer zone,* in which the Republican party was dominant as indicated by 60 percent or more of the vote being cast for the Republican candidate; and (4) the *zone of competition,* in which neither party received more than 60 percent of votes (Kasperson, 1971: 403).

In the 1951 election the winning Democratic candidate's core area of support was located in the populous heart of the city, and the zone of competition was located north and south of the inner zone. Subsequently, this particular Democratic mayor fell from favor, and the Democratic party ran Richard Daley for mayor. He faced weak opposition, and the core Democratic area expanded from a basic 7 wards to 19 wards, while all but 3 of the remaining wards were classified as the inner zone; that is, Daley received 60 percent or more of the vote in these wards. Kelley and others (1967: 375) suggested that the Daley organization in Chicago manipulated the vote by varying the *convenience of registering.* The Republican candidate did not receive 60 percent of the vote in any of the 50 wards.

Kasperson (1971: 405) claimed that the voting zones of the city of Chicago during this era definitely follow the Burgess concentric zone theory of land use and city growth described in Chapter 7. The majority of Democratic support was in the core and workers' home areas and in zones with incomes lower than the average for the city as a whole. These zones also included a low percentage of homeowners and a high percentage of minorities and foreign-born. In addition, these areas were those that began to lose substantial population between 1950 and 1960.

These population losses are working hard toward undermining the traditional Democratic support in the wards, and the rapid population increase in outer areas of competition is decreasing the influence of traditional core areas. These population increases and losses mean that the politician is becoming torn more and more between his obligation to the core and the inner zones and the need to obtain votes from outer zones to remain in office (Kasperson 1971: 406). Thus, candidates must increasingly tailor their appeals to voters of markedly different regions in the city. In the core and inner city politicians stress *tangibles* such as jobs and increasing educational opportunities, while in

"WHAT ARE YOU LAUGHING AT? TO THE VICTOR BELONG THE SPOILS."

Cartoonist Thomas Nast used satires like this one to attack political corruption in old New York. The notorious Tweed Ring became expert in the art of tailoring their appeals to specific groups of voters in distinct zones of the city — namely, immigrants in the slums. Modern politicians often encounter the dilemma of keeping obligations toward core zones of a city while soliciting needed votes from suburbanites interested in their own affairs.

the outer zone *intangibles* are stressed in appeals to "good government," "reform," and "law and order." Thus support in the core and inner city may be patronage jobs, local favors, lack of code enforcement; their opposite, of course, may be retribution.

The question of stability in voting patterns by area is an important one. How flexible is the vote? If the ward or area consistently votes one way, it may be taken for granted and the candidate will make appeals more to the zone of competition voters who may hold swing votes in a close election. Whatever the result, the Chicago study showed quite clearly that the political behavior of individuals located in various wards is translated into rather consistent, enduring patterns that politicians take into account and utilize in making their appeals to voters. Whether these areas "cause" voters to act as they do or whether there is some other explanation has not yet been determined.

Social Area Analysis and Political Behavior in St. Louis

The population of St. Louis is, on the average, higher in urbanism and lower in social rank than its suburbs (Greer and Orleans, 1968). Both of these dimensions are associated with a lower degree of localized social participation in the city, that is, neighboring and participation in local political organizations. The predominant mode of political involvement in the suburbs is personally oriented, with neighbors and local organizations being influential. Residents of suburban areas are more likely than city residents to rely upon other people for political information, to be involved in political affairs, and to have a higher level of political competence.[1] Personal influence, then, is more important in the suburbs than in the city. Residents of the city rely more upon mass media and nonlocalized organizations outside of the political sphere for information, and so on. Political behavior and knowledge are broader gauged in the city, going beyond the immediate local residential community. But in the suburbs they are more likely to be related to the local community.

In the percent of votes for candidates and/or issues and the percent of voter turnout in the same elections, the major social area dimension was social rank, although the urbanization index was quite important and negatively associated with voter turnout in a sewer district election. Lower turnout by the urbanization index suggests overall that voters living in such areas had less interest and stake in this election than those living in areas characterized by less urbanization since sewers were already in and available for those social areas with a higher urbanization index. Of those who did turn out, residents of areas of high urbanization were more likely to have voted for sewers, thus suggesting that "metropolitanites" live in areas with a higher urbanization index. Similarly, it appears that "localities" live in more familism-oriented areas and feel that the city and the suburbs have little in common. Thus the voting in highly familistically oriented social areas is more likely to be less favorable toward sewer bonds even though a positive vote may have been in their own self-interest. In fact, it may be the increase of populations with strong neighborhood

---

[1] In the Greer and Orleans study this probably should have been more correctly called knowledge, since the measure used is ability to name leaders in the local community.

commitments that generates much of the "metropolitan problem," since the development of such neighborhood orientations may make the solution of metropolitan problems less feasible when they require popular support, for example, voter consent (Kaufman and Greer, 1960).

The proportion of city and suburban residents completely uninvolved in the political process is comparable (approximately one out of five), but the extent of high involvement is much greater in the suburbs: Further, involvement by city residents is more likely to be limited to voting, whereas involved suburban residents do more than merely vote. In both the city and the suburbs persons who are involved with neighboring, local organizations, and so on, are more likely than isolates to be politically active. That is, those who participate extensively outside of the political sphere are more likely than nonparticipators to be politically involved (Greer and Orleans, 1968).

In summary there is less political participation — voting, taking a position on local issues, persuading others on local issues, attending meetings, and so on — by residents of lower-ranking areas and of those characterized as being higher in urbanism (lower on familism), although urbanism is an even more consistent and powerful differentiator with respect to political involvement.

Other Cities and Voting Behavior

A study of Baton Rouge, Louisiana, showed that there were three homogeneous voting areas in the city divided along two dimensions: occupational (manual versus nonmanual) and race (white versus black). Also, in some elections white laborers versus upper white nonmanuals was an important factor. Of the elections studied a somewhat consistent pattern emerged, with a trend toward support of conservative condidates (Howard et al., 1971: 50). In Seattle, Washington, the association between the Democratic vote and mean rental of housing units by precincts was very high. Once again, as in many of the studies previously discussed, social class seemed to be a predominant factor.

A Note on Social
Class and Political Behavior

Virtually all studies discussed in this chapter set out to explain political behavior from a variety of perspectives. However, no matter what aspect was examined, social class emerges as a common and predominant explanatory factor. Other factors are mentioned, but not nearly so often, and they do not have the force of conviction behind them. Some have argued that the predominance of social class has declined over the years; yet a review of a number of studies over the past several decades suggests that social class is as important now as it ever was in determining political behavior, and there are some indications that it is becoming more important (Alford, 1963). Obviously, in particular elections at particular times and places other facets may be important. Certainly, urban and rural residence, religion, moral issues, and ideology, inasmuch as it can be separated from social class, influence some election outcomes (for a discussion of these and other factors see Lipset, 1960).

The Suburbs
and Voting Behavior

In general it has been consistently reported that overall metropolitan areas predominantly vote Democratic. Even during the Eisenhower and Nixon years urban congressional districts for the most part remained Democratic, and Congress was controlled by Democrats. Nevertheless, it has also been systematically noted that suburbs of metropolitan complexes predominantly vote Republican. Several reasons for this have been advanced. First, suburban Republicanism is a product of the population redistribution that is taking place in metropolitan areas. "The upper income and status groups most likely to vote Republican have moved from the cities, taking their political preferences with them" (Greenstein and Wolfinger, 1958–1959: 220). This explanation does not attribute to suburbs the converting of Democrats to Republicans, which is, of course, the gist of the second hypothesis — the conversion thesis. That is, a move to the suburbs is accompanied or followed by a switch from the Democratic to the Republican party as a result of the Republican political climate there. A third hypothesis is that a move to the suburbs indicates a preselective process whereby those Democrats who live in the city are already in the conversion process — the move to the suburbs solidifies their basic larger set of attitudes in which a shift to the Republican party is implicit.

In their attempt to unravel the explanation for Republican suburbs, Greenstein and Wolfinger (1958–1959) suggested that a combination of self-selection and/or environmental conversion takes place. Thus Democrats move to the suburbs and then change as a result of exposure to environmental pressures, for instance, Republicanism. Suburban Democrats are prone to cross-pressures unlike Democrats in the city who are the dominant political party. The data from this study, however, did not support the thesis that it is the upwardly mobile who converted from the Democratic party to the Republican party; rather upwardly mobile individuals maintained their original familial party loyalties.

Most early suburbs were the locus of Republican party strength; but with the advent of post–World War II mass-produced suburbs, better-paid white-collar, industrial, and other workers became suburbanites. Would the traditionally Republican nature of the suburbs become substantially changed as a result of this influx of people, many of who were, at least formerly, Democrats? Some believed that occupation, religion, previous party affiliation, and so on, would mitigate against conversion and that the movement would reflect only those characteristics of suburban movers. If they had formerly been Democratic, they would remain Democratic, and the character of suburbs would change as a result of different kinds of people moving in. "Consequently, one would not expect political party preference to be upset by movement to the suburbs" (Lazerwitz, 1960: 30).

In testing some of the implications of suburban movement, Lazerwitz (1960) examined central, suburban, and adjacent residential belts of metropolitan complexes. According to his data, the central city residential belt had the largest percentage voting Democratic. Interestingly, the suburban belt was more Republican than the outer belt beyond the suburbs in 1948, but by 1952 there was virtually no difference between the suburban and outer adjacent belt; by 1956 the suburban belt was more Democratic than the most distant belt of the metropolitan complex. Thus, over the time span of this study, suburbs became increasingly Democratic. The size of the metropolitan complex has some bearing on these relationships, however, since in smaller complexes Democratic voters for both the President and members of Congress decreased during this period. Thus "residential belts of the large population group are consistently more Democratic than the corresponding belts of the small population group" (Lazerwitz, 1960: 35). It should be noted that larger suburban residential areas are more typical of larger cities.

Some have suggested that the suburban electorate is becoming rather erratic in nature. That is, in the 1950s it was increasingly Republican in national elections but was increasingly Democratic on the state and local levels. As a result, Wallace (1963) studied Westport, Connecticut, a city located about 50 miles from New York City and characterized by relatively rapid growth after World War II and up through 1960. New arrivals contrasted with older residents; the inmovers were in the communications industry, were well-educated, and had relatively high incomes. Moreover, in contrast to many other suburbs, Westport was rather open in regard to religious minorities—about 20 percent of the population was Jewish at the time of this study.

In Westport it appears there has been very little change in party voting for the president year by year. "If one is a Republican, he votes for the Republican candidate—no matter who. If one is a Democrat, he votes for the Democrat—no matter who" (Wallace, 1963: 164). Thus about 8 out of every 10 members of a political party voted for their party's candidate, no matter who the candidate was or what the circumstances were. Among the unaffiliated, 44 percent *always* voted Republican, 20 percent *always* voted Democrat. In Westport little change in party affiliation was related to suburban movement or to the theory that suburbs make for Republicans. Of the changes that did occur, Protestants were slightly more likely, and Jews much more likely, than their parents to be Democratic, while Catholics were somewhat more likely to be Republican than their parents. Overall, then, the picture in Westport was one of political stability, with little change among individuals from one election to another and even from one generation to another.

The changes that occurred in Westport were a gradual step-by-step movement away from the Republican party, and there was some suggestion

Dwight Eisenhower's personal influence temporarily abated the general trend toward Democratic Party hegemony in Washington. Studies such as those by Manis and Stine argue that the growth of suburban Republicanism cannot be taken at face value during the years in which "Ike" dominated national politics.

that this disaffection was picking up steam. The greatest losses were among strong Republicans (note that this was long before Watergate and related incidents). The changers had already indicated some disaffection with the Republican party by switching votes during earlier elections and by having parents who at times also were switchers and/or unaffiliated Republicans. Thus Wallace (1963: 166) states: "Those who changed most readily are more nearly like the followers of the party to which they moved."

One aspect that grows out of the rigidity of many Republicans and Democrats in their voting patterns is that the effective power of the less interested and less partisan minorities is enhanced far beyond their numbers, since they are the swing votes in any closely contested election. In Westport, for example, religion is related to political party stability in voting: Protestants are generally more Republican than Catholics and especially Jews. It should be noted that when party change is occurring, however, Protestants are more likely to become Democrats, whereas Catholics are more likely to become Republicans; however, Jews are becoming increasingly Democratic. The most stable Democrats are Jews and members of other minority religions.

In another test of the suburban-residence and political-change hypothesis, Manis and Stine (1958–1959) studied a suburb of the city of Kalamazoo, Michigan. The residents of this suburb had consistently voted Republican election after election. The researchers found that about one out of every nine persons interviewed had changed his or her party preference. Of the 23 persons changing their party affiliations, 20 changed from Democrat to Republican. But most of these changes were made during 1951 and 1952, with virtually no changes taking place since then. Thus it is argued that virtually all of these changes were related to the "Eisenhower theory" of an individual person rather than party. In other words, Eisenhower, rather than suburban influence, is credited with having brought about these changes. The researchers concluded that suburban residence did not have any other appreciable effect upon voting or changes in party preference. Rather, they attributed the change to Eisenhower at the national level and to occupational changes and religious affiliation of the residents. Manis and Stine concluded then that their study does not confirm the hypothesis that moving to the suburbs changes Democrats to Republicans.

Thus it appears that suburban areas over time have tended to favor Republican candidates, although in more recent years there have been substantial Democratic gains in some suburbs. The conversion and preselection hypotheses have not been verified in that most suburban movers from the city have tended to express the political characteristics of their previous residences. It certainly remains to distinguish among different types of suburbs and migration streams to suburban areas and to determine how they affect voting patterns (Boskoff, 1970: 266).

Race and Ethnicity

Orum (1966) noted two contrasting perspectives in regard to the political participation of blacks. The first and most popular perspective maintains that blacks are less likely than whites to participate in the political process. The second point of view, in contrast, argues that blacks are hyperactive political participators. The first, or social isolation, perspective assumes that most blacks are apathetic, ignorant, and indifferent to civic affairs; Orum added that this may be quite true, but the real question is whether blacks are any more apathetic, ignorant, and indifferent than the majority of whites.

Unfortunately, the evidence is somewhat mixed, so that no definitive answer can be given. For example, in Detroit during the decade 1930–1940, blacks were reported as becoming "politically average." That is, their political participation was reported to be growing and approximating that of the general population; they were becoming less rigid in party affiliation and occasionally supported third-party candidates. Subsequently, blacks in Detroit were reported as being more likely to belong to political organizations than whites, with 12 percent of blacks and 2 percent of whites belonging (Orum, 1966: 38–39). Virtually identical percentages were reported for a national sample (Hausknecht, 1962: 75). Nevertheless, in some cities and nationwide it appears that blacks are less likely than whites to vote. The trend since 1952, however, has been for more and more blacks to participate at least minimally in the political process by voting; and in Chicago, St. Louis, and several other northern industrial cities during the 1950s and 1960s substantial proportions of blacks voted, even though the proportions were somewhat below that of whites (Glantz, 1960). Some analyses suggest that while at the national level blacks are less likely than whites to vote when social class and/or education is controlled, their voting behavior is substantially the same. That is, lower-class whites and blacks vote in about the same proportions, so that the overall discrepancy in voting patterns is a social class rather than a racial phenomena. This is consistent except for the southern region, where blacks are less likely to vote regardless of social class and more likely to report that they are "ineligible" to vote.

There is city variability in chicano political participation; 56 percent of Los Angeles chicano respondents compared with 77 percent of the general population, reported that they were registered to vote, in that city. But 46 percent of San Antonio chicanos, compared with 43 percent of the general population for that city, reported that they were registered. In both cities the highest proportion of those registered were of middle age, and the proportion registered increased with income. In actual voting behavior chicano participation was below that of the general population and lower in San Antonio than Los Angeles. However, the chicano vote in San Antonio has been translated into chicano candidates winning elections primarily because the chicano population is more concentrated (or segregated) there than in Los Angeles. This concentration has lead to enough bloc voting, so that chicano candidates win elections, and, in fact, it "has been great enough to overcome the adversity of the social milieu and of the more stringent election rules in Texas" (Grebler et al., 1970: 565–566).

Finally, the study of the political participation of the many other ethnic populations in the United States has for the most part been neglected. Recently, it was shown that there is great variability among ethnic populations such as the French, German Catholics, the Spanish speaking, Jews, Italians, and Poles in this country in regard to education and political participation. Similarly, ethnic identification or consciousness differentially affects political participation. Much research is needed to explain adequately the different patterns of ethnic political participation (Greeley, 1974).

Chicanos are participating more and more in political actions other than voting, as illustrated by this United Farm Workers organizational meeting in Rio Grande, Texas. Most political researchers agree that, all other considerations aside, the most vital ingredient in political action is a belief that each citizen can indeed affect the outcome of a contest.

Elections Other
than President or Mayor

As we noted earlier, the evidence indicates that the voting behavior of individuals located in different situations or areas tends to follow a regular pattern, for instance, Republican or Democrat. These studies also show a relationship between lower social class or status and Democratic voters and between higher socioeconomic class or status and Republican voters. Uyeki (1966) noted that these generalizations are based primarily upon presidential and/or mayoralty elections. He suggested that there are a number of other issues upon which voters make decisions — welfare levies, park bonds, referendums, and so on. There may be different factors affecting voting on these kinds of issues in contrast to presidential elections. For example, voters of high socioeconomic status are more likely to vote in favor of such issues than are Democratic voters. While the preceding conclusions are based upon *individuals* and their voting patterns, do individuals similarly situated in the metropolitan complex have similar voting patterns — and over time? Thus the focus can be directed to social areas of the metropolis and voting other than presidential or mayoralty elections.

Uyeki (1966) carried out such a study for Cleveland and 21 other cities in the SMSA, ranging in size from the central city's 876,050 residents to Brooklyn's (Cleveland, Ohio, SMSA) population of 10,733. There was a wide range in sociodemographic characteristics in these cities except for the nonwhite (primarily black) population that resided in the central city. Uyeki arranged the various cities along the *social area* dimensions described in Chapter 7: social rank, urbanization, and segregation. Voting decisions studied included (1) county tax levies for welfare, (2) county bonds for physical improvements (road, zoos, sewers, etc.), (3) good-government issues (i.e., to create a state board of education, add more judges, etc.), and (4) elections for the governor, senators, and the President. In the Cleveland SMSA during the time period studied, social rank was clearly related to 90 percent of the voting pattern, urbanization to about 42 percent, and segregation to 20 percent of the election results. The segregation measure is related very strongly to election patterns for state and national offices but only weakly to the other three categories of elections.

Persons residing in higher-class areas voted systematically over time for improving the buildings and capital of the community and for governmental machinery thought to provide greater efficiency. In addition, residents of higher-status suburbs also voted consistently for public improvements and welfare monies, for lower-income people. Also, on the other hand, ethnic areas had a variegated pattern of voting on buildings, welfare, and other issues but were consistent in voting (e.g., Democratic) for candidates in state and national elections (for additional information about such elections in the Cleveland metropolitan area, see Norton, 1963). Another study of a California voter decision over housing discrimination reported the following as the underlying resistance to housing intergration: "Persons of equal status tend to live in the same neighborhood. Negroes have a lower social status than whites. Therefore, if Negroes move into a previously white neighborhood in any numbers, either the Negroes gain in status, the whites lose, or both." Those who voted for eliminating housing discrimination tended to be the minority groups and upper-level people in professional and managerial positions who were thus relatively secure in their social status. Those rejecting equal housing included the adherents of Goldwater drawn from all socioeconomic levels.

Nonpartisan Elections

Nonpartisan elections, in which a ballot is used containing no party designations, probably make up over one-half of the total number of elections in the United States. Adrian (1959) has described four different types: First, there are nominally nonpartisan elections in which the only candidates who normally have a chance of being elected are those directly supported by a major political party organization. This type of election is relatively rare. Second, some nonpartisan elections are held in which the candidates are supported by a variety of groups, among them political party organizations. These elections also are relatively rare, accounting for about 10 percent of nonpartisan elections. A third type of nonpartisan election is one in which the candidates are supported by various interest groups, but political parties have little or no part in campaigns. Adrian cites a study that reported that 42 percent of the elections in 192 cities in California fit this model. The fourth type is perhaps the type of nonpartisan election reformers had in mind when they proposed the nonpartisan ballot, since these elections have no political parties or campaigns involved. About one-half of nonpartisan elections are classified as "true" nonpartisan elections of this kind. There may be a direct correlation between size of community and this type of nonpartisan ballot, with most elections in cities under 5000 population falling into this classification.

The essential arguments for nonpartisan elections are that they eliminate partisan consideration for essentially nonpolitical tasks of administering local city and town affairs and that national parties work to the detriment of local situations. Further, the nonpartisan ballot is supposed to eliminate the prejudices and other drawbacks of national parties that are irrelevant to the operation of local government. In addition, candidates may abdicate responsibility when a partisan ballot exists, which in turn leads to a party hierarchy (Orleans, 1968: 288). Arguments cited *against* nonpartisan ballots and elections are that national parties provide an organizational context against which diverse local interests can be coordinated and positions on politics can be clarified in a larger context than the local one. Similarly, a partisan ballot is more advantageous than a nonpartisan ballot because it adds the discipline of the national political party to the candidate and ultimate accountability to the electorate (Orleans, 1968: 288).

Nonpartisan elections in the United States tend to favor Republicans, because they mobilize the business interests of "Main Street" in such elections. However, most research has been conducted in smaller cities and towns, so that the politics of nonpartisan elections in larger cities and metropolitan complexes may be different. In larger cities, then, the heterogeneity of the population may militate against any significant degree of organization without a party label identification and hence Democrats may come out ahead (Orleans, 1968: 296–297).

Generally, research has shown that election results in cities that have nonpartisan elections are influenced by the proportion of foreign-born and their descendants. For example, "Bay City," Massachusetts was reported to have a political split between native-born Yankee Protestants and foreign-born Catholics (Freeman, 1958). Several studies of New Haven, Connecticut have shown the impact of the foreign-born upon organizations and political cleavages in the community (Minnis, 1959; Wolfinger, 1965). Similarly, much of New York City's politics reportedly revolves around immigrant loyalties. In a more elaborate study of several hundred cities Gordon (1970), using election results beginning in 1930 and ending in 1960, showed the different impacts that immigrant populations had and have on voting turnout.

One basic hypothesis derived from the studies of immigrant voting is that hard-fought elections and those that the public assumes it has a stake in will result in higher voter turnout on Election Day. In nonpartisan elections in cities having substantial immigrant populations, for example, candidates are put up who represent not only other interests but also the foreign-born immigrant population. This generates interest in the election. The lack of such interest in partisan elections is explained by assuming that ethnic loyalty becomes party loyalty, so that ethnicity then becomes less of an issue or identifying mechanism (Pomper, 1966: 91). Thus, cities with small immigrant populations have about the same voter turnout as cities with partisan elections, suggesting that in nonimmigrant cities political parties are organized on bases other than the foreign-born, for example, on social class or some other relevant factor (Gordon, 1970: 679).

Perhaps the major exception to the relationship between ethnicity and larger voter turnout is a matter of region. Southern cities, for instance, generally have lower turnouts than cities in other regions; this may be partially a carry-over of the fact that blacks in the South were disenfranchised for many years and in some areas may still be effectively disenfranchised (for another point of view see Kelley et al., 1967). Excluding blacks and chicanos, there is a strong tendency for immigrants to live in eastern cities, not in midwestern or western cities; therefore, the impact of immigrants upon election turnout is greater in these "older" cities than in "newer" cities of the Midwest and the West.

Alford and Lee (1968) also embraced the notion that nonpartisan elections reduce voter turnout; for example, in California cities turnout in partisan elections was 50 percent, while it was only 30 percent in nonpartisan cities (also see Kelley et al., 1967). Several other factors appear to be related to lower voter turnout, and the authors asked whether or not the turnout reflected underlying characteristics of the cities. They also noted, however, that higher turnout quite typically is associated with "negative voting"—that is, rejection of referendums, and so forth. Another factor associated with higher turnout is the form of local government: Cities with a mayor-council form of government and partisan elections have higher turnouts than those with a council-manager form of government and nonpartisan elections.

After studying data for some 282 cities spread throughout all regions of the United States, Alford and Lee (1968) showed that voting turnout is generally higher in cities with both or either partisan elections and/or a mayor-council form of government and with a more clearly delineated social class and/or ethnic distributions. In contrast to some other studies, they reported that voting turnout is higher in cities with less well educated populations. Similarly they noted that voting turnout is higher in cities with more residentially stable populations and that cities with larger turnouts are also more responsive to various social groupings in the community than are reformed cities. They cited others who believe that this is so because reformed election procedures such as the nonpartisan ballot have removed the basic party influence and thus the effects of social composition and cleavages are better able to be articulated in unreformed cities—mayor-council and partisan-election cities.

There are several questions that can be asked in regard to a greater voter turnout. First, is this turnout translated into better services and programs for the neighborhood and individuals, or does it merely reflect the ability of parties to get out the vote? Second, does a larger voter turnout have any impact in the city upon the larger social structure and thereby result in better services and programs?

Alford and Lee do not address the first question at all and only briefly allude to possible answers for the second one. Thus, according to them, a high voting turnout may allow a city to apply leverage extralocally so that bargains can be struck between local leaders and state and national leaders—for example, demonstrated ability to deliver the vote. On the other hand, they also noted that a highly active community may result in social cleavages that lead to a stalemate in local decisions.[2] As a result, little would be accomplished locally, statewide, or nationally because of it. They did not resolve this question and left it open to further research. Finally, they noted that cities with higher levels of education have lower turnouts than those with lower levels of education. This does not necessarily mean that *individuals* in either high- or low-turnout cities reflect this trend; the better educated in all cities may be more likely to turn out than those with lower-level education, but this individual effect is lost in studies using the city as a unit of analysis.

Following up Adrian's typology of nonpartisan elections outlined earlier, Williams and Adrian (1959) studied four middle-sized cities in the Midwest and suggested that voting for nonpartisan candidates was similar but not the same as voting for political party candidates. They concluded that "the similarity of voting patterns in the two political areas casts doubt on their complete separability." They proposed that the nonpartisan ballot in reality is not and in fact is heavily influenced by party. In the three cities that had citywide elections, the areas that normally voted for Republican candidates had better turnout records for nonpartisan elections; this gave them a dispropor-

[2] Earlier, in Chapter 11, we pointed out that countervailing power blocks can lead to stalemate and community inaction.

tionate influence upon the selection of municipal officials in the nominally nonpartisan election. But even in these cities the nonpartisan ballot does permit some recruitment of Democratic and minority-party members onto the ballot, and a few of them get elected from time to time.

SOME OTHER FACTORS RELATED TO URBAN POLITICAL BEHAVIOR

Generally, parents are more politically involved than their children, and there is a positive relationship between parents and children in political perspectives (Uyeki and Dodge, 1964). In addition, political interest typically increases from young adulthood to old age (Glenn and Grimes, 1968). There is some suggestion too that occupational mobility, either upward or downward, is associated with change in political party. While some believe that the upwardly mobile are more inclined to vote Republican (Boskoff, 1970: 266), most available research evidence demonstrates that the upwardly mobile either do not change or become less conservative and hence more likely to vote Democratic than Republican (Hopkins, 1973). It also is interesting to note that only 4 percent of voluntary-association members belong to political and pressure group organizations; and women are twice as likely as men to belong to these types of organizations (Hausknecht, 1962: 57). Participation in voluntary associations, community events, and church activities are related to voting. But the extent of interaction with friends and neighbors is not related to whether a person votes or not. Thus it may be that active involvement in various kinds of nonpolitical organizations — voluntary associations, special-interest groups, the church, and so on — helps increase knowledge, develop skills, and bring such participants into contact with the issues, actors, and affairs of politics. Even though they may have little formal connection with politics, "All of these factors then combine to propel individuals to the polls" (Olsen, 1972: 331).

Overall, blacks are apathetic about politics, but they are not too much different from whites in this regard, since neither race participates extensively in political decision making beyond the mere marking of a ballot (Orum, 1966: 45). Of course, some issues and candidates in the black community do evoke more political response and voter activity than others. Middleton (1962) evaluated the hypothesis that civil rights issues are of prime importance in the determination of presidential votes by southern blacks but not by whites. His study of an unnamed southern city of about 50,000 tends to confirm this hypothesis. Kennedy in the 1960 election received a greater proportion of the black vote than did Stevenson in 1956 primarily because blacks saw Kennedy as being stronger on civil rights (a conclusion that may have been false). During this campaign, however, whites were less influenced by the civil rights issue and voted for Kennedy on the basis of party loyalty and stands on other issues. Interestingly, in the 1968 general presidential election, Goldwater took a much larger share of the white vote in the South, while Johnson took an estimated 95 percent of the black vote in contrast to the 46.9 percent Kennedy had received.

The Future

Changes in the electoral college have been suggested for presidential elections. They would decrease the influence of the larger urban states, metropolitan centers, blacks, catholics, and low-income persons. Thus in the future we may see political conflict developing over procedures that will wipe out the advantages that larger urban and metropolitan populations now have in such elections. If this were to happen, rural areas would not only have advantages in the Congress, where they already control most of the important committees by virtue of seniority, but they would also benefit by selecting the President at the expense of the urban population (Spilerman and Dickens, 1974).

Then too the impact of Watergate and related incidents must be considered. Will it cause a reversal similar to that of the Eisenhower years, when many Democrats converted to Republicanism? Another plausible alternative is more extensive apathy of former adherents of both parties.

A DISCONCERTING CONCLUSION

"Scholarly studies of American voting are but twenty years old, yet already they have largely demolished the myth of Rational Man in the democratic process: the alert voter who sees issues, seeks knowledge about them, weighs alternatives, and comes to an intellectual decision on the merits of the case" (Wallace, 1963: 163).

BIBLIOGRAPHY: Articles

Adrian, Charles R., "A Typology for Non-Partisan Elections," *Western Political Quarterly,* 12 (June 1959): 449–458.

Alford, Robert R., "The Role of Social Class in American Voting Behavior," *Western Political Quarterly,* 16 (March 1963): 180–194.

Alford, Robert R., and Eugene C. Lee, "Voting Turnout in American Cities," *American Political Science Review,* 62 (September 1968): 796–813.

Alford, Robert R., and Harry M. Scoble, "Sources of Political Involvement," *American Political Science Review,* 62 (December 1968): 1192–1206.

Anon., "California Voters and Housing Discrimination," unpublished paper, n.d.

Cox, Edward F., "The Measurement of Party Strength," *Western Political Quarterly,* 13 (December 1960): 1022–1042.

Cutright, Phillips, and Peter H. Rossi, "Party Organization in Primary Elections," *American Journal of Sociology,* 64 (November 1958): 262–269.

Eldersveld, S. J., "Theory and Method in Voting: Behavior Research," *Journal of Politics,* 13 (February 1951): 70–87.

Glantz, Oscar, "The Negro Voter in Northern Industrial Cities," *Western Political Quarterly,* 13 (December 1960): 999–1010.

Glenn, Norval D., and Michael Grimes, "Aging, Voting, and Political Interest," *American Sociological Review,* 33 (August 1968): 563–575.

Gordon, Daniel N., "Immigrants and Municipal Voting Turnout: Implications for the Changing Ethnic Impact on Urban Politics," *American Sociological Review,* 35 (August 1970): 665–681.

Gosnell, Harold F., and Normal Pearson, "The Study of Voting Behavior by

Correlational Techniques," *American Sociological Review,* 4 (December 1939): 809–815.

Greeley, Andrew M., "Political Participation Among Ethnic Groups in the United States: A Preliminary Reconnaissance," *American Journal of Sociology,* 80 (July 1974): 170–204.

Greenstein, Fred I., and Raymond E. Wolfinger, "Suburban Political Behavior," *Public Opinion Quarterly,* 22 (Winter 1958–1959): 473–482.

Heberle, Rudolf, "On Political Ecology," *Social Forces,* 31 (October 1952): 1–9.

Heberle, Rudolf, "The Ecology of Political Parties," *American Sociological Review,* 9 (August 1944): 401–414.

Hopkins, Andrew, "Political Overconformity by Upwardly Mobile American Men," *American Sociological Review,* 38 (February 1973): 143–147.

Howard, Perry H., William J. Long, and Gene A. Zdrazil, "An Ecological Analysis of Voting Behavior in Baton Rouge: From Strom Thurmond to George Wallace," *Social Forces,* 50 (September 1971): 45–53.

Kaufman, Walter C., and Scott Greer, "Voting in a Metropolitan Community: An Application of Social Area Analysis," *Social Forces,* 38 (March 1960): 196–204.

Kelley, Stanley, Jr., Richard E. Ayres, and William G. Bowen, "Registration and Voting: Putting First Things First," *American Political Science Review,* 61 (June 1967): 359–377.

Knoke, David, "A Causal Model for the Political Party Preferences of American Men," *American Sociological Review,* 37 (December 1972): 679–689.

Lazerwitz, Bernard, "Suburban Voting Trends: 1948 to 1956," *Social Forces,* 39 (October 1960): 29–36.

Litchfield, Edward H., "A Case Study of Negro Political Behavior in Detroit," *Public Opinion Quarterly,* 5 (June 1941): 265–274.

Maccoby, Herbert, "The Differential Political Activity of Participants, in a Voluntary Association," *American Sociological Review,* 23 (February, 1958): 524–532.

MacRae, Duncan, Jr., "Occupations and the Congressional Vote, 1940–1950," *American Sociological Review,* 20 (June 1955): 332–340.

Manis, Jerome, and Leo Stine, "Suburban Residence and Political Behavior," *Public Opinion Quarterly,* 22 (Winter 1958–1959): 483–489.

Middleton, Russell, "The Civil Rights Issue and Presidential Voting Among Southern Negroes and Whites," *Social Forces,* 40 (March 1962): 209–215.

Norton, James A., "Referenda Voting in a Metropolitan Area," *Western Political Quarterly,* 16 (March 1963): 195–212.

Olsen, Marvin E., "Social Participation and Voting Turnout: A Multivariate Analysis," *American Sociological Review,* 37 (June 1972): 317–333.

Orum, Anthony M., "A Reappraisal of the Social and Political Participation of Negroes," *American Journal of Sociology,* 72 (July 1966): 32–46.

Pomper, Gerald, "Ethnic Group Voting in Non-Partisan Municipal Elections," *Public Opinion Quarterly,* 30 (Spring 1966): 79–97.

Salisbury, Robert H., and Gordon Black, "Class and Party in Partisan and Non-Partisan Elections: The Case of Des Moines," *American Political Science Review,* 62 (September 1963): 584–592.

Sheingold, Carl A., "Social Networks and Voting: The Resurrection of a Research Agenda," *American Sociological Review,* 38 (December 1973): 712–720.

Spilerman, Seymour, and David Dickens, "Who Will Gain and Who Will Lose Influence Under Different Electoral Rules," *American Journal of Sociology,* 80 (September 1974): 443–477.

Uyeki, Eugene S., "Patterns of Voting in a Metropolitan Area, 1938–1962," *Urban Affairs Quarterly,* 1 (June 1966): 65–77.

Uyeki, Eugene S., and Richard W. Dodge, "Generational Relations in Political Attitudes and Involvement," *Sociology and Social Research,* 48 (January 1964): 155–165.

Wallace, David, "Some Functional Aspects of Stability and Change in Voting," *American Journal of Sociology,* 69 (September 1963): 161–170.

Williams, Oliver P., and Charles R. Adrian, "The Insulation of Local Politics Under the Non-Partisan Ballot," *American Political Science Review,* 53 (December 1959): 1052–1063.

Wolfinger, Raymond E., "The Development and Persistence of Ethnic Voting," *American Political Science Review,* 59 (December 1965): 896–908.

BIBLIOGRAPHY: Books

Alford, Robert F., and Harry M. Scoble, *Bureaucracy and Participation,* Chicago: Rand McNally & Co., 1969.

Bean, Louis H., *Ballot Behavior,* Washington, D.C.: American Council on Public Affairs, 1940.

Berelson, B. R., Paul F. Lazarsfeld, and W. N. McPhee, *Voting,* Chicago: University of Chicago Press, 1954.

Boskoff, Alvin, *The Sociology of Urban Regions,* New York: Appleton-Century-Crofts, 1970.

Campbell, Angus, Gerald Gurin, and Warren E. Miller, *The Voter Decides,* Evanston, Ill.: Row, Peterson & Company, 1954.

Easton, David, *A Framework for Political Analysis,* Englewood Cliffs, N.J.: Prentice-Hall, 1965.

Ewing, Cortez A. M., *Congressional Elections: 1896–1944,* Norman, Okla.: University of Oklahoma Press, 1947.

Grebler, Leo, Joan W. Moore, C. Guzman, and collaborators, *The Mexican-American People: The Nation's Second Largest Minority,* New York: The Free Press, 1970.

Greer, Scott, and Peter Orleans, "The Mass Society and the Parapolitical Structure," in Scott Greer, Dennis L. McElrath, David W. Minar, and Peter Orleans (eds.), *The New Urbanization,* New York: St. Martin's Press, 1968, pp. 201–221.

Hausknecht, Murray, *The Joiners.* New York: Bedminster Press, 1962.

Heberle, Rudolf, *Social Movements,* New York: Appleton-Century-Crofts, 1951.

Kasperson, Roger E., "Toward a Geography of Urban Politics: Chicago, a Case Study," in Larry S. Bourne (ed.), *Internal Structure of the City,* New York: Oxford University Press, 1971, pp. 400–410.

Key, Valdimer O., Jr., *Southern Politics in State and Nation,* New York: Alfred A. Knopf, 1950.

Lazarsfeld, Paul F., Bernard Berelson, and Hazel Gaudet, *The People's Choice,* New York: Duell, Sloan, and Pearce, 1944.

Lipset, Seymour M., *Political Man: The Social Bases of Politics,* Garden City, N.Y.: Doubleday, 1960.

Lipset, Seymour M., "Political Sociology," in Hans L. Zetterberg (ed.), *Sociology in the United States of America,* (ed.), UNESCO, 1956, pp. 43–55.

Minnis, Mhyra S., "The Patterns of Women's Organizations: Significance, Types, Social Prestige Rank, and Activities," in Marvin B. Sussman (ed.),

Community Structure and Analysis, New York: Thomas Y. Crowell, 1959, pp. 269–287.

Orleans, Peter, "Urban Politics and the Non-Partisan Ballot: A Metropolitan Case," in Scott Greer, Dennis L. McElrath, David W. Minar and Peter Orleans (eds.), *The New Urbanization,* New York: St. Martin's Press, 1968, pp. 287–298.

Rice, Stuart A., *Quantitative Methods in Politics,* New York: Russell and Russell, 1969 (reprint of 1928 ed.).

Rice, Stuart A., *Farmers and Workers in American Politics,* New York: Columbia University Press, 1924.

Rossi, Peter, "Four Landmarks in Voting Research," in Eugene Burdick and Arthur J. Brodbeck (eds.), *American Voting Behavior,* Glencoe, Ill.: The Free Press, 1959.

Titus, Charles H., *Voting Behavior in the United States,* Berkeley, Calif.: Publications of the University of California at Los Angeles in Social Sciences, v. 5, No. 1, University of California Press, 1935.

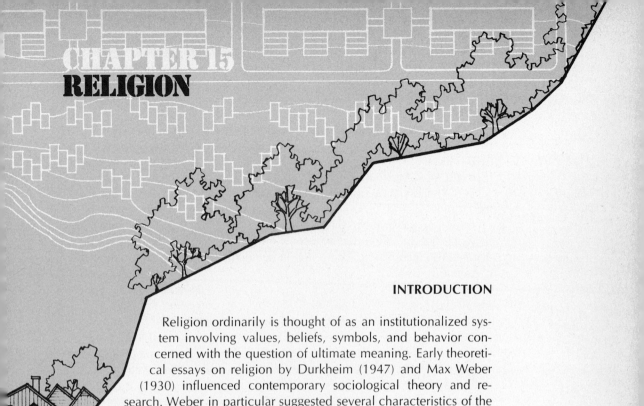

CHAPTER 15
RELIGION

INTRODUCTION

Religion ordinarily is thought of as an institutionalized system involving values, beliefs, symbols, and behavior concerned with the question of ultimate meaning. Early theoretical essays on religion by Durkheim (1947) and Max Weber (1930) influenced contemporary sociological theory and research. Weber in particular suggested several characteristics of the "spirit of capitalism" that should have relevance for contemporary urban society:

1. Work is a worthwhile activity in its own right.
2. Economic judgments should be made on purely rational grounds.
3. One should not indulge in personal vanities.

In addition, Weber assumed the following: (1) Every major religious group develops its own distinctive orientation toward *all aspects of life,* and these orientations profoundly influence the daily actions of its adherents and hence the institutional structure of society. (2) These orientations are assumed to be partially independent of the social situation of groups. On the basis of the foregoing assumptions, religion should influence behavior in all spheres of one's everyday life (Lenski, 1963: 8).

On the other hand, major perspectives on urbanism point to alternative conclusions as a result of the following:

1. Urban conditions bring people of diverse backgrounds into constant and close contact with one another. As a consequence, the diffusion of ideas results in religious assimilation as well as in other spheres of activities; *tolerance* and *secularism* inevitably arise.

2. Associated with urbanism is *specialization* and *compartmentalization.* As a result, life is viewed in parts unrelated to each other rather than as a whole. Religion, then, may become compartmentalized.

Throughout history many important cities have been, and some remain, religious centers, for example, Rome, Jerusalem, Mecca, and Salt Lake City. Cox, in *The Secular City* (1965), argued that factors related to urbanization hasten secularization. As a theologian, he suggested that rationality is possible only in the liberating atmosphere of an urbanizing society and that the two—rationality and urbanization—have freed religion from its traditional handicaps, superstitions, and misconceptions.

Pfeffer (1958) noted three phases of religion in the United States: (1) the colonial period, in which conflicts over dogma and theology dominated; (2) from colonial times to the early twentieth century, which was marked by religious bigotry and prejudice against individuals, and (3) the present, with a decline in religious prejudice but with competition among major religions on basic public issues.

Only 1 of every 10 people in the United States was a church member in 1776; 1 out of 5 was in 1800. Today over 60 percent of the people in the United States belong to a church or synagogue (Lipman and Vorspan, 1962: 293). In 1776 fewer than one person in 25 was Catholic and less than 1 per 1000 was Jewish. Thus the United States earlier was a Protestant (and nonaffiliated) nation. Protestants, on the face of it, insisted on a separation between state and religion. However, they also insisted on certain violations of this separation, for example, Thanksgiving, "In God We Trust" on coins, government-paid ministers in the armed forces, and so on.

Most writers on religion in contemporary United States agree with Cox that there has been an increase in the secularization of society in recent decades despite the fact that church membership has increased faster than the population (Yinger, 1963), at least until very recently. Cox also believes that secularization is aiding rather than hindering religion. Many writers on religion imply that secularization and urbanization are one and the same process, but rarely is a direct statement made to this effect. Ordinarily, *secularization* is defined as the separation of religion from other aspects of life. There is a conflict between those who believe that the increasing secularization of religion has led it to a "lowest common denominator" (Yinger, 1963) and those who argue that it is becoming more sophisticated as a result of secularization. With these conflicts and points of view in mind, Lenski (1963) reported that not only has there been an increase in church membership but also religious organizations are vigorous and influential in the daily lives of individuals and in secular institutions.

"God is concerned with the whole of men's lives: on at least this one point all the churches agree." He is concerned with human beings' activities everyday: their work, play, politics, and family life. Does this belief really hold in the contemporary highly secularized environment of the modern metropolis in the United States? Is there *really* a difference between the believer and the unbeliever? Does the type of religious commitment make a difference? If there are differences, are they a result of the influence of religion or of something else? (Lenski, 1963: 1).

The spiritual leader of Roman Catholics—the largest single denomination in the United States—is the Pope. Here, Paul VI is being carried down the steps of St. John's Basilica in Rome.

These questions and others have been asked but only partially answered. Probably less systematic sociological research has been devoted to religion than any other major institution of our society. Even rarer are studies interrelating religion with other aspects of urban life.

PROTESTANT—CATHOLIC—
JEW—AND ? IN THE URBAN UNITED STATES

Catholics are now the largest single denomination in the United States, with a membership three times as large as that of the Methodists. In 1962 there were about 62 million Protestants in over 225 denominations, 40 million Roman Catholics, 2.5 million Eastern Orthodox, and 5.25 million Jews. Seldom discussed is how many "disbelievers" and nonaffiliated there are in the United States. While they are in the majority, they are unorganized and as such are second-class citizens in regard to how much and what kinds of religion may be reflected in the public schools and in other public institutions. In 1957 it was estimated that 68 million people in the United States did not belong to a church.

Roman Catholics make up approximately 38 percent of the population in larger metropolitan areas (200,000 and larger); white Protestants, 39 percent; black Protestants, 11 percent; and Jews, 8 percent. Jews represent about 3 percent of the total population, yet the vast majority of them live in cities. For example, it has been estimated that 2.25 million Jews live in New York City. In some metropolitan areas Jews have abandoned the central city for specific suburbs that have become predominantly Jewish in composition. While cities in the United States contain a majority of the population, they more and more contain a minority of Protestants. In fact, of the 10 cities studied by Lipman and

These Catholic rioters are using corrugated iron sheets to advance upon British troops in Belfast, Ireland, an area where severe religious cleavages among Catholics and Protestants has led to continuous bloodshed.

Vorspan (1968), only two of them—Muncie and Nashville—were predominantly Protestant.

Population growth and mobility have made Roman Catholics the major religious group in virtually every large city in the United States (Lipman and Vorspan, 1962: 301). Within Roman Catholicism there is a developing pluralism, with varying points of view being at least partially related to ethnicity (e.g., Irish and Italian), regional variability, and social class. In most cities Catholics do not participate in the ministerial association because of their separatism aims; thus most ministerial associations are actually made up of ministers representing a minority of the religious population. Similarly, in some cities, parallel Protestant and Jewish ministerial associations exist, suggesting even less interaction and more fragmentation.

Lipman and Vorspan (1968: 338–342) claimed that cities in the United States are becoming triple religious ghettos. That is, there are neighborhoods primarily inhabited by Jews, Catholics, or Protestants, with little intermixing. Further, adherents of various religions tend to have friends of the same religion and to belong to organizations primarily with members of the same faith. Although the suburbs may be white, therefore, they also may be religiously segregated. Triple ghettoization may not appear to be as potentially threatening on the surface as in actual practice. For example, if some trends noted in other societies were to become prevalent in the United States, severe cleavages along religious lines could develop into open conflict. Ireland is the most obvious contemporary example where Protestants and Catholics are in open warfare. Similarly, in contemporary Holland and Lebanon life follows religious divisions.

Religious tension and conflict are widespread in cities in the United States (Lipman and Vorspan, 1962: 292) because major religious denominations often disagree on public matters: Christmas in the public schools, tax funds for sectarian purposes, religious services in the schools, birth control, so on. Nevertheless, religious denominations share some enemies—secularism, materialism, apathy, intellectual superficiality, nihilism, and communism (Lipman and Vorspan, 1962: 299). Religious pluralism is a way of life in this country, and it appears that this will be the case in the future.

At the turn of the century the U.S. Census Bureau collected "religious information." But, since 1936, questions on religion have been eliminated from the census. Only limited data are available in regard to characteristics of believers and nonbelievers, the impact of urbanization, and characteristics of communities having high and low religious participation. Thus many statements regarding religion in this chapter must be regarded as tentative.

Urban conditions bring about secularism because they require cooperation and close association among people of diverse backgrounds and religions. Similarly, the specialization and the compartmentalization required in the urban environment influence religious institutions and lessen their impact upon the everyday life of people living in urban regions (Lenski, 1963: 11). This point of view has been challenged by those who note that urban conditions may be generating communal as opposed to associational religion. The *associational* aspect of religion is the frequency of attendance at worship services; *communal* involvement, on the other hand, is the degree to which primary relations are among members of the same religious group (Lenski, 1963: 23–24).

Communal religion meets the need for communal relationships outside the family; churches are increasingly filling people's need for "communal identification" and belongingness (Lenski, 1963). "In brief, the specialization and compartmentalization inherent in the urban way of life drive men to transform their religious groups from narrow, specialized associations into groups which are more communal in character" (Lenski, 1963: 11).

Like Lenski, Herberg (1956) agreed that urban conditions promote communal rather than associational religion. He noted that communal religion is broader than the family but narrower than the total society. Associational religion is viewed as being segmentalized and compartmentalized, whereas the communal type is much broader based. Lenski suggested the paradigm shown in Table 15-1 for the associational and communal aspects of religion.

Herberg believed that religious groups are becoming a more important feature of American life—hence more communal in nature. This is perhaps a result of the need for identification. Many older traditional ethnic communities are disintegrating, and the church is replacing them in importance, after several generations' decline. Herberg hypothesized that the Americanization process

TABLE 15-1
**Relative Strength of Associational and Communal Bonds
in the Four Major Socioreligious Groups**

| | STRENGTH OF BONDS | |
SOCIORELIGIOUS GROUP	ASSOCIATIONAL (FREQUENCY OF ATTENDANCE)	COMMUNAL (PRIMARY-GROUP RELATIONS)
Jews	Weak	Strong
White Catholics	Strong	Medium
White Protestants	Medium	Medium
Black Protestants	Medium	Strong

(defined by number of generations in the United States) is linked to a strengthening of religious associations. Lenski (1959) reported no decline, however, and even a strengthening of religious ties. These findings apply to migrants from other countries but also to white Protestant migrants of southern birth. Activity in churches, then, seems to be most frequent among those who are most Americanized but also the most urbanized (Nelsen and Allen, 1974).

Substantial religious communality, as measured by intrareligious friendships, religious self-identification, religious participation, and intermarriage attitude, is strong in Protestant City, Catholic City, and Mormon City (Anderson, 1968). The most marked form of communality was in Mormon City, with Protestants being somewhat more communally oriented than Catholics.

URBAN CHARACTERISTICS AND RELIGION

Information available from the 1957 Current Population Survey in which a question on religion was asked demonstrated substantial differences in population distribution by religion among various regions in the United States and between urban and rural residence. Similarly, studies tend to show that there are regional differences in the growth of church membership, but growth is largest where the general population as a whole is increasing (Douglass and Brunner, 1935; Taylor and Jones, 1964). Churches have moved with people from the farm to the city and from the city to the suburb. Also, Table 15-2 shows that rural districts have the lowest percentage of church members, while cities of 25,000 to 50,000 people have the highest percentage of members, although not much more than the very largest cities. Douglass and Brunner (1935: 41) reported that Protestantism does better in agricultural areas than in industrial settings, whereas just the opposite is true of Catholicism. In other words, rural areas should be more likely to have more Protestant adherents, whereas urban areas with industrial capability are more likely to be heavily Catholic.

More recently, Dynes (1959: 254) argued that a religious organization

TABLE 15-2
Distribution of Church Members According to Urban Groupings — 1920

	PERCENT	
CITY SIZE	CHURCH MEMBERS	NOT CHURCH MEMBERS
300,000 and over	59	41
100,000–300,000	59	41
50,000–100,000	57	43
25,000–50,000	60	40
Small Cities	55	45
Rural Districts	52	48

Source: Douglass and Brunner, 1935. Used by permission.

can only be understood in terms of its social context — the community in which it is located. The community and its resources — such as its people and their characteristics — are the factors that determine the potentiality and limits of a religious program. Using this idea as a takeoff point, Dynes systematically characterized the context and characteristics of urban areas. He found that the larger the community, the greater the proportion of non-Protestants. Ninety-nine percent of Jews and 85 percent of Catholics live in communities of over 2,500 population size. Seventy-seven percent of Jews and 28 percent of Catholics live in cities over 500,000 population. Part of the reason for the concentration of Jews and Catholics in the larger urban areas is related to the early settlement pattern of the United States. Most of the initial colonizers of this country who were believers were Protestants, and they settled in scattered expanding frontier rural areas. During the great immigration and the growth of cities in the mid-1800s, Catholics and Jews from Ireland and Central Europe trekked to the United States and for the most part settled in selected urban areas. This immigration changed the religious character of many large cities from Protestant to non-Protestant. Since that time, then, as the size of a community increases, the proportion of Protestants to non-Protestants decreases. "The older established Protestant denominations either have a greater proportion of their members in rural areas or tend to approximate the national distribution of the United States' population in communities of various sizes — rural areas, small towns, as well as cities" (Dynes, 1959: 259).

Urban areas also have a variety of offshoot religious groups of the main denominations, and the city is a fruitful area for the creation of new independent religions, for example, the Christian Science Church. Cities also have been the scene of cults that mix mystical and esoteric beliefs with some traditional religious elements thrown in for good measure. Many of these cults draw upon the excess female population in the cities (Dynes, 1959: 259).

The proportion of blacks in a city is positively related to the proportion

Off-shoots of the major religions exist in most cities. Examples range from itinerant preachers on busy streetcorners to this storefront church of obscure denomination.

of Protestants in a city, and it is estimated that well over 90 percent of black church members are Protestants, with their special denominations of Protestantism. Other racial and ethnic populations, of course, tend to belong to one or another particular denomination based on the religion brought with them from the mother country. Social classes also are unequally spread out among various denominations. Dynes (1959: 260) noted that national samples typically show that Methodists, Presbyterians, Lutherans, Episcopalians, and Congregationalists are overrepresented in the middle classes and Presbyterians, Episcopalians, Unitarians, and Congregationalists in the upper classes.

''The larger the community, the larger the average size of the church'' (Dynes, 1959: 261). Churches in one census of religious bodies showed that the average size of churches in New York and Chicago was over 1000 members; in smaller cities such as Kansas City and Louisville the average size of churches was around 600 members. Based upon a study of Methodist churches in six states, Dynes (1959) reported that church size reaches its peak in cities of 10,000 to 50,000 people and drops after that. However, this may be a denominational rather than a churchwide phenomenon.

Older cities and metropolitan areas in the United States appear to have a higher proportion of church members than newer ones. In larger metropolitan areas, when a city experiences suburbanization, "churches do not move out of the downtown areas as readily as do stores or families" Dynes (1959: 261). Larger churches continue to draw their parishoners from a wide geographical area, and they are able to continue active programs. Subsequently, when suburban churches are constructed and begin to attract suburbanites, downtown churches begin to decline, especially in those areas in which former residential areas are converted for offices, commercial land use, and so on.

Chapin (1957: 505) reported that for 16 cities the variation in growth of Protestant churches corresponds positively with population growth and negatively with the age of the city. "The greater the proportion of the population of higher socio-economic status in the community, the larger the average size of the church" (Dynes, 1959: 262).

Churches tend to have a homogeneous population, and this leads to a host of additional ideas—that is, the more diverse the community, the more churches it will have; the more homogeneous a community, the fewer churches it will have (Dynes, 1959: 263). "Similarly,the fewer the churches of a particular denomination in a community, the more residentially dispersed will be their parishoners." In surveying several studies testing this hypothesis, Dynes reported one on Methodism in 30 cities. It showed that over 60 percent of church members lived within a mile of the local church. Another study of 1350 metropolitan Protestant churches showed that 53 percent lived within a mile of the church and thus lived in a compact parish. Compact churches, then, will have a relatively homogeneous membership, whereas a dispersed membership will be heterogeneous.

Generally, more women than men participate in church activities. This has led Dynes (1959: 265) to hypothesize that church participation will be greater in cities or in areas within them where women outnumber men. The 1936 Census of Religious Bodies indicated that for every 78.5 men there were 100 women who were members of a church, and more women than men are on Protestant and Catholic membership lists. The exceptions to this generalization are "male immigrant" oriented churches such as the Buddhist and Greek Orthodox. Older individuals are more likely to attend church than either middle aged or young people, especially young single persons (Lazerwitz, 1961: 304). Families with children, particularly those five years old and over, have a rather high church affiliation.

Smaller communities generally have greater religious participation than do larger ones; but there is no evidence that participation continues when people leave a smaller place and move to a larger one. Longer duration of residence in the same place of residence is associated with frequent church attendance. Rural migrants to the city and migrants to larger places from smaller places take a long time to approximate the level of participation of those having a long duration of residence (Zimmer, 1955).

Religious organizations lag in creating churches in new communities, for example, suburbs, and this lag helps account for former in-town cities retaining their membership for some time. Evidence suggests that churches follow population trends; that is, as the anglo population begins to leave the central city for the suburbs, churches, after some delay, begin to follow their original parishoners to the suburbs, thus keeping close to the majority of their members. There are fewer churches in newly settled suburban communities than there are in the older parts of the metropolitan complex. Dynes (1959: 263) thus says that "the more recent the settlement of a community, the fewer churches it will have."

VARIATIONS WITHIN URBAN AREAS AND RELIGION

By accident of birth into a family, an individual inherits an organized and functioning religion or lack of religion.

The major religious groups in Detroit are as follows:

	PERCENT
White Protestants	41
White Catholics	35
Black Protestants	15
Jews	4
Other	5

Protestants can be viewed in the following manner:

FUNDAMENTAL SECTS (DEVOTIONAL)	CONSERVATIVE-ORTHODOX CHURCHES	LIBERAL PROTESTANTS
Four-Square Church	Church of Christ	Methodists
Nazarene	United Brethren	Presbyterians
Pentecostal	Christian	Disciples of Christ
Assembly of God	Seventh-Day Adventists	Congregationalists
Evangelical	Latter-Day Saints	Episcopalians
Holiness Churches	Jehovah's Witnesses	Evangelical-Reformed
	First Church of God	First Christian
	Lutherans	United Pilgrim
	Baptists	Religious Science

AGNOSTIC OR SEMI-RELIGIOUS GROUPS	PROTESTANT—NO DENOMINATION	OTHERS
Unitarian	—	Greek Orthodox
Universalist		Bahai
		Subud

FIGURE 15-1
A Classification of City Churches

TYPE I	TYPE II
A Widely Dispersed Parish	A Compact Parish
A Selected Clientele	A Dominant Neighborhood Penetration
Downtown church	Traditional church
Prestige church	Institutional church
One-of-a-kind church	"Storefront" church
Church for the handicapped	Sect church
	Foreign-language church
	Suburban church

CHURCHES IN TRANSITION[a]

A Semidispersed Parish
An Unstable Constituency

Local church merger
Bilingual background
Merged denominations
Theological eccentricity
Stranded church
Relocated church
Federated church

[a] Churches in transition occupy an intermediate status, are currently in transition, and cannot be considered as types at all. Eventually, the seven situations will yield Type II churches. However, this eventually can be realized only at the end of a process of settling down and emergence from the intermediate status.

Source: Shippey, 1960.

As already noted, it appears that both religious and secular activities are segregated along racial lines.

As shown in Figure 15-1, Shippey (1960) made a distinction between "metropolitan" and "neighborhood" churches, with a greater dispersion of membership for metropolitan churches, whereas neighborhood churches are just that—their members live in the local neighborhood.

The distribution of people belonging to different religions in Detroit is not random; that is, concentrations of people belong to similar churches (Lenski, 1963: 77). This is true even though some earlier concentrations of the Irish, French, Italians, and Germans have been dispersed. Thus Lenski's analysis revealed that socioreligious populations are unevenly distributed in most sections of Detroit. He divided the urban complex into 12 different areas and noted, in all but two areas, that in each "one or another of the four socioreligious groups constituted a majority of the residential population, despite the fact none of the groups enjoys a majority in the community as a whole."

Black Protestants are in the majority in two Detroit inner-city areas; Catholics make up the majority in two different areas—the southern suburbs and the outer east side of the central city. Catholics are a plurality in another area that is in transition from a white to a black neighborhood. Jews are the most concentrated religious population in several areas adjacent to each other. White Protestants are a majority in the western portion of the outer city and in all suburban areas except one southern suburb in which Catholics make up the majority.

The least concentrated religious populations are white Protestants and Catholics, with black Protestants and Jews being about equally concentrated in several specific areas. Lenski (1963: 79) noted that the greater concentration of Jews than black Protestants is remarkable, since blacks are severely limited in their choice of housing both by finances and outgroup hostility (also see McAllister et al., 1972). Lenski concluded, therefore, that the concentration of blacks is involuntary, while that of Jews is voluntary and related to the value they place on religion (and culture?). Finally, he pointed out that differences in the residential location of religious populations are closely linked to the social class structure. Growing churches in 16 cities that Chapin (1957) studied were located in "better territory," while average or declining churches were located in "poorer territory." Churches with scattered memberships tend to be located in lower-class areas, whereas those with local memberships are located in middle- and upper-class areas. Those churches that are declining the most, both in poorer and better territories, have the most compact membership.

Zimmer and Hawley (1959) found a strong association between place of residence and religion. Churches tend to take on the character of the neighborhood in which they are located. In a study by Warner and others (1949) they identified six social classes in Yankee City: (1) the upper upper class, (2) the lower upper class, with the total upper class consisting of about 3 percent of the population, (3) the upper middle class, (4) the lower middle class, with a combined total of about 39 percent in the middle classes, (5) the upper lower class, and (6) the lower lower class, with about 58 percent in the lower classes (also, see Hollingshead, 1949). The upper classes predominately belonged to the Unitarian and Episcopalian churches; the Unitarian church drew most heavily from upper-middle-class families, and these persons made up the majority of the membership of the Baptist, Congregational, and Christian Science churches. Lower-middle-class families tended to belong to the Congregational and Episcopal churches. The lower classes were made up of various ethnic groups whose origins were primarily European. Upper-lower-class families primarily attended the Roman Catholic Church. The major Protestant denomination with substantial lower class membership was the Methodist. Some lower-lower-class families were Catholic, but there were also a few Baptists and Congregationalists.

Religious conflict in Paper City (Holyoke, Massachusetts) was studied extensively by Underwood (1957). The city — a company city — has quite clear ecological areas, such as areas for homes of workers, managers, and owners. These areas were planned before construction began. Subsequent growth has taken all of one side of the river and followed the general guidelines specified in the original plan. Underwood noted that this ecological pattern of social classes is simple — "a social ramp from the working tenements in the Lowlands up the hill to the well-to-do residents" (p. 195). The social class division in the city follows Catholic parish lines quite closely; thus parishes represent the social class structure of the city with little variation, and there is little mixing of Catholics by classes. This results in social class homogeneity by parish and compact geographical parishes. On the other hand, the membership of Protestant churches in Holyoke tends to be more scattered and to include a few members from different social classes. Nevertheless, Protestant churches, in general, have gradually drifted away from working-class neighborhoods of the city.

In a study of the spatial distribution of religious preference in Wichita, Kansas, Cowgill (1960) noted that Wichita has been called a city of churches and, according to a religious census, part of the "Bible Belt." Nevertheless, Wichita has a percentage of Catholics and Jews that is below the national standard (at least at the time of the last national religious census in 1957).

In Wichita, income and status differences are reflected in the spatial distribution of Protestant churches. Those who prefer the Episcopal church, for example, live almost exclusively in higher-income sections of the city. There is an Episcopal church in the black section, but the proportion of Episcopalians living there is low. Residents preferring Congregationalist and Presbyterian churches also tend to live in upper-class areas in Wichita. On the other hand, Methodists make up the majority in most areas (census tracts) with average or slightly above-average incomes. Methodists are fewer in the wealthiest sections of the city and fewest in the poorest sections. Thus Methodism in Wichita is strictly a middle-class phenomenon.

Persons who perfer the Pentecostal Church are primarily from the lower classes. Other denominations in Wichita that draw primarily from the lower classes are the Nazarene, Adventist, Baptist, Assembly of God, Church of Christ, Church of God, and United Brethren. Thus virtually all Protestant churches in Wichita are associated with certain social classes and residential areas. On the other hand, the Roman Catholic Church in Wichita, unlike in Paper City, cuts across all social class and residential areas, including black and chicano residential areas. The Jewish population evidently has been highly mobile in Wichita, since the population is relatively scattered and has moved away from the location of its synagogues.

The most highly concentrated areas of religious preference, however, consist of those families preferring the African Methodist Episcopal Church; adherents of this faith live exclusively in the black residential area of the city.

Similar concentrations are found for the Christian Methodist Episcopal and the National Baptist churches, whose memberships are predominantly black.

Based upon his study of Protestant churches in Des Moines, Northwood (1958) claimed that segregation in churches is a result of internal factors — such as how the congregation reacts and the minister's beliefs and influence — and several external factors — such as the spatial location of the church, as for instance, in or near a black residential area. In Des Moines all churches with black members were located in the transition zone or adjacent to a residential area having a black population. Integration of blacks into the churches was not universal, with only about one out of every three churches in such locations having black members. Integration of blacks into formerly all-white churches was facilitated when other characteristics such as occupational and educational levels and incomes were similar. Almost all black members of predominantly white churches were upwardly mobile. Overall, "church size, location, and stability area external conditions which affect the decisions of the congregation on social segregation" (Northwood, 1958: 160).

Lest a wrong impression be given, at the time of this study of Des Moines only a fraction of 1 percent of the total membership in sample churches was cross-racial. Northwood (1958: 159) concluded that the church in Des Moines, for the most part, is a "conservative, change-resisting institution."

One of the cities that Lipman and Vorspan (1962) studied was Muncie, Indiana, better known as Middletown to social scientists. Muncie is an industrial city with a number of large plants; its population is primarily native-born, with a small percentage of blacks who live in two distinct residential areas. At the time of this study the city was predominantly Protestant, with very few Catholics and Jews. There are few openly expressed tensions among the religions in Muncie; intolerance is reserved for "nonbelievers." Under the surface, however, religious tensions exist, the most serious one being between Christians and Jews. Lipman and Vorspan (1962) reported that restrictive covenants have been used to keep Jews out of some neighborhoods. On the other hand, cooperative efforts existed among youth and in human relations endeavors, but they did not attack or help solve the social problems of the city.

Probably because of residential proximity, there is a great deal of denominational homogeneity in marriage. Data derived from both the 1957 Current Population Survey and a study of June 1961 college graduates show that well over 80 percent of spouses in both of these surveys belonged to the same religion (Greeley, 1970: 950). Further, well over 80 percent of marriages within the major Protestant denominations take place within a specific denomination. The data could have been a result of religious conversion to the faith of the spouse after the marriage; however, except for Lutherans who had some modest success in conversion before marriage, these denominational marriages represent not conversions but within-faith marriages (Greeley, 1970). Some recent research in Indiana suggests, however, "that there is a lessening of religious constraints upon the marriages of today" (Monahan, 1973: 203).

Religion and Social Class

Differences in the geographical locations of people in a community are usually linked to their placements in the *class structure*. Barber (1957: 157) pointed out that church affiliation is used as a symbol of social class position. People may even select their church affiliations in terms of the social class positions to which they belong or aspire to belong. Churches, however, serve only as rough indicators of social class position. There is a fairly strong relationship between being middle class and belonging to a church. Members of sects, however, are more likely to come from the lower classes. Church membership for the upper classes is considered as representing selective participation in a socially favored activity. For many it has become a secular activity that requires a minimum of obligation—unlike the many other voluntary organizations that are competing for the individual's time. "The greater the proportion of population of lower-socioeconomic status in a community, the smaller average size of the church." While there are fewer participants in some churches, especially sect churches, there is more participation in all aspects of the church by its members. The church "is the most meaningful association and source of friendship" (Dynes, 1957: 331–334).

Churches and various denominations have great variation with respect to occupational, income, and educational composition of their memberships. Overall differences between Protestant and Catholic churches hide substantial variations within Protestant denominations. For example, well over one-third of the members of Episcopal and Unitarian churches are professionals, while only 8 percent of Lutherans are, and some churches (Assembly of God and the United Brethren) have no members who are professionals. Nevertheless, while people who belong to churches tend to group themselves according to certain social traits, churches are probably more heterogeneous than any other social grouping in the United States (Bultena, 1949: 386).

In citing several early studies relating religion to various measures of social class, Gockel (1969) showed that in 1945–1946 Congregationalists, Episcopalians, Presbyterians, and Jews occupied the four top positions on measures of social class, while Methodists, Lutherans, Catholics, and Baptists made up the lower half of the ranking. Lenski (1963) reported the following religious and social class structure for Detroit:

RELIGIOUS GROUP	NONMANUAL (PERCENT)		MANUAL (PERCENT)	
	UPPER MIDDLE	LOWER MIDDLE	UPPER WORKING	LOWER WORKING
Jews	43	30	9	17
W-Protestants	19	25	31	25
W-Catholics	12	27	35	25
B-Protestants	2	10	19	69

Many Jewish families in the United States conscientiously keep religious laws and customs passed down virtually unchanged from generation to generation. Here, a family celebrates the first day of Passover.

Generally it appears that Protestants are more likely than Catholics of similar occupational origin to have professional and business-level occupations, while Catholics are more likely than Protestants of the same occupational origin to have white-collar occupations. Also, Protestants are more often sharply upwardly mobile than are Catholics. These differences hold when a variety of controls are applied including size of community of origin (Jackson et al., 1970). Nevertheless, while at the end of World War II Protestants had higher incomes, occupations, and educational attainment than Catholics, since that time Catholics have gained and even surpassed Protestants in most aspects of status (Glenn and Hyland, 1967: 85). The major reason advanced for this more rapid advancement of Catholics is "their heavy concentration in the larger non-Southern metropolitan areas, where earnings, occupational distributions, educational opportunities and rates of upward mobility are more favorable than in the typical home communities of Protestants" (Glenn and Hyland, 1967: 85).

These findings derived from a series of national surveys suggest that religious influences do not handicap Catholics in their competition for "worldly success" with Protestants but that other factors, for example, the characteristics and the location of places of residence, are more important. However, it also should be noted that Jews "are maintaining a wide lead over other religious categories and apparently have improved their relative standing since World War II" (Glenn and Hyland, 1967: 85).

In the 1957 Population Survey Jews occupied higher occupational positions than did either Protestants or Catholics, with Protestants being intermediate between Jews and Catholics (Goldstein, 1969). However, Episcopalians and Presbyterians closely resemble Jews in their socioeconomic level. Nevertheless, generally the large differences reported among major religious categories in income is a result of urban-rural residence education, and occupational level (Goldstein, 1969: 631). Similarly, using sophisticated statistical techniques, Gockel (1969) showed that most income differences by religious affiliation disappear or are substantially reduced when race, region, and size of place are controlled. Only three religious affiliations depart substantially from this finding—Congregationalists, Episcopalians, and Jews, whose income is higher than the others even though other variables have been considered and their effects removed.

Jews in Urban Areas

The Jewish faith can be thought of as being urban in nature. About three-fourths of the American Jewish population live in the 12 largest metropolitan regions in the United States, typically in concentrated areas with a relatively high density or in the most "urban" areas of the metropolitan complex. Massarik (1959: 241) noted that this urban Jewish population has been undergoing transformation like the rest of the population and the movement of some segments of people to suburbia has affected it, although the trend has varied from city to city. He found that the Jewish community in San Francisco, at least up until the time of his study, had remained well-integrated and stable. On the other hand, the Buffalo Jewish ghetto has virtually disappeared, and the Jewish population has intermingled with other populations throughout the city. In other cities the outward movement of population has resulted in Jewish suburbs such as in Newark.

In Los Angeles Massarik (1959) noted trends that are widely representative of other cities: (1) a dense Jewish urban area, (2) Jewish suburbia, and (3) Jewish population scatter. At the time of his study, as well as currently, two adjacent areas of relatively high urban density were areas of Jewish population concentration. Jewish suburbia is similar to other suburbs except for its Jewishness. Finally, there is a widespread scattering of Jews in Los Angeles, especially in the San Fernando Valley. Interestingly, scattered Jews represent a more heterogeneous lot than do those concentrated in the dense Jewish areas, while suburban Jews primarily are in the child-rearing years.

The changes in and the location of the Jewish ghetto across several generations was traced in a "Gilded Ghetto" of a northern city (Kramer and Leventman, 1961). The first settlement of Austrian, German, and Hungarian Jews was on the north side of the city, with over 80 percent of Jews living in this area of the city. Native-born, second-generation children spread out more than their parents, and those who had financial success began the gilded ghetto on the opposite side of the city, although still maintaining the integrity of their religion and culture. Finally, third-generation Jews appear to be "melting" into the general population, with a movement away from the north side to southside suburbs; accompanying these moves are social relationships outside of the Jewish faith. Eventually, of course, these extended social relationships should lead to an increase in intermarriage, a loss of the Jewish heritage, and an even greater dispersal of the adherents of the Jewish faith in this northern city.

The Black Church in Urban Areas

The importance of the church in black life has been well documented and reported to be the strongest black institution (McCord et al., 1969: 107). For example, according to a study of a national representative sample, 35 percent of blacks belong to church-related organizations, more so than any other kind of organization (Hausknecht, 1962: 75). Frazier (1964) noted that while Christianity brought about a loss of the African cultural heritage, it also played a major role in creating solidarity among blacks from a variety of tribes and cultures in Africa who lacked social cohesion and a structured social life under slavery conditions in the New World. While the early black clergy were uneducated, they still served along with religion as effective agents of social control (Frazier, 1964: 32; Scanzoni, 1971: 49). Later, even though more secularized, churches served as the prime institution or means whereby blacks became assimilated into urban life (Frazier, 1964: 50–52). On the other hand, black churches have historically functioned to sustain or lead black revolts (McCord et al., 1969: 108). Part of the confusion over the part that the black church may play in social change and racial protest may be related to different points of view within the black community and the black church. For example, Marx (1967) presents evidence that "religious involvement may be seen as an important factor working against the widespread radicalization of the Negro public" (p. 72). Nevertheless, as he noted, there are many militant blacks who are religious. He believes that the "otherworldly" orientation by some religions and their adherents inhibits protest, whereas "temporal" religious groups concerned with the here and now may be highly supportive of racial protest and militant strategies. These contrasting points of view become important because, as Cone (1970: 54) noted, there can be no black revolution without the masses, and the black masses are in the churches.

Scanzoni (1971: 51) reported that as of 1964–1965 over 80 percent of blacks in Indianapolis remained, to some extent, involved in church, and Babchuk and Thompson (1962: 650) reported that 87.5 percent of Lincoln, Nebraska, blacks were affiliated with a church. However, Scanzoni also noted that the affiliation with church is not as true for younger blacks, and Hannerz (1969: 109–117) found that the church "habit" in Washington, D.C.'s Winston Street area is declining.

This view of a Baptist church in Kinlock, Missouri, shows the typical enthusiasm and dominant female composition of many black churches.

McCord and others (1969: 109–117) dichotomized churches into those that stress the "other world"—salvation—and those that stress "this world." Members of this-world-oriented churches tend to have members who are in higher-level occupations, better educated, and middle aged. They, along with their ministers, were in the forefront of the civil rights movement. The authors further reported that this-world church participants have been more likely than the other-world oriented to believe in violence and self-defense, admire black personalities rather than white personalities, be highly critical of the police, more "pushy," less trusting, and suffer more psychosomatic complaints.

In the Near Northeast (Washington, D.C.) churchgoing is of major importance as elsewhere because it constitutes a great part of visible community activity. Vidich and Bensman (1960) estimated that church-related activities constitute at least one-half of all organized social activities of the white community they studied. This included religious fellowship as well as the vast array of activities that appeals to a wide variety of interests. In the Near Northeast about 60 percent of adults and 51 percent of teenagers belong to a church. In both instances, *of those who belong* just under 60 percent attend church regularly, which is again similar to Vidich and Bensman's estimate that only about one-fourth of the community actively participates in church activities.

Thus only about 30 percent of Near Northeast adults and teenagers attend church regularly, which is somewhat in contrast to blacks in Indianapolis (Scanzoni, 1971: 286), where 51 percent attend church at least once a week.

Unfortunately, these studies do not indicate who belongs to which kind of church, whether this- or other-world oriented, storefront (Frazier, 1964: 53–55), palatial, or otherwise, nor were reasons for church attendance determined. In contrast to some other studies that suggest a difference in church attendance by younger persons (Scanzoni, 1971: 51), adults and teenagers in the Near Northeast spend about the same amount of time in church activities. Hannerz (1969: 46, 96) discovered that churches around Winston Street are filled with middle-aged and older women and female and male children. The congregation always has a great majority of women who express puritanical views even though they may not practice them. Most black churches, not too surprisingly, are female oriented. Many of them stress the trouble that they believe men cause their women. In addition, preachers stress righteousness and *cautiousness* (Hannerz, 1969: 65–66). However, there is a growing cynicism over ''preaching'' and a decline in church attendance by younger persons. Also, Frazier (1964: 71) has argued that the black church is a major barrier to integration of blacks into the mainstream of life in the United States (for recent substantiating evidence see McCord et al., 1969: 89).

In the Near Northeast (Chapin et al., forthcoming) the 30 percent of adults and teenagers who attend church get there by different ways, spend varying amounts of time in church activities, and attend churches spread throughout the neighborhood and the district. Adults are more likely than teenagers to go to church by automobile (their own or somebody else's), and the churches adults go to are, in many instances, farther away than those that teenagers attend. For adults, there are no differences by working status in church membership, hours spent in church activities, or the number of minutes it takes to get to church. However, working adults are more likely to use their ''own car'' to get to church, while nonworking adults are more likely to get to church by bus or to walk.

Goode (1966: 103) has summarized a great deal of literature with the generalization that ''the higher the class level, the greater the degree of church participation; the lower the class level, the less the degree of church participation.'' Scanzoni (1971: 52) agreed with this position and reported that poorer blacks attend less often than those who are better off. When income per household members is used as an indicator of social class, however, Near Northeast adults do not follow this pattern. Lower-income adults are more likely than higher-income adults to be regular church attendees. For teenagers no large differences in church membership, attendance, hours spent at church, or distance to the church are evident by income levels. The only major difference by income level for teenagers is in the mode of transportation to church: Lower-income teenagers are more likely to walk to church or go in someone else's car, whereas higher-income teenagers are more likely to go in their own cars or by bus. Also, teenagers from nonworking families are more likely than those from working families to belong to a church and to attend regularly.

Many ghetto residents attend church because it helps them in obtaining suitable marriages, in getting ahead, and in making social adjustments (Scanzoni, 1971: 120–123). On the other hand, this getting-ahead form of participation may reflect an overall middle-class pattern, whereas the religious participation of Near Northeast residents is more akin to working-class participation, which is religious in character rather than organizational or secularized (Goode, 1966: 111). The proportion of regular church attendees evidently has been dropping, and Hannerz (1969: 41) has pointed out that it is no longer necessary for a person to belong to a church to be "respectable." Nevertheless, it appears unwise to dismiss the church as no longer being an important black institution. The church remains a major part of the black perspective, and it seems that it will continue to be a primary institution well into the future (Hannerz, 1969: 147; McCord et al., 1969: 107).

Drake and Cayton (1945) examined the status structure and social system of blacks in Chicago during the 1930s. He divided the black community into the upper (5 percent), middle (30 percent), and lower classes (about 65 percent). In the upper class only a small number of black families or individuals belonged to a church; those who were members typically belonged to the Congregational, Episcopalian, or Presbyterian churches. Younger members of the middle class belonged to the Baptist and Methodist churches but were infrequent attenders. Older middle-class blacks in Chicago of the era were the churchgoers of the middle class. Lower-class churches were the Baptist, Holiness, and Methodist churches, and almost one-half of the lower-class population belonged to a church. Attendance was another matter, however, with a much smaller proportion frequently attending church.

Church Attendance in Urban Areas

Women's organizations in New Haven represent the cleavages of the community and, according to Minnis (1959), exist in a complex pattern of interlocking networks. The most rigid cleavage in organizations in New Haven is by race, with 90 percent of the organizations excluding people outside their own race. The few racially mixed organizations that do exist are primarily church affiliated or veterans' organizations. About three-fourths of organizations are religiously exclusive and thus reveal major cleavages among Protestants, Catholics, and Jews. Interestingly, many organizations apparently unrelated to religion, for example, the Veterans of Foreign Wars, had severe religious restrictions on membership. Further, some organizations restricted membership along racial, ethnic (Polish, Italian, etc.), and religious bases simultaneously, and one wonders how the organizations ever find qualified members.

Comstock and Partridge (1972) reported that the frequency of church attendance varies by denomination, sect, age, social class, and place of residence. According to them, members of conservative religious groups attend church more often than members of liberal sects. Men attend less frequently than women, and the middle aged more frequently than the young or the old. Frequency of church attendance appears to be highest in the middle class, with poorest attendance figures reported for lower social classes. Social class variations are not clearly understood, however, and reported patterns differ by age and rural-urban residence.

If individual reports of church attendance are taken at face value, on any given Sunday in Madison, Wisconsin, "about 10 percent of the no-church people, 43 percent of the Protestants and 80 percent of the Catholics attend church" (Bultena, 1949: 388). About equal proportions of people from various social classes belong to churches, and their average attendance does not differ significantly (Bultena, 1949: 386). However, Dillingham (1967: 110) showed that when members and nonmembers of churches are examined, social class has a positive association with church attendance, since more people in the lower classes do not belong and, therefore, they seldom, if ever, attend church. Further, among members of the *same* Protestant denomination there is a relationship between social class and church attendance, but *among* denominations there is a negative relationship. That is, across denominations, lower-class people who belong to a church participate more frequently than those from the upper levels who belong to one; yet proportionately more people from upper classes than lower classes belong to a church.

Most studies show that migrants to an urban community generally attend church less often than natives, although the differences are small. This is true despite the argument that churchgoing is a meaningful activity in rural areas and that rural migrants should be more experienced in this type of activity than in more distinctly urban activities, such as formal voluntary organizations. Jitodai (1964: 246) argued that the reason more urban than rural migrants participate in church affairs is because the urban church performs different functions than the rural church. He viewed the urban church as being another secondary association performing integrative functions much like all other formal voluntary associations. It is as foreign to rural migrants as are other voluntary associations (also see Lenski, 1963: 46). Those who migrated early from rural to urban areas supported churches that were familiar to them. These churches were one mechanism by which ruralites adapted to an urban way of life in terms of a familiar institution. Similarly, churches in the suburbs may help to foster social integration there.

A survey of Catholic mass attenders in Montreal showed that the level of church attendance increased as people moved from the central areas of the city to the periphery; however, the higher rate of church attendance in the suburbs represents mainly *nominal religious* participation (mass only), whereas those who participate in taking communion or in devotional religious practices is greater in central city areas. Thus religious participation in the suburbs may be viewed as *attachment* to a serving institution rather than as *commitment* to a basic institution (Carlos, 1970). It has been interpreted as having utility for community integration and identification rather than for religious purposes. In addition, religious participation in the suburbs is believed to be more geographically bound than in the city. Further, suburban church participants are a population that would not be attracted to the church under different circumstances (Carlos, 1970: 756). Additionally, years ago it was noted that while the residentially mobile may participate less in religious activities than the residentially stable, the lower religious participation by the geographically mobile may be related to their younger age and lower probability of being married and having young children (Fichter, 1954: 105).

Christian women go to church more than Christian men, and this does not change when women are in the labor force (Lazerwitz, 1961). In addition, a study of a variety of areas in New York City with varying incomes and lifestyles revealed that "the older the metropolitan male becomes, the less likely he is to turn to the church" (Bahr, 1970: 70). The trend was for disaffiliation rather than affiliation with church as men grew older, except for skid-row men, who were least likely to give up their ties to the church. This may be because the church is the "last link" between these men and the larger society. "The findings seem to indicate a compatibility that does not exist for other voluntary organizations" (Bahr, 1970: 71).

Religiosity

In a review of literature on religiosity Dittes (1969) noted that social scientists have increasingly differentiated between believers for whom religion is a thoughtful commitment and those for whom it is a formalized and external response. The ambiguous results reported in many studies on religion may well be the result of failing to make this distinction. Evidence suggests that individuals holding presumably the same beliefs and carrying out the same religious practices can differ radically on how religion affects their lives. When responses on social and religious attitudes of the two groups are separated, the data give significantly different results on variables such as prejudice, intolerance, and so on. There is considerable agreement on the distinction between these two: (1) the *extrinsic* religious orientation, which focuses on the more explicit, the more formalized, and the more institutionalized aspects; and (2) the *intrinsic* religious orientation, which consists of the more internalized set of dominant attitudes that may affect behavior and attitudes in diffuse roles and activities, not just those connected with designated traditional forms.

Using different measures of religiosity, Goode (1966) concluded that church participation for Protestants means different things for persons in white-collar occupations than it does for those in lower-level, working-class occupations. For white-collar workers, church activity has become so secularized that it is only another form of associational membership. Working-class church members, on the other hand, actually participate less in some church activities than white-collar workers, but their religious activity is much less likely to have

Religious rites are important in the practice of most religions; however, rites are external responses and do not necessarily show a thoughtful commitment to religious precepts.

been secularized: It is more specifically "religious" in nature. From a national representative sample it appears that when religious commitment is measured by the feeling that religion is "very important" and by frequent attendance at church, Catholics are more committed than Protestants. Also, it appears that religious commitment has an impact upon participation in voluntary organizations, since Catholics who are religiously committed are less likely to belong to them than Protestants, whose religious commitment is associated with more voluntary-organization participation (Hausknecht, 1962: 54–55). Social class influence may be operating, of course, since Catholics tend to be of the lower class and lower-class individuals in general tend not to participate as much in voluntary organizations as middle- and upper-class individuals.

CONCLUSIONS

The relationship between religion and urban phenomena is a relatively neglected area of research. As a result, there are few studies with controls for other dimensions—especially social class and denomination in the broader Protestant category. Few studies have examined nonattenders or nonbelievers and their influence upon results; this may very directly be reflected in statements made about church attendance and religion (Dillingham, 1967), as well as for other relationships. For example, Comstock and Partridge's report (1972) of the association between church attendance and mortality indicates a higher relative risk among nonattenders of the 1963 residents of Washington County, Maryland: The relative risk was 2.1 for arteriosclerotic heart disease, 2.3 for pulmonary emphysema, 2.1 for suicide, and 3.9 for cirrhosis of the liver. In the field of mental health, religious attendance has been reported to be positively correlated with personal adjustment in old age (Moberg, 1956).

Finally, it also appears that if major religions have different value and behavioral systems, their influence should be variously distributed throughout the metropolitan complex, since major religious populations tend to be concentrated in different areas.

BIBLIOGRAPHY: Articles

Anderson, Charles H., "Religious Communality Among White Protestants, Catholics, and Mormons," *Social Forces,* 46 (June 1968): 501–508.

Babchuk, Nicholas, and Ralph V. Thompson, "The Voluntary Associations of Negroes," *American Sociological Review,* 27 (October 1962): 647–655.

Bahr, Howard M., "Aging and Religious Disaffiliation," *Social Forces,* 49 (September 1970): 59–71.

Bultena, Louis, "Church Membership and Church Attendance in Madison, Wisconsin," *American Sociological Review,* 14 (June 1949): 384–389.

Carlos, Serge, "Religious Participation and the Urban-Suburban Continuum," *American Journal of Sociology,* 75 (March 1970): 742–759.

Comstock, G. W., and G. B. Partridge, "Church Attendance and Health," *Chronic Diseases,* 25 (1972): 665–672.

Cone, James H., "Black Consciousness and the Black Church: A Historical-Theological Interpretation," *Annals of the American Academy of Political and Social Science,* 387 (June 1970): 49–55.

Cowgill, Donald O., "The Ecology of Religious Preference in Wichita," *Sociological Quarterly,* 1 (April 1960): 87–96.

Dillingham, Harry C., "Rejoinder to 'Social Class and Church Participation,'" *American Journal of Sociology,* 73 (July 1967): 110–114.

Dittes, J. E., "Psychology of Religion," *Handbook of Social Psychology,* 5 (1969): 602–659.

Dynes, Russell R., "The Consequences of Sectarianism for Social Participation," *Social Forces,* 35 (May 1957): 331–334.

Glenn, Norval D., and Ruth Hyland, "Religious Preference and Worldly Success: Some Evidence from National Surveys," *American Sociological Review,* 32 (February 1967): 73–85.

Gockel, Galen L., "Income and Religious Affiliation: A Regression Analysis," *American Journal of Sociology,* 74 (May 1969): 632–647.

Goldstein, Sidney, "Socioeconomic Differentials Among Religious Groups in the United States," *American Journal of Sociology,* 74 (May 1969): 612–631.

Goode, Erich, "Social Class and Church Participation," *American Journal of Sociology,* 72 (July 1966): 102–111.

Greeley, Andrew M., "Religious Intermarriage in a Denominational Society," *American Journal of Sociology,* 75 (May 1970): 949–952.

Jackson, Elton F., William S. Fox, and Harry J. Crockett, Jr., "Religion and Occupational Achievement," *American Sociological Review,* 35 (February 1970): 48–63.

Jitodai, Ted T., "Migrant Status and Church Attendance," *Social Forces,* 43 (December 1964): 241–248.

Lazerwitz, Bernard, "Some Factors Associated with Variations in Church Attendance," *Social Forces,* 39 (May 1961): 301–309.

Lenski, Gerhard E., "Religion and the Modern Metropolis," *Review of Religious Research,* 1 (Summer 1959): 24–29.

McAllister, Ronald J., Edward J. Kaiser, and Edgar W. Butler, "Residential Mobility of Blacks and Whites: A National Longitudinal Survey," *American Journal of Sociology,* 77 (November 1972): 445–456.

Marx, Gary T., "Religion: Opiate or Inspiration of Civil Rights Militancy Among Negroes," *American Sociological Review,* 32 (February 1967): 64–72.

Moberg, David O., "Religious Activities and Personal Adjustment in Old Age," *Journal of Social Psychology,* 43 (May 1956): 261–267.

Monahan, Thomas P., "Some Dimensions of Interreligious Marriages in Indiana, 1962–67," *Social Forces,* 52 (December 1973): 195–203.

Nelsen, Hart M., and H. David Allen, "Ethnicity, Americanization, and Religious Attendance," *American Journal of Sociology,* 79 (January 1974): 906–922.

Northwood, Lawrence K., "Ecological and Attitudinal Factors in Church Desegregation," *Social Problems,* 6 (Fall 1958): 150–163.

Shippey, Frederick A., "The Variety of City Churches," *Review of Religious Research,* 2 (Summer 1960): 8–19.

Yinger, Milton, "Religion and Social Change," *Review of Religious Research,* 4 (Spring 1963): 129–148.

Zimmer, Basil G., "Participation of Migrants in Urban Structures," *American Sociological Review,* 20 (April 1955): 218–224.

Zimmer, Basil, and Amos H. Hawley, "Suburbanization and Church Participation," *Social Forces,* 37 (May 1959): 348–354.

BIBLIOGRAPHY: Books

Barber, Bernard, *Social Stratification,* New York: Harcourt, Brace and Co., 1957.

Chapin, F. Stuart, Jr., Edgar W. Butler, and Frederick A. Patten, *Blackways in an Inner City,* Urbana, Ill.: University of Illinois Press, forthcoming.

Chapin, F. Stuart, "The Protestant Church in an Urban Environment," in Paul K. Hatt and Albert J. Reiss, Jr. (eds.), *Cities and Society,* Glencoe, Ill.: The Free Press, 1957, pp. 505–515.

Cox, Harvey, *The Secular City: Secularization and Urbanization in Theological Perspective,* New York: Macmillan, 1965.

Douglass, H. Paul, and Edmund S. Brunner, *The Protestant Church as a Social Institution,* New York: Harper and Brothers, 1935 (reissued in 1972, New York: Russell and Russell).

Drake, St. Clair, and Horace R. Cayton, *Black Metropolis,* London: Jonathan Cape, 1946.

Durkheim, Emile, *The Elementary Forms of Religious Life,* trans. by J. W. Swain, Glencoe, Ill.: The Free Press, 1947.

Dynes, Russell R., "The Relations of Community Characteristics to Religious

Organization and Behavior," in Marvin B. Sussman (ed.), *Community Structure and Analysis*, New York: Thomas Y. Crowell Co., 1959, pp. 253–268.

Fitchter, Joseph, S. J., *Social Relations in the Urban Parish*, Chicago: University of Chicago Press, 1954.

Frazier, E. Franklin, *The Negro Church in America*, Liverpool, England: Liverpool University Press, 1964.

Hannerz, Ulf, *Soulside*, New York: Columbia University Press, 1969.

Hausknecht, Murray, *The Joiners*, New York: Bedminster Press, 1962.

Herberg, Will, *Protestant-Catholic-Jew*, Garden City, N.Y.: Doubleday, 1956.

Hollingshead, August B., *Elmtown's Youth*, New York: Wiley, 1949.

Kramer, Judith, and Seymour Leventman, *Children of the Gilded Ghetto*, New Haven, Conn.: Yale University Press, 1961.

Lenski, Gerhard, *The Religious Factor*, Garden City, N.Y.: Doubleday Anchor Books (paperback), 1963.

Lipman, Eugene J., and Albert Vorspan (eds.), *A Tale of Ten Cities*, New York: Union of American Hebrew Congregations, 1962.

McCord, William, John Howard, Bernard Friedberg, and Edwin Harwood, *Life Styles in the Black Ghetto*, New York: W. W. Norton and Company, 1969.

Massarik, Fred, "The Jewish Community," in Marvin B. Sussman (ed.), *Community Structure and Analysis*, New York: Thomas Y. Crowell Co., 1959, pp. 237–252.

Minnis, Mhyra S., "The Patterns of Women's Organizations: Significance, Types, Social Prestige Rank, and Activities," in Marvin B. Sussman (ed.), *Community Structure and Analysis*, New York: Thomas Y. Crowell, 1959, pp. 269–287.

Pfeffer, Leo, *Creeds in Competition*, New York: Harper & Brothers, 1958.

Scanzoni, John N., *The Black Family in Modern Society*, Boston: Allyn and Bacon, Inc., 1971.

Taylor, Lee, and Arthur R. Jones, Jr., *Rural Life and Urbanized Society*, New York: Oxford Press, 1964.

Underwood, Kenneth, *Protestant and Catholic*, Boston: Beacon Press, 1957.

Vidich, Arthur J., and Joseph Bensman, *Small Town in Mass Society*, Garden City, N.Y.: Anchor Books, 1960.

Warner, W. Lloyd, et al., *Democracy in Jonesville*, New York: Harper & Bros., 1949.

Weber, Max, *The Protestant Ethic and the Spirit of Capitalism*, trans. by Talcott Parsons, London: Allen and Unwin, 1930.

URBAN PROBLEMS

SECTION FIVE

The nature of social problems is such that some explanation needs to be given of what conditions constitute a social problem and, particularly, urban social problems. The first fact we must face is that not everyone in the United States agrees on what constitutes an urban social problem. In this section of the book we shall examine environmental hazards; physical and mental illness; slums, poverty, and housing; government and services; and crime, suicide, and violence. This list, of course, reflects the author's judgment as to the important problems facing cities and metropolitan areas in the United States, and some individuals would perhaps deny some or all are problems. The point is that what conditions constitute a problem is socially determined.

Therefore, part of the consideration in any particular discussion of urban social problems is to discover to whom the conditions are undesirable and according to what values. The use of drugs and alcohol is *the* major social problem to some; others believe that divorce and nuclear-family disintegration are the most critical problems facing Americans. Others believe that war and/or segregation in our cities are the major problems. But all of these are, or not, major problems depending upon who is making the evaluation.

Problems are evaluated human behavior and conditions, and people may evaluate any given behavior and/or conditions differently. If you and I consider some condition or behavior as a problem, it is only recognized as such when a large number of others, especially influentials, also consider it as a problem. The conditions may be the same, but the human evaluation of them is the key to determining whether or not a social problem exists. Segregation of minorities in cities *is* a problem to many social scientists and others; however, to many others the *real* problem is the tinkering by social scientists and/or militants with the social system that has been devised to keep minorities "in their place."

Once it is decided that an urban social problem exists, another consideration is whether or not to do anything about it. *If* something should be done about the problem, the next question is what. There are numerous possibilities of what should be considered as a solution to any particular social problem, and once again values play an important role in what any particular individual believes is an acceptable solution.

Most social scientists agree that there are certain types of problems broadly characteristic of cities and metropolitan areas in the United States. The majority of them are the product of basic conditions of our society. Whenever patterns of undesirable conditions appear in many metropolitan areas, but they do not appear to be the difficulties of any particular metropolitan area, probably something is wrong with the system.

Characteristic types of problems of contemporary metropolitan areas in the United States include: (1) indebtedness of cities and taxes, (2) urban blight and slums, (3) lack of adequate housing, (4) economic dependence of a large segment of the population, (5) poorly financed and staffed schools, especially in the inner city, (6) high delinquency and crime rates, (7) inadequate provisions for the mentally and physically ill, (8) the plight of the aged, (9) a need for jobs, (10) conflict over expenditures for services, including charity and welfare, (11) transportation and traffic congestion, (12) air pollution, (13) water pollution, and (14) waste disposal.

There are two contrasting approaches to these problems: First, they may be part and parcel of contemporary United States and of a dynamic society; second, each problem may be taken out of its situational context and treated in isolation from the basic conditions that produced it. So far, the second approach has been favored. Many of these problems probably are not solvable at the local level or on an individual basis; any given local effort has little effect against the tide of the larger society. Nevertheless, some of these problems were brought about by a loss of local autonomy to the larger society — including corporations, state government, and the federal government.

Factors working against the solution of these problems are the lack of identification with the local community, apathy, residential mobility — here today, gone tomorrow, and alienation or anomia — normlessness, estrangement from the dominant value system.

As we have already indicated, there is the conflict over whether or not the problems exist, what society *can* and *should* do about them. Alleviative measures may actually, inadvertently, make the situation worse than it was previously. Finally, as some people believe, the problem may be too large and complex to deal with or it simply reflects human nature, which cannot be changed.

Currently, there is a lack of public knowledge concerning the extent of urban problems in the United States and solutions for them; and it appears that there is a lack of willingness to undergo social change to solve them. Accordingly, we can expect these urban social problems to be with us well into the future.

CHAPTER 16
SLUMS, POVERTY, AND HOUSING

INTRODUCTION

A metropolitan complex is made up of a mosaic of commercial, industrial, park, residential, and other kinds of areas. Among the least understood, although perhaps one of the most extensively studied, is the slums. *Slums* ordinarily are those areas of the city that are characterized by blight and obsolete housing and occupied by a poverty-stricken population. Many slums are located in areas of transition from one type of land use to another, for example, a former residential area located near the CBD in the process of becoming converted to commercial or industrial use. There are also areas located elsewhere in the metropolitan complex that were built decades ago and the housing has deteriorated because of age and other factors. Thus, while slums are primarily located in transitional areas near the CBD, there are pockets of them located elsewhere in the metropolitan complex, such as in older suburban areas; and an occasional "rural-fringe" slum is known to exist.

Gans (1962) suggests that a distinction needs to be made between low-rent areas and slums: low-rent areas are those that have a fully organized social life, for example, the West End, Italian neighborhood in Boston, as opposed to a slum, in which "social disorganization" exists. Hannerz (1969: 11) also has noted that the term "ghetto" is commonly used to identify areas of the inner city that others call slums. In this chapter these terms are used interchangeably, and by them we mean to convey only that the areas and people living in them have some characteristics in common. In one instance the common characteristic is poor housing and living conditions; in another, any particular ghetto or slum may be composed of a population of a certain ethnicity or skin color (e.g., black). Little attention will be paid to anglo suburban ghettos or to high-rise "gilded" Jewish ghettos in this particular chapter. Two of the most prominent features of slums and ghettos examined extensively in this chapter are the prevailing poverty and blighted housing that exist there.

POVERTY

Poverty does not only mean low incomes but also the despair and hopelessness found in slums, where there are large numbers of unemployed or underemployed workers, large families with reduced or minimal resources, and, in some instances, missing males. When we consider poverty, we must take into account *relative position in society*. In other words, although a family in the United States may have more resources than a family in some other society, it still may be relatively poor in our society. Further, the question of basic needs and their relative costs must be taken into account in any definition of who is and who is not poor. Poverty is inherited, not genetically, but culturally. The byproducts of poverty include ignorance, disease, delinquency and crime, alienation, and indifference.

Historically, the period between 1929 and 1947 showed a reduction in the inequality of the distribution of income; since 1947 the inequality of income has not changed significantly (Haley, 1971: 19). Nevertheless, if today's poor are compared with those of 1960, they are relatively worse off because of the decreased buying power of their income.

Who Are the Poor?

How to determine who is poor is not an easy decision in a rapidly changing pluralistic society. There probably is not one generally acceptable and uniform measure of who is poor. Nevertheless, "if it is not possible to state unequivocally 'how much is enough,' it should be possible to assert with confidence how much, on an average, is too little" (Orshanksy, 1965: 3). Under criteria adopted by the Social Security Administration, it was estimated that in 1963 a total of 7.2 million families and 5 million individuals living alone or with nonrelatives "lacked the wherewithal to live at anywhere near a tolerable level." Thus the combined number of poor, in 1963, totaled some 37.5 million persons.

Orshansky (1965: 4) pointed out that

> 1 in 7 of all families of two or more and almost half of all persons living alone or with nonrelatives had incomes too low in 1963 to enable them to eat even the minimal diet that could be expected to provide adequate nutrition and still have enough left over to pay for all other living essentials.

Thus somewhere around one-fourth of all citizens in the United States are living at or below the poverty level. Orshansky (1965: 4–5) indicated that the populations most vulnerable to the risk of inadequate income have long been identified and of late much publicized, but they make up only a small part of all the nation's poor.

Families headed by a woman are subject to a risk of poverty three times that of units headed by a man, but they represent only one-fourth of all persons in families classed as poor. Indeed, almost three-fourths of poor families have a man as the head. Children growing up without a father must get along on less than they need far more often than those living with both parents. In fact, two-thirds of them are in families with inadequate income. But two-thirds of all the children in the families designated as poor do live in a home with a man at the head.

Many of the aged have inadequate incomes, but almost four-fifths of poor families have someone under age 65 at the head. Even among persons who live alone, as do so many aged women, nearly one-half of all individuals classified as poor have not yet reached old age. Nonwhite families suffer a poverty risk three times as great as white families do, but 7 out of 10 poor families are white.

And, finally, in our work-oriented society, those who cannot or do not work must expect to be poorer than those who do. Yet more than one-half of all poor families report that the head currently has a job. Moreover, one-half of these employed family heads — representing almost 30 percent of all the families classified as poor — have been holding down full-time jobs for a whole year. In fact, of the 7.2 million poor families in 1963, 1 in every 6 (1.3 million) was the family of a white male worker who worked full time throughout the year. Yet this is the kind of family that in our present society has the best chance of escaping poverty. All told, of the 15 million children under age 18 counted as poor, about $5\frac{1}{3}$ million were in the family of a man or woman who had a full-time job all during 1963.

In addition, as reported by the Council of Economic Advisers (1964), the poor in the United States can be characterized as follows:

- One-fifth of our families and nearly one-fifth of our total population are poor.
- Of the poor, 22 percent are nonwhite; and nearly one-half of all nonwhites live in poverty.
- The heads of over 60 percent of all poor families have only grade-school educations.
- Even for those denied opportunity by discrimination, education significantly raises the chance to escape from poverty. Of all nonwhite families headed by a person with 8 years or less of schooling, 57 percent are poor. This falls to 30 percent for high-school graduates and to 18 percent for those with some college education.
- But education does not remove the effects of discrimination: when nonwhites are compared with whites at the same level of education, the nonwhites are poor about twice as often.
- One-third of all poor families are headed by a person over 65, and almost one-half of all families headed by such a person are poor.
- Of the poor, 54 percent live in cities, 16 percent on farms, 30 percent as rural nonfarm residents.

—Over 40 percent of all farm families are poor. More than 80 percent of nonwhite farmers live in poverty.

—Less than one-half of the poor are in the South; yet a southerner's chance of being poor is roughly twice that of a person living in the rest of the country.

—One quarter of poor families are headed by a woman; but nearly one-half of all families headed by a woman are poor.

—When a family and its head have several characteristics frequently associated with poverty, the chances of being poor are particularly high: A family headed by a young woman who is nonwhite and has less than an eighth-grade education is poor in 94 out of 100 cases. Even if the female head is white, the chances are 85 out of 100 that she and her children will be poor.

Therefore, although most poor people are white, nonwhite families are more likely to be poor than are white families, and about one-half of all poor families are headed by women, an older person, or a disabled person.

Not only do the poor have less income, they have to, in the words of Caplovitz (1967) "pay more" for the goods and services that they receive. This includes professional services that in some instances, at least theoretically, could be free to the poor. Thus Caplovitz pointed out that differences between the poor and the better off are not only a matter of economics but also one of recognizing that a problem exists, that there are experts who can handle such problems, and that the poor person must feel secure in the company of the person who is to provide the service. He concluded that most poor people are ill prepared to cope with consumer problems. This lack of preparedness has led to many illegal and quasi-legal consumer practices that result in the poor paying more.

Similarly, other pressures lead to the poor paying more than for comparable goods available elsewhere. For the providers of goods and services in poor neighborhoods pressures include higher per-unit costs, higher insurance rates, higher theft losses, and so on, and each of these higher costs is passed on legitimately to the consumer in poor neighborhoods. Also, there is a general lack of knowledge about where or to whom to go in case of consumer fraud; many others who are aware of potential assistance believe that the agency or person would not intervene effectively if called upon for help. This perhaps incorrectly would be called apathy; perhaps it is more of a *realistic expectation* that the system will not operate in a favorable manner for the poor— an expectation based upon previous experience.

The poor spend, on the average, one-third of their available dollars for food (Orshansky, 1965: 8). The approximately 35 million identified as poor in 1963 needed a total income of $28.8 billion to cover their basic living requirements. Interestingly, Orshansky (1965: 14) estimated that the public assistance received by 7¾ million persons, from federal, state, and local funds, accounted for only about a quarter of their incomes—$4.7 billion. Even then, their total income only totaled about $17.3 billion, and it covered only 60 percent of their estimated needs.

Poverty and Employment

A basic value of our society is that individuals should work, and it is especially incumbent upon the unemployed poor to have the desire to find work (Sussman, 1964: 397). Not considered in this value is the increasing probability that even if the poor individual is motivated, industrious, and ambitious, there are insufficient job openings for those who want them, since there are structural conditions that mediate these individual characteristics — whether or not jobs are available and the individual is trained for the position.

One current hypothesis in regard to the urban poor is that "the uneducated and unskilled poor have been left behind in a rapidly advancing and automated technology and hence have failed to operate successfully in the newly emerging job market" (Bluestone, 1968: 410). A more persuasive argument is that many people with adequate skills are simply not being provided with adequate jobs, a hypothesis supported by the data on underemployment. *Underemployment* refers to those persons who work at a full-time job but who are not making enough money to survive above the poverty level. For example, almost one-third of all families living below the poverty level as defined by the U.S. government in 1964 were headed by a person who worked 50–52 weeks throughout the year at a full-time job. These working poor spend nearly one-half of their waking hours at arduous, numbingly repetitous jobs devoid of opportunity for occupational mobility (Bluestone, 1968: 410). The underemployed represent nearly one-fifth of the employed labor force.

Approximately one-third of underemployed persons are black, although because of their greater absolute number more whites than blacks are in the working poor category. Over one-half of the working poor are in the prime work years between 25 and 54. Ninety percent of all families among the working poor are male-headed households, although in one-fifth of these households the wife also worked at least part time; even so, the sum total of the two incomes failed to raise the family income above the poverty line. The working poor (and many of the unemployed) have enough education and adequate skills, so that the problem is not a lack of preparation, but rather the inability to find jobs. They cannot find jobs because the jobs do not exist.

What are the solutions to under- and unemployment? One suggestion points to training, retraining, and education and sending individuals into the highly specialized American labor force presumably equipped to function in it. Yet as we have pointed out, the problem may not be one of adequate education and training (although, of course, they are important); the trouble may be that the economy cannot furnish an adequate number of jobs above the poverty level. Since there are several million families in poverty despite the fact that the family head is always working, stress needs to be placed not only upon increasing the numbers of jobs for the poor but also to make sure that there are increasing advancement opportunities and better-paying positions so that a full-time worker and his family will not remain at a poverty level of living.

A number of other specific measures have been suggested as being necessary to eliminate low wages: (1) permit closed-union shops; (2) have unions take on the task of organizing the unorganized lower-wage earners; (3) broaden and increase the level of minimum-wage legislation; (4) ensure that jobs at a guaranteed minimum-income level are available, and let the government act as an employer of last resort; (5) implement a negative income tax; and (6) create jobs that not only ensure a minimum-income level but also utilize a person's creativity. This last suggestion may call for a re-creation of the value of all kinds of work (Bluestone, 1968: 418–419).

Poverty and Education

Recently a study of 12 of the larger cities in the United States showed that high-school graduation for whites is worth about $25 per week, while for nonwhites the difference is only $8.33. High-school graduation, therefore, has about a three-times higher payoff for whites than for nonwhites (Harrison, 1972: 804). Nevertheless, this particular study showed that education facilities the entry of both whites and nonwhites into new occupations and, at least for ghetto whites, greater occupational mobility. It also suggested that it is much easier for poor whites than nonwhites to move out of poverty, to obtain higher-paying jobs, and to be occupationally mobile than it is for nonwhites.

One aspect of this study shows that the expected inverse relationship between education and unemployment and labor force participation did not materialize.[1] Thus

> perhaps education increases the expectations and standards of ghetto workers which, when unmet to discriminating or otherwise exploitative employers, leads to frustration. This in turn may reduce the job attachment of the worker. If presently employed, he or she may display greater absenteeism, more frequent recalcitrance when given orders by foremen, or less patience with what is perceived as racist behavior on the part of coworkers. If the ghetto resident is not presently employed, then — although he is indeed searching for work — the change in his standards or expectations may lead him to increase the wages expected before employment will be accepted. If the offered positions do not meet his standards, then he will reject the job and search further, or turn to other income-generating activities such as public welfare or "the hustle." In this way, he may remain unemployed for a relatively long period of time [Harrison, 1972: 808].

[1] It should be noted that there may be conflict between this study and research results reported in Chapter 10 that claimed that blacks suffered no such limitations.

Finally, it has been suggested that "unless a Black high school student is certain that he will complete college, he may be better off (in terms of his lifetime income) by dropping out of the educational system before finishing high school" (Harrison, 1972: 810).

Urban and Rural Differences in Poverty

Twenty-four percent of poor whites live in central cities, whereas 44 percent of the nonwhite poor live there. In 80 percent of poor families with a younger male head, he works; most of these men worked at least 40 weeks out of the year (Jackson and Velten, 1971: 95). The earnings of the poor were highest in the central cities and lowest in the suburbs. Poor white males earn more on the average than do poor black males.

Poverty Areas Within Metropolitan Complexes

Nonwhite families are concentrated to a much larger extent in poverty areas of the larger metropolitan areas than are white poverty families. Similarly, the Bureau of the Census (1966: 1) reported that "nonwhite families comprised about 12 percent of all families in SMSA's of 250,000 or more but made up 42 percent of all families in Poverty Areas and only 6 percent of all families in Nonpoverty Areas."

Poverty and Children

Around 15 million of the poor in 1963 were children, or more than one child in every five in families. Of these, only 3.1 million needy children were receiving assistance in the form of aid to families with dependent children, the public program specifically designed for them (Orshansky, 1965: 15–16).

Himes (1964: 448–449) also found that there are cultural deprivations that lower-class black youths face in regard to work: (1) irrelevant job models, (2) exclusion from the prevailing work ethic, and (3) alienation from the culture of the modern factory and office. Lower-class black children are denied the experience of daily association with workers who inadvertently, through the socialization process, introduce the child to the role of the worker and the world of work. These young children do not learn that there is a linkage between effort and advancement; when they do begin to work in offices or factories, they quickly become alienated to the structured situation because they have not been prepared for what to expect in the work situation.

Herzog and Lewis (1970) exposed a number of myths surrounding children of poor families. One is that the matriarchal family dominates. The authors pointed out that this partially represents some families but is not even the desired mode in these families. Similarly, to characterize poor parents as being apathetic in regard to the future of their children is fallacious. Finally, the most damaging myth is that the children of the poor cannot and will not be able to take advantage of opportunities if they are presented to them.

These children live in a housing tenement in Chicago's "Black Belt." According to Himes, such children are not likely to experience a socialization process that will assure their adaptation, later in life, to the work climate of a modern office or factory.

Conclusions

There are many persons in the United States who lose out on their chances of ever rising above the poverty level because they have been denied the most basic needs and opportunities. Past social policies have not been effective in alleviating their condition, and more creative and innovative approaches are necessary. As Orshanksy (1965: 26) has pointed out: "The poor have been counted many times. It remains now to count the ways by which to help them gain a new identity." To eliminate the cycle of poverty requires an elimination of un- and underemployment, changing a welfare system that rewards a father for leaving the household, developing expanded opportunities for persons born under poverty circumstances, and developing mechanisms to restore the strength and vigor of families that are too weak to cope effectively with contemporary society.

Further, there is ample justification for the position that education and training programs without a supply of jobs are unlikely to have any major impact upon unemployment and poverty. They will have a positive impact when involuntary part-time employment and substandard wages are eliminated. The remedy must be the opening up of new and better-paying jobs. They should be physically accessible to ghetto residents, their availability must be made known, and promotional possibilities must be made available. Only then will training and education bear fruit. The emphasis must be directed away from alleged individual and family defects and redirected toward the social structure and how it might be altered to eliminate constraints upon ghetto employment and job opportunities.

SLUMS AND HOUSING

Wilson (1965: 2) has stated that housing in the United States, and in big cities especially, has been improving over the past 20 or 30 years. According to him, this improvement "has been one of this country's most significant yet often underalded achievements." In fact, he goes so far as to claim that the United States does not have an urban or a housing problem. Rather, there are "problems of the people in those cities," and they are poverty, race, and culture. By culture Wilson means the problems of establishing a cultural and educational basis for a sound, stable family life that will prepare people to take advantage of the opportunities that confront them.

But in reality hard-core slum areas continue to deteriorate, and the residents who live in them have little opportunity to obtain adequate housing, since most of the construction after World War II has been for upper-middle-class and upper-income families. Little low-income housing has been built since the mid-20s, and almost a half-century of rapid changes in our cities — including the great black urban migration — has passed with hardly any housing construction for low-income families.

Currently, the poor in the United States, for the most part, live in deteriorated and dilapidated housing that would be, or has been rejected, by those with adequate incomes. In addition, even a housing shortage of inadequate housing exists. Minorities live in poor housing for two basic reasons: (1) The vast majority of them have an income problem, and (2) personal and institutional racism operate to keep in the slums those minorities with adequate incomes. There are several other reasons why blacks in particular have not taken advantage of the open-housing market that does exist: A lack of knowledge about potential housing is one inhibiting factor; an unwillingness to leave the friendship patterns and relationships established in the ghetto is another.

Barth and March (1962) reported a project in Seattle, Washington, that had as its goal interviewing white homeowners who had advertised an intention to sell to determine whether they would object to showing or selling their homes on a nondiscriminatory basis. The authors asked the homeowners for their permission to make their addresses and names available to agencies servicing nonwhite home seekers. Eighteen percent were willing to do so, and 32 percent more showed a willingness to sell their houses on an open market.

At the time of this Seattle study, realtors played a substantial role in blocking blacks' access to purchasing homes on the open market. First, they publicly opposed open-housing legislation both at the local and state levels. Second, a majority of them refused to service blacks in the housing market. This meant that blacks were effectively cut off from even those white homeowners (at least 18 percent) who would sell their homes on an open market. In addition, several local organizations provided open-housing listings but blacks

At least one woman in this picture of an apartment building on New York's West Side appears to believe that this building warrants repairs. Whether the others — including the touring assemblyman — share her opinion is another question.

in general believed that these houses were inferior or otherwise they would not have been listed. Barth and March concluded that poor communication is a major barrier to blacks finding adequate housing. It is partially self-imposed and partially a result of the discriminatory practices of some realtors and others involved in the housing market. The authors suggested that some mechanism must be established whereby black home seekers and potential anglo home sellers can communicate with each other.

Evidence is accumulating that shows that what people want in housing is not related to their socioeconomic levels but to their values, family patterns, life styles, and stages in the life cycle (Michelson, 1974). One's stage in the life cycle is independent of socioeconomic level, and yet it has certain implications for desired housing. For example, during the child-rearing years high-rise apartments make it difficult for low-income families to supervise their children adequately outside of the apartments. A high rise is more suitable for some older persons as long as its location gives them full access to a variety of medical, shopping, and other services. Similarly, family type may be important in housing preferences: Nuclear families (father, mother, and children) typically have a preference for single-family housing units located away from the inner city; extended families — with multiple generations in the household — are more likely to prefer and to have experienced high-density neighborhoods and indeed may feel socially deprived when living away from such familiar surroundings (Gans, 1962: 22–23).

Life styles, which are to some degree associated with family patterns, also are related to housing preferences. They revolve substantially around the *use of time*. Most people believe that the nuclear-family pattern requires a single-family housing unit, preferably located elsewhere than the inner city; likewise, a person who is career oriented rather than family oriented may prefer a centrally located apartment. Also, a person interested in culture may want to live close to the core of the city where most cultural facilities are located.

Finally, values come into play in housing preferences, designs, and locations. One dominant feature of many new high-rise apartment buildings and some newer suburbs is *safety*. Others prefer high density with a maximal emphasis upon the potential for interaction. Some people prefer privacy and thus lower densities, while others give preference to location over housing characteristics.

Housing Variation
Within Metropolitan Complexes

A paradox of American cities is that land values decrease with distance from the center while family incomes tend to increase with distance from the center. Thus typically the poor are living on the most expensive land, whereas those who are better off occupy less expensive land. Newer housing generally is being built in expanding suburbs, while older housing in the inner city, as well as in other older areas in the city and the metropolitan complex, is "filtering" down to the poor. In the filtering theory of housing, as housing grows older or is out of style or located in a neighborhood that is becoming less desirable, it will be passed down to families of lower income. For the theory to work, more desirable housing is made available for those who want and can afford it, thus freeing older, less desirable homes for the filtering-down process.

Current housing problems are a result of the early growth of cities. The greatest proportion of poor-quality housing in the United States is located in the central cities of metropolitan areas. This housing was filled by immigrants from other countries, and more recently in most cities this same housing has been filled by southern blacks, in some cities by Puerto Ricans, and in others by persons of Mexican descent. Housing in central cities is much more likely to be rented than owned, in contrast to the suburbs, where ownership dominates. Generally, owned housing is in better condition than rental units. Of those persons living in the central city, minorities are more likely than anglos to be renters. Further, whether owned or rented, housing utilized by minorities in cities tends to be housing in the most deteriorated and dilapidated condition.

Several factors account for the extent of deteriorated and dilapidated housing in the central city: (1) Typically, the housing is older — that is, the housing stock was built decades ago; and (2) there is a lack of maintenance, especially by absentee landlords. The new construction in housing that has taken place since World War II has been primarily in the open-land suburbs, which make large-scale production feasible.

When the housing stock of a whole area or neighborhood in a city becomes deteriorated and dilapidated and pretty much beyond repair, the area is considered as a slum. "The housing in such an area is a detriment to physical well-being. Usually such areas lack sunlight and fresh air, adequate water supplies, and sewage control, and often there are fire and accident hazards, as well as severe overcrowding" (Beyer, 1965: 338). The population of slums includes older people with inadequate incomes and of minority status. Also, rates of illiteracy, physical and mental abnormalities, and other impairments are higher in the slums than elsewhere. Neighborhood facilities and services are usually inadequate.

Some areas characterized by deterioration and dilapidation can be rehabilitated. Generally, rehabilitation, renewal, or redevelopment of areas in cities has been left up to governmental action rather than individual families or private contractors, probably because it is not economically feasible for the latter to carry out such enterprises.

Two oversimplifications currently hinder the solving of inner-city slum problems. First is the belief that all slum dwellers are alike in their population characteristics, for example, unemployment, race, and attitudes and behavior. Actually, slum dwellers have different characteristics, and some are employed full time in good jobs, but some are underpaid; some are underemployed or unemployed and looking for work; others are no longer in the labor force — that is, they have given up looking for a job. Similarly, there are a variety of different kinds of people living in the slums; for example in a Chicago slum, Italians, blacks, chicanos, and Puerto Ricans live in close proximity to each other (Suttles, 1968). In a Washington, D.C., slum a variety of family patterns were found (Hannerz, 1969) and various life styles were also reported to exist in the black community in Houston (McCord et al., 1969). Similarly, substantial variations in life styles, family types, socioeconomic levels, and behavioral and attitudinal differences were reported in a Near Northeast black community in Washington, D.C. (Chapin et al., forthcoming).

While this street may not be typical of all slum areas, the lack of garbage pickup is notable; the area does appear to have fire protection, but there seems little municipal interest in removing abandoned automobiles from the street.

A second hindrance to solving inner-city slum problems is that most remedial action has been concentrated upon a single substandard condition. "Any effective ghetto-improvement strategy must concern itself with at least jobs and employment, education, housing, health, personal safety, crime prevention, and income maintenance for dependent persons" (Downs, 1970: 31).

PUBLIC HOUSING
AND URBAN RENEWAL

"A decent home and suitable living environment for every American family" has been a stated national objective since passage of the Housing Act of 1949. Subsequently, the Housing and Urban Development Act of 1968 authorized a variety of new programs and refinements in existing programs in an effort to come to grips with the housing problems that continued to exist in this country, particularly as they relate to lower-income families. These housing acts represent a major effort to bring together the talent, expertise, and resources of the public and private sectors of the country. The Housing Act provides incentives for people to help themselves become better citizens, self-supporting and not dependent on government welfare. It recognizes that the problems to be resolved involve more than just providing housing for lower-income families. Thus it provides that, to the greatest extent feasible, opportunities for employment and contracts for work arising in connection with the construction or rehabilitation of housing under special programs be given to lower-income persons and business concerns located in the areas where such housing will be built.

In most cities, separate agencies are concerned with redevelopment, zoning, subsidized housing programs, zoning enforcement, and so on. Some cities have established housing authorities. Within the general guidelines set by federal public housing laws and by the Housing Assistance Administration (HAA), which administers low-rent public housing programs, local housing authorities have much room for constructive action. Local housing authorities may plan projects, determine specific criteria for admission to leased housing, and issue other administrative regulations. Unfortunately, rents must cover maintenance, housing authority staff, and the creation of a reserve fund for expenditures such as major repairs. If the authority increases its services, it must either pay for them out of current rent collections or raise rents. This builds in a tendency to defer maintenance or to favor the admission of tenants in the higher ranges of eligible income categories, since they generate more rental income and tend to demand less in the way of managerial costs and time. This institutional arrangement has produced controversy as local authorities resist the admission of lower-income tenants or those with greater social problems.

A widely criticized feature of the public housing law is the upper limit on tenant income. In most cases, when income rises above certain levels, tenants are required to move. They are often pushed into housing markets where they can find nothing but grossly inadequate housing at the prices they previously paid for leased housing. Tenants are forced to choose between not increasing their incomes and staying in leased housing or increasing their incomes and moving into inadequate housing.

Too often in the past, local housing authorities have built and leased massive, unattractive, institutional projects that are clearly different in shape, size, and character from ordinary apartments and housing developments. As a result, in many cities public housing is referred to not by an address, nor even by a name, but as "the project." Some people consider residence in such projects a sign of second-class citizenship.

Local housing authorities also may lease new or existing houses and then sublet them to tenants. The authority pays to the owner the difference between the approved economic rent and the amount the tenant can pay. This program makes it possible for low-income families to live in neighborhoods where other residents are not receiving subsidies. In effect, it is a rent supplement program under another name, with the likely potential of producing more housing for low-income occupants. An important step that a local housing authority might take is to involve persons in the target community in every stage of the redevelopment program, including planning, construction, operation, and employment. It has not been the general practice of housing authorities to emphasize citizen and/or tenant participation.

Another manner of dealing with substandard housing is to enforce housing codes strictly and to create ordinances that pertain to "good house-keeping." Although code enforcement is only one tool that can be used in the elimination of slums, it is probably the most effective in guaranteeing a decent house and a suitable living environment. It can prevent blight from spreading to areas with standard housing and can upgrade basically sound and restorable communities. However, strict code enforcement has some built-in problems such as:

1. Coercion of tenants by landlords to move if the former complain about substandard conditions.
2. Lack of understanding of codes by tenants and landlords.
3. Financial inability of lower-income owners to rehabilitate.
4. Code regulations that restrict new building innovations and techniques.
5. Lack of knowledge by owners and tenants as to what financial assistance is available to them.

Section 117 of the Housing Act of 1949 authorizes federal grants to cities, counties, and municipalities to cover part of the costs of concentrated code enforcement programs in designated areas of the localities, including administration, relocation assistance, section 312 rehabilitation loans and section 115 grants, and the provision and repair of necessary streets, curbs, sidewalks, streetlighting, tree planting, and similar improvements.

Section 312, added by the Housing and Urban Development Act of 1964, authorized direct federal loans at 3-percent interest rates to low- or moderate-income owners of residential and business property in urban-renewal areas, code enforcement areas, and to low- or moderate-income owner-occupants of residential property in areas designated for rehabilitation within a reasonable time. These loans also are made to enable owners to bring the structures up to code requirements. Section 115 grants and section 312 loans are made by local agencies or through a private, nonprofit group. Such agencies also can now operate directly in rehabilitating housing in urban-renewal areas.

While improving the existing housing stock is a worthwhile endeavor, substantial portions of the housing stock in most cities are beyond repair and need to be replaced. In addition, there is vacant land suitable for housing developments and isolated vacant residential lots available for building sites. The federal government has several programs that assist local governments to subsidize housing. These programs are viewed as one mechanism, along with private enterprise, that may assist in building additional housing.

Providing the housing needs of low- and low-middle-income families requires the provision of low-cost publicly subsidized housing, which includes renovating older housing as well as constructing new housing. Subsidized housing is a necessity, since these families are unable to obtain adequate housing in the standard, privately financed housing market. The following alternatives have been suggested (Johnson: 1965: 7) as providing a solution to the slum housing problems:

— Providing rent supplements for families across a wide range of lower- and moderate-income brackets so that they can afford decent housing.
— Providing rent supplement assistance to those forced out of their homes by code enforcement and all forms of federally assisted government action, from highways to urban renewal.
— Using both urban-renewal funds and public housing funds to rehabilitate existing housing and make it available to low- and moderate-income families. There is no reason to tear down and rebuild if existing housing can be improved and made desirable.
— Emphasizing residential construction and rehabilitation on a neighborhood-wide scale in the urban-renewal program.

Several arguments advanced for public housing are that newly constructed housing invariably is financially out of the reach of families with low incomes; housing that low-income families can afford is being removed from the housing market faster than it is being replaced; diseases and hazards are more difficult to control under poor housing conditions; and, finally, all families should be able to live comfortably in adequate housing. In addition, the justification for slum clearance and the construction of public housing has been that the slums themselves as well as the social problems accompanying them will be eliminated by such programs.

"Unfortunately, the contention that slum clearance is a solution to a multitude of social problems may detract from more basic arguments for providing adequate housing for the less fortunate and their families" (Shannon, 1966: 1). In fact, Wilson (1965) has contended that urban renewal is either irrelevant or disadvantageous for these kinds of problems — "urban renewal has bypassed the real problems, or, in some cases, made them worse."

Public housing projects do not always involve large-scale housing removal, since there are many projects that involve rehabilitation of individual residences and piecemeal removal dependent upon individual housing-unit condition. Most urban-renewal or redevelopment programs, however, involve mass removal and the clearance of housing that force people to move out of the destroyed neighborhood. Similarly, the typical urban-renewal project prevents the original residents from returning to the old areas of residence; even if they should be able to return, churches, schools, kin, and friends are no longer in the neighborhood. In addition, rent typically increases for over two-thirds of those involved in urban-renewal programs (e.g., in one study over 50 percent). Further, many residents of inner cities are not aided by urban renewal in many instances because they are forced to move to large factorylike skyscrapers of public housing; these facilities have not solved the housing problem and may have intensified social problems.

In an area of Akron, Ohio, destined for urban renewal, the residents had a generally favorable view of government and their neighborhood; but they were divided in regard to the desirability of the proposed urban renewal. Those residents who were middle class—relatively well educated, mobile, well paid, and knowledgeable about the project—tended to favor it; also, younger persons tended to favor it. On the other hand, persons who were older, less well educated, homeowners, not knowledgeable about the project, and currently less capable of independent action tended to be negative about the project. In addition, those residents who were negative tended to have more friends and relatives living in the neighborhood, though they visited them less often than those who were positive about the urban-renewal project. Those who were positive tended to visit with people more both in and out of the neighborhood. Race of the resident was not a factor in positive and negative appraisal of the urban-renewal project. One cautionary note was added by the authors of this study when they pointed out that they questioned residents about urban renewal in the abstract; after the project begins, their attitudes and behavior might change drastically.

Public Housing and Quality of Life

A basic assumption related to the construction of public housing projects is that the rehousing of families will improve their quality of life. In one of the first tests of this hypothesis a study of Sumner Field Homes in Minneapolis was carried out in 1939 and 1940 (Chapin, 1940). This particular study very carefully developed an experimental group—those who moved into the public housing project—and a control group—much like the experimental group in regard to race, employment of husband, occupational classification, number of persons in the family, and income, except they still lived in the slums. At the beginning of the housing project dwellers and slum residents were substantially similar in *morale, general adjustment, and social participation*. One year later they were still similar in morale and general adjustment. However, the public housing residents were substantially more active in social participation than slum residents, gained more in social status, had better furnishings in the living room, and had reduced their crowding in the dwelling unit. Thus this particular study showed that there are possible definite positive social effects of good housing.

Rumney (1951) compared a low-income population, formerly slum residents living in a public housing project, and another low-income population residing in a deteriorated area of Newark, New Jersey. He found that illnesses and accidents were lower among public housing families than among slum residents; for example, the tuberculosis rate per 10,000 persons was 29 for public housing residents and 59 in areas of substandard housing. Similarly, he reported that in Pittsburgh the infant mortality rate in public housing projects was 42, while it was 71 in areas of substandard housing. In addition, juvenile delinquency rates per 10,000 population were 383 in public housing and 570 in the slums.

A somewhat similar study was carried out in Baltimore between 1955 and 1958 (Wilner et al., 1962). Comparisons were made between low-income black families living in a public housing project and a control sample residing in an unrehabilitated area of the city. Families were matched on size of dwelling unit, age of female head of household, age of oldest child, presence of husband, number of children, and so on. A number of hypotheses were examined in regard to these varying housing and living environments. In general, rehoused families were better off than slum families.

Results of this study showed that illness rates were lower for rehoused families than for slum families. This was the case for persons under 35, especially for children. Disabilities from childhood communicable diseases were lower in the housing project than in the slums, and illnesses for males and females in the age range of 35–59 were lower for rehoused families. Residents of the housing project were somewhat better psychologically adjusted than slum families. Rehoused families had a substantial increase in neighboring and mutual-assistance activities, such as helping with household tasks or in times of illness. Rehoused families had fewer quarrels and arguments, had more mutually shared activities in household tasks, and shared more leisure-time activities than was true of those still living in substandard housing. The rehoused also had more pride in the neighborhood, spent more time in improving it, and expressed more satisfaction with their style of life, living conditions, and the neighborhood.

Rehoused women improved their morale, had more favorable self-images, and experienced reduced anxieties. Children in the housing project did better in school than those remaining in the old neighborhood. However, there was little difference noted between the results of intelligence and achievement scores of the rehoused and the slum dwellers. In addition, in this study some effects of the changed environment might not have been discernible for a longer period of time, and presumably these changes would also favor those who had been rehoused.

More recently, a study conducted in New Haven, Connecticut, examined the impact that moving large, low-income black families into privately owned homes or apartments located in various parts of the city had upon family functioning (Weller and Luchterhand, 1973). These homes were "vastly superior to the former residences" and were made possible by an 80-percent subsidy paid by the city. The research included two sets of control families that were compared with relocated families to evaluate the impact of improved housing. The relocated families had more living space, more bedrooms, a reduced number of housing deficiencies, and fewer families had to walk through bedrooms to get to bathrooms. In addition, subsidized relocated families moved to better neighborhoods. However, the results of the New Haven study do not offer any clear-cut findings of the impact upon relocated families, other than improved housing. As the authors pointed out, though, change was measured over a very short period of time, so that there may be lag effects. Also, it appears that relocated families were not given a choice of residence but were given one that they had to take; thus the element of a predetermined selection of a house and neighborhood may have been detrimental and attenuated any possible impacts. Further, given the economic situation of the family, it may be that other problems are so overwhelming that improved housing alone is not enough. It may have to be buttressed by a job or a better-paying job that will permit the family to live a life style similar to that of their new neighbors — if they so desire.

In a study of public housing needs in Des Moines, Shannon (1966: 26) noted that rather than the kinds of houses being built, the city needed low-rent duplex and quadruplex units or townhouses rather than high-rent large, multiple-unit structures. "The need is for appropriate units in appropriate locations for low income renters." He estimated that 4000 or 5000 would be needed to house adequately those in Des Moines who needed low-cost housing; however, he estimated, and even then only tentatively, that the city might construct between 500 and 1000 units, or about one-fourth the total need. These units could be built in one or two housing projects on a scattered-site basis. Maintenance costs go up with scattered units, but if integration of the poor and minorities is desirable, scattered rather than clustered sites are needed.

Wolf and Lebeaux (1967) noted that most studies of slum clearance by urban renewal have been of "old-style ethnic" areas, for example, not low-income black neighborhoods in which most contemporary urban renewal is taking place. Accordingly, they studied a predominately black area of Detroit in regard to potential effects if urban renewal were to take place there. They reported that only about one-fourth of the residents had "predominantly positive feelings" about the neighborhood. Almost two-thirds were "thinking about moving" or said that they would like to move away if they could. No strong emotional or symbolic attachment to the neighborhood was found; and, in fact, there was a great deal of fear and a large amount of "rowdy, violent, and delinquent behavior on streets and playgrounds." Thus the results of this study contrast markedly with some other studies of ethnic slum areas. Nevertheless, the authors pointed out that urban renewal even in these kinds of areas tends to have deleterious effects, primarily the destruction of strong and meaningful social and kinship ties.

Conclusions

While there can be no doubt that there are serious poverty, health, service, and housing problems in the slums, the assumption that rehousing the poor will automatically solve other problems is not supported by available evidence. If changes are to occur, they will occur not only because of rehousing but also because of a reorganization of the social life and perspectives of the slum dwellers and through altering societal conditions so that adequate job opportunities and incomes are available to them. There is a need to reconcile what is done to the physical shells of cities with what is done for the people who live in them (Wilson, 1965: 7), since one of the major problems associated with large-scale slum clearance is the destruction of established patterns of social interaction with relatives, neighbors, and friends as well as with churches, schools, shopping centers, and recreational facilities, and so on. It does appear that up until now "when all is said and done, political factors, rather than need, probably have the greatest weight in determining whether or not Public Housing is constructed" (Shannon, 1966: 22).

The Future

Downs (1970: 40) suggested that alternative ghetto futures can best be accomplished by focusing upon the major choices relating to the following three questions:

1. To what extent should future minority population growth be concentrated within central cities?
2. To what extent should minority and nonminority populations be residentially segregated from each other in the future?
3. To what extent should society redistribute income to relatively depressed urban areas or populations in society as a process of enrichment?

He summarized a number of different possibilities into five different strategies:

1. *Present Policies:* concentration, segregation, and nonenrichment.
2. *Enrichment Only:* concentration, segregation, enrichment.
3. *Integrated Core:* concentration, integration in the core only, enrichment.
4. *Segregated Dispersal:* dispersal throughout the metropolitan area but in segregated districts, enrichment.
5. *Integrated Dispersal:* dispersal and integration throughout the metropolitan complex, enrichment.

He opted for *integrated dispersal* with the added feature of enrichment. His reasoning included the belief that future jobs will be available primarily in suburban areas, and there will be a need to bring workers and jobs closer together. There is also a need to end the clustering in schools of lower-income children in order to improve their education; the development of an adequate housing supply and the provision of free choice for lower-income and black families require the construction of such housing in the suburbs. Continuing concentration of the poor—especially blacks—in the central cities leads to unacceptably high levels of crime and violence; and, finally, continuing concentration of the poor and blacks in central cities will result in a highly segregated society.

BIBLIOGRAPHY: Articles

Barresi, Charles M., and John H. Lindquist, "The Urban Community: Attitudes Toward Neighborhood and Urban Renewal," *Urban Affairs Quarterly,* 5 (March 1970): 278–290.

Barth, Ernest A. T., and Susan March, "A Research Note on the Subject of Minority Housing," *Journal of Intergroup Relations,* 3 (Autumn 1962): 314–319.

Bluestone, Barry, "The Poor Who Have Jobs," *Dissent,* 15 (September–October 1968): 410–419.

Chapin, F. Stuart, "An Experiment on the Social Effects of Good Housing," *American Sociological Review,* 5 (December 1940): 868–879.

Bureau of the Census, "Characteristics of Families Residing in 'Poverty Areas,' March, 1966," Series P-23, No. 19, August 24, 1966.

Harrison, Bennett, "Education and Underemployment in the Urban Ghetto," *American Economic Review,* 62 (December 1972): 796–812.

Herzog, Elizabeth, and Hylan Lewis, "Children in Poor Families: Myths and Realities," *American Journal of Orthopsychiatry,* 40 (April 1970): 375–387.

Himes, Joseph S., "Some Work-Related Cultural Deprivations of Lower-Class Negro Youths," *Marriage and the Family,* 26 (November 1964): 447–451.

Johnson, Lyndon B., "Message on Cities," The White House, March 2, 1965.

Orshansky, Mollie, "Counting the Poor: Another Look at the Poverty Profile," *Social Security Bulletin,* January 1965.

Rumney, Jay, "The Social Costs of Slums," *Journal of Social Issues,* 7 (1951): 77–83.

Sussman, Marvin B., "Postscript," *Journal of Marriage and the Family,* 26 (November 1964): 395–398.

Weller, Leonard, and Elmer Luchterhand, "Effects of Improved Housing on the Family Functioning of Large, Low-Income Black Families," *Social Problems,* 20 (Winter 1973): 382–389.

Wilson, James Q., "Urban Renewal Does Not Always Renew," *Harvard Today,* (January 1965): 2–8.

Wolf, E. P., and Charles N. Lebeaux, "On the Destruction of Poor Neighborhoods by Urban Renewal," *Social Problems,* 15 (Summer 1967): 3–8.

BIBLIOGRAPHY: Books

Beyer, Glenn H., *Housing and Society,* New York: MacMillan Co., 1965.

Caplovitz, David, *The Poor Pay More,* New York: The Free Press, 1967.

Chapin, F. Stuart, Jr., Edgar W. Butler, and Frederick C. Patten, *Blackways in the Inner City,* Urbana, Ill.: University of Illinois Press, forthcoming.

Council of Economic Advisers (1964), "The Problem of Poverty in America," in James G. Scoville (ed.), *Perspectives on Poverty and Income Distribution,* Lexington, Mass.: D. C. Heath and Co., 1971, pp. 66–73.

Downs, Anthony, *Urban Problems and Prospects,* Chicago: Markham Publishing Company, 1970.

Gans, Herbert J., *The Urban Villagers,* New York: The Free Press, 1962.

Haley, Bernard F., "Changes in the Distribution of Income in the United States," in James G. Scoville (ed.), *Perspectives on Poverty and Income Distribution,* Lexington, Mass.: D. C. Heath and Company, 1971, pp. 17–40.

Hannerz, Ulf, *Soulside,* New York: Columbia University Press, 1969.

Jackson, Carolyn, and Terri Velten, "Residence, Race, and Age of Poor Families in 1966," in James G. Scoville (ed.), *Perspectives on Poverty and Income Distribution,* Lexington, Mass.: D. C. Heath and Co., 1971, pp. 89–99.

McCord, William, John Howard, Bernard Friedberg, and Edwin Harwood, *Life Styles in the Black Ghetto,* New York: W. W. Norton & Company, 1969.

Michelson, William, "Social Insights to Guide the Design of Housing for Low Income Families," in Charles Tilly (ed.), *An Urban World,* Boston: Little, Brown and Co., 1974, pp. 421–429.

Shannon, Lyle W., *An Assessment of the Need for Public Housing in Des Moines,* University of Iowa, Iowa Urban Community Research Center, 1966.

Suttles, Gerald D., *The Social Order of the Slum,* Chicago: University of Chicago Press, 1968.

Wilner, Daniel M., et al., *The Housing Environment and Family Life,* Baltimore: Johns Hopkins Press, 1962.

CHAPTER 17
MORTALITY AND ILLNESSES IN URBAN AREAS

INTRODUCTION

In this chapter we are concerned with mortality and illnesses — physical and mental. Little historical data are available that indicate variations in mortality and illnesses in early cities and urban regions or areas within them in the United States. Nevertheless, it is quite clear that urbanization, urban conditions, and variation in spatial patterning of various populations in cities and urban areas have influenced illness and mortality.

Early cities no doubt were unhealthy places. Sanitation was primitive, and the incidence of disease and death probably were higher in the cities than in rural areas. At times epidemics would sweep the populations of some cities. More recently, the clear distinction between urban and rural areas in the incidence of disease and death rates has become less clear. Most contemporary metropolitan regions in the United States have adequate sanitary facilities, which include the disposal of solid wastes. Foodstuffs and dairy products are produced under much more sanitary conditions than previously. In addition, health care facilities tend to be much more extensive and accessible in urban areas than in rural areas.

A decline in infant mortality rates has been primarily a result of the rigid inspection of milk and the use of sterilized milk. Reducing the infant mortality rate in urban areas substantially reduced urban-rural differences in mortality, because it was primarily at the earlier ages when the difference in mortality was greatest. In other words, early high mortality rates in cities primarily reflected infant mortality rates. Currently, some of the highest incidences of illness and rates of mortality are in rural areas — among migrant laborers and Indians living on reservations.

Like so many other social phenomena, most of what is reported in this chapter depends upon social definitions. This is perhaps most clearly illustrated in the studies of mental disorders. If the definition and the delineation of mental disorder vary both over time and by political and geographic jurisdictions, the variations observed may be partially or entirely explained by how mental disorder is defined—rather than by any changes attributable to urbanization, industrialization, changing population distributions, or whatever. This is a major problem that should be kept in mind during the reading of this chapter.

In addition, case finding techniques need to be considered. There are three main methods in case finding, each of which may result in the discovery of varying levels of disorder (Mercer et al., 1964). First, some places have developed case registers that include all persons identified and labeled by official agencies. Second, some studies in the United States have surveyed both public and private agencies and hospitals to develop a register similar to that in the first method, but the reported rates are typically higher than those reported by the first method. Both of these techniques may result in systematic biases, since they only include those cases or persons who have some official contact with public and/or private agencies or have been hospitalized. The biases generally are such that the lower social classes and minority populations are over-represented. The field survey, a third method, may include all of the population in a given area, or it may involve a *sample* of some specified universe, such as a city, county, or some specified region within a metropolitan complex—for example, a health district. The main distinction between this approach and the first two is the entire universe or a representative sample come under scrutiny and typically result in higher rates than by register methods. This means either actually or potentially every person in the specified universe will have been investigated for possible indications of illness. The results of studies conducted by these methodological approaches may differ radically. In any event, it is absolutely necessary that it be specified which of these approaches is being used in any given study, since the procedures result in different conclusions about causation and the nature of society.

MORTALITY
Urbanization and Mortality

Throughout most of recorded history there have been high birth and death rates that offset each other and lead to small population increases and decreases (Antonovsky, 1967). From at least Greco-Roman times through the eighteenth and nineteenth centuries, life expectancy was between 20 and 30 years and now in the United States it is approaching 70.

A. F. Weber (1899: 343–367) showed that for New England in 1892 the death rate was lowest in rural parts and steadily increased with the size of city. Mortality was heavier in the city than in the country in every period of life (i.e., by every age category). Part of the "excessive urban mortality," according to Weber, was related to technology in that city occupations at that time were more dangerous than rural occupations. In addition, excessive urban mortality was supposedly due to a lack of pure air, water, and sunlight, "together with uncleanly habits of life induced thereby." "Part cause, part effect, poverty often accompanies uncleanliness: poverty, overcrowding, high rate of mortality, are

This crowded graveyard in Brooklyn, New York, is a quiet place in the metropolis. Adna Weber believed that urban mortality depends more on cultural background and sense of community than on population density alone.

usually found together in city tenements." However, Weber was careful to note that it may not necessarily be poverty and/or density in the city that creates higher mortality but that the reaction of different populations of varying cultural backgrounds to poverty and crowded conditions in the city may overcome or intensify this problem. He gave several specific examples of Russian and Polish Jews who were among the poorest people in New York City in the mid-1890s and who lived under extremely crowded conditions; yet their infant mortality rate was relatively low. He noted that there is but one answer: These particular people were extremely careful in observance of sanitary laws. They strictly observed the Mosaic laws regarding cleanliness, the cooking of food, habits of eating, drinking, and so on. He suggests, then, that there is no inherent reason that people should die faster in larger communities than in smaller places, "provided they are not too ignorant, too stupid, or too selfishly individualistic to cooperate in the securing of common benefits."

Type of Metropolitan Complex and Mortality

Altenderfer (1947) studied 92 cities in the United States having populations of 100,000 or more in 1940. He found that, by income categories, lowest-income cities had higher death rates than those in middle- and high-income cities. In a study comparing city size and rural-urban mortality for heart disease in the United States (1940), the rate for mortality declined as the size of city decreased. There were clear and substantial urban-rural differences, with the rural mortality rate being only about two-thirds of that of the urban figure. In addition, reportedly there was an association between rheumatic fever and rheumatic heart disease and urbanization, overcrowded housing, and nutritional deficiency, and, of course, poverty.

Variation Within Metropolitan Complexes and Mortality

Sheps and Watkins (1947) studied deaths in New Haven from 1930 to 1934 and reported that death rates vary inversely with social class of area. Similarly, a study of Buffalo using 1939–1941 death data shows an inverse gradient for both male and female death rates (Yeracaris, 1955). The largest differences occur among the lower-income categories; that is, the difference in death rates between the lowest social class and the next lowest social class is greater than the difference between the highest social class and the next lowest social class. The author of the Buffalo study noted that if the death rate of the highest-income area had prevailed throughout Buffalo, 19.1 percent of deaths would not have occurred. A study of death rates in Pittsburgh for both 1940 and 1950 showed similar death rate differentials by economic level of residential area (Patno, 1960). Similar findings were reported for Baltimore as of 1950 (Tayback, 1957).

Of particular interest is the study made by Ellis (1958) of death rates in Houston in 1949–1951. He used a modification of the Shevky and Williams' social rank index (see Chapter 7) to examine several different death rate measures. His findings were similar to the others cited previously with the exception that males in the lowest-class areas have a lower death rate than those in the next highest level. Ellis offered as a possible explanation the availability of free medical treatment for the residents of areas of lowest social rank. If this explanation if a plausible one, of course, it strongly suggests that if medical care is effectively utilized, death rates can still be lowered. Ellis further analyzed mortality data for the seven leading diseases in Houston (1949–1951), and these data revealed an inverse relationship between mortality and socioeconomic status for both infectious and chronic diseases, with that of infectious diseases most pronounced. He also found that socioeconomic differentials in mortality are *increasing* insofar as chronic diseases are concerned (Ellis, 1958). Stockwell's study (1963a and 1963b) of Providence and Hartford during the same time period as the Houston study, also based on a modified form of the Shevky-Williams' social rank index, showed similar results.

In summary, most of these studies suggest a proposition that *death rates vary by ecological area of residence and that this relationship is inversely related to social class.* In other words, as social class of the area declines, death rates increase. However, at least one study has suggested that even in the lowest-class areas death rates may be reduced by having adequate medical care readily available.

Social Factors and Mortality

Societies in which life expectancy is low and death rates are very high are characterized by a lack of social differentiation. The decline in death rates probably first occurred in the upper social classes because they were first able to improve their environment through sanitation. Similarly, they were the first people who were able to afford the most up-to-date medical care available in any particular historical epoch. Therefore, any society that has different levels of sanitation within it and various levels of medical care available to segments of the population leads one to suspect that in that society there will be life expectancy and death rate variation.

With the emergence of modern sanitation and medical practice in the United States, the life expectancy of the middle and upper strata increased at a rapid rate. On the other hand, there is some evidence to suggest that the lower-classes' life expectancy may have even declined somewhat with the beginning of industrialization. The beneficial changes wrought by industrialization appeared in the upper strata of society, then slowly percolated downward resulting in increasing social class differentials, in life expectancy and death rates. Quite consistently, occupational differences in death rates have also been reported. In general, socioeconomic differentials rather than specific occupational hazards are crucial in the relationship between social class and mortality. Further, this relationship appears to hold in a variety of places, despite the multiplicity of methods and the different kinds of indexes used to obtain the data. In other words, the evidence is quite conclusive that there are social class differences, and, given the structure of metropolitan areas in the United States, ecological differences in life expectancy and mortality.

Antonovsky (1967) hypothesized that in the future the lower classes may be in an even more disadvantageous position. He based this hypothesis on the argument that the gap between social classes has been closing as a result of the triumph over infectious diseases, especially through modern sanitation techniques and mass innoculations. Now, however, access to medical care, preventive medical care, health knowledge and practice, and the increasing relation of chronic disease to mortality will result in lower-class people becoming increasingly disadvantaged, hence once again increasing class differences. It should be noted that he did *not* argue that the life expectancy in the lower social classes is going to decrease or that the death rate of the lower class is going to increase. Rather, he proposed that the *relative difference* between social classes is going to become greater again in the future.

Several other factors may add to the death rates of certain areas within the metropolitan complex as well as explain variation in death rates among cities. The age structure of a city or some subdivision within a city has some bearing on the death rate. Obviously, retirement communities, even those that are relatively affluent, may have a higher death rate than a poorer city populated by younger persons by virtue of its age composition; that is, a larger

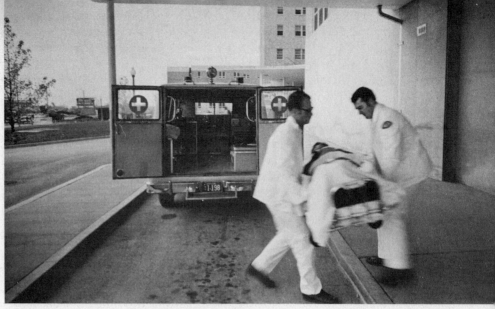

Since the range of city services and the speed at which they are available varies according to social class, class differences figure prominently in recovery and mortality statistics.

proportion of the population has a high risk of mortality. Similarly, metropolitan complexes as well as areas within them may have differing levels of environmental hazards, which means that population segments are differentially exposed to these hazards (see Chapter 19). The simple fact is that in contemporary United States knowledge about life expectancies and death rates by metropolitan complexes and by areas within them is almost nonexistent!

PHYSICAL ILLNESSES
Urbanization and Physical Illnesses

Earlier we noted that until the advent of modern sanitation practices, cities were unhealthy places in which to live. Yet little evidence exists that directly demonstrates that urban people are inherently (to use A. F. Weber's phrase) more likely to become physically ill than rural people.

Social Factors and Physical Illnesses

Bauer (1972: 1–2) reported that in the United States in 1968 it was increasingly certain that low-income persons had less access to medical care and that what access they had was to a lower quality and range of services. Fewer services existed in the immediate residential area of low-income persons, and the ratio of doctors (other than certain specialists) to the population was much lower in cities than in suburbs. She summarized the results of her analysis as follows:

> The data in this report show that low-income persons
> continue to be multiply disadvantaged in health. Persons with

incomes of less than $5,000 have more limitation of activity, more disability, and more hospital episodes than the total population. Unfortunately they have fewer resources for obtaining medical care: fewer have hospital insurance and of course they have less cash to pay expenses on their own. Within the low-income group, aid recipients have poorer health than nonrecipients. On all health measures, they have higher rates than nonrecipients—in many cases, twice as high.

In a review of 40 studies of the effects of housing on health, a majority (26) of them "showed a *positive* association between housing and health, or housing and social adjustment." Poor housing tended to go with poor health and adjustment, better housing with better health and adjustment (Wilner and Walkley, 1963: 215). The researchers noted that housing is related to a number of personal characteristics of the inhabitants—education, income, cultural background—and the utilization of medical facilities.

In an attempt to unravel the effects of housing and personal characteristics, Wilner and Walkley conducted a study in Baltimore of (1) a *test* sample of 300 families (1341 persons) who had originally lived in a slum area but had subsequently moved to a new public housing project and (2) a *control* sample of 300 families (1349 persons) who remained in the slum. In virtually every comparison made, the families who moved into the new public housing project were better off than those who remained behind.

When they compared morbidity rates for the test and control samples, "test rates were regularly lower than control rates in three categories: infective and parasitic conditions, mainly the communicable diseases of childhood; digestive conditions; and accidents." The occurrence of accidents was one-third lower in the housing project as contrasted with the slum. In general, test rates also were lower than control rates in respiratory conditions and for allergic and metabolic episodes. It should be noted, however, that during the resettlement period—the first five months in the housing project—test rates of illness and disability for almost everyone under age 20, regardless of sex, were *higher* than control rates. This suggests that a *change of residence* for children may at first lead to a higher incidence of the more common communicable diseases.

In this Baltimore study test families were more satisfied with their housing and available space, had more personal relations with neighbors, more common family activities, showed more pride in their neighborhood and community, and gave far more favorable views regarding the neighborhood as a place to live and to raise children. Test respondents were more likely than controls to "indicate felt improvement in position in life, and to report themselves as rising in the world." The psychological state of the test sample was better than the controls insofar as general morale was concerned. For children test performance scores remained similar for both tests and controls, but test children "were considerably more likely to be *promoted* at a normal pace, control children being held back more often for one or more semesters." One explanation for this difference is that test sample children were more likely than the controls to attend school daily. That is, having fewer illnesses provides the opportunity for regular attendance, another indirect benefit of improved housing quality.

In a study (Gordon, et al., 1960) of coronary artery disease in the rapidly growing suburb of Bergen County, New Jersey, patients who survived an acute cardiovascular accident for six months were significantly different in social backgrounds than those who did not survive. Major features of their differences are as follows:

(1) Among those who survived at least six months, the self-employed, professional and managerial class patients tended to have significantly more coronary attacks and at younger ages. Skilled laborers who had attacks tended to be older. The intervening social and economic group was intermediate in age.

(2) Socially and economically higher and geographically more mobile ethnic groups (particularly younger patients of the Jewish faith, who are significantly more upwardly mobile newcomers to Bergen County) had an earlier and higher morbidity.

(3) Economic, social and ethnic features were significantly correlated with each other.

(4) Higher social and economic position was associated with survival, particularly among the younger cardiac patients. Newcomers tended to survive. Longer-residents did not tend to get early attacks but were significantly less likely to survive.

Among 129 expectant mothers seeking antenatal class guidance and 516 psychiatric outpatients requiring psychotherapy, social psychological features were again significantly correlated:

(1) Higher economic groups sought help more readily.

(2) The main upwardly mobile newcomer group to the Bergen County area, those of Jewish religious background, predominated.

(3) Ethnic features, suburban migration, education and intelligence were significantly intercorrelated with each other.

(4) These correlated features were related to therapeutic response.

Certain types of occupations were much more frequently associated with morbidity and mortality, both among the younger as well as the entire groups of patients. From these findings it might be concluded that the following circumstances were associated with mortality:

(1) Greater supervisory stress. Supervisors and managers were worse off than workers, operators, and salesmen.

(2) Size of the business. Executives in large firms (which are generally competing more successfully than smaller business) did better than managers and owners of small business. Large firms often can provide better economic and social arrangements for ill executives.

(3) Financial insecurity. Managers of the small businesses were worse off than owners. Workers, protected by their union plus unemployment and sickness benefits, were better off than supervisors, who often received neither management nor union protection.

(4) Necessity for continued direct personal involvement in the business. Men in construction work, or running establishments in which they personally provided a service (cleaners, tailors, and so on) did not do as well as merchants. The latter presumably could employ a manager to run the store if they became ill or wanted a vacation.

Quite clearly, then, living in a changing, rapidly growing suburban area is associated with extensive social mobility, loosening of family and community ties, and this in turn tends to decrease the psychological and economic security of some individuals. Some of these persons then are highly susceptible to depression, emotional, and physical illnesses. Many times their emotional and psychosomatic disorders are not treatable, and some commit suicide and others develop fatal coronary artery disease (Gordon et al., 1960).

Finally, Gordon and colleagues summarized the results of their study as follows:

> The evidence gathered thus far would indicate that the rapidly advancing socially mobile younger newcomer groups tended to develop coronary artery disease, emotional and psychosomatic disorders earlier. They sought help quickly, and tended to respond satisfactorily. Many less successful individuals were of local birth. Their life situations were more likely associated with chronic frustration and possibly with economic decline. They tended to develop disorders later. But they frequently had more severe emotional and physical problems. They were more likely to succumb from coronary artery disease. Middle-aged men and women in particular were victims of this disease. They also tended to suicide.

Unfortunately, no comparisons with stable suburbs or other types of areas within the metropolitan complex were carried out.

Kadushin (1964) accepted the position that in earlier times the lower social classes had high rates of physical illness due to the character of their everyday lives. But he argued that this previous relationship between class and illnesses has largely been eliminated by modern medical research and practice and that whatever difference that does currently exist is a result of people in the lower classes being more likely than others to be concerned about and report symptoms of physical illness. Mechanic (1968: 259–266) disputed this point of view and claimed that there remain definite social class differences in physical illness, especially chronic ones.

Recently, Conover (1971) examined both of these positions by using data gathered by the National Health Survey (84,000 families representing 268,000 individuals from a national sample interviewed between July 1965 and June 1967). He reported that "for whites and non-whites, with age adjusted or not, there is a strong relationship between income and measures of chronic disease." Further, the impact of income on chronic disease is more dramatic at the lower ranges of the social class scale. In addition, he found that families of lower income have 50 percent or more problems than do families of higher income, whether white or nonwhite. He concluded that chronic illness is so widespread that about one-half of all people in the United States have some chronic illness (85 percent for those over age 65). He further noted, however, that only 11 percent claim any limitation of activity as a result of these illnesses. Some illnesses are age related, and some are cumulative with age. Conover felt that race differences are rather minor and that when the relationship between social class and specific diseases are analyzed, it appears to hold for all the illnesses included except for diseases of the thyroid gland. The evidence, then, contradicts the hypothesis that there are no social class differences in chronic diseases. In fact, it suggests that the relationship between social class and the more severe measures of chronic disease are clear and of great magnitude.

Given the importance of age and social class in chronic disease, it should come as no surprise that there are substantial differences in rates of illnesses within metropolitan areas. Little evidence suggests that similar differences will be found by comparing metropolitan complexes. If there is substantial variation in social class and age structure of two separate cities, however, perhaps it is reasonable to expect these individual characteristics to carry over into rates between them.

MENTAL ILLNESS
Urbanization and Mental Illness

Urban life has often been assumed to lead to higher rates of mental disorder than rural life, and, in fact, admission rates to mental hospitals in urban places have been higher than in rural areas (Rose and Stub, 1955). In general, however, studies comparing urban and rural areas on this aspect remain inconclusive because of the varying definitions of mental disorders, the degrees of accessibility to hospital facilities, and the differing abilities of urban and rural families to care for their own mentally ill. The one study ac-

While most mental hospitals are no longer the grotesque prisons they once were, it is still not clear if they are anything more than custodial institutions.

complished over time, using similar definitions of mental disorders (though the terminology may have differed somewhat), reported a relative consistency in accessibility to a mental hospital (Goldhamer and Marshall, 1953). The authors found that as urbanization took place in the state of Massachusetts between 1840 and 1940, rates of admission for psychoses rose from 41 per 100,000 in 1840–1845 to 85 per 100,000 in 1941. As urbanization occurred, then, so did increases in mental disorders; however, when they controlled for age, admissions for those between 20 and 50 were the same later as earlier. Older people accounted for the increase in hospitalization rates, probably as a result of two factors: (1) more people live to an older age; and (2) formerly probably more of the older mentally ill were cared for at home in rural areas than in urban areas. Therefore, as urbanization of the population occurred, there were more older people who were more likely than previously to be hospitalized when they had a mental illness.

Lin (1959) asked the questions "does urbanization constitute a threat to mental health" and "is modern civilization responsible for the alleged increase of mental ill-health in the present world?" The answer he gave is that the data are inconclusive because of the difficulty involved in measuring and analyzing "the intricate relationship of the human psyche to the environment." Many early studies revealed that primitive or underdeveloped societies had virtually no mental illness. Subsequently, however, other observers claimed that mental disorder does not vary greatly by time culture and society. This point of view is expressed primarily by those who believe in the role of physiology; those stressing cultural variation tend to emphasize sociocultural influences. "There is good evidence that certain types of mental disorder are related to certain environmental (sociocultural) factors, and this deserves careful attention in order to understand the effect of urbanization on mental health . . . ." (Lin, 1959: 25). Further, Lin stated that there is evidence that the rate of neuroses increases with urbanization and industrialization. In addition, the rates of psychosomatic diseases—such as hypertension, nonarthritic rheumatism, gastritis, peptic ulcers, exophthalmic goiter, diabetes, and so on—are believed to increase with urbanization.

Nevertheless, the data are conflicting, and no definitive answer can be given at this time as to whether or not the urbanization of society influences the rates of serious mental disorders. The question is still an open one.

Type of Place and Mental Illness

Schroeder (1942) reported variance in rates of mental disorders in St. Louis, Milwaukee, Omaha, Kansas City, and Peoria and that such variation "could be expected in communities of varying size and situation." Unfortunately, he did not give specific rates for each of these cities, so that no specific comparisons can be made.

According to Jaco (1959: 396–397), most ecological studies of mental disorders have been confined to commercial-industrial types of urban places. He reported that a replication of these studies in a "political-type" place, and the pattern of highest rates being in the CBD and decreasing toward the periphery was not found. He hypothesized that as the type of urban place varies, so does the distribution of mental disorders.

Variation Within
Metropolitan Areas and Mental Illness

Virtually every study of mental disorders has shown that they are not found evenly distributed throughout the metropolitan complex, but rather that they are concentrated or clustered in certain areas. Also, there appears to be systematic variation in the areal distribution of different types of mental disorders. For example, manic depressives are distributed rather evenly throughout the metropolitan complex, while schizophrenics follow the clustering pattern shown by all types of people with mental disorders as a whole. The highest rates cluster around the center of the city, and rates progressively decline at greater distances from the center. Early studies of mental disorders in Chicago, Providence, St. Louis, Milwaukee, Omaha, Kansas City, and Peoria all reported this pattern (Faris and Dunham, 1939; Schroeder, 1942). The only exception to the general pattern in these early studies was that in older, outlying deteriorated areas of the metropolis, rates were high, much like those in the city center.

TABLE 17-1
Percentages of Mental Disorders of Austin, Texas, Compared with the United States and Chicago

MENTAL DISORDERS	(1) AUSTIN (1946–1952)	(2) U.S.A. (1949)	(3) CHICAGO (1922–1934)
Schizophrenia *(Dementia Praecox)*	16.1	22.7[a]	36.8[a]
Manic Depressive	11.4	5.8[a]	8.0[b]
Senile	19.7	11.5[a]	3.9[a]
Cerebral Arteriosclerosis	6.6	15.5[a]	11.9[a]
Involutional Psychosis	1.4	4.6[a]	—
General Paresis	6.4	3.7[a]	0.1[b]
Psychoneuroses with Organic Changes of the Nervous System	5.9 4.3	4.2 1.1[a]	— —
With Mental Deficiency	2.8	2.4	—
Without Psychosis	18.0	14.2[b]	0.04[a]

[a] $P < 0.01$.

[b] $P < 0.05$.

Source: Used by permission from: Belknap and Jaco, 1953: 237.

Each major subclassification of mental disorder appears to have its highest incidence in areas with specified characteristics. The concentration of paranoid schizophrenics that Faris and Dunham found in Chicago rooming-house areas led them to suggest that communication with others is necessary for normal mental stability and that social isolation leads to mental breakdown. They noted that mental disorders appear to be more prevalent in areas of high residential mobility and with a heterogeneous population than in areas where residential stability and homogeneity are standard. On the other hand, they reported higher rates of manic-depressive psychoses in areas with higher-valued rentals. They also showed rates of psychoses varied by race, nationality, socioeconomic status, and occupation.

Belknap and Jaco (1953) studied mental illness in Austin, Texas, during the period from January 1946 to June 1952. They chose this particular city partly to determine whether the ecological approach to the study of mental disorders resulted in different distributions of the mentally disordered in a political-type city as opposed to the typical industrial-commercial type cities that had been studied by others. They argued that "if the ecological approach to the study of mental disorders is valid, then it follows that cities with different ecological bases should have different mental disorder rates and distributions." Also, they note that other sociological characteristics may vary either independently or dependently with ecological variations.

Their findings indicated that Austin's first admission rates were substantially different from those reported by Faris and Dunham for Chicago. These data are shown in Table 17-1. Also reported in the table are the results of a 1951 national study. The overall incidence rate was less than that of the United States for 1949. Nevertheless, significantly higher rates of manic-depressive psychoses, senile psychosis, general paresis, psychoses with organic change of the nervous system, and cases without psychosis were found in Austin when compared with the rest of the United States. Rates for schizophrenia, psychosis with cerebral arteriosclerosis, and involutional psychosis were significantly lower in Austin. No differences were found for psychoneurosis and mental deficiency (Belknap and Jaco, 1953: 241).

The ecological distribution of rates differed from those reported for commercial-industrial type cities in that no pattern of decreasing rates from the center to the periphery was found. However, the authors did find higher rates in the CBD, but they also found high rates near the edge of the city that did not appear to be randomly distributed. Somewhat similar departures were reported by Schroeder (1942) for the six cities he studied. These variations may be reconciled by further knowledge of the individual cities; that is, probably these atypical peripheral sections within the urban complex were older areas, even though they are located on the periphery. Their sociological character, then, is hypothesized as being similar to central city areas where high rates have been systematically found. This particular study also reinforced earlier reported studies in that systematic ecological relationships were found between high rates of mental disorder and age, sex, color, social class (as measured by average rental value), patient's and father's occupational situs.

An unusual feature of this particular study was that actual church membership figures were obtained from a local agency and related to the ecological distribution of mental disorders. Baptist, Methodist, Lutheran, Christian, and Church of Christ church affiliates had higher incidence rates; Catholic and Episcopalian affiliates had lower rates; and Presbyterian and Assembly of God church affiliates had rates neither higher nor lower than their proportions in the sample (Belknap and Jaco, 1953: 239–240).

Since they found varying ecological distributions and rates of several major mental disorders, and these results were somewhat different than those typically reported for commercial-industrial type cities, Belknap and Jaco concluded that the ecological approach is "probably valid" and that cities with different ecological bases will have a different spatial distribution of mental disorders. If this is true, they further urged that research in the distribution of mental disorders should always take into consideration the ecological base; care should also be exercised in extending findings based upon one type of city to other types. Care should also be taken to consider other factors: Austin, for example, is a much smaller city than Chicago, and hence city size as well as age and other factors may lead to differential ecological patterns. Despite some dissent, it does appear that the ecological variation in the distribution of mental disorders in American metropolitan centers is fairly uniform.

Building upon the earlier study of Austin, Jaco (1959) classified areas by all first admissions of diagnosed functional psychoses to the local state hospital for a period of 12 years to determine high- and low-rate areas. In the high- and low-rate areas he selected a representative sample of *all residents* to determine whether characteristics of areas are associated with the onset as well as the incidence of mental disorders. Except for church membership, residents of high-rate areas had less knowledge of neighbors' names, fewer personal friends and acquaintances, visited friends less often, visited outside of the neighborhood and town less often, and were less likely to hold a membership in voluntary organizations such as lodges, fraternal organizations, and occupational groups and to vote than were residents of low-rate areas. In addition, economic instability and downward social mobility were very important factors, with residents of high-rate areas exhibiting more economic instability and downward mobility than those of low-rate areas. Further, he noted that high-rate areas had *less* spatial mobility, which may throw some doubt on the "drift hypothesis."

Finally, Jaco reported that disruption of the family, that is, divorce and female employment, also was more prevalent in high- than in low-rate areas. He concluded that persons who live in areas with high rates of mental disorders encounter more stressful life conditions than those who reside in areas with low rates. If *individual* factors are considered as relatively constant in these areas, "then those communities whose inhabitants possess a high degree of social isolation, downward social mobility, economic instability, and family dislocation should exhibit higher incidence rates of the functional psychoses than those communities where these conditions exist to a significantly lesser extent" (Jaco, 1959: 409).

In a survey of community agencies that dealt with "various types of mental-hygiene" problems in Baltimore's Eastern Health District, Lemkau and others (1941, 1942a, 1942b) found that both the incidence and the prevalence of hospitalized psychosis in 1936 were about 25 percent above national averages, and they added that this is "not surprising considering the urban character of the district." In comparing the nonhospitalized with the hospitalized, they noted that the race distribution was similar but that older-aged and female psychotics were more likely to be kept at home than younger-aged and male psychotics. The number of psychotics in the community was estimated to be one-third of the number in the hospital, and child neurotics showed a different demographic pattern than adult neurotics. Finally, supporting other studies, they reported that both psychoses and neuroses appear to be most prevalent among the lowest socioeconomic classes of the white population. Most of these cited studies of mental disorders in urban environments utilized hospitalized cases in calculating rates. However, a number of general household surveys conducted subsequently indicated that a substantial number of those who are psychotic never enter a mental hospital. Potentially, nonhospitalized psychotics may be distributed differently in the metropolitan complex than those who are hospitalized.

As a result of their study (1956) of the incidence of hospitalized and nonhospitalized psychotics in an above-average-level socioeconomic suburban area of Boston (Wellesley) and the Whittier Street area of the city of Boston, which was below average in socioeconomic status, Kaplan and others noted that the rate of hospitalized psychotics was higher in the Whittier Street area than in suburban Wellesley. They regarded these findings as a confirmation of other studies that suggested an inverse relation among socioeconomic level, social environment, and mental disorders. Further comparisons of totals of hospitalized and nonhospitalized psychotics in each area reduce the relationship between socioeconomic status and mental disorders somewhat but do not change the overall conclusion that mental-disorder rates vary by socioeconomic level and area of residence. More nonhospitalized cases were discovered in Wellesley than in the Whittier Street area. As a result, the authors claimed that there are more nonhospitalized cases in Wellesley because a greater proportion of people there than in Whittier Street hold a negative attitude toward state hospitals. It should be noted that the findings from this study using both hospitalized and nonhospitalized cases continue to support the notion that areas within metropolitan complexes have substantially different rates of mental disorders (also see Srole et al., 1962).

Social Factors and Mental Illness

Faris and Dunham (1939) hypothesized that social isolation may be a determining factor in some types of mental disorders. In particular, they suggested a relationship between mental disorders and living in areas of high residential turnover. They gave several possible explanations for the concentration of the mentally ill in certain parts of the metropolitan complex but emphasized stress factors associated with living under dense, crowded conditions in housing and neighborhoods that are deteriorated and dilapidated and in areas characterized by anonymity and social isolation.

A second approach is based upon the speculation that individuals with specific types of mental illness "drift" into certain parts of the urban complex and thereby contribute to high rates of mental disorders in them. That is, the character of the area of residence is not viewed as a causal factor as in the first case but is only associated with mental disorders as a result of many individuals drifting or moving into the area. In addition, the mentally disordered are assumed to have moved to these deteriorated neighborhoods because they are downwardly mobile. Finally, proponents of this approach argue that a precipitating factor in a mental disorder may be in the difficulties a residentially mobile person has in adjusting to new situations.

Clausen and Kohn (1954: 141), in their critique of the ecological approach to the study of mental disorders, stated that "without question" the high concentration of alcoholics in cheaper rooming-house areas represents a downward sifting of individuals whose life patterns and personalities were formed years earlier in other residential settings. Clausen and Kohn felt that this was significant, since they were concerned with the "causes" of mental disorders and tended to question the importance of ecological factors as deter-

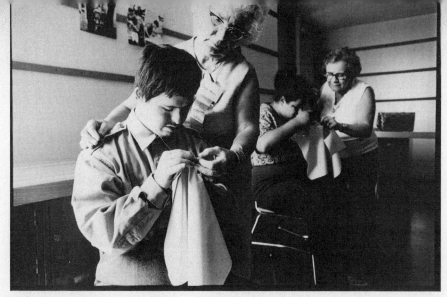

These impaired children are typical of many individuals in our society who have been labeled "retarded." There is no conclusive evidence that urban living is any more conducive to impairment than is rural living.

minants of these causes. They suggested that if the drift hypothesis is accepted, it is more appropriate to obtain "data on area of residence in early childhood or at the time of the first clear sign of overt disorder" rather than on current place of residence. Despite the criticism by Clausen and Kohn, it should be noted that the clustering of the mentally disordered apparently exists in most cities. Any explanation of the causes and consequences of mental disorders should consider this fact or be rejected.

Besides the notion that environmental conditions may lead to distinctive subcultures that are related to the incidence of mental disorder, Clausen and Kohn (1954: 142–143) pointed out that area of residence might also affect the probability of whether or not a person with similar characteristics will be "labeled" as having a mental disorder. They also proposed that there may be social class differences in the degree to which children are vulnerable to potential stress and mental disorder and in the degree to which adults are exposed to actual stress that may lead to mental disorder. Anyone who has visited or lived in certain areas of the city is aware that some areas are more "stressful" than others; again, then, it is no surprise that rates of mental disorder vary by areas within the metropolitan complex. Finally, people who do not "fit" in an area may be more prone to mental illness than those who do (Wechsler and Pugh, 1967).

IMPAIRED COMPETENCE
"Mental deficiency," "mental retardation," and "impaired social competence" are terms that have been used at different times in the United States to categorize individuals who do not function adequately under some definition or measure of social adequacy. Each of these terms has an emphasis on social competence attached to it. Lemkau and others (1942b: 278)

suggested that definitions of mental deficiency were originally based upon social competency, but diagnosis has become dependent upon results of tests designed to evaluate the intellectual dimensions of the personality. The use of intelligence tests has led to view mental deficiency as an inability to perform certain set tasks, rather than an inability to discharge the responsibilities of living in society.

The use of intelligence tests, or its equivalent, is associated historically with the term "mental retardation." More recently, a return to the notion of "social competency" has resulted in the use of the terms "impaired competence" or "maladaptive behavior," which once again emphasizes the ability of an individual to get along satisfactorily in the community rather than performance on IQ tests. In the sections that follow, these terms will be used, and it behooves the reader to note which emphasis is stressed at any particular time or for any particular study, since these varying points of view and definitions have very real ramifications for those who are and are not labeled.

Urbanization and Impaired Competence

Little evidence is available that indicates one way or another that urbanization has affected the rate of mental retardation or impaired competence. Urban-rural differences in impaired competence are confounded by varying definitions, services, and resources utilized in case findings (Farber, 1968: 74). In Maine (as reported by Farber) the rate was higher in urban than rural school systems. The latter reported more "doubtful" cases and a higher excess of males than did the urban school systems. On the other hand, Farber reported an opposite finding in Illinois with higher rates of trainable severely retarded, and slow learners in rural areas. In smaller school systems, the impaired are more visible and there is less reliance on "formal case-finding procedures"; both of these factors lead to more doubtfuls, who are treated as impaired.

Others have suggested that those persons who migrate out of rural areas are more intelligent than the population left behind. Farber (1968: 77–79) partially tested this selective migration hypothesis and concluded that "intellectually retarded people tend to remain as residual population." Similarly, Klineberg (1935) showed that the longer southern-born black children lived in New York City, the higher their IQ test scores were. Subsequently, in Philadelphia Lee (1951) replicated Klineberg's study and reported similar results: The younger southern migrant black children were when they entered the Philadelphia schools, the greater was their increase in IQ.

Most of these studies then point toward the proposition that currently there are rural-urban differences in rates of mental retardation. The implication of these studies is that higher rates should be found in rural areas as a result of selective migration to urban areas by the more intelligent population. None of these studies sheds any light upon whether or not rates of impaired competence have increased as a result of the urbanization of society.

Type of Place and Impaired Competence

The first important investigation of mental retardation in the United States was accomplished in the 1930s in Baltimore (Lemkau et al., 1942b). This study primarily relied upon agency files and records and IQ scores to classify a person as mentally retarded, although some untested persons with an official history of mental retardation also were included. A prevalence rate of 12.2 per 1000 population was reported. A curvilinear relationship with age was shown, with an increasing prevalence through adolescence and a steady decline thereafter. Unfortunately, data were not given for subdivisions within the larger area of Baltimore that served as the context for this particular research.

Farber (1968: 55–56) reviewed a number of other prevalence studies that "took place in large cities, others in rural dominated countries and sparsely settled areas, still others in states with much industry and widely differentiated economic areas." He found a "marked similarity in the prevalence rates produced by these investigations" and noted that this is remarkable because of both the widely varying environmental conditions and the wide variety of case-finding procedures and measurement techniques used.

Variation Within Metropolitan
Areas and Impaired Competence

In another study Lei and others (1974) reported different utilization rates of mental-retardation services by type of agency in Riverside, California. They reported a similar distribution and concentration of labeled mental retardates between public school nominees and those named by other public agencies. Quite a different picture emerged from the geographic distribution of the users of private agencies. These different distributions illustrate quite clearly the variation in utilization of agencies by the mental retardates in this city. Areas with the highest rates of retardates labeled by public schools and other public agencies were characterized by concentrations of minority families (chicano and black) and by families of lower socioeconomic status, by poorly educated households, poor housing quality, old and deteriorated housing, and *greater* duration of residence in the community. Users of private agencies tended to cluster in areas of predominantly anglo (white, nonminority) middle-class families, better housing quality, and newly developed residential neighborhoods.

In another study related to the one reported previously, and in the same city, Riverside, California, Butler and others (forthcoming) reported on a household field survey of intellectual and behavioral impairments. It supported the notion that there are differential concentrations of the intellectually and behaviorally impaired in metropolitan areas. These areas are characterized by ethnic minority populations, poor housing, overcrowded conditions, and inadequate neighborhood services. Interestingly, although the methods and data bases used in this household survey study differed from those used in the previous agency study of mental retardation, the clustering of retardates identified by public agencies parallels almost exactly the ecological patterns reported in this study of intellectual and behavioral impairments.

Even though the ecological approach has been used extensively in the study of mental illness, its bearing on the use of facilities for the mentally retarded is not too well known. Jenkins and Brown (1935), using data gathered between 1925 and 1934, studied the incidence of mental deficiency in various areas of Chicago. They found that the incidence of mental deficiency among children corresponded negatively with a gradient of socioeconomic status (as measured by rents) and positively with measures of community disorganization such as juvenile delinquency. They also reported that mental deficiency rates were highest in deteriorated areas of the city where poverty and dependency were common. Thus it should be noted that Jenkins and Brown reported findings similar to those of Faris and Dunham for the same city. Likewise, the Castle and Gittus (1957) study of Liverpool, England, revealed the existence of residential clusters in which feeble-mindedness was apparent to a decidedly greater extent than elsewhere in the city. Again, these areas were concentrated in the inner-city residential areas that bordered on the industrial and commercial core. In reviewing rates at *two different times,* they reported that the same parts of the city carried the highest incidence of social problems as those that, at an earlier time, had the highest rates (also see Jackson, 1974).

In another study conducted in Chicago, concentrations of candidates (e.g., the mentally retarded) for "ungraded classrooms" were found in the underpriveleged sections of the city (Mullen and Nie, 1952). In this same study, for the students "excused from school" they obtained quite a different picture. The results showed that the excused persons as a whole represented a more serious degree of mental retardation than the ungraded candidates, with excused persons scattered throughout the city without showing any obvious ecological concentration.

In view of the foregoing studies, there seems to be a general concensus that users of specialized services for mental retardation are disproportionately distributed among various sections of the metropolitan complex and that high-rate areas are characterized by lower-socioeconomic status, poverty, and deteriorated and dilapidated housing and neighborhoods.

Social Factors and Impaired Competence

From the very earliest studies more males than females have been reported as being mentally deficient, and the rate of blacks is typically nearly four times that reported for whites; however, this difference appears primarily at the younger ages. Similarly, more chicanos than anglos are reported as being impaired. Rates also are higher in the lower-socioeconomic class. All of the studies cited in this chapter also have reported that mental deficiency is greater among children than among adults. Most of the adult rates probably are composed of the most severely retarded or incompetent, while for younger people the rates are usually composed primarily of those who have been labeled by a local school system. Evidently, these incompetents "disappear" into the "normal" population when they become adults!

A follow-up study comparing persons of "normal and subnormal intelligence" in Baltimore reported that normal persons move to other parts of the same metropolitan complex more often than subnormals; however, another follow-up study of normals and retardates showed that the latter moved more within the metropolitan area but within rather restricted areas of the city (Baller, 1936). Selective movement within a metropolitan complex, of course, could influence the rates of mental retardation, especially when it is within narrowly restricted neighborhoods as suggested by Baller. In all of the other studies, however, there does not seem to be a great deal of support for an explanation that relies on the drift of impaired persons toward the clustering areas. On the contrary, Mullen and Nie (1935: 777) suggested that the debilitating nature of "pauperism, slumism, and their concomitants" appear to be the main causal factors.

INTERRELATIONSHIP OF
MORTALITY, ILLNESSES, AND IMPAIRMENTS

Faris and Dunham (1939) showed that urban areas characterized by high rates of social pathology were also characterized by high rates of mental disorders. Schroeder (1942–1943) too reported that the areas of concentration of pathologies in the six cities he studied were similar to those of mental disorders. As an example, he found that the correlations between mental disorders and other measures of social pathology in Peoria were: 0.81 — adult crime, 0.74 — juvenile delinquency, and 0.65 — suicide. In addition, correlations are rather substantial for social pathologies and indicators of lower social status and deteriorating neighborhoods. He claimed that there are "insanity" areas in cities comparable to the delinquency areas of Chicago that Shaw (1929) reported.

A mental illness is more likely to be discovered in a mentally deficient person than in one of normal intelligence because the mentally deficient person is likely to be seen by those who are capable of recognizing the presence of the illness (Lemkau et al., 1942b: 279). Probably, then, a higher rate of mental illness is reported for the mentally deficient than for the general population, although real levels for both may be similar.

SUMMARY

Differences in mortality and illnesses appear to be systematically related to variation in types of metropolitan complexes; moreover, there are substantial variations in mortality and illnesses in various areas within the metropolitan complex, which in turn suggests the importance of ecological factors. Higher rates of mortality and illnesses appear to be systematically related to certain features of urban areas and their neighborhoods: social class, ethnicity, poverty,deteriorated housing, and so on.

BIBLIOGRAPHY: Articles

Altenderfer, Marion E., "Relationship Between Per Capita Income and Mortality, in the Cities of 100,000 or More Population," *Public Health Reports*, 62 (November, 1947): 1681–1691.

Antonovsky, Aaron, "Social Class, Life Expectancy and Overall Mortality," *Milbank Memorial Fund Quarterly*, 45 (April 1967): 31–73; also in E. Gartley Jaco (ed.), *Patients, Physicians and Illness*, 2nd ed., New York: The Free Press, 1972, pp. 5–30.

Baller, Warren R., "A Study of the Present Social Status of a Group of Adults, Who, When They Were in Elementary Schools, Were Classified as Mentally Deficient," *Genetic Psychology Monographs*, 18 (June 1936): 165–244.

Butler, Edgar W., Tzuen-jen Lei, and Ronald J. McAllister, "Impaired Competence in an Urban Community: An Ecological Analysis," *Urban Affairs Quarterly*, forthcoming.

Castle, I. M., and E. Gittus, "The Distribution of Social Defects in Liverpool," *Sociological Review*, 5 (1957): 43–64. Also reprinted in George A. Theodorson (ed.), *Studies in Human Ecology*, New York: Harper & Row, Publishers, 1961, pp. 415–429.

Clausen, John A., and Melvin L. Kohn, "The Ecological Approach in Social Psychiatry," *American Journal of Sociology*, 60 (September 1954): 140–151.

Conover, Patrick W., "Social Class and Chronic Illness," paper presented to the Southern Sociological Society, 1971.

Gordon, Richard E., J. E. McWhorter, and Katherine K. Gordon, "Coronary Artery Disease in a Rapidly Growing Suburb," *Journal of the Medical Society of New Jersey*, 57 (December 1960): 677–683.

Jackson, Robin, "The Ecology of Educable Mental Handicap," *British Journal of Mental Subnormality*, 20 (No. 1, 1974): 18–22.

Jaco, E. Gartley, "The Social Isolation Hypothesis and Schizophrenia," *American Sociological Review*, 19 (October 1954): 567–577.

Jenkins, R. L., and Andrew W. Brown, "The Geographical Distribution of Mental Deficiency in the Chicago Area," *Proceedings of the American Association on Mental Deficiency*, Chicago, 1935, pp. 291–307.

Kadushin, C., "Social Class and the Experience of Ill Health," *Sociological Inquiry*, 34 (Winter 1964): 67–80.

Kaplan, Bert, Robert B. Reed, and Wyman Richardson, "A Comparison of the Incidence of Hospitalized and Non-Hospitalized Cases of Psychosis in Two Communities," *American Sociological Review*, 21 (August 1956): 472–479.

Lee, Everett S., "Negro Intelligence and Selective Migration: A Philadelphia Test of the Klineberg Hypothesis," *American Sociological Review*, 16 (April 1951): 227–233.

Lei, Tzuen-jen, Louis Rowitz, Ronald J. McAllister, and Edgar W. Butler, "An Ecological Study of Agency Labelled Retardates," *American Journal of Mental Deficiency*, 79 (July 1974): 22–31.

Lemkau, Paul, Christopher Tietze, and Marcia Cooper, "Mental-Hygiene Problems in an Urban District," *Mental Hygiene*, 25 (October 1941): 624–646.

Lemkau, Paul, Christopher Tietze, and Marcia Cooper, "Mental-Hygiene Problems in an Urban District—Second Paper," *Mental Hygiene*, 26 (January 1942a): 100–119.

Lemkau, Paul, Christopher Tietze, and Marcia Cooper, "Mental-Hygiene Problems in an Urban District—Third Paper," *Mental Hygiene*, 26 (April 1942b): 275–288.

Lin, Tsung-Yi, "Effects of Urbanization on Mental Health," *International Social Science Journal,* 11 (1959): 24–33.

Mercer, Jane R., Edgar W. Butler, and Harvey F. Dingman, "The Relationship Between Social Developmental Performance and Mental Ability," *American Journal of Mental Deficiency,* 69 (September 1964): 195–205.

Mullen, Frances A., and Mary M. Nie, "Distribution of Mental Retardation in an Urban School Population," *American Journal of Mental Deficiency,* 56 (April 1952): 777–790.

Patno, Mary E., "Mortality and Economic Level in an Urban Area," *Public Health Reports,* 75 (September 1960): 841–851.

Schroeder, Clarence W., "Mental Disorders in Cities," *American Journal of Sociology,* 48 (July 1942): 40–47.

Sheps, Cecil, and J. H. Watkins, "Mortality in the Socio-Economic Districts of New Haven," *Yale Journal of Biology and Medicine,* 20 (October 1947): 51–80.

Stockwell, Edward G., "A Critical Examination of the Relationship Between Socio-Economic Status and Mortality," *American Journal of Public Health,* 53 (June 1963a): 956–964.

Stockwell, Edward G., "Socio-Economic Status and Mortality," *Connecticut Health Bulletin,* 77 (December 1963b): 10–13.

Tayback, Matthew, "The Relationship of Socio-Economic Status and Expectation of Life," *Baltimore Health News,* 34 (April 1957): 139–144.

Wechsler, Henry, and Thomas F. Pugh, "Fit of Individual and Community Characteristics and Rates of Psychiatric Hospitalization," *American Journal of Sociology,* 73 (November 1967): 331–338.

Yeracaris, Constantine A., "Differential Mortality, General and Cause-Specific, in Buffalo, 1939–1941," *Journal of the American Statistical Association,* 50 (December 1955): 1235–1247.

BIBLIOGRAPHY: Books

Bauer, Mary Lou, *Health Characteristics of Low-Income Persons,* Rockville, Md.: U.S. Department of Health, Education, and Welfare, Vital and Health Statistics, Series 10, No. 74, July 1972.

Belknap, Ivan, and E. Gartley Jaco, "The Epidemiology of Mental Disorders in a Political-Type City, 1946–1952," in *Interrelations Between the Social Environment and Psychiatric Disorders,* New York: Milbank Memorial Fund, 1953, pp. 235–243.

Ellis, John M., "Socio-Economic Differentials in Mortality from Chronic Diseases," in E. Gartley Jaco (ed.), *Patients, Physicians and Illness,* New York: The Free Press, 1958, pp. 30–37.

Farber, Bernard, *Mental Retardation: Its Social Context and Social Consequences,* Boston: Houghton Mifflin Company, 1968.

Faris, Robert E. L., and H. Warren Dunham, *Mental Disorders in Urban Areas,* Chicago: University of Chicago Press, 1939.

Goldhamer, Herbert, and Andrew W. Marshall, *Psychosis and Civilization,* Glencoe, Ill.: The Free Press, 1949, 1953.

Jaco, E. Gartley, "Social Stress and Mental Illness in the Community," in Marvin B. Sussman (ed.), *Community Structure and Analysis,* New York: Thomas Y. Crowell Company, 1959, pp. 388–409.

Klineberg, Otto, *Negro Intelligence and Selective Migration,* New York: Columbia University Press, 1935.

Mechanic, David, *Medical Sociology,* New York: The Free Press, 1968.

Rose, Arnold M., and H. R. Stub, "Summary of Studies on the Incidence of Mental Disorders," in Arnold M. Rose (ed.), *Mental Health and Mental Disorder,* New York: Norton 1955, pp. 87–116.

Shaw, Clifford R., *Delinquency Areas,* Chicago: University of Chicago Press, 1919.

Srole, Leo, Thomas S. Langner, Stanley T. Michael, Marvin K. Opler, and Thomas A. C. Rennie, *Mental Health in the Metropolis: The Midtown Manhattan Study,* New York: McGraw-Hill, 1962.

Stern, Bernhard J., "Socio-Economic Aspects of Heart Disease," in E. Gartley Jaco (ed.), *Patients, Physicians and Illness,* 1st ed., New York: The Free Press, 1958, pp. 24–30.

Weber, Adna Ferrin, *The Growth of Cities in Nineteenth Century,* New York: The Macmillan Company, 1899.

Wilner, Daniel M., and Rosabelle Price Walkley, "Effects of Housing on Health and Performance," in Leonard J. Duhl (ed.), *The Urban Condition,* New York: Simon and Schuster, 1963, pp. 215–228.

CHAPTER 18

CRIME, RIOTS, AND RACIAL VIOLENCE

INTRODUCTION

The material presented in this chapter assumes that the distribution of crime and delinquency, riots, and racial violence in time and space are associated with and vary according to the physical structure and social organization of different metropolitan complexes, as well as by areas within them. These areas coincide for some offenses but not for others. The importance of the relationship of social class to crime is stressed in substantial literature cited in this chapter; however, strong evidence indicates that the degree of stability in an area may be equally as important as social class in influencing the crime rate. It should be noted that few longitudinal studies of crime rates for cities exist, so most of the material in this chapter relies upon cross-sectional research.

Fortunately, more longitudinal data exist on riots and racial violence in U.S. cities. The evidence shows quite clearly that riots in earlier times were not racially motivated. Instead, they concerned conflicts between workers and management and between more recent immigrants (e.g., the Irish) and resident anglo groups. Only since World War II have riots had truly racial connotations. There is some dispute over the influence of city characteristics upon contemporary riots, racial violence, and riot severity. The research surveyed in this chapter is admittedly inconclusive; much more research is needed before racial violence in U.S. cities will be adequately understood.

CRIME AND DELINQUENCY

Most ecological studies of crime rely upon official crime statistics. But peculiarities in each locale may result in differential reporting that affects the comparability of data.

(1) for one reason or another, crimes frequently are not reported at all; (2) there may be differential reporting of crime from one area to

another, which may distort in varying degree and direction the derived crime rates for different parts of the city; (3) there may be differential reporting of crime according to the type or nature of the crime; (4) sometimes the police, in order to make a good showing or to protect the name of a community, may suppress or alter official crime records; (5) the policy of the police in making arrests, as well as the assignment of greater proportions of officers to certain areas, may bias recorded statistics [Schmid, 1960b: 675].

Early studies tended to focus on where violations *occurred* and to neglect where violaters *lived*. As it turns out, for some crimes these areas are the same, while for others they are distinctly different. High crime rates in some instances may only represent greater opportunities and conditions favorable for committing certain kinds of crimes. An example that Schmid presents (1960b: 676) is shoplifting, which occurs primarily in CBDs. In Seattle during 1949–1951, 22 persons were arrested for "carnal knowledge," and 18 of these arrests took place in the CBD; yet only one of the persons arrested for this crime actually lived in the CBD. Similarly, many people "drift" to skid row, and most of those who are arrested there—for vagrancy, lewdness, drunkenness, and so forth—are people who live in the area.

Two contrasting positions have been hypothesized as explaining some kinds of criminal and delinquent behavior. The "differential association" notion suggests that if a criminal or delinquent subculture dominates in a particular area or areas within the metropolitan complex, then there should be a large number of crimes committed in the area or elsewhere by the residents who adhere to that delinquent subculture. On the other hand, others have argued that crime rates are high in areas characterized by isolation, anonymity, personalization, and anomie (Schmid, 1960b: 677). Both of these hypotheses may help explain high crime rates, but each is obviously different in its orientation and may help explain high crime rates in different kinds of areas.

Urbanization and Crime

Historically, rates for crimes known to the police (except for crimes of violence) are higher in urban areas than in rural areas and higher in metropolitan areas than in smaller urban areas. Murder rates are higher in rural areas than in metropolitan areas as is forcible rape (Uniform Crime Reports, 1973).

Ogburn (1935: 31) noted that new and rapidly growing towns are *supposed* to attract the adventurous and the lawless. In his study of 62 cities, however, he found that cities with slowing rates of growth have higher crime rates than cities with increasing rates of growth. He suggested that this difference is primarily a result of economic factors associated with declining economic opportunity in slower-growing cities, whereas faster-growing cities have more opportunities and less unemployment. Clinard (1942; 1960), who carried out studies in Iowa and in Sweden concerned with the relation of urbanism to criminal behavior, found that urban offenders were more likely than rural offenders to perceive themselves as criminal and to belong to and/or accept a "criminal culture." Offenders who lived in smaller places had some features of the criminal culture, but rural offenders had few of its traits—such as differential association with criminal norms and delinquent gangs. In summarizing his earlier study and a doctoral dissertation based upon his subsequent work in Iowa, Clinard (1960: 253–254) made the following observations:

1. There is a progressive rate of increase in property crimes when measured by residence types indicative of urbanism, with the rates varying directly with the degree of urbanism.
2. Rural offenders are more residentially mobile, not as well integrated in their home communities, and more impersonal in their attitudes toward others than nonoffenders.
3. Earlier, but not currently, rural offenders more often committed their offenses where they were anonymous, that is, outside of the home community.
4. Differential association with criminal norms, particularly those of delinquent gangs, is not as important in the development of rural and small-town offenders as among more urban offenders; however, delinquent gangs are playing a more significant role among rural offenders than previously as society becomes increasingly urbanized.
5. There is a marked difference between offenders from areas of varying degrees of urbanism in the age at which they began criminal activities and in progression in seriousness of crimes committed, with urban offenders beginning at younger ages.

In replicating his Iowa studies in Sweden, Clinard concluded that there are few differences and general agreement on all the preceding points.[1]

Rural-suburban-urban differences in crimes were illustrated by a *Los Angeles Times* article dated January 14 1973, which reported a national study conducted by the Gallup poll in December 1972. According to the article, one of three persons in center cities reported that they had been victims of one or more crimes during the previous year, while one in five in the suburbs and only about one in eight in rural areas reported being victims.

Type of Metropolitan Complex and Crime

Ogburn, in the study (1935) referred to earlier, eliminated southern cities from his research because of the high percent of black population. Of the remaining regions he reported that cities west of the Mississippi River have higher crime rates than cities east of it. In addition to finding regional dif-

---

[1] Clinard actually makes it quite clear in his 1960 article that he is focusing on the relation of crime to the degree of urbanism—impersonality, extensive mobility, and differential association. He was comparing offenders in three types of residential areas that were then related to increasing amount of urbanism: slight (farm), moderate (village), and extensive (city). Thus his study was *not* concerned directly with the process of urbanization as necessarily implied by the heading to this section.

ferences in crime rates, he analyzed a whole array of other dimensions and hypothesized that there are several clusters of factors that help explain crime rate variation.

One cluster includes primarily the foreign born and their descendants. Cities with factors centering around immigrants have lower crime rates as a result. A second cluster is a set of factors indicating economic conditions in the city. This cluster includes changes in rates of city growth and in wages, and monthly rentals. Higher economic status—for instance, faster-growing cities, wages and rentals increasing—is associated with lower crime rates. The third factor is the sex ratio: The greater the proportion of males in a city, the higher the crime rate. Statistically, using multiple correlational techniques, Ogburn found that the seven dimensions included in the three clusters just mentioned account for about one-half of the variation in crime rates among cities. Some of the dimensions not important in explaining variation in crime rates are population size of the city, the percent of blacks (excluding southern cities, however), police–general-population ratio, homeownership, percent of apartment dwellers, age, and so on.

In a later study (1950) conducted of all U.S. cities of 100,000 population or more, many of the same variables were used as in the earlier Ogburn study. Again, factor analysis was used as the statistical tool to determine whether there were underlying dimensions that would help account for variation in city crime rates (Schuessler, 1962). This study described five different factors. One was tentatively identified as "degree of social frustration" and includes positive associations with percent nonwhite, overcrowding, and murder and assault (crimes against the person) and negative relations with percent of native white and those with higher incomes. This study leads to the hypothesis that because of racial segregation and living in dense, overcrowded conditions, aspirations will be more frequently thwarted in cities with high proportions of nonwhites and there will be more violence in those types of cities.

Another factor was described as "degree of institutional control" and was characterized by the police-population ratio, percent of married males, percent of foreign-born males, percent of owner-occupied dwelling units, and average value of dwelling units. A third factor he labeled "degree of industrialization." It included median school years completed, percent of families of two or three persons, percent in manufacturing occupations, and the average dwelling-unit rental costs. This factor is *negatively* related to each of the specific offense rates. "It would thus appear that massive industrial employment tends to create and reinforce a community environment which mitigates against those offenses which become part of the official police record."

The author discounted two other factors as not being important, one on statistical grounds and another on the basis of its composition. One included property crimes—robbery, burglary, grand larceny, petty larceny, and auto theft. Two interpretations are suggested for this factor: (1) Theft is independent of all other social circumstances; or (2) it is tied to variables outside of the ones included in the study. The author chose the latter explanation and labeled it the X factor—that is, it is an unknown.

Both the Ogburn and Schuessler studies reported that cities in which there are ample economic opportunities have lower crime rates, thus reminding us that crime may not be solved on an individual basis alone but that the solution may require a larger social structure or ecological perspective.

These studies also demonstrate that variation in city crime rates may be "resolved into general statistical factors which possibly correspond to basic social dimensions that are integral to crime causation" (Schuessler, 1962: 323). Finally, it should be explicitly noted that none of these studies related crime rates to the *typologies* of cities described earlier, and this may be where the next advance in the study of variation in city crime rates will be made.

Variations in Crime Rates
Within Cities and Metropolitan Complexes

Studies of within-urban and metropolitan variation in crime rates have consistently shown striking differences from one part of the city to another. Generally, central areas show the highest concentration of crime rates with contrasting low areas in peripheral and suburban residential areas.

Shaw (1929) was one of the first to report that delinquency rates decline from the CBD to peripheral areas of the city. In this earlier study rate declines were apparent whether residences of offenders, mile-square sections of the city, or radials outward from the CBD, or zones were used. Thus, as for truants, the rate of delinquency varies inversely with the distance from the CBD. These rate differences reflect significant variation in the types of communities through which the radial lines pass (Shaw, 1929: 62). Similarly, he reported a strong relationship between juvenile delinquency and male adult measures of crime, as well as for female offenders. It also was quite clear that recidivism rates are highest in central areas of the city and decline toward peripheral areas of the city.

Shaw reported, as have all those who have subsequently accomplished this type of research, that high crime rates occur in areas characterized by physical deterioration and declining populations. In addition, he stressed the importance of immigrant populations. However, this was during large-scale immigration to the United States, and most of the immigrants lived in areas of the city that subsequently were taken over by other disadvantaged persons. This dimension has not been found to be as important in subsequent studies. In a continuation of the 1929 study Shaw and McKay (1942) found that in the 21 Canadian and American cities they studied, crime and delinquency rates were highest in inner zones and slums. Similarly, they reported a general belief that prostitution is more extensive in the city core and slums than elsewhere.

In a study of Baltimore (1939–1942) replicating a great deal of the earlier Shaw and McKay work, Lander (1954) reported that almost three-fourths of recorded delinquency took place within a two-mile radius of the city center. Viewing juvenile delinquency in Baltimore by zones did not result in a gradual decline but a precipitous drop after the first two zones. However, several areas beyond these first two zones with high rates had a high percent of blacks. Lander had high correlations between the same variables that Shaw and McKay found in their studies but felt that if more sophisticated statistical techniques are used, many of the highly correlated variables with delinquency become unimportant, indicating no substantive relationship between them and delinquency — that is, they are spuriously related. He used the example of substandard housing and overcrowding as illustrations of two variables that have been systematically related to juvenile delinquency. However, with more sophisticated statistical techniques of analysis, such as partial-correlation analysis, he argued that they are spuriously related to delinquency or are not important in explaining high rates.

Lander also carried out a factor analysis and reported two factors important in explaining high crime rates: The first is anomie, or normlessness — the breakdown and weakening of the fabric of society. Variables indicative of anomie, according to him, are high delinquency rates, the percent of nonwhites (i.e., blacks), and the percent of nonhomeowners or renters. The second factor is economic and includes the median years of education completed, median rentals, the percent of overcrowding, and the percent of substandard housing. Lander concluded therefore, that his factor analysis clearly demonstrates that delinquency in Baltimore is fundamentally related to the *stability* or *anomie* of areas and is not a function of, nor is it basically associated with, the economic characteristics of areas (p. 59). Thus one would predict a low delinquency rate for a *stable* community even though it was characterized by poverty, bad housing, and overcrowding.

As a result of his analyses, Lander rejected the notion that distance from city center is significant in the prediction and understanding of delinquency rates (p. 74). He did note wide variations but that some areas near the core have low delinquency rates, while others on the periphery have high rates. Again, he uses the notion of anomie, or a lack of social cohesion or stability, in an area as the key factor in high and low delinquency rates. In addition, he rejected the notion that a high percentage of blacks in an area necessarily means that there will be a high delinquency rate in the area. He claimed that in areas with extremely high proportions of blacks who have resided there for a long period of time — namely, stable areas — and in spite of a lower socioeconomic level, the delinquency rate will be low.

Somewhat later in time, Schmid utilized several different methodological approaches to describe the basic dimensions of crime areas, all of which showed a rather close relationship to each other and a variety of individual kinds of criminal behavior. One approach he used to elicit the "underlying social and demographic dimensions in the distribution of crime as well as in identifying and describing crime areas" was to utilize the statistical technique of factor analysis. According to Schmid's (1960a) factor analysis of 1950 U.S. census data and crime reports for the years 1949–1951 in Seattle, the 38 individual variables he used represented 8 major factors:

Factor I: Low Social Cohesion—Low Family Status
This factor represents low social cohesion, with weak family life and older, declining, lower-status neighborhoods. Associated with it are high rates of automobile theft, theft from automobiles, indecent exposure, shoplifting, nonresidential robbery, and check fraud.

Factor II: Low Social Cohesion—Low Occupational Status
Low occupational and educational measures, obviously, are suggested as well as related measures of income; in addition, this dimension contains large percentages of laborers, blacks, unemployed, foreign-born whites, older housing (constructed prior to 1920), and a high percentage of males. Fighting, robbery (highway and car), nonresidential burglary, and disorderly conduct-miscellaneous characterize the high crime rates.

Factor III: Low Family and Economic Status
This factor reflects a large proportion of males, the unemployed, and a low proportion of the married population. High crime rates are common drunkenness, vagrancy, drunkenness, lewdness, petty larceny, fighting, and robbery (highway and car). "In the light of the present data, this constellation represents the urban crime dimension *par excellence.*"

Factor IV: Popular Mobility
Factor IV is described primarily by high residential mobility with no other dimension added; associated crimes are shoplifting, check fraud, burglary of residence by night, attempted suicide, burglary of residence by day, automobile theft, and theft from automobile.

Factor V: Atypical Crime Pattern
This factor consists primarily of bicycle theft, indecent exposure, and nonresidential burglary.

Factor VI: Low Mobility Groups
No crime variables are represented in this factor. This factor has population stability, but also a high rate of population growth, foreign-born white population, owner-occupied dwelling units, older population, and proprietors, managers, and officials.

Factor VII: Ambiguous
A factor difficult to interpret—thus it has been discarded.

Factor VIII: Race

This factor is characterized by blacks, nonresidential robbery, and nonresidential burglary.

Schmid noted that it is important to know how these factors are related to specific areas within the larger urban complex; therefore, he determined which census tracts in the city were unusually related to these factors. Upon examining the CBD, skid row, and contiguous areas, he found that these sections of the city had the highest crime rates, although each area was characterized by different crimes. The CBD was highest on Factors III and IV; therefore, crime in the CBD is primarily characterized by high rates of check fraud, shoplifting, residential burglary, automobile theft, theft from automobiles, and attempted suicide. Demographic characteristics associated with Factors III and IV are high population mobility and a high proportion of unmarried and unemployed males. In contrast, areas *contiguous* to the CBD are more related to Factors I and VII. Thus this area, which contains rooming and apartment houses, with some single-family dwellings and business establishments, is characterized by higher rates of automobile theft, theft from automobiles, indecent exposure, shoplifting, nonresidential robbery, and check fraud. Separate from these Schmid reported that skid-row areas include a large number of cheap rooming houses and hotels and are characterized by high rates of fighting, robbery (highway and car), nonresidential burglary, and disorderly conduct-miscellaneous crime rates.

Another interesting cluster of areas are representative of Factor V, the atypical crime pattern. These areas all are located contiguous to Woodland Park and Green Lake, and there is a large bicycle rental agency, extensive use of bicycles, especially on the bicycle path around Green Lake and at several parks and bathing beaches; this may help account for the high rate of bicycle theft and perhaps for the high rates of indecent exposure and nonresidential burglary.

In another approach in determining "concise, generalized spatial configurations of various types of crimes" Schmid (1960b: 666–670) computed rates on the basis of the total population in each of six one-mile zones radiating outward from the point of highest land value (located in the CBD) to portray differences in crime by areas within Seattle. As indicated previously, this technique also shows that most crimes decrease, more or less, in direct proportion to distance from the city center. Embezzlement is the most pronounced in this tendency, with shoplifting, theft from a person, rape, sodomy, and burglary also showing a marked change in the rate of occurrence from inner to outer zones of the city. As before, bicycle theft is the only crime that has a higher rate in the outermost zone than in the city center. "The differentials between inner and outer zones, however, for peeping tom, obscene telephone calls, indecent liberties, and carnal knowledge are relatively small." Since most crimes conform to the gradient pattern, the generalized "total index crimes" for Seattle during 1960–1970 shown in Figure 18-1 represents the spatial distribution of

These bicycles offer a great opportunity to bicycle thieves. Schmid's factor analysis ties the local rate of bicycle theft to the rates of indecent exposure and nonresidential burglary.

most crimes in that city (Schmid and Schmid, 1972) during this time period, as well as earlier.

Fortunately, Schmid (1960*b*) also related crime rates to some variables used to delineate several of the urban typologies described in Chapter 7. In that chapter we noted that typologies delineate various areas within metropolitan complexes on the basis of information available in published reports of the U.S. census conducted every 10 years. The techniques used to derive their typologies are somewhat different. For example, the Tryon typology derives three dimensions, labeled *family life, assimilation,* and *socioeconomic independence.* Shevky uses the terms "urbanization" (although some adherents use the term "family status"), "segregation," and "social rank." As we reported in Chapter 7, Schmid interrelated the results of each of these typologies using his Seattle information and concluded that they are statistically similar in their results. Further, Schmid (1960*b*: 672) reported that the two typologies are alike in their relationship to the 20 crimes he examined in Seattle. These results are shown in Table 18-1 which is taken from the Schmid study. These data, again, suggest a systematic relationship between types of areas and crime rates, and, as before, the only major departure is that of bicycle theft, which takes place in outlying residential areas of the city. Finally, Schmid noted that the results using Tryon and Shevky typologies "show a marked coincidence with the findings based on factor analysis in the first part of this study."

Polk (1957–1958) studied juvenile delinquency in San Diego in 1952 within the framework of social area analysis; he discovered that the relationships are such that no support could be given to the popular notions that one social class is more delinquent than another or that juvenile delinquency is an indication of a breakdown in family life. The main social area factor related to juvenile delinquency in San Diego is ethnicity. This may be explained by "social conditions under which the Negro is forced to live" that are conducive to criminality and other types of pathology, or "the observed relationship between ethnic status and delinquency in our study may be due to differential treatment by law enforcement officers." That is, there may be a tendency for the police to arrest more black and chicano young people than youth of anglo ancestry regardless of their behavior (Polk, 1957–1958: 215–216).

Noting some of the discrepancies in the literature about the influence of social class, Clark and Wenninger (1962) hypothesized that "rates of illegal conduct among the social classes vary with the type of community in which they are found." They expected differences in illegal behavior among differing communities within a metropolitan complex. Within a given community, however, they expected crime rates to be similar for all social classes within that area. They studied four populations in the "northern half of Illinois" (p. 827): (1) a *rural farm* population, (2) a *lower urban* sample drawn from a crowded, largely black area of Chicago, (3) an *industrial city* of about 35,000 people and a relatively autonomous c ty outside of the Chicago metropolitan complex, and (4) an *upper urban* sample of a very wealthy suburb of Chicago. To measure illegal behavior they used an inventory of offenses, that was administered to all of the members of the sample. Thus their measure of offenses is *reported behavior*. Clark and Wenninger failed to detect significant differences in illegal behavior rates among social classes of rural and urban areas. However, lower-class areas had higher serious-crime offense rates. Differences within a larger area by social class were generally insignificant. The authors suggested that the pattern of illegal behavior within small communities or within "status areas" of a large metropolitan center is determined by the predominant class of that area. Finally, they hypothesized that there are area-wide norms to which juveniles adhere regardless of their social class. But they did not deal with *how large* an area of this kind is, though they did indicate that size as well as other dimensions should be examined in future studies.

According to this study, then, a "delinquent subculture" emerges only in large metropolitan places, where social classes are found in large, relatively homogeneous areas. Similarly, in areas of social class heterogeneity, those who

Figure 18-1. Total Index of Crimes and Offenses Reported, Seattle (1960–1970). The data on this map represent cases reported to the police during the eleven-year period 1960 to 1970. Cases have been allocated according to census tracts. There are certain areas in the city, such as Fort Lawton, Sand Point Naval Air Station, and the University of Washington where normally the Seattle police do not have jurisdiction. Accordingly there are no cases recorded for such areas. The total number of cases represented on this map is 311,143. *From Schmid and Schmid (1972: 150).*

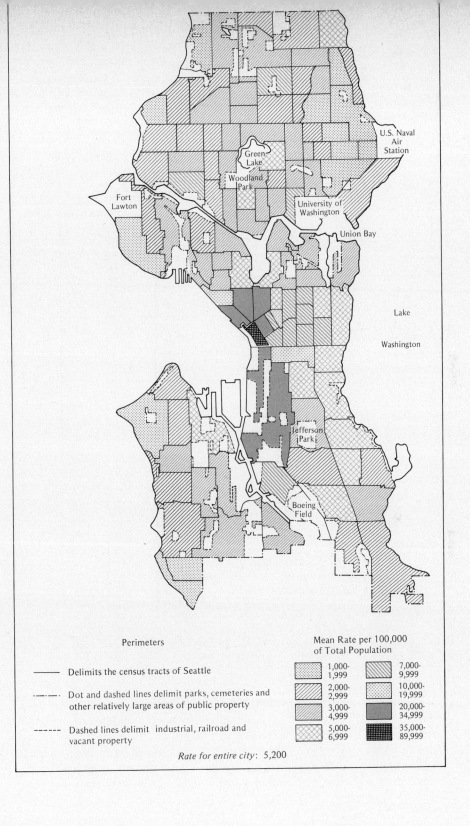

U.S. Naval
Air
Station

Green
Lake

Woodland
Park

Fort
Lawton

University of
Washington

Union Bay

Lake

Washington

Jefferson
Park

Boeing
Field

Perimeters

———— Delimits the census tracts of Seattle

—·—·— Dot and dashed lines delimit parks, cemeteries and
other relatively large areas of public property

— — — — Dashed lines delimit industrial, railroad and
vacant property

Rate for entire city: 5,200

Mean Rate per 100,000
of Total Population

	1,000-1,999		7,000-9,999
	2,000-2,999		10,000-19,999
	3,000-4,999		20,000-34,999
	5,000-6,999		35,000-89,999

TABLE 18-1
Correlation of Crime Variables with Dimensions of Shevky and Tryon Typologies and with Selected Census Variables, Seattle

CRIME VARIABLES		Variable Number	SHEVKY TYPOLOGY[a]		
			URBAN-IZATION	SEGRE-GATION	SOCIAL RANK
Suicide	Attempted	1	−.460	−.304	−.295
	Completed	2	−.463	−.339	−.242
Drunkenness	Drunk	3	−.262	−.349	−.324
	Common Drunk	4	−.182	−.312	−.287
Disorderly Conduct	Fighting	5	−.256	−.499	−.342
	Other	6	−.299	−.462	−.363
Vagrancy	Vagrancy	7	−.225	−.395	−.319
Sex Offenses	Lewdness	8	−.275	−.444	−.302
	Indecent Exposure	9	−.405	.065	−.035
Larceny	Petty Larceny	10	−.257	−.421	−.331
	Shop Lifting	11	−.373	−.330	−.189
	Bicycle Theft	12	.193	.076	−.092
	Auto Theft	13	−.535	−.136	−.219
	Theft from Auto	14	−.492	−.306	−.313
Fraud	Check Fraud	15	−.366	−.087	−.153
Burglary	Residence, Day	16	−.286	−.258	−.232
	Residence, Night	17	−.279	−.232	−.157
	Non-Res. Day & Night	18	.011	−.182	−.249
Robbery	Highway & Car	19	−.277	−.447	−.371
	Non-Residential	20	−.256	−.489	−.168

Source: Schmid (1960b: 673).

[a] It has been necessary to reverse the signs of the Shevky indexes of "urbanization" and "segregation" to make them comparable with the Tryon indexes of "family life" and "assimilation."

are in the social class minority will take on the prevailing norms of the area, whether they reflect a delinquent subculture or have a middle-class orientation. That is, "those who are taught to occupy middle class positions apparently take on lower class illegal behavior patterns when residing in areas that are predominantly lower class." Further, "area patterns of behaviors obviously exist and must be handled in some manner." Within the inner core,

TRYON TYPOLOGY			SINGLE CENSUS VARIABLES					
FAMILY LIFE	ASSIMI-LATION	SOCIO-ECON. IND.	P.C. MALE	P.C. 14 YRS. AND OVER	P.C. MAR-RIED	MEDIAN INCOME	P.C. UN-EMP.	P.C. NEGRO
−.582	−.524	−.396	.709	.480	−.618	−.561	.750	.167
−.591	−.471	−.250	.561	.587	−.673	−.595	.713	.132
−.421	−.469	−.321	.814	.467	−.529	−.472	.820	.216
−.327	−.388	−.257	.740	.398	−.437	−.393	.734	.196
−.425	−.597	−.315	.812	.418	−.519	−.511	.833	.376
−.464	−.562	−.331	.808	.462	−.547	−.530	.846	.325
−.376	−.477	−.296	.773	.423	−.484	−.455	.782	.280
−.433	−.546	−.276	.831	.439	−.530	−.478	.820	.300
−.367	.006	−.157	−.114	.254	−.292	−.241	.079	−.086
−.430	−.508	−.299	.831	.500	−.547	−.489	.851	.278
−.413	−.530	−.248	.478	.339	−.507	−.420	.525	.262
.252	.131	−.009	−.195	−.015	.178	.135	−.210	−.008
−.632	−.333	−.343	.477	.505	−.548	−.464	.579	.011
−.625	−.546	−.400	.769	.576	−.682	−.577	.800	.160
−.429	−.360	−.282	.556	.352	−.480	−.348	.501	.009
−.394	−.483	−.296	.724	.350	−.488	−.398	.671	.168
−.362	−.465	−.199	.668	.328	−.490	−.365	.599	.147
.042	−.208	−.113	−.080	.003	.027	−.079	−.033	.219
−.444	−.592	−.345	.843	.459	−.554	−.531	.852	.316
−.273	−.374	−.098	.082	.245	−.288	−.320	.300	.474

crime rates may vary; Rumney (1951) found that the juvenile delinquency rate in a public housing project (383/10,000) was less than in nonpublic housing areas in the slums (570/10,000).

Kobrin (1951: 653) noted that less than one quarter of the boys in the urban areas having high numbers of delinquents are actually court charged as delinquents. From some points of view this could invalidate the notion that delinquency is primarily a cultural phenomenon rather than a result of personality or psychological processes. Kobrin showed, however that the official crime rate is only the minimum appropriate measure of the actual crime rate in an area. He demonstrated with more inclusive records available in Chicago that "not one-fifth but almost two-thirds of the boys in delinquency areas may be regarded as official delinquents" (p. 655). Thus most of the studies we have reported so far use relatively unrefined statistics and only show the minimum crime that takes place. More efficient recordkeeping *and* reporting by victims would result in much higher crime rates than those now available. This also has been demonstrated by the Clark and Wenninger study and a number of others that have used questionnaires to measure reported "hidden" criminal or delinquent behavior.

Schmid (1960*b*: 678) has said that

> urban crime areas, including areas where criminals reside *and* areas where crimes are committed, are generally characterized by all or most of the following factors: low social cohesion, weak family life, low socioeconomic status, physical deterioration, high rate of population mobility, and personal demoralization as reflected by attempted and completed suicide, drunkenness, and narcotic violations.

To develop an adequate integrative theory of crime it will be necessary to relate to role of individual behavior to specific areas of the large city. In his statement, Schmid differentiated between areas where criminals reside *and* those where crimes are committed. This separation leads to another approach for examining crime patterns that has been explored by Boggs (1965) in her study of St. Louis in 1960. Research previous to hers led to the conclusion that areas where offenders reside are not necessarily the same areas where most crime occurs, since, typically, CBDs have the highest crime rates while the typical offender lives in lower-class, nonwhite, anomic neighborhoods. Thus there is a discrepancy between *crime offender* and *crime occurrence* rates. The *standard crime rate* is computed as the number of crimes relative to the number of persons living in the area of occurrence. According to Boggs, a *valid* rate would be based on risks appropriate for each crime category. This notion leads to the necessity of considering, for example, the number of untended parked cars in auto theft rates, the number of occupied housing units in residential burglary rates, and so on, rather than only the population of the area (p. 900). From this approach, then, environmental opportunities for different kinds of crime vary from neighborhood to neighborhood. These varying opportunities are expected to be reflected in different occurrence rates, and it can be determined which areas are exploited at higher rates for certain crimes.

To determine whether a few general factors explain the relationships among the crime variables, Boggs carried out a factor analysis with 12 occurrence and 6 offender variables. Four factors appear to describe these crimes: (1) residential day and night burglary occurrence, homicide-aggravated assault oc-

A substantial amount of shoplifting takes place in most stores in the United States. Here a woman has an opportunity to steal a necklace. Schmid notes that shoplifting is particularly characteristic of the CBD. Boggs would argue that this woman probably doesn't live in the CBD and that crime offender rates should be differentiated from crime occurence rates at any specific location.

currence, burglary offenders, and homicide-aggravated assault offenders; (2) business crime occurrence characterized by business robbery, nonresidential day and night burglary, auto theft, and grand larceny with no offender variables; (3) forcible-rape occurrence, larceny offenders, and miscellaneous robbery occurrence; (4) besides being part of the third factor, larceny offenders and miscellaneous robbery also are part of the fourth factor, along with offender variables of forcible rape, larceny and auto theft, and highway robbery occurrence.

Boggs related her factor analysis of crimes to the social areas of St. Louis, since she was concerned with the question, "do high rates of crime occur among residential populations characterized as lower-class, non-white and anomic?" This is not the same as asking whether high rates of crime are committed by persons with these same characteristics. In using the social area analysis framework, she used the urbanization (familization) component as an indirect measure of anomie. Her results indicate that the first factor is directly associated with the segregation component (the percent of black) regardless of its social rank or the extent of urbanization. In addition, high occurrence rates in high offender neighborhoods indicate that familiarity between offenders and their victims is a shared characteristic of these offenses. Boggs noted that her conclusions are similar to those of Schuessler, which we described earlier in the chapter. Bullock (1955) also noted that black homicides tend to occur on the block on which both the assailant and the victim live.

Boggs' second factor is similar to Schuessler's property crimes factor, and it appears that "the most intensively exploited business crime targets are those located in high-rank neighborhoods adjacent to offender areas" (p. 907). Forcible rape and miscellaneous robbery are randomly distributed among social areas—thus no distinguishable pattern in the metropolis is apparent. She noted that this factor is very similar to the one we described earlier in Schmid's study of bicycle theft, indecent exposure, and residential burglary in Seattle. Boggs' fourth factor, composed primarily of offender variables, suggests that offender neighborhoods are also neighborhoods of high occurrence, even though the offenders may not reside in the same areas in which they commit their crimes.

Boggs concluded that crime occurrence rates vary by the "environmental opportunities" specific to each crime category. In this view CBDs are *not* the most intensively exploited crime areas in the city. Further, crimes do not always take place within the area in which the offender lives, but the scene of a crime varies extensively by type of crime and area. Criminal offenders and victims may reside in the same area, even on the same block; yet data on other crimes show that the offender and the area of occurrence are widely separated.

Longitudinal Studies of Crime in Urban Areas

In the revised edition of Shaw and McKay (1969), several chapters are devoted to crime and delinquency rate differentials in cities other than Chicago. These cities included Philadelphia (1926–1938), Boston (1927–1930 and 1931–1934), Cincinnati (1927–1929), Cleveland (1919–1931 and 1928–1931), and a substantially different type of city outside of the manufacturing belt, the old, southern city of Richmond, Virginia (1927–1930). Each of these cities showed patterns of crime and delinquency similar to that exhibited in Chicago, and, in addition, there appeared to be little change over time in these rates.

Few current studies exist of changing crime patterns over time for specific areas within metropolitan complexes. Part of the reason, of course, is the paucity of reliable and comparable data over time for one city, let alone for several cities. Aside from these problems, Shaw (1929: 161–174) reported that the relationship between juvenile delinquency rates in the same areas of the city in 1900–1906 and 1917–1923 was extremely high (r = 0.84), as were recidivism rates between the two time periods. Given these high rates in the same areas for over a 30-year period, "it should be remembered that relatively high rates have persisted in certain areas notwithstanding the fact that the composition of population has changed markedly" (Shaw, 1929: 203).

In the revised edition of their earlier work Shaw and McKay (1969: 329–358) included rates for Chicago "for a period of 65 years, which is something more than one-half of the life of the city." During this time, the population of Chicago doubled (between 1900 and 1930), whereas between 1930 and 1960 the increase was minimal—5 percent. The suburban areas increased little before 1930 but very rapidly between 1930 and 1960. In comparing delinquency rates for 1934–1940, 1945–1951, 1954–1957, 1958–1961, and 1962–1965, they found the distributions to be remarkably similar. "The great suburban development, significant changes in the composition of the population, and the expansion of industry, *together,* seem not to have changed very significantly the number of different types of delinquency-producing areas in Chicago" (p. 345).

There were a few exceptions in which rapid increases and rapid decreases occurred in rates. *In both rapidly increasing and decreasing areas,* the population was predominantly black. The downward trend occurred in areas *"in which Negro population has been concentrated for several decades"* (p. 377). In addition, these data covering over 60 years reveal that areas of high rates in delinquency typically also are those most disrupted by incoming populations. Finally, Schmid (1960*b*: 669–670) compared offenses in Seattle for two different periods, 1939–1941 and 1949–1951, and he reported that they "manifest a substantial correspondence." He found differences in absolute rates, partly a result of changing definitions and classifications, but the basic configurations for various crimes by zones in the city show a marked similarity (also see Schmid and Schmid, 1972).

Kobrin (1951: 656–660) suggested that, at the polar extremes, delinquent areas within metropolitan complexes can be thought of as those in which integration between the conventional and criminal value systems occurs. "Areas range from those in which integration is well advanced to those in which it is minimal." In the areas in which the conventional and criminal cultures are well articulated, criminal and delinquent activity is learned behavior, and younger persons are trained in skills related to violence, concealment, evasion of detection, and the buying off of policemen, judges, and so on. This, of course, represents the socialization process of becoming a professional criminal—the differential association hypothesis. On the other hand, Kobrin described another criminal extreme in which there is little integration into the conventional crime culture; criminal behavior in these areas is characterized as being "hoodlum" in nature, and violence, theft, and so forth, are almost a form of recreation and there is an "unending battle against all forms of constraint." Kobrin is well aware that most delinquency areas fall somewhere in between these polar extremes but they all express one form or another of these basic characteristics.

Conclusions

Research following the procedures set down by Shaw has confirmed the association of juvenile delinquency and crime with the physical structure and social organization of the city and metropolitan complex. Short (in the introduction to the revised edition of Shaw and McKay, 1969:xxvii) noted that "the association of delinquency with specific social conditions seems less important than the general pattern of association and the existence of areas within cities in which a variety of social ills are concentrated." Schmid (1960a: 542) claimed that while

sweeping inferences are not waranted by a single study, it seems very likely on the basis of this investigation—as well as other research on the ecological structure of the urban community by the present author and his colleagues—that similar patterns are to be found in other American cities.

As we have seen in this chapter, the argument advanced by Schmid and his colleagues and others is well founded. Finally, Shaw and McKay (1969: 101–107) reported that in Chicago delinquency rates are associated with infant mortality rates (1927–1933, $r = 0.75$), tuberculosis rates (1931–1934, $r = 0.93$), and mental disorder rates (1922–1933, $r = 0.72$). On the basis of these data they hypothesized that delinquency is not an isolated phenomenon but is closely associated, area by area, with rates of truancy, adult crime, infant mortality, tuberculosis, and mental disorder. They believe that if other problems had been considered, a similar relationship would have been found.

RIOTS AND RACIAL VIOLENCE
Riots in the early part of the twentieth century in cities of the United States have been reviewed by Grimshaw (1960), who reported that in some of these early riots entire black areas were eliminated by white violence, arson, and looting. Since then there have been time periods of relative calm, but in the late 1960s once again violence came to the fore and approximated that of previous times in the history of the United States. The Commission on Civil Disorders found that most of the deaths that had occurred during these riots were a result of the use of force by the police and the National Guard. Student riots also occurred during the 1960s, although they certainly were not as widespread as many people believe. Most campus disturbances did not involve violence to persons or major damage to property. Nevertheless, an extensive concern about student rioters continues to this day. Major campus disturbances appeared to have declined since the 1968 Democratic convention in Chicago.

Underlying the ecological approach to riots is the assumption that social structure and ecological setting influence to some degree the behavior of individuals. Ordinarily, riots are distinguished from others forms of violence and activities in that they are not attempts to seize state power, nor are they planned and organized revolutionary activity. In other words, they are spontaneous, unplanned, and disorganized, with little thought given to seizing the political power of the state (Bowen and Massotti, 1968: 14–15). In the remainder of this section we shall focus on riots and violence in the cities and metropolitan areas of the United States because more information about them is available and they appear to be more systematically related to the ecology of the city and the metropolitan complex than student disturbances and some other types of violence.

The school desegregation decision of 1954 and the Civil Rights Act of 1964 were made during a period of few large-scale race riots; in August 1965, however, riots erupted in the Watts area of Los Angeles. Hundreds of people

Because of attacks upon the buses and their black pupils by whites, Boston police are escorting this school bus to South Boston High School.

were injured, 34 deaths occurred (mainly blacks), and over $35 million in property damage was reported. By the end of the year 1967, 8 major disturbances, 33 major and 119 minor disorders had been reported in the United States. These disturbances and disorders occurred in cities of all different sizes. Government reports suggest that major grievances felt by blacks then were police practices, unemployment, lack of housing, education, and recreational opportunities, and the political structure, which was perceived as being oppressive.

The typical rioter, according to these reports, was better educated and among those better off economically and a long-time resident of the area where the riots occurred. Thus the "criminal riff-raff and hoodlum theory of riot participation" receives little support from most research data (for a review of one such riot—the Watts riot of 1965—see Oberschall, 1968). Further, the outside-agitator, conspiracy notion has been seriously questioned by the lack of outside-area residents arrested during riots. In the 1965 Watts riot poor police-black relations played a major part as well as the election during the previous November in which the white Southern California population had voted by a 2-to-1 margin to repeal the fair housing act while virtually all black voters had voted to retain it. The Watts riot was leaderless and according to Obserschall "was structurally and behaviorally similar to the Negro riots in other cities during the Summers of 1964, 1965, and 1966."

Intermetropolitan Variation and Riots

Grimshaw (1960) has noted that the question of why some cities have riots and others do not cannot be answered until data have been collected on at least four types of areas: those characterized by combinations of high or low social tensions with weak or strong external forces of constraint. Of course, he

TABLE 18-2
Immediate Precipitants of Race Riots, 1913–1963

Rape, murder, attack, or hold-up of white women by black men	10
Killings, arrest, interference, assault, or search of black men by white policemen	15
Other inter-racial murder or shooting	11
Inter-racial fight, no mention of lethal weapons	16
Civil liberties, public facilities, segregation, political events, and housing	14
Black strikebreakers, upgrading, or other job-based conflicts	5
Burning of an American flag by blacks	1
No information available	4
Total Number	76

Source: Lieberson and Silverman (1965: 889).

assumed that social tension and constraint forces are the key variables and cities should be studied on these bases; however, it may be more realistic, given our current ignorance, to concentrate on broader types enumerated in earlier chapters and relate riots and the lack of them to these city typologies.

Lieberson and Silverman (1965), using a variety of data sources, examined the immediate precipitants and underlying conditions of 76 race riots between 1913 and 1963. They were especially concerned with "why riots occur where they do rather than in some other cities of comparable size and location." The immediate precipitants of the 76 race riots they examined are shown in Table 18-2. Most immediate precipitants of riots involved interracial bodily injury and violations of interracial segregation taboos.

Four major categories of conditions within cities were examined by Lieberson and Silverman as possible "underlying causes" of racial riots: (1) population growth and composition, (2) work situation, (3) housing, and (4) government. They noted that the rapid influx of blacks into cities is a frequently cited reason because it is assumed that the disruption of the social order creates problems that lead to race riots. However, in pairing cities of the same size and in the same region of the country, one of which had a riot or riots while the other did not (a control city), they found that the results clearly do *not* support this hypothesis. In addition, no differences in racial composition are apparent between riot and control cities. Therefore, the percent of black and the rate of growth of the black population in a city evidently have no relationship to whether or not a riot occurs there.

On the other hand, when the work situation is examined in riot and control cities, black male workers in the former are more likely to hold higher-level jobs than in the latter. As Lieberson and Silverman pointed out, "encroachment of Negroes in the white occupational world evidently tends to increase the chances of a riot, although we must also consider the possibility that Negro militancy increases as Negroes move out of their traditional niche." Further, the results of this study suggest that neither low black income nor even relatively large differences between black-white incomes are likely to result in race riots in a city. Unemployment, whether white or black, does not increase the chances of a riot, and differences between storeownership by blacks in riot and control cities are rather slight. Further, they reported that there is no tendency for housing quality to be associated with riots. Thus housing and demographic characteristics of cities in general do not seem to be the underlying conditions associated with race riots. White (1968: 163) explained that the following structural characteristics of cities help predict (ex post facto) which cities will have a riot: the percent of blacks, total population size, density (unspecified as to which measure of density), and family income.

Lieberson and Silverman placed most of their emphasis on conditions related to local government. They reported that the police force composition influences the likelihood of a riot. Not too surprisingly, cities without a riot had more black policemen per 1000 blacks than did cities with a riot. The way in which the city council was elected also appeared to be important, since "the more direct the relation between voter and government, the less likely are riots to occur." Therefore, the authors believe that the functioning of local government is extremely important in lessening the stress between races and reducing the likelihood of race riots.

Spilerman (1970), however, argued that while city characteristics may have been important factors in riots prior to the 1960s, he believes that conditions conducive to riots have been pervasive since that time and that city characteristics are no longer important riot variables. Thus in the 1960s "all cities shared an identical probability of experiencing a disorder." That is, local conditions do not differ significantly enough by city for them to overcome the exposure of blacks to various stimuli that lead them, as individuals, to develop black solidarity and to foster a consciousness of identity that transcends geographic and social class boundaries. He rejected the hypothesis that "cities which experienced racial disturbances in the 1960's are either structurally or demographically different from cities which did not have such disorders." In addition, he claimed that if he had followed the Lieberson and Silverman (1965) procedure of pairing riot and nonriot cities, the results would have been the same as he reported—that is, no difference.

Nevertheless, Spilerman reports that "racial disorders are more likely to occur where the level of life for the Negro is least oppressive according to objective measures." That is, there are more disturbances where blacks, relative to whites, are better off than other blacks living elsewhere and where black educational attainment is also greater than that of other blacks living elsewhere. Finally, disorder-prone cities tend to have stable populations and better-quality housing. Further, following Lieberson and Silverman's analysis, he showed that disturbances are more likely in high-population-per-councilman cities and in cities where there is a mayor-council structure. In spite of this evidence, Spilerman then used some rather sophisticated statistical techniques to state that "the *only* community variable related to the location of disorders'' is the number of blacks. This, then, once again led him back to the explanation that blacks

> in all cities have come to share in a riot ideology to mean that an individual's proclivity to riot is not influenced by community conditions, and we further assume that characteristics such as age and sex, which are known to affect participation, are distributed in substantially the same way in every community.[2]

The conclusion Spilerman reached, then, is that the racial disorders of the 1960s were not responses to conditions in local cities. But he did vacillate in stating that

> Disorder-prone cities do differ from their less traumatized neighbors in many significant respects. Racial violence is more likely where Negroes are better situated in occupational status, in education and income, and where the rate of population growth is small. However, these conditions have little to do with a community being prone to racial disorder, and are instead the incidental characteristics of cities with large Negro populations [p. 645].

In a critique of Spilerman's analyses, Mazur (1972) argued that

> In sum, one could assert the following about Black urban riots in the 1960s without being grossly inconsistent with available evidence: National disorder-proneness increased from the early 1960s to the late 1960s and then decreased markedly by 1971. The location of riots within any one year may largely have been a matter of chance; however, there was an additional systematic tendency for cities with large Negro populations to have a high number of riots. This may be explained by the fact that these large cities are close to sources of riot contagion and/or by their large Negro population size per se. There is some evidence that the occurrence of rioting in a city increases (reinforces) the probability of a future riot there. Riots may be caused, in part, by underlying community conditions. In short, the causes of Black riots are complex and not well understood.

In spite of the foregoing, Spilerman (1972: 499) remained unconvinced and stated that he must insist that community characteristics and conditions are insignificant in the outbreak of protests and riots. The evidence to date, including his own, suggests otherwise.

In a recent study Butler (1974) found data that show an inverse associ-

---

[2] It should be noted here that the age distribution in a community is a question that can be answered by the use of census data. Contrary to Spilerman's argument, it should *not* be assumed that there are no differences in this regard.

ation between residential segregation of blacks and both the number and intensity of race riots in the first nine months of 1968. In expanding upon this notion, he examined whether the degree of black political organization and the degree of interaction and communication between blacks and whites as a result of working together in city welfare organizations had similar influences upon both the number and intensity of race riots. Using a sample of 118 cities, he showed that cities in which there were more extended black and white relations, for instance, in political organizations, riots were more likely to occur than where black political organization was more highly developed. The explanation offered for this finding is that "some degree of contact or interaction between two different groups is necessary in order for there to be conflict between them." Thus in highly segregated cities there is less contact and hence less likelihood of conflict. Black political organization has a dampening effect upon possible conflict by disciplining individuals to work within organizations and to plan strategy rationally. Again, therefore, the likelihood of riots is lessened; however, in the future, in these very same cities, it is possible that planned conflict may develop.

Intrametropolitan Variation and Racial Violence

Grimshaw (1960: 116–118) reported that two types of ecological locations within metropolitan places are focal points of race riots. First, transfer points of public transportation, particularly where members of one race have to pass through the territory of the other. Second, government buildings have figured prominently in past racial violence. Grimshaw found that, after 1960, racial condlict appeared in a previously unexperienced form, and he suggested that ecological focal points of the past will decline in importance and subsequently that participants in racial violence will not be populations residing in the affected areas as previously.

In examining early racial riots and violence in East St. Louis, Washington, D.C., Chicago, Tulsa, and Detroit, Grimshaw noted that they all had sharp increases in black population in the years immediately preceding major interracial disturbances, and there were accompanying strains in the accommodative structure (Grimshaw, 1960: 109). He also discovered that while there are sharp disagreements about most facets of urban race riots prior to the end of World War II, they converge in descriptions of their ecology. For example, *black residential areas with no or a minimal number of business establishments* had few racial incidents. These particular areas where no riots occurred contained populations in which income, years of education, and occupational status were above those of the larger black population. Similarly, *white higher-class residential neighborhoods* on the periphery of the city were virtually free of any kind of racial violence, although at times youths from these neighborhoods "prowled in automobiles in search of stray Negroes" to beat up.

The major race riots have been concentrated in black slums, and many of these slums were completely or partially destroyed during the riots. Grim-

shaw showed that violence typically began in the CBD, and blacks then re-
treated to their own sections. Black victims accounted for the largest share of
riot-related deaths in Springfield, Illinois (1908), East St. Louis (1917), and Tulsa
(1921). Arson was widespread in each instance, and in Tulsa and East St. Louis
the black areas were almost totally destroyed. The Harlem, New York, riots
(1935 and 1943) were limited to black areas, and "physical clashes were
usually between the resident population and the police" (p.112).

Discounting the existence of *stable mixed neighborhoods* (areas in
which blacks and whites have lived amicably for long periods), Grimshaw instead believes that *contested areas,* "areas previously dominated by whites undergoing racial transition and those which, although not yet penetrated, are in
the line of movement of the Negro population and anticipating invasion" are
more typical of urban areas. Although it is not completely clear,[3] it appears that
in these transitional areas physical assaults took place on individuals, but there
was a lack of major violence in them. In *white-dominated areas not contested
by blacks* only one major riot was reported, and Grimshaw claimed that this
one took place strictly as a result of peculiar circumstances that are not likely to
happen again. Black workers in a section of Chicago in 1919 had to pass
through the all-white stockyards district to get home; ordinarily, they would
have used public transportation to get through the area to go home; however, a
transportation strike resulted in many blacks having to travel through this hos-
tile territory on foot to get home. Of those who attempted to do so, "many were
beaten, and several slain." In fact, Grimshaw has stated that in this riot 34 percent received their injuries in the black belt and 41 percent in the stockyards
district.

Blacks, like other people, have a variety of social groupings that tend
to congregate in different areas within the ghetto. Examining two wards of
Rochester, Schulman (1968: 267) concluded that the conditions that give rise
to alienation are endemic throughout the ghetto. However, it remains to be answered whether the alienated are also those who participate in riots. No evidence is given in this study to suggest that this is a valid generalization. In contrast to the Rochester study, in examining variation in riot behavior *within* the
black ghetto of Watts, Abudu and others (1972) assumed that there was
variability in riot behavior in different areas of the ghetto. As a result of their
analysis, they concluded that the frequency of riot-type events is highly variable among subareas of the ghetto. The number of fires correlated with factors
of blackness and the lower level of education and with what they called the fer-
tile-ground factors—office and commercial enterprises. It is primarily in areas
of the ghetto characterized previously that "there develops the sociodemographic fertile ground for massive, violent protest" (p. 423). Their analyses,
therefore, coupled with other results, suggest that while the proportion of
blacks in a city may not be important in determining whether or not a riot de-

[3] See Grimshaw's comments on p. 114 versus his statement on p. 115.

velops, the extent of blackness within the ghetto is influential in determining where the most severe rioting behavior will occur. There evidently must be a critical mass for the riot to develop, and this mass does not occur randomly in the ghetto.

"Neighborhood status modality" has an important influence upon who does and who does not participate in riots (Warren, 1971). Persons who had a higher status modal position than their neighbors were more active in rioting than persons congruent with or below their neighbors. In addition, in black neighborhoods in which there is a great deal of social integration, for example, visiting with neighbors, rioting was less likely. On the other hand, this relationship was further specified because "where visiting is extensive, and a negative orientation to neighbors exists, non-modals (both high and low) show the highest level of rioting of any subgroup analyzed. By contrast, "non-modal"-lows riot least where there is little neighborhood visiting and a positive commitment to the neighborhood."

Lieberson and Grimshaw (1965: 898) emphasized that race riots are frequently misunderstood and are blamed on "communists," "hoodlums," or "rabble-rousers." The community fails to see riots in terms of how well or how poorly the institutional structure is functioning and that there are conditions in which the social institutions do have influence.

From this perspective, Abudu and colleagues (1972: 408) argued that the stoning of white-driven automobiles, the taunting of police and firemen, and the looting and burning of white-owned commercial establishments in the ghetto "may be considered more specific responses than either voting for, or writing to an office-holder who has little or no discernible or direct relationship to these ghetto experiences." According to them, black riots in the cities are *politically* motivated and represent attempts to demonstrate viability in the trade-offs of politics.

Riot Severity

Wanderer (1969) developed an "index of riot severity" using the following items: killing, calling out the National Guard, calling in the state police, sniping, looting, interference with firemen, and vandalism. These items, in the order given here, formed a Guttman Scale with a Coefficient of Reproducibility of 0.92, which means that, excluding about 8 percent error, these dimensions formed a scale that was ordered in that each scare on the scale indicated what kinds of other events took place during the riots. A scale type of 5, for example, meant that vandalism, interference with firemen, and looting occurred in that riot but not sniping, using the state police and the National Guard, or the killing of a law officer.

City characteristics associated with the riot severity index were the *percentage increase of blacks*, not percentage of blacks in the city. The greater the percentage increase of blacks, the greater the severity of the riot. However, the racial composition of the city was found to be unrelated to the presence or absence of riots and to the severity of the riot index. Housing, in general, appears to be unrelated to riot severity. Further, median black rent, median value of black place of living, or median percentage of black homeowners did not show any relationship to riot severity, nor did population density (although it is difficult to tell from Wanderer's work what measure of population density he used). Similarly, no relationship between two measures of previous criminality, larceny and assault, and severity of riots was found. Finally, no relationship between police preparation and riot severity was noted. It was unfortunate that Wanderer did not build upon previous studies and include the population-police ratio.

The results of research on the riot severity index suggests that events that make up riots are patterned, and the severity of riots is linked to certain characteristics of cities. But further specification is needed before the generalizations arising from this research can be wholeheartedly accepted.

Conclusions

Five general explanations of black protests have appeared in the literature (Geschwender, 1964). The "vulgar Marxist hypothesis" suggests that as blacks experienced a worsening of their conditions of life, they became increasingly dissatisfied until they rebelled. The "sophisticated Marxist hypothesis" or "relative-deprivation hypothesis" assumes that as blacks experienced an improvement in their life conditions, they simultaneously observed whites experiencing a more rapid rate of improvement and thus became dissatisfied and rebelled. A third and somewhat related hypothesis might be called the "rising-expectations hypothesis," which notes that as blacks experienced an improvement in their life conditions, they also experienced a rise in their desires. Desires increased more rapidly than improved life conditions, resulting in dissatisfaction and rebellion. The "rise-and-drop hypothesis" rests upon the assumption that as blacks experienced an improvement in life conditions, a sharp reversal occurred and thus they became dissatisfied and rebelled. Finally, the fifth hypothesis is called the "status inconsistency hypothesis" and suggests that blacks possess a number of different status attributes that are differently ranked on the various status hierarchies, which in turn leads to dissatisfaction and rebellion.

In evaluating these hypotheses, Geschwender rejected immediately on the basis of contrary evidence the vulgar Marxist hypothesis because "the position of the Negro is improving educationally, occupationally, and incomewise." It might be instructive, however, to ask black male ghetto residents whether or not they agree with the "fact" that their life conditions are improving, thus calling into question the vulgar Marxist hypothesis. Geschwender also rejected the rise-and-drop hypothesis, since he believes that blacks are steadily improving their levels of education, occupation, and income.

Geschwender further believes that the three remaining hypotheses are closely related in that the sophisticated Marxist hypothesis and the status inconsistency hypothesis both have relative deprivation as their essence. He has also noted that the rising-expectations hypothesis sees blockages of legitimate aspirations as a key variable and thus again results in a notion of relative deprivation. Whatever explanation may ultimately be accepted, the fact remains that racial violence and riots in the past have been fairly consistently located in certain ecological areas of the metropolitan complex. Many observers expect a broader ecological base in the next series of riots that occur in U.S. cities.

Flaming and Palen (1972: 275), in summarizing the results of their analysis of the efficiency of the 1967 riots in Watts and Milwaukee, reported that their data indicate that whites continue to ignore the "message of the riots" — the problems of health, rat control, poor housing, under- and unemployment, and discriminatory law enforcement continue to exist in these areas. They further showed that other life conditions subsequently have actually deteriorated in these riot-torn areas. If past experience is any guide, when future race riots and violence occur in the United States, they will once again be highly localized within specific areas of the metropolitan complex despite some contrary beliefs.

Finally, our description of riots in the United States more or less summarizes the state of current knowledge on the subject. Even though violence and riots have occurred extensively in the United States during the twentieth century, empirical knowledge about riots is still very meager and answers to some of the most basic and elementary questions still do not exist.

BIBLIOGRAPHY: Articles

Abudu, Margaret J. G., Walter J. Raine, Stephen L. Burbeck, and Keith K. Davison, "Black Ghetto Violence: A Case Study Inquiry into the Spatial Pattern of Four Los Angeles Riot Event-Types," *Social Problems,* 19 (Winter 1972): 408–426.

Boggs, Sara L., "Urban Crime Patterns," *American Sociological Review,* 30 (December 1965): 899–908.

Bullock, Henry A., "Urban Homicide in Theory and Fact," *Journal of Criminal Law, Criminology and Police Science,* 45 (January–February 1955): 564–575.

Clark, John P., and Eugene P. Wenninger, "Socio-Economic Correlates of Illegal Behavior Among Juveniles," *American Sociological Review,* 27 (December 1962): 826–834.

Clinard, Marshall B., "A Cross-Cultural Replication of the Relation of Urbanism to Criminal Behavior," *American Sociological Review,* 25 (April 1960): 253–257.

Geschwender, James A., "Social Structure and the Negro Revolt: An Examination of Some Hypotheses," *Social Forces,* 43 (December 1964): 248–256.

Grimshaw, Allen D., "Urban Racial Violence in the United States: Changing Ecological Considerations," *American Journal of Sociology,* 66 (September 1960): 109–119.

Kobrin, Solomon, "The Conflict of Values in Delinquency Areas," *American Sociological Review,* 16 (October 1951): 653–661.

Lieberson, Stanley, and Arnold R. Silverman, "The Precipitants and Underlying Conditions of Race Riots," *American Sociological Review,* 30 (December 1965): 887–898.

Los Angeles Times, "Many Didn't Report Crimes, Poll Finds," January 1, 1972.

Mazur, Allan, "The Causes of Black Riots," *American Sociological Review,* 37 (August 1972): 490–493.

Oberschall, Anthony, "The Los Angeles Riot of August, 1965," *Social Problems,* 15 (Winter 1968): 322–341.

Ogburn, William F., "Factors in the Variation of Crime Among Cities," *Journal of the American Statistical Association,* 30 (March 1935): 12–34.

Polk, Kenneth, "Juvenile Delinquency and Social Areas," *Social Problems,* 5 (Winter 1957–1958): 214–217.

Rumney, Jay, "The Social Costs of Slums," *Journal of Social Issues,* 7 (1951): 77–83.

Schmid, Calvin F., "Urban Crime Areas: Part I," *American Sociological Review,* 25 (August 1960a): 527–542.

Schmid, Calvin F., "Urban Crime Areas: Part II," *American Sociological Review,* 25 (October 1960b): 655–578.

Schuessler, Karl, "Components of Variation in City Crime Rates," *Social Problems,* 9 (Spring 1962): 314–323.

Spilerman, Seymour, "Strategic Considerations in Analyzing the Distribution of Racial Disturbances," *American Sociological Review,* 37 (August 1972): 493–499.

Spilerman, Seymour, "The Causes of Racial Disturbances: A Comparison of Alternative Explanations," *American Sociological Review,* 35 (August 1970): 627–649.

Wanderer, Jules J., "An Index of Riot Severity and Some Correlates," *American Journal of Sociology,* 74 (March 1969): 500–505.

Warren, Donald I., "Neighborhood Status Modality and Riot Behavior: An Analysis of the Detroit Disorders of 1967," *Sociological Quarterly* 12 (Summer 1971): 350–368.

BIBLIOGRAPHY: Books

Bowen, Don R., and Louis H. Massoti, "Civil Violence: A Theoretical Overview," in Louis H. Massoti and Don R. Bowen (eds.), *Riots and Rebellions,* Beverly Hills, Calif.: Sage, 1968, pp. 11–31.

Flaming, Karl H., and J. John Palen, "Urban Violence: A Question of Efficacy," in J. John Palen and Karl H. Flaming (eds.), *Urban American Conflict and Change,* New York: Holt, Rinehart and Winston, Inc., 1972, pp. 270–276.

Lander, Bernard, *Towards an Understanding of Juvenile Delinquency,* New York: Columbia University Press, 1954.

Schmid, Calvin F., and Stanton E. Schmid, *Crime in the State of Washington,* Olympia: Washington State Planning and Community Affairs Agency, 1972.

Schulman, Jay, "Ghetto Area Residence, Political Alienation, and Riot Orientation," in Louis H. Masotti and Don R. Bowen (eds.), *Riots and Rebellion,* Beverly Hills, Calif.: Sage, 1968, pp. 261–284.

Shaw, Clifford, *Delinquency Areas,* Chicago: University of Chicago Press, 1929.

Shaw, Clifford R., and Henry D. McKay, *Juvenile Delinquency and Urban Areas,* rev. ed., Chicago: University of Chicago Press, 1969.

Uniform Crime Reports for the United States, U.S. Federal Bureau of Investigation, 1973.

White, John G., "Riots and Theory Building," in Louis H. Masotti and Don R. Bowen (eds.), *Riots and Rebellions,* Beverly Hills, Calif.: Sage, 1968, pp. 155–165.

CHAPTER 19
ENVIRONMENTAL PROBLEMS

INTRODUCTION

Each metropolitan region has natural environmental features and manmade alterations of that natural environment. Recent technological innovations have reduced substantially the time required by human beings to alter the natural environment. The configuration of the natural environment and the manmade alterations of it may produce hazards such as air and water pollution, noise, fires, floods, and earth slides (Van Arsdol et al., 1964: 145), which are inimical to health and/or result in economic loss. Varying natural and manmade conditions result in areas *within* any given metropolitan complex having different environmental hazards. Environmental hazards may be determined in several different ways. First, objective measurements may be made of hazards such as air pollution, noise, and so forth. Second, it is quite another matter if one is concerned with the degree of public awareness of the hazard, since objective measures and public awareness may or may not match. Further, attitudes about environmental conditions may change over time. For example, "a generation ago belching smokestacks were welcomed, as indicators of full employment, whereas today they are more likely to be taken as symbols of technological obsolescence and management irresponsibility" (Ayres, 1969: 10).

AIR POLLUTION

"The air over a city is both a lifeline and a sewer" (Rydell and Schwarz, 1968: 119). Urban air is a scarce commodity, and the quantity of unpolluted air in an urban complex changes over time. Human alterations of the natural environment may intensify the effects of temperature inversions associated with air pollution and its associated health problems. Leighton (1966) has pointed out quite succinctly that air pollution currently is not particularly severe in some locales such as the Granby Basin in Colorado and the Piedmont region of North Carolina. But with an increasing population base and man-

A variety of air pollutants from manufacturing are shown in this photograph. The second major cause of air pollution is the automobile.

made alterations of the natural environments in those locales, they, along with others, have a great potential problem because of extremely strong inversion layers. In addition, metropolitan areas and cities generate substantial heat and thus facilitate the development of inversion layers that keep pollutants suspended above the city (Lowry, 1967).

In service center cities air pollution is primarily a byproduct of automobiles, whereas in manufacturing-type cities industrial pollution would be added to that produced by automobiles. Thus the type of city may have an affect upon the level of air pollution when the severity of inversion layer is controlled.

Distribution of Air Pollution

Air pollution is widely diffused in many metropolitan regions, although certainly there are areas *within* the metropolitan complex with much heavier concentrations of air pollution for longer periods of time than other areas within the same metropolitan region. In Los Angeles County, for example, in 1962 air pollution was widely diffused but tended to concentrate in more central sections and along the base of mountains to the east. Approximately 50 percent of the population in Los Angeles County at that time lived in heavily polluted areas. Concentration of the heaviest levels of air pollution was in areas of older housing, which were further characterized by heavily traveled streets and freeways, concentrations of industrial and commercial activities, low rent, low-status ethnics and minorities, physical deterioration and aging housing (Van Arsdol et al., 1964). Unfortunately, objective data on air pollution distribution in other metropolitan centers are noticeably lacking. However, Van Arsdol and others are convinced that their findings hold for other metropolitan complexes as well.

Air pollution problems may be increased in certain urban areas by the overall spatial and temporal arrangement of buildings, streets, and so forth (Rydell and Schwarz, 1968: 115). "Once pollutants are released into the atmosphere their dispersion and transportation is caused by the urban microclimate, in particular the wind speed and the vertical temperature gradient" (p. 115). Hence one mechanism available for controlling air pollution in urban complexes is the city's form, which can be used to spread the pollution to surrounding rural areas. Obviously, this is not a long-term solution, since air pollution might build up in suburban and rural regions. Nevertheless, man-made changes in the urban environment could help to alleviate part of the problem by proper designing of buildings and streets to facilitate the spread of the pollution. Similarly, locating air-pollution-producing industry downwind from the city would lessen urban air pollution but increase suburban and rural pollution. New methods of transporting people and goods also could help in alleviating urban air pollution, as would more efficient allocations of open space and other land uses (Rydell and Schwarz, 1968).

Generally, air quality criteria have been derived from: (1) citizen awareness and complaints, (2) impact of air pollution upon health, and (3) the economic analysis of the costs of air pollution and control measures. (Rydell and Schwarz, 1968: 119).

Awareness of Air Pollution

The study of the perceptual awareness of air pollution is based on the assumption that humans are the creators of the condition, the measurers of the problem, and the sources of its solution. The fact that air pollution exists and is relative to human perception has some important implications. The first is to what degree air pollution is tolerable, and second is to what extent toleration varies by different population segments. Differential perceptual awareness may lead to varying behavioral and organizational responses by human beings. The perception, or lack thereof, of air pollution is not necessarily related to its involuntary effects, that is, the health and mortality impact upon individuals can exist whether or not a person perceives the air pollution. In fact, the literature suggests that air pollution has its most adverse effects on older persons; yet it is these same persons who least perceive the problem. The point is that air pollution is an urban social problem only when it is perceived as such, even though it still may have negative health consequences. Further, probably only those persons who are aware that air pollution is a serious problem are likely to attempt to do anything about it: Only an aware and awakened public will support effective control programs.

Previous studies of the perceptual awareness of air pollution have focused primarily on the following:

1. Awareness of the nature and extent of air pollution as a problem (Medalia, 1964).
2. Where knowledge about air pollution is obtained.
3. The perceived causes of air pollution.
4. Attitudes about air pollution as a problem.
5. What, if anything, should be done about air pollution.
6. The programatic elements persons would accept and support in efforts by local, state, and federal governments to overcome air pollution.
7. How accurately individuals perceive air pollution.
8. Whether or not awareness of air pollution has galvanized the individual into behavioral responses.
9. The perceived causes of air pollution.

Whether or not air pollution is perceived by populations and monitored by agencies depends primarily upon the meaning given air pollution by people (Molotch and Follett, 1970).

In Los Angeles County in 1962, 28.1 percent of a representative sample population believed that they lived in a neighborhood in which air pollution was a problem. This may be compared with the slightly over 50 percent who actually lived in heavily polluted areas by objective measurements. A national urban study conducted in 1966 and a follow-up of the same respondents in 1969 showed figures almost identical to the 1962 Los Angeles County study (Butler et al., 1972). In 1966, 30.2 percent reported air pollution as a serious problem in their neighborhood; by 1969 the percentage of *the same persons* who reported air pollution as a serious problem in their neighborhood had increased only slightly, to 31.2 percent. Interestingly, in the 1966 survey, 56.4 percent believed that air pollution was a problem at the metropolitan level! Apparently, many people believe that air pollution is a serious metropolitan problem but not a problem in their particular neighborhood (Butler et al., 1972). This may be because air pollution awareness depends substantially upon its perception. It is difficult to perceive air pollution in some areas because buildings, telephone poles, and so on, block long-range vision and thus makes air pollution less noticeable. Of course, some pollutants are not visible.

Yet Degroot et al. (1966: 246) studied air pollution in Buffalo, New York, and reported that "conventional differentiating variables, such as age, sex, race, socioeconomic status and education were not significantly related to concern about air pollution. The over-riding variables, without exception, was the actual air quality in the areas of residence." Also, Rankin (1969) reported similar attitudes about air pollution in West Virginia, as did Schusky (1966) when she reported public awareness and concern about air pollution in the St.

Louis metropolitan area. On the other hand, in a study of public concern about air pollution in Durham, North Carolina, only 13 percent thought that air pollution was a serious problem in that city, although 74 percent said it was a serious problem throughout the United States (Murch, 1971).

In their study of the perception of various environmental hazards, Van Arsdol and others (1964: 152) reported that ". . . while non-whites are concentrated in smog areas, the intrusion of social hazards in such areas and the concern of such populations with other social problems may have obscured their perception of environmental hazards." Membership in a visible ethnic minority, then, may be such a pervasive and all-encompassing fact that it is the determining factor in matters of attitude formation. The entire social milieu of the ghetto or barrio makes it very unlikely that a rather remote societal problem such as air pollution would be even close to one's top priorities. The data suggest that poor lower-class anglos are considerably more likely than ethnic minority individuals to feel that air pollution is salient. This reinforces the possibility that it is not status or class but the overwhelming reality of being black or brown in a dominant anglo society that is the most important factor in their relative lack of concern about air pollution.

Thus ethnicity has strong effects upon the saliency of air pollution that do not disappear when social class, income, and education are controlled. This is especially important since much of the non-anglo population in Los Angeles lives in older residential areas where smog is more heavily concentrated because of heavily traveled freeways and nearby industrial sources of air pollution. These data analyses suggest that air pollution is not highly salient in *any* ethnic group; however, it is relatively much more salient to anglos than to blacks or chicanos; and this relationship is apparently not the result of education, income, or SEI correlates of ethnicity.

Little research has explored the question of where knowledge about air pollution is obtained. Some reports indicate that the population correctly perceives that industry and automobiles are the principal contributors to the problem. Nevertheless, there is a population segment that believes that even without industry and automobiles, air pollution would exist, that is, that it is a natural phenomenon. Little public concensus exists as to what should be done about air pollution: Suggestions include controlling industry and/or automobile exhausts, mandatory automobile inspections, gasoline rationing, money for research, and the development of mass rapid transit. Further, there is little agreement as to who should spearhead reduction in air pollution — suggestions range from the local, state, and federal governments to universities, industry, and the individual.

Air pollution may restrict behavior such as the amount of physical exertion that is deemed desirable (i.e., in schools physical education may be terminated if air pollution reaches a specified level); other restrictions are improper breathing, eye and/or nose and throat irritations, and generally feeling so poorly that the individual does not become involved in physical activities.

Under severe air pollution conditions, visibility may be so markedly reduced that normal community activities must be halted or altered. However, air pollution may affect human behavior regardless of whether or not it is perceived. Under less severe conditions, then, visibility impairment may not even be noted by an individual but, in fact, is reduced to such a degree that irritability, and so on, lead to more automobile accidents. Another obvious response to air pollution is to avoid it by moving to pollution-free location—if one can be found (Butler et al., 1972).

Behavior by individuals contributes to the total air pollution problem as well as their own specific likelihood of being affected. For example, persons in some occupations are likely to be exposed to severe polluted conditions for long periods of time and, accordingly, have an unusually high-risk factor of morbidity and mortality. Occupations such as traffic officer, automobile mechanic, and truck driver immediately come to mind. In addition, cigarette smoking, the use of fireplaces, some methods of cooking, and the use of certain aerosol sprays all contribute to *individualized* air pollution.

Effects of Air Pollution on People

Air pollution has a variety of effects upon people. Some have hypothesized that it might influence residential location, although the research done so far suggests that the impact that air pollution has upon population distribution is minimal (Butler et al., 1972). Others have suggested that air pollution may affect a variety of household activities such as how often one washes the automobile, upkeep of the dwelling unit, interior housecleaning, and leisure activities. Some of these affects, it should be noted, may be more indirectly than directly attributable to air pollution.

Perhaps the most attention of the effects of air pollution upon man has been concerned with the health, morbidity, and mortality aspects (Lewis, 1965). Goldsmith (1968) has pointed out that "a man can live for five weeks without food, for five days without water, but only five minutes without air." He further suggested that before health effects of air pollution can be determined, the following requirements must be met: (1) Pollution, or an index of it, must be measured; (2) one or more effects must be measured; and (3) a relationship between the two—pollution and its effects—must be shown.

While streets may be quiet, uncongested, and safe from crime and violence, because of pollutants life there may not be as safe as some believe (Esposito, 1970: 8). Among the major pollutants, carbon monoxide is the most lethal. Other pollutants, in large enough quantities, can and do produce death; however, most exposure to pollutants is not sufficiently great to cause death. But illness and malaise are rather commonly related to pollution. Auerbach (1967) reported that people who live in the northern part of Staten Island, New York, adjacent to industrial Bayonne-Elizabeth, New Jersey, have a high "excess-death" rate (the number of deaths over and above the number normally expected). That is, for males over 45 the respiratory cancer death rate is about 15 per 100,000 greater there than for males to the south, where the air is not badly polluted. The respiratory cancer excess-death rate for women is even larger, since twice as many women die from respiratory cancer in the polluted area as opposed to women living elsewhere on Staten Island. Esposito (1970: 8) cited a study that reported an estimate of 100 to 2,200 excess deaths occurred in New York City between 1960 and 1964 because of *episodic* high levels of sulfur dioxide in the air.

Using sootfall as a measure of urban air pollution, both Cincinnati and Pittsburgh had the highest levels in low-lying areas of river bottoms (Mills, 1943: 131). Both statistically and graphically this study showed that there was a close relationship between high pneumonia and tuberculosis rates (white males only) and sootfall. "In the cleaner air of the higher suburban districts little difference exists between male and females' pneumonia or tuberculosis rates, but in the polluted air of the bottom districts, the increase in male rates is almost twice as great as that of the female" (p. 136). This indicates that air pollution is a key factor in high pneumonia and tuberculosis rates and primarily affects males rather than females (Mills, 1954: 18).

Similarly, "If the low pneumonia rates of the cleaner suburbs could be made to prevail over the whole city, Chicago would each year have over 500 fewer deaths from this one cause alone" (Mills, 1954: 102). The Loop district is Chicago's dirtiest area, and the measure of sootfall decreases in all directions outward from it. Sootfall in the Loop is 150 tons per square mile per month but drops to 11 tons per square mile per month in the most northwesterly suburb. This variation is matched by similar variations in deaths due to pneumonia (white males). Thus pneumonia death rates were highest in the Loop and progressively decreased toward the suburbs; Loop rates for white males were over 10 times higher than those in the suburbs. Similar contrasts between the dirtier Loop and the cleaner suburbs were noted for pulmonary tuberculosis, with the Loop rate being 360 and that in the cleanest outlying districts being roughly 25. The death rate for cancer of the air passages and lungs was only one-third as high in the suburbs as in the Loop. Since these rates might have been affected by social class of the neighborhood, an analysis was carried out to determine whether this was a contributing variable. This hypothesis was discarded, however, when it was noted that death rates by sex varied substantially in the Loop and suburban areas, with the main effect being upon white males, while females were relatively unaffected by dirtier air, much as in the Pittsburgh study. Male laborers having the longest outdoor exposure to polluted air and inhaling greater amounts of it because of their physical activity had the highest lung cancer and pneumonia rates in both the dirty and clean parts of the city, although, again, laborers in the Loop had much higher rates than those in the suburbs (Mills, 1954: 113).

In another study of Chicago air pollution using the amount of SO_2 (sulfur dioxide) as a measure of air pollution, symptoms and precipitation of acute respiratory illness coincided substantially with high daily levels of air pollution, especially among elderly persons with advanced bronchitis (Carnow et al., 1969: 776). Similarly, a study of air pollution in Nashville indicated that for several categories of infant deaths, dustfall, either alone or in combination with other factors such as socioeconomic status, is a key factor (Sprague and Hagstrom, 1969). Also, while mortality from respiratory disease generally varied inversely with socioeconomic class, in the middle class respiratory disease mortality was directly related to the degree of exposure to sulfation (Zeidburg et al., 1967), as was asthmatic attack rates for adults (Zeidburg et al., 1961).

Several problems exist in measuring air pollution's effect upon mortality. First, ordinarily a very large population is necessary so that excess deaths can be estimated, unless there is a "disaster" such as the ones in Donora, Pennsylvania in 1948 (Roueche, 1953), London in 1948 and 1952 (Mills, 1954), New Orleans in 1955, and the worldwide one in 1962 (Goldsmith, 1968). Second, the intermittent nature of a substantial proportion of a population precludes precise estimates of the effect of air pollution in a region upon the mortality rate. The mortality that does occur also will vary substantially by urban type and by areas within metropolitan complexes because population age structure is highly variable. Research suggests that the aged are the most susceptible to pollution mortality (Pond, 1950), as are infants and those with an antecedent history of respiratory and/or heart problems.

Low-level exposure to air pollution may lead those who are susceptible to an earlier death than expected. But, in addition, many others have their health affected without immediate death. As Esposito (1970: 10) has pointed out, an individual may have grown accustomed to seeing air pollution, but this does not necessarily mean the body has adapted to it. Thus substances floating about in the air may cause ill health as well as affect the subsequent quality of future generations: *Mutagens* damage genetic capabilities and cause mutations, and *teratogens* interfere with normal fetal development and result in deformed babies.

Ethyleneimines (from insecticides, solid rocket fuels, emissions from textile and printing industries, and other industrial processes), benzo-a-pyrene (primarily an automobile byproduct), hydrocarbons (from incomplete engine combustion), carbon monoxide (from automobiles, etc.), and particulate matter (from burning coal, oil, and asbestos from automobile brake linings and clutch facings, and building materials) all have been linked to birth deformities, cancer of the lung, stomach, esophagus, prostate, or bladder and to heart strain and aggravation of existing heart trouble. In addition, Carr (1965) has suggested that many automobile accidents routinely ascribed to drunkenness may actually be attributable to excess inhalation of carbon monoxide.

The few studies accomplished to date suggest that premature infants and the infirm are highly susceptible to air pollution. Most susceptible, however, are the aged. Goldsmith further listed effects of air pollution other than those described previously and argued that they are differentially distributed among persons of different ages and medical statuses: (1) acute sickness or

This view of Webster, Pennsylvania, was taken one year after the 1948 disaster, when mortality near the zinc works at Donora skyrocketed because of fatal air pollution levels. The pall of smoke and soot shown here was typical of conditions when the zinc works operated at full blast.

death; (2) chronic diseases, shortening of life, or impairment of growth; (3) alteration of important physiological functions such as ventilation of the lung, transport of oxygen by hemoglobin, dark adaptation (ability to adjust eye mechanisms for vision in partial darkness), or other functions of the nervous system; (4) other symptoms, such as sensory irritation, which in the absence of an obvious cause might lead a person to seek medical attention and relief; (5) sufficient discomfort, odor, impairment of visibility, or other effects of air pollution to lead individuals to change behavior, residence, or place of employment.

Sufficient exposure to air pollution appears to be a factor in chronic bronchitis and emphysema, although probably it is not the only causal agent. There is some evidence that cigarette smokers are more susceptible than nonsmokers in a common polluted environment. Furthermore, there is evidence suggesting a link between air pollution and asthmatics. The available studies are not definitive because few of them have sorted out *individual* air pollution from *community* air pollution. One obvious solution is to study young children. When this has been done, the studies indicate "a strong case for adverse effects of air pollution on lower respiratory tract conditions" (Goldsmith, 1968).

Little data exist that establish a relation between air pollution and mental well-being. However, a series of studies conducted in California during 1956–1961 indicates that perception of air pollution is associated with feelings of overall malaise as well as physical symptoms such as eye irritation, asthma, nose complaints, headaches, and chest pains. Further, these complaints were more prevalent during air pollution episodes than when more favorable weather conditions existed.

In studying the foregoing human responses to air pollution, Goldsmith (1968) presented a cogent argument for the most sensitive measuring instruments possible, since a level of air pollution that may have a minimal effect upon some individuals will seriously affect others. Therefore, an additional problem is ferreting out the characteristics of persons with different thresholds of tolerance to air pollution. Goldsmith concluded that individual pollution, cigarette smoking, and the like, are major causal factors in lung cancer, whereas community-wide air pollution is, to date, only a suspected factor.

Economic Costs of Air Pollution

Any discussion of the costs of air pollution must make explicit that social values are inherent in the concept of costs (Teller, 1967). To estimate costs we need reliable and valid measures—even so, these estimates will vary according to the point of view of who is making them. Further, trade-offs and alternative control management programs only make sense when one considers this fact. "Emitters" of air pollution and "receptors" do, in fact, have different views of the necessity of risks and how much should be spent to avoid certain levels of risk.

Monetary costs for converting old plant equipment and transportation vehicles to acceptable levels (by whose standards?) and for the building of new plants and vehicles can probably be estimated fairly accurately. However, the social and health costs of air pollution are virtually impossible to measure with any great amount of precision. For example, in regard to the effects upon health and mortality, how does one measure the cost of a father or a mother to their children? What effect does air pollution have on present and future earnings, length and severity of temporarily disabling and efficiency-reducing capabilities, permanent disabilities, increased probability of morbidity and mortality from other diseases, and absenteeism from work and school? Further, how can one estimate air pollutant costs in their impact on the size, composition, and distribution of the population and its income? Finally, how much would it cost to find and treat victims, and what costs accrue to those who attempt to avoid air pollution by moving (Weisbord, 1961; Butler et al., 1972)?

At a somewhat different level, how much does air pollution cost in regard to house values (Nourse, 1967), to the need to paint house exteriors more often, to the time spent in routine cleaning, to the frequency of doing laundry and buying detergents and washing the car? How willing is the public to pay for the amelioration of air pollution and, finally, what is the cost of air pollution upon property and rental values? All of these questions suggest that air pollution has costs other than those ordinarily anticipated (Ridker, 1967).

Organization of the Human Population and Air Pollution

Air pollution has implications for the organization of the human population. The environment, technology, and human population structure (spatial distribution, etc.) and organization are uniquely related to air pollution. Through its use of the environment and its impact upon the environment through technology, the human population is responsible for most of the air pollution that exists. Human beings are the only species that can do anything about overcoming the air pollution problem.

People residing in large population concentrations are ordinarily organized around urban life forms, for example, Southern California and the Los Angeles metropolitan area; they use the environment in certain ways and through their technology—freeways—produce air pollution. This air pollution may drift and be added to locally produced oxidants. Broadly, then, the entire metropolitan complex, as well as the state and the nation, are important in the study of the air pollution problem. A study of the political impact and influence various individuals, groups, organizations, and industries have upon decision making at the local, state, and federal levels in regard to air pollution, its control, management, and effects is imperative in researching the organization of the human population and its impact upon the environment.

On a different and more localized scale, a study of the ways in which the problems of air pollution can erect barriers or precipitate effective local and extralocal public action is important. The communication and determinants of public information and consequent attitudes toward various alternative solutions are substantially a product of the social organization of the population. The population's response to air pollution in local communities may be to organize and to attempt to influence local, state, and federal officials in the use of power, management techniques, and so forth, in order to overcome the problem. Will these organizations have an influence upon regulatory measures with respect to controlling technology? Will there be effective attempts by individuals and organizations to influence management systems in regard to air pollution? How will the management systems be brought into being, who manages the management systems, and how effectively will they implement controls? All of these aspects need to be examined at the local level and tied to state and federal power structures as they are related to enforcement.

Currently, there are few local organizations in metropolitan areas that are concerned with air pollution. There have been attempts by a few individuals to combat pollution but no large-scale organized efforts to influence local, state, and federal officials in attempts to overcome air pollution. Given the heavy damage from air pollution that is expected to become highly visible over the next few years, it may be expected that in many metropolitan regions local organizations will be formed to combat air pollution.

The forms that organizations may take are varied, and the impetus for them may be local or extralocal. With the aid of "experts" in air pollution, organizations may be formed that essentially require local "voluntary" participation. Discussion groups and educational meetings should be helpful in educating local persons in regard to the air pollution problem and what they can do about it. Another community organization approach is to focus more on conflict rather than discussion and education, and organizations can stress the external nature of the "enemies" and how local residents may combat them. Hostility toward outsiders, including government and industry, is apparent in this approach to meeting the problem. In both instances, organizations might be formed that would act as "watchdogs" over industry and public agencies that are charged with air pollution control and management.

Molotch (forthcoming) argued, however, that the problem of air pollution is not simply obtaining the right kinds of information and acting upon it, but rather determining who has vested interests in the continuation of air pollution and attacking the problem at that level. Controlling air pollution from this perspective assumes that the use, control, and knowledge of *social power* is the only way that technology, which is producing air pollution, can be effectively managed and brought under control. A mobilized and organized public wielding its power would be a factor to be reckoned with and would make air pollution more than a symbolic issue. Thus as Gilluly (1970: 273) has pointed out, the Ninth Amendment to the Constitution, which states: "The enumeration in the Constitution of certain rights, shall not be construed to deny or disparage others retained by the people," and the Fourteenth Amendment, which states: "Nor shall any state deprive any person of life, liberty, or property without due process of law," could be construed as protecting the public against environmental hazards. However, the courts have not yet been challenged to determine whether these amendments apply to environmental polluters. That is, if these and other laws were enforced, they would have a real impact upon the control of air pollution.[1]

Differences in the elements and mix of air pollutants varies among metropolitan complexes and by areas within any individual metropolitan region. Therefore, the effects of air pollution are highly mixed since such differential levels of exposure exist. In addition, *it is highly probable that only a fraction of the actual pollutants that have harmful effects on human beings have been identified to date!*

Technically, the control of air pollution is now possible; however, the extent of control desired greatly influences the costs. Currently, little systematic effort is made in most metropolitan areas in the United States to control air pollution. One of the major reasons for this is related to the lack of cooperation among various cities and other governmental units within the metropolitan area. As Hawley (1971: 248) has noted,

> Most proposals for the correction of environmental pollution treat the problem as a simple matter of man's misbehavior. The complexity that is recognized lies mainly on the environmental side of the equation. There is insufficient awareness of the fact that the misbehavior in question is invariably embedded in a highly ramified

[1] For a discussion of legal and other ways of combating pollution and polluters, see Saltonsall (1970); Landau and Rheingold (1971); and Cox (1970).

system of relationships. Man's relation to his physical environment has been developed and is maintained through the organization he has achieved and not by each individual taken separately. If there is to be any hope of a lasting solution to environmental misuse, it will have to begin in the social structure of the community and society [also see Duncan, 1961].

The recent experience of Pittsburgh suggests that it is possible to some extent to clean up the air!

NOISE POLLUTION

Noise levels vary remarkably by neighborhoods within metropolitan complexes. Most noticeable is the noise level in areas adjacent to airports that accommodate jets and other large commercial aircraft. In addition, neighborhoods adjacent to freeways, thruways, industry, and heavily traveled streets make up the total package of noise pollution that pounds the ears of many urban residents (Prestemen, 1968). There is some indication that high noise levels attributed to automobiles and industry can be substantially reduced. Knudsen and Plane (1973) have noted that wider sidewalks and streets substantially reduce traffic noise. An even greater reduction could be made by using sound-absorbent street and sidewalk surfacing and groundcover plants. In combination these measures would reduce current noise levels by three-fourths. Additional reductions in noise levels could be made by covering lower levels of buildings with acoustical tile and by tilting lower floors of buildings. These suggestions are primarily practical, obviously, in newer, developing areas; however, they could be gradually implemented in already existing cities as new construction and redevelopment take place—that is, given the will, substantial changes in building codes, and economic resources.

The effect of noise upon human beings has been studied from several different approaches. One survey study examined the impact of airport noise upon residents living near the Los Angeles International Airport. Through in-depth interviews it was ascertained that the major effect of aircraft noise was upon activities involving active or passive communication such as talking on the telephone or television viewing. Other findings from this study indicated that a majority of respondents were not bothered or were only slightly disturbed by aircraft noise, that few persons made a formal complaint about it, and that there was limited awareness of noise abatement by community residents. Also, this study showed that a majority of residents were aware of the noise before they moved in, that their property value had not decreased as a result of it, and that few persons were willing to make any personal expenditure to eliminate aircraft noise (Burrows and Zamarin, 1972)![2]

In contrast to this study, an extensive survey of the effects of noise on

---

[2] It should be noted that the authors of this article were employees of the Douglas Aircraft Company.

Residents of neighborhoods adjacent to major airports are constantly exposed to high noise levels. The development of supersonic jetliners—with twice the decible level of noise as older craft like the one pictured here—has only exacerbated the problem.

people produced the following results: (1) Noise can permanently damage the inner ear, with resulting hearing losses that can range from slight impairment to nearly total deafness; (2) it can result in temporary hearing losses, and repeated exposures to noise can lead to chronic hearing losses; (3) noise can interfere with speech communication and the perception of other auditory signals; (4) it can disturb sleep; (5) it can be a source of annoyance; (6) noise can interfere with the performance of complicated tests and, of course, can especially disturb performance when speech communication or response to auditory signals is demanded; (7) it can reduce the opportunity for privacy; and (8) it can adversely influence mood and disturb relaxation (Miller, 1971). On the bright side, however, noise has not yet been positively linked to excess deaths, shortened life span, or incapacitating illness.

Several other studies give other evidence of the impact of noise upon people (Farr, 1967). One such study used sophisticated measuring instruments such as electroencephalographic (EEG) and behavioral measures and concluded that jet aircraft sounds resulted in physiological effects that outlasted the physical presence of the auditory stimulus, that is, the noise itself. In addition, "it was possible to note both behavioral and EEG changes during waking performances subsequent to nights disturbed by the jet aircraft fly-overs which were not apparent during performances subsequent to undisturbed nights" (LeVere et al., 1972: 384). Even limited exposure to nocturnal noise, then, can produce significant changes in an individual's pattern of sleeping and has a carry-over in physiological disturbance, as measured by EEG devices. Several other studies have linked aircraft noise to increased admission rates to psychiatric hospitals (Herridge, 1972; Abey-Wickrama et al., 1969) and to stress resulting in lowered reading achievement and so on (Glass et al., 1973).

Thus it can be concluded that airports contribute substantially to noise pollution in some areas within the metropolitan complex, and residential areas located in low-level flight routes receive more than their share of noise pollution. This has been especially true since the advent of jet-powered aircraft in the late 1950s. Noise from these jets soon became a major complaint of airport neighbors. Nevertheless, Graeven (1974) has pointed out that there is relatively little research that explores the effects of airplane noise on the prevalence of health problems. Borsky (1970) suggested that possible human responses to noise include an awareness of the noise, disruption of normal everyday activities, annoyance reactions, and complaints about the noise. In his study of areas in Foster City, part of which lies under the landing path to San Francisco International Airport, Graeven divided the city into four noise impact areas according to an objective level of exposure to airplane noise. He concluded that persons who lived in the high exposure area were more likely to report that they were exposed to airplane noise, to feel like complaining about it, and to report disruptions of normal everyday activities than were persons in less exposed areas. He reported no systematic relationship between age, sex, and so on, and airplane noise. He further noted that persons who lived in less exposed areas spent more time at their places of residents than did those who lived in high exposure areas. Finally, he found that awareness of noise and annoyance reactions to it were systematically related to health problems, although the relationship between level of exposure to noise and health problems was minimal. Thus his research suggests that people who are aware of noise and annoyed by it are more likely to have health problems than those whose exposure to noise may be similar, but they are not perceptually aware of it. Since noise pollution is differentially distributed within the metropolitan complex, area and individual perceptions of the noise must interact to produce health problems.

Solutions to airplane noise pollution to date have included introducing quieter engines and steeper glide patterns, but these remedies have not resulted in adequate reduction in noise level. Another solution has been land acquisition around airports. When Los Angeles International Airport was to be expanded, for example, almost 10 percent of the $500-million cost was allocated to land acquisition (McClure, 1969: 119–120). Van Arsdol and others (1964: see especially the map on p. 147) reported the incidence of noise around Los Angeles International Airport. From their work it is apparent that it would be impossible to acquire all of the land near that airport that has severe noise pollution.

Recent proposed solutions to airplane noise include removing airport facilities from metropolitan to rural areas or, in some instances, to offshore platforms (Miles, 1972). In both instances the problems of access to airports are intensified and result in greater ground traffic. In addition, other problems are associated with these proposed solutions. For example, Dulles International Airport was built in the countryside, some distance from Washington, D.C.; however, in accordance with some of the classic land development principles of Hoyt, which were examined in Chapter 7, the land around the airport and between the facility and the city is rapidly becoming filled in with industry, office buildings, and residential subdivisions. This encroachment problem obviously would not accompany the offshore construction of airports. But offshore construction is expected to cost some $7 to $13 billion compared to an approximate $1-billion cost for a land-based airport. Interestingly, in Los Angeles County in the early 1960s there were three airports for which exact sound data were available indicating that there was virtually no correspondence between areas of heavy aircraft noise pollution and heavy air pollution (Van Arsdol et al., 1964).

WATER POLLUTION

The movement of water is much more predictable than the movement of air. Nevertheless, water-related problems—both obtaining it and disposing of it—are substantial for most cities in the United States. Water supplies for cities, of course, are primarily lakes and streams, and though they may contain abundant water, they may be reduced by pollution engendered by using them as waste disposal sites.

The major sources of water pollution are organic sewage, infectious agents (e.g., typhoid), plant nutrients that wash off from sewage and fertilizers, organic chemicals like pesticides and detergents, inorganic chemicals such as sludges and chemical residues, land sediments from soil erosion, radioactive substances, and waste heat from electric and nuclear power plants and industry (Revelle, 1968; Gilluly, 1970b).

As we pointed out in Chapter 3, animals roamed the streets and served as garbage disposals in early cities. Thus it is not too surprising that early cities were characterized by periodic epidemics and high rates of illness because of inadequate sewage disposal. Similarly, water was polluted by the disposal of sewage and trash into lakes and streams, and the water used in early cities was many times taken from these very same polluted sources. One of the first departments of sewers was created in New York City in 1849. Currently, however, "It is no longer the simple matter of a city's running a pipe out into a nearby lake or stream and taking in the water it needs with no more than elementary filtering and chlorination, or of dumping its sewage through an outfall line with no thought of treatment" (Fisher, 1971: 485). In addition, while at least 83 percent of the urban population in the United States is served by sewers, only 63 percent have available in their cities sewage treatment facilities. Fortunately, virtually every city and town in the United States now has water purification plants.

One important aspect of water pollution in American cities is the apparent unwillingness of local governments to enforce conformity to water purification standards (Hawley, 1971: 246). Part of this reluctance is the result of a fear that industry in the city will relocate elsewhere. Generally, both obtaining water and disposing of it must be considered a problem too large for an individual city and as such probably requires at least a regional authority to cope with it.

Finally, water also is used for recreational activities such as fishing, boating, and swimming. Millions of dollars have been allocated to make rivers useful once again for such purposes—for example, the $300–$400-million program to make the Potomac River in the Washington, D.C., area and the Hudson River in New York swimmable.   .

OTHER ENVIRONMENTAL HAZARDS

In addition to air, noise, and water pollution, other environmental hazards exist in some metropolitan complexes and in areas within any given metropolitan complex (Widener, 1970). Fires, earth slides, floods, tornadoes, and hurricanes are examples of episodic environmental problems. Again, using Los Angeles County to illustrate, fires (primarily brush fires) and earth-slide areas are located in the hilly sections of the metropolis, while floods are just the opposite taking place in lowland areas devoid of adequate storm drains and elsewhere along bodies of water subject to storms. In contrast to air and noise pollution, which affect large population segments, environmental hazards such as fires, earth slides, and floods in the 1960s affected only about 2 percent of the population in the Los Angeles metropolitan complex (Van Arsdol et al., 1964). Technology has changed since this study was conducted, however, and many hills formerly not usable for housing are now being flattened, and thousands of houses are being built upon them on stairlike pads, and the potential for earth slides has thus increased. Similarly, thousands of houses have been built in low-lying ground that was extensively flooded during the late 1930s. Since that time no large-scale floods have occurred because of additional storm drains being built *and below-flood-level rainfalls*. However the *potential* of earth slides and floods to affect larger segments of the population has increased markedly during the 1960s and the early 1970s. Floods generally result from particularly high spring temperatures rapidly melting winter snow or extremely heavy rain over a brief period of time. Heavy rainfall may result in flash floods that develop quickly and take communities by surprise ("Mortality . . .," 1974: 6). The two major flood disasters over the past several years have been the flash flood of June 9, 1972, in Rapid City, South Dakota, which took 237 lives, and the "most extensive floods in United States history, unleashed by Hurricane Agnes, which caused at least 117 deaths on the eastern seaboard during June, 1972" (p. 6). By geographical division, the North Atlantic and Missouri areas had the most deaths by floods during the years 1965–1974.

Flood control is a complex problem that involves a variety of measures (Burton and Kates, 1964). Reforestation of water sheds, construction of reservoirs and flood walls, diversion of rivers, improved techniques for forecasting

These people in West Alton, Missouri, are among many residents who refused to leave their homes during this 1973 flood of the Missouri and Mississippi Rivers. Studies such as Kates' indicate that many residents of flood areas fail to consider the dangers of flood seriously.

rising river levels, and, finally, recent legislation that requires local governments to implement building codes aimed at reducing housing developments in flood plains—all should result in less flood damage and loss of life in future years ("Mortality . . .," 1974: 6–7). On the other hand, mitigating against such positive appraisal is a result of a recent study of residents of 15 different sites along the coast from North Carolina to New Hampshire that suggests that a "high proportion of coastal dwellers take minimal steps to reduce their hazard," and many of them elect to live at considerable risk rather than reduce their seaward amenities by conservation measures (Kates, 1967: 68–69). Similarly, many have opposed construction of seawalls and others have knowingly lowered sand dunes in order to improve views and accessibility to beaches (p. 69).

 Other kinds of problems and potential hazards in cities of the United States are solid-waste disposal, pesticides, and disfigurement of the urban environment. To some extent solid wastes have been useful as landfill. However, in general, especially in larger cities, discarding solid wastes is a large-scale enterprise involving scores of trucks, workers, and shifting landfill locations. Pesticides "used in excess or applied sloppily not only can damage the countryside and the ponds, but also can be harmful to city people" (Fisher, 1971: 488). Similarly, disfigurement of the environment resulting from poor planning, lack of architectural controls, poor construction, undisciplined city management and civic behavior also lead to environmental hazards in the city (pp. 488–489) in addition to visual pollution (McEvoy and Williams, 1970). These types of hazards have been little explored but appear in many cities in the United States.

CONCLUSIONS

It was pointed out earlier in this chapter that air pollution is the most frequently reported environmental hazard. In addition, over one-fifth of the individuals sampled in a national study of all persons residing in metropolitan areas of the United States in 1966 believed that water pollution was a serious metropolitan problem, although only about one-half that many believed it to be a problem in their immediate neighborhoods. Around 7 percent reported airplane noise as a serious problem both at the metropolitan and neighborhood levels (Butler et al., 1972).

The effects of floods, fires, and earth slides upon human beings are of a different magnitude than those of air pollution, water pollution, and noise, since they are mainly episodic rather than chronic. The impact of noise in urban areas upon individuals has only recently become a subject of serious investigation. Thus data so far are not conclusive but imply that being subjected to high noise levels not only damages hearing capabilities but also is associated with a higher level of mental disorders and behavioral problems in certain areas within the metropolitan environment. Little scientific knowledge is available concerning the impact that water pollution and other environmental hazards have upon residents of metropolitan areas.[3] Each of these environmental hazards is related, more or less, to the mental and physical health of the population. While little direct evidence exists in this regard, there is no doubt expressed by any knowledgeable authority about their impact, only the degree.

Since these environmental hazards safely can be assumed to be related to the health of the population and all of them are amenable to some degree of correction given contemporary technology, it is a fair question to ask why they continue to exist as urban problems. They undoubtedly continue to exist because at least part of the solution lies outside of the direct relationship between human beings and the environment (Kates, 1971). The vagaries of nature's whims are an important factor, therefore. Probably much more important, however, is the social and power influence that has been exerted against those who attempt to solve environmental hazard problems.

In conclusion, environmental hazards are differentially distributed both between and within metropolitan areas. Some population segments are more likely to be exposed to the chronic problems of air pollution and noise, while others are more likely to be exposed to episodic hazards such as fires, floods, and earth slides. It is doubtful that any of these environmental hazards

[3] For a general treatment of environmental problems, their origin, treatment, and possible control, see *Environmental Quality* (1970).

in metropolitan regions and areas within them will be alleviated during the next several decades.

BIBLIOGRAPHY: Articles

Aby-Wickrama, M. F. a'Brook, F. E. G. Gattoni, and C. F. Herridge, "Mental-Hospital Admissions and Aircraft Noise," *The Lancet,* (December 1969): 1275–1277.

Auerbach, Irwin, "The Pall Above, the Victims Below," *Medical World News,* 8 (February, 1967): 60–69.

Ayres, Robert U., "Air Pollution in Cities," *Natural Resources Journal,* 9 (January 1969): 1–9.

Boffey, P., "Smog: Los Angeles Running Hard, Standing Still," *Science,* 161 (September 1968): 990–992.

Burrows, Alan A., and David M. Zamarin, "Aircraft Noise and the Community: Some Recent Survey Findings," *Aerospace Medicine,* 43 (January 1972): 27–33.

Burton, Ian, and Robert W. Kates, "The Floodplain and the Seashore: A Comparative Analysis of Hazard-Zone Occupance," *Geographical Review,* 54 (July 1964): 366–385.

Butler, Edgar W., Ronald J. McAllister, Edward J. Kaiser, "Air Pollution and Metropolitan Population Redistribution," paper presented at the American Sociological Association, New Orleans, August 1972.

Carnow, Bertram W., Mark H. Lepper, Richard B. Shekelle, and Jeremiah Stamler, "Chicago Air Pollution Study," *Archives Environmental Health,* 18 (May 1969): 768–776.

Cox, Jeff, "They Go to Court to Protect the Environment," *Organic Gardening and Farming,* (September 1970): 78–81.

Creer, Ralph N., "Social Psychological Factors Involved in the Perception of Air Pollution as an Environmental Health Problem," unpublished master's thesis, University of Utah, August 1968.

Crowe, Jay, "Toward a Definitional Model of Public Perceptions Toward Air Pollution," *Journal of Air Pollution Control,* 18 (March 1968): 154–157.

De Groot, Ido, "Trends in Public Attitudes Toward Air Pollution," *Journal of Air Pollution Control,* 17 (October 1967): 679–681.

De Groot, Ido, et al., "People and Air Pollution: A Study in Buffalo, N.Y.," *Journal of Air Pollution Control,* 16 (May 1966): 245–247.

Duncan, Otis Dudley, "From Social System to Ecosystem," *Sociological Inquiry,* 31 (Spring 1961): 140–149.

Farr, Lee E., "Medical Consequences of Environmental Home Noises," *Journal of the American Medical Association,* 202 (October 1967): 171–174.

Fisher, Joseph L., "Environmental Quality and Urban Living," in Larry S. Bourne (ed.), *Internal Structure of the City,* New York: Oxford University Press, 1971, pp. 483–490.

Gilluly, Richard H., "Taking Polluters to the Courts," *Science News,* 98 (September 26, 1970a): 273–374.

Gilluly, Richard H., "Finding a Place to Put the Heat," *Science News,* 98 (August 1, 1970b): 98–99.

Glass, David C., Sheldon Cohen, and Jerome E. Singer, "Urban Din Fogs the Brain," *Psychology Today,* 6 (May 1973): 93–99.

Graeven, David B., "The Effects of Airplane Noise on Health: An Examination of Three Hypotheses," *Journal of Health and Social Behavior,* 15 (December 1974): 336–343.

Haagen Smit, A. J., "Man and His Home," *Vital Speeches,* 36 (July 1970): 572–576.

Herridge, C. F., "Aircraft Noise and Mental Hospital Admission," *Sound,* 6 (1972): 32–36.

Jeffries, Ronald, Edgar W. Butler, and David Gold, "Salience and Intensity of Public Attitudes Toward Air Pollution," Riverside, Calif.: Unpublished paper, August 1972.

Kates, Robert W., "Natural Hazard in Human Ecological Perspective: Hypotheses and Models," *Economic Geography,* 47 (July 1971): 438–451.

Knudsen, Vern O., and Vern C. Plane, "Model Studies of the Effects of Motor Vehicle Noise on Buildings and Other Boundaries Along Streets and Highways," paper presented at the Acoustical Society of America, Boston, Mass., April 1973.

Leighton, Phillip A., "Geographical Aspects of Air Pollution," *Geographical Review,* 56 (No. 2, 1966): 151–174.

LeVere, T. E., Raymond T. Bartus, and F. D. Hart, "Electroencephalographic and Behavioral Effects of Nocturnally Occurring Jet Aircraft Sounds," *Aerospace Medicine,* 43 (April 1972): 384–389.

Lowry, William P., "The Climate of Cities," *Scientific American,* 217 (August 1967): 15–33.

Medalia, Nahum Z., "Air Pollution as a Socio-Environmental Health Problem: A Survey Report," *Journal of Health and Human Behavior,* 5 (Winter 1964): 154–165.

Miles, Marvin, "Floating Airport: Answer to L.A.'s Jet Noise Problem?" *Los Angeles Times,* June 4, 1972.

Mills, Clarence A., "Urban Air Pollution and Respiratory Diseases," *American Journal of Hygiene,* 37 (January–May 1943): 131–141.

Molotch, Harvey, and Ross C. Follett, "Air Pollution: A Sociological Perspective," *Project Clean Air Task Force Assessments,* Vol. 3, Riverside, Calif.: University of California, 1970.

"Mortality from Tornadoes, Hurricanes, and Floods," *Statistical Bulletin,* 55 (December 1974): 4–7.

Murch, Arvin W., "Public Concern for Environmental Pollution," *Public Opinion Quarterly,* 35 (Spring 1971): 100–106.

Nourse, Hugh O., "The Effect of Air Pollution on House Values," *Land Economics,* (May 1967): 181–189.

Plane, Vern C., and Vern O. Knudsen, "Model Studies of the Effects of Motor Vehicle Noise on Shapes and Arrangements of Buildings Along Urban Streets, III. Roadside Barriers," unpublished paper, Department of Physics, University of California, Los Angeles.

Pond, M. Allen, "Environmental Health and the Aging Population," *American Journal of Public Health,* 40 (January 1950): 27–33.

Prestemen, D. R., "How Much Does Noise Bother Apartment Dwellers?" *Architectural Record,* 143 (February 1968): 155–156.

Rankin, Robert E., "Air Pollution Control and Public Apathy," *Journal of Air Pollution Control,* 19 (August 1969): 565–569.

Rapoport, R., "Los Angeles Has a Cough," *Esquire,* 74 (July 1970): 83–85.

Rydell, C. Peter, and Gretchen Schwarz, "Air Pollution and Urban Form: A Review of Current Literature," *Journal of the American Institute of Planners,* 34 (March 1968): 115–120.

Schusky, J., L. Golner, S. Z. Mann, and W. C. Loring, "Methodology for the Study of Public Attitudes Concerning Air Pollution," *Journal of Air Pollution Control,* 14 (November 1964): 445–448.

Schusky, Jane, "Public Awareness and Concern with Air Pollution in the St. Louis

Metropolitan Area," *Journal of Air Pollution Control,* 16 (February 1966): 72–76.

Sprague, Homer A., and Ruth Hagstrom, "The Nashville Air Pollution Study: Mortality Multiple Regression," *Archives of Environmental Health,* 18 (April 1969): 503–507.

Teller, Azriel, "Air Pollution Abatement: Economic Rationality and Reality," *Daedalus,* 96 (Fall 1967): 1082–1098.

Van Arsdol, Maurice D., Jr., Georges Sabagh and Francesca Alexander, "Reality and the Perceptions of Environmental Hazards," *Journal of Health and Human Behavior,* 4 (Winter 1964): 144–153.

Zeidburg, Louis D., Robert J. M. Horton, and Emanuel Landau, "The Nashville Air Pollution Study: V. Mortality from Diseases of the Respiratory System in Relation to Air Pollution," *Archives of Environmental Health,* 15 (August 1967): 214–224.

Zeidburg, Louis D., Richard A. Prindle, and Emanuel Landau, "The Nashville Air Pollution Study: I. Sulfur-Dioxide and Bronchial Asthma. A Preliminary Report," *American Review of Respiratory Diseases,* 84 (October 1961): 489–503.

BIBLIOGRAPHY: Books

Borsky, P. N., "The Use of Social Surveys for Measuring Community Responses to Nose Environments," in J. D. Chalupnik (ed.), *Transportation Noises: A Symposium on Acceptability Criteria,* Seattle: University of Washington Press, 1970, pp. 219–227.

Carr, Donald E., *The Breath of Life,* New York: W. W. Norton and Company, 1965.

Esposito, John C., *Vanishing Air,* New York: Grossman, 1970.

Environmental Quality, The First Annual Report of the Council on Environmental Quality, Washington, D.C.: U.S. Government Printing Office, August 1970.

Goldsmith, J. R., "Effects of Air Pollution on Human Health," in Arthur C. Stern (ed.), *Air Pollution,* 2nd ed., New York: Academic Press, 1968, pp. 547–615.

Hawley, Amos H., *Urban Society,* New York: Ronald Press, 1971.

Kates, Robert W., "The Perception of Storm Hazard on the Shores of Megalopolis," in David Lowenthal (ed.), *Environmental Perception and Behavior,* Chicago: Department of Geography Research Paper No. 109, University of Chicago, 1967, pp. 60–74.

Landau, Norman J., and Paul D. Rheingold, *The Environmental Law Handbook,* New York: Ballantine Book (Friends of the Earth), 1971.

Lewis, Howard R., *With Every Breath You Take,* New York: Crown Publishers, 1965.

Loveridge, Ronald O., "The Environment: New Priorities and Old Politics," in Harlan Hahn (ed.), *People and Politics in Urban Society,* Urban Affairs and Annual Reviews. Beverly Hills, Calif.: Sage Publications, 1972.

McClure, Paul T., *Some Projected Effects of Jet Noise on Residential Property near Los Angeles International Airport by 1970,* Santa Monica, Calif.: Rand Corporation Report P-4083, April 1969.

McEvoy, James, and Sharon Williams, *Visual Pollution in the Lake Tahoe Basin,* Davis, Calif.: Tahoe Research Group, University of California, 1970.

Miller, James D., *Effects of Noise on People,* Washington, D.C.: U.S. Environmental Protection Agency, 1971.

Mills, Clarence A., *Air Pollution and Community Health,* Boston: Christopher Publishing House, 1954.

Molotch, Harvey, "Pollution as a Social Problem," in Jack D. Douglas (ed.), *Social Problems,* New York: Random House, forthcoming.

Revelle, Roger, "Pollution and Cities," in James Q. Wilson (ed.), *Metroplitan Enigma,* Cambridge, Mass.: Harvard University Press, 1968, pp. 107–120.

Ridker, Ronald G., *Economic Costs of Air Pollution,* New York: Praeger Press, 1967.

Roueche, Berton, *Eleven Blue Men,* Boston: Little, Brown and Company, 1953.

Saltonsall, Richard, Jr., *Your Environment and What You Can Do About It,* New York: Walker and Company, 1970.

Watson, Goodwin B., *Social Psychology — Issues and Insights,* New York: J. B. Lippincott Company, 1966.

Weisbord, Burton, *Economics of Public Health,* College Park, Pa.: University of Pennsylvania Press, 1961.

Widener, Don, *Timetable for Disaster,* Los Angeles: Nash Publishing, 1970.

CHAPTER 20
GOVERNMENT AND SERVICES

INTRODUCTION

Originally in the United States, counties, municipalities, and townships[1] were the governmental jurisdictions first set up to form the local governmental system. Later, school districts also became prominent. Counties and municipalities, of course, served to aid the state government in carrying out some of its obligations in the legal system, conducting elections, and in providing services. Generally, states were divided into counties to facilitate such activities at the local level. Municipalities were organized to supply local services in more densely populated places. While counties covered the entire population, municipalities were concerned primarily with residents in urban areas and included only a small portion of the state. School districts originated "because of the strong conviction that public education was of such importance to the society as to warrant its own local financing and its freedom from the politics of other local governments" (Bollens and Schmandt, 1975: 48). Thus while counties and municipalities were primarily administrative units, school districts came into being to serve a particular purpose.

Nonschool special districts came into being to meet needs that were not being met by traditional forms of government. Other than schools, these special districts primarily are a twentieth-century development, especially since the end of World War I. Many early municipalities that were geograhically distinct units have been joined together through expanding populations and interstitial areas filling in with population. Municipalities have partially incorporated this population into the city by annexing territory and population adjacent to their old boundaries, although this is less prominent now than formerly. Municipality boundaries, therefore, have tended to expand over time as urban population growth has occurred. Similarly, many states subdivided counties into more units as population increased.

---

[1] Generally, townships in the New England states combine some of the elements of both counties and municipalities and in some instances these townships included the school district.

There has been a proliferation of the many special districts, especially school districts and others, to meet the needs of the expanding urban and suburban population. As population grew in and around urban centers, the increasing number of municipalities, school districts, special districts, and unincorporated areas all increased the complexity of metropolitan area government. Currently, there is little resemblance to the original state, county, and township or municipal government approach of the early days. Many laws made it more easy to incorporate places than to annex area and population to already established cities. Thus the legal code had great impact upon current metropolitan governmental structure. Also, it should be noted that many people in current urban complexes live outside of municipalities; they live in a distinctly urbanized metropolitan area but in unincorporated territory.

After World War II the annexation process once again began in earnest, although more recently it has fallen into disfavor. In recent times the number of counties in most states has remained virtually the same. In some places county governments contract out services to smaller municipalities. There have been a few consolidations of cities. The development of metropolitan government that has appeared in Nashville and Miami-Dade County, Florida, may be indications of the future. Similarly, substantial unification has taken place in school districts, with former elementary-school districts merging with each other, as have some junior-high and high-school districts. In some places all these levels of schools have been unified, and in a few places the unified school districts include the junior-college level.

Special districts have proliferated in urban regions, and there appears to be no abatement in this process. While many of these special districts cover only a small portion of the urban complex, others cover the entire metropolitan area, and, in some instances extend beyond it — mass transit districts, airport or harbor districts. These larger special districts have some elements of metropolitan-wide government and again may be indicative of the future as more and more consolidation and unification take place.

MULTIPLE LOCAL GOVERNMENTS

In most metropolitan regions there is a complexity of governmental jurisdictions. As Table 20-1 illustrates, in 1972 there were a total 22,185 local governments in the 264 SMSAs of the United States. This means that the average number of local governments was 86.4 per metropolitan area. These are major independent units such as cities, school districts, special districts, and so on, and these do not include the various smaller agencies, departments, and other units of each of these larger individual governmental units. Each of these local governments has

> its own corporate powers such as the right to sue and to be sued and to acquire and dispose of property, its own officials, and its own service delivery system, and its own ability to raise revenue through taxation or charges. Each thus wears the potent mantle of

TABLE 20-1
SMSAs by Total and Average Number of Local Governments, 1972

SMSA SIZE GROUP (1970 POPULATION)	NUMBER OF SMSAs	NUMBER OF LOCAL GOVERNMENTS	AVERAGE NUMBER OF LOCAL GOVERNMENTS
All SMSAs	264	22,815	86.4
1,000,000 or more	33	8,847	268.1
500,000–1,000,000	36	3,307	100.2
300,000–500,000	51	3,213	89.3
200,000–300,000	84	2,784	54.6
100,000–200,000	27	3,505	41.7
50,000–100,000	33	529	19.6

Source: Census of Governments: 1972, Vol. 1, *Governmental Organization*, Washington, D.C.: U.S. Bureau of the Census, 1973.

public authority, which embraces financial extraction from the citizenry and the means of affecting people's lives beneficially or detrimentally. Since each is a separate unit and legally independent, it may (and sometimes does) act unilaterally and without concern for the needs and wishes of or the effect on residents in neighboring localities [Bollens and Schmandt, 1975: 42].

There is some regional variation in the number of local governments, with the South generally having fewer jurisdictions than metropolitan regions in the Northeast and North Central regions. Similarly, it appears that "the greater the population of the area, the more local units are likely to be found" (Bollens and Schmandt, 1975: 43). Generally, the larger urban complexes have a greater number of local governments, with the largest metropolitan areas having the most governmental jurisdictions. There is some variation within metropolitan size ranges, with some larger places, such as Baltimore, having fewer jurisdictions than other cities its size. On the other hand, Portland, Oregon, and Madison, Wisconsin, have many more local governmental jurisdictions than do other cities and metropolitan complexes of their size.

Special districts and municipalities make up more than 60 percent of local governmental units within metropolitan regions. School districts make up a substantial portion — about one in every five units. Many incorporated places in urban regions are relatively small, with populations under 2500. Some have populations less than 1000, and many of them are small in overall land size.

OVERLAPPING LOCAL
GOVERNMENTAL JURISDICTIONS

While many local governmental jurisdictions in urban regions cover separate geographic areas, many also have overlapping geographical boundaries. The most obvious ones occur in school districts and special districts. Thus there may be several elementary-school districts that send children to a junior-high-school district that overlaps several of the elementary schools, while several junior-high-school districts may be overlapped by one or several high-school districts. Cutting across all of these school boundaries may be a junior-college district that encompasses all of them plus many elementary-, junior-high-, and high-school districts. Overlapping all of these school boundaries will be city boundaries, unincorporated areas, special-district boundaries — perhaps sewage, fire, or disposal districts, with perhaps a regional airport or port commission thrown in, not to mention the county government.

SERVICES

One of the major distinctions made in meeting the service needs of city and urban residents is the extent to which the service should be a local or an areawide function. Currently, there is no satisfactory mechanism whereby services are allocated on a local or an areawide basis. This, of course, suggests that the allocation of services is not based upon a systematic approach to their delivery, but rather more on the basis of historical precedent in any given city or metropolitan area. An Advisory Commission on Intergovernmental Relations (*Performance*, 1963) suggested that air pollution control and water supply and sewage disposal (among others) should be areawide services, whereas fire protection and public education should be more locally administered functions. In between these, for example, were parks and recreation and public welfare, which presumably could be administered either locally, areawide, or in some other manner. In any case, the commission attempted to show how the delivery of important urban services could be optimized by utilizing different levels of governmental administration — for instance, local versus areawide levels.

A very real problem in developing an optimal distribution of services within the metropolitan complex is the resistance of local governments and their adherents to developing areawide services units. Generally, this reluctance is based on the fear that areawide jurisdiction will leave the local unit little voice in the delivery of such services. In addition, some persons are unwilling to lose the power they have over the administrative unit.

Water Supply

''Urban areas require water for a variety of purposes including human consumption, waste disposal, manufacturing and recreation'' (Bollens and Schmandt, 1975: 146). The need for water in urban areas has increased as a result of population growth, improved living conditions, and the needs of industry. There are regional differences in water: Quantities are ample in some places, but water is of poor quality; other metropolitan areas, though, have a water deficit, but the water they do have is of adequate quality. Thus while the United States as a whole has adequate water resources, distributing of high-quality water to places where it is needed remains a crucial problem.

These water towers illustrate an old solution to the problem of providing urban areas with adequate water supply.

Currently, providing water in metropolitan areas is an extremely diversified function involving multiple tiers of government and in some instances private agencies. Municipal ownership is dominant in some metropolitan regions such as Minneapolis-St. Paul, while special districts or contractual relations between a larger city and its smaller suburban places also exist. Over 1000 special water districts serve a variet of communities in the metropolitan complex. The Metropolitan Water District of Southern California, the largest of these districts, services multiple SMSAs in Southern California cutting across a number of county lines from the Colorado River bordering on Arizona and flowing into Mexico. This district brings water from central and northern California through viaducts over 500 miles long to serve this multiple metropolitan complex area with its huge population. The complexity of this water district is shown by its implications for interstate relations (e.g., California and Arizona) and international relations (e.g., United States and Mexico). Similarly, the relationship between Chicago, bordering states, and Canada shows how complicated the supply of water can become in contemporary urban complexes.

Sewage Disposal

At least 50 million people in the United States are drinking water that does not meet public health standards (U.S., 1967: 13). Much of this water does not meet minimum standards because of improper sewage disposal that

In addition to sewers, the collection and disposal of garbage is a major undertaking in all cities in the United States. Burning dumps in many areas have been replaced by huge landfills which are rapidly exhausting their potential for holding refuse.

contaminates what otherwise might be safe water. Legislation concerning sewage disposal came after World War II and in 1956; however, it was not until 1972 that amendments to earlier legislation allowed some of the basic problems to be attacked. Among these were the ability to regulate discharges at the points where they occur. Thus feedlots, industry, and municipal treatment plants all had to obtain permits that in effect controlled the constituents of effluents and a schedule for achieving compliance with the new, stiffer regulations.

A variety of mechanisms currently is used in sewage disposal administration. A majority of cities have joint operations that include both collection and treatment facilities. Contractual agreements between larger cities and their suburbs are rather common, although some metropolitan areas still have a large number of smaller, inefficient districts. A few metropolitan areas have split the responsibility between local units and a regional agency. To date, no metropolitan region has been able to integrate all of its units into one system (Bollens and Schmandt, 1975: 150–151). Finally, evolving in the field of sewage disposal is a municipal handling of the construction and operation of local sewage-collection facilities, with the metropolitan level furnishing the major interceptor sewers and treatment plants and with the state and national governments establishing the policy framework, especially in regard to minimum water purity standards, and providing financial assistance.

The newest of the mass transit systems in the United States is located in San Francisco and Oakland—the Bay Area Rapid Transit (BART). The private automobile dominates most urban transportation largely because only a half dozen American cities have ever developed efficient mass transit.

Transportation

There can be no denial that the automobile is extremely popular with Americans in general. Since its inception around 1900, the automobile has resulted in a remaking of the shape of urban landscape. As the population became able to purchase automobiles, they did so in large numbers. As the number of automobiles increased, so did the number of roadways, parking lots, freeways, and drive-in theaters, banks, eating places, motels, and so on. Thus the United States is now an automobile-oriented society. With the increase in the number of automobiles and automobile-related activities and services, mass transit, except in a very few cities, declined markedly. As an example, Figure 4-4 showed the Pacific Electric Railway in the Los Angeles metropolitan area just prior to its decline. If the map was overlaid by another map of the freeway network in the Los Angeles basin, they would correlate almost perfectly; in fact, some of the freeways are built over the old railway bed.

With the exception of perhaps Boston, Chicago, Cleveland, New York, Philadelphia, and the San Francisco-Oakland metropolitan areas, no other city in the United States has anywhere near an adequate mass transit system. Yet even today most transportation money in these cities as well as virtually all others continues to be poured into roadways and associated services rather than into the development of a balanced metropolitan transit system. As shown in Chapter 9, few people in the United States travel to work by mass transit; similarly, few people use it to go into the central city for shopping and other activities. This is at least partially because the mass transit does not exist; where some semblance of mass transit does exist, the facilities may be outdated, with uncertain schedules, and old equipment, and the use of such mass transit is restricted to those who have no other option.

Recently, the responsibility for transportation in the United States has been increasingly transferred from local levels to more areawide levels, and in some instances, to the federal level; an example is development of the Interstate Highway System. Many metropolitan region transportation commissions and authorities are now in operation, with the likelihood of more being created in the near future. Some of the regional authorities have little power, and most do not have the power to raise funds other than through fares or contributions from local governmental units. Some funds are available from the federal level, but they are minimal and are generally available only for ''demonstration'' projects. As such, then, they do not meet the basic problem and needs of the metropolitan regions involved.

Other recent trends involve the development of specialized transportation modes for specific categories of people. These include mini-busses to take people around downtown areas, such as in Washington, D.C., and Los Angeles; dial-a-bus for shopping, visiting hospitals, doctors, and so on; meditrans, which has specific routes to carry people to various medical facilities; corporations, colleges, and universities that organize their own satellite transportation modalities to get people to work and/or to downtown, and so on. Perhaps one of the most important developments in transportation is the recent federal legislation that *allows* up to $800 million of the some $5 billion annually collected from federal gasoline taxes to be used in the development of mass transit. It should be noted that this law only allows this expenditure for three consecutive years. Since the law does not mandate the expenditures and has a limited time span, it will be interesting to see whether the strong automobile lobbyists will be able to halt the expenditures and extension of this bill.

Finally, it should be noted that it is increasingly becoming recognized that transportation is an areawide function. This does not necessarily mean that all transportation-related activities must come under the jurisdiction of an areawide commission or authority. It does imply, however, that local streets and highways need to be articulated into the mass transit system. Only such a broad-gauged approach to the metropolitan transportation network can successfully meet the transportation needs of people living in the metropolis. Regional planning is one mechanism that possibly might overcome some of the difficulties in transportation in the metropolis. Funds, of course, would help. Ultimately, however, the transportation networks within most urban complexes will remain as problems until it is recognized that an efficient, well-balanced transportation system is of benefit to all metropolitan residents and, as such, any given modality cannot provide all of the necessary transportation. This may mean too that some elements in the system may not be able to, on the face of it, pay their own way and must be subsidized.

Police and Law Enforcement

Crime in the United States over the past decade has been rising at a faster rate than the population. This may be partially a result of better reporting procedures and more willingness by citizens to report crimes; however, after

Traffic control and monitoring is a major task of most police departments in the United States. Here a young woman keeps traffic moving in Lucerne, Switzerland. Americans have only recently begun to realize the potential of police personnel specialized for noncrime functions.

discounting these factors, crime apparently still has risen faster than the population has increased. Thus it is no surprise that many people in this country express fear about crime and report it as one of the major problems facing our society.

In the United States the protection of people and their property is a highly complex and specialized undertaking. Police departments are a 24-hour service agency and have responsibility for maintaining law and order in all parts of their political jurisdiction. Yet it is obvious that law enforcement officers are differentially perceived in different parts of the metropolis. In minority neighborhoods, police officers are typically viewed as an "occupation force," while in at least some other neighborhoods they are viewed as "protectors."

Most often police are viewed as being concerned with maintaining law and order and initiating action — for example investigation and arrest — against lawbreakers. On the other hand, they also spend as much if not more time in other activities, including traffic control, providing information, resolving marital and other kinds of interpersonal conflicts, and participating in a variety of other kinds of noncriminal-related activities. Yet most police officers have been trained only in traditional law enforcement procedures and these other activities that actually may take up more than one-half of their time have been entirely neglected in training programs.

Some police departments have become aware of this past neglect and have attempted to compensate for it (for an example see Butler and Cummins,

Community services, such as dealing with a lost child, may take more than half the day of a police officer's time. The "cops and robbers" image of all police work is slowly being replaced by more realistic appreciations.

1967). Nevertheless, many of the programs that on the surface appear to be "community services" programs end up being public relations programs. The latter as such probably will fail to convince skeptical citizens of the serious intent of police departments. More likely to be successful are programs that emphasize that the police are public servants and that they do in fact spend substantial parts of their everyday working hours on what should be broadly conceived of as community services rather than on law enforcement.

Most police departments in the United States are localized units; there are few special police districts. As with fire protection, police departments are highly variegated in size, competence, and the extent of volunteerism. Some law enforcement is carried out on a contractual basis, with a larger central city or county contracting out service to a smaller political jurisdiction. The variability in police departments is much more serious than that in fire fighting, since law violaters may quickly travel from one jurisdiction to another. Thus communication among police units is necessary, and records must be kept in such a manner that they can be quickly sent from one jurisdiction to another. "Inadequate law enforcement in one community can have important social costs for the remainder of the area" (Bollens and Schmandt, 1975: 160). As a result, there have been some changes in police work over the past few years. These changes have partially resulted from federal legislation that encouraged, by monetary rewards, more elaborate planning on a statewide basis, centralization of communications, improved records, laboratory facilities, training standards, and so on.

A problem of our society, of course, is how to have adequate law enforcement without losing our freedoms. This is not an easy issue to come to grips with, and no obvious panaceas now exist to resolve the dilemma.

Fire Fighting and Fire Prevention

The range of fire fighting and fire-prevention activities in cities and metropolitan areas apparently is highly varied. The range is from volunteer fire departments in smaller urban places to large-scale departments and highly specialized equipment in larger cities with tall office buildings, apartment houses, and varied kinds of industrial plants. Fire-prevention activities are seldom carried out in smaller places with volunteer fire departments, while in larger places it is extremely difficult to oversee all of the city in meeting fire-prevention codes.

Fire fighting is extremely hazardous, and the number of injuries and deaths among fire fighters is higher than for any other work. Fire protection is generally a highly localized activity. That is, the local fire protection district is not likely to extend beyond the town or city limits. This is partially a result of the local nature of most fires; fires seldom go beyond a single political jurisdiction and there are few special fire-fighting districts. In some places a smaller city may contract with a larger unit, such as the central city or county, for fire-fighting services, but these services are located locally in the contracting place rather than in the larger political jurisdiction. In the future, it is highly likely that fire fighting and prevention will remain highly localized activities with a wide range of effectiveness.

Social Services

Social services tend to be carried out at the county or state level, with substantial federal legislation and funding influencing their administration.

Fire fighting is a dangerous profession that requires elaborate equipment in larger metropolitan centers. The higher the buildings, the more sophisticated—and expensive—does fire-fighting become.

There is an apparent lack of coordination, gaps in services, and evaluation of services. For example, a city may have multiple private and public agencies dealing with family planning. Yet each agency may not be aware of the others and their services, the extent to which there is overlapping clientele, and gaps in meeting needs. Similarly, no place in the United States has adequate knowledge of the incidence or prevalence of drug abuse, the extent that the need for services is being met, or how effective existing programs are in meeting service needs and solving problems. These two examples can be duplicated with every kind of social service in virtually every city and urban place in the United States. This is true despite the fact that millions of dollars are spent each year on such services.

A CONCLUDING NOTE

Perhaps the most often proposed solution to urban problems has been the unification or consolidation of local governments into one jurisdiction. Friesema (1968) has made explicit at least four assumptions made by those in favor of consolidation (Greer, 1962; Sofen, 1963). These assumptions are as follows:

1. Local intergovernmental relations among the jurisdictions within metropolitan areas are ad hoc and sporadic.
2. While other sectors of the metropolitan community are becoming increasingly interdependent, the political integration of the metropolitan area is standing still.

3. Political integration is considered as a synonym for formal unification. It is a state to be achieved rather than a continuing process.
4. Special districts, service agreements, and other contractual arrangements for solving individual metropolitan area problems are not satisfactory solutions to the many problems of our metropolitan areas, at least in comparison to complete governmental unification.

Friesema evaluated each of these assumptions and argued that to date there is scant evidence to show that unification will solve the problems facing cities and urban places. While one may agree or disagree with his conclusions, his analysis is especially useful because he made explicit the *implicit* assumptions of a proposed solution to major urban problems. In addition, he critically examined these assumptions. The guidelines he has set up will probably be the first necessary steps for solving urban problems—if they are to be solved.

Finally, not one single city, urban complex, or metropolitan region in the United States has identified the extent of social service needs, what local unit has responsibility in meeting these needs, how much overlap there is in various public and private jurisdictions in meeting these needs, what services and needs are being adequately or inadequately met, how effective the delivered services are, and whether they can be more effectively delivered at a local, neighborhood, city-wide, urban-area, metropolitan complex, or wider regional basis. While this is a sad commentary upon the current state of affairs, there is little prospect that there will be major changes over the next few decades.

BIBLIOGRAPHY: Books

Bollens, John C., and Henry J. Schmandt, *The Metropolis: Its People, Politics, and Economic Life,* 3rd ed., New York: Harper & Row Publishers, 1975.
Butler, Edgar W., and Marvin Cummins, *Community Services Unit: First Report and Preliminary Evaluation,* Winston-Salem: Winston-Salem Police Department, July 1967.
Census of Governments: 1972, Vol. 1, *Governmental Organization,* Washington, D.C.: U.S. Bureau of the Census, 1973.
Friesema, H. Paul, "The Metropolis and the Maze of Local Governments," in Scott Greer, Dennis McElrath, David W. Minar, and Peter Orleans (eds.), *The New Urbanization,* New York: St. Martin's Press, 1968, pp. 339–354.
Greer, Scott, *Governing the Metropolis,* New York: John Wiley and Sons, 1962.
Performance of Urban Functions: Local and Areawide, Washington, D.C.: Advisory Commission on Intergovernmental Relations, 1963.
Sofen, Edward, *The Miami Metropolitan Experiment,* Bloomington, Ind.: Indiana University Press, 1963.
U.S. Department of Health, Education, and Welfare, Task Force on Environmental Health and Related Problems, *A Strategy for a Livable Environment,* Washington, D.C.: Government Printing Office, 1967.

PLANNING AND THE FUTURE

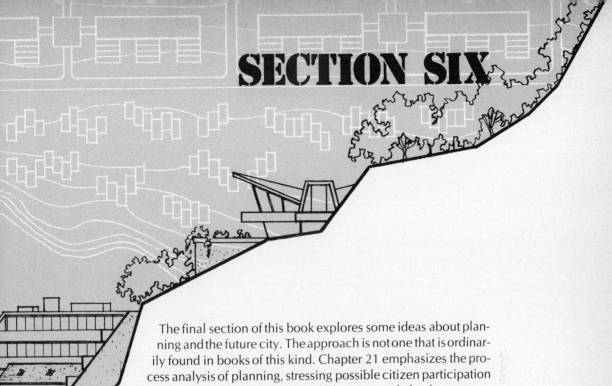

SECTION SIX

The final section of this book explores some ideas about planning and the future city. The approach is not one that is ordinarily found in books of this kind. Chapter 21 emphasizes the process analysis of planning, stressing possible citizen participation and input to help establish general planning goals for the community and neighborhood and delineating specific doable objectives within delineated time frames. Also, some of the assumptions of the planning process that are involved when it concerns *active* citizen participation are made explicit. The approach thus is somewhat removed from traditional perspectives or principles available in standard city planning and urban sociology textbooks.

Chapter 22, on the future, also is somewhat different from what one might expect. This is because the focus is more upon some *possible viable alternatives* rather than on "pie-in-the-sky" or utopian approaches so often described in the literature. While certainly utopian perspectives on future cities and urban places have their place, it also is necessary to inject a note of realism into evaluating what the urban future will be like so that we have some idea of the possible kind of urban environment we may be facing in the future.

CHAPTER 21
URBAN PLANNING

INTRODUCTION

Historically, evidence of planned cities exists as far back as Babylon. Similarly, early Greek cities had regular patterns, suggesting that they too were planned. Roman cities and towns were systematically built into rectangular blocks planned by military engineers. Planning appeared not to change much from the Greek and Roman period up to the building of Versailles. The gardens, palaces, and the city of Versailles were considered as one unit by the group of architects that designed it. Several hundred years later, Napoleon III had substantial portions of the Paris slums replaced by broad avenues, long sweeping boulevards, plazas, and vistas of the city. Much like other slum clearance projects of today, of course, this perhaps first, large-scale slum clearance did not rebuild all of Paris, and vast sections remained as they were previously. Another notable achievement of this era was the plan by Christopher Wren for rebuilding London after the fire of 1666.[1]

In colonial United States[2] new towns were being built. Some of them had no plan, whereas others, such as Savannah, Georgia, followed a rectangular-block grid pattern, with some plazas or open areas, much like early Greek and Roman cities. On the other hand, originally Washington, D.C., was to have followed the gridiron plan, but L'Enfant was hired to revise Jefferson's proposed grid plan. He did so by including sweeping diagonal avenues cutting across the grid and placing monuments and important buildings at major intersections. While one result of this plan was the facilitation of traffic in and out of the city, it also created confusion for those who remained in the city because of the crosscutting diagonals overlaid on the grid system. Similarly, many triangular lots and unusual intersections exist because of this plan. Nevertheless, many

---

[1] For illustrations of city form throughout these historical eras, see Bacon (1967) or Morris (1972).

[2] For an extended historical review of city planning in the United States since 1890, see Scott (1969).

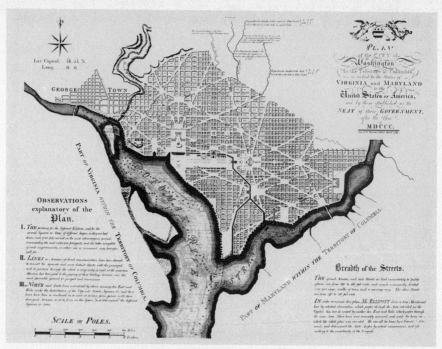

This engraving of Pierre L'Enfant's plan was made by Andrew Elliot in 1792. It was the final plan adopted by Congress for the federal city of Washington, D.C.

credit L'Enfant's plan for the development of what has been called the "city beautiful" movement that dominated planning in the United States up until World War I.

Subsequent city planning in the United States has emphasized "the master plan," which sets forth the goals of a particular city over the next 10 years or so. Earlier, these plans typically developed under the direction of a semi-independent planning commission. But gradually this function was taken over by professional planners under the direction of the chief executive of the city—either a mayor or city manager. A typical master plan contains extensive statements and illustrations about land use and zoning, where open space and parks are or should be located, and generally presents the requirements for future development and alteration for every neighborhood in the city. The master plan invariably contains statements and maps illustrating where what kinds of housing may be built, for example, single-family or multiple-family units, how much land space must be set aside for each living unit, specifies where commercial, industrial, and other land uses may or may not be allowed, establishes building codes that must be adhered to in new construction and in rebuilding, and generally has substantial implications for future slum clearance and/or rehabilitation of neighborhoods. Overall, there are direct statements about the

This view of Lake Ann in Reston, Virginia, is typical of a development with a recreational focal point and with commercial activity relegated to the periphery of the community.

transportation network as well. But even when these are not included in the master plan, it nevertheless has implications for the transportation networks in the city by virtue of its specifying zoning, street location, size, and composition.

More recent developments in city planning have centered on the development of "garden cities." They have a central business and civic center surrounded by residential areas, with industry located at the periphery—all of which is surrounded by a greenbelt to delineate and separate the city from other cities, rural areas, and so forth. Somewhat related to the concept of garden cities has been the development of garden suburbs: Homes face the garden, and a recreational area is located in the center and is surrounded by homes. Streets are at the periphery so that no automobile traffic is allowed around homes or in the centralized recreational area (see Morris, 1972: 53 for similar developments in the Roman Empire).

CONTEMPORARY URBAN PLANNING

"The planning of cities is regarded variously as an ivory-tower vision, a practical and necessary program for development, or an undesirable interference with the citizen's freedom to do as he wishes with his own property" (Thomlinson, 1969: 201). While there is a variety of definitions of planning, at its simplest level it is a thoughtful consideration of purposes and means to future changes. All planning involves *value* judgments. Thus the political nature of planning must be recognized, and the question of what values and whose values planners will seek to implement becomes crucial for residents of the local community and the metropolitan region.

Evolving criticism of planning by some does not question whether or not it is necessary but questions instead the orientations of some planners. "The concepts and methods of civil engineering and city planning suited to the design of unitary physical facilities cannot be used to serve the design of social change in a pluralistic and mobile society" (Webber, 1968: 1093). Similarly,

> Our greatest potential, however, lies in our cities, which are collapsing not only because the people who live in them have lost faith in their future but also because the cities no longer evidence the realities of these times. Almost all of our cities were created to serve the production and transportation needs of the now vanishing industrial age. Indeed, our planning continues to be based on the assumption that the functions of production and transportation are still the most important ones for a city to fulfill [Theobald, 1968: 137].

Types of Planning Agencies

There are three major types of planning agency organizations: (1) the semi-independent planning commission, (2) the executive staff agency, and (3) the legislative staff agency (Ranney, 1969: 49). First, planning was done in semi-independent agencies — planning commissions. The main reason for them was to remove planning from the sphere of politics. In most cities a planning commission or agency still exists. In some cities the planning commission hires professional planners who work for it. Thus the power of planning decisions resided with the commission. Many cities continue to have such commissions, but they have become "advisory" rather than decision-making bodies. The main reason why the planning commission approach fell into disfavor is because many felt that it had too many weaknesses to make effective plans and to carry them out. Another reason advanced for the failure of the planning commission approach was that while "respected citizens" had expertise in certain areas of endeavor, they did not know how to develop city plans. Proponents of the professional staff agency argue that only professionals know how to develop master plans and how to implement them. In order to implement plans, so the argument goes, planners should be located in the executive branches of local governments so that plans can be integrated with the rest of governmental functions. Further, along with the change in orientation from semi-independent to staff agencies, the appointment of full-time planning directors has passed from the planning commission to the city manager or mayor (Ranney, 1969: 59).

Orientations of Planners

Planning has been carried out from various points of view. From a primarily physical point of view, planning results in blueprints or designs for fu-

A substantial amount of planning time and taxpayers' dollars go into attempts at re-vitalizing deteriorated and dilapidated downtowns. This urban shopping mall is located in the "model city" of Poughkeepsie, New York. Unfortunately, except under unusual circumstances, these attempts have failed.

ture development and master and general plans, and it recommends courses of action for the achievement of them in the future. Some have called this *deductive planning* (Petersen, 1966).

Most planners in staff agencies are single-purpose planners (Gilliam, 1967: 1142). They assume that whatever is planned—whether it be an industrial plant to produce goods, a highway to move traffic, or a nuclear plant to produce power—has effects only upon that element of the environment. However, they influence more than perhaps they intend: They influence all of the people and the total environment of the urban complex. Thus if a highway is to be built, broader concerns than moving traffic such as the disruption of neighborhoods, the displacement of homes, higher air pollution, the destruction of jobs, the scarring parks or scenic areas, and so on, also could be considered as important elements in planning. This latter perspective requires multipurpose planning. *Multipurpose planning* takes a broader view of the planning process and the requirements beyond the physical master plan or immediate construction of a highway, plant, or factory. Thus multipurpose planning expands the myopic world view of single-purpose planning and more realistically helps maintain the environment. Of necessity, it must draw upon natural, physical, and social scientists, as well as the public, to generate and carry out adequately such a multifaceted plan.

Planning in most cities still reflects a physical bias. However, a broader point of view has taken hold in some places. It includes the recognition that social process and behavior, economic factors (such as property values, employment opportunities, productivity, and transportation costs), the political and power structure systems, and the environment all influence planning. Thus *social* planning places more emphasis on these factors as well as recognizing the importance of evolving goals based upon local community and neighborhood value systems (Chapin, 1965). Hence in more recent planning there is an attempt to coordinate public policies in a variety of spheres. This approach has come to be known as *inductive* or social planning (Petersen, 1966).

Planning from the social perspective appears to include the following (Petersen, 1966):

1. It is more concerned with process rather than state, and it is concerned with moving from the present rather than only to some idealized future.
2. While the physical character of the city or region is important, it is only one element in a complex web of relationships in cities involving a complex relationship between social, economic, and political factors.
3. As a corollary of point 2, relevant skills needed by planners are varied as are the problems the planner must deal with; thus demography, economics, architecture, and the full range of the social sciences are necessary in planning.
4. Various points of view are necessary to realize a broad overall plan.
5. The choice of competing goals can be greatly facilitated by extending the principles of the market and of cost accounting to new uses. Costs to human welfare, social welfare benefits, and so on, must be considered in decision making in regard to the selection of planning goals.

Finally, *utopian planning* has been a focus of some work; most planners dismiss utopian perspectives as the "abandonment of reason" (Petersen, 1966). Nevertheless, what is considered utopian by one person may not be considered as such by another. In fact, probably many current activities in planning would, at a previous time, have been thought of as being utopian in nature.

Almost universally, planners desire to correct or avoid certain social and urban problems through organized, concerted, well-thought-out programs. Physical planners believe that the manipulation of the physical environment, along with provision of employment and recreation opportunities, will result in a lessening of urban social problems. Social planners and sociologists tend to stress the importance of the social milieu. They both emphasize employment, but other aspects attached to physical planning are still debated. In fact, physical design may only temporarily affect, or perhaps even hinder, social interaction. Social planners urge that residents be included in the planning process as a means of assuring that the latter's needs and desires are taken into consideration. Thus recent planning in some cities involves collaboration with people in the community, that is, planning *with* people rather than *for* them. Therefore, the planner becomes a counselor-participant in community life rather than an observer-recorder or a master planner (Goschalk and Mills, 1966).

THE PLANNING PROCESS[3]

Planning, as we saw earlier, is a conscious attempt to influence the future. It is generally a *creative* effort to overcome perceived problems rather than an immediate *reaction* to a crisis. As a creative, conscious effort to control future events, planning involves the following:

1. Controlling events and delineating viable options (maximizing future options/alternatives).
2. Minimizing future uncertainty.

It should be noted, however, that there are always unexpected or serendipitous results of planning decisions that must always be considered in evaluating or relying on a plan to solve the problems it is designed to solve. Several steps may be utilized to establish a useful plan. They include clearly knowing the *purposes* of the plan, having *goals* firmly stated, having specific measurable *objectives* for each goal delineated, generating needed *information,* and knowing how the plan can be *adopted* and *implemented.*

Purpose of the Plan

The purpose of the plan needs to be clearly stated: What is its function? Is it a master plan for a city or a neighborhood, a program, or what? Many plans evolve without ever having a clearly explicated purpose. Much like beginning a scientific research project, a plan will probably be more meaningful if its *purpose* is carefully considered and consistently carried out.

Goals of the Plan

Goals must be delineated: What are the general goals of the plan in terms of achievement, performance, or aspirations? (Fitch, 1967: 33). Ordinarily, the plan will be more meaningful if goals are *doable* and can at least be partially met within a specified time limit. "Initiation of many planning goals leads to untenable positions in terms of action" (Boyce, 1963: 250). Similarly, there appears little justification for accepting many goals of planners, since they may not have been tested in the real world.

Most current planning efforts—even though they are related to improvements in transportation, building construction, and so on—are designed

---

[3] Much of this section is a revision of material presented in Armstrong and Butler (1974).

more to restrict change than to facilitate it. As a result, city and urban planning may be too important to be left exclusively to the planners. With their too often restricted world view, they are handicapping the development of the urban complex and hindering the application of new technology and the points of view of the citizens. Thus the goals of the plan are of extreme importance, since they reflect the value system and orientation that will be set forth and possibly implemented in the future.

Objectives of the Plan

For each goal specific objectives must be clearly stated. They should be expressed in measurable terms and set within specified time limits. Objectives then become the mechanism whereby goals are met and the functions of the plan are fulfilled. Stating specific measurable objectives in a time frame allows a test of whether or not the goals of the plan are being met and also a guide to what priorities must be set.

Information Collecting

Invariably, the planning process as outlined so far requires the generation of information. At the minimum, the following are needed:

1. Research plan preparation; formation of committees to determine data and/or surveys needed in land use, employment, education, transportation (public and private), health, the physical, social, and economic environment, and so on.
2. Research (assessment of conditions by means of inventory, surveys, and compilation of existing data) on the physical environment, socioeconomic environment, public facilities, unique features, assistance programs, and so on.
3. Analysis: Review and consideration of findings.

Plan Adoption

Different mechanisms are necessary for plan adoption, depending upon the purposes, goals, and objectives of the plan. Obviously, the sponsoring agency or unit will influence the plan adoption process. But plan adoption does not necessarily mean that the plan will be implemented.

Plan Implementation

A plan, by virtue of its statements of goals and objectives, suggests that if in the future, specific actions, behavior, and so forth, are accomplished, certain events will be controlled through the exercise of viable options. That is, expectations of the future will be met. One major problem pointed out earlier is that there probably will be unanticipated factors at work that will mitigate these expectations. Indeed, occasionally there are instances when completely opposite results occur, so that the plan appears to have created more problems than it has solved.

Professional Planners

Professional planners have in the past emphasized the *physical environment*. They have typically assumed that their values represented those of the public and others for whom they were doing the planning. Similarly, they believed that their standards and objectives were also those desired and wanted by the general public, at least by vested interests. All these assumptions were made on the basis of limited evidence.

Citizen Participation

Citizen participation in the planning process involves different assumptions and values. First, it must be assumed that citizens can effectively make creative input into the planning process. Citizens do not usually come to the planning process with as many constraints in regard to what may or may not be a desirable plan. For example, citizen involvement almost invariably means a lessened emphasis on the physical environment and a primary focus on the *social* and *economic environment*.

One basic assumption of citizen involvement in the planning process is that primary attention must be given to the needs, desires, and goals of the people involved. In one such development of a plan the following assumptions were paramount (Armstrong and Butler, 1974: 24–26):

1. People have the right to participate in decisions that affect their well-being.
2. Participatory democracy is a useful method for conducting community affairs.
3. People have the right to strive to create the environment that they desire.
4. People have the right to reject an externally imposed environment.
5. Maximizing human interaction in a community will increase the potential for humane community development.
6. Effective community planning assists human beings in meeting and dealing with their environment.

A corollary of these assumptions is that if residents in a community have the right to participate in decisions that affect their well-being, then mechanisms must be prepared to facilitate this participation. Plans or programs drawn in the privacy of offices and subsequently taken to people in the community for acceptance cannot be considered a community plan. Citizen participation in the community planning process begins with people where they are, in the community. There are certain human needs—food, clothing, shelter, and so forth. How these needs are met is culturally defined; people may fulfill the same need in many different ways, none of which is absolutely right or wrong.

The concept of need has opened up a whole area for manipulation. The present rush toward planning is a good example. It has been determined that orderly growth is desirable in most cases. To achieve it planning is necessary. Citizens are informed — and generally agree — that they need planning so that they can live in an orderly society. To define citizens' needs and desires, free and open discussion and ample consideration of viable alternative goals and objectives is necessary so that questions can be asked about an issue before it is settled.

In a true community plan developed with citizen participation there may be a need for a facilitator whose major role is to motivate citizens to examine their total environment with a view to seeing how it might be enhanced or improved. The facilitator should encourage people to analyze their situation and to set goals and objectives that provide a basis for future planning and for changing the physical and social environment as need be. A predetermined program by a city, a county, or a regional commission, and so on, imposed upon community residents defeats the very purpose of citizen planning. Planners cannot assume that common geographic proximity always leads to the development of common interests. When citizens participate in a community plan, they tend to support what they have helped create and in the process may develop common interests in the community plan. The facilitator can help motivate citizens to define their own problems and to search for systematically and to discover courses of action that may be implemented; he or she can also help by focusing attention on long-range planning rather than the short-sighted *reaction* to immediate situations.

The process of community planning with citizen participation, in accordance with realistic community goals and objectives, requires a common understanding on the part of citizens and governmental agencies. One mechanism to assure the best possible recommendations for improvement is to form citizens' advisory committees representing all population elements of the community so that no group is excluded.

A citizens' advisory committee will, of necessity spend many hours in meetings, gathering material, making and evaluating recommendations, and carrying out the many phases of the research inventory and planning effort. When citizens of different backgrounds, interests, and cultures come together, they bring to the total a wealth of variety. The citizens then can begin to examine themselves and their community and determine their needs and desires. Although it may be very difficult to achieve a situation in which citizen participation in public decision making is free and open to all interested persons, effort can be made to involve those people most concerned or directly affected by decisions. The belief that broadened representation and increased breadth of perspective are conducive to community planning can have a major impact upon the outcome of the community plan and lead to even more extensive community involvement.

A discussion of what representation is and is not can be never ending. The one who can best represent an individual is that same individual. For many reasons it is obvious that community planning is not going to involve physically all of the residents of a community. It is, therefore, important that mechanisms be instituted so that no viewpoint be excluded from the community planning process. One mechanism facilitating citizen participation is to hold community workshops in the local area. These workshops can help determine the main problems facing residents of a community, develop suggestions for solving them, determine the adequacy of services and facilities in the community, outline needed services and current needs, and evaluate how residents view public officials and their concern about the community or local area. An important facet of such workshops is to ask elected officials, the mayor, officials in the city's council or assembly, agency personnel, and others living outside the community or local area to attend these workshops and answer the same questions as do community residents. Additional workshops might deal primarily with possible *solutions* to the problems elicited in the first workshop. Similarly, community surveys and workshops in schools and with local businesspeople may prove useful and enlightening.

Use of Data or Information

Various research reports, commission reports, especially reports compiled by city planning departments, and block group data from the U.S. census make possible both an analysis of the demographic composition of the community and also some evaluation of the extent or need for employment, education, welfare, and so on (see Chapter 2). Such data and factual information can serve only as a guide, since planning is both value-laden and normative. The combination of communal values held by the residents of a community should determine what kinds of information should be gathered. Additional available sources of data and information such as government data books, census materials, and so forth, are not generally known by citizens. A facilitator can serve an important function by supplying information about sources of data as well as giving instruction regarding the handling data and making it usable. Data and information can be distributed to citizens, thereby enhancing the quality of citizen decisions. Data and information can be inserted into ongoing decision-making processes in such a manner so as not to impair the process of search and discovery by citizens. If data are presented in such a manner that decisions are forced, discussions stifled, or alternatives overlooked, then the principles of citizen planning have been violated.

Role of Citizens' Advisory Committees

Sifting through substantial amounts of information is a major undertaking. A citizens' advisory committee can play an important role by continually keeping the community as a whole involved in the planning process and by assuring constant feedback to the community. After recommendations are made by the community and the committee, additional community workshops could be held in which each recommendation is explicated and evaluated. Following this process, many hours probably will be spent in developing recommendations, and it should be clear that some of them will evolve only after an extensive discussion, evaluation, and compromise. Also, in any planning process or the evolution of a plan, *values* — as indicated by what people believe to be true and good — clearly are inherent whether or not one considers planning necessary and in what goes into a plan if one is considered a necessity.

FUTURE PLANNING ISSUES

Future planning will involve many issues that some thought had been resolved in the past and other issues that are just now becoming topics of discussion. Among them are: (1) a continuation of the physical-versus-social-planning controversy; (2) optimum city size and density of areas within cities and urban regions; (3) whether cities should be compact or whether sprawl should be permitted to continue; (4) boundary integrity and maintenance, especially as they affect solutions to urban problems; (5) the extent to which citizen participation should be encouraged and facilitated; (6) a revival of the controversy over where planning agencies and staff should be located — for example, staff agencies under the city manager or mayor, semi-independent, or completely independent agencies; and (7) the acquisition of funds for planning and implementation.

Physical Versus Social Planning

The struggle between physical and social planners is just now in its infancy and can be expected to intensify over the next several decades. It should be recognized that if problems facing cities and urban regions are to be solved, it will be necessary for social planners to win this struggle.

Optimum City Size and Density

The discussion over optimum city size has been a continuing one since the days of early Greek philosophers. The solution is no closer to being found at the moment than it was then. City size and density both rely upon adherence to certain value systems and beliefs about what is good and true. As such, the optimum city size will depend upon other factors such as whether or not compact cities come into being, whether sprawl continues as it has in the recent past, developing transportation technologies, and so forth. Apparently, then, this is a controversy that is expected to continue well into the future.

Compactness Versus Sprawl

General arguments against urban sprawl center on the increased costs of serving a more scattered population versus the costs of serving a more compact population (Boyce, 1963: 245). While obviously the increased costs of sprawl is a deficit, it also has many advantages. Among them are more open space and lower population density, more commercial and industrial development in outlying areas made more accessible to more people, and more flexibility for future development possibilities (Boyce, 1963). A corollary of a com-

Part of the struggle between physical and social planning will be over the need for and location of nuclear power plants such as this one near Portland, Oregon. Such plants have already been the subject of vehement controversy.

pact city is high density. Currently, most people are opting for more privacy and places for children to play, which to date has meant that families, when given the opportunity, have selected relatively low-density suburban living as opposed to higher-density apartment living. However, given future city designs (see the next chapter) now in the developmental stages for compact cities, perhaps this antipathy of the general public for high-density living will be overcome.

Boundary Maintenance

As local boundaries within larger metropolitan and urban regions become more and more meaningless insofar as human activities are concerned, attempts to deal with urban problems on the basis of a restricted boundary probably will result in failure. Recognizing this currently, more and more plans are made on a *regional* basis. Regional planning has been made necessary by the development of large SMSAs in which it is difficult to determine when one is leaving one city and entering another one. Nevertheless, there has been substantial resistance to this notion, since many smaller jurisdictions are wary of losing control over the planning in their cities or communities.

Citizen Participation

Despite the legal requirements of many pieces of current legislation, citizen participation to date has been rather slight in planning activities. Many cities have a "pseudo-citizen participation" by forming committees or commissions and occasionally holding "public hearings"—generally during hours when the general population is at work and unable to attend. Thus, to date, citizen participation in planning endeavors has been minimal. This minimal par-

Most developments planned with the future in mind appear to stress compactness—as does "Habitat," built on Mackay Pier in Montreal for the world's fair in 1967.

ticipation may be a result of a lack of interest by the public, or it may be that the proper facilitating mechanisms have not been established for effective citizen participation. A discussion of the planning process in this chapter demonstrates one way of ensuring citizen participation (Armstrong and Butler, 1974). However, this process requires dedication to the point of view that citizen participation is desirable, useful, and productive even though it may require more effort. It is apparent that in many cities citizens are demanding and receiving the opportunity for input into the planning process. The pressure is expected to continue and to grow in the future.

Locus of Planning Agencies

Early planning agencies primarily were under the jurisdiction of the planning commission. However, as we pointed out earlier, subsequently planning activities became more and more incorporated into staff agencies under the direction of the city manager or mayor. City managers and mayors are reluctant to give up their planning departments. But in the future there will be increasing pressure to remove planning functions from the city executive's office to either a semi-independent agency or a completely independent one. In an effort to offset this removal many cities have been joining together in associations, at least partially concerned with planning functions. However, urban research shows that when effective, creative, innovative plans are successful, they do *not* originate among city officials but are the result of a coalition of individual citizens who band together to pressure city hall. It may be assumed that if creative and innovative planning is to be accomplished in the future, different mechanisms will have to be developed to remove the planning process from the staff agencies and the city executive's office. Otherwise, static master plans will continue to be generated — plans that will not help solve the crisis of our cities.

Funds for Planning and Implementation

Cities constantly plea for more money to meet their needs — planning and otherwise. Actually, ample funds are available in the United States for developing meaningful plans for and by citizens. However, it will be necessary to reorder priorities, to evaluate where current expenditures are fulfilling real needs, to examine every program to determine whether it is efficient *and* meeting real human needs, and to eliminate unneeded and ineffective services if these funds are to be reallocated. There is on the horizon a development of a perspective that will require government at all levels to demonstrate the basic *need* for the program, that it is meeting that need effectively, and that some desirable outcomes are being generated. This means that planning agencies will be required to demonstrate the need for planning, that the planning has accomplished its goals and objectives, and that it has led to desired outcomes — as evaluated by influential leaders, planners, or citizens, or some combination of these.

BIBLIOGRAPHY: Articles

Boyce, Ronald R., "Myth Versus Reality in Urban Planning," *Land Economics,* 39 (August 1963): 241–251.
Gilliam, Harold, "The Fallacy of Single-Purpose Planning," *Daedalus,* 96 (Summer 1967): 1142–1157.
Goschalk, David R., and William E. Mills, "A Collaborative Approach to Planning Through Urban Activities," *Journal of the American Institute of Planners,* 32 (March 1966): 86–95.
Petersen, William, "On Some Meanings of 'Planning,'" *Journal of the American Institute of Planners,* 32 (May 1966): 130–142.
Webber, Melvin M., "The Post-City Age," *Daedalus,* 97 (Fall 1968): 1091–1110.

BIBLIOGRAPHY: Books

Armstrong, DeVonne W., and Edgar W. Butler, *Eastside Community Plan,* Riverside, Calif.: City of Riverside, January 1974.
Bacon, Edmund N., *Design of Cities,* New York: The Viking Press, 1967.
Chapin, F. Stuart, Jr., *Urban Land Use Planning,* 2nd ed., Urbana, Ill.: University of Illinois Press, 1965.

Fitch, Lyle C., "Social Planning in the Urban Cosmos," in Leo F. Schnore and Henry Fagin (eds.), *Urban Research and Policy Planning,* Beverly Hills, Calif.: Sage Publications Inc., 1967, pp. 329–358.

Morris, A. E. J., *History of Urban Form,* New York: John Wiley and Sons, 1972.

Ranney, David C., *Planning and Politics in the Metropolis,* Columbus, Ohio: Charles E. Merrill Publishing Company, 1969.

Scott, Mel, *American City Planning: Since 1890,* Berkeley and Los Angeles: University of Californis Press, 1969.

Theobald, Robert, *An Alternative Future for America,* Chicago: Swallow Press, Inc., 1968.

Thomlinson, Ralph, *Urban Structure,* New York: Random House, 1969.

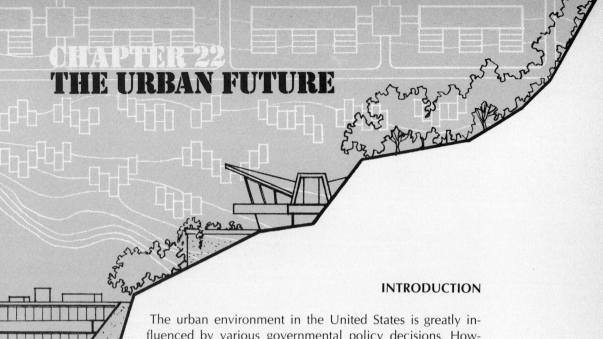

CHAPTER 22
THE URBAN FUTURE

INTRODUCTION

The urban environment in the United States is greatly influenced by various governmental policy decisions. However, it is also quite clear that there are really no goals and objectives set at the national level that are consistent with the development of blueprints for future American cities. The Housing Act of 1949 came closest to defining a goal for future cities in the United States. It promised a suitable living environment for every American family, although no time frame was specified. No other readily discernible goals and objectives exist, despite the fact that in a variety of programs there are frequent references to community renewal, redevelopment and, of course, community master plans.

"The latent model in most planning and most considerations of the future city is curiously restricted to the traditional version of the multipurpose city — a static conglomeration of commercial enterprise, industrial production and distribution points related to material transportation and warehousing" (McHale, 1968: 90). It has not been seriously considered that the future city may stop evolving as a multifunctional aggregate as it has in the past and that it might take many special forms for varied social purposes. Currently, in our urban society there is a proliferation of life styles that requires an increasing number of different perspectives on living. This increasing range of urban life styles and their flexibility are key issues in the development of any typology of future cities. Many of the developing urban life styles revolve around age, occupation, and institutions. Each will influence the physical, psychophysical, and social aspects of the future city. Currently, those who have a highly mobile and differentiated life style are people such as airline flight personnel, corporate staffs, scientists, technologists, and others whose occupational/residential location often varies from year to year, with a great deal of mobility between conventions, meetings, projects, talks, and so forth. Also among these new lifestyles are the new property class of professionals who travel constantly

This new Florida development is an emerging specialized community that soon will be filled with elderly persons in full- or semi-retirement.

to different geographical locations and consult with others in businesses, universities, corporations, and so forth. Students also are an economically identifiable lifestyle group, as are persons involved in the new leisure activities that include the increased use of recreational and travel facilities (McHale, 1968: 93).

If certain of our present urban trends continue by the year 2000, water and air will be dangerously polluted. Increasing pollution at the rates now characterizing some of our larger cities will make relatively pure air and water among the most scarce and costliest of all natural resources. In addition, traffic congestion in the air over cities will be horrendous. Open space close to where people live will become so scarce that the use of park and other recreational facilities will have to be rationed. Central cities, if current trends continue, will become more segregated than ever, and most of them will contain a majority of blacks while surrounding suburban areas will be virtually all white. Slums will still exist and will be expanding, while central cities will continue to be the gathering ground for minorities, the aged, and other disadvantaged people.

Some of the larger cities will have all the appearances of being "ungovernable" (Perloff, 1967). The gap between suburban communities and central cities with all their problems, including limited tax capacity, will be greater than ever. Some new towns will be built that will cluster around major metropolitan areas, thereby providing attractive environments for residents, but obviously they will be beyond the reach of most lower- and middle-income families. In addition, there possibly will be some very impressive greenbelts to keep undesirables out of the new towns. New superhighways, parking structures, and so forth will be criss-crossing cities, and yet intown transportation will continue to be a major headache. All of this, of course, is based upon the assumption that trends now obvious will continue into the future. The grossest failures probably will be recognized as such, and some changes will be made. But it is relatively certain that some conditions *probably will get worse.*

Perloff (1967) believes that if any of these particular problems are to be solved in the future city, certain kinds of questions must be asked: How much do we believe in having unpolluted resources such as water and air? Should from one-half to two-thirds of urban land be used for the movement and storage of cars? If so, where are streets to be placed — underground, on the surface, or above ground? And most importantly, what is to happen to the space over urban land? That is, how high can buildings be built? Should highways and airways be permitted over the ground, and to what extent can polluted air be tolerated? Similarly, questions will have to be asked about to what degree water should be clean or unpolluted for consumption, recreation, and production purposes.

Moreover, the problems of the ghettos and the slums will remain. It will take tremendous resources, imaginative new solutions, and effective political infighting to reverse or dent the trends now apparent. At this point, no one knows where the necessary resources are to come from, where the new solutions are to be found, or who is willing to do the political infighting necessary to reverse present trends. The creation of new communities and new towns would broaden the alternatives that many people have to live diverse urban life styles. Nevertheless, it also should be emphasized that new towns and new communities almost universally are beyond the economic resources of lower-middle-class and lower-class families. Finally, rather typically, few offer mechanisms whereby changes can be accomplished.

FUTURE URBAN POPULATION

Projections of future urban population growth in the United States suggest that by the year 2000 about 90 percent of the population in this country will be living within existing metropolitan regions. As shown in Figure 22–1, two continuous urban conurbations appear to be developing along the East and West coasts and strip cities along the Gulf Coast, the Great Lakes, and possibly

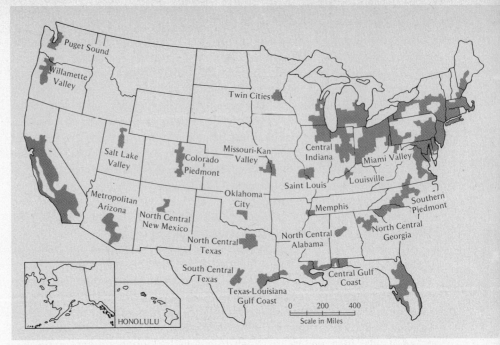

Figure 22-1. Urban Regions, 2000. *From Dimensions of Metropolitanism and Appendices, Research Monograph 14 and 14A (1967 and 1968) by Dr. Jerome P. Pickard. Reprinted with permission of the Urban Land Institute.*

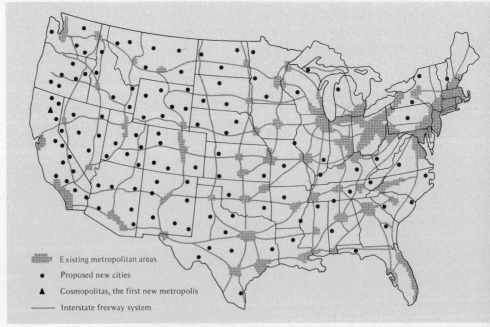

Existing metropolitan areas

• Proposed new cities

▲ Cosmopolitas, the first new metropolis

—— Interstate freeway system

Figure 22-2. The New Urban Frontier. *Used by permission of Daniel W. Cook and the New Mexico Quarterly, 1968.*

Caged automobiles in this downtown parking lot in Salt Lake City, Utah, may represent the wave of the future. Such an approach may indeed facilitate parking, but it is not likely to ameliorate transportation headaches during rush hour — a classic case of treating the symptom instead of the illness.

along the Rocky Mountains, with Denver as the nuclei (Pickard, 1967 and 1968).

One possibility for taking care of an expanding population, estimated to be between 250 and 350 million, and a population increasingly living in urban complexes, is to develop planned and new scattered metropolitan regions. One such possibility focuses on the development of between 100 and 500 new "metro-cities" in diverse locations throughout the United States (Cook, 1968). They could be developed on federal public domain lands in the western states, and the Interstate Highway System would be an effective link between them.

> The concept of the Cosmopolis is that of a cosmopolitan city, conceived in the Space Age, with finitive limits. Its economy would be organized upon the principle of private property ownership for all, equal opportunity for all to participate in the ownership of capitalistic production, and hence economic and social justice. It could be a city of universal affluence [Cook: 1968: 84].

The distribution of existing and such proposed new cities is shown in Figure 22-2.

The cost of the cities with an average population of 1 million would border at least around $1000 billion, which is a large sum, yet not as much as the costs for a total urban-renewal effort. According to Cook (p. 86), this program, if imaginatively executed, could do the following:

1. Increase the efficiency of our economy by adapting production to marker areas rather than tying it to natural-resource deposits or cheap transportation areas.
2. Create millions of new property owners, jobs, and entrepreneurial opportunities.
3. Decentralize the concentrated pattern of decision making now prevalent in our society. The concentration of economic power and political authority is a danger to political and economic freedom. Big government and big business directly and indirectly account for about 80 percent of the jobs, and nearly 70 percent of all productive activity of the United States is lodged in the top 500 corporations. The Cosmopolis program, with its attendant economic reforms, could distribute economic and political power more widely.
4. Compete with existing cities and metropolitan areas, thereby accelerating action for massive improvement in all our major cities, as well as slowing their growth by attracting part of their populations to new urban centers.
5. Distribute minority groups more evenly throughout the United States, and provide new ground-floor opportunities for the disadvantaged to participate in the economy.

At this time, of course, it is highly unlikely that such a program will be undertaken.

TYPES OF FUTURE CITIES

An Experimental City project has been proposed by Spilhaus (1967). It would have an optimum size determined by research yet to be carried out. According to this view, a city of 100,000 may be too small for the diversity of cultural, recreational, and educational, health-care, and work opportunities that make for a functional self-contained community. However, an 8- or 10-million population has been amply shown to be too much. Somewhere in between lies the optimum number. Once the city's optimum size is determined, the answer to preventing the uncontrolled growth that led to today's urban problems is *not* to control individuals but to design a mix of industrial, commercial, and other employment opportunities that keeps the population in a "healthy equilibrium."

While Spilhaus sees the experimental city being planned in as much detail as possible, he also believes that it should be designed and built so that it can be changed easily. Technological innovations would be used to reduce physical restraints within the city and hopefully to allow residents more freedom to thrive and move about. It would be necessary to remove pollutants, filth, noise, and congestion from the city and hope that this will give city residents diversity and choice in the selection of activities. Improved communications would consist of two-way, point-to-point video and other kinds of communication, which would remove the necessity for substantial amounts of travel. Utilizing current technology, the experimental city would be a leader in the concept of modern preventive medicine—"instead of healing the sick, doctors would contribute to the public-health concept that emphasises the building up and banking of a capital health and vigor while young, and a prudent spending of this capital over a lifetime without deficits of ill-health" (p. 1136).

One of the obvious needs of the experimental city will be a mass transportation system that retains all the advantages of the automobile to a common destination. The city's airport would be located at such a distance and in such a direction that landing patterns would not be over the city but over a noninhabitated insulating belt. Main public utilities would be accessible in vehicular and other underground tunnels, thereby eliminating the noisy digging up and remaking of streets currently common in the U.S. These utility tunnels would double as traffic tunnels and utility trenches for the transport of heavy freight, for telephone lines, for power and gas lines, water and sewer mains, and for the rapid transit of emergency vehicles—police, fire, and medical rescue.

In the experimental city there should be a total optimum environment without a hampering diversity of architectural forms and combinations. Thus there should be experiments with enclosing portions of the city within a dome that would have controlled conditions of temperature, humidity, fumes, and light. Since not everyone would want to live in such a perfectly controlled environment, other areas would be left as they are now, which would still involve exposure to the elements and thus variation in climate.

The location of an experimental city creates problems, since it should be far enough from other urban areas to develop self-sufficiency and not be hampered by restrictive practices of a dominant neighboring city. Obviously, extremes in climate could provide a kind of all-weather test facility needed for experimenting with technological innovations. There must be enough land for an insulating belt around the city, otherwise conventional and uncontrolled encroachments or such developments would soon abrogate the experiment. Spilhaus suggested that no private ownership of land be permitted, with publicly owned land being leased to various persons. Revenues to manage the city would come from leases rather than from state taxes. The experimental city will be a kind of participatory democracy.

A broad-gauged typology of future cities has been suggested by McHale (1968: 94–97); according to him, the following typology might describe cities of the future.

1. The *ceremonial city*—a type of city now observable in political and administrative capitals but also one in the future that may revolve around public observances and events such as the Olympic Games or a world's fair.

Brasilia, the capital of Brazil, may be a prototype of the future ceremonial city. It was built from jungle expressly as the administrative capital of the country.

2. The *university city* — many currently exist. It is expected that in the future more will come into being as society becomes more technologically complex and requires centralized research and other kinds of equipment.

3. The *scientific city* — usually an outgrowth of the university city but focuses on an aggregate of research development efforts. A currently developing example is the Research Triangle in North Carolina, between Raleigh, Durham, and Chapel Hill.

4. The *festival or art city* — is obviously related to university or ceremonial capitals but also is in an evolutionary state in such places as Edinburgh, Venice, and Salzburg. There are also some contemporary places such as Cannes, where an annual film festival takes place. Similarly, other cities are developing festival calendars and art festivals.

5. The *recreation or "fun" city* — is probably already in existence in its purest form in Las Vegas, but the coast of the Côte d'Azur, the Costa Brava, and Miami strip are other examples. Developing in the future probably will be ski cities, boating cities, and theater and opera cities.

6. The *communication city* — a developing example of a communication city is the core area of New York City.

7. The *convention/conference city* — is already in existence and again many core areas of major cities, which include their large

hotels, railroads, air networks, and ancillary services, approximate this type of future city.

8. The *museum city* — is a city steeped in art, history, and archeological finds. A current example in the United States is Williamsburg, Virginia. The museum city or restored archeological site also may become a kind of a psychological-physical time machine in which individuals or groups may choose to reenact or reexperience the human condition in a variety of historical periods.

9. The *experimental city* — as indicated earlier, has been suggested. There are developments of experimental cities in the desert of Arizona, and other utopian-type communities and architectural developments in a variety of places all can be called experimental cities.

In these future cities communications, education, and research will become increasingly important. For example, Theobald (1968: 138) believes that the future city will be organized around communication modalities, and thus no one will move themselves or goods except when they choose to; rather, the important element in these cities will be production, distribution, and movement of information. An implication of this approach is that *power* will be the ability to participate in the defining of issues, how effectively the issues are posed, and who influences the answers or has the information to answer the questions. Therefore, knowledge and the generation of knowledge will make future cities serving these functions extremely important. University cities will include traditional kinds of teaching but also education in its broadest sense, including adult and continuing education, and professional schools and research complexes (Graubard, 1967).

THE IDEAL FUTURE CITY

A number of perspectives have been developed that could influence the ideal future city. Among their proponents are LeCorbusier, who has already extensively influenced contemporary cities, Soleri, Jacobs, and compact-city adherents. In addition, a number of others, such as Abrams, have proposed dominant themes and areas of concern that future cities must be like if they are to be fit places to live.

The Radiant City

LeCorbusier has influenced the work of all serious contemporary architects and city planners (Anthony, 1966: 279). "With his elevated highways and stilted buildings, LeCorbusier was the first man to develop fully and defend the theme of complete separation of vehicular from pedestrian traffic, the first man to treat the pedestrian with the respect and honor we now accord only to the automobile" (p. 279). He advocated freeing the ground of cities for pedestrians by lifting buildings and roads above ground level, with the whole ground level becoming large uninterrupted parks. He visualized tall buildings within self-contained areas with a proposed density of 300 persons per acre and an optimum population of 3 million persons. When this figure was exceeded, additional new cities were to be built to take care of the excess population. Another of his proposals was that "all land in the city should be public property in order to avoid land speculation and to make easier the city's organic and logical development" (Anthony, 1966: 281). For the most part, he ignored the practical problems of carrying out his city designs. Such problems as how to adjust landownership and the availability of resources were up to others to study and solve. LeCorbusier's ideas have been utilized in existing cities such as Brasilia and Chandigarh (capital of Punjab, India) and in sections of other cities. The main feature of his perspective includes tall apartment buildings; however, most people in the United States do not find such units desirable. Nevertheless, most "models" of future cities include LeCorbusier's ideas, ignoring as he did problems of costs and individual preferences (LeCorbusier, 1967).

Miniaturization

The compact rearrangement of space is Soleri's (1969) means of bringing beauty, harmony, efficiency, and spaciousness to cities. This process would allow human beings to enjoy the city without destroying the countryside. This frame of reference holds that miniaturization is the key to all life and that current cities violate this principle. Thus they must become more compact to reduce time and space obstacles to human activity. They can be made more compact through more efficient utilization of various dimensions, especially the vertical one. Following the principles of miniaturization and utilization of the third dimension called *verticality,* once again *Homo sapiens* will be in tune with nature and the nature evolutionary patterns of miniaturization that are being violated in today's cities.

Diversified Use of Space

One of the most ardent critics of most city planning practices is Jacobs (1961). She was unhappy with city planning practice on the basis of its uncritical acceptance of the "open-space" concept. More open space for what? she asks. For open space to be useful, it must be used by ordinary people, and it will not be used just because it is there. Rather, Jacobs would prefer that streets be the focus of interaction, leisure, and other activities—especially people watching the activities of other people, which she believes is the most reasonable solution for making streets "safe" from muggings, crimes, and so on.

One of the most important conditions for a lively, active, safe city, according to Jacobs, is the assurance of an intricate and close-grained utilization of streets, open spaces, and other public places the give each other constant mutual support, both economically and socially. Further, children should have available "lively streets" where they might be raised under the unstructured

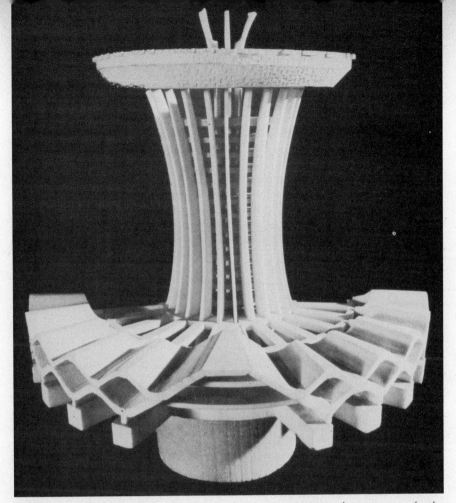

P. Soleri's model community stresses a compact arrangement of space, use of solar energy, and the development of completely different lifestyles. This model of "Babel" depicts a futuristic community encompassed by a single structure almost 4000 feet high and covering an area of 3000 acres. Babel would support a population of 800,000 at a density of 263 per acre. The gigantic "base" shown at the bottom would allow construction on marshy land where more conventional cities would be unthinkable. The central sections are primarily residential and commercial, and the "cap" would develop solar energy for municipal use.

surveillance of meaningful adult activities. This is in contrast to garden cities, apartment complexes, and urban-renewal projects with their "enclosed park enclaves with blocks," which are boring places that children do not use after the age of six.

City diversity is the keystone upon which Jacobs believes lively neighborhoods are built. According to her, "diversity itself persists and stimulates more diversity." From this perspective, supermarkets, delicatessens, bakeries, foreign groceries, and so on, all make up a diverse neighborhood just as the standard movie houses, art movies, and so on, do. Diverse people and diverse elements in the city protect it against the "Great Blight of Dullness."

In summary, Jocobs' point of view includes at least four conditions for the building or rebuilding of lively cities:

1. Cities need areas with mixed primary uses so that people who go outdoors on different schedules, who are there for different purposes, but who may use many common facilities, have available the necessary facilities.
2. Blocks should be short with many opportunities to turn corners.
3. A lively neighborhood should have buildings that vary in age and condition and have a good proportion of older buildings.
4. The neighborhood must include residents but also a sufficiently dense concentration of people who are there for other purposes to ensure population diversity.

The Compact City

An attempt at bringing together the LeCorbusier Jacobs, and Soleri perspectives was carried out by Dantzig and Saaty (1973). They utilized two dimensions that this book has explored systematically in cities — space and time. Space and time, they noted, cut across all perspectives of city planning, of utopian communities, and of cities proposed by LeCorbusier, Jacobs, and Soleri. Thus they found that while Los Angeles currently utilizes approximately 35 percent of its land surface for transportation-related use, if Los Angeles were "stacked" vertically, its land surface would correspondingly shrink depending upon the height of the stack. This vertical stress would make the city more compact. Similarly, they noted that most, if not all, human activities take place within a time rhythm or cycle. Joining time and space dimensions should allow a more meaningful compact city to be constructed that brings into play the views of LeCorbusier and Soleri but also allows the diversity so dear to Jacobs.

As shown in Figure 22-3 the general plan for Dantzig and Saaty for a compact city includes a population base of 250,000 residing in an area of 2.2 square miles. The city could expand to a size of 2 million people. It would have a radius of 3,000 feet, with a population of 250,000, and 4,420 feet, with a population of 2 million persons. The shape chosen is circular with a radius eighteen times its height" (p. 37). Figure 22-3 also shows five distinct rings: (1) core; (2) core edge, (3) inner residential area, (4) mid-plaza, and (5) outer residential area. The core, of course, contains shops, churches, hotels, and elements ordinarily thought of as being associated with the core of a city, while its edge would serve primarily as a parking area and contain ramps for ascending and descending to various levels. Also, the core edge would have a promenade with small parks and recreational areas. Beyond the inner residential area would be the mid-plaza, which would provide local facilities such as elementary schools, clinics, neighborhood shops, and play areas. Connecting the

Figure 22-3. Top and Side View of Compact City. Population: 250,000. Base area: 2.2 square miles. As the city grows to 2 million people its height and diameter are expanded to dimensions double those shown. *Used by permission of George B. Dantzig and Thomas L. Saaty and The W. H. Freeman Company, 1973.*

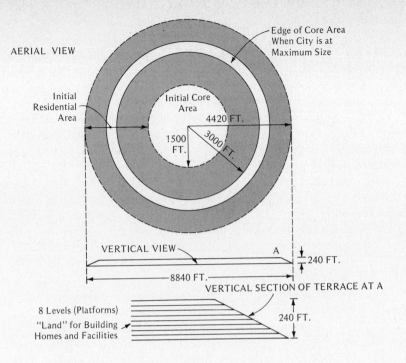

AERIAL VIEW

Edge of Core Area When City is at Maximum Size

Initial Residential Area

Initial Core Area

4420 FT.

1500 FT.

3000 FT.

VERTICAL VIEW

A

240 FT.

8840 FT.

VERTICAL SECTION OF TERRACE AT A

8 Levels (Platforms)

"Land" for Building Homes and Facilities

240 FT.

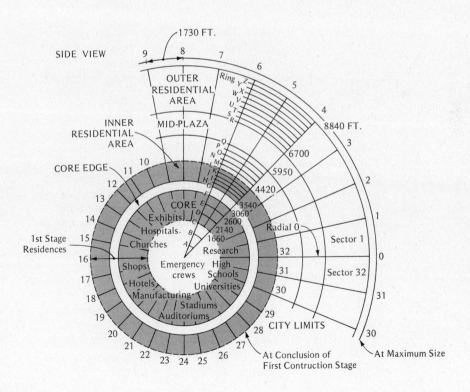

SIDE VIEW

1730 FT.

9 8 7 6 5 4 3 2 1 0 31 30

OUTER RESIDENTIAL AREA

Ring Z Y X W V U T S R

8840 FT.

MID-PLAZA

INNER RESIDENTIAL AREA

Q P O N M L K J I H G F E D C B A

6700

5950

4420

3540

3060

2600

2140

1660

CORE EDGE

10 11 12 13 14 15 16 17 18 19 20 21 22 23 24 25 26 27 28 29 30 31 32

CORE

Exhibits

Hospitals

Churches

Shops

Hotels

Manufacturing

Stadiums

Auditoriums

Emergency crews

Research

High Schools

Universities

Radial 0

Sector 1

Sector 32

1st Stage Residences

CITY LIMITS

At Conclusion of First Contruction Stage

At Maximum Size

outer residential area, as well as all of the other areas, are two-way roadways that radiate from the core edge like spokes of a wheel; cross-streets are alternating one-way roads. Automobiles would be electric powered but probably would not be used very much because of the compactness of the city.

Some of the advantages of the compact city would be more available time and opportunity because of the increased accessibility to all parts of the city and the fitting of the city to the rhythm of the people who live there. Criticisms of the compact-city approach revolve around the extensive crowding and increased density of the population, the lack of sunlight, the sameness, and vulnerability. Each of these criticisms, of course, involves a value system about how one should live. Dantzig and Saaty present arguments against each of these potential criticisms and believe that the potential benefits make the negative consequences pale in comparison.

The Livable Future City

The ideal future city will be free of slums, poor planning, billboards, and pollution. A resident of this ideal future city will consider it as extending to the limits of a 100-mile radius, which will include districts with 25,000–50,000 population separated by continuous parks from other parts of the urban region (Lovelace, 1968: 52). This future city will serve the people who live in it in contrast to current American cities, which do not. A number of suggestions for such future cities are as follows:

1. A major objective of the city of the future must be to maximize relationships among people–to promote human interaction by persuasive elements in the physical environment.
2. Small urban cells should be created in the larger settlement. These should be the fundamental units of the community. Cluster design may be used to create them.
3. More sophisticated urban design should be used to bring about both higher population densities and more open space. The design should permit privacy for the individual and the family but at the same time allow the opportunity to mix with others.
4. The city design should combine the small "cells" into neighborhoods and then into districts, which then combine to form the metropolis. The objective is an arrangement that permits one to know oneself and where he or she fits into the life of the city. Further, the individual should be able to see these patterned relationships outdoors, and the city should cease being visually chaotic.
5. The city should be built on a human scale. Grandiose, baroque concepts should go.
6. The city should be livable. The superhuman scale that characterizes major technological improvements such as highways, rapid transit lines, and airports should be mitigated by careful design that respects the human scale.

This model shows what a realistic and livable future city may be like. Note that most features of present urban technology—private cars, parking lots, high-rise apartments—still exist in modified form. The model is evolutionary rather than revolutionary, and thus is likely to come into being.

7. Educational facilities should become a more dominant feature of the physical city.
8. There should be more open space, and it should fit in with the new pattern of the city, winding through it everywhere rather than existing here and there haphazardly as isolated chunks.
9. There should be no barriers in the city that express any distinctions of class or race.
10. The new city should be natural in design without any ostentation or faking, with an emphasis on the qualities and the amenities that promote human well-being. The existing areas that reduce well-being or create tension—such as stereotyped high density, all high-rise residential areas (the Pruitt-Igoe housing project in St. Louis, for example), dilapidated or rundown areas, residential neighborhoods without parks or those next to heavy industries—all would be eliminated.
11. The person would have priority over the automobile: Each would have separate paths, and crossings would be minimized. Separation of human and vehicular traffic would also be characteristic of shopping areas.

In summary, the new city would be orderly, attractive, and intimate, with the most offensive products of today's technology (pollution, billboards, overhead wires, litter, and dirt) no longer tolerated. Design would be given new importance. Habitations would be built with a view toward the relations of the individual building to the whole structure of the city. Livability and technological problem solving would go hand in hand (Lovelace, 1968: 54–55).

Most of these recommendations involve the construction of new cities. What about old cities or currently existing ones? Under this proposal a regional arrangement of places would be split up into a number of smaller parts, each of the size to foster personal interaction. Each of these smaller parts would have a population of 25,000–50,000 persons. Older metropolitan areas then, of course, would be divided into a large number of such parts (Lovelace, 1968: 60). Within these parts of 25,000–50,000 people there would also be urban cells of approximately 500–1,000 people. In newer developing cities these would be subdivisions or groups of blocks, but in older neighborhoods it would require the development of cells in block groups within the communities of 25,000–50,000 people. Finally, then, the 25,000–50,000-person cities would make up a great metropolitan region that might involve thousands of square miles and large numbers of counties (Lovelace, 1968: 61).

REFORMATION OF CURRENT CITIES

A considerable disillusionment with twentieth-century urban reform has developed over the past few years. As a result, Meyerson (1968: 1425 ff.) proposed several different themes around which reform in the future might achieve some measure of agreement so that coalitions of forces might be formed to achieve urban reform. Among them are:

1. Urban services and facilities should be responsive to their users, customers, or clients. For example, parks and playgrounds in the past have been designed for recreation workers rather than the users. Services in the future should become essentially user based.
2. Decisions should be decentralized, bringing them closer to those affected by them.
3. User orientations and decentralization probably will result in greater diversity in programs that may differ radically from those now in existence, and these variations should be tolerated.
4. There will be a necessity for decreasing administrative rules and regulations and less utilization of scarce resources in overhead expenses.
5. Diversity of choice in housing, transportation, municipal services, and other functions will increase, and some of these functions may be consolidated and carried out by different jurisdictions than currently.
6. The voluntary sector may grow dramatically, especially in the

areas of health, education, job development, and in religion and recreation.

7. Experimentalism in attempting to solve urban problems should replace "canned" programs exported to all cities regardless of their problems or unique situations. Thus alternative approaches will be developed, and the lessons learned from each demonstration will allow a fuller range of options in meeting urban problems.

8. There should be a growth of urban research to achieve a more useful knowledge base upon which to make decisions and to develop knowledge about the intended and unintended consequences of them.

9. More attention should be placed upon the senses as they relate to the development of the city and urban region; thus the senses of sight, smell, and sound all become part of the expectations and aspirations of people about their urban environment.

10. While the quantity of education will continue to grow, emphasis must be placed upon the quality of education: Students should be helped to understand the urban environment in which around 90 percent of them will live and the policy options available; better education will aid them in making relevant choices so that meaningful change can take place.

Another set of themes was proposed by Abrams (1965: 287 ff.). He set out a variety of plans to bring about more desirable future urban environment. Among the considerations that he set forth are the following:

1. Cities should set an example of better design and comfort in publicly assisted improvements. Among the elements involved in better design is the fact that current urban renewal and other development programs take up a whole block or, at times, large numbers of blocks, and this obviously then has an impact upon the future design of the city. Depending upon what the city builds today, therefore, the city faces these buildings and these developments in the future. Urban architecture generally falls into two broad classifications: In the first one price is no object, which generally includes public buildings, institutional investments such as universities, museums, temples, prestigious office buildings, and so on; the second, balance-sheet architecture, is related to building housing with the profit motive in mind—if an investor or a builder does not properly build within these constraints, he or she will lose the investment.[1] Abrams pointed out a current problem in developing better designs is that many city codes and regulations overemphasize safety. In many instances

---

[1] It should be added that although Abrams did not mention it as a third classification, urban public housing developments are neither price-no-object architecture nor balance-sheet architecture oriented toward making a profit. Rather, these developments are massive housing areas built at the lowest possible cost, often architecturally unaesthetic, not too functional, and not profitable.

they are carry-overs from a previous time and are no longer functional. While the city planning commission exhorts good architecture, less density, and small coverage, the same city's tax assessor exacts a premium for each of them (p. 291). Similarly, it has been noted that public housing projects are built for the poor, and the law is written so they will be poorly designed. Not only the poor, of course, are affected by the projects, but the projects become part of the city's ambiance and thus affect everyone in the city. Finally, Abrams added that the architecture of *discomfort* appears on streets, parks, and in public places. He believes that a comfort station living up to its name cannot be found anywhere in the United States. Public privies of any kind, comfortable or otherwise, are absent in virtually all cities of the United States. According to him, the main reason for this lack of amenities, as well as the lack of small parks and playgrounds and social centers, is our exaggerated concern with profit making. On the contrary, the city and its residents should be concerned with the aesthetic, functional aspects, and there should be inducements provided to make them possible. Otherwise, as Abrams has pointed out, "mediocrity will continue on our urban horizons" (p. 294).

2. Cities should utilize the natural features within them and reclaim them wherever possible. Most cities in the United States were originally blessed with good landscapes and waterscapes. Most of these blessings were destroyed during the industrial surge, and lakes, rivers, and streams were polluted, old trees were felled, and hills leveled for factories, houses, or speculative developments. In virtually every large city in the United States waterfronts have been cut off from the population and no longer serve as useful vistas and/or recreational centers. This has been accomplished by housing developments, industrial sites, and high-speed highways.

3. Cities should multiply the number of trees, parks, and green spaces. Street trees and small parks supply reprieve from the steel and cement facades dominating city scapes. Unfortuantely, virtually no city in the United States has a greenbelt or wedges of green going through them as do cities such as Copenhagen and London. The small parks that run through London or the green walks of Paris have not been duplicated in any American city. It should be noted that trees serve not only aesthetic purposes but also provide ventilation and shade, absorb noise and dust; and recent evidence suggests that they also can help to reduce air pollution and to improve the city's weather. Abrams believvs that if city neighborhoods are to be rebuilt properly, all federal programs should include provisions for space for parks, playgrounds, within and around developments, and there should be money made available for public acquisition of areas for small parks and playgrounds not only in the cities but also in suburbia, which in many instances is bare of parks.

4. Cities should be made more attractive for tourism, diversion, and leisure. Abrams pointed out, interestingly enough, that when tourists from the United States go abroad, they generally head for Paris, London, Rome, and so forth. Yet when they go on a vacation in the United States they move toward

the mountains, lakes, or national parks. The main reason for this is that European cities have things to offer the tourist, whereas American cities do not. Abrams attributed this lack of tourist interest in cities as being due to "our growing urban and suburban dullness" (p. 302). One of the main reasons for this lack of tourism in cities in the United States is that *streets* are not interesting. They should be among the cities' best assets—for walking, recreation, and diversion. The federal government pays 90 percent of the cost of interstate highways, but it does nothing to improve city streets for the people who live there or who might want to live there. Perhaps one of the reasons that theaters, dance halls, and nightclubs are declining is that people—both suburbanites and tourists—are no longer willing to visit the city where they are located. Similarly, art galleries, museums, restaurants, and so forth, require visitors to the city if they are to survive. They also make the city an interesting place for the local resident.

5. Cities must salvage the CBD. Without it, according to Abrams, there are only neighborhoods left, and with only neighborhoods there are no contrasts, no alternatives, no easy escape, and no real freedom of movement. He pointed out that cities with pulsating downtowns are those that thrive and are recognized throughout the world. Again he points, for examples, to the cities of Rome, London, and Paris (and perhaps San Francisco), where people still go and which are remembered for their downtowns and various exhibits. A downtown area lives or dies as a whole, not piecemeal as many people and planners in the United States prefer to believe. He also stressed the fact that many cities in the United States cater to drivers and not to pedestrians. If the downtown or the CBD is to survive, it must be planned as a place to spend the day, not an hour, in an environment where people can spend an evening walking, visiting, eating, obtaining recreation, and so forth. Interestingly, Abrams believes that strict immigration quotas have helped make our downtowns and cities dull. In contrast to many who see ethnic neighborhoods as being detrimental, he believes that they are a plus, especially when they are located near the downtown CBD.

6. Cities must build upon the existing values of neighborhoods rather than destroying them. Neighborhoods in most cities of the United States include the good and the bad insofar as housing conditions are concerned. As so often pointed out by social planners, Abrams believes that housing conditions alone should not be the sole determinant of what deserves to stay or what must be torn down. He also pointed out that a neighborhood of bad houses is not always made better by leveling it and reshuffling the inhabitants to other areas. Thus slum clearance also is slum transference. In many cities some of these older houses are of better quality than the new private and public multiple dwellings that replace them. What neighborhoods may need is not necessarily physical improvement but the addition of key amenities that bring out hidden values or generate new ones. Abrams espouses this approach primarily because he believes that the neighborhood is a voluntary formation of people,

each of who has his or her own good reasons for electing to move into it. The reasons may vary but may include proximity to friends, parents, or work, access to rent that fits the budget, to the right church, and proper playmates for children, or just plain sentiment (p. 315). Finally, Abrams noted that perhaps what is needed in many older neighborhoods is not their destruction or slum transference, but more realistic federal programs so that homeownership in slum areas is more readily available. Thus, perhaps this would increase the incentive to improve homes and dwellings in the neighborhood without a complete physical overhaul.

7. Cities should leave room for people to contribute to their own environments. Most current projects in the United States, because of their large size, do not have allowance for people living in the neighborhood to make changes they desire. Thus people of a neighborhood do not have the chance to add their own creative ideas to the environment, and, accordingly, the project is destined to remain as cold and dull as when it was built. In addition, the needs of neighborhood residents cannot all be known in advance. Abrams proposed that more property should be required for a project than is required for immediate development. Then after the community has been settled, people can decide whether there is a need for a community or social center, a playground, a library, schools, or whatever other improvements they think are necessary. According to Abrams, the contributions of individuals and families to the neighborhood are as important as public additions.

8. Cities should give people a sense of belonging to their neighborhoods. In projects, organizations that bring people together have been discouraged for fear that they might give management trouble. This situation contrasts with that of many neighborhoods in the city in which people come together to interact and have joint activities. This does not mean, of course, that all areas within the city should become a neighborhood; some people do not want to know their neighbors (including the people who live next door), and this preference too should be granted. Similarly, Abrams argued that various facilities in a neighborhood should be make available to the people living there; for example, public schools should serve multiple functions — not only as a place for educating children but as a social meeting place, a theater, a dance center, a forum. Similarly, churches should serve more than their religious functions.

9. Cities should encourage commercial clusters. According to Abrams, clusteration can be one of the most effective devices for revising neighborhoods. A cluster can be a wholesale or retail center; it can be areas where the focal points are the purchase of wares, entertainment, or services. It can be an area of antique shops, second-hand bookshops, art/movie areas, and so forth. Whatever these clusters may be, Abrams believes that they should not only be allowed but encouraged to exist and to give variety to the city.

10. The city should be made a great center for adult education. The reduction of working hours and the availability of more free time, longer life

span, increasing technology, and preparation of married women for tasks outside the home, all imply a greater need for adult education opportunities. Little effort has been expanded in attempting to bring together the necessary institutions, resources, and so forth, for adult education.

11. Cities need to develop a *realistic* mass transportation program. As most city dwellers in the United States are aware, no city in the United States currently has developed such a program. The main element in such programs up until now appears to be thruways, freeways, more mammoth garages for storage of automobiles, and vast complexes for trucks. Yet a big city's main line of defense against the automobile and highway glut is mass transportation. Currently, neither the railroads nor trolley cars nor other means of transportation used long ago are giving city passengers the service they used to. If anyone wants to visit the downtown area, the business district, they almost have to go by automobile. As a result, two-thirds of downtown Los Angeles is devoted to freeways, streets and off-street parking. Finally, it should be noted that mass transit is not only a large central city problem but is related to getting to and from suburbs into the city and to and from various areas in the metropolitan region as well as from one city to another.

12. Cities should enhance their walkability. One of the major elements of the cities that are regarded as true cities (e.g., Rome, London, Paris) is that there are many walkable sections within them. Few cities in the United States are now considered walkable. Yet there are cities that have illustrated that the automobile is not indispensable for the good life and that, in fact, walking areas are most attractive and may draw more customers to shopping areas. Thus the development of malls in some cities and in larger areas, the development of shopping malls under large buildings, which may be a block long at least, have some element of a trend back to a walkable city.

13. Cities should be made more livable for females. Abrams believes that current cities in the United States inhibit females and, as a result, they have lost population because they have lost the confidence of the female—as one seeking love, as a wife, a career woman, and a mother.

14. Cities must improve public schools. The decline of the city's public school system has been associated with the massive black immigration into cities and the segregation that it has brought about in these cities. Many of these black migrants have come from the South and are considered culturally deprived. In addition, many white families that have elected to remain in the city have been withdrawing their children from the public school system and enrolling them in private schools. Thus an increasingly greater proportion of central city schoolchildren are black. This makes it more difficult to hire good teachers for the segregated schools. Similarly, it puts a great strain on the finances of cities in their efforts to meet the added social-economic burdens that segregation and poverty impose. Abrams believes that the solution to this problem is not enforced desegregation, nor is it sending a few black children on long bus rides to white schools or white children to black schools. Rather, it

is the development of neighborhoods in cities and suburbs in which people may live regardless of their skin color; thus these neighborhoods would be more likely to offer an equal opportunity for a good education.

15. Cities should concentrate more effort on improving the environment for children. Little that the city offers is oriented toward children. There are few playgrounds and few parks, and thus pavements and sidewalks have become play spaces because they happen to be there. In the overall delineation of priorities, children's needs are forgotten and the space left to them is minute. Abrams believes that one part of the reason for this lack of concern with children is that city planning deals with the environment as emphasized by housing while ignoring the neighborhood. According to him, both must be improved. Up until now most inputs in cities in relation to children and poverty have been inconsequential. If the city is to be a better place for children, it must be a better place for everyone, black and white, and in every aspect of its environment, since these are the only real answers to the welfare of the city child in the long run.

According to Abrams when the city faces the future there are other factors that need to be taken into consideration, and these "require a change in the nation's philosophy" (p. 361). The new philosophy must acknowledge that there are values worth preserving in cities as there are in the suburbs; it must acknowledge that the central city and the suburbs are an entity, that each depends upon the other for job opportunities, services, recreation, escape, variety, and progress. The new philosophy needs to redefine state and federal functions in providing for the general welfare, which includes clear and definable lines of jurisdiction among the federal government, state, and local governments. Further, the new philosophy needs to assure all citizens of the right to live wherever they choose; similarly, it should provide that low-income families be entitled to the opportunity to own homes and to own them without fear of losing them when unemployment, illness, or death intervenes. Finally, this new philosophy should be concerned with poverty as a national problem.

Obviously, the new philosophy of Abrams requires substantial *value* changes and thus is not likely to be acceptable to most people in the United States. This, of course, has great implications for what the American city of the future will be like.

AN INJECTION OF REALISM

Both wittingly and unwittingly some city rulers exploit the city and its inhabitants with public investments that are costly and wasteful (Long, 1972: 159–160). Instead, they should be investing in making the local economy viable; a local economy that does not support itself is, in fact, living on welfare. Therefore, each city must "pursue a vigorous policy to restore the viability of its local economy" and to rid itself of economic dependence to one of a trading partner with equal stature.

To accomplish a goal of independence and economic viability a city must undertake a "systematic inventory of its assets and its liabilities. A start can be made by inventorying the employed and employable population" (Long, 1972: 162). One of the most important tasks that can be undertaken in a city is to improve its state of employment, which is related to inadequate housing. Long (1972: 170) believes that a realistic approach to the housing problem in the cities has only three real alternatives: (1) increase people's incomes, (2) decrease housing costs, and/or (3) review the standards of housing decency (in this instance, standards would be downward).

Long (1972: 162) has said that "It seems scarcely credible that, after all the funds that have been spent on planning, the city should still lack an inventory of its human resources." Further, city expenditures on planning, health, education, and other services may not only prove to be unproductive but, in some instances, counterproductive; thus services, their costs, and their outcomes need to be seriously examined but rarely have been.

Similarly, few individual cities have examined the future in terms of realistic potential opportunity for utilizing their economic, manpower, and physical resources. For example, in some locations, one potential utilization is in health care.

> The health industry also offers a major opportunity to utilize the city's unused and underutilized plant. Nursing homes, geriatric care, child care—all the health services that require nursing and some medical supervision can, in principle, make use of the city's stock of apartments and large older buildings. If the city would both promote the development and stringently supervise the quality of the services, it could command a growing, better met market for this kind of health care. As a health center with a rounded complement of capabilities, from multiphasic automated health-testing to produce economies of scale with medical parks and residence neighborhoods for doctors, nurses, technicians and other employees to research and development efforts mounted by universities, hospitals, and industry to produce new bioelectronic and other technology, the city has a major interest in pushing health and the health industry aa a major use of its people, plant, and location Long, 1972: 180–181].

Other opportunities certainly must exist; but without evaluating the need, without an inventory of its human resources and an orientation toward effective social planning, these potential opportunities cannot be fulfilled.

While it is potentially possible to carry out some of the ideas advanced about the location of future cities, the building of them, and the revitalization of present cities, it is highly unlikely that such changes will be made in our lifetimes. Some elements, to be sure, may be changed, but the massive changes implied by all of the approaches surveyed in this chapter require at least the following: (1) costs beyond imagination—much more than $160-billion tab of the

Vietnam War; (2) overcoming the hold that traditional physical planning concepts have upon planners, city officials, and the general public; (3) the elimination of rigid construction codes, many of which are based upon outmoded building and construction concepts; (4) economic incentives for individuals and cities to readjust their thinking in regards to what cities can and should be like; and (5) recognizing that all of these are ingrained in the dominant value system of the population in the United States and appear highly resistant to change.

The last point is perhaps the most important one. It stresses that in the United States there has not been a substantial commitment to rebuilding older cities, constructing new cities, or altering the environment in a really meaningful manner because *funds* are spent elsewhere, presumably for higher-priority items. Some progress has been made in overcoming the traditional emphasis of physical planning with a neglect of the social. Nevertheless, the real test will come when it will be necessary to commit economic resources to carry out such social plans. Currently, for example, millions of dollars of revenue-sharing allocations are spent on capital expenditures — buildings; virtually no revenue-sharing resources are spent on social planning or social services. This is the case in spite of the fact that revenue-sharing funds are perhaps the only resources cities and counties receive that are available for both kinds of expenditures.

Similarly, it is highly unlikely that, in the future, rigid construction codes and outmoded construction concepts will be changed, since both the building industry and unions have a vested interest in maintaining such codes. Further, master plans and traditional planning concepts support the present codes. In addition, it is improbable that the legal code will be rewritten so that economic or other kinds of incentives will be made available for cities and individuals to change their living environments radically.

Finally, it should be noted that any realistic assessment of the next few decades cannot depend upon or assume that there will be substantial changes in the composition of the central city, since it is highly unlikely that the minorities and the aged composition of cities will change drastically, nor the problems facing them in the future. Thus any discussion of future cities is fruitless without recognizing these realities.

BIBLIOGRAPHY: Articles

Anthony, Harry A., "LeCorbusier: His Ideas for Cities," *Journal of the American Institute of Planners,* 32 (September 1966): 279–288.

Cook, Daniel W., "Cosmopolis: A New Cities Proposal," *New Mexico Quarterly,* 38 (Summer 1968): 83–89.

Graubard, Stephen R., "University Cities in the Year 2000," *Daedalus,* 96 (Summer 1967): 817–822.

Lovelace, Eldridge, "Communities for a New Generation," *New Mexico Quarterly,* 38 (Summer 1968): 52–62.

McHale, John, "The Future City(s): Notes on a Typology," *New Mexico Quarterly,* 38 (Summer 1968): 90–97.

Meyerson, Martin, "Urban Policy: Reforming Reform," *Daedalus,* 97 (Fall 1968): 1410–1430.

Perloff, Harvey S., "Modernizing Urban Development," *Daedalus,* 96 (Summer 1967): 789–800.

Spilhaus, Athelstan, "The Experimental City," *Daedalus,* 96 (Winter 1967): 1129–1141.

BIBLIOGRAPHY: Books

Abrams, Charles, *The City Is the Frontier,* New York: Harper & Row, 1965.

Dantzig, George B., and Thomas L. Saaty, *Compact City: A Plan for a Livable Urban Environment,* San Francisco: W. H. Freeman and Company, 1973.

Jacobs, Jane, *The Death and Life of Great American Cities,* New York: Random House, 1961.

LeCorbusier, *The Radiant City,* New York: Grossman-Orion Press, 1967 (English translation of the 1933 French version).

Long, Norton E., *The Unwalled City: Reconstituting the Urban Community,* New York: Basic Books, 1972.

Pickard, Jerome P., *Dimensions of Metropolitanism,* Research Monograph 14 and 14A, Washington, D.C.: Urban Land Institute, 1967 and 1968.

Soleri, Paolo, *Arcology, the City in the Image of Man,* Cambridge, Mass.: M.I.T. Press, 1969.

Theobold, Robert, *An Alternative Future for America,* Chicago: Swallow Press, Inc., 1968.

AUTHOR INDEX

Italic page number indicates full reference citation.

SUBJECT INDEX